Workin

WORD

FOR WINDOWS™

MW01687052

Working with

WORD

FOR WINDOWS™

Russell Borland

Microsoft PRESS®

The Authorized Edition

PUBLISHED BY
Microsoft Press
A Division of Microsoft Corporation
One Microsoft Way
Redmond, Washington 98052-6399

Copyright © 1990 by Russell Borland
All rights reserved. No part of the contents of this book
may be reproduced or transmitted in any form or by any means
without the written permission of the publisher.

Library of Congress Cataloging-in-Publication Data
Borland, Russell, 1946–
Working with Word for Windows / Russell Borland.
p. cm.
Includes index.
ISBN 1-55615-163-2 : $22.95
1. Microsoft Word for Windows (Computer program) 2. Word
processing. I. Title.
Z52.5.M523B67 1990 89-12574
652.553--dc20 CIP

Printed and bound in the United States of America.

1 2 3 4 5 6 7 8 9 FGFG 3 2 1 0 9

Distributed to the book trade in Canada by General Publishing Company, Ltd.

Distributed to the book trade outside the United States and Canada by Penguin Books Ltd.

Penguin Books Ltd., Harmondsworth, Middlesex, England
Penguin Books Australia Ltd., Ringwood, Victoria, Australia
Penguin Books N.Z. Ltd., 182–190 Wairau Road, Auckland 10, New Zealand

British Cataloging-in-Publication Data available

Apple® and LaserWriter® are registered trademarks of Apple Computer, Inc. IBM®, PC/AT®, and PS/2® are registered trademarks of International Business Machines Corporation. Windows™ is a trademark and Microsoft® and MS-DOS® are registered trademarks of Microsoft Corporation.

Project Editor: Barbara Olsen Browne **Technical Editor:** Gerald Joyce

Berta, for inspirational ikebana 'n' stuff
Basti, my relaxation teacher
Fred, even though he still isn't singing again
And the Inn of Lalazar Head

Contents

Acknowledgments

I acknowledge Claudette Moore, former Acquisitions Editor for Microsoft Press. Claudette not only had a practical and exciting vision of this book but also shared my enthusiasm for the product and believed in the rightness of my writing this book.

I thank Bryan Loofbourrow, Development Lead for Word for Windows, Peter Jackson, Technical Lead, and Adrian Wyard, Associate Program Manager, for making Word for Windows as exciting, as powerful, and as fun and easy as it is. The efforts of these three and the team of programmers and testers made this product great and this book possible.

For struggling with and conquering the manuscripts I left behind with them, I acknowledge the editors of the documentation that comes with Word for Windows—Laurie Boehme, Mary Deaton, Monica Harrington, Darlene Rudd, and Charles Brod.

And I acknowledge the brilliant efforts of the people at Microsoft Press, who did their damnedest: in particular, Jerry Joyce, who provided technical review and never tired of finding and correcting flaws; Becky Geisler-Johnson, who turned my Miróesque sketches into intelligible conceptual art; and Brianna Morgan and her team of nitpicky proofreaders, who took at least the bristles off my sow's-ear sentences. Of course, no book could or should get finished without an editor. Mine made sure I really wrote a book instead of a shambles, and she puts up with a lot.

All of which leaves me to confess that more often than not I was "stetting" when I should have been sliding—that is, despite the fine efforts of these people and all the rest of those at Press who touched this book, mistakes are mine, and you can't take that away from me.

Introduction

Microsoft Word for Windows has led the way into a new generation of word processing—a generation that breaks down the barrier between word-processed text and graphics.

Word is a powerful word processor that can combine text with imported paint-type and draw-type graphics, spreadsheets, and charts—all in the same file. As you work, your text and graphics appear on the screen as they'll look on the printed page.

Word is an exciting program to work with because it matches the needs and wishes of people who create documents. I saw evidence of this fact at a recent conference, in a session about desktop publishing. The following is what the 25 people in attendance said they wanted from a desktop-publishing program:

- Control of layout changes
- The ability to produce a more readable page
- Efficiency
- WYSIWYG (What You See Is What You Get) or at least a preview mode
- Reasonable cost
- A variety of fonts and type sizes
- Typeset-quality printing
- Reasonable word-processing capabilities
- Global styles, with the ability to make local changes
- The ability to insert graphics easily
- Automated functions for indexes, tables of contents, page numbers, tables, and equations
- Electronic archiving for final drafts
- A straightforward user interface that makes learning easy
- Excellent on-line help

As I listened to the participants compile this list, I grew increasingly excited because Word can do every one of these tasks—and more. This book will show you how to tap these Word features.

Word takes advantage of Microsoft Windows to give the user a straightforward interface—drop-down menus, dialog boxes, and icons—that makes it easy to jump in and get started. In addition, Word lets you customize the interface. For each type of document that you work on, you can have a hand-tailored set of menus, keyboard assignments, styles, glossary entries, and macros. You need not have Microsoft Windows to use Word; the Word program includes the Windows software you'll require.

Although you do not have to probe deeply into Word to get up to speed on the product, you'll find plenty of features to investigate down the road. Fields generate contents for you, such as the current date or the result of a calculation. Macros combine commands and actions, and Word includes an embedded BASIC programming language that you can use to create programs that extend Word's functionality.

What You Can Get from This Book

Although this book starts with a brief explanation of the basics of using Word, it moves quickly to the foundation of the program—Word's four most power-packed features, which I call its four pillars: styles, fields, macros, and templates. Throughout the book, you'll find descriptions of the concepts that underlie these four features. And you'll find clear directions for when, where, and how to apply these features to your work. Hands-on examples lead you through the procedures. I also give you tips about how to get even more out of the four pillars and out of the Word product in general. This inside information comes from my having been a member of the Word product design team, working alongside the developers since the project began.

This book is primarily for the user who has some experience with Word for Windows. You should already know the basics of Word for Windows. Or you should feel that you can pick up the basics from the brief refresher at the beginning of the book, which reviews starting and quitting Word, the basic Windows interface, and creating and refining documents. If you do not feel that you can pick up the basics quickly, you might want to work through the on-line tutorial that comes with Word or read *Learn Word for Windows Now* by Michael Boom, also published by Microsoft Press.

This book does not describe in detail Word's advanced programming aspects. But it does introduce those topics to readers who want to learn how to create advanced macros.

How This Book Is Divided

This book is divided into three parts. Part I begins with starting and quitting Word and then takes a look at the Windows interface, walking you through creating, editing, and printing a document, followed by formatting, polishing, and saving it. If you're familiar with these basics, either you can work through Part I as a quick refresher or you can skip it. If you're not familiar with the basics but can pick them up quickly, Part I teaches you what you need to know to get the most out of Parts II and III.

Part II makes up the bulk of the book and describes styles, fields, macros, and templates. You'll learn how to format using styles and how to insert text and graphics using fields. The discussion includes information about linking text and graphics within documents, across documents, and across Windows programs. These chapters also explain how to automate tasks by using macros and how to create templates, which set up standard documents for you instantly.

Part III explains additional Word features that can make the document creation process both easier and more powerful. You'll learn how to store and retrieve standard pieces of formatted text and graphics in glossaries. And you're in for a pleasant surprise when you read the chapter about tables because Word makes creating any size or type of table easy, even when your tables include spreadsheet-like calculations. In another chapter, you'll read about how to preview your documents to see the final page makeup plus how to make final text edits and how to position objects on the page. The final two chapters explain how to merge print—which helps you to create form letters, address lists, and so on—and how to create mathematical and scientific formulas and equations. An appendix gives you additional in-depth information about fields.

System Requirements

Like any program, Word is designed to run in a minimal hardware and software environment. Although running at the minimum might be less costly, it usually doesn't deliver the optimum operating results. The first of the following two lists shows the minimum system you need to run Word. The second list explains how you can soup up your computing environment for maximum Word performance.

Minimum System Requirements

Word requires the following minimum system to operate:

- 80286-based system (AT, AT-compatible)
- 640 KB of memory
- EGA video display card

NOTE: *Word will run on a CGA video display card, but the appearance is usually unsatisfactory. Also, the Word on-line tutorial will not run satisfactorily on a CGA system.*

- Local hard disk or connection to a network file server

NOTE: *The file server is intended for storing document files—and not Word program files—because the performance across networks is usually not fast enough.*

- MS-DOS 3.0 or later
- Optional: mouse

NOTE: *Microsoft Windows is not required. Word includes a run-time version of Windows 2.11. You can use this Windows version to run Word, but you cannot use it to run other applications at the same time or to transfer data between applications.*

Recommended System for Top Performance

If you'll be using Word heavily or if you want to run Word and other Windows applications at the same time (especially large applications such as Microsoft Excel), you'll want to enhance your computer system by following the recommendations listed on the next page. Your system will run faster and display fewer low-memory messages. The following enhancements are listed in the order in which you should add them:

- If you do not have a full version of Windows, buy one (version 2.11). The run-time version you received with Word provides the Windows interface for a single application only, including the Control Panel, Clipboard, and Spooler. With a full version of Windows, you can run more than one application at a time and transfer data from one application to another.
- If you have a full version of Windows, upgrade your copy to version 2.11. Word's Setup program provides an upgrade to Windows version 2.11. This version requires less memory and also does a better job of managing memory. To run Windows version 2.11, you need MS-DOS version 3.2 or later.
- Install at least 2 MB of memory (preferably expanded memory).
- After you have additional memory, run MEMSET.EXE from MS-DOS, which sets up 512 KB of memory as a disk cache with the SMARTDRV.SYS device driver. If you use RAMDRIVE.SYS to set up an emulated disk drive in memory, be sure you have version 2.10 or later. You see the version number when you start up your computer.
- Upgrade your equipment to an 80386-based system. Have at least 2 MB of memory installed.
- If you do not have a mouse, add one.
- Upgrade your keyboard to one with 12 function keys so that you'll have additional keys (8 combinations) for choosing commands and actions easily.
- For aesthetic reasons, upgrade your display to at least an EGA video display card that has 256 KB of memory. VGA provides additional display refinement.

PART I

Getting the Basics Down

If you need a quick review of the basic skills that are required to use Word for Windows, this is the place to begin.

Part I reviews setting up Word, choosing commands, moving around in a document, and selecting text. You also learn how to adjust Word to suit your working style and your word-processing tasks. The choices you'll have as you work with Word will become more clear to you as you read Part II, but this introduction will make working with Word more comfortable from the beginning. Part I also reviews the basic document process. You create a document that contains text and graphics, proofread and edit the document, and then print it. To finish, you reorganize and format the example document, preview it before you print it, add a table of contents and an index, and save the document. You also learn how to find documents on disk and how to open more than one document at a time. When you finish Part I, you'll be ready to learn about the features that make Word for Windows special and to advance to an intermediate level of use.

Chapter 1

Setting Up, Starting, and Quitting

Here's a brief look at how to run the Word for Windows Setup program and what happens during setup, plus how to start and quit Word.

Setting Up Word

Word comes with a Setup program. You run the Setup program to copy the files you need and to set up your computer's memory for maximum performance from Word. The Setup program also sets up your printer to work with the Word for Windows program.

To set up Word:

1. Be sure you're in MS-DOS and that drive A is active.
2. Insert the Setup disk in drive A and type *Setup*.
3. Press the Enter key, and follow the directions that appear on your screen.

The Setup program copies the following files to the directory you specify or to a default directory:

- Word program
- Hyphenation file
- Dictionary and program files for the speller, the thesaurus, and on-line help

- Documentation files of sample documents and templates
- Conversion program files for converting files between the Word for Windows file format and the file formats of the leading word-processing programs (check your Word package for possible notice of additional conversions for which you can send)
- Graphics-import programs for importing graphics from Lotus and several computer-aided design (CAD) programs
- Printer-driver files and other Windows files if the version of Windows installed on your machine is earlier than 2.11

TIP

Making Your Word Directory Cleaner

If you leave the setup as it is after you run the Setup program, you can run Word with no problems. Your Word program directory will be cluttered with files, however, which makes it harder to isolate various types of files. Word gives you a tool for isolating file types—a special section in the file named WIN.INI, which is in the directory that contains your Windows program. Files that end with the extension INI contain information that directs the file's related program during the program's start-up phase. For example, an INI file might contain settings for windows, user preferences such as the choice of printer, colors, and modes of operation. You can edit most INI files (although not the INI file for Word, named WINWORD.INI) using any text editor or word processor that can save a file as plain text (ASCII file format); therefore, you can use Word to edit the WIN.INI file. To add instructions to WIN.INI and isolate file types in their own directories, open WIN.INI and find the heading "Microsoft Word" enclosed in square brackets. Under the heading, type the following three lines:

```
ini-path=
dot-path=
util-path=
```

After the equal sign (=) in each of those lines, type the pathname to indicate where you want to store these types of files.

If you do not specify a directory, Setup proposes \WINWORD on your computer's first hard-disk drive (usually drive C). The Setup program also copies a run-time version of Windows onto your disk if you do not have Windows installed. This run-time version of Windows allows you to use Word in the Windows environment but not to run more than one application at a time or to transfer data from one application to another. The run-time Windows files that the Setup program copies include screen, keyboard, mouse, and printer-driver files. Setup might alter your AUTOEXEC.BAT file to add the directories for Windows and Word to your PATH variable—a command that tells MS-DOS where to look for files—but will not destroy your current PATH.

```
[Microsoft Word]
Status=1
LookHelp=1
MaxApp=1
MaxDoc=0
LoadCoreCode=yes
ini-path=c:\winword\ini
dot-path=c:\winword\dot      ├ Path entries
util-path=c:\winword\util
```

The INI path is for the WINWORD.INI file, which stores the Word settings. You'll learn more about these settings in Chapter 3, "Personalizing Word for Windows." By using this line in your WIN.INI file, you direct Word to create and store its WINWORD.INI file in the directory in which you want it, instead of in the directory in which you store the Word program. The DOT path is for template files. You'll learn more about templates in Chapter 6, "Using Word's Four Pillars: Styles, Fields, Macros, and Templates," and in Chapter 11, "Templates." If you create this entry, be sure to move all files that have DOT filename extensions from your Word program directory to your new DOT directory. The UTIL path is for spelling, hyphenation, thesaurus, conversion, and help files. Be sure to move these files from the Word program directory to your new UTIL directory. If you need more information about MS-DOS directories and how to create them, see your MS-DOS user documentation.

A special feature of the Setup program also helps you set up your computer's memory to get the best performance from Windows and Word. Setup might alter your CONFIG.SYS file by adding a "DEVICE=" line for SMARTDRV.SYS. SMARTDRV.SYS is a device driver that controls a special area in computer memory—called a disk cache—that stores parts of the Word program so that the program runs faster.

Starting Word

You can start Word either from MS-DOS or from Windows. When you start Word from the MS-DOS prompt, you type *winword* followed by start-up variations that tell Word what kind of task you want to accomplish. When you start Word from Windows, you take either of two approaches. You can select WINWORD.EXE, choose the Windows File Run command, and type any start-up variations in the File Run dialog box. Or you can double-click WINWORD.EXE or any Word for Windows document name shown in the MS-DOS Executive window. Whether you start Word from MS-DOS or from Windows depends on how you like to work and what you're doing on your computer when you decide to start Word.

When Word starts, you see the screen shown below:

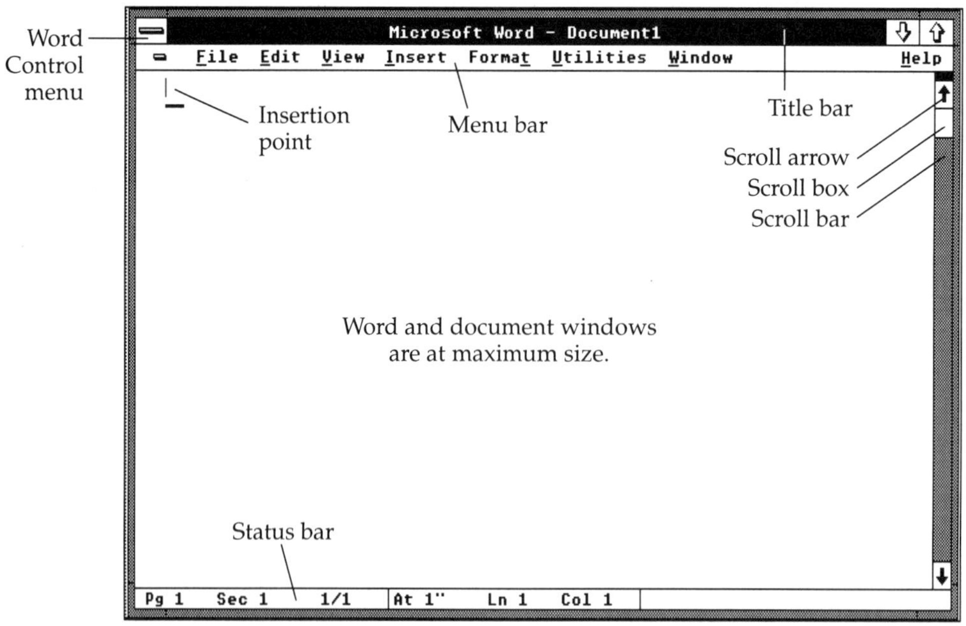

Chapter 3, "Personalizing Word for Windows," explains screen elements in addition to those shown above and shows how you can alter the screen.

Starting Word from MS-DOS

Before you start Word, change to the directory in which you want to store documents. Be sure to store your documents in a directory other than the Word program's.

If you're starting Word from MS-DOS, you type *winword* followed by any variations you might want and press the Enter key. The following sections explain the variations you can choose from. If you type no variations, Word creates a blank new document named Document1.

To start and run the tutorial

Type *winword /t* and press the Enter key to start Word and run the online tutorial.

To start with no document

Type *winword /n* and press the Enter key to start Word with no document. Use this approach only if, without first having a document open, you want to run or record a macro; open, create, or find a file; run the tutorial; or read help information.

To start and open an existing document

Type *winword document-name* and press the Enter key to start Word and open an existing document. You can type up to nine document names, and Word will open them all, in the order in which you typed them. For a document that is not in the active directory, you can type the name of the directory in which the document is stored (pathname). For example, you could type the following line:

```
winword report c:\document\status letter
```

If a document does not exist, Word displays a dialog box that includes three buttons: Open, New, and Cancel. If you choose the Open button (Alt+O), Word displays the File Open dialog box. If you choose the New button (Alt+N), Word displays the File New dialog box. And if you choose the Cancel button (Esc), Word creates a generic document (Document1), as if you had started Word without a document name.

To start and run a macro

Type *winword /mmacro-name* and press the Enter key to start Word and run a macro. You must precede each macro name with the /m switch, leaving no space between the /m and the first letter of the macro name. You can type as many macro names as you want, and Word will run them all, in the order in which you typed them. For example, you would type the following to run two macros named file1 and Reset Menu:

```
winword /mfile1 /mResetMenu
```

If you mix document names and macro names, Word opens all the documents first and then starts running the macros. For example, you would type the following to open a document named report and run two macros named file1 and Auto Exec:

```
winword report /mfile1 /mAutoExec
```

Starting Word from Windows

When you start from Windows, you have the same options as when you start Word from MS-DOS: You can type multiple document and macro names or a mixture of the two. Word opens all the documents in the order in which you typed them and then runs any macros that you specified.

To start and create a new document

Double-click WINWORD.EXE to start Word with a blank new document named Document1. You can also use the alternative method: Select WINWORD.EXE, choose the File Run command, and then choose OK.

TIP

Getting the Best Performance from Expanded Memory

If you have expanded memory installed in your computer, you can start Windows a special way for best performance. Start Windows by typing *Win /n* and pressing the Enter key. Then, start Word using one of the methods described above for "Starting Word from Windows." Note, however, that if you will be running other applications at the same time as Word, you must start Windows without the /n switch.

To use File Run to start

Choose the File Run command when you want to start Word and do any of the following: open an existing document, run a macro, start with no document, or run the on-line tutorial.

After you choose File Run and the File Run dialog box appears, type *winword* and a space in the Run box. Then, type one of the following, depending on what you want to do: a document name, */m* followed by a macro name, */n* (no document), or */t* (tutorial). Precede each macro name with the /m switch, leaving no space between the /m and the first letter of the macro name. Choose OK. For documents that are not in the active directory, you can type the full pathname. This approach works in the same way as starting Word from MS-DOS. You can type as many document or macro names as you want, or mix the two, and Word opens all documents and then runs any macros. For an idea of what you might type in the File Run dialog box, see the two entry examples in the earlier section "Starting Word from MS-DOS."

Quitting Word

How you quit Word depends on whether you want to quit to Windows or to MS-DOS. When you quit, Word checks to see whether you've saved the changes to all open documents. If you have not saved your changes, Word asks if you want to save them.

To quit from Word to Windows, use any one of the following methods:

- Choose the File Exit command.
- Choose the Word Control Close command.
- Press the Alt+F4 keys.

You're now in MS-DOS Executive.

TIP

Running Word Under Windows Version 3.0

If you are running Word with version 3.0 of Microsoft Windows, add the line *files=60* to your CONFIG.SYS file. If you already have a "files=" line in your CONFIG.SYS file, be sure the number is no lower than 60. But unless you have a specific reason to set the number higher than 60, use 60 to keep your system as fast as possible.

To quit from Word to MS-DOS, press the Alt+Esc keys until MS-DOS Executive is active. Then, use any one of the following methods to return to MS-DOS:

- Choose the File Exit command.
- Choose the Windows Control Close command.
- Press the Alt+F4 keys.

This second method is a shortcut because it lets you use MS-DOS Executive to quit Word and Windows at the same time.

Chapter 2

Word for Windows Essentials

To use Word for Windows effectively, you need to be familiar with a few essentials: how to use commands from both the menus and the keyboard, how to move around in a document quickly, and how to select text for such tasks as editing and formatting. This chapter explains how to accomplish these tasks in Word. If you need more information about Windows, see *Microsoft Windows, Basic Skills for Windows Applications,* which came with your copy of Word.

Keep in mind that Word, like all Windows programs, is based on an object-action model—that is, you select an object and then choose an action that affects that object, as Figure 2-1 on the next page shows. In Word, the object you select is text, a graphic, or a table. The action you choose is a command.

Although this chapter explains the methods you use to choose commands, it does not describe the commands themselves. You'll find descriptions of specific commands throughout this book.

Using Commands

Word has two kinds of commands: those that perform an action as soon as you choose the command and those that ask for more information first. Some commands you choose from a menu. Other commands you

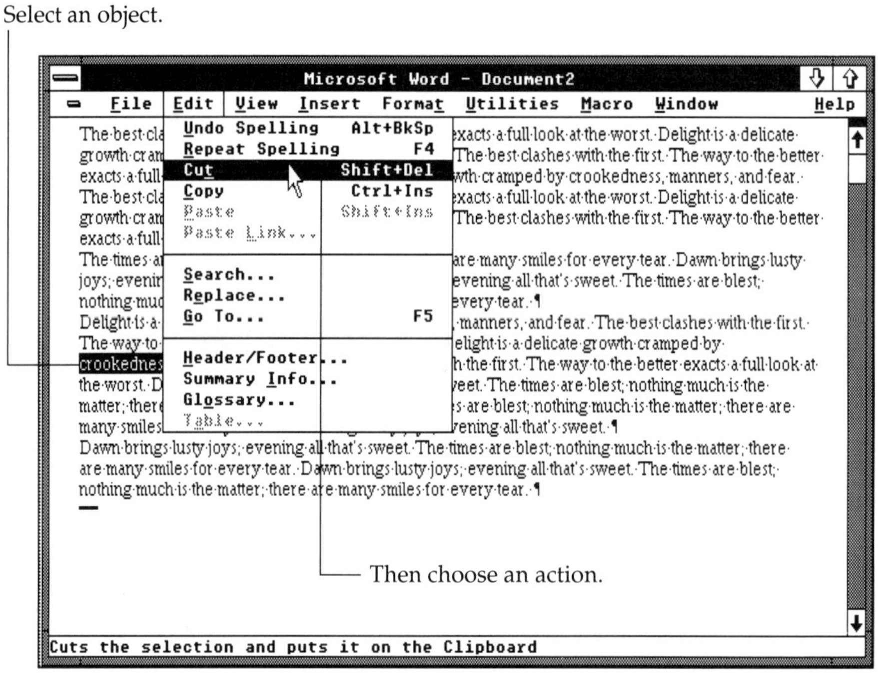

Figure 2-1.
Object-action model.

choose by pressing the key(s) to which these commands are assigned, called keyboard shortcuts. (You can find available keyboard shortcuts in the menus, to the right of the command names.)

When you choose a menu command whose name is not followed by an ellipsis (...), Word performs the action immediately. When you choose a menu command whose name is followed by an ellipsis, Word displays a dialog box in which you give additional information, and then Word carries out the action. If you choose a command using a keyboard shortcut and Word needs more information, a message appears in the bottom-left corner of the screen. For most keyboard shortcut commands that show messages, you can display a dialog box by using the same keyboard shortcut a second time. Later in this chapter, "Commands Assigned to Keys" explains more about keyboard shortcuts.

Pressing the Esc key gets you out of most commands. If it's too late to use Esc—that is, if the command has already finished its work—you can usually use the Edit Undo command (Alt+Backspace) instead if you choose it immediately. Edit Undo restores your work to the way it was before you chose the command that you want to reverse. Esc and Edit Undo do not always work, however. For example, you cannot use Esc or Edit Undo after you start to save a file or start to quit Word.

Opening and Using Menus

To open a menu, position the mouse pointer on the menu name and click the left mouse button. You can also use the keyboard both to open a menu and to choose a command: Press the Alt key, and then press the key for the underlined letter in the menu name. For example, press Alt,F to open the File menu, and then press the S key to choose the Save command. For the Word Control menu, press Alt,spacebar to open the menu. And for the Document Control menu, press Alt,hyphen key.

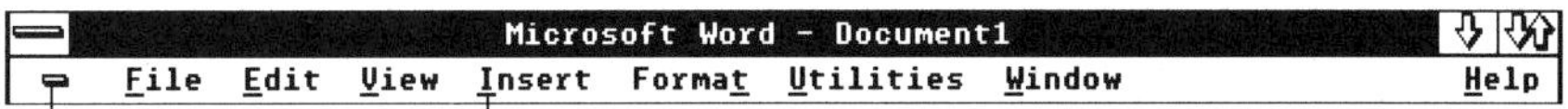

Document Control menu

Underline indicates key that opens menu.

Word has two sets of menus—short menus and full menus. To see which set of menus you currently have, scan the menu bar for the Macro menu. If you do not see it, Word is set up in its short menus mode. If you do see it, Word is set up in its full menus mode. You can also open the View menu to see which set of menus is displayed:

Press Alt and then press V to open the View menu.

Press the down arrow key to highlight a command name.

At the bottom of the View menu, you see either the Full Menus or the Short Menus command—whichever of the two you're not currently using. The short menus set is designed primarily for beginning users and excludes the more sophisticated commands. The full menus set displays all commands on the menus and gives you access to all Word features.

To move from menu to menu, press the left or right arrow key. Notice the commands on each menu. Now, return to the View menu and choose either the Full Menus or Short Menus command (whichever is displayed) to see the other menu set. Activate the menu bar again by pressing the Alt key or by clicking a menu name using the mouse. Look through the menus again to see the difference.

When you finish exploring the menu sets, be sure that the full menus are selected because the descriptions in this book assume that you're using full menus. The View menu should show the Short Menus command.

Using a dialog box

After you choose a command that displays a dialog box, you'll find in the dialog box various boxes and buttons (called controls) for collecting information and for helping you make your choices. Often, all controls in a dialog box are already set, so if you're satisfied with the settings, you can leave them as they are. Or you can change only those settings that currently need changing.

When you finish setting the dialog box controls, choose the OK button, and the command does its task. But if you decide not to carry out the command after all, choose the Cancel button to cancel the command and close the dialog box.

The following examples show the parts of a dialog box:

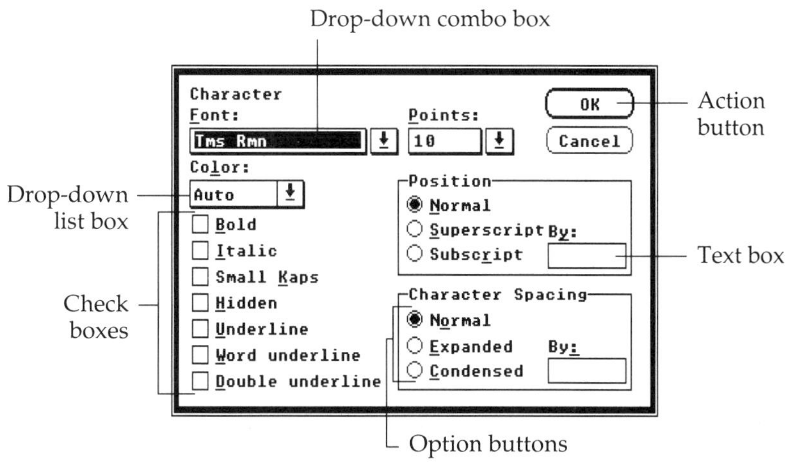

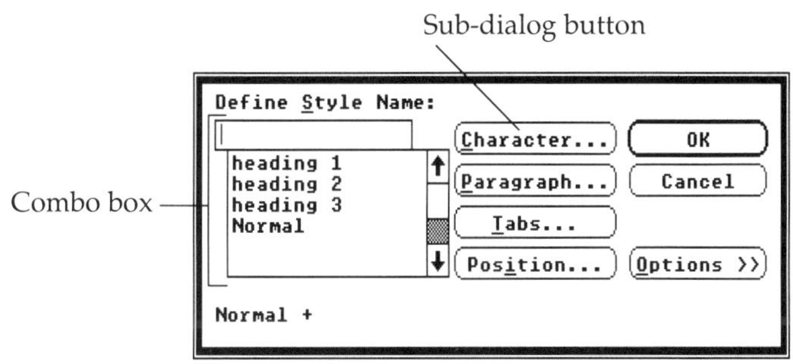

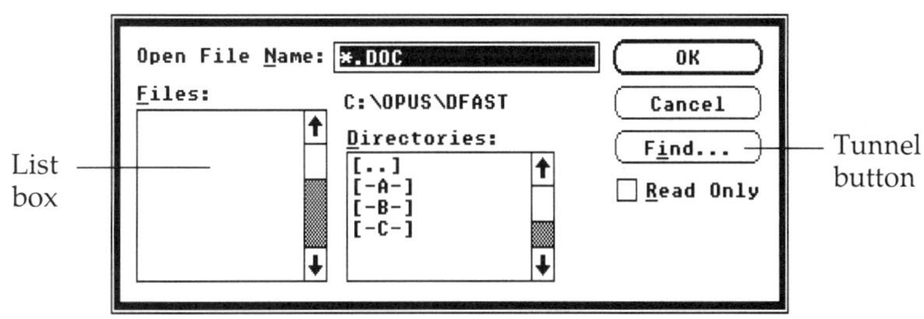

Text box. In a text box, you type a response, such as a name or a measurement.

Command buttons. You use the following three types of command buttons to perform an action or to display another dialog box: action, tunnel, and sub-dialog.

Action button. You press an action button to perform such standard actions as OK, Cancel, Close, Options (displays the full dialog box), Define, Insert, and Delete.

Tunnel button. You use a tunnel button to close the active dialog box and to open another dialog box that's closely related to the first. This button is a convenience that lets you bypass the menu, as if you were going through a tunnel to another dialog box. A tunnel button's name includes an ellipsis.

Sub-dialog button. A sub-dialog button opens another closely related dialog box, called the sub-dialog box, without closing the first dialog box. When you close the sub-dialog box, the original dialog box becomes active again. You use sub-dialog buttons primarily when you define, rename, or merge items in the original dialog box—for example, when you work with styles. A sub-dialog button indicates that a dialog box has a dialog box of its own, in the same way that some commands have dialog boxes. A sub-dialog button's name includes an ellipsis.

List box. A list box lists all your choices. If the list contains more items than can be displayed at one time, the list box includes a scroll bar. Press a key that matches the first character of an item in the list to select and highlight that item. Press the key again to select the next choice that matches, and so on.

Drop-down list box. A drop-down list box also lists all your choices. To drop the list so that you can see the items it contains, click the down arrow box to the right of the current choice, press the Alt key and the down arrow key together, or press F4. Press these keys or click the down arrow box a second time to close the list. The current choice is shown in the box when the list is not dropped down. When it is dropped down, the selected item is highlighted. Again, press a key that matches the first character of a choice in the list to select the first choice that matches, regardless of whether the list is closed or dropped down. Press the key again to select the next choice that matches, and so on.

Combo box. A combo box lists possible choices and lets you type your own response if what you want is not in the list. A combo box is a combination of a text box and a list box. Press the down arrow key to select an item from the list. The selected item is then highlighted.

Drop-down combo box. A drop-down combo box also lists possible choices and lets you type your own response. To drop down the list so that you can see the items it contains, click the down arrow box to the right of the current choice, press the Alt key and the down arrow key together, or press F4. Pressing these keys or clicking the down arrow box a second time closes the list. The current choice is shown in the box when the box is not dropped down. When the list is dropped down, the selected item is highlighted. If you type part of a choice and then drop the list, Word selects the first choice that matches what you typed.

Check box. You use a check box to turn on or turn off an option. When a check box is turned on, it has an X inside it. You can turn on any combination of check boxes in a dialog box.

Option button. Option buttons show all your choices when the number of choices is limited to usually no more than three or four choices. When you choose an option button, a black dot appears inside it. Within a single group of options, you can select only one option button at a time. A dialog box might contain more than one group of option buttons.

Gray settings in dialog boxes

If you select a block of text and want to review any settings regarding that text, you can choose the command you want and then check the settings in the dialog box. This approach works well if the entire block of text is set up in the same way. (“Selecting Text,” later in this chapter, explains how to select text in Word.)

Occasionally, however, you select text that contains more than one setting. For example, you might select text only part of which is boldface. When a selection contains a number of settings, the dialog box cannot show all of them, so it shows you that there's a mixture by filling check boxes with gray; by leaving option buttons, text boxes, and combo boxes blank; and by showing no highlighted settings in lists. If enough memory is available and the mixture of settings is not complex, however, Word grays only the settings that are actually mixed and shows the settings that are not mixed.

For example, suppose you select italicized text that also contains some boldface, as in the following:

> ***First*** *things first*

The Format Character dialog box shows the following settings:

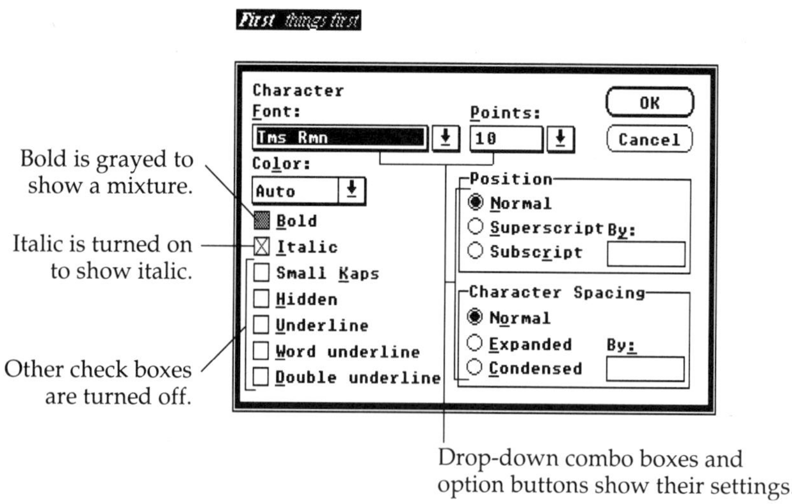

When a dialog box contains gray settings, you have several choices. You can leave the gray settings as they are, which retains the mixture in the selection, or you can change any setting as you normally would. If you change a gray setting, you make that setting the same for all the selected text.

TIP

Double-Clicking Your Choices

You can double-click an option button to choose it and to close the dialog box in one quick action. This approach is the same as choosing the option and then choosing OK.

Moving around in a dialog box

After a dialog box is open, you can press the Tab key to move forward through the controls (for example, boxes, lists, buttons) one at a time and the Shift+Tab keys to move backward. You use the spacebar to turn on or turn off check boxes or to choose the selected command button. For option buttons, use the arrow keys to cycle through the options. In a dialog box that contains many controls, using Tab and the spacebar can be tedious. Instead, you can move directly to any control or setting and activate it by using either the mouse or the keyboard. Using the mouse, click the box, list, or button that you want. Using the keyboard, press the Alt key and the letter that's underlined in the control's name.

Commands Assigned to Keys

You've already seen how you can choose commands from menus by pressing the Alt key. For example, pressing Alt,E,C first displays the Edit menu and then chooses the Copy command. To the right of the Copy command in the menu, a keyboard shortcut is listed: Ctrl+Insert. If you press Ctrl+Insert, you save a step because you bypass the Edit menu and choose Copy directly.

Some Word commands that appear on menus have keyboard shortcuts. For example, Ctrl+Insert is a shortcut for the Edit Copy command, and F5 is a shortcut for the Edit Go To command. Word also contains commands that are assigned only to keys and that do not appear on a menu. For example, the MOVE command is assigned to F2, and the

TIP

Getting to a Dialog Box

Any keyboard shortcut command that displays a message on the screen opens the related dialog box if you use the same keyboard shortcut a second time. For example, if you press the Ctrl+F keys so that you can enter a font name and the ribbon is not turned on, the message "Which font name?" appears. You can type the name of the font you want to use, if you're sure of the spelling (including uppercase and lowercase letters) and its availability. If you press Ctrl+F a second time, Word displays the Format Character dialog box, which contains a list of the available fonts.

SEARCH AGAIN command is assigned to the Shift+F4 key combination. Some of these key commands and shortcut keys need additional information, but instead of displaying a dialog box, they display a message at the bottom-left of the screen. That message lets you know what to do next or what information to type.

Word also contains keyboard commands that toggle operational modes. For example, the Ins key toggles between inserting text between characters and inserting text over characters as you type (called overtype mode). Such toggle keys turn on indicator labels in the status bar at the bottom of the screen to show the current mode. (If the status bar is turned off, you will not see the indicator labels.)

The following table shows the mode keys and their indicators:

Key(s)	*Indicator*	*Mode*
F8	EXT	Extends the selection
Ctrl+Shift+F8	COL	Selects a column
Ins	OVR	Switches between overtype and insert
CapsLock	CAPS	Types letter keys to insert capital letters
NumLock	NUM	Types numeric keypad keys to insert numbers

Moving Around in a Document

To move the insertion point around in your document, you use keys, the mouse, or the Edit Go To command. All actions take place from the insertion point. When you begin typing again, Word inserts the characters at the insertion point, which appears as a blinking vertical bar. If you select text or a graphic, the insertion point is at one end of the selection.

Moving Around Using Keys

When you use keys to move through a document, you're simply moving the insertion point. You use the cursor keys, which are the numeric keypad keys shown in the table below. Some keyboards have an additional set of cursor keys, located between the keypad and the typing keys. The NumLock key toggles the keypad between inserting numbers (numeric keypad) and moving the insertion point (cursor keys). The extra set of cursor keys between the numeric keypad and the typing keys lets you leave the NumLock key turned on (numeric keypad), which is handy if you like to use the numeric keypad to type a lot of numbers.

Key	*Action*
→	Moves right one character (same line)
←	Moves left one character (same line)
↓	Moves down one line (same column)
↑	Moves up one line (same column)
Home	Moves to the beginning of the line
End	Moves to the end of the line
PgDn	Moves down one windowful
PgUp	Moves up one windowful
Ctrl+→	Moves right one word
Ctrl+←	Moves left one word
Ctrl+PgUp	Moves to the top line of the window
Ctrl+PgDn	Moves to the bottom line of the window
Ctrl+↑	Moves to the beginning of the current paragraph
Ctrl+↓	Moves to the beginning of the next paragraph
Ctrl+Home	Moves to the beginning of the document
Ctrl+End	Moves to the end of the document

Moving Around Using the Mouse

If you scroll through your document using the mouse, the insertion point does not move. You'll find this approach handy if you want to see something elsewhere in your document and then continue typing where you were. If you start scrolling with the mouse and then press a key or choose a command that moves the insertion point, however, the insertion point moves to the first character in the current windowful of text. In this way, you can mix mouse and keyboard scrolling.

Keys and commands that move the insertion point are the arrow keys, the REPEAT SEARCH key combination (Shift+F4), the NEXT FIELD key (F11 or Alt+F1), the PREVIOUS FIELD key combination (Shift+F11 or Alt+Shift+F1), the GO TO key (F5), the Edit Go To command, the Edit Search command, and the Edit Replace command.

The following table shows what to click on the screen to scroll using the mouse:

Click Here	*To Scroll Document*
Up scroll arrow	Up one line
Down scroll arrow	Down one line
Right scroll arrow	Right one column
Left scroll arrow	Left one column (Hold down the Shift key while you click the left scroll arrow to scroll into the left margin.)
Scroll bar between scroll box and scroll arrow	One windowful in the direction of the scroll arrow
Horizontal scroll box	Back from the left margin so that the zero point on the ruler lines up with the edge of the window (normal position)

Moving by percentage using the mouse

You can also use the mouse to scroll a percentage of the way through a document by dragging the scroll box in the vertical scroll bar to a position that represents the percentage that you want. For example, to scroll halfway through the document, drag the vertical scroll box to the middle of the vertical scroll bar.

TIP

Returning to the Original Insertion Point After Mouse Scrolling

Suppose you use the mouse to scroll to another part of a document and then want to continue typing at the insertion point. To do so, you need to return the text that contains the insertion point to the window. Press the GO BACK key combination (Shift+F5) to quickly return to the insertion point.

Moving Around Using the Edit Go To Command

When you want to move the insertion point to a specific destination in a single bound, use the Edit Go To command. You can also choose Edit Go To by pressing the GO TO key (F5). If you press F5 a second time, the Edit Go To dialog box appears.

After you choose Edit Go To, you specify a destination by either typing the destination or selecting a bookmark name. A destination can be one of the following:

- A specific destination, such as L330, which takes you to line 330
- A relative destination, such as P+30, which takes you forward 30 pages
- A percentage destination, such as 25%, which takes you to a point one-quarter of the way into the document

Specific destinations

Each specific Go To destination has three parts: a section number, a page number, and an item number. The item number can be a line number, a footnote number, or an annotation number, as shown in the following illustration:

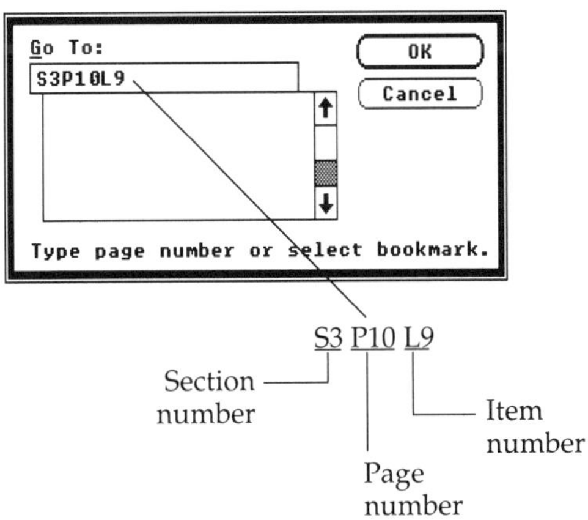

You can include all three parts of the Go To destination in any order, or you can omit any part—but what you include determines how Word looks for your destination. For example, if you type *S3P10L9*, Word looks for the ninth line on the tenth page of the third section. But if you leave out the section and page information and then type *L109*, Word looks for the 109th line in the document, even if lines 1 through 109 contain more than one section.

Relative destinations

You can also use the Edit Go To command to move the insertion point relative distances. For example, if you type *P–10* you can move the insertion point back 10 pages. Type *L+100* to move the insertion point forward 100 lines. If a destination contains two or more parts, only the largest part of the destination address can be relative. So, although S–4P5 works (tells Word to go back four sections and then find the fifth page in that section), S10P–5 does not work. It does not work because only the larger part—the section, in this case—can be relative.

Percent destinations

The Edit Go To command also lets you move a percentage of the way through your document. Type any percentage, and Word moves the insertion point that far. For example, type *33%* to move about one-third of the way into a document. If you type a percentage greater than 100%, Word moves the insertion point to the document's end.

You cannot use percentages and the other types of destinations together.

Bookmark destinations

A bookmark is a name you assign to a piece of text or to a particular place in a document so that you can find that text or place again. In

TIP

Combining "Go To" Jumps

If you're unsure about which page you want to go to but you know that it's near a specific location in your document, you can do a jump in two steps. First, go to the specific destination. Then, go to the relative destination. For example, to go to the fifth page before the beginning of Chapter 4 (Section 4) in your document, choose the Edit Go To command to jump to S4 and then choose Edit Go To again to go to P–5.

Word, a bookmark is like a combination of a paper bookmark and the ink highlighting that you might use in a book.

You can jump to specific text by using a bookmark name as the Edit Go To command's destination. When you specify a bookmark, Word jumps to the location and selects the text that is marked by the bookmark. A bookmark can mark either an insertion point or any size selection. When you choose Edit Go To or press the GO TO key (F5) twice, you see a list of all bookmarks in the document. You can type or select any name in the list.

You cannot use bookmarks and the other types of destinations together.

A summary of Go To destinations

The following lists show the section, page, and item destinations that you can type in the Edit Go To dialog box. You can also mix destination parts, as the examples following these lists show.

Section Destinations	*Go To*
S, S+, or S+1	Start of next section
S– or S–1	Start of previous section
S*n*	Start of section number *n*
S+*n*	Start of section, *n* number of sections after the current section
S–*n*	Start of section, *n* number of sections before the current section

Page Destinations	*Go To*
P, P+, or P+1 (or leave the dialog box blank)	Start of next page
P– or P–1	Start of previous page
P*n*	Start of page number *n* of whole document
P+*n*	Start of page, *n* number of pages after the current page
P–*n*	Start of page, *n* number of pages before the current page

Line Destinations	*Go To*
L, L+, or L+1	Beginning of next line
L– or L–1	Beginning of previous line
L*n*	Beginning of line number *n* of whole document
L+*n*	Beginning of line, *n* number of lines after the current line
L–*n*	Beginning of line, *n* number of lines before the current line

Footnote Destinations	*Go To*
F, F+, or F+1	Next footnote
F– or F–1	Previous footnote
F*n*	Footnote number *n* of whole document
F+*n*	Footnote, *n* number of footnotes after the current footnote
F–*n*	Footnote, *n* number of footnotes before the current footnote

Annotation Destinations	*Go To*
A, A+, or A+1	Next annotation
A– or A–1	Previous annotation
A*n*	Annotation number *n* of whole document
A+*n*	Annotation, *n* number of annotations after the current annotation
A–*n*	Annotation, *n* number of annotations before the current annotation

You can mix these destination parts. For example, type *SnPn* to move the insertion point to the start of page *n* in section *n*. Or you can type *S–2L10* to move the insertion point to the tenth line from the beginning of the section that's two sections before the current section. And type *69L2* to move the insertion point to the second line on page 69. If you type *FS* in the Edit Go To dialog box, the insertion point moves to the first footnote of the next section. If you type *FS2P3*, the insertion point moves to the first footnote on the third page of Section 2. And if you type *P+10A8*, Word moves the insertion point to the eighth annotation on the tenth page after the current page.

Selecting Text

You select text when you want to do something to it—for example, format it or copy it. To select text means to expand a highlighted area from the insertion point across all the characters you want. If you use the keyboard to select, hold down the Shift key while you move the insertion point. If you use the mouse, you can click, double-click, or drag to select, with or without Shift.

Using the Keyboard to Select Text

Along with the Shift key, you use the EXTEND SELECTION key (F8), the SHRINK SELECTION key combination (Shift+F8), and the COLUMN SELECTION (Ctrl+Shift+F8) key combination when you use the keyboard to select text.

Hold down Shift while pressing the arrow keys that move the insertion point. When the highlight includes all the text and graphics that you want to select, release Shift. For a review of which keys move the insertion point, see "Moving Around Using Keys" earlier in this chapter.

If you're selecting to a faraway spot in a document or if you want to select text that Word recognizes as a text unit (word, sentence, and so on), use the EXTEND SELECTION key (F8). When you press F8, "EXT" appears in the status bar, and you can select without holding down the Shift key. You can also select by pressing any character key; the selection extends to the next character that matches the one you type, including jumping to the next paragraph mark when you press the Enter key.

If you press F8 again, the selection expands to the next larger unit of text. For example, if you press F8 and begin selecting words, pressing F8 again selects sentences. The extend mode is canceled whenever you press the Esc key or choose a command that affects the selection. Pressing Esc, however, does not remove the selection.

The counterpart to the EXTEND SELECTION key (F8) is the SHRINK SELECTION key combination (Shift+F8). When you press Shift+F8, the selection shrinks to the next smaller unit of text. If you extend the selection using the EXTEND SELECTION key, the SHRINK SELECTION key combination shrinks the selection back through the same selections the EXTEND SELECTION key made. If you did not use the EXTEND SELECTION key, Word shrinks to the first unit in the selection that's the next smaller size. For example, if you select a paragraph and then press Shift+F8, the selection shrinks to the first sentence in the paragraph.

Sentence selected; press F8 twice to extend selection to paragraph.

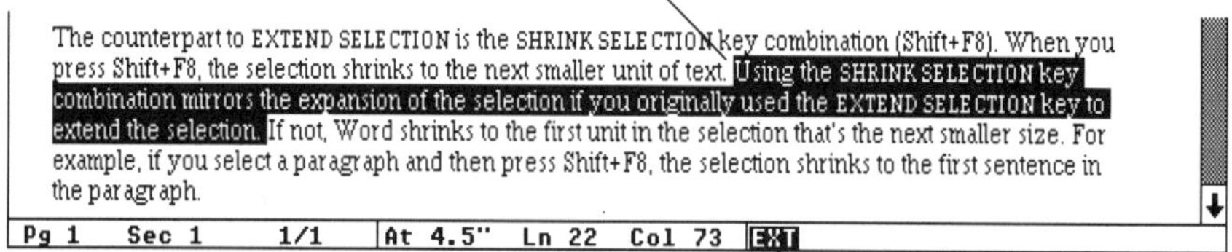

EXT is displayed in status bar.

Paragraph selected; press Shift + F8 to shrink selection.

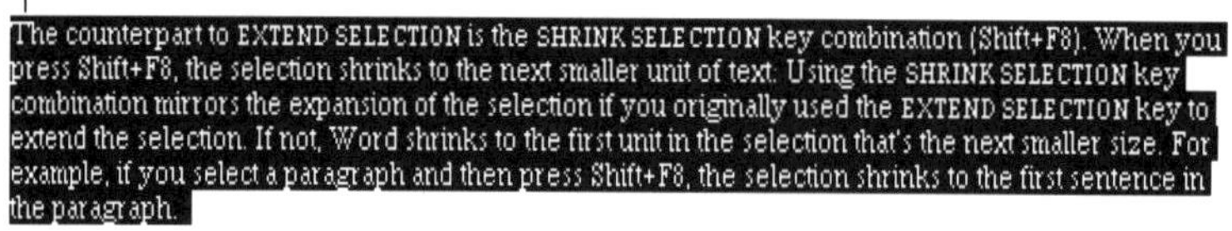

Selection has shrunk to previously selected sentence.

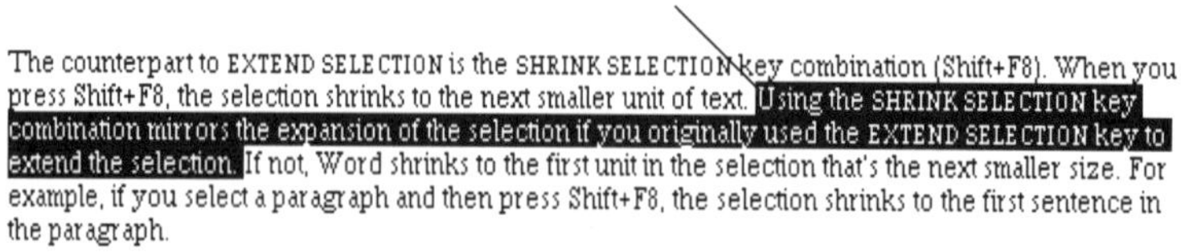

For tables, columns of text that contain tab stops, and even regular text, you can select in columns. First, position the insertion point at a corner of the column, and then turn on the column select mode by pressing the COLUMN SELECTION key combination (Ctrl+Shift+F8). Then, move the insertion point to the opposite corner of the column. You can select up or down, or you can select right or left. The column select mode is canceled whenever you press the Esc key or choose a command that affects the selection. Pressing Esc, however, does not remove the selection.

Using the Mouse to Select Text

Perhaps the greatest benefit of having a mouse is using it to select text. You can use the mouse along with the Shift key or the Ctrl key—or with the COLUMN SELECTION key combination (Ctrl+Shift+F8)—to select text. You can also use the mouse alone to select by clicking, double-clicking, and dragging. You can use these mouse methods in document text and in the selection bar, which is an invisible column along the left edge of the window. The selection bar is explained in greater detail on the next page in "Using the mouse with the selection bar."

Clicking and double-clicking the mouse to select text

Hold down the Shift key, and then click anywhere in the document to select from the insertion point to the spot at which you click. To select a sentence, hold down the Ctrl key and then click anywhere in the sentence. To select a word, double-click anywhere in the word.

Dragging the mouse to select text

Move the mouse pointer to the start of the text that you want to select, hold down the mouse button, and then move the mouse to expand the selection in any direction you want. The selection expands character by character.

To select by words or by sentences instead, select a word or a sentence but continue to hold down the mouse button and then drag. For example, hold down the Ctrl key, hold down the mouse button, and then drag to expand the selection by sentences.

Using the mouse with the selection bar

The selection bar is an invisible column along the left edge of the window. You know when the mouse pointer is in the selection bar because the pointer changes shape to an arrow that points upward and to the right. You can click, double-click, and drag in the selection bar to select the text you want.

To select a line, click in the selection bar. To select a paragraph, double-click in the selection bar. To select the whole document, hold down the Ctrl key while you click in the selection bar.

When you drag in the selection bar, how the selection expands depends on what your original selection was. For example, if you double-click but hold down the mouse button after the second click, dragging in the selection bar expands the selection by paragraphs.

Using the mouse to select by columns

To select by columns when you select with the mouse, use the COLUMN SELECTION key combination (Ctrl+Shift+F8). Position the insertion point at any corner of the column that you want to select, press the Ctrl+Shift+F8 keys to turn on column select mode, and then point to the opposite corner of the column and click either mouse button. You can also position the mouse pointer at one corner of the column, hold down the right mouse button, and drag to the opposite corner of the column to select by columns.

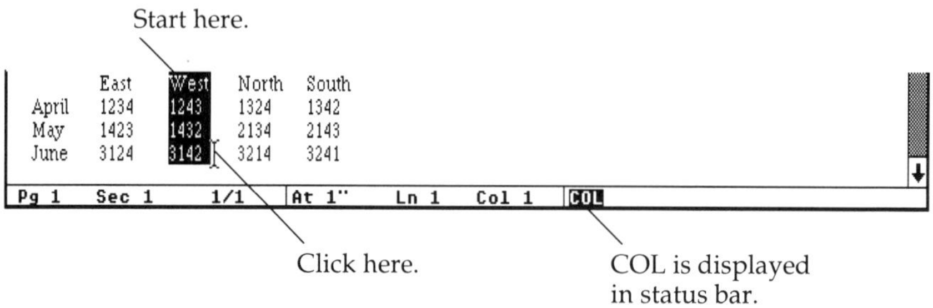

For fun, you can turn on column select mode by pressing the Ctrl+Shift+F8 keys and then point somewhere away from the insertion point, hold down the mouse button, and move the mouse in a circle to make the column selection rotate around the insertion point.

Using the Mouse in Windows

When you use a Windows application such as Word, special areas on the screen respond to mouse actions. These areas are in addition to those areas on the screen that you use to choose commands, to move around your document, and to select. The following sections give you a quick look at these screen areas, which you click, drag, or double-click to produce the response you want.

Areas that you click

The following are the areas of the screen that respond when you use the mouse to click them:

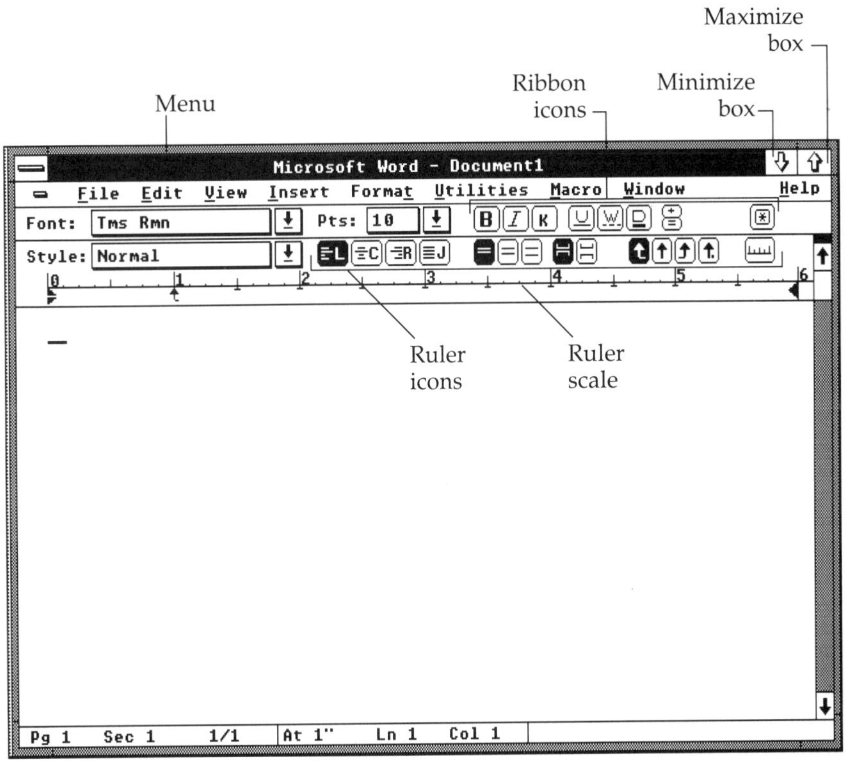

Menu. Clicking a menu opens the menu.

Ruler and ribbon icons. Clicking these icons applies the formatting. Clicking the combo boxes on the ruler and on the ribbon activates these controls so that you can type or select an item.

Ruler scale. Clicking on the ruler scale sets a tab stop.

Maximize box. Clicking the maximize box expands the window to its maximum size. When the window is enlarged to its maximum size, the restore box replaces the maximize box.

Minimize box. Clicking the minimize box shrinks the window to its minimum size.

Areas that you drag

You can use the mouse to drag in the following areas:

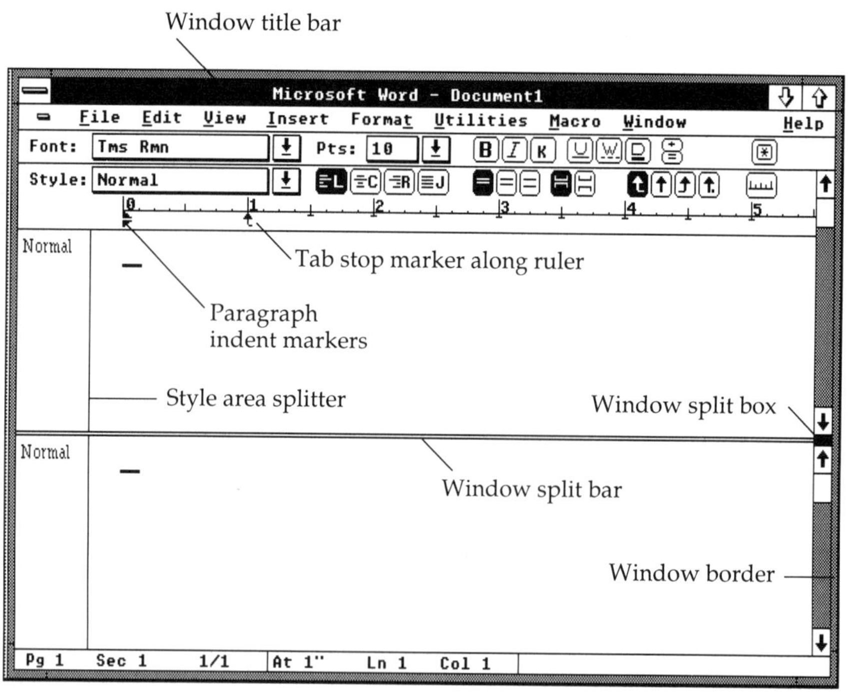

Paragraph indent marker. Dragging a paragraph indent marker sets a new paragraph indent. (For alternative views and areas to drag on the ruler, see the illustrations of the ruler below.)

Tab stop marker along ruler. Dragging a tab stop marker along the ruler sets a new tab stop position. Dragging a tab stop marker off the ruler clears the tab stop.

Window split bar. Dragging a window split bar splits the document window to show two views of a document. Hold down the Shift key while splitting to open the footnote pane. Hold down the Ctrl key while splitting to open the annotations pane.

Window split box. Dragging a window splitter resizes the two panes. Drag to the top or bottom of the window to close the pane.

Style area splitter. Dragging a style area splitter resizes the style area or closes it.

Window border. Dragging a window border resizes the window.

Window title bar. Dragging the window title bar moves the window.

Ruler column marker. Dragging a ruler column marker sets a new column width for the selected rows in a table. To see column view, click the ruler view icon while the insertion point and the selection are within a table.

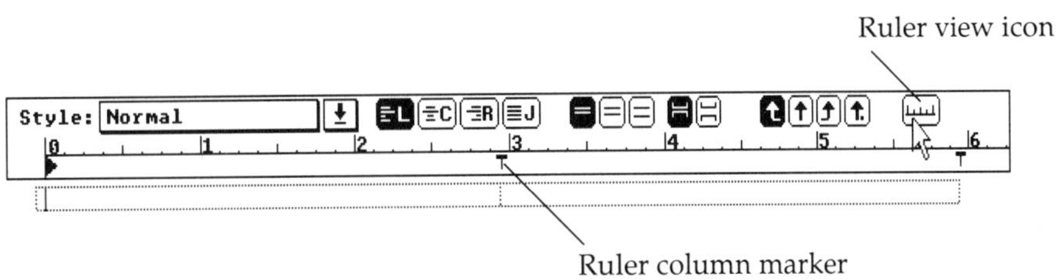

Ruler margin marker. Dragging a ruler margin marker sets a new margin for the document.

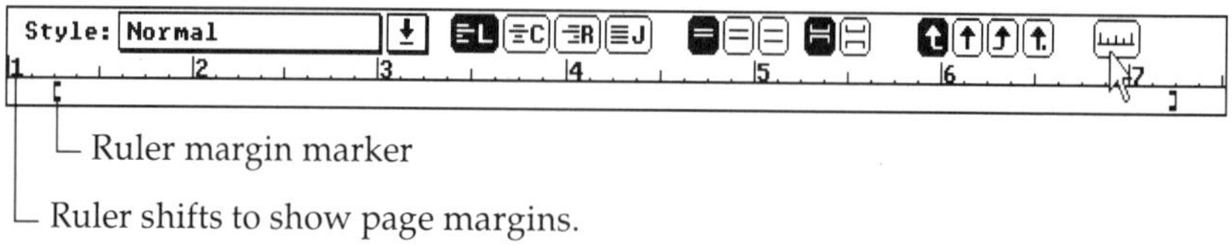

Areas that you double-click

Double-clicking these areas using the mouse makes them respond as explained below:

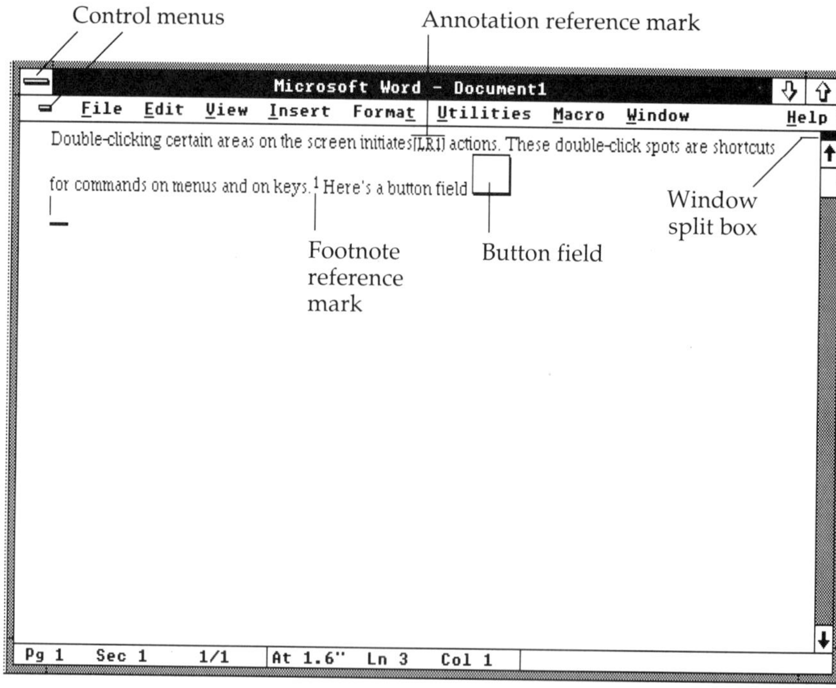

Control menus. Double-clicking a control menu closes that window.

Window split box. Double-clicking a window split box splits the window in two or closes the window split.

Footnote reference mark. Double-clicking an automatic footnote reference mark opens the footnote pane (if in a document) or closes the footnote pane (if in the footnote pane).

Annotation reference mark. Double-clicking an annotation reference mark opens the annotation pane (if in a document) or closes the annotation pane (if in the annotation pane).

Button field. Double-clicking a button field makes the field perform its task.

Double-clicking any one of these areas using the mouse tells Word to display a dialog box:

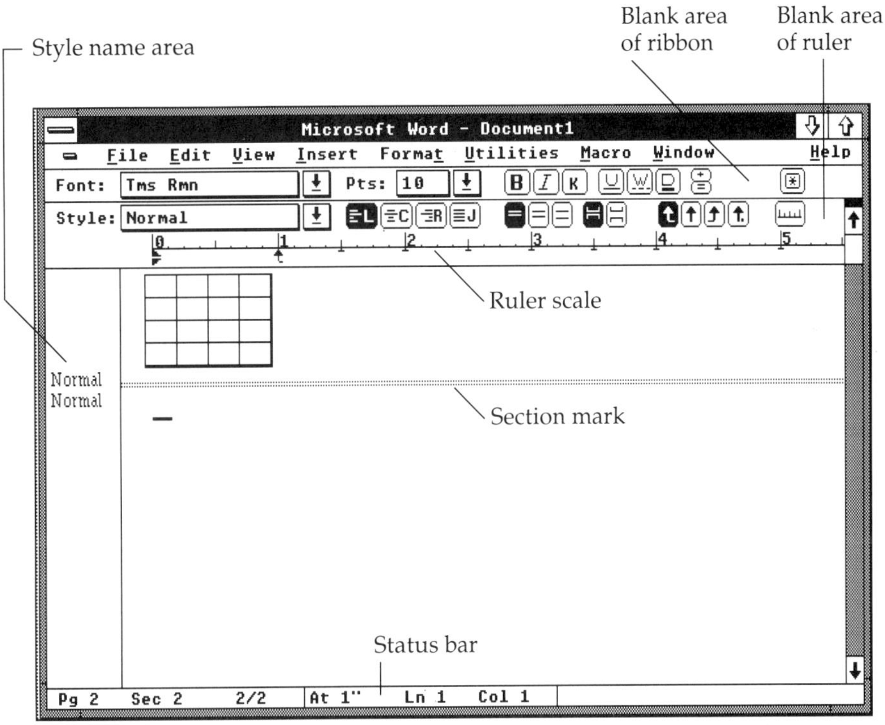

Style name area. Double-clicking a style name area opens the Format Styles dialog box.

Blank area of ribbon. Double-clicking a blank area of the ribbon opens the Format Character dialog box.

Blank area of ruler. Double-clicking a blank area of the ruler opens the Format Paragraph dialog box.

Ruler scale. Double-clicking the ruler scale opens the Format Tabs dialog box.

Section mark. Double-clicking a section mark opens the Format Section dialog box.

Status bar. Double-clicking the status bar opens the Edit Go To dialog box.

Corner marks. Double-clicking a corner mark opens the Format Document dialog box (in Page View only).

Chapter 3

Personalizing Word for Windows

If you've ever struggled with a word processor that was set up awkwardly, you'll be relieved to know that Word for Windows gives you control over much of how your screen looks and how the Word for Windows program operates. By adjusting the window displays and some of the functioning, you can build a personal word processor that suits the way you work and that even adjusts to each type of document you work on.

Personalizing Begins with Your Name

Personalizing begins the first time you start Word, when a dialog box requests your name and initials:

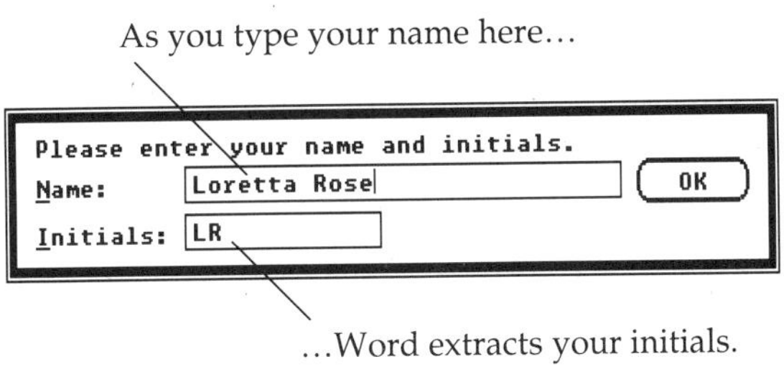

As you type your name, Word fills the Initials box with the first character of each part of your name. You can accept the initials Word extracts or type any initials you want.

Word inserts the name you type here in two other dialog boxes: Edit Summary Info and Utilities Customize. (Word also inserts your initials in the Utilities Customize dialog box.) In the Edit Summary Info dialog box, Word inserts your name in the Author box to make it easy to find a document by searching for it by the author's name. In the Statistics subdialog box of the Edit Summary Info dialog box, your name identifies who created, who last saved, and who last printed the document. If you include a name in a document's summary information, it'll be easier to find the document again by searching for it by the name of the author or by the name of the person who worked on the document. Word uses your initials from the Utilities Customize dialog box for annotations (that is, editorial comments) so that the author can identify who made the comments.

You can change the name that's entered in these two dialog boxes. For example, you can change the name in the Edit Summary Info dialog box when you work on a document authored by someone else. Or you can change the name and initials in the Utilities Customize dialog box when you use someone else's workstation but want your name in the summary information and your initials in the annotations.

After you stamp your name on Word, you're ready to personalize the part of Word that you'll spend the most time with: the screen.

Personalizing the Screen

Because Word offers so many ways to adjust the screen, it would be a shame if you did not take the time to set up the most congenial screen you can. Some changes that you can make to your screen—such as window size or colors—affect how all windows look in any Windows application, and not only in Word for Windows. Other changes personalize only Word for Windows. For example, you can choose to use short, full, or customized full menus in Word. Still other changes—such as displaying tab characters and paragraph marks—affect only the document you're currently working on. This section describes the three kinds of screen changes.

Changes That You Can Make for All Windows

The most noticeable changes you can make to the screen are changes to the windows. You can adjust the colors used in windows on a color monitor (or the shades of gray on a monochrome monitor), the width of the border around windows, the window size, and the window position.

Changing window colors

Using the Windows Control Panel, you can adjust the hue, brightness, color, and texture of many different parts of the windows, including their backgrounds, menu bars, title bars, and scroll bars. Play with each adjustment, and see how you like the results. A sample window in the dialog box shows you the effects of your changes before you apply them to your screen. If you decide you do not want the changes you made to the screen, choose the Reset button to return the screen colors to their previous settings.

To change the colors used in the window, choose the Word Control Run command (Alt,Spacebar,U). The Run dialog box appears. Select the Control Panel option (Alt+P), and then choose OK. The Control Panel window appears.

Next, choose the Preferences Screen Colors command (Alt,P,S). From the list in the Preferences Screen Colors dialog box, select the part of the window that you want to change and then adjust the slider bars for Hue, Bright, and Color. Note the changes in the Sample window. When you're satisfied with these changes, select another part of the window, if you want, and adjust the slider bars for that part.

When you finish adjusting the screen colors, choose OK, and then choose the Control Panel Close command (Alt,spacebar,C) to put away the control panel.

Changing window border width

Every window has an adjustable border. You use the border when you change the window's size, as the next section, "Changing window size," explains. You can make the window's border as thin as one pixel (one dot on the computer screen) or as thick as you want.

When considering what width you want for the window border, keep in mind how wide a border you'll need to make adjusting window size easy and how much of the screen you're willing to give up to window borders. The default window border width is five pixels.

To adjust a window's border width, choose the Word Control Run command (Alt,spacebar,U). The Run dialog box appears. Select the Control Panel option (Alt+P), and then choose OK. The Control Panel window appears.

Next, choose the Preferences Border Width command (Alt,P,W), type the number you want (in pixels) in the Preferences Border Width dialog box, and then choose OK. Choose the Control Panel Close command (Alt,spacebar,C) to put away the control panel.

Changing window size

If you like to see as much of your document as possible, use the Control Maximize command to set your windows to their maximum sizes. At its maximum size, a single window takes up the entire screen. You can also set a window to minimum, restored, custom, or arranged (tiled) size.

The Control menu includes the Minimize command, which changes the Word window into an icon. To return a window to its previous size and location—to the way it was before you used Control Maximize or Control Minimize—use the Control Restore command (Alt,spacebar,R). If the window is at maximum size, you can also click the Restore box, which is a box in the top-right corner of the window:

Restore box

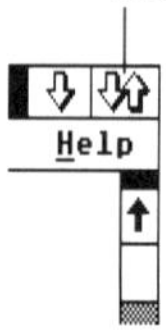

TIP

Deciding On a Border Width Setting

Because I do not adjust window size often, I usually set the border width to one pixel. This setting allows the maximum amount of space for displaying a document. If you adjust window size often, however, you'll probably want to leave the setting at the default of five pixels. It's easier to position the mouse pointer on a wider border.

To customize the size of your window by hand—to the height and width you want—use either the Control Size command or the mouse.

To custom size the active window using Control Size, choose Word Control Size (Alt,spacebar,S). A four-headed arrow appears. Press one of the arrow keys to move the four-headed arrow to the border that you want to adjust. Press the arrow key for the direction in which you want to move the border. A shadow border indicates the new window size as you press the arrow key. Press the Enter key to redraw the window at its new size. Repeat the preceding steps for any other sides that you want to adjust.

To resize a window by using the mouse, move the mouse pointer onto the window border or corner that you want to reposition. The mouse pointer changes into a two-headed arrow. Hold down the left mouse button and drag the border to its new position, and then release the mouse button.

If you want to make all document windows equal in size and tiled (that is, not overlapping), use the Window Arrange All command. This command positions all open windows so that their borders interlock in the work space, all title bars are visible, and no windows overlap or have blank space between them, as shown in Figure 3-1 on the following page.

TIP

Sizing Two Sides of a Window at One Time

After you choose the Control Size command and press an arrow key to place the four-headed arrow on a border, you can press an arrow key to move the two-headed arrow to a corner of the window. For example, if you move the four-headed arrow to the right border, press the up arrow key to move the two-headed arrow to the top-right corner. By moving the two-headed arrow when it is on a corner, you can simultaneously adjust the two sides of the window that meet at that corner.

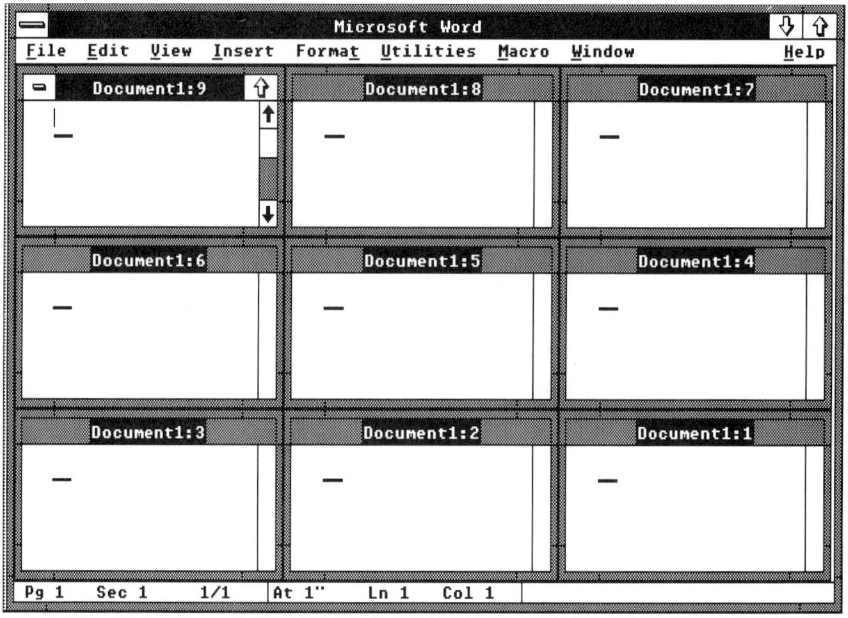

Figure 3-1.
Use Window Arrange All to make all document windows tiled.

Changing window position

When windows are smaller than their maximum allowable size, you can reposition them on the screen. Window positioning can be especially handy when you have two or more windows that you want to position side by side to compare their contents. You can move document windows anywhere within the Word window. And you can move the Word window in any available space on the screen. To position a window, you use the mouse or the keyboard.

To use the mouse, drag the window's title bar. This method also works for dialog boxes that have title bars.

To use the keyboard, choose either the Word Control Move command (Alt,spacebar,M) or the Document Control Move command (Alt,hyphen,M), press the arrow keys for the directions in which you want to move the window, and then press the Enter key when the window is positioned where you want.

Changes That You Can Make to Word Windows

After you set up the color, size, and arrangement of your windows, you might want to personalize the Word window. The changes you make affect how you use Word. For example, you can change to short or full menus, or you can open a second window into the same document.

Choosing from short, full, or customized full menus

As explained in Chapter 2, "Word for Windows Essentials," you can choose from either short or full menus when you use Word. You can also customize the full menus to accommodate the way you work.

The first time you run Word, you see the short menus. This reduced set of commands focuses on the basic features you need to produce simple documents. If you will not be creating tables of contents or indexes, writing or recording macros, or needing such tools as a thesaurus or complex styles, you might want to use only the short menus. The short menus never change, and you cannot customize them.

You change to full menus by choosing the Full Menus command from the View menu. Turning on full menus adds more commands to

TIP

Dragging Windows and Dialog Boxes

If you want to play with the mouse and practice your mouse technique, you can move a window by dragging its borders individually.

You can use the mouse to drag dialog boxes that have title bars. Alternatively, you can use the Control menu to move those dialog boxes. You might be able to move any dialog box that does not have a title bar by pressing Alt+F7, which is a keyboard shortcut for the Control Move command. Not all dialog boxes will respond to this trick, however; you'll have to experiment. A four-headed arrow appears, as it does when you choose the Control Move command. Press the arrow keys to move the dialog box; you'll see a shadow border, which indicates the new position. When the dialog box is positioned where you want it, press the Enter key to move the dialog box to the position that the shadow border indicates. You can now continue to work with the dialog box. Be aware that this technique is unlikely to work in any Windows application other than Word.

the menus and also adds a menu called Macro. With full menus turned on, you can build your own custom menus. As you read this book and run Word, use the full menus.

To customize the full menus, you can add and remove commands and macros from any menu. For example, if you think a command would be better placed on another menu, you can move it to there. If a command name seems unintuitive, you can change it to a more descriptive name.

You can also create a macro that modifies a command's behavior. For example, if you want the Print command to print one copy of the active document as soon as you choose the command, you should create the macro, give it a name such as FilePrint, and then add your new macro to a menu. Your macros override Word's built-in commands. And you can create a set of menus for each type of document you work on. For more information about customizing menus, see "Assigning a Macro to a Menu" in Chapter 10 and "Advanced Technique: Creating a Template from Scratch" in Chapter 11.

Displaying the character-formatting ribbon

If you choose the Ribbon command from the View menu, Word displays a character-formatting ribbon in the Word window. The ribbon shows which keys to press to apply various type styles in your document. If you have a mouse, you can click the ribbon's icons to apply the styles. In addition to its use in applying type styles, the ribbon shows you the current formatting of the selected text so that you can review formatting you already applied:

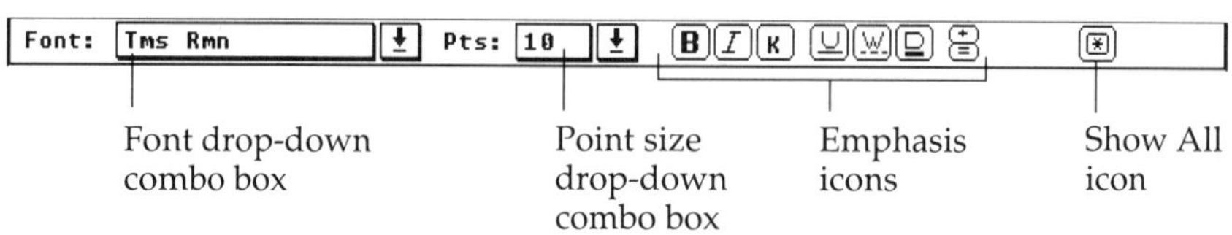

You can turn the ribbon on or off. Its initial setting is off to reduce the number of elements on the screen and to give you the maximum vertical space for displaying your document.

Displaying the status bar

The status bar displays the position of the text that's in the window in relation to the whole document. It also shows the page number, number of pages, section number, line number, the measurement from the top of the page to the insertion point, and the status of several keys and of macro recording:

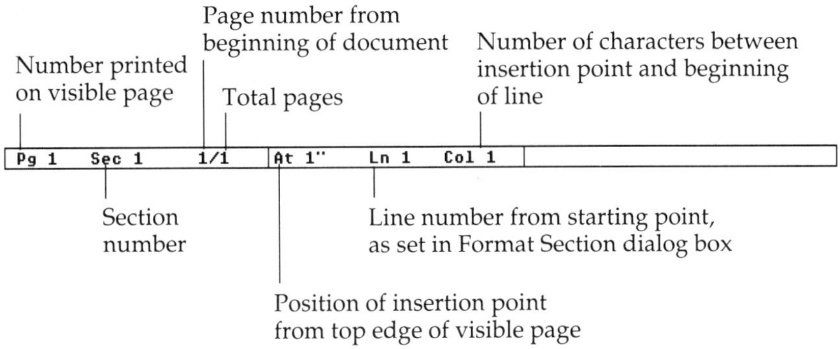

The "At" and "Ln" information will appear only if the Display as Printed option in the View Preferences dialog box and the Background Pagination option in the Utilities Customize dialog box are turned on. In addition, the page and section information is up to date if the Background Pagination option is turned on; this information is also up to date immediately after you choose the Utilities Repaginate Now command.

In extend mode (F8), Word displays "EXT" in the status bar, and in column select mode (Ctrl+Shift+F8), Word displays "COL". Pressing the CapsLock key causes Word to display "CAPS" in the status bar. Word displays "NUM" in the status bar when the NumLock key is on. If you press the Insert key to turn on overtyping, Word displays "OVR" in the status bar. And Word displays "MRK" when you choose the Utilities Revision Marks command to turn on revision marking. Choosing the Macro Record command to record a macro causes Word to display "REC" in the status bar.

You can turn the status bar on and off by using the View Status Bar command.

Opening new windows

A document appears in a window, and each window can be divided into two panes. Usually, each pane displays a portion of the document's contents. Word also has panes for footnotes, headers and footers, and annotations, as explained in "Splitting a window into panes" later in this chapter.

When the two panes contain document contents, shown in normal editing view or in Page View, each pane scrolls independently of the other pane, giving you views of two different parts of one document. If one pane is in Outline View and the other is in normal editing view, however, scrolling one pane scrolls the other pane.

Word lets you open another full-size window into the active document. This additional window scrolls independently of any other windows that show the same document. To open another window into the same document, choose the New Window command (Alt,W,N) from the Window menu.

You can use Window New Window in conjunction with the Document Control Split command, which splits a window horizontally into two panes, or parts. For example, to see four views of the same document, create a second window into the document and then split each of those windows. "Splitting a window into panes," later in this chapter, explains how to split a window into two panes.

TIP

Choosing Which Multiple Views to Display

When you either open a new window or split a window into panes, you see at least two views of your document. Choose Window New Window to open new windows when you want to see more than two views of your document or see the parts side by side. But to see only two views of the document when a horizontal arrangement of the views meets your needs, choose the Document Control Split command to split the window.

Two other methods open an additional window into a document: choosing the File Open command or selecting the document name from the bottom of the File menu. In any case, you must resize the window, or use the Window Arrange All command, to make the original window visible at the same time.

Changes That You Can Make to the Document Window

With your work space set up, you're ready to turn your attention to spicing up the document windows. For example, you can split a document window into two panes or set the view to display tab and paragraph marks. You can make most of the changes to only one pane if you want, leaving the other pane unchanged.

Splitting a window into panes

You split a window into panes when you want to simultaneously see two views of a document. For example, you can use split panes to see the Outline View of the document in one pane and the normal editing view in the other. You can make the panes equal in height, or you can adjust one pane to any size and let Word adjust the other pane to fill the rest of the document window. You can split the window yourself.

You use either a command or the mouse to split a window. To use a command, choose the Document Control Split command (Alt,hyphen,T), press the up or down arrow key to position the split bar, and then press the Enter key. Using the mouse, double-click the split box, which is the black box at the top of the vertical scroll bar. You could alternatively drag the split bar to the position you want and then release the mouse button.

The other commands and actions shown below also split the window, as long as the window is not in Page View:

- Choosing the Edit Header/Footer command to view or edit headers and footers
- Choosing the Insert Footnote command or the View Footnote command to insert, view, or edit footnotes
- Double-clicking an automatically numbered footnote reference mark or holding down the Shift key and dragging down the split box to insert, view, or edit footnotes

- Choosing the Insert Annotation command or the View Annotations command; double-clicking an annotation reference mark; or holding down the Ctrl key and dragging down the split box to insert, view, or edit annotations

Displaying the ruler

If you choose the View Ruler command, Word displays a paragraph-formatting ruler in the active document window, as shown in Figure 3-2 below. Each document window can have its own ruler, and you can turn the ruler on or off for each window.

The ruler contains icons that you can drag to set the positions of indents and tab stops. It also contains icons that you can click to set the paragraph alignment, line spacing, paragraph spacing, type of tab stop, and ruler view mode. And the ruler includes a drop-down combo box that shows the selected paragraph's style and a list of all the styles defined in the document.

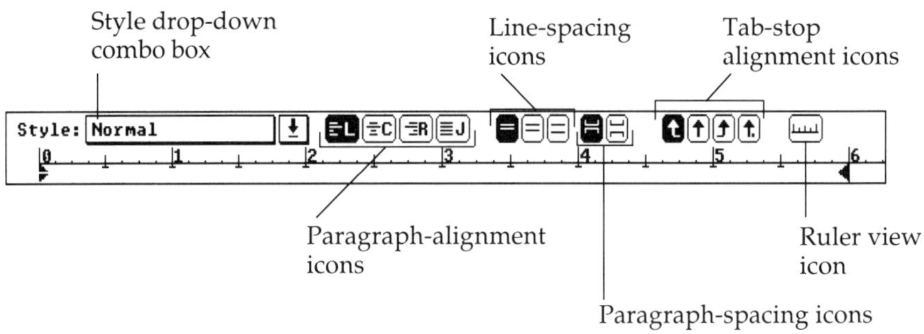

Figure 3-2.
Word's ruler for paragraph formatting.

"Formatting paragraphs using direct formatting," in Chapter 5, describes how to use the ruler icons.

You can change the ruler scale by changing the default unit of measure setting in the Utilities Customize dialog box. Initially, Word uses inches as its default unit of measure setting. The unit of measure setting affects the scale that appears on the ruler—note in Figure 3-2 that the ruler shows inches and portions of inches. The unit of measure setting also affects the units of measure in dialog boxes.

For example, if you type *0.5* in the From Left box under Indents in the Format Paragraph dialog box, Word translates 0.5 to 0.5". If you change the default unit of measure setting to centimeters and then type *0.5*, Word translates 0.5 to 0.5 cm. In addition, the scale marks on the ruler change to reflect a centimeter scale, as shown below:

To change the unit of measure setting, choose the Utilities Customize command (Alt,U,U), choose a new Unit of Measure setting, and then choose OK.

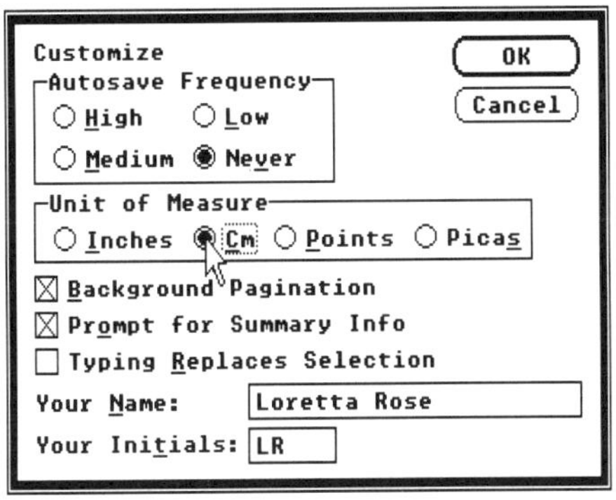

Later in this chapter, you'll learn about the rest of the options that are available in the Utilities Customize dialog box.

Displaying a document in Outline View

Choose the View Outline command to display the document in outline format. If you have applied any of the heading styles to paragraphs in your document, these paragraphs are indented in this view to show their levels in the document's outline organization and in its hierarchy. (Three heading styles are always visible in the ruler's Style combo box.)

You can use Outline View to create and organize your documents. Plus, if you set a paragraph to a level in the outline (level 1 through level 9), Word applies the corresponding heading style (heading 1 through heading 9) to the paragraph to format your headings for you.

In outline format, you can use Outline View in one pane and the normal editing view or Page View in the other pane. This arrangement lets you see, simultaneously, the underlying structure and the text as it will print. Also, when you scroll the outline while the other pane is in normal editing view, you direct Word to scroll the other pane at the same time, which makes using Outline View a quick way to travel through a document to a specific place. In addition, if you switch to Outline View, you can quickly select a whole section of a document by double-clicking the mouse in the selection bar that's next to the section heading. For more information about using Outline View, see Chapter 5, "Refining Documents."

Displaying documents in Draft View

If you choose the View Draft command, Word displays all open documents in all windows and panes in the system font. The system font in Windows is a monospace font (that is, all the characters are the same width). Draft View is the only one of the four views that affects all the panes and windows. Using Draft View gives you this advantage: Word can display documents, typing, and editing faster than it can in normal editing view because Word can more easily calculate how many characters to put on each line. Also, Draft View is handy if you use small fonts that are not easy to read on the screen. Draft View displays all characters in an easily read 12 points. Text to which character formatting has been applied is underlined on the screen.

Displaying a document in Page View

Choose the View Page command when you want Word to display the document as it will appear when printed, with the text at full size. This view shows only part of a page at a time (unless you have a large monitor). Using this view means that you can see snaking (that is, newspaper-style) columns in a side-by-side arrangement; headers, footers, and footnotes in place; and graphics in their final positions with text wrapped around them. You can also edit all these elements as a final cleanup before printing. You can switch both panes to Page View or switch to Page View in one pane and leave the other pane in either normal editing view or Outline View. For more information about using Page View, see Chapter 14, "Previewing and Perfecting Page Layout."

Setting your view preferences

Choose the View Preferences command to display a dialog box whose controls you can use to turn on or off parts of the window. You can also use this dialog box to display elements such as marks for tab characters and for hard line breaks. By turning on these controls, you can more easily distinguish among visual elements that might otherwise appear similar on the screen. For example, if you see blank space on the screen, you might wonder what causes that space. By turning on the controls in the View Preferences dialog box, you can see that some blank space is caused by marks for tab characters, and some by different kinds of spaces. You can also distinguish among different types of hyphens, see where paragraphs end, and see where hard line breaks are. The following discussion gives a closer look at each control and what it does for you.

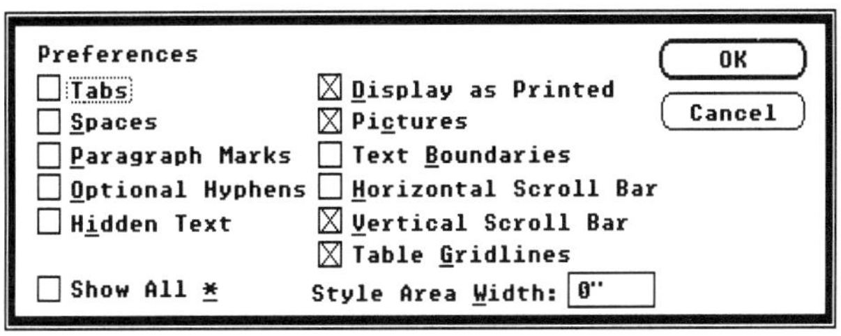

All the controls in the first column of the View Preferences dialog box are initially turned off. In the second column, the Text Boundaries and Horizontal Scroll Bar options are initially turned off, the Style Area Width option is set to 0, and the other controls are turned on.

The Tabs option displays a tab character as →. The Spaces option displays a regular space as a dot halfway up the line height (·) and a nonbreaking space as a degree symbol (°). The Paragraph Marks option displays a paragraph mark as ¶, a new line character as ↵, and a cell mark and a row mark in a table as ¤. (A cell mark appears as an x for point sizes that are 10 points and smaller.) Turning on the Optional Hyphens option displays a regular hyphen as a hyphen (-), an optional hyphen as a logical NOT symbol (¬), and a nonbreaking hyphen as a long hyphen (—). The Hidden Text option makes visible any text to which you applied hidden character format and adds a dotted underline to indicate the hidden text formatting. Annotation reference marks and fields for table of contents entries (TC), fields for index entries (XE), and fields for referenced documents (RD) are examples of hidden text. The Show All option turns on all the controls above it plus the Text Boundaries and Table Gridlines options. The Show All option also shows automatically numbered footnote reference marks and footnote continuation marks inside dotted boxes and turns on the View Field Codes command. When you turn off the Show All option, the other controls affect the display according to their settings in the View Preferences dialog box.

If you turn on the Display as Printed option in the View Preferences dialog box, the type styles for your text are displayed on the screen only as your printer can print them. To also see on the screen the fonts, sizes, and type styles that your printer cannot print, turn off the Display as Printed option.

The Pictures option displays the graphics that your document contains. When you scroll or type, Word blanks out graphics to increase scrolling speed and then displays the graphics when you stop. As a result, your document's graphics flash off and on, blank and visible. To stop the flashing, turn off the Pictures option. Your graphics appear as correctly sized empty boxes.

If you're in Page View, turn on the Text Boundaries option in the View Preferences dialog box to identify text areas by displaying dotted boxes around them.

The Horizontal Scroll Bar option turns the horizontal scroll bar on or off. Because most documents are not wider than the window, this control is initially turned off; turn it on if you use wide paper or work with tables in which you want to insert columns. The Vertical Scroll Bar option turns the vertical scroll bar on or off. Even if you do not have a mouse, the vertical scroll bar is useful because it shows how far you are from the beginning of the document.

The Table Gridlines option displays dotted boxes around all the cells in a table. These gridlines do not print. Turn the Table Gridlines option off if you want to see the table without these lines. This option does not affect table cell borders that you turn on in the Format Table dialog box. For more information about table cell borders, see "Formatting Cells and Tables" in Chapter 13.

The entry in the Style Area Width box adjusts the width of the area that shows style names along the left edge of the screen. You can make the style name area as wide as half the width of the document window.

Using the View Field Codes command

Fields are special instructions for calculating and inserting contents in a document. Chapters 6, 8, 9, and the Appendix explain more about using fields. For now, you need to know that fields can appear in two forms. You see either the fields' instructions, called codes, or the fields' results, which are text, graphics, or numbers that the instructions calculate and insert. The View Field Codes command sets the display of all fields in a document to either the codes or the results. To see field codes and results at the same time, you can split the document window into two panes. By doing so, you can edit the codes and see the effects of your changes as you work.

You can also use the TOGGLE FIELD key combination (Shift+F9) to switch between field codes and results in individual fields. If you switch several fields and have a combination of codes and results in a single pane, you can choose View Field Codes to display all the fields in the pane in a single form.

Personalizing Operations

Personalizing Word also involves changing some of the ways that Word operates. You can use the Utilities Customize dialog box, shown below, to control four types of operations: automatic saving, pagination, summary information, and typing to replace selected text.

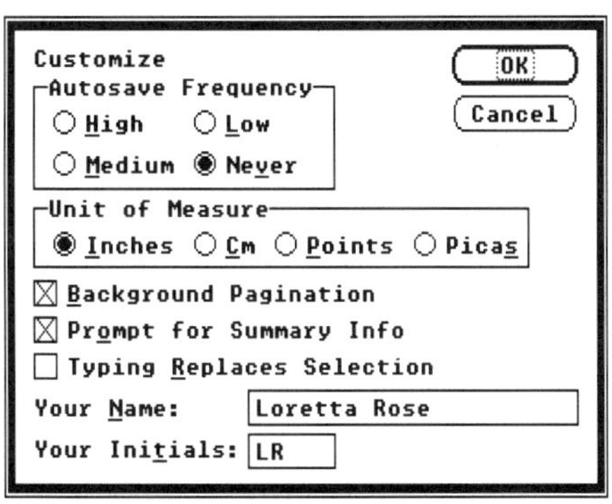

Autosave Frequency

If you have trouble remembering to save your document, you might want to turn on the Autosave option in the Utilities Customize dialog box. This feature does not save your document for you; it displays a dialog box at set time intervals to remind you to save your work. When the dialog box appears, you can choose to save, postpone saving, or restart the autosave clock on a new time interval of Low (30 to 60 minutes), Medium (20 to 45 minutes), or High (10 to 30 minutes). The exact time for each interval depends on how many changes you make. If you make many changes, Word shortens the time between reminders; if you make few changes, Word lengthens the time.

Background Pagination

If you want the page breaks in your documents to be visible at all times, you can turn on the Background Pagination option in the Utilities Customize dialog box. When background pagination is on, Word breaks pages when you pause in your actions—during pauses in typing, editing, formatting, and so on. If you have a minimum system configuration (640 KB total memory), however, you might want to turn off background pagination to increase response speed and reduce the number of times Word reads from and writes to the disk. When background pagination is turned off, choose the Utilities Repaginate Now command whenever you're ready to repaginate. Background pagination is initially turned on.

Prompt for Summary Information

You can add summary information to any document, including the document's author, title, subject, keywords (to identify the topics), and any additional comments. You can use these pieces of information along with the File Find command to retrieve a document or a group of documents. To help you add summary information to a document, Word is initially set up to display the Summary Info dialog box when you save a document for the first time. Turn off this control if you do not want the dialog box displayed. If you choose Summary when you use the File New command and if you provide summary information at that time, the Summary Info dialog box does not reappear when you save the document for the first time.

Typing Replaces Selection

Word initially inserts whatever text you type or paste, even when text is selected. But if you turn on the Typing Replaces Selection option in the Utilities Customize dialog box, typing or pasting replaces the selected text. The Backspace key is included in this scheme, which means that Backspace can be used as a delete key in addition to the Delete key. Typing Replaces Selection can be handy if you have a piece of text that you want to replace with another piece of text in a one-step operation. Turn off the Typing Replaces Selection option if you want to insert your typing and pasting even when you have a selection. Also turn off this option if you want to avoid accidentally deleting text.

Personalizing Resources

As you process your documents, many resources available in Word help you work, including glossaries (for storing text and graphics), dictionaries, and document templates. These resources are described below and explained in greater detail in later chapters.

Glossary Entries

Glossary entries store text and graphics that you want to reuse. For example, you can store a graphic in a glossary entry and then insert that same graphic in a number of different documents. Alternatively, you can construct an entire document by inserting text and graphics that are stored in various glossary entries.

You can set up a group of glossary entries for each type of document you prepare. These specialized glossaries make it easy to recall standard text for specific types of documents and for specific topics. Word lets you create, change, and delete glossary entries. Chapter 12, "Glossaries," explains more about how to use glossary entries in Word.

Styles

Styles store paragraph formatting that you want to reuse. By using styles, you can create documents with consistent formats. Then, for example, if you want to change the format of all paragraphs that use a particular style, you can simply change the style, and Word changes all paragraphs for you. Chapter 7, "Styles," explains how to use styles in your Word documents.

Additional Spelling Dictionaries

You can create additional spelling dictionaries to store personal and specialized terms that you want to use in addition to the words included in Word's main spelling dictionary. For example, you might include company names, product names, and staff names in the standard user dictionary, which is a supplement to the main dictionary.

You can use a second supplementary dictionary for terms that belong to a particular discipline or to a particular type of communication. This second supplementary dictionary is the one you'll switch to if you work on a document that deals with a special topic. This feature allows you to segregate and collect terms in specialized dictionaries. This way you avoid cluttering the main dictionary, and you speed up locating suggestions to replace misspelled or mistyped words. After your dictionaries are set up, you can select the specialized dictionary you want whenever you check spelling. "Spelling Checking," in Chapter 4, explains more about using spelling dictionaries.

Macros

A macro stores a sequence of actions, including choosing commands, pressing keyboard command keys, typing, and any other actions that you can take in Word except mouse actions. You can use a macro to record repetitive tasks. You can then assign that macro to a key or a menu for easy access and then run the macro when needed, rather than repeating the individual actions. Chapter 10, "Macros," explains macros in detail.

Document Templates

A document template can store text, macros, styles, glossary entries, page formatting, and menu and key assignments. Using templates makes it easy to create documents that consistently match your standard style, design, and layout. Templates also help you customize Word for each type of document on which you work. For more information about the many ways in which you can use templates, see Chapter 11, "Templates."

Fonts

A font is a set of characters of uniform shape and design. Windows and Word for Windows come with a set of fonts, which the Setup program installs for you. You choose the fonts as you work in Word. Using the Windows Control Panel, which you display by choosing the Word Control Run command (Alt,spacebar,U), you can add or delete fonts to choose which type styles are available for each of your documents. For more information about using fonts, see your *Microsoft Windows User's Guide.* Also see *Microsoft Windows Basic Skills for Windows Applications,* which is included in your Word package.

Printers

Printers provide Word with important information for the screen display as well as for printing. Word uses the printer information for adapting the display to match your printer's capabilities so that what you see on the screen is what you get when you print. You can install, change, and remove printers from Windows. And you can choose both a printer and a font cartridge (if font cartridges are available) in Word when you're ready to print. If several printers are available—including those available via a network—you can choose the printer that best fits your document. For more information about using printers in Windows, see your *Microsoft Windows User's Guide.* Also see the *Microsoft Windows Basic Skills for Windows Applications* or the *Microsoft Word for Windows Printer Guide,* both of which are included in your Word package.

Chapter 4

A Walk Through Creating Documents

Because the easiest way to learn is by doing, this chapter walks you through the process of creating a document in Word for Windows. Here you can practice the basics and get a glimpse of many Word features. You create a document by creating its contents and then proofreading, editing, printing, and saving them.

The next chapter, "Refining Documents," goes a step further by showing you how to organize ideas, format text, preview and revise the document, add a table of contents and an index, and so on. After you read these two chapters, you'll have the skills you need to use the more advanced features explained in Parts II and III of this book.

Creating a Document

You can create a document either by starting Word or by choosing a command after Word is running. When you start Word, a document, titled "Document1," is created for you. When Word is running, choose the File New command to create a document. That document is titled "Document," followed by a new number. The number identifies the document in relation to other documents in the current session. Documents are numbered consecutively.

Creating Document Contents

To insert text into a document, you either type the text you want or paste it from the Clipboard. To insert graphics, you paste them from the Clipboard, where you can temporarily place artwork from files created in such graphics programs as Microsoft Excel or Windows Paint. You can also use the Insert Picture command to insert graphics from files that were created using other graphics programs. "Pasting Text and Graphics," on the next page, describes Insert Picture.

Typing Text

To see what happens when you type in Word, and to produce practice text, type the text that follows on the next page. Use the Backspace key

TIP

Documents Created from Templates

Choose the File New command, and take a look at the File New dialog box:

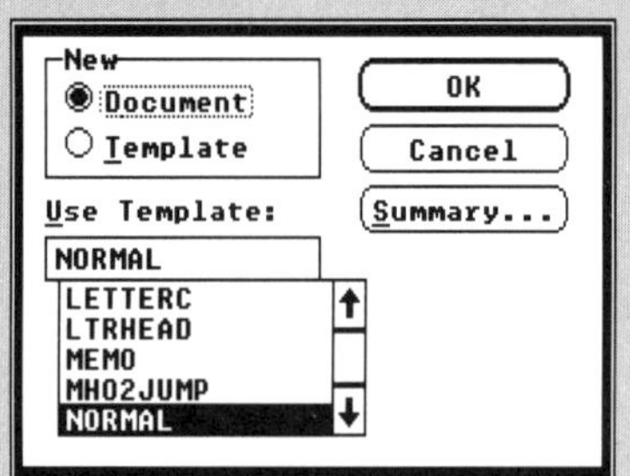

Note the Use Template label and, in the list, the name NORMAL. When you create a document, it's based on a model document called a document template. NORMAL (the file is named NORMAL.DOT) is the default document template that Word uses for any document for which you do not specify a document template. Templates contain text, formatting, and many other elements that make creating documents easy. Chapter 6, "Using Word's Four Pillars: Styles, Fields, Macros, and Templates," includes an overview of templates, and Chapter 11, "Templates," describes templates in detail. When you're ready to experiment with using templates, select a template name and choose OK in the File New dialog box.

to erase any typing mistakes. Note that when text reaches the right margin, Word breaks between two words to start a new line.

The best clashes with the first. The way to the better exacts a full look at the worst. Delight is a delicate growth cramped by crookedness, custom, and fear.

Be sure to type a space after the last period.

Press the REPEAT key (F4). Word repeats the sentences you typed. F4 repeats your last action, whether you typed, chose a command, or pressed keys. (The Edit menu also includes a Repeat command that you can choose if you prefer using menus.) Then, press F4 four more times until you have a long paragraph of text, and then press the Enter key to start a new paragraph. Next, type the additional text shown in the second paragraph below:

The best clashes with the first. The way to the better exacts a full look at the worst. Delight is a delicate growth cramped by crookedness, custom, and fear. The best clashes with the first. The way to the better exacts a full look at the worst. Delight is a delicate growth cramped by crookedness, custom, and fear. The best clashes with the first. The way to the better exacts a full look at the worst. Delight is a delicate growth cramped by crookedness, custom, and fear. The best clashes with the first. The way to the better exacts a full look at the worst. Delight is a delicate growth cramped by crookedness, custom, and fear. The best clashes with the first. The way to the better exacts a full look at the worst. Delight is a delicate growth cramped by crookedness, custom, and fear. The best clashes with the first. The way to the better exacts a full look at the worst. Delight is a delicate growth cramped by crookedness, custom, and fear.

Dawn brings lusty joys; evening all that's sweet. The times are blesst; nothing much is the matter; there are many smiles for every tear.

Start a new paragraph, and type this text.

Pasting Text and Graphics

Before you can paste text and graphics into your document, you must have something on the Clipboard to paste. Start by selecting the last two sentences that you typed in the example above. Then, choose the Edit Copy command (Alt,E,C) or press the Ctrl+Insert keys, as a shortcut, to copy the text to the Clipboard.

To see what's on the Clipboard, choose the Word Control Run command (Alt,spacebar,U) and press the Enter key. The Clipboard window shows the copied text. Close the window (Alt,spacebar,C) to return to the document. Now, to paste the contents of the Clipboard into the document, position the insertion point at the beginning of the second paragraph and choose the Edit Paste command, or press the Shift+Insert keys.

Move the insertion point to the end of your text by pressing the Ctrl+End keys. Then, press the REPEAT key (F4) three times to insert copies of the Clipboard contents into your document.

To insert graphics into a document, you can choose from a couple of methods. You can copy and paste graphics via the Clipboard from a Windows program that creates graphics, such as Microsoft Excel (charts) or Windows Paint (pictures). To insert graphics created using computer-aided drawing (CAD) programs or from scanned images, Word provides the Insert Picture command.

If you have a Microsoft Excel and a chart file that you want to insert into a document, start Microsoft Excel, open the chart file, select the chart, copy it to the Clipboard, and then quit Microsoft Excel. (If you do not have a Microsoft Excel chart file, use a picture created with Windows Paint instead.) Now, position the insertion point where you want the chart (or picture) to appear in your Word document. Either choose the Edit Paste command (Alt,E,P) or press the PASTE key combination (Shift+Insert) to insert the chart into the Word document.

Using the Clipboard to copy and paste graphics works for any graphics programs that run under Microsoft Windows. Word can also import graphics from other graphics programs, including:

- Any TIFF file
- Lotus PIC
- HPGL
- AutoCAD ADI binary
- AutoCAD ADI ASCII
- Micrografx Draw!
- CGM Graphics
- Zenographics Mirage
- Video Show
- Windows Metafile

For files created using these programs, you use the Insert Picture command to insert the graphics into a Word document. First, choose the Insert Picture command (Alt,I,P). Then, in the Insert Picture dialog box, select a TIFF file (a file with the file-name extension TIF)—or type the name of a graphics file that's in a format different from TIFF—and then choose OK. If no TIFF files appear in the Insert Picture dialog box list, switch to the directory that contains the Word on-line tutorial files (the WINWORD.CBT directory). This directory contains some TIFF files that you can use to practice inserting graphics into a document. If you set up Word without the on-line tutorial and have no graphics files, choose the New Picture button in the Insert Picture dialog box to insert an empty picture frame into your document. The frame reserves space so that you can later glue a graphic in that position.

See "Formatting Graphics" in Chapter 5 for information about changing the size of a graphic and adding a border to it. See Chapter 14, "Previewing and Perfecting Page Layout," for information about positioning graphics on a page. And see the Appendix, "Field Types and Their Instructions," for details about the IMPORT field, which Word uses to insert and process graphics from graphics files.

Proofreading and Editing Your Document

As you review the contents of your document, you'll probably want to make some changes in it. You might want to delete or move text, for example, or check spelling and hyphenation. But before you begin proofreading and editing, you need to decide whether to keep track of these changes by having Word mark your revisions.

Revision Marking

Have you ever received a revised document and wondered what was changed? In Word, you can mark text changes so that anyone reading a document can see at a glance what was added or deleted.

When you first turn on revision marking in the Utilities Revision Marks dialog box, Word marks with an underline any text you add and marks with a strike-through line any text you delete. A revision bar in the outside margin indicates any lines that contain changes. If you prefer not to use an underline to mark added text, the Utilities Revision Marks dialog box gives you the following choices:

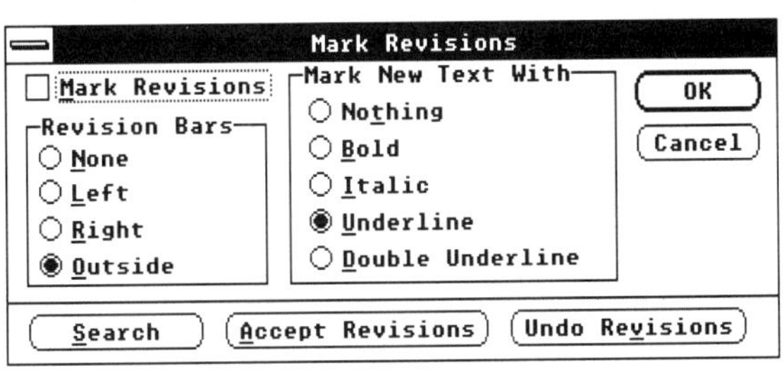

To turn on revision marks, choose the Utilities Revision Marks command (Alt,U,M) and choose the Mark Revisions option in the Utilities Revision Marks dialog box (Alt+M). Take a look at the choices you have for the placement of revision bars and for the type of mark Word will use to identify new or deleted text. If you want options other than the defaults, choose them. Then, choose OK to start revision marking. "MRK" appears in the status bar to show that revision marking is turned on; you create and edit as usual, and Word marks the text accordingly.

To turn off revision marking, you choose Utilities Revision Marks (Alt,U,M), turn off the Mark Revisions option (Alt+M), and then choose OK. You'll take a closer look at what you need to consider before you turn off revision marking later in this chapter in "Reviewing Your Revision Marks." (For now, leave revision marking turned on.) In that section, you'll also see how to accept or undo your revisions. Keep in mind that revision marks affect line and page breaks, word count, and so on, so you'll want to remove the revision marks when you need to know exactly how your final document will look.

Deleting, Moving, and Copying Document Contents

As you work with document contents in Word, you might want to delete, move, and copy the text or graphics. You can use the Edit menu's Cut, Paste, and Copy commands. You can also use the keyboard equivalents for those commands: Shift+Delete for the Cut command, Shift+Insert for the Paste command, and Ctrl+Insert for the Copy command. And when you move or copy contents, Word has two special keys that combine the two processes.

Deleting contents

Word gives you a number of methods to choose from to delete contents, as the following list shows. Which method you use depends on how much you want to delete, what you want to do with the contents after they're deleted, and what your preferences are as you work. Because Word "sees" a graphic as a single character, methods that delete a character can also delete a graphic.

- Pressing the Backspace key deletes the character to the left of the insertion point.
- Pressing the Delete key deletes the character to the right of the insertion point. To delete a larger amount of document contents, select the contents you want to delete and then press Delete; Word deletes the entire selection.
- To put the contents that you delete onto the Clipboard, select the contents and either choose the Edit Cut command (Alt,E,T) or press Shift+Delete.
- To replace text character by character as you type, turn on the Overtype mode by pressing the Insert key.
- To replace the selection with the first character you type, turn on the Typing Replaces Selection option in the Utilities Customize dialog box, select the contents you want to replace, and then type; the Backspace key also deletes the selection.

To practice deleting, try some of the above methods in your example document, which should look like the following:

The best clashes with the first. The way to the better exacts a full look at the worst. Delight is a delicate growth cramped by crookedness, custom, and fear. The best clashes with the first. The way to the better exacts a full look at the worst. Delight is a delicate growth cramped by crookedness, custom, and fear. The best clashes with the first. The way to the better exacts a full look at the worst. Delight is a delicate growth cramped by crookedness, custom, and fear. The best clashes with the first. The way to the better exacts a full look at the worst. Delight is a delicate growth cramped by crookedness, custom, and fear. The best clashes with the first. The way to the better exacts a full look at the worst. Delight is a delicate growth cramped by crookedness, custom, and fear. The best clashes with the first. The way to the better exacts a full look at the worst. Delight is a delicate growth cramped by crookedness, custom, and fear.
Dawn brings lusty joys; evening all that's sweet. The times are blesst; nothing much is the matter; there are many smiles for every tear. Dawn brings lusty joys; evening all that's sweet. The times are blesst; nothing much is the matter; there are many smiles for every tear. Dawn brings lusty joys; evening all that's sweet. The times are blesst; nothing much is the matter; there are many smiles for every tear. Dawn brings lusty joys; evening all that's sweet. The times are blesst; nothing much is the matter; there are many smiles for every tear. Dawn brings lusty joys; evening all that's sweet. The times are blesst; nothing much is the matter; there are many smiles for every tear.

Select the last sentence of the first paragraph, and choose the Edit Cut command. The sentence is placed on the Clipboard and marked with a strike-through line as a deletion. If you did not have revision marking turned on, deleting using Edit Cut removes the sentence rather than marking it. But in either case, because the sentence is placed on the Clipboard instead of being discarded, you can paste it back into the document using the Edit Paste command or the Shift+Insert keys.

Moving contents

You can move contents by cutting and pasting, but cutting contents to the Clipboard erases whatever you're currently storing on the Clipboard. You might find that you prefer using the MOVE key (F2) instead of the cutting-and-pasting method. Using F2 lets you move document contents as if you were cutting and pasting them. F2, however, does not store on the Clipboard the contents that you're moving, so you'll find this key particularly handy when you have Clipboard contents that you want to keep.

Try moving the first sentence of the second paragraph: First, select the sentence, and then press the MOVE key (F2). The message in the status bar asks "Move to where?" Move the insertion point in front of the last sentence in the first paragraph (the one you deleted in the preceding section). The insertion point is now a dotted, blinking bar to show that you're in the middle of a move. Press the Enter key to move the sentence. The sentence is marked with a strike-through line at its previous location and is underlined at its new location, and the insertion point is positioned where you set it during the move action.

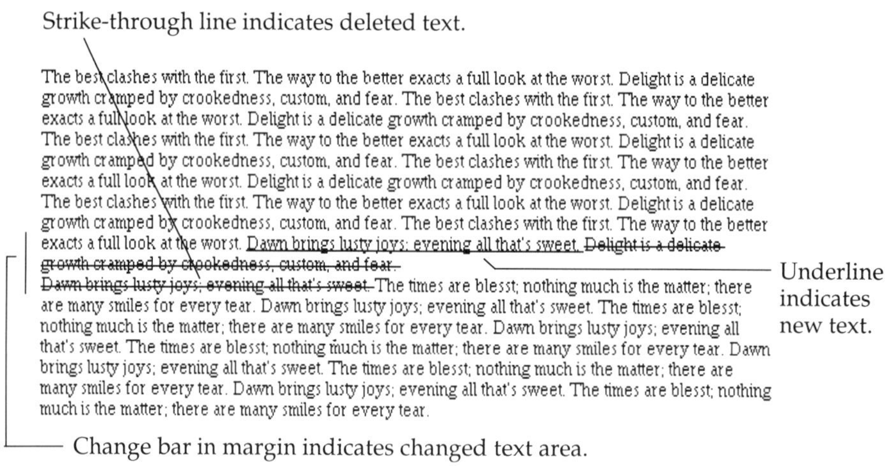

You just performed a "move to" action. You might also want to use the "move from" action to move contents to the insertion point. For this example, leave the insertion point where it is and press the MOVE key (F2). This time, the message in the status bar asks "Move from where?" Select the third unmarked sentence in the second paragraph. Selections you make during a move are marked with a dotted underline. Then, press the Enter key to move the sentence. The sentence is marked with a strike-through line at its previous location and underlined at its new location, and the insertion point remains at its original position.

The best clashes with the first. The way to the better exacts a full look at the worst. Delight is a delicate growth cramped by crookedness, custom, and fear. The best clashes with the first. The way to the better exacts a full look at the worst. Delight is a delicate growth cramped by crookedness, custom, and fear. The best clashes with the first. The way to the better exacts a full look at the worst. Delight is a delicate growth cramped by crookedness, custom, and fear. The best clashes with the first. The way to the better exacts a full look at the worst. Delight is a delicate growth cramped by crookedness, custom, and fear. The best clashes with the first. The way to the better exacts a full look at the worst. Dawn brings lusty joys; evening all that's sweet. The times are blesst; nothing much is the matter; there are many smiles for every tear. ~~Delight is a delicate growth cramped by crookedness, custom, and fear.~~

~~Dawn brings lusty joys; evening all that's sweet.~~ The times are blesst; nothing much is the matter; there are many smiles for every tear. Dawn brings lusty joys; evening all that's sweet. ~~The times are blesst; nothing much is the matter; there are many smiles for every tear.~~ Dawn brings lusty joys; evening all that's sweet. The times are blesst; nothing much is the matter; there are many smiles for every tear. Dawn brings lusty joys; evening all that's sweet. The times are blesst; nothing much is the matter; there are many smiles for every tear. Dawn brings lusty joys; evening all that's sweet. The times are blesst; nothing much is the matter; there are many smiles for every tear.

This text was moved up.

Copying contents

The COPY key combination (Shift+F2) offers the same advantages as does the MOVE key. You can copy contents using the COPY key combination (Shift+F2) instead of the Copy and Paste commands. Shift+F2 does not store on the Clipboard the contents you copy, so your Clipboard contents are not disturbed.

Select the first unmarked sentence in the second paragraph, and press the COPY key combination (Shift+F2). The message in the status bar asks "Copy to where?" Move the insertion point in front of the last sentence in the first paragraph (the sentence you deleted earlier). The insertion point is now a dotted, blinking bar that shows you're in the middle of a copy. Press the Enter key to copy the sentence. The sentence is underlined at its new location but is unmarked at its original location, and the insertion point is positioned where you set it during the copy action.

You just performed a "copy to" action. You might also want to use the "copy from" action to move contents to the current position of the insertion point. For this example, leave the insertion point where it is and press the COPY key combination (Shift+F2). This time, the message in the status bar asks "Copy from where?" Select the third unmarked sentence in the second paragraph. Selections you make during a copy are marked with a dotted underline. Then, press the Enter key to copy the sentence. The sentence is underlined at its new location but is unmarked at its original location, and the insertion point remains at its original position.

Spelling Checking

Before you send out a document for others to read, you'll want to let Word check the spelling for you. By comparing words in your document against one or more dictionaries, Word can check your spelling

TIP

Moving Contents to and from the Insertion Point

Keep in mind that you move contents either to a new insertion point or from another location to the existing insertion point. Because you use the same MOVE key (F2) for both of these actions, you need to remember when the key moves contents to a new insertion point and when it moves contents from another location:

- If you start with a selection, F2 moves contents to the new insertion point you choose.

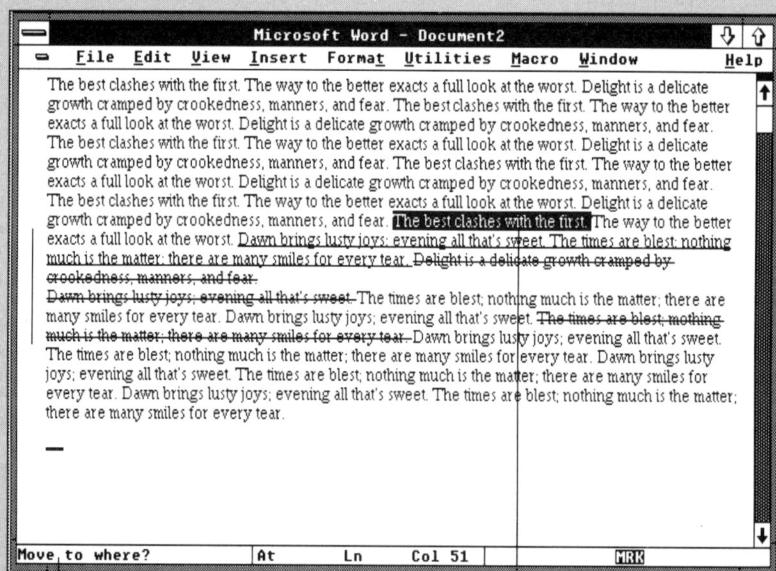

Note message in status bar.

Text that's selected when F2 is pressed

and alert you to possible mistakes. For each word that Word cannot find in a dictionary, the program asks what you want to do. You can choose to do any of the following: Change the spelling of the word, ask for suggested changes, leave the word as it is, or add the word to a dictionary. Word also checks for words that are incorrectly capitalized and for repeated words.

To do spelling checking, Word uses as many as three dictionaries. The first dictionary, which is the main dictionary, contains about 100,000 words. Microsoft supplies this dictionary file as the basis for spelling

- If you start with an insertion point, F2 moves contents from another location to the insertion point.

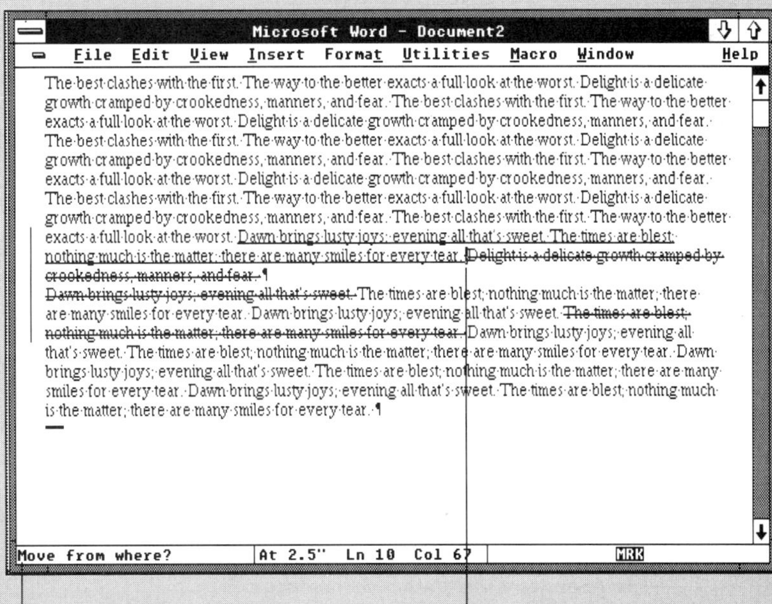

These same guidelines also hold true for the COPY key combination (Shift+F2).

checking; you cannot alter this dictionary. You can, however, add new words to a second dictionary, which acts as a supplement to the main dictionary. This second dictionary is called STDUSER.DIC. Think of this supplemental dictionary as an amendment, or update, dictionary for the main dictionary. As it does with the main dictionary, Word uses STDUSER.DIC for every document that you check.

You can use a third dictionary for specialty words. This dictionary applies to a single document or to a series of documents about a specific topic or area that has its own jargon and technical terms. For example, you might select a legal dictionary to check legal documents, a medical dictionary for medical reports, and a dictionary of customer names for a mailing list. Although Word always uses the main dictionary and STDUSER.DIC, you can select a third dictionary from among any number of other supplemental dictionaries. And you can easily create new supplemental dictionaries.

Word will check all the words in your document, only a selection of words, or a single word. Spelling corrections are marked as revisions whenever the Mark Revisions option is turned on in the Utilities Revision Marks dialog box.

Checking the spelling in your whole document

To check the spelling in your whole document, first be sure you have an insertion point and not a selection of text. Then, choose the Utilities Spelling command (Alt,U,S). You see the Check Spelling dialog box:

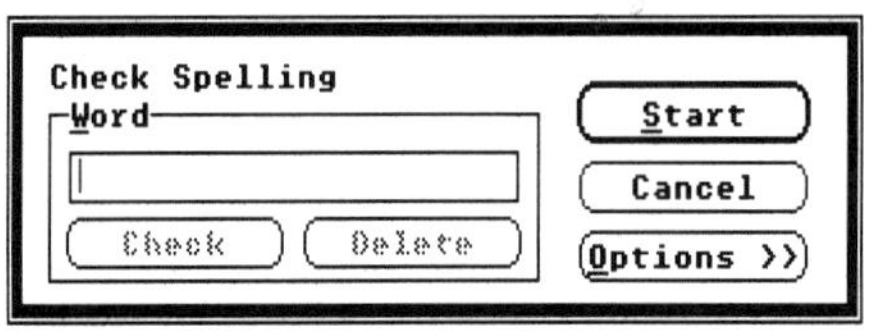

The next section, "Checking the spelling of a single word," explains how to use this dialog box when you want to check only one word. For now, choose the Start button (Alt+S) to start checking all words in your document.

When Word finds the word "blesst" in your document, you see the Spelling dialog box because "blesst" is not in any of the active dictionaries. This dialog box offers a number of options to solve your spelling dilemma:

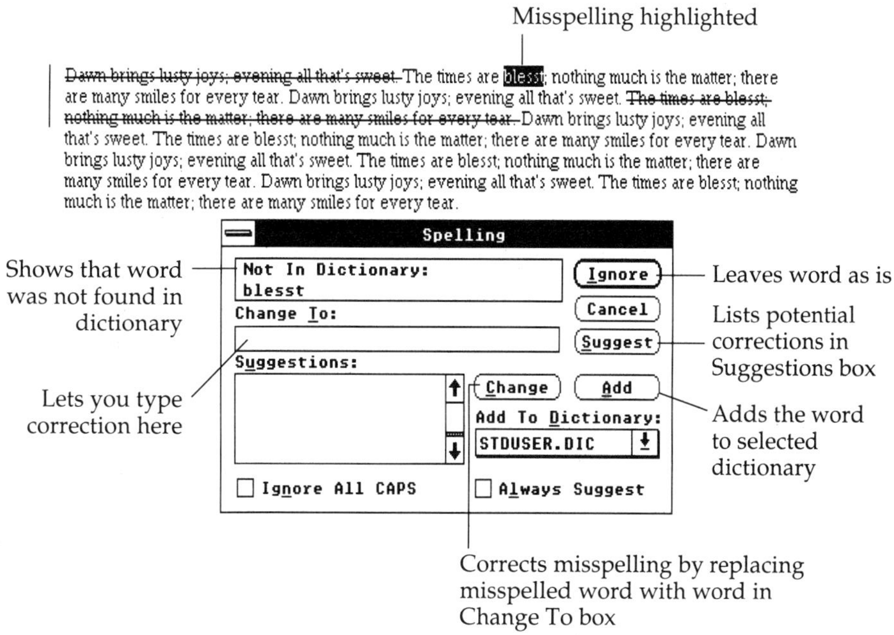

To see a list of suggested spellings, choose the Suggest button (Alt+S) and review the spellings listed in the Suggestions box. For this example, select "blest" from the list and then choose the Change button (Alt+C). Whenever the word you want is not in the Suggestions list, type your own correction in the Change To box and then choose the Change button. You can also add the word to a dictionary by selecting the dictionary you want in the Add to Dictionary list and then choosing the Add button (Alt+A). If you started spelling checking anywhere other than at the beginning of the document, when Word reaches the end of the document, you're asked if you want to continue checking spelling from the beginning.

Checking the spelling of a single word

You can check a word's spelling either before or after you type the word in your document. To check a word before you type it, choose the Utilities Spelling command (Alt,U,S). You see the Check Spelling dialog box:

Type word to be checked.

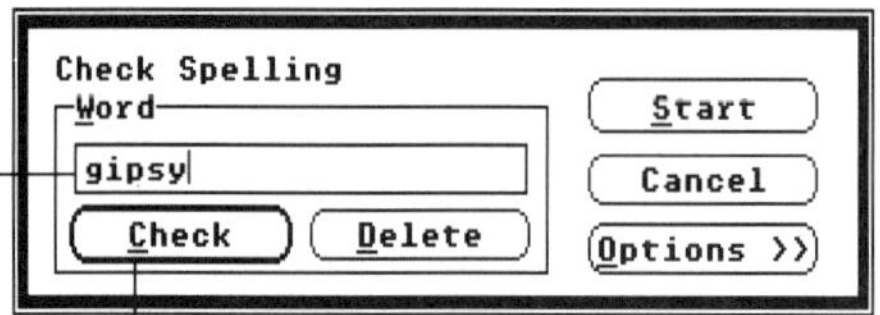

Then, choose Check.

In the Word box, type the word you want to check, and then choose the Check button (Alt+C). If you typed a word that's included in one of the spelling dictionaries, you see the message "Word was found in *name* dictionary"; *name* will be "Main," "Main update" (STDUSER.DIC), or "user" (your chosen supplemental dictionary). The Check Spelling dialog box returns in case you want to check another word.

If Word could not find the word you originally typed, you see the Spelling dialog box, in which you can ask for spelling suggestions and add the word to either the Main update (STDUSER.DIC) or the other supplemental dictionary. You add it by selecting the dictionary name from the Add To Dictionary list and then choosing the Add button (Alt+A).

TIP

Selecting or Creating a Dictionary

When you want to either select a particular dictionary to use for spelling checking or create a new dictionary, choose the Utilities Spelling dialog box, choose the Options button, and then open the Supplemental Dictionaries list. In addition to using the Main and Main update dictionaries, you can select one user dictionary. If the dictionary does not exist, type its name in the Supplemental box and Word will create it for you. You can change from one dictionary to another in the Check Spelling dialog box. While you check spelling in the Spelling dialog box, you can add a word to either the Main update or the other supplemental dictionary.

To check a word that you already typed in a document, select the word and then press the SPELLING key (F7). If the word is included in a Word dictionary, you see the message "Spell Check Completed" in the status bar. If Word could not find the word, you see the Spelling dialog box, where you can ask for spelling suggestions or, again, add the word to one of the two supplemental dictionaries.

Using the Thesaurus

Using precise language in writing is always a challenge, which is why many people turn to a thesaurus. In Word, you can use the internal thesaurus that Microsoft licenses from Houghton Mifflin, publishers of a printed thesaurus. You can look up words based on any of the following: an insertion point, a single selected word, or a word that you type in the Utilities Thesaurus dialog box. And you can use the thesaurus to replace all occurrences of a word.

To try using the thesaurus, select the first occurrence of the word "custom" in your example text. You can select the word by placing the insertion point anywhere within the word or immediately to the right of the word. You can also select the word by highlighting it. Then, either choose the Utilities Thesaurus command (Alt,U,T) or press the THESAURUS key combination (Shift+F7). Word displays a dialog box that lists synonyms for "custom," based on the highlighted definition of the word in the Definitions box:

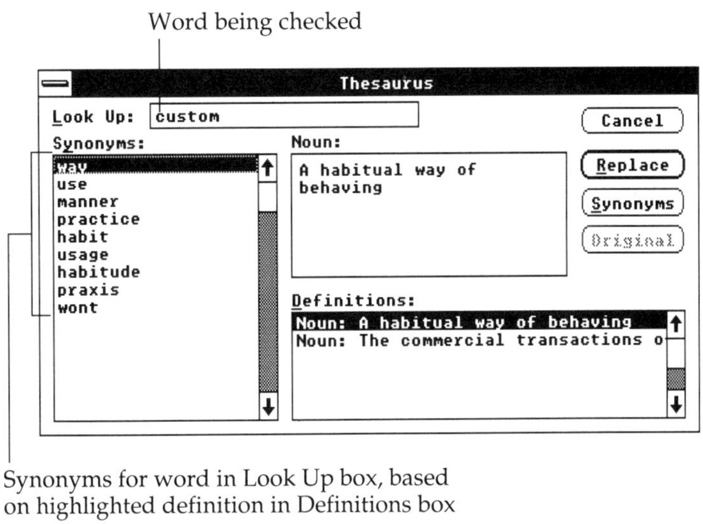

To see a list of synonyms for another definition, select the definition and note the changed Synonyms list. So far, neither Synonyms list has shown an alternative word that has a clearer meaning than "custom" in your example's context.

To find a word that makes the meaning of "custom" clearer to modern readers, change the word in the Look Up box. Move to the Look Up box (Alt+L), and change the word slightly by changing "custom" to "customs": Press the End key, type *s*, and then choose the Synonyms button (Alt+S). Word makes each of the words in the Synonyms list plural. From the list, choose "manners," and then choose the Replace button (Alt+R). The Replace command replaces the word "custom" in your document with the word "manners." "Custom" is marked with a strike-through line, "manners" is underlined (and appears in front of "custom"), and both words are selected.

Reviewing Your Revision Marks

By now your screen shows many revision marks—for the text you moved and copied and for the changes you made using spelling checking and the thesaurus. Before you go on to the finer points of polishing your document, you should review these changes, accept or undo the revisions, and turn off revision marking. The marked-up text in your document affects line breaks, page breaks, word count, hyphenation, and so on, so you'll want to get rid of the marks and the text marked for deletion when you're sure they're no longer needed and you want to see how your final document looks.

Start by choosing the Utilities Revision Marks command (Alt,U,M) and then choosing the Search button (Alt+S). Word finds and selects the first segment of text that contains revision marks. To accept all the

TIP

Replacing All Occurrences of a Word

When you want to replace all occurrences of a word rather than only one, use the Edit Replace command. For example, in your sample document, be sure that no text is selected, choose the Edit Replace command (Alt,E,E), type *custom* in the Search For box and *manners* in the Replace With box, turn off the Confirm Changes option (Alt+C), and then choose OK. All instances of "custom" are replaced with "manners."

revisions in the selected text, choose the Accept Revisions button (Alt+A). The underlining disappears from the new text, and the text that contains strike-through marks for deletion is removed.

To find the next segment of marked text, choose the Search button (Alt+S) again. If the text is behind the dialog box, you can move the dialog box out of the way: Either choose the Control Move command (Alt,spacebar,M) and use the arrow keys and the Enter key or drag the dialog box with the mouse. This time, try undoing the revisions by choosing the Undo Revisions button (Alt+V). The new text is removed from the document, and the strike-through lines disappear from the previously deleted text, which remains in the document.

For the rest of your document, you can continue to search for marked text and accept or undo each revision in this way. You can also accept or undo all remaining revisions at one time by closing the Mark Revisions dialog box, choosing the Utilities Revision Marks command (Alt,U,M) again, and then choosing either the Accept Revisions button (Alt+A) or the Undo Revisions button (Alt+V). For example, to accept the rest of the revisions in your example text, choose the Close button (Esc), be sure you have an insertion point, choose Utilities Revision Marks (Alt,U,M), and then choose the Accept Revisions button (Alt+A). When a dialog box appears, choose Yes to accept all revisions. Now that you have finished marking revisions, turn off the Mark Revisions option (Alt+M) in the Utilities Revision Marks dialog box and choose OK.

TIP

Marking Revisions with Revision Marking Turned Off

Even if you forget to use revision marking when you revise a document, you can still compare the original document and the revised version to review most changes. First, open the revised version of the document. Then, choose the Utilities Compare Versions command (Alt,U,V). In the Utilities Compare Versions dialog box, select the name of the original, unrevised document and choose OK. Word compares the two documents and, in the revised document, places a change bar in the margin next to each paragraph that has changed. Word does not mark new text with underlines, and deletions are no longer in the file for Word to mark with strike-through lines. To see individual revisions such as these, you must use the Utilities Revision Marks command to turn on revision marking during editing.

Your document now contains no revision marks, all the deleted text has been removed, and revision marking is turned off.

Using Hyphenation

One sign of a polished document is a minimum of raggedness at the right margin. Although you might not want to justify text—that is, make it flush with both the left and right margins—you might want to keep the line length in each paragraph fairly uniform. The easiest way to achieve uniformity is to hyphenate your document. Even where you do justify text, you might want to use hyphenation to reduce the amount of space that's added between words.

Word provides three methods for hyphenating words:

- You insert hyphens manually.
- Word inserts hyphens semiautomatically (it lets you approve the placement of each suggested hyphen).
- Word inserts hyphens automatically where needed.

Semiautomatic and automatic hyphenation break words at appropriate places and insert optional hyphens when the lines do not have enough space for whole words.

For semiautomatic and automatic hyphenation, you can adjust a Hot Zone at the right margin. The Hot Zone is explained later in this section.

Manual hyphenation

You can manually insert three different kinds of hyphens: regular, nonbreaking, and optional. Use a regular hyphen, which is always visible, if you want the word to have a hyphen regardless of its position in the line. Use a nonbreaking hyphen, which is always visible, if you want to prevent Word from starting a new line immediately before or after the hyphen. An optional hyphen appears only if the hyphen is needed at the end of a line. Use an optional hyphen if you want to permit Word to place at the end of the previous line the part of the word that's before the hyphen.

To insert a regular hyphen (-), simply type the hyphen. To insert a nonbreaking hyphen, press the Ctrl+Shift+hyphen keys. To insert an optional hyphen, press the Ctrl+hyphen keys.

Semiautomatic hyphenation

To hyphenate semiautomatically, first be sure you have an insertion point anywhere in the document. Then, choose the Utilities Hyphenate command (Alt,U,H). You see the Hyphenate dialog box. To start the hyphenation process, choose OK. Word displays a word in the Hyphenate at box; all appropriate breaks for the word are shown with hyphens.

A blinking square shows the suggested position for the hyphen. To select a different hyphenation point in the word, press the right arrow key or the left arrow key or click with the mouse. Selecting a hyphenation point to the right of the dotted, vertical bar in the word has no effect because the part of the word to the left of the hyphen is too long to fit at the end of the preceding line. To insert an optional hyphen at the point shown by the blinking cursor and then find the next word for hyphenation, choose Yes. To bypass the word and find the next word for hyphenation, choose No. And if you want to stop hyphenation altogether, choose Cancel.

When Word finishes hyphenating your document, you see a message that tells you it has completed hyphenation. Choose OK. Word also selects all the text between the starting and ending points of the hyphenation process. To cancel the selection, press an arrow key or click the mouse.

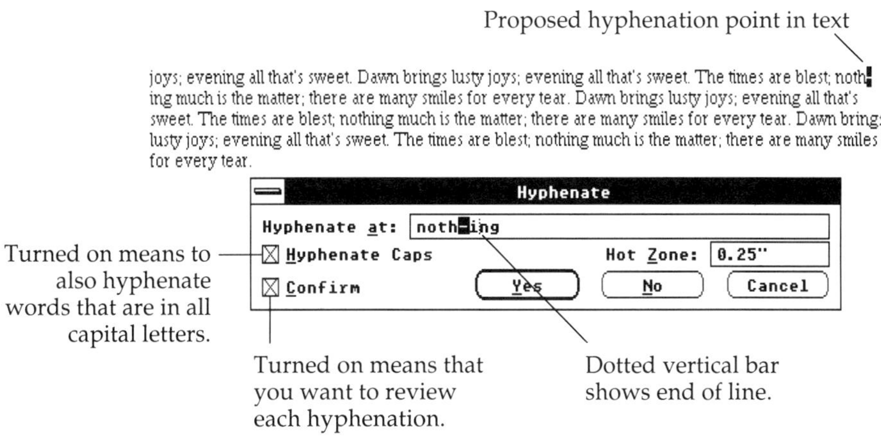

Figure 4-1.
Word's Utilities Hyphenate dialog box.

The Utilities Hyphenate dialog box, shown in Figure 4-1, contains a box labeled Hot Zone. This box shows a measurement for the area at the right margin in which you want words hyphenated. Word tries to hyphenate when the amount of blank space at the end of a line is greater than the measurement you type in the Hot Zone box. You use this box to increase or decrease the amount of raggedness at the right margin, and thus the number of hyphens that Word inserts. If you type a smaller measurement, Word inserts more hyphens and the lines are less ragged at the right margin. If you type a larger measurement, Word inserts fewer hyphens and the lines are more ragged at the right margin. The default measurement of one-quarter inch (0.25") is a good compromise for the Hot Zone width. You might want to decrease that measurement if you print in more than one column, or increase the measurement if Word inserts too many hyphens for your taste.

Numbering Paragraphs

Word lets you number paragraphs with automatic numbers. The number for each paragraph changes as you move, insert, or delete paragraphs with automatic numbers. In addition to automatic numbering, you can use two other forms of numbering: sequential and manual. Sequential numbering lets you number groups of items, such as graphics or tables, throughout a document. Chapter 8, "Fields: Facts and Functions," explains fields and sequential numbering.

Manual paragraph numbers are text, rather than fields, that Word inserts at the beginning of selected paragraphs when you choose the Utilities Renumber command (Alt,U,R). For a description of manual paragraph numbers, see the tip "Numbering Paragraphs in a Table" in Chapter 13.

To see how automatic numbering works, choose the Utilities Renumber command (Alt,U,R). Word displays the Renumber Paragraphs dialog box:

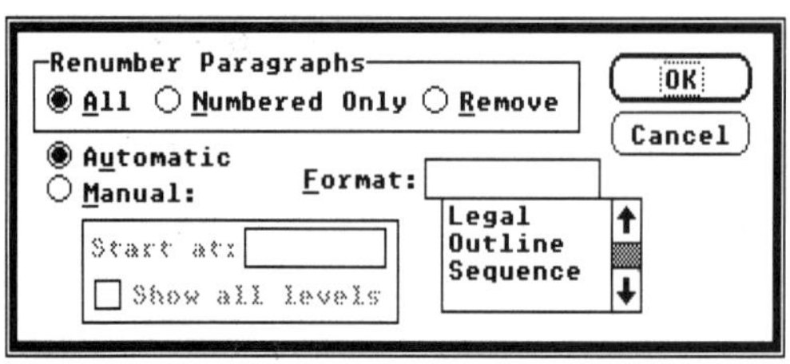

In the Format box (Alt+F), select Sequence (S,F4). Then, choose OK. Each paragraph now begins with a number followed by a period and a tab. If you see "{autonum}" instead of a number in the document, check to be sure that the View Field Codes command is turned off and that the Show All option is turned off in the View Preferences dialog box. Start another paragraph to check that adding new paragraphs does not affect numbering: Position the insertion point in the middle of the first paragraph and press the Enter key; Word adds an unnumbered paragraph.

To add a number in front of the new paragraph, choose Utilities Renumber again. In the Renumber Paragraphs dialog box, select Sequence in the Format box (Alt+F,S,F4), and then choose OK.

Position the insertion point in the middle of the third paragraph, and press the Enter key (to start another paragraph). To number this new paragraph, follow the same steps: Choose the Utilities Renumber command (Alt,U,R), select Sequence in the Format box, and then choose OK.

To see the numbers change, move the third paragraph so that it precedes the second: Select the third paragraph, press the MOVE key (F2), press the Ctrl+up arrow key to position the insertion point at the beginning of the second paragraph, and then press the Enter key. The paragraph moves, and the numbers change.

In the middle of an automatically numbered sequence, you can insert paragraphs that do not have numbers. These paragraphs do not affect the sequence of existing numbers.

Automatic paragraph numbering is based on your document's outline. All paragraphs to which the same heading level (heading 1 through heading 9) styles have been applied are numbered consecutively, between headings at a higher level, as shown in Figure 4-2 on the following page.

Using Annotations

When your document is in the shape you want, you might need to send it out for review. In Word, you can lock your document so that other users can add comments in the form of annotations but cannot change the text itself. When you receive the annotations, you can choose to incorporate them into your text, edit them, ignore them, or delete them. Typically, you would not annotate your own documents, although you

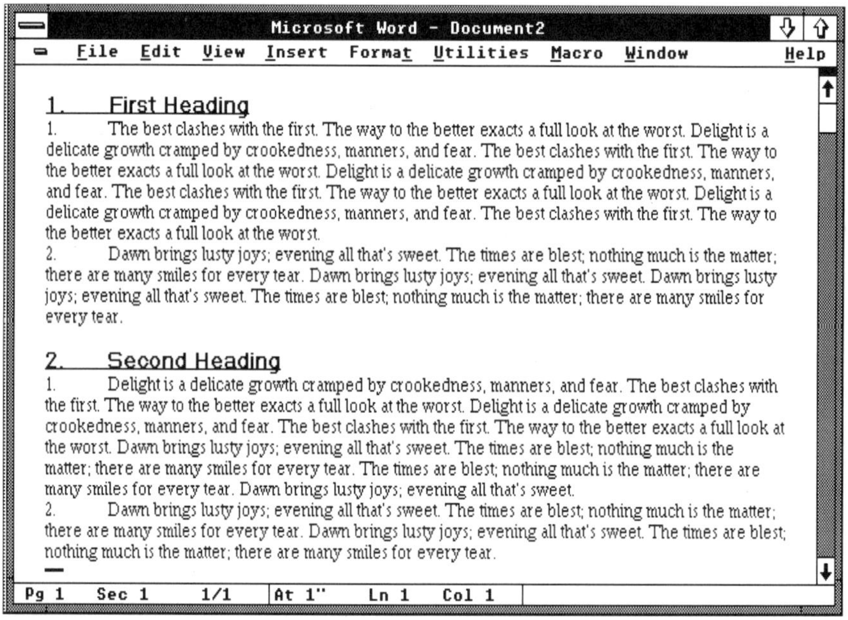

Figure 4-2.
Automatic paragraph numbering is based on your document's outline.

could use annotations as notes to yourself about revisions that you still want to make to your document. Figure 4-3 shows a document that contains an annotation.

To lock your document and then insert and delete annotations, start by choosing the File Save As command (Alt,F,A). In the File Save As dialog box, type a name for the document, choose the Options button (Alt+O), turn on the Lock for Annotations option (Alt+L), and then choose OK. Because you are the document's author, you will not notice any difference in the ways in which you can work with your document. You can change it in any way that you want. If other users were to open the document now, however, they would find that they could insert and view annotations but could change nothing else. For example, choose the Utilities Customize command (Alt,U,U), change your name in the dialog box to another name, choose OK, close the document, and then open it again. Take a look at the menus: Now only a few commands are available. From the Insert menu, for example, you can choose the Annotation command (Alt,I,A) only.

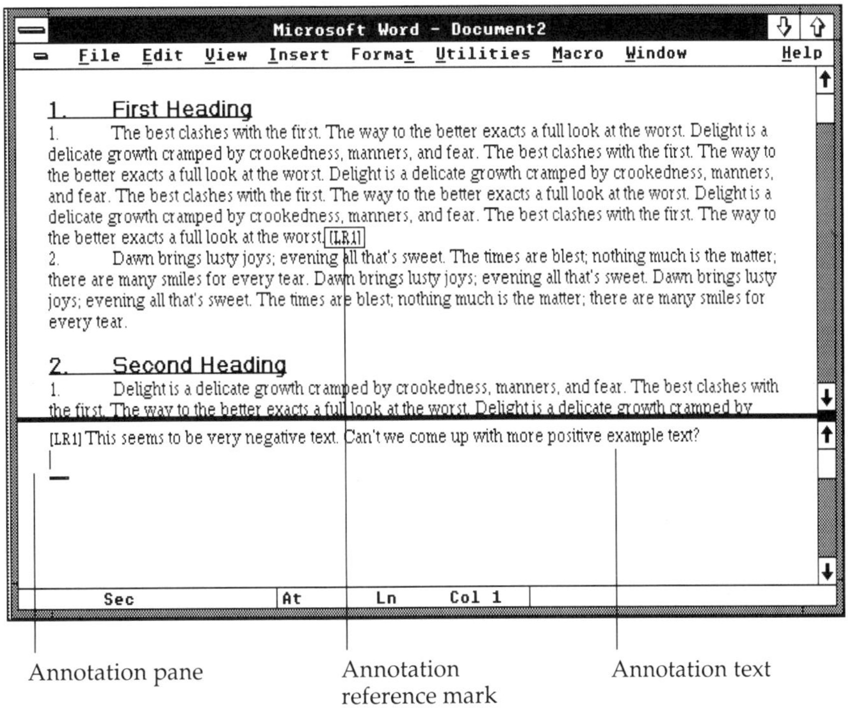

Figure 4-3.
A document that contains annotations.

Now, choose the Insert Annotation command (Alt,I,A). Word splits the window and inserts your initials, followed by a sequential annotation number, in the document pane and in the annotations pane.

Type a comment of any length. You can format an annotation's characters and paragraphs any way you want, but you cannot use styles: Word assigns a special style to annotations. When you finish the comment, press the NEXT PANE key (F6) to return to the document pane. Position the insertion point where you want to insert the next annotation, choose the Insert Annotation command (Alt,I,A) again, and then type and format your next comment.

Choose the File Save command (Alt,F,S) to save the document after you finish inserting annotations. Word saves your annotations on disk, along with the document.

To see a document that contains annotations as it appears when a reviewer returns it to you, choose the Utilities Customize command (Alt,U,U). Change the name back to your own, choose OK, close the document, and then open it again. The full menus are now restored, and the annotation reference marks are no longer visible because they are formatted as hidden text, and the Hidden Text option is turned off in the View Preferences dialog box.

When you're ready to review the annotations, open the annotations pane by choosing the View Annotations command (Alt,V,A). The window splits, and the annotations appear in the lower pane. The annotation reference marks are again visible in the document because View Annotations also turns on the hidden text option for as long as the annotation is displayed.

To act on an annotation, you can delete it, copy it to the document, change the document based on the annotation, ignore the annotation but leave it intact, or edit the annotation by adding your own note to it.

TIP

Making Groups of Annotations Distinguishable at a Glance

You might find it difficult to see at a glance all of one person's annotations. To make it easier to distinguish among different reviewers, each reviewer can use a different color.

After annotating the document, the reviewer can select the annotation text in the annotation pane and apply a color to it. A reviewer or an author applies color either by choosing the Format Character command or by pressing the COLOR key combination (Ctrl+V), typing the name of the color, and then pressing the Enter key.

Word assigns special annotation styles to both annotation reference marks and annotation text. (Chapter 5, "Refining Documents," explains more about using styles.) To prevent changes to a document, Word does not let you change style formatting in the document pane while the document is locked. As a result, you cannot change the color of the annotation reference marks in the document pane unless you're the author. But either the author or the reviewer can change the color of both the annotation reference marks and the annotation text in the annotation pane.

As you review annotations, you'll find that the most convenient way to move from one annotation reference mark to the next is to use the Edit Go To command (Alt,E,G) or the GO TO key (F5). Either choose Edit Go To or press F5, type *a*, and then press the Enter key to jump to the next annotation reference mark. You jump from the document pane to the annotation text in the annotation pane by pressing the NEXT PANE key (F6).

You delete an annotation by jumping to the annotation reference mark in the document pane, selecting it, and then pressing the Delete key. Word deletes the annotation text when you delete an annotation reference mark.

After you finish reviewing and deciding what to do with the annotations, you might need to unlock the document so that others can make changes. To unlock your document, choose File Save As (Alt,F,A), choose the Options button (Alt+O), turn off the Lock for Annotations option (Alt+L), and then choose OK.

Printing Your Document

Before you can print, your printer must be set up and ready. This process involves both hardware and software: the printer hardware, the printer's physical connections to your computer, and the printing software. After your printer is physically set up and connected, see the next section for a summary of the steps that you follow to set up the printer software. Then you'll be ready to print your document.

Setting Up Your Printer

If you installed Word using the Setup program that came with your copy of Word, your printer software is probably set up. If you chose not to set up your printer during installation, you need to either go through the setup process again, skipping the parts you've already completed, or follow the steps that are summarized here. You also need to follow this procedure if you've added or changed printers since you ran the Setup program. *Microsoft Word for Windows Printer Guide* and the *Microsoft Windows Basic Skills for Windows Applications* manual that came with your copy of Word contain more information about setting up your printer software.

Setting up your printer involves three basic procedures: installing your printer in Windows, setting your printer options, and choosing from among the installed printers.

To install a printer:

1. Choose the Word Control Run command. (You can use Alt,spacebar,U.)
2. Select the Control Panel option (Alt+P), and then choose OK.
3. Choose the Installation Add New Printer command (Alt,I,N).
4. Type the name of the disk drive and directory in which the printer-driver files you want are located, and then choose OK.
5. Choose the printer you want to install or add, and then choose the Add button (Alt+A).
6. If you want to copy the printer-driver file to your printer-driver directory, choose the Yes button (Alt+Y).

   If the printer-driver file is already in the directory in which you want it, choose No (Alt+N).
7. Choose the Setup Connections command (Alt,S,C).
8. Select a printer and a connection. If another printer is already using the connection you want to use, change that printer's connection to NONE and then connect the new printer. Choose OK.
9. Choose the Setup Printer command (Alt,S,P).
10. Select the printer you want to use most often, and then choose OK.

    This is the printer Word will use when you choose the File Print, File Print Merge, or File Find command to print documents. You can change the printer selection by using the File Printer Setup command.
11. If you have a serial printer, choose Setup Communications Port (Alt,S,M).

12. Type the number you want in the Baud Rate box, choose the other communications settings that are appropriate, and then choose OK.
13. Close the Control Panel (Alt,spacebar,C).

To select or change a printer:

1. Choose File Printer Setup (Alt,F,R).
2. Select the printer you want to use.
3. Choose the Setup button (Alt+S), select a specific printer in the dialog box, adjust any printer settings that you need to change, and then choose OK in each dialog box until all dialog boxes are closed.

The contents of the Setup dialog box change depending on which printer driver you selected and which printer you use with that printer driver. For PostScript drivers, you can select from among many different printer makes and models. You can also set options for header files, error reporting, and handshaking. For information about these options, consult *Microsoft Word for Windows Printer Guide*, along with your Windows and printer documentation. For Hewlett-Packard LaserJet printers and similar laser printers, you can select from among the various makes and models and the available cartridges and soft fonts and according to the amount of memory in the printer. For printers that Windows does not support, Word contains a special printer driver named PRDDRV.DRV. This driver lets you print with printers that use the PRD printer files that Microsoft supplies with its MS-DOS version of Microsoft Word. For information about this printer Setup dialog box and about using the MS-DOS version of Word's PRD files, see *Microsoft Word for Windows Printer Guide* and your printer documentation.

Printing

Printing a Word document is an easy task when your printer is ready to use. You can print additional parts of a document—such as annotations—either along with or instead of the document text.

To print a document and its annotations, start by choosing the File Print command (Alt,F,P). In the File Print dialog box that's shown on the following page, you can specify both the number of copies and the specific pages to print.

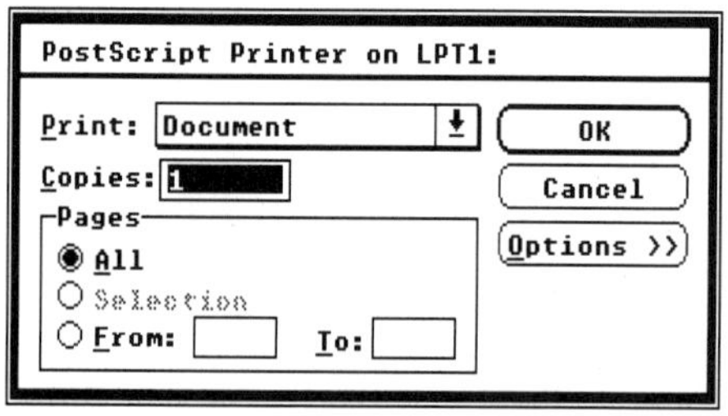

Choose the Options button to open the rest of the dialog box:

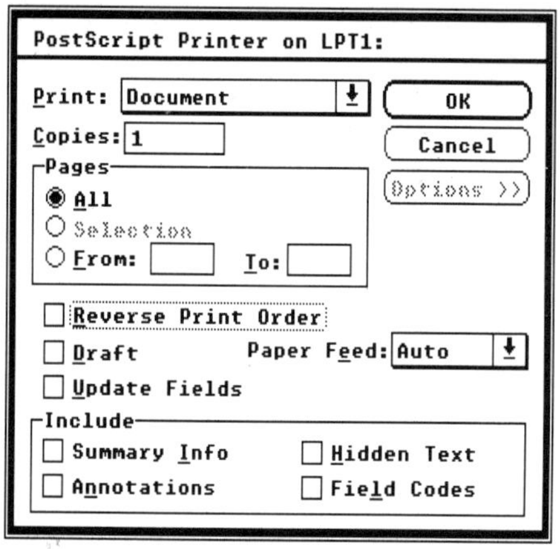

Turn on the Include Annotations option (Alt+N). This option also turns on the Hidden Text option, which tells Word to print hidden text. As mentioned earlier in this chapter, annotation reference marks are formatted as hidden text and will not print unless the Hidden Text option in the File Print dialog box is turned on. To start printing, choose OK. Word prints the entire document first and then prints the annotations. The annotation reference marks appear where reviewers inserted them in the document text.

Saving After Printing

After you finish printing, choose the File Save command (Alt,F,S) to save the document before closing it or quitting Word. After you save the document, you can be sure that it exactly matches the printed document. You might be saving only the new page breaks, but saving this information could become important later if you want to make changes based on your printed copy.

Chapter 5

Refining Documents

After you create a document, you'll probably want to refine it by making such changes as formatting text, modifying page breaks, and adding a table of contents and an index. This chapter walks you through the processes of refining a draft document in Word for Windows and previewing before you print.

Organizing Ideas

Suppose you recently attended a seminar and made a list of a few important items. So that you can follow the examples in this chapter, create a new document that includes the following list, with one item per paragraph:

Public relations means making converts.
Making the business case requires understanding the customer's case.
Never reinventing the wheel means being content with the Stone Age.
Memory enriches life and work.
Never leave well enough alone.
It needs brains to be a real fool.
Innovate! Innovate! Dance on the rubric!
While those who ignore history may be doomed to repeat it, those who study history are usually only looking for precedent.
Compatibility means shared mistakes.

Now suppose that you want to organize these ideas into a coherent, polished report. The following sections explain how.

Outlining to Structure Your Documents

Some might remember outlining as a boring, pointless task that one had to perform for the English teacher. Often people do not use outlines because of such negative memories or because they believe that outlining takes time away from writing. In Word, outlining is integrated with the whole process of creating a document, so any time you spend creating an outline is actually time spent adding material to your document. Beyond using an outline to structure your documents, you can use outlines to order your thoughts and to quickly reorganize a document, to emphasize your major points by making them into headings that can be used as entries in a table of contents, and to provide a framework that lets you move through your document with ease.

To get a taste of using outlining in Word, organize the list items you just typed by putting them into logical order and adding headings to group them: Start by positioning the insertion point anywhere in the second item, and then press the following outline keys: Alt+Shift+up arrow key. The second item in the list moves up to become the first:

Making the business case requires understanding the customer's case. — Pressing the Alt+Shift+up arrow keys moved this line up.
Public relations means making converts.
Never reinventing the wheel means being content with the Stone Age.
Memory enriches life and work.
Never leave well enough alone.
It needs brains to be a real fool.
Innovate! Innovate! Dance on the rubric!
While those who ignore history may be doomed to repeat it, those who study history are usually only looking for precedent.
Compatibility means shared mistakes.

The Alt+Shift+arrow keys are Word's outline keys. The up and down arrow keys move paragraphs up and down in the outline. The right arrow key demotes a heading one level by assigning the appropriate heading style to it, and the left arrow key promotes a heading one level. Later in this section, you'll find a summary of all the outline keys in "A summary of the outline keys."

You can make all these changes to the outline in normal editing view. In Outline View, you can use these outline keys or the mouse to make changes. And Outline View shows you the structure of the outline by indenting the various heading levels. To switch to Outline View, choose the View Outline command (Alt,V,O).

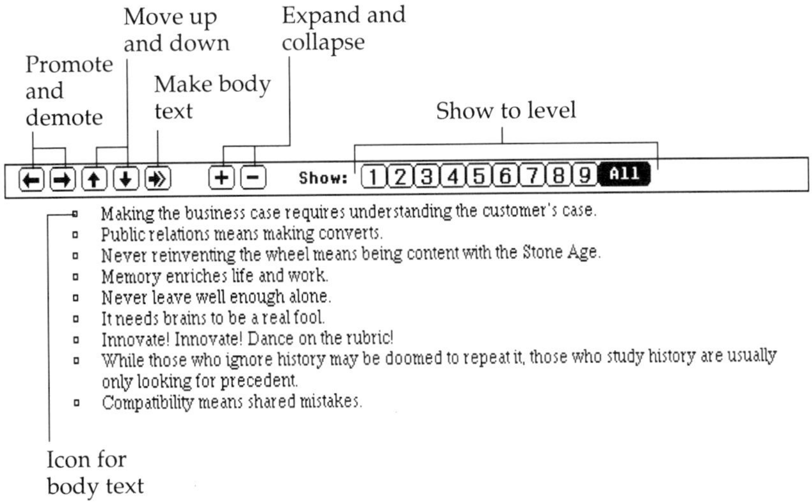

If you have a mouse, you can click the icons on the icon bar to manipulate the outline. You'll find this approach especially handy when you want to move two or more consecutive paragraphs that are at the same heading level to a new location in your document. To move the paragraphs, select them and then click the up icon or the down icon on the icon bar. If you do not have a mouse, press the Alt+Shift+up arrow or down arrow keys. For example, select the last two list items. Note that you can select any amount of text within one paragraph. But when a selection crosses into a second paragraph, you can select only whole paragraphs. Click the up icon on the icon bar or press Alt+Shift+up arrow key until the selected items are third and fourth in the list, below "Public relations means making converts."

You can also move your list items by dragging the icons that are next to the individual paragraphs. For example, point to the icon for the next-to-last item. The mouse pointer changes to a four-headed arrow, as illustrated on the following page.

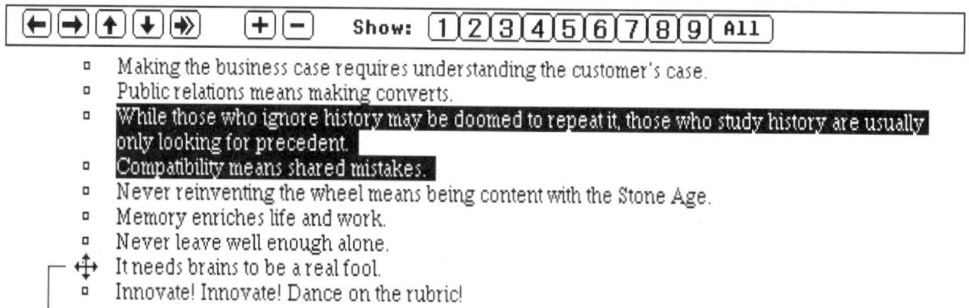

Four-headed arrow indicates ready to drag with mouse.

Drag the icon downward until the dotted horizontal line that appears is at the bottom of the list, and then release the mouse button—that item is now the last in the list. You can also drag a paragraph icon upward by dragging until the dotted horizontal line is positioned where you want to move your selected list item, between the two paragraphs. You can drag only one heading level at a time. But when you start to drag a heading, all its subtext—including any subordinate headings and body text—is selected and moves with the heading.

Exactly as you can click the up and down icons on the icon bar to move paragraphs upward and downward, you can click the promote and demote icons on the icon bar to promote and demote headings, and you can click the demote-to-body-text icon to demote headings to body text. You can also drag headings to the right and left to demote and promote them. Use the icon bar to promote and demote multiple paragraphs that are at the same level, and use dragging to promote and demote a heading and its subtext. If you do not have a mouse, you can use the Alt+Shift+left arrow keys to promote a heading, the Alt+Shift+right arrow keys to demote a heading, and the Alt+Shift+5 keys (5 on the numeric keypad) to convert a heading to body text.

In your example text, select all the list items and then click the promote icon on the icon bar, or press the Alt+Shift+left arrow keys. You have assigned the heading 1 style to the items. To see the heading style, choose the View Preferences command (Alt,V,E), move to the Style Area Width box (Alt+W) in the View Preferences dialog box, type *0.6*, and then choose OK. The style names appear in a column along the window's left side. Styles named "heading" plus a number indicate heading paragraphs. Styles named "Normal" or anything other than "heading" indicate body text.

Style area shows level of each heading.

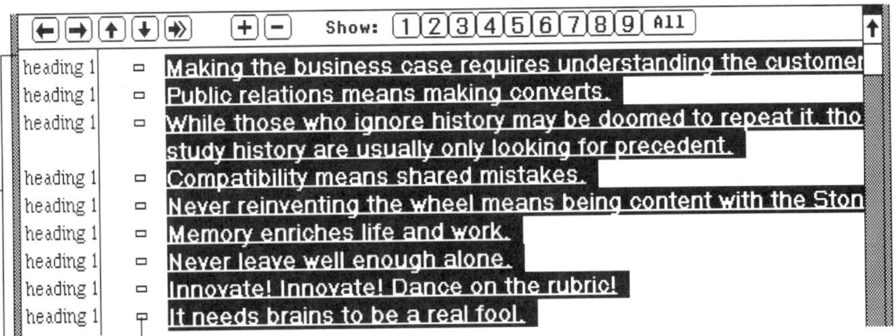

Icon for heading without subtext

Now, add a couple of new paragraphs—these will become major headings for grouping the existing list items. Start by positioning the insertion point in front of the first item, pressing the Enter key to start a new paragraph, and then moving the insertion point back up to the new paragraph. The new paragraph is also heading level 1. Type the following text for the new heading:

Customers are the Business

Next, add another paragraph between the two sentences that begin with "Public relations means" and "While those who ignore." Move the insertion point to the end of "Public relations means making converts," press the Enter key to start a new paragraph, and then type the following text for the new heading:

Creativity is the Product

Demote the second and third paragraphs to heading level 2 by dragging each item's icon to the right, by selecting the text and clicking the demote icon on the icon bar, or by selecting the text and pressing the Alt+Shift+right arrow keys. Also demote to heading level 2 all the headings that are below the second heading you just inserted ("Creativity is the Product").

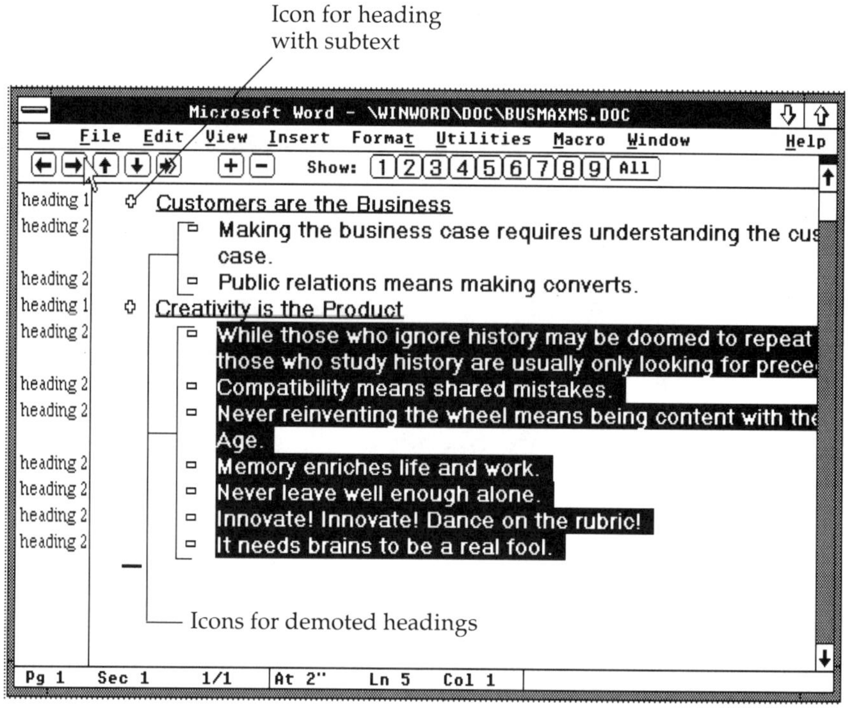

Under the heading that begins with "Never reinventing the wheel," add some body text: Start by positioning the insertion point at the end of the "Never reinventing the wheel" paragraph and then pressing the Enter key to create a new heading level 2 paragraph. Demote that heading paragraph to body text by dragging the paragraph icon to the right until it snaps to the left and stays there, by clicking the body text icon on the icon bar, or by pressing the Alt+Shift+5 keys (5 on the numeric keypad). Then, in a paragraph by itself, type each of the items as shown on the following page.

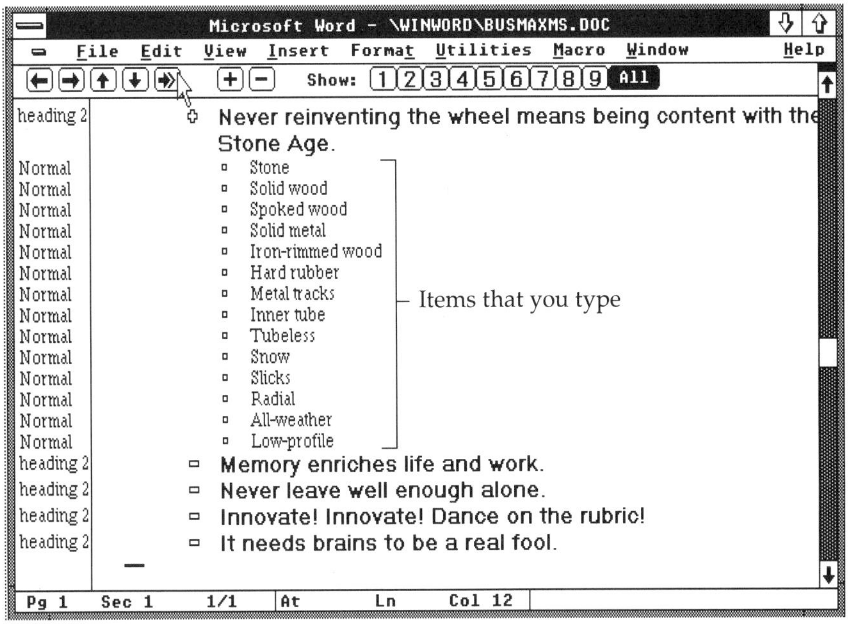

You'll work with the above list of items later in the chapter. For now, collapse the outline so that the list is hidden and you can see more of the whole outline. To collapse an outline, position the insertion point in the heading that begins with "Never reinventing the wheel," and then use one of the following methods:

- Double-click the paragraph icon.
- Click the collapse icon on the icon bar.
- Press the minus sign key (–) on the numeric keypad.
- Press the Alt+Shift+minus sign keys (using the minus sign key either on the numeric keypad or above the letter keys).

Note that the paragraph icon changes from a minus sign to a plus sign and that Word displays a gray underline beneath the heading. The plus sign indicates that the heading has subtext. The gray underline indicates that the subtext is collapsed.

Next, to see how Word displays tables in Outline View, add a table to your outline. This example also shows you that you can move a table in a document in the same way that you move a paragraph of text. (Chapter 13, "Tables the New, Easy Way" explains in detail how to use tables in Word.) Position the insertion point at the end of the heading that begins with "Making the business case," press the Enter key, and then demote the new paragraph to body text. Choose the Insert Table command (Alt,I,T), and then choose OK in the Insert Table dialog box to insert a two-column table. After you type each piece of information as shown in Figure 5-1, press the Tab key to move to the next column of the table, as indicated by the → symbol. Word adds another row to the table when you press the Tab key at the end of a row.

Indicates press Tab to move to next cell
(arrows will not appear on screen)

Version →	Units shipped (K) →
1.0 →	64 →
1.1 →	100 →
1.5 →	87 →
2.0 →	50 →
2.1 →	99

Figure 5-1.
Units Shipped table.

At this point you should save your document, using the File Save (Alt,F,S) command. Because you're saving this document for the first time, Word displays the File Save As dialog box. Type a name for the document and choose OK. Word also displays the Edit Summary Info dialog box the first time you save a document. You use this dialog box to give Word summary information about the document—information that will help you to find the document again. Fill in the summary information now so that you'll have an example of this summary information to use later in the chapter when you try the File Find command. Fill in the dialog box as shown on the following page, and then press the Enter key.

Author's name is filled in by Word (but you can edit the name).

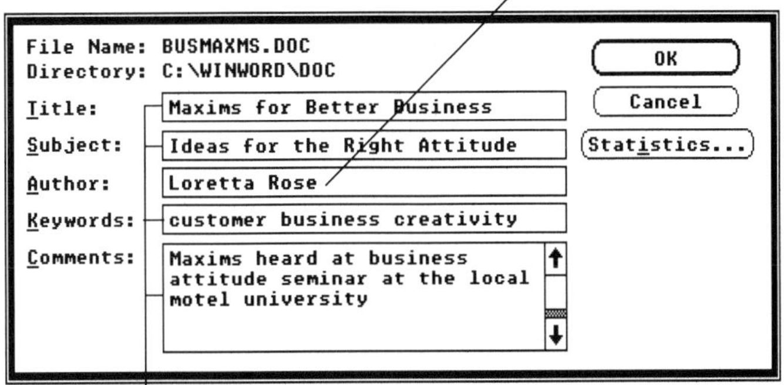

Fill in other boxes as appropriate.

A summary of the outline keys

The table below shows the keys that you use as outline keys. Except as noted, the outline keys work in normal editing view, in Outline View, in Draft View, and in Page View.

Keys	*Action*
Alt+Shift+left arrow key	Promotes heading; applies next higher heading style
Alt+Shift+right arrow key	Demotes heading; applies next lower heading style
Alt+Shift+5 (numeric keypad)	Demotes to body text; applies Normal style
Alt+Shift+up arrow key	Moves paragraph to above next visible paragraph
Alt+Shift+down arrow key	Moves paragraph to below next visible paragraph
Alt+Shift+1 through 9	Shows headings at level specified (in Outline View only)
Alt+Shift+A, or * on the numeric keypad without Alt+ Shift	Expands outline to show all headings and body text (Outline View only)
Alt+Shift+F	Shows full body text or only first line (toggle; in Outline View only)

(continued)

continued

Keys	*Action*
Alt+Shift+plus sign key (+), either on the numeric keypad or above the letter keys; you can also press + on the numeric keypad without pressing Alt+Shift	Expands the selected headings to show next level of subtext (in Outline View only)
Alt+Shift+minus sign key (–), either on the numeric keypad or above the letter keys; you can also press – on the numeric keypad without pressing Alt+Shift	Collapses the selected headings to hide next level of subtext (in Outline View only)

Sorting Information in Your Document

You might want to arrange some types of information in your documents alphabetically, numerically, or chronologically. Lists, for example, often contain numeric information. In Word, the Utilities Sort command will arrange your information for you.

You can choose to arrange the information in either ascending or descending order—from A to Z, 1 to 9, or earliest date to latest; or from Z to A, 9 to 1, or latest date to earliest. You might arrange alphabetic and historic lists in ascending order, for example, and lists of quantities in descending order.

Alphabetic sorting in a document outline

To see how easy it is to sort an alphabetic list quickly, try this example. You'll also see how you can use sorting to reorder whole sections of a document. Start by checking to see whether you're still in Outline View—if not, choose the View Outline command (Alt,V,O). To make only heading levels 1 and 2 visible, click the 2 on the icon bar or press the Alt+Shift+2 keys (2 above the letter keys). Select all the items that follow the "Creativity is the Product" heading, but do not select the heading itself. Choose the Utilities Sort command (Alt,U,O), and then choose OK in the Utilities Sort dialog box. Word arranges the items in alphabetic order. If the list of items under the heading that begins with "Never reinventing the wheel" expands, click the 2 on the icon bar again or press Alt+Shift+2 (2 above the letter keys).

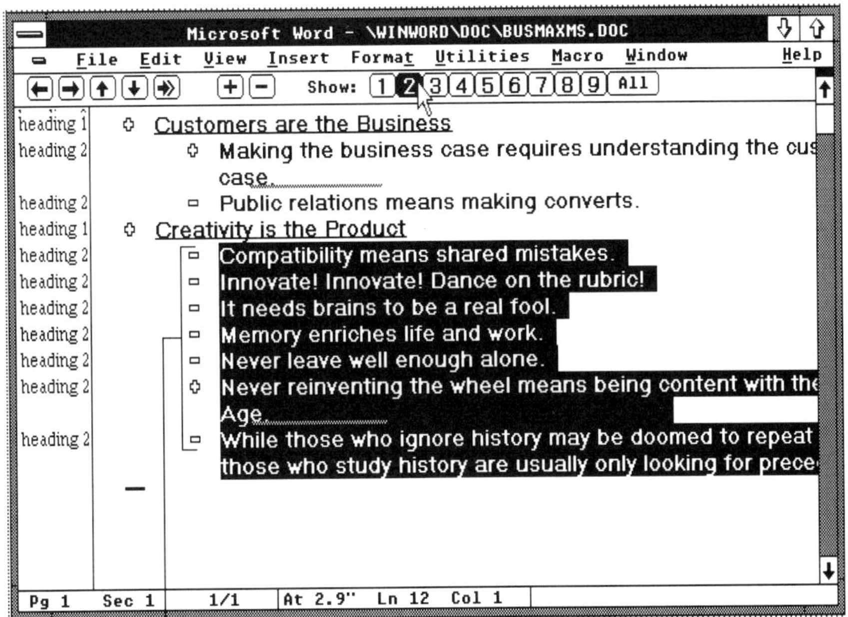

Headings are now in alphabetic order.

Sorting in tables

You also have the option of sorting the information in a table, based on any of the table's columns. Chapter 13, "Tables the New, Easy Way," explains in detail how to sort columns in tables. In Figure 5-2, you see a simple example of numeric sorting in a table.

In the table you added to your example document, the information lists the versions in ascending order:

Ascending order

Version	Units shipped (K)
1.0	64
1.1	100
1.5	87
2.0	50
2.1	99

Figure 5-2.
Table of versions in ascending order.

To see which versions were most popular, you might instead want to see the information in descending order of the number of units shipped. To sort the table based on the second column, "Units Shipped (K)," switch from Outline View back to normal editing view. You want to switch from Outline View so that you can select a column; in Outline View, you can select only whole rows in a table. Next, select rows 2 through 6 of the table, excluding the column headings, and choose the Utilities Sort command (Alt,U,O).

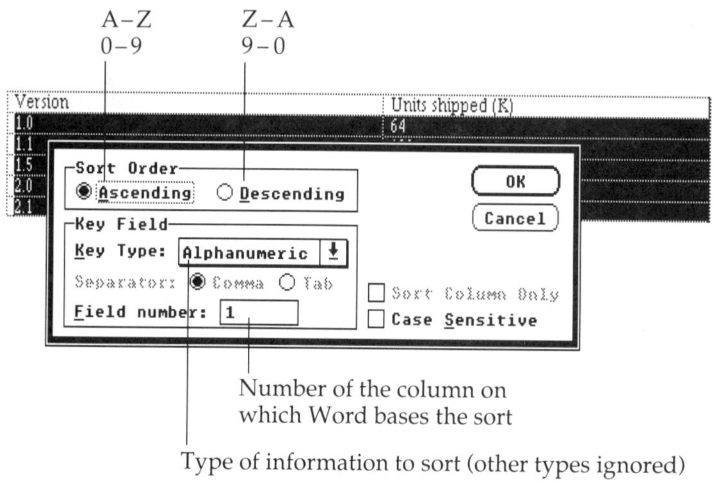

In the Utilities Sort dialog box, choose the Descending option for Sort Order (Alt+D), move to the Key Type box (Alt+K) and select Numeric (press N), move to the Field number box (Alt+F) and type 2 to indicate the second column, and then choose OK. Word sorts the list so that the version number with the most units shipped is at the top.

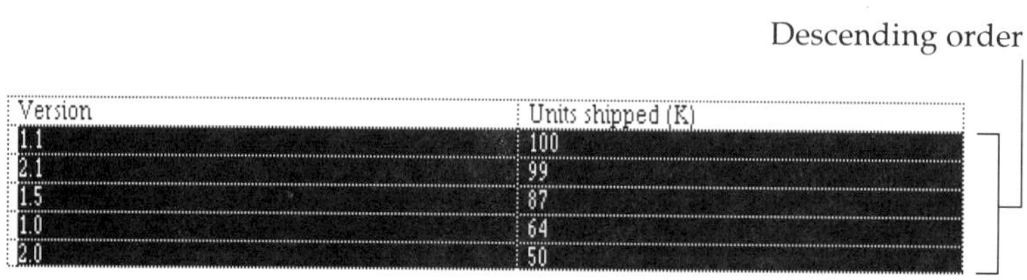

At this point, choose the File Save command (Alt,F,S) to save the document again.

Formatting the Document

As you create and refine your document, you'll want to decide on the appearance of the document's contents. You can format text characters, graphics, lines, and pages.

Formatting Characters

Formatting the text characters means setting the type style and size of the letters and words, setting the vertical position of the character relative to other characters in the line (for superscript and subscript), and setting the amount of spacing between characters (similar to kerning). You use the mouse, the keyboard, or the Format Character command to format text. When you use the mouse or the keyboard to format, you change only one formatting element at a time. For example, to format text as boldface and italic, you change it to boldface and then use the mouse or the keyboard a second time to change it to italic. When you use the Format Character command (Alt,T,C) to format, however, you make all the text formatting changes at one time in a dialog box. On the next page, "A summary of combination keys for character formatting" provides a summary of all the key combinations that are available when you use the keyboard to format characters.

To try character formatting, select the top row of column headings in your table. To make the selection boldface, use one of the following methods:

- Using the mouse, click the "B" (boldface) icon on the ribbon. If the ribbon is not displayed, choose the View Ribbon command (Alt,V,B) to turn it on.
- Using the keyboard, press the Ctrl+B keys.
- Using the Format Character command (Alt,T,C), turn on the Bold option (Alt+B) in the Format Character dialog box, and then choose OK.

Without changing the selection, make the text italic as well, using one of these methods:

- Using the mouse, click the "I" icon on the ribbon. If the ribbon is not displayed, choose View Ribbon (Alt,V,B) to turn it on.

- Using the keyboard, press the Ctrl+I keys.
- Choose the Format Character command (Alt,T,C), turn on the Italic option (Alt+I) in the Format Character dialog box, and then choose OK.

The text is now both italic and boldface:

Version	***Units shipped (K)***
1.1	100
2.1	99
1.5	87
1.0	64
2.0	50

Anytime you add one text format to another, the new and the existing text formats are combined. Select the heading "Creativity is the Product," and remove the underlining using one of the following methods:

- Using the mouse, click the "U" icon on the ribbon. If the ribbon is not displayed, choose the View Ribbon command (Alt,V,B) to turn the ribbon on.
- Using the keyboard, press the Ctrl+U keys.
- Using the Format Character command (Alt,T,C), turn off the Underline option (Alt+U) in the Format Character dialog box, and then choose OK.

As this example shows, the basic steps you follow to apply or to remove a text format are the same. You toggle between the on and off format settings.

A summary of combination keys for character formatting

When you use the keyboard for character formatting, you can use the following Ctrl key combinations:

Ctrl Key Combination	*Applies*
Ctrl+B	Boldface
Ctrl+I	Italic
Ctrl+U	Underline (does not break between words)
Ctrl+W	Word underline (breaks between words)
Ctrl+D	Double underline (does not break between words)

(continued)

continued

Ctrl Key Combination	*Applies*
Ctrl+Shift+ equal sign key (=)	Superscript by 3 points (1 point = 1/72 inch)
Ctrl+equal sign key (=)	Subscript by 3 points
Ctrl+H	Hidden text format
Ctrl+K	Small capitals
Ctrl+F	Font change
Ctrl+P	Point size change
Ctrl+V	Color change
Ctrl+spacebar	Removes all text formatting applied and lets only paragraph style determine text format

Formatting Graphics

After you insert a graphic, you have several formatting options: Add a border around the graphic, crop it (that is, cut off part), and scale it (enlarge or reduce its image size). Move the insertion point to the end of the heading "Public relations means making converts," press the Enter key, and insert a graphic. See "Creating Document Contents" in Chapter 4 for information about how to insert graphics.

To add a border to a graphic, first select the graphic: If you use a mouse, either click the graphic or drag across it. If you use the keyboard, select the graphic as you would select a single character of text.

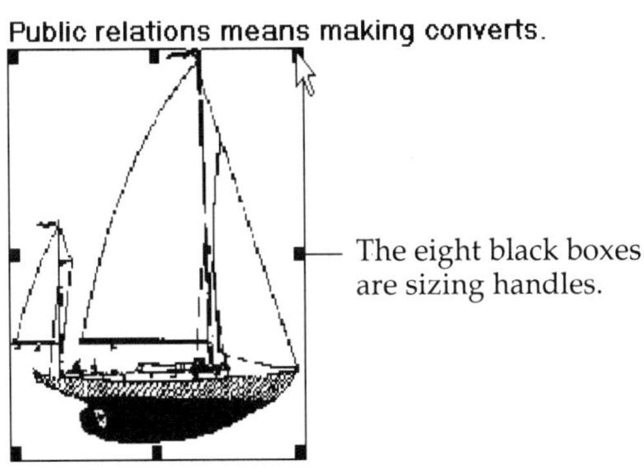

Choose the Format Picture command (Alt,T,R), select a Picture Border style, and then choose OK.

To crop or scale a graphic, use the mouse or the Format Picture command. First, select the graphic. To crop a graphic using the mouse, drag any one of the sizing handles. Dragging into the graphic crops part of the image. Dragging away from the graphic adds white space along that side of the image. To scale a graphic using the mouse, hold down the Shift key while you drag a sizing handle. When you press Shift and drag into the graphic, you scale down (decrease the size of)

TIP

Displaying Text in Color

To add pizzazz to your display and to take advantage of a color printer if you have one, you can format your text in one of eight colors: black, white, red, blue, cyan, magenta, yellow, or green. Word applies color to text in the same way it applies boldface or any other formatting.

Auto color display is another option. If you choose the Auto option in the Format Character dialog box, Word displays text in the default text color that you set using the Preferences command in the Windows Control Panel. You can change the color of any amount of text—a character, word, sentence, paragraph, and so on. And you can use all eight colors in a single document. If you have a color printer, Word prints your text in the colors you apply. If you do not have a color printer, Word prints your text in the printer's single color, as if you had not applied color.

To try applying color to text, select the heading "Customers are the Business." Choose the Format Character command (Alt,T,C), move to the Color box (Alt+L) in the Format Character dialog box, select one of the colors, and then choose OK. The heading text is now displayed in the selected color.

You can also use the COLOR key combination (Ctrl+V) to apply color to text. Select the text you want to color, press the Ctrl+V keys, type the name of the color, and then press the Enter key. Note that when you type a color name, you need type only the first letter of the color, except when you choose black or blue. For black or blue, type at least the first three letters so that Word knows which of the two colors you want. If you forget which colors are available, press the COLOR key combination (Ctr+V) again to see the Format Character dialog box.

the image. When you press Shift and drag away from the graphic, you scale up (increase the size of) the image. To crop and scale a graphic using the Format Picture command, choose Format Picture (Alt,T,R).

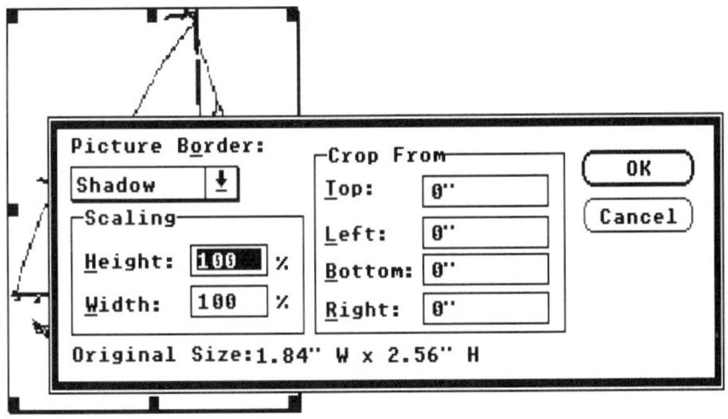

Figure 5-3.
Format Picture dialog box.

To scale a graphic, type a percentage in the Scaling Height and Width boxes. Typing a number that's less than 100 scales down the image size. Typing a number that's greater than 100 scales up the image size. To crop a graphic, type a measurement in the appropriate Crop From box(es): Top, Left, Bottom, and Right. A positive measurement cuts off part of the image. A negative measurement adds white space along that side of the image. If you also want to add a border around the graphic, select a Picture Border style. When you have assigned all desired formatting, choose OK.

Note that the Format Picture dialog box displays the graphic's original size (see Figure 5-3 above). To return a graphic to its original size after you crop and scale it, type *100* for each of the Scaling percentages and *0* (zero) for each of the Crop From measurements in the Format Picture dialog box. To use the mouse to return a graphic to its original size, hold down the Ctrl key while you double-click the graphic. This mouse method resets scaling to 100 percent and cropping to 0. See Chapter 14, "Previewing and Perfecting Page Layout," for details about positioning and moving graphics on pages. And see the Appendix, "Field Types and Their Instructions," for information about the IMPORT field, which Word uses to insert and process graphics from graphics files.

Formatting Lines Using Paragraph Formatting

When you format a paragraph, you primarily position lines. Paragraph boundaries extend to both side margins and from the bottom of the previous paragraph (or the top margin) to the paragraph mark. Within those boundaries, you control the line length, the alignment of lines at the left and right boundaries, the amount of space between lines, the amount of space above and below the paragraph, and the placement of text at tab stops.

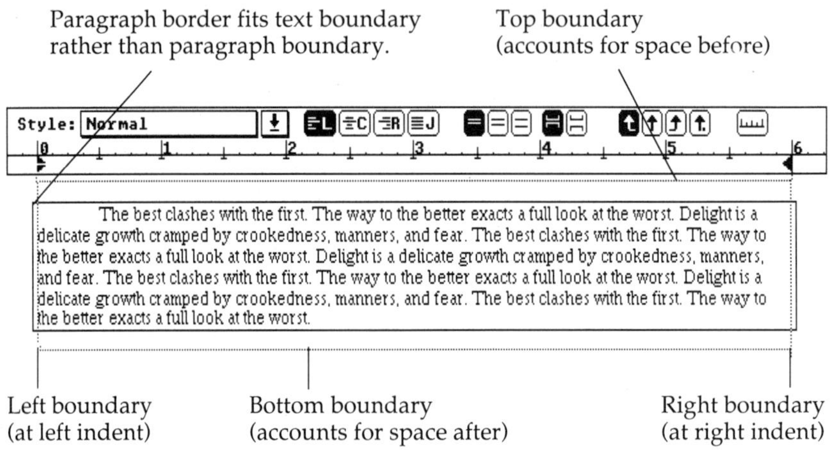

Paragraph formatting lets you set the left indentation of a paragraph's first line different from that of the rest of a paragraph so that your first line can have either a standard or a hanging (to the left of the rest of the paragraph) indent. Even though the command and the dialog box that you use to set tab stops are different from the ones that you use for the rest of paragraph formatting, you do set tab stops for each paragraph. To emphasize the connection between paragraph formatting and setting tab stops, the Format Paragraph dialog box contains a Tabs button. You choose Tabs to display the Format Tabs dialog box and to finish formatting a paragraph. So it makes sense to include tabs stops as part of your paragraph formatting—particularly because you do not need to use tab stops to create tables in Word. (See Chapter 13, "Tables the New, Easy Way," for information about creating tables.)

You can use two methods to format paragraphs: direct formatting or styles. When you use direct formatting, you apply formatting to your paragraphs individually, exactly as you did to characters, using the mouse, the keyboard, or the Format Paragraph command. When you use styles, you apply a formatting name to a paragraph. Styles allow you to apply the same style name to any number of paragraphs and be confident that those paragraphs will be formatted consistently. To change the paragraphs' formatting, you change only the formatting that's assigned to the style, and Word changes the formatting of all the paragraphs.

Formatting paragraphs using direct formatting

To apply direct paragraph formatting to your example text, select the heading that begins with "While those who ignore history." Indent the heading one-half inch, using one of the following methods. Later in this section, you'll find summaries of the key combinations and ruler mode keys that are available when you use the keyboard to format.

- Using the mouse, drag the left-indent icon to the ½-inch tick mark on the ruler. If the ruler is not displayed, choose the View Ruler command (Alt,V,R) to turn it on.

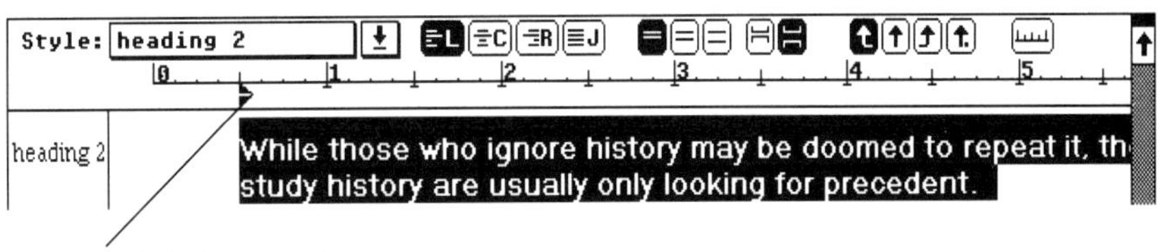

Left-indent marker

- Using the keyboard, press the Ctrl+N keys.
- Using the Format Paragraph command (Alt,T,P), move to the Indents From Left box (Alt+F) in the Format Paragraph dialog box and type *0.5"*, and then choose OK.

Select the heading "Customers are the Business," and center it using one of these methods:

- Using the mouse, click the "C" (center) icon on the ruler. If the ruler is not displayed, choose the View Ruler command (Alt,V,R) to turn it on.
- Using the keyboard, press the Ctrl+C keys.

- Using the Format Paragraph command (Alt,T,P), choose the Center option for Alignment (Alt+C) in the Format Paragraph dialog box, and then choose OK.

A summary of combination keys for paragraph formatting

When you use the keyboard for direct paragraph formatting, you can use these Ctrl key combinations:

Ctrl Key Combination	*Applies*
Ctrl+L	Left alignment
Ctrl+C	Center alignment
Ctrl+R	Right alignment
Ctrl+J	Justified alignment
Ctrl+1 (1 above the letter keys)	Single spacing
Ctrl+2 (2 above the letter keys)	Double spacing
Ctrl+5 (5 above the letter keys)	One-and-one-half-line spacing
Ctrl+O (letter O)	One line of space inserted above paragraph
Ctrl+E	All space eliminated above paragraph
Ctrl+N	Left indent increased to next tab stop (default is ½ inch); first-line indent moved by same amount
Ctrl+M	Left indent decreased to previous tab stop (default is ½ inch); first-line indent moved by same amount
Ctrl+T	Left indent increased to next tab stop (default is ½ inch); first line still indented to its current position
Ctrl+G	Left indent decreased to previous tab stop (default is ½ inch); first line still indented to its current position
Ctrl+X	Paragraph formatting reset to the style that's applied to it; any direct formatting removed
Alt+Shift+5 (5 on the numeric keypad)	Normal style applied to paragraph

A summary of ruler mode keys for paragraph formatting

If you're using the keyboard to format, you can press the Ctrl+Shift+F10 keys to turn on and activate the ruler. Press the right and the left arrow keys to move the ruler cursor small distances (¼ inch or ½ centimeter), the Ctrl+right arrow and Ctrl+left arrow keys to move the ruler cursor larger distances (1 inch or 2 centimeters), the Home key to move the ruler cursor to the 0 point, or the End key to move the ruler cursor to the right margin. Position the ruler cursor where you want to set an indent or a tab stop. (The ruler cursor is the box in the bottom line of the ruler.) To move the ruler cursor to the left of the left margin, hold down the Shift key while you move the ruler cursor. To apply these settings to the selected paragraphs, press the appropriate keys from the following list and then, after you make all the settings you want, press the Enter key.

Ruler Mode Key	*Action*
L	Sets left-indent marker to ruler cursor position; moves first-line indent by same amount and in same direction as left indent
R	Sets right-indent marker to ruler cursor position
F	Sets first-line indent marker to ruler cursor position
1	Selects left alignment for new tab stops
2	Selects centered alignment for new tab stops
3	Selects right alignment for new tab stops
4	Selects decimal alignment for new tab stops
Insert	Inserts a tab stop at ruler cursor position
Delete	Deletes tab stops selected by ruler cursor
Esc	Cancels ruler mode and discards any changes you made
Enter	Ends ruler mode and applies ruler settings

Formatting paragraphs using styles

Formatting paragraphs using styles gives you additional formatting power that you can apply with a minimum of effort. Chapter 7, "Styles," explains styles in detail. Here you get a quick demonstration of how you apply styles to format paragraphs in your document.

Word supplies four styles: Normal, heading 1, heading 2, and heading 3. Normal is the basic style that's assigned to all paragraphs as a default setting. Heading 1, heading 2, and heading 3 format your document's headline paragraphs. You've seen the Normal and heading styles in action earlier in this chapter in "Outlining to Structure Your Documents." The table on the next page describes these four styles.

Style Name	*Formatting*
Normal	Font: Tms Rmn 10 Point, Flush left; plus the following settings that do not appear in the style's description in formatting dialog boxes: no indents, single line spacing, no space before or after, no keep together or keep with next paragraph, no border, no page break before, default tab stops (every ½ inch)
heading 1	Normal + Font: Helv 12 Point, Bold Underline, Space Before 1 line
heading 2	Normal + Font: Helv 12 Point, Bold, Space Before 0.5 line
heading 3	Normal + Font: Tms Rmn 12 Point, Bold, Indent: left 0.25"

To apply styles to a paragraph, position the insertion point in the paragraph that you want to format or select either a portion of text or the entire paragraph. Then use the mouse, the keyboard, or the Format Styles command:

- Using the mouse in normal editing view, turn on the ruler if it's not on already by choosing the View Ruler command (Alt,V,R). Or press the Shift+Ctrl+F10 keys. On the ruler, click the down arrow at the right end of the Style box and select the style you want to apply.
- Using the mouse in Outline View, click the promote icon or the demote icon until the paragraph has the heading level you want. You can also drag the paragraph icon to the left or to the right to the appropriate heading level.
- Using the keyboard in normal editing view, press the Ctrl+S keys, type a style name, and then press the Enter key. Or, if the ruler is turned on, press Ctrl+S, press the Alt+down arrow keys, and then select a style from the styles list.
- Using the keyboard in Outline, normal editing, Draft, and Page views, press the Alt+Shift+left or right arrow keys to promote or demote the heading level, or press Ctrl+S and type the style name.

- Using the Format Styles command (Alt,T,Y), choose a style name from the list of names in the dialog box, and then choose OK.

To position a paragraph in your example text and set its width, first select the heading "It needs brains to be a real fool." Then, choose the Format Position command (Alt,T,O). In the Horizontal box, choose the Center option. Move to the Vertical box (Alt+V), and choose the Center option. Next, move to the Paragraph Width box (Alt+W), type 2, and then choose OK. When you look at the page in Page View, in Print Preview, or when printed on paper, the paragraph is centered on the page and the rest of the text flows around it:

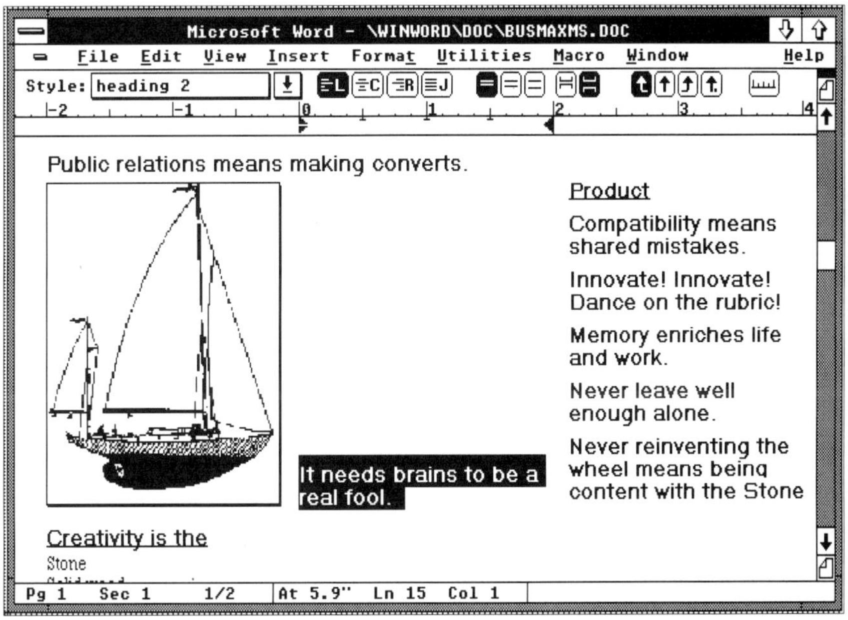

For information about Page View and Print Preview, see "Previewing and Revising" later in this chapter.

Copying Character and Paragraph Formatting

Occasionally, you'll want to reuse some of your character and paragraph formatting to save yourself time and effort. In Word, you can copy character and paragraph formatting from one place to another—

in the same document or between documents. This technique is primarily for the mouse. Because the action is performed by a built-in command, however, you can also assign the action to a key combination. For more information about assigning a command or a macro to a key combination, see Chapter 10, "Macros."

To copy text formatting using the mouse, first select the text to which you want to copy formatting. Then, point to any character in the text whose formatting you want to copy. Hold down the Ctrl+Shift keys while you click the left mouse button.

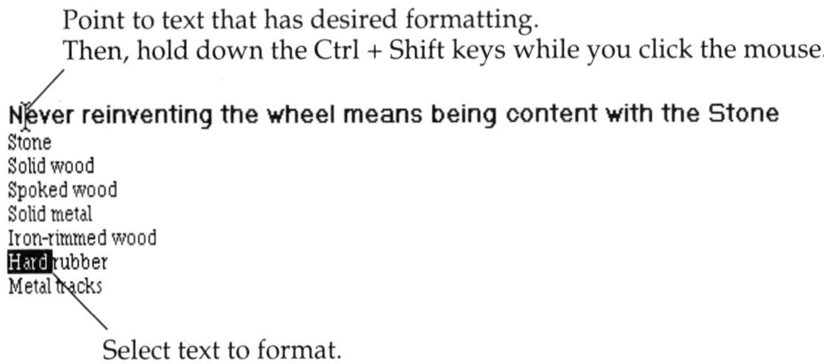

To copy paragraph formatting using the mouse, first select the paragraph to which you want to copy formatting. Then, move the mouse pointer into the selection bar beside the paragraph whose formatting you want to copy. Hold down the Ctrl+Shift keys while you click the left mouse button.

TIP

Something Special: Positioning Objects

When you print a document, you'll want the advantage of being able to put text, graphics, or tables anywhere on a page and have the rest of the text flow around it. Word lets you position an object on the page, set its size, set the space between the object and the text that flows around it, and give the object borders to further set it off. Position formatting applies to paragraphs, as do tab stops and alignment. The procedure on the preceding page gave you practice positioning a paragraph and setting its width.

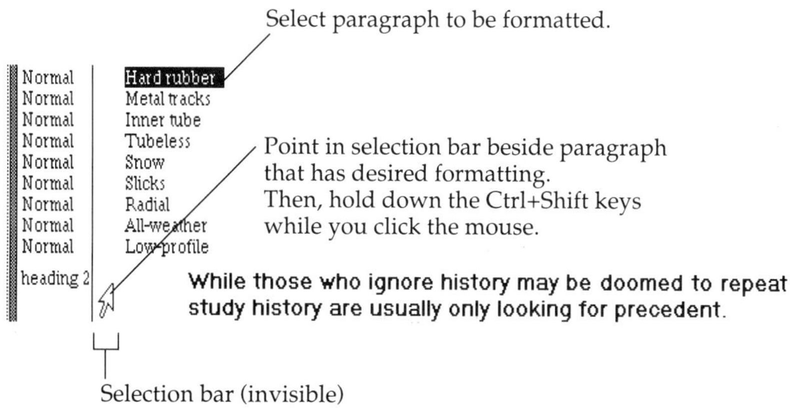

Pages: Section and Document Formatting

Formatting for pages comes in two varieties: section and document. Section formatting is special page formatting for only a part of the document. Document formatting is general page formatting for the whole document.

Section formatting

A section is a part of a document in which you want some aspect of page formatting to be different from the rest of the document: a different number of columns; different headers or footers; or individualized page, line, and footnote numbering. The last page of a section can also be a place to collect a whole section's footnotes. The following material shows you how to insert section breaks, format a section in multiple columns, and turn on a section's line numbering.

Multiple columns in section formatting. You use the Format Section command to change the number of text columns in a section. To try this procedure, first position the insertion point in front of the word "Stone," which is in the list under the heading that begins with "Never reinventing the wheel." Choose the Insert Break command (Alt,I,B), choose the Continuous option for Section Break (Alt+T) in the Insert Break dialog box, and then choose OK. Word breaks the text into a separate section and inserts a section mark, which looks like a row of colons stretching across the screen, as illustrated on the next page.

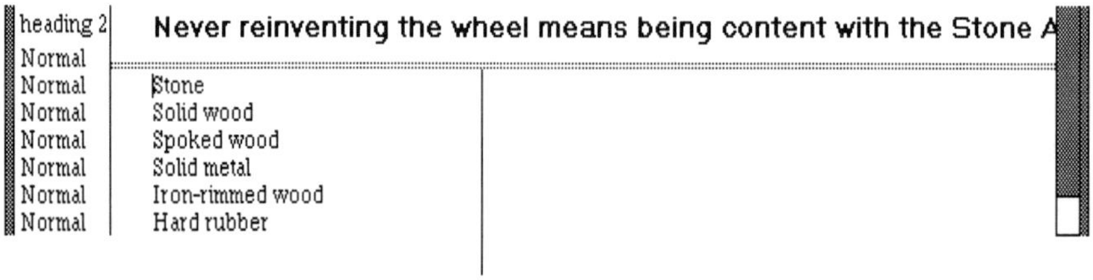

Section mark

Position the insertion point in front of the heading that begins with "While those who ignore history," choose Insert Break (Alt,I,B), choose the Continuous option for Section Break (Alt+T) in the Insert Break dialog box, and then choose OK to insert a second section mark. Now you can format the list alone in two columns. To change the list to two columns with a line between the columns, position the insertion point above the second section mark and choose Format Section (Alt,T,S). (You can also double-click the mouse on the second section mark.) In the Format Section dialog box, type *2* in the Number box for Columns, turn on the Line Between option (Alt+L), and then choose OK. You will not see the two columns until you switch to Page View or to Print Preview or until you print the document. For more information about previewing options, see "Previewing and Revising" later in this chapter.

Line numbering in section formatting. You might want to use line numbers for some types of documents. To add line numbers to the first section of a document, move the insertion point to above the first section mark and choose the Format Section command (Alt,T,S). In the Format Section dialog box, turn on the Line Numbering option (Alt+I) and then move to the Count By box (Alt+B) and type *5* (to show a line number on every fifth line, as in 5, 10, 15, and so on). Choose OK. The line numbers do not appear in normal editing view or in Page View. They appear illegibly in Print Preview but are legible in the printed document.

Document formatting

Some page formatting is the same throughout a document: page size, margins, and the placement of footnotes. In Word, however, you can set the starting page number and footnote number for a document, which is handy when a document consists of two or more separate document files and you want the numbering to be consecutive. The following sections explain how to set the page size, margins, and placement of footnotes for a whole document.

Setting page size and margins. To practice setting the page size and margins for a document, start by choosing the Format Document command (Alt,T,D). In the Format Document dialog box, note that the Page Width is 8.5" and the Height is 11", which reflects the most commonly used paper size in the United States. You can leave these settings as they are. Also note the measurements for the Margins: The Top and Bottom are 1" and the two sides are 1.25". Change the Left and Right margins to 1" by moving to the Left box (Alt+L) and typing *1* and then to the Right box (Alt+R) and typing *1*. Then, choose OK. Word displays the reduced side margins, which in turn give you longer text lines:

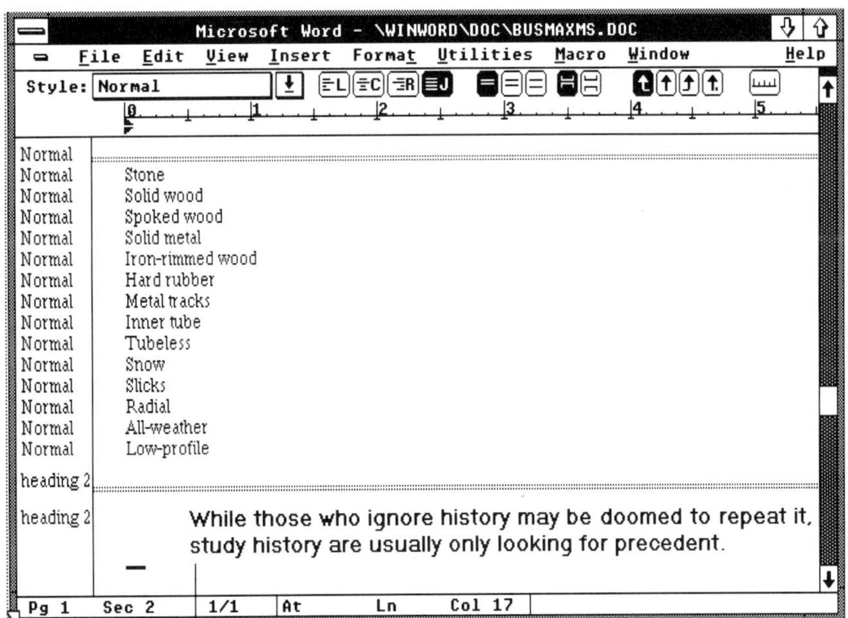

Compare line break for this heading with that of a previous illustration.

Setting the placement of footnotes. You can, of course, add footnotes to the text in your Word documents. But, more important, you can choose where Word prints the footnotes—on the same page as the footnote reference, at the end of a section, or at the end of a document. Try the following procedure to practice inserting footnotes and printing them at the end of the section.

In your example text, position the insertion point at the end of the words "Iron-rimmed wood." Choose the Insert Footnote command (Alt,I,N), and then choose OK in the Insert Footnote dialog box. Word inserts an automatically numbered footnote reference and opens the footnote pane so that you can type the following footnote text:

The following items are types of wheel coverings.

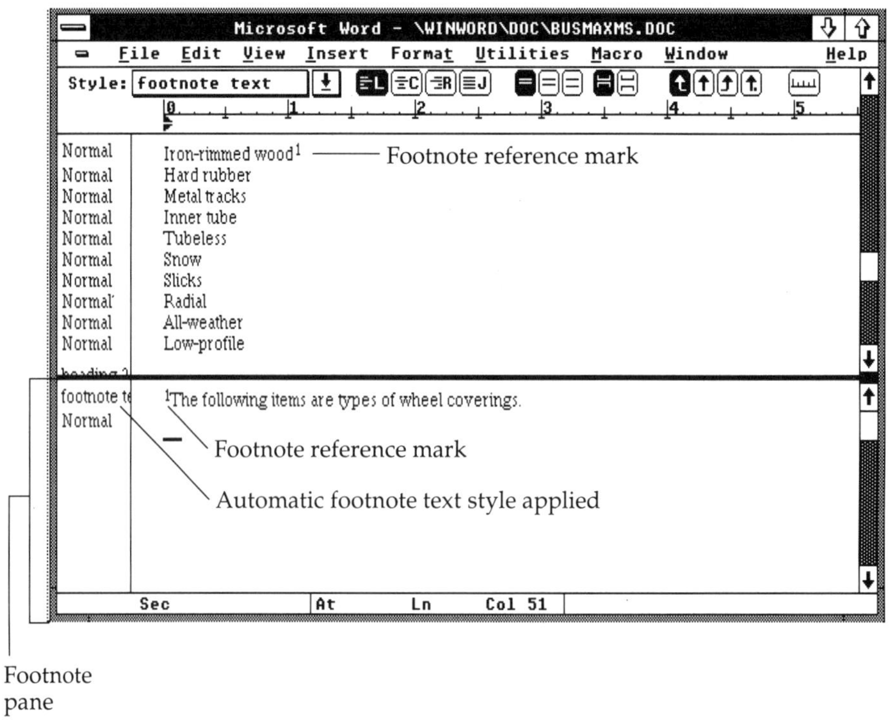

When you finish typing the footnote text, press the F6 key or click in document pane. Then, position the insertion point at the end of the word "Snow," choose Insert Footnote again, choose OK, and type the footnote shown on the following page.

The following items are treads for rubber tires.

Close the footnote window by pressing the Alt+Shift+C keys or by choosing the Control Split command (Alt,hyphen,T), pressing the PgUp or the PgDn key, and then pressing the Enter key. Or you can use the mouse to drag the split box to the top or bottom of the window. Now tell Word to print the footnotes at the end of the section: First, choose the Format Document command (Alt,T,D). Move to the Print at box under Footnotes (Alt+A) in the Format Document dialog box, and select End of Section. Then, choose OK. When you look at the page in Page View or in Print Preview or when you print the page, the footnotes appear at the end of the list. The end of that list is the end of the section. If a section spans more than a page, the footnotes print where the section ends.

TIP

Printing Footnotes on a Separate Page at the End of a Section

A section does not always end neatly at the bottom of a page, so footnotes that are printed at the end of a section will often be printed in the middle of the page. To print the footnotes on a separate page at the end of a section instead, position the insertion point in front of the section mark and then press the PAGE BREAK key combination (Ctrl+Enter) to insert a page break as the last character before the section mark.

Also note that you can collect footnotes that are formatted in the Format Document dialog box to print at the end of a section. This dialog box contains an option named Include Footnotes, which is turned on by default. If you turn off Include Footnotes in the Format Section dialog box, Word collects that section's footnotes and adds them to the footnotes in the next section. By selectively turning off the Include Footnotes option, you can tell Word where to print the footnotes. For example, to print the footnotes at the end of the document but in front of the index, you would turn off the Include Footnotes option for all the document's sections except the last section, which contains only the index. If you used the End of Document position to print footnotes, Word would print the footnotes following the index.

Previewing and Revising

Word lets you see what your document will look like before you actually print it so that you can correct errors and save the time and expense of extra printing cycles. In normal editing view, you see text formatting, line breaks, and paragraph alignment as they'll appear when you print the document. (Except for the practice in Outline View, you've been working in normal editing view.) You do not see headers, footers, footnotes, columns, and positioned objects in place in normal editing view. To see the page as it will look when printed, use one of Word's two preview options: Print Preview and Page View.

Print Preview shows you an overview of the entire page's layout. You see margins; the general shape of paragraphs; the positions of headers, footers, and footnotes; where positioned objects will print; and how text will flow around those objects. Except for footnotes, you can adjust the positions of all these elements and the margins and page breaks by using the mouse or the keyboard to move them. Page View shows you an exact on-screen image of the printed page. Because the screen displays a page at actual size, you see only a portion of the page at a time unless you have a full-page monitor. You can edit and format text and graphics in Page View using the same methods you use in normal editing view. You can also reposition various page elements using the normal formatting methods, as opposed to using special procedures as you do in Print Preview.

Using Print Preview

To see a whole page at a time, choose the File Print Preview command (Alt,F,V). In Print Preview, as illustrated on the next page, you cannot read the text unless you have a full-page monitor because the text is in 4-point type, which an EGA resolution screen cannot show legibly. Also, you cannot edit text in Print Preview—but you can edit it in Page View. The next sections give you practice in switching between one-page and two-page views and in changing margins and page breaks.

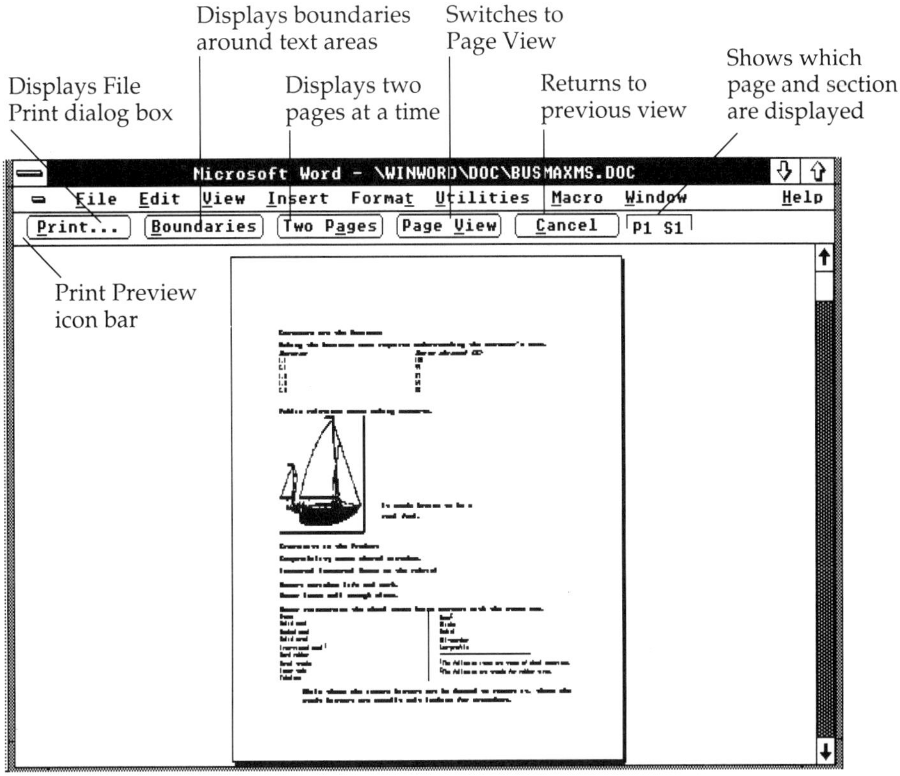

Switching between one-page and two-page views in Print Preview

You can see either one or two pages at a time in Print Preview. If you have a full-page monitor, you can read the text in the one-page view. To switch from the one-page to the two-page view, click the Two Pages button on the icon bar or press the A key. To switch back to the one-page view, click the One Page button, as illustrated on the next page, or press the A key.

Displays one page
at a time

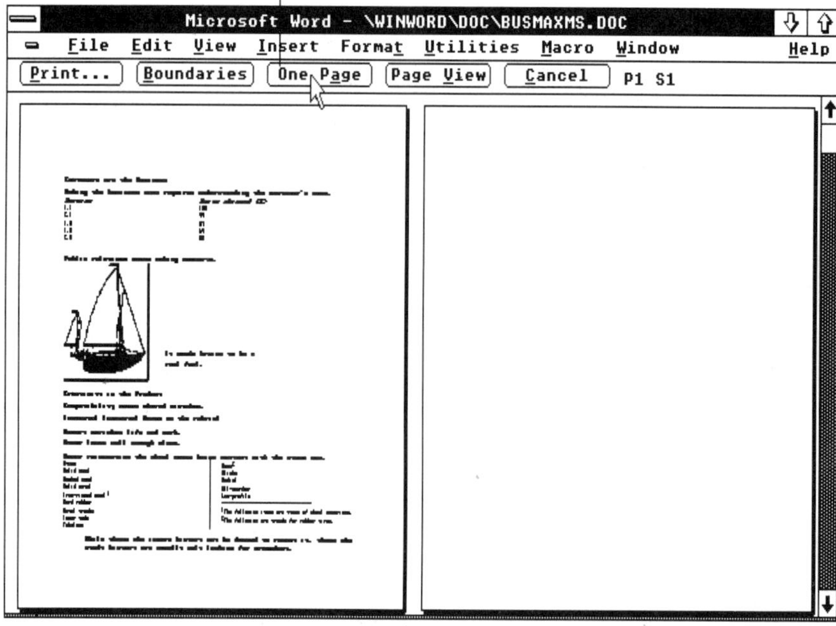

Changing margins in Print Preview

If you have a mouse, you can drag the page margins to new positions while you're in Print Preview. You can also use the Tab key and the arrow keys to reposition margins. As you move the margin icons, Word displays a margin's measurements at the right end of the icon bar, in place of the page number. Remember that margins affect the entire document, so when you adjust the margins on one page, you're adjusting the margins on all pages.

To start, click the Boundaries button or press the B key. Dotted lines mark the page's margins. To move the margin using the keyboard, press the Tab key one time; the left-margin icon line seems to disappear, which means that the line is selected. Press the right arrow key until the measurement on the icon bar shows "1.25"". Or, using the mouse, drag the left margin's dotted-line icon toward the center of the page to 1.25". The illustration on the next page shows the new margin position.

Now use the keyboard to move the right margin. Press the Tab key until the right margin seems to disappear. Press the left arrow key to

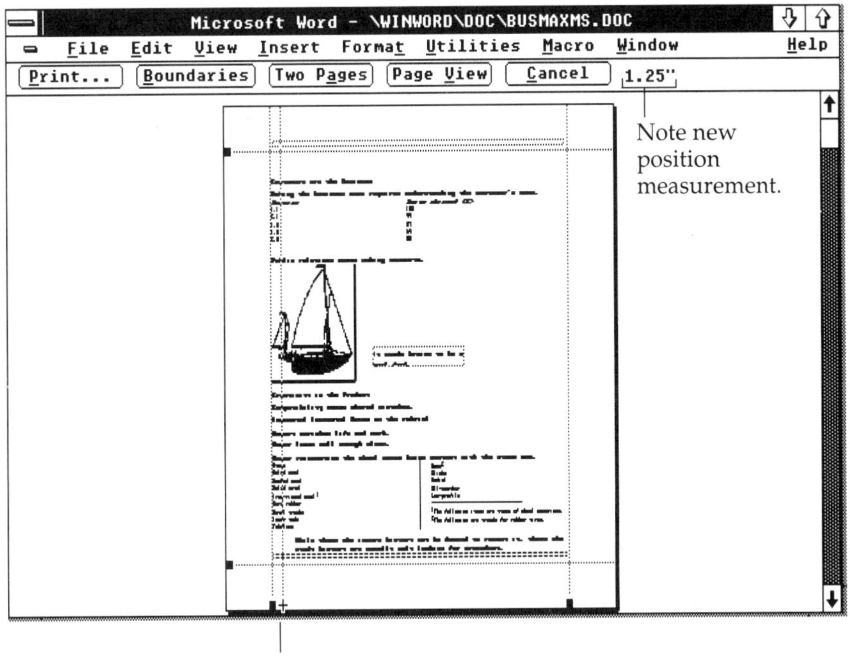

move the right margin's dotted-line icon toward the center of the page to the 1.25" position, and then press the Enter key to freeze the icon at the new margin position, as shown in Figure 5-4 on the next page. Then, either click anywhere outside the page or press Enter again to tell Word you're finished moving margins, and Word reformats the page, using the new measurements.

Changing page breaks in Print Preview

If you review a page in Print Preview and do not like the page break position, you can use the mouse or the arrow keys to move the break. First, click the Two Pages button or press the A key to display two pages, and then click the Boundaries button or press the B key to display the margin boundaries. Press the Tab key until the mouse pointer (+) is on the page break's dotted-line icon. Press the up arrow key to move the page-break icon up, and then press the Enter key. Or, using the mouse, drag the page-break icon for the left-hand page up to a break between paragraphs. Note that when you change a page break, Word reformats the page immediately, as Figure 5-5 on the next page shows.

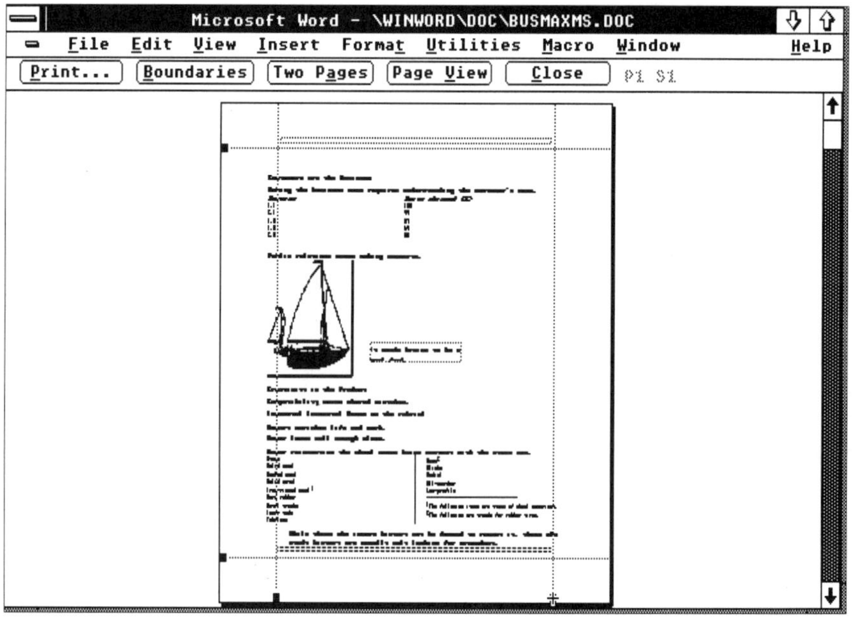

Figure 5-4.
Right margin moved.

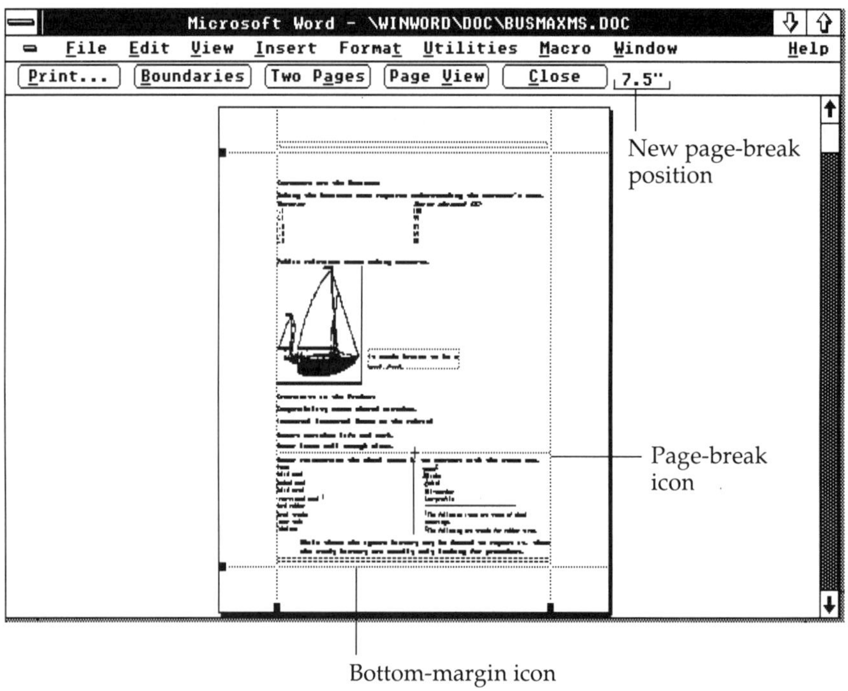

Figure 5-5.
Page break changed.

Using Page View

To see a page in Page View, choose the View Page command (Alt,V,P). As a shortcut when you're in Print Preview, click the Page View button or press the V key.

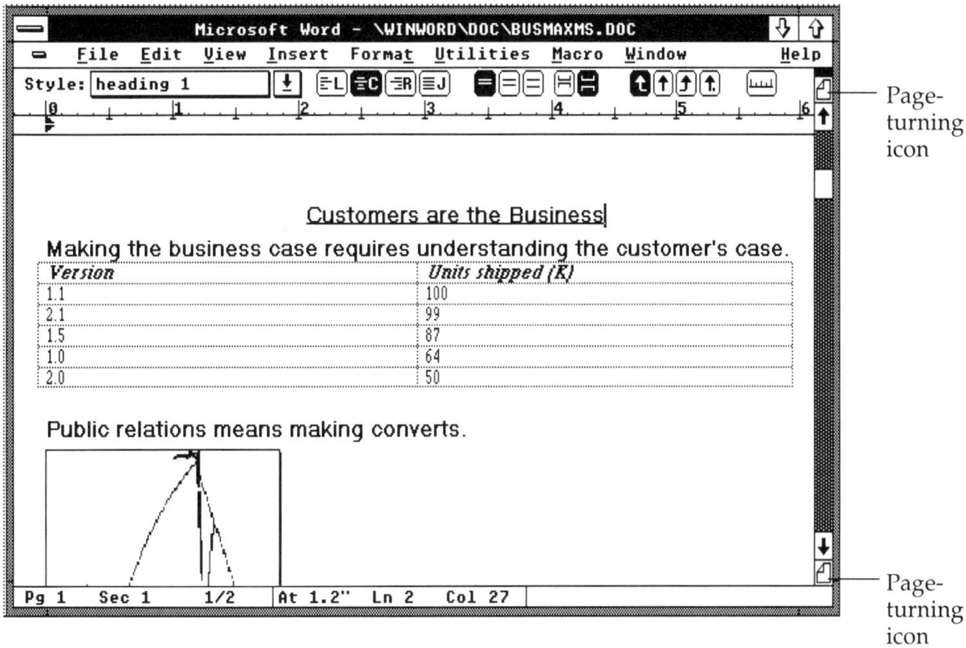

The page-turning icon jumps to the next or the preceding page. The scroll bar scrolls within the page that's displayed.

The following two sections explore two of the features that you can use in Page View: editing and formatting text, and adding headers and footers.

Editing and formatting text in Page View

In Page View, you can add any amount of text within the current text boundaries. Adding text in Page View is the same as adding text in normal editing view: You position the insertion point and then type. You can also delete, replace, move, copy, and format text as in normal editing view. You'll probably want to limit your editing and formatting in Page View to final polishing, however, because of the time that Word requires to reformat the pages. Scrolling from page to page is slower in

Page View, and it takes longer to move text or graphics from one place to another. If you insert enough text to cause a page break when you're in Page View, you have to wait for Word to reformat the page. To avoid these slowdowns, switch back to normal editing view when you type a lot of text. In normal editing view, you do not need to wait for page reformatting, and pagination can occur in the background.

To see some of the effects of editing and formatting text in Page View, try the following: Position the insertion point in front of "Iron-rimmed wood" in your example text, and press the Ctrl+Shift+Enter keys to insert a column break. Now, position the insertion point at any spot in the document and start typing. Type enough text to allow you to see some reformatting. A good place in your example text to practice is in the middle of the list of wheels and tires, after "Solid metal." Now, select the text you just typed and apply justified alignment to it:

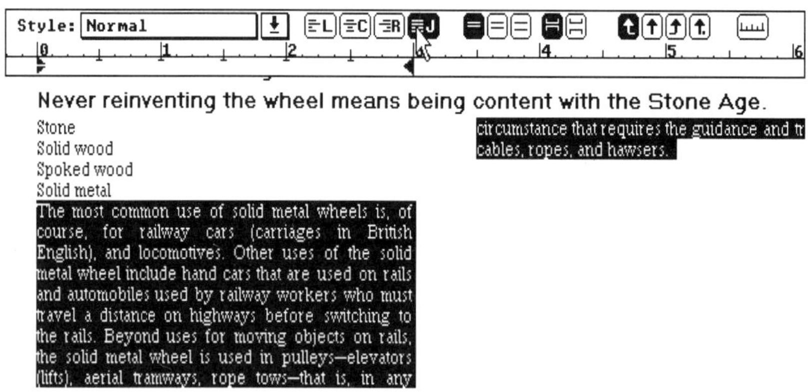

Adding headers and footers in Page View

Header and footer text is text that appears on every page—a header appears at the top (head) of a page, and a footer appears at the bottom (foot) of a page. Headers and footers are often page numbers, names or numbers of chapters, names of documents, authors' names, or chapter section names. Chapter 8, "Fields: Facts and Functions," explains more about inserting header and footer text in documents. Here you get a brief look at inserting the author's name, the page number, and the date in a header. You also see how to control the position of a header or footer on the page.

First, choose the Edit Header/Footer command (Alt,E,H). Because Header is selected by default in the Edit Header/Footer dialog box, choose OK. The page scrolls, and the insertion point appears at the beginning point of the header text area. Then, insert the author's name, the page number, and the date: To insert the author's name, press the INSERT FIELD key combination (Ctrl+F9), type *author*, and then press the UPDATE FIELD key (F9). To insert the page number, press the End key, press the Tab key, and then press the INSERT PAGE NUMBER key combination (Alt+Shift+P). When you use this key combination, Word updates the field and displays the result for you. To insert the date, press End, press Tab, and then press the INSERT DATE key combination (Alt+Shift+D).

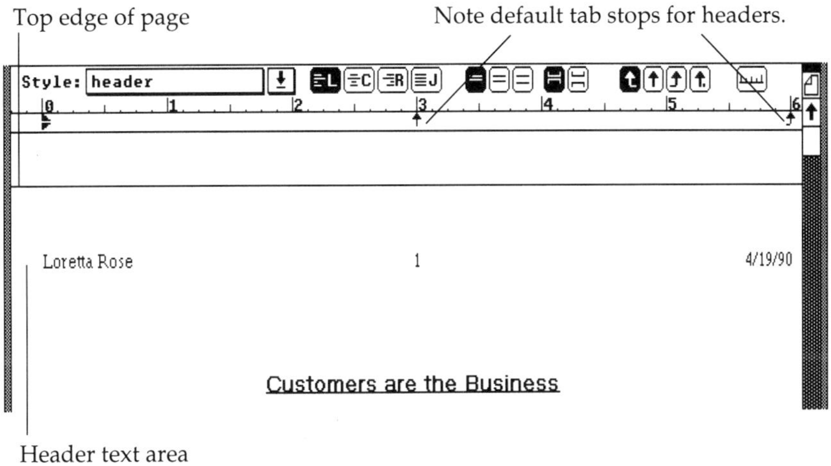

To position the header and footer, choose the Edit Header/Footer command (Alt,E,H) again. In the Edit Header/Footer dialog box, choose the Options button (Alt+O), move to the Header box (Alt+H) under Distance From Edge, type *0.75"*, and then choose OK. The header now starts at ¾ inch from the top edge of the page. If the header is taller than the space that's available between the top of the header and the top margin, Word adjusts the top margin so that the header fits. Word also makes the same adjustment for footers. Now that you have made a number of changes to the document, it is a good time to save the document again: Choose the File Save command (Alt,F,S), or press the SAVE key combination (Shift+F12 or Alt+Shift+F2).

Finishing by Adding a Table of Contents and an Index

After you finish entering and formatting the text in your document, you might want to insert a table of contents, an index, or both. The following sections give you practice inserting these elements in a document.

Inserting a Table of Contents

Because you used the heading styles (heading 1, heading 2, and heading 3) in your example text, you've already done the groundwork for inserting a table of contents. Now you simply direct Word to insert a table of contents, and it's done on your approval.

Begin by positioning the insertion point where you want the table of contents to begin. Choose the Insert Table of Contents command (Alt,I,C), and then choose OK. Word collects copies of the heading text and its page numbers and inserts the table of contents:

Customers are the Business........1
    Making the business case requires understanding the customer's case........1
    Public relations means making converts........1
Creativity is the Product........1
    Compatibility means shared mistakes........1
    Innovate! Innovate! Dance on the rubric!........1
    It needs brains to be a real fool........1
    Memory enriches life and work........1
    Never leave well enough alone........1
    Never reinventing the wheel means being content with the Stone Age........1
    While those who ignore history may be doomed to repeat it, those who study history are usuall
    only looking for precedent........2

If you change the document in ways that might affect the table of contents—for example, by adding or deleting text or changing formatting—you can update the table of contents quickly. Simply position the insertion point anywhere within the table of contents and press the UPDATE FIELD key (F9). Word collects the entries for the table of contents again and inserts the table of contents in the same position. If you choose Insert Table of Contents when your document already contains a table of contents, Word asks if you want to replace the existing table of contents. Choose Yes when you want Word to delete the existing table of contents and insert a new one at the insertion point. Choose No when you want Word to cancel the Insert Table of Contents command.

In the Insert Table of Contents dialog box, additional choices are available, as illustrated on the next page.

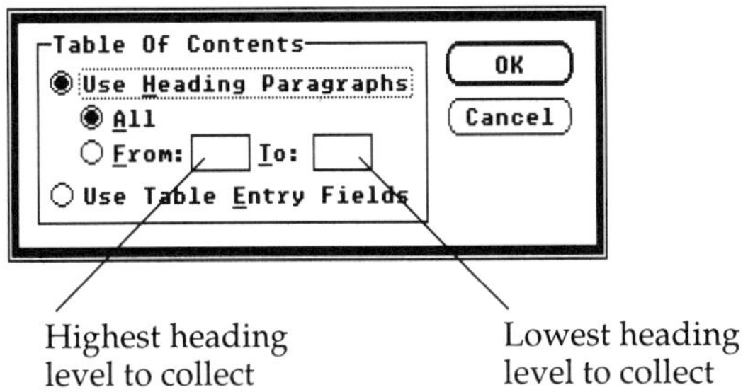

Because you used all the headings for your example table of contents rather than only some of them, you did not need the options shown in the dialog box above. When you use headings for the table of contents, however, you can specify that only certain headings be collected. This option lets you limit the table's scope to a specific level of information.

Chapter 8, "Fields: Facts and Functions," describes how to use the Use Table Entry Fields option, which is shown above in the Insert Table of Contents dialog box.

Inserting an Index

An index gives your readers a handy tool for quickly finding information in your documents. To create an index, you insert index entries throughout your document and then collect those entries in an index. The process is much like creating a table of contents.

You can create an index entry from text that's already in your document or from additional text that you type in the Insert Index Entry dialog box. You'll speed this editing process if you return to normal editing view: Choose the View Page command (Alt,V,P). To insert both types of index entries, select the word "Stone" in your example text. Choose the Insert Index Entry command (Alt,I,E), and then choose OK. For "Solid wood," "Spoked wood," and "Solid metal," repeat this process by selecting the text, choosing Insert Index Entry (Alt,I,E), and choosing OK. You can also choose Insert Index Entry and, in the Insert Index Entry dialog box, type additional index entries that are not part of the document text. Position the insertion point at the end of "Spoked wood," choose Insert Index Entry (Alt,I,E), type *Wood:spoked*, and then choose OK. This step inserts an entry for your index that will appear as shown on the next page.

Regular index entries

```
Stone{xe·"Stone"}¶
Solid·wood{xe·"Solid·wood"}¶
Spoked·wood{xe·"Spoked·wood"}{xe·
"Wood:spoked"}¶
Solid·metal{xe·"Solid:metal"}¶
```

Multiple-level index entry
(created by colon)

The colon between the two words tells Word that the first word is a main entry and the second word is a subentry. Each subentry must be preceded by a colon. If you want to have multiple subentries that are at the same level, insert a separate, complete index entry for each subentry. You can have up to seven index entry levels: a main entry and up to six subentry levels, separated from each other by a colon.

After you insert your index entries, position the insertion point where you want the index to start, choose the Insert Index command (Alt,I,I), and then choose OK. Word collects copies of the index entry text and the page numbers and inserts a normal, indented index:

```
Solid metal, 2
Solid wood, 1
Spoked wood, 2
Stone, 1
Wood
    spoked, 2
```

If you change the document in ways that might affect the index (for example, by adding or deleting text, by changing formatting, or by inserting or deleting index entries), you can update the index quickly. Simply position the insertion point anywhere within the index and press the UPDATE FIELD key (F9). Word collects the entries for the index again and inserts the index in the same place.

If you choose Insert Index when your document already contains an index, Word asks whether you want to replace the existing index. Choose Yes if you want Word to delete the existing index and insert a new one at the insertion point. Choose No if you want Word to cancel the Insert Index command.

The following additional options are available to you in the Insert Index dialog box:

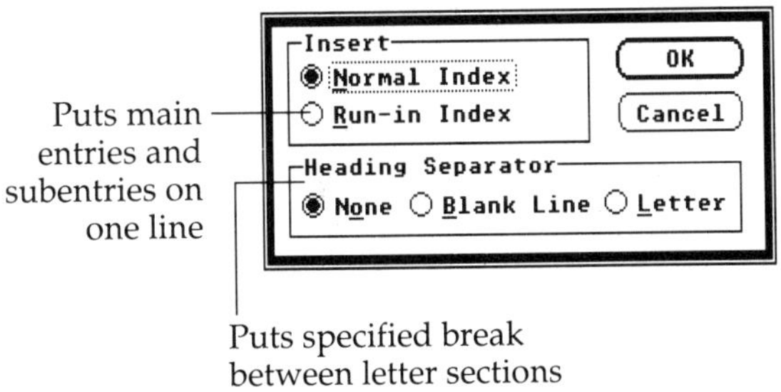

A run-in index lists on a single line all the subentries for a main entry, wrapping to additional lines if necessary. A heading separator differentiates each letter section of the index. The separator can be a blank line at the beginning of each letter section, or it can be the letter of the following section.

Storing and Finding Documents

After your document is completed and polished, you'll want to save it using a name that allows you to easily find it again. And for those documents that you do have trouble finding again later, Word includes a document retrieval facility that finds and sorts documents based on a variety of criteria: author, date, contents, and the document's summary information.

When you save a new document, fill out the summary information as completely as you can. The more information you supply, the easier it will be later to find the document.

Saving Documents

Save an existing document with a different name so that you can also preserve an original copy: Choose the File Save As command (Alt,F,A), and type a new file name in the File Save As dialog box, as shown on the following page. The dialog box also gives you the options of storing the document in a different directory and file format and of making a backup copy.

Type a new file name here.

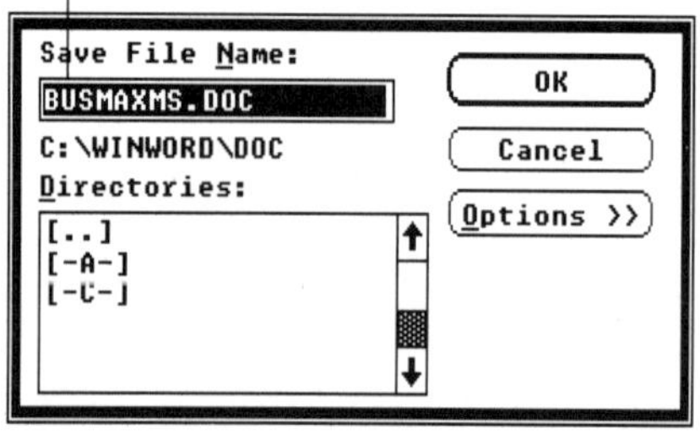

When you change a document's name by saving it using the File Save As command, Word displays the Edit Summary Info dialog box, where you can change the summary information to fit the revised document. Fill in the dialog box as shown below and then choose OK:

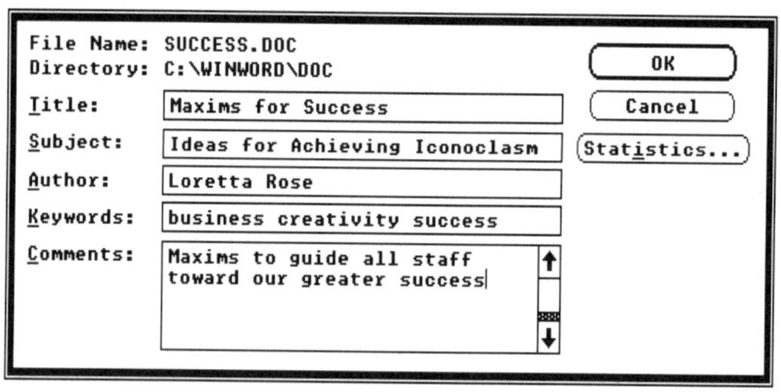

Finding Documents: File Find and Summary Info

If you cannot find a document by name quickly, choose the File Find command (Alt,F,F) to use Word's document retrieval facility. When you choose File Find for the first time in a work session, Word compiles a list of all files on your current drive that have the file name extension DOC. To compile a list of files that were saved today, choose the Search button (Alt+S) in the File Find dialog box. In the Date Saved From box (Alt+M), type today's date. Leave the Date Saved To box blank to tell Word to look through all documents between the Dated Saved From date and today. In this case, the two dates are the same. Choose OK, and the File Find dialog box lists all documents that were last saved with today's date. From the dialog box, you can now open any of the documents listed, as shown on the next page.

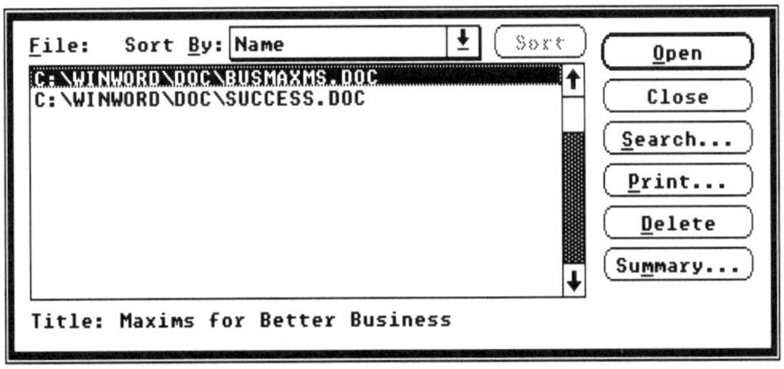

Using File Find to Open Multiple Documents

After you use the File Find command to collect a list of documents, you can select and open as many as nine documents at a time. Files that match the options that you specified in the File Find Search box appear in the list in the File Find dialog box. Select from the list the files that you want to open.

Using the mouse, hold down the Shift key and click the document names you want. Using the keyboard, hold down Shift and press the down arrow key to select a series of files. If you go too far down the list, continue holding down Shift and press the up arrow key to deselect files. To skip files in the list, hold down the Ctrl key instead of Shift, press the up and the down arrow keys to move the dotted box to the name of the file you want to select, and then press the spacebar to select the file. To deselect a file from a list after you release Shift, or to deselect a file from the middle of a list, hold down Ctrl, press the up and the down arrow keys to move the dotted box to the file you want to deselect, and then press the spacebar:

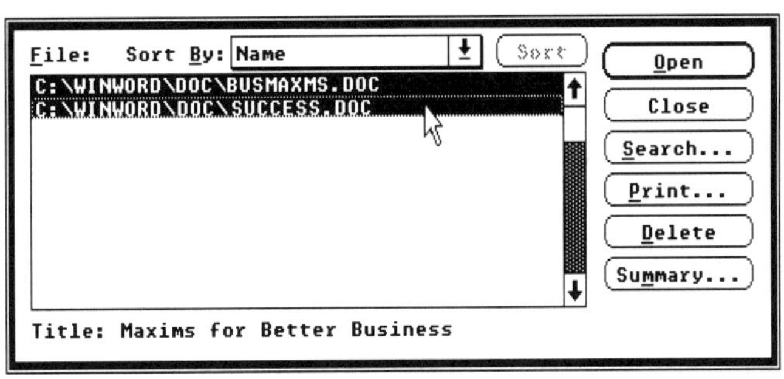

After you select the files you want to open, choose the Open button (Alt+O) to open all the selected documents. Then, choose the Window Arrange All command (Alt,W,A) to see all the documents at one time, in equal-size windows:

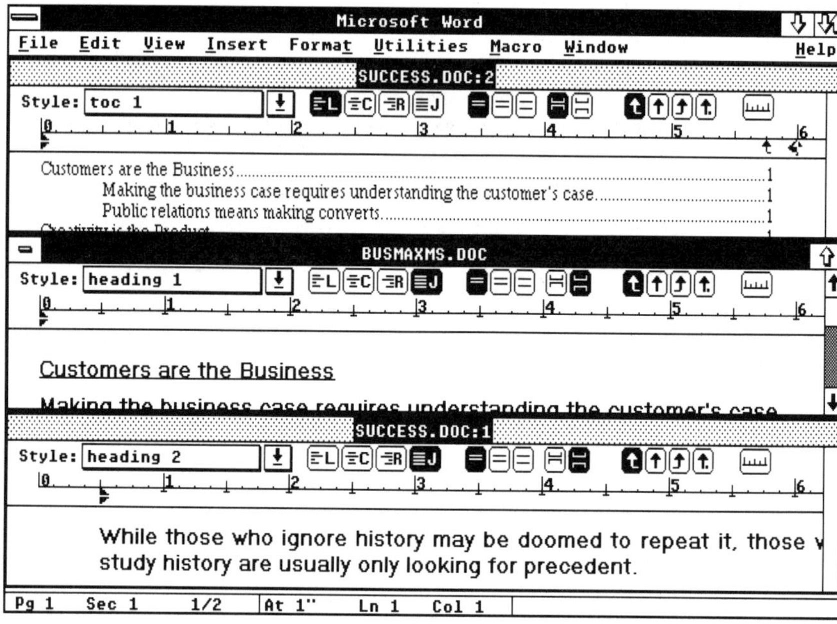

PART II

Four Pillars of Word for Windows

Part II describes the heart of Word for Windows: what makes it unique, what makes it powerful, and what makes it a major advance in document processing.

We begin with an overview of Word's four pillars—styles, fields, macros, and templates. Then individual chapters describe each pillar in detail.

Styles Add Formatting Power

Anytime you work with Word for Windows, you use styles, even if you're not aware of it. Word automatically applies styles to every element in a document, including paragraphs, headings, and the table of contents. And you can change those styles whenever you want. Styles provide a convenient way to format so that you can concentrate on creating the best document you can, knowing that Word is taking care of the formatting for you in a consistent way that you prescribe.

Fields Insert and Update Contents for You

A computer can often generate and update information faster than you can. In Word, you can use fields to generate and update information in your documents. Fields can pull in text and graphics from other files and programs, calculate page numbers and cross-references, build tables of contents and indexes, turn a table into a miniature spreadsheet, and more. Fields help you insert contents in a document in a variety of ways and let you keep the inserted contents up to date with little effort.

Macros Can Remove Tedium from Your Work

Creating, editing, and publishing a document can mean enduring repetitive editing tasks. But in Word, you can use macros to record a series of actions and play them back later when you need them rather than repeat the same actions. You can also write macros yourself, using Word's built-in BASIC programming language.

Templates Create Standard Documents Easily

Many documents, such as memos and reports, have a standard form and content. Their appearance and boilerplate text are always the same. To save the time spent creating the standard format and contents of such documents over and over again, Word uses document templates. These templates are on-line document models that work like preprinted forms, providing all the standard text and formatting for you. Word comes with templates, which you can either use as they are or modify. And you can create templates of your own. You use templates to personalize Word for Windows for each of the document tasks you perform.

Chapter 6

Using Word's Four Pillars: Styles, Fields, Macros, and Templates

The four pillars that make Word for Windows unique are styles, fields, macros, and templates. This chapter introduces these pillars and provides steps for quickly and easily applying each pillar to your documents. Then Chapters 7 through 11 take you more deeply into each of these four features, including examples that you can work through.

Chapter 7, "Styles," explains how to use styles. That information comes first because styles can be used—either directly or indirectly—in each of the other three pillars. Chapters 8, "Fields: Facts and Functions," and 9, "Fields II: Creating Special Effects," explain fields. Fields are covered next because they can unite many parts of a document and can also be used in macros and templates. (A complete description of fields and their instructions appears in the Appendix, "Field Types and Their Instructions.") Using macros is explained in Chapter 10, "Macros." Macros are also easy to use, and they provide your first step into the functional program-like areas of Word. Finally, Chapter 11, "Templates," tells you how to use templates. This discussion is last because using templates combines all four pillars plus a number of other aspects of Word.

First, It's a Matter of Context

Context is a term used in Word to describe when certain features are available for you to use. Word has three contexts: document, template, and global. In document context, the sphere of effect is within a single document; in template context, it's only in documents that were created from the same document template; and in global context, it's in all documents.

Each context has a set of features, many of which are shared by two contexts, as Figure 6-1 shows. You can select the context for features—especially for text, styles, macros and their assignments, and glossary entries—when you define, create, or assign those features.

Word favors the document context over the template, and the template context over the global. For example, any document formatting you've set up for a specific document overrides the global document formatting. Document context is the main context in which you work. Word selects the default context for each element shown in the table below. But when you define, create, or assign elements, you have a chance to place the elements in another context.

Document	*Template*	*Global*
Text	Text	(Text)
Document formatting		Document formatting
Styles	Styles	(Styles)
	Glossaries	Glossaries
	Macros, menu arrangements, keyboard assignments	Macros, menu arrangements, keyboard assignments

Figure 6-1.
Table of contexts for document elements.

Styles

A style is a set of paragraph formatting instructions that are stored under a style name so that you can reuse that same formatting quickly, easily, and consistently.

Each paragraph has its own style, which can be the same or different from the paragraphs around it. If you create a document and start typing without being concerned about styles, Word applies the Normal style to all your paragraphs. Normal is the basic style—it forms the structure for all other styles. To use a style other than Normal, you must specifically apply it. Also in this chapter you learn how to apply a style, how to create a style by formatting a paragraph, and how to change a style.

Applying a Style

You apply a style name to a paragraph. As you can do when you apply paragraph formatting, you can simply position the insertion point in the paragraph or select part or all of the paragraph before you apply the style. Use any one of the following methods to apply a style:

- Choose Format Styles (Alt,T,Y), type or select a style name in the Format Styles dialog box, and then choose OK.

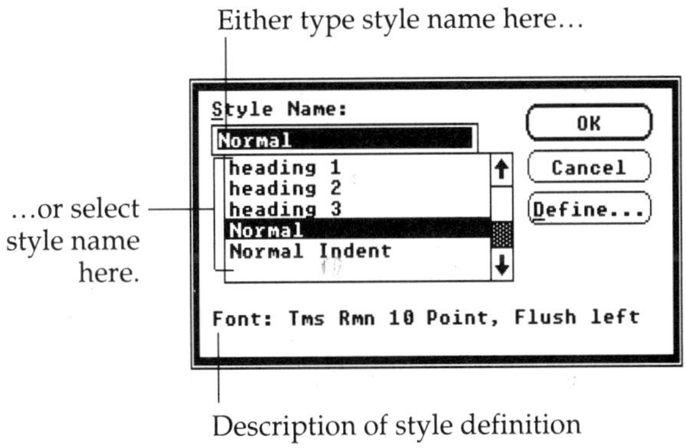

- Press the Ctrl+S keys. If the ruler is visible, the Style box is active. Type or select the style you want to apply. Press F4 to drop down the list. Then, if you used the keyboard to select the style, press the Enter key. If the ruler is not visible, you see the message "Which style?" in the status bar. Type the name of the style you want to apply, and then press Enter. Pressing Ctrl+S is usually the quickest way to apply a style.

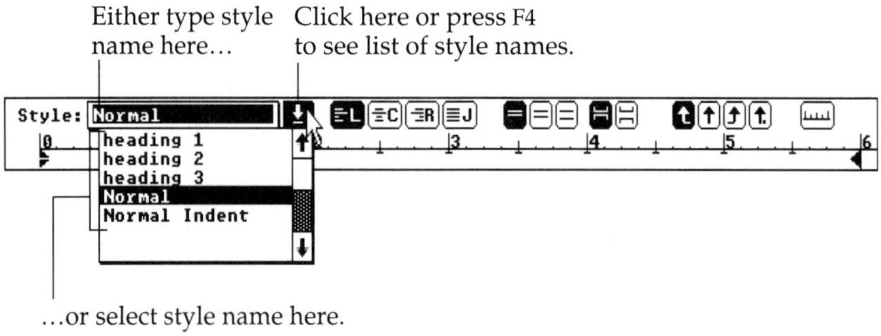

- If the ruler is visible, click the down arrow at the right side of the Style box, and select the style you want to apply.
- In normal editing view, Outline View, Draft View, or Page View, press the Alt+Shift+left arrow keys to apply the next higher heading style (heading 1 through heading 8 styles), the Alt+Shift+right arrow keys to apply the next lower heading style, or the Alt+Shift+5 keys (5 on the numeric keypad) to apply Normal style for body text.
- In Outline View only, drag a heading to the left to apply the next higher heading style (heading 1 through heading 8 styles), to the right to apply the next lower heading style, or to the far right to apply Normal style for body text.
- In Outline View only, click the promote icon to apply the next higher heading style (heading 1 through heading 8 styles), the demote icon to apply the next lower heading style, or the body text icon to apply Normal style for body text.
- Copy paragraph formatting from a paragraph that has a style applied to it: Using the mouse, select the paragraph you want to apply the style to, move the mouse pointer to the selection bar next to the paragraph whose style you want to copy, and then hold down the Ctrl+Shift keys while you click the left mouse button.

Select the paragraph you want to format.

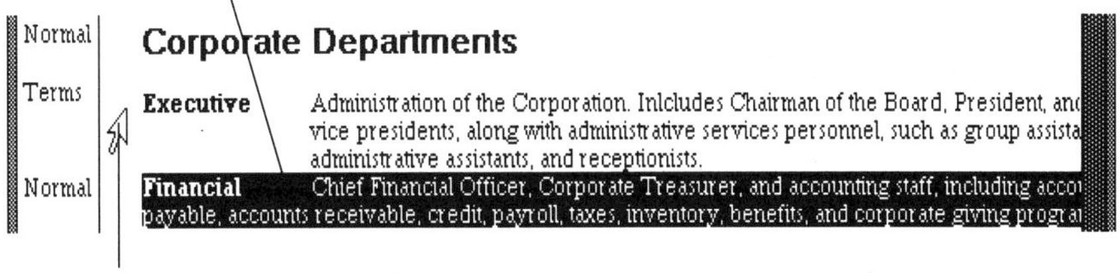

Point in the selection bar beside the paragraph that has the style you want.

Creating a Style from Paragraph Formatting

The easiest way to create a style is to format a paragraph the way you want it—including the text formatting—and then capture the paragraph's formatting as a style. Start by formatting the lines and text of a paragraph.

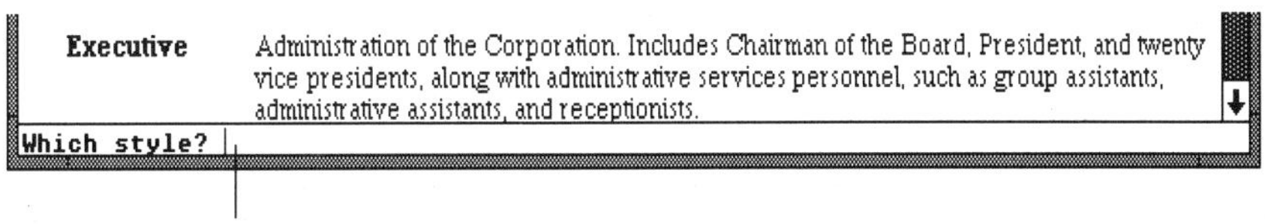

Type new style name.

Press the Ctrl+S keys, and if the ruler is visible, type the name you want for the new style in the Style box. If the ruler is not visible, type the style name in the status bar when prompted, as shown above. Choose Yes when Word asks if you want to define the style based on the selection. When you save the document, Word also saves the style.

Using the Ctrl+S keys is the quickest way to create a style from paragraph formatting. You can also use the Format Styles command or the ruler, as explained in the preceding section, "Applying a Style."

Changing a Style from Paragraph Formatting

You can also change a style based on a particular paragraph's formatting. For example, type some text for a paragraph. Then, press the Alt+Shift+left arrow keys to format the text as a heading 1 paragraph; the text is now larger, boldface, and underlined. Select the heading, and then press the Ctrl+U keys to turn off underlining. Now, to change the style that is based on this paragraph, press the Ctrl+S keys, press the

Enter key, and then choose Yes when Word asks if you want to redefine heading 1 based on the selection. All heading 1 paragraphs in your document lose their underlining, and any new heading 1 paragraphs you add to the document are not underlined.

If you want a style change such as this one to apply to all new documents you create, add the style to your templates. Chapter 7, "Styles," and Chapter 11, "Templates," explain how to add styles to templates.

Fields

Fields are instructions to Word that are enclosed between special characters, which appear on the screen as braces. The instructions tell Word to perform an action and generate some text, numbers, or graphics and then display the result at the field's location in the document.

For example, you can insert a DATE field to display the current date in a memo. All fields are inserted in the same way, and all field codes have a similar appearance:

Date field code	Time field code	Page field code
{date}	{time}	{page}

Questions About Fields

The paragraph above already answers the question "What is a field?" The following questions and answers fill you in further about what fields can do and how you use them.

What can fields do? Fields can insert dates, times, page numbers, authors' names, and summary information about a document. On letters and form letters, fields can insert names and addresses. Fields can be set up to insert contents from other documents and other programs and to insert cross-references to topics and page numbers. Fields can also number paragraphs and lists and can generate tables of contents, indexes, and lists of photos, charts, and illustrations. And fields can jump to other parts of a document and run macros. The Appendix, "Field Types and Their Instructions," provides a complete list of field types and what they do.

Why would you want to use fields? Fields allow you to insert in your document contents that might change from time to time. For example, you can use a field to insert your company logo graphic in a document. If you need to change the logo, you change it only once in your graphic file, and all fields that you use in the future to insert that graphic will insert the new version. (In Chapter 5, "Refining Documents," you used fields to generate paragraph numbers, a table of contents, and an index.) Form letters, address labels, and all types of merge printing use fields. Because many document elements are based on fields, you'll probably want to use fields often; most have been set up for easy use.

Can using fields speed up my work? In addition to the times when you must use fields—such as for page numbers, dates, tables of contents, and indexes—fields can help you automate many other tasks that are involved in creating and completing a document. For example, you might want to use fields to prompt you to insert information at a particular place in a document—perhaps the name and address in a letter or the author's name in a memo.

FILLIN field asks
for author's name.

{author {fillin "Type the author's name"}}

Where can I use a field? You can use a field almost anywhere in a document; only a few fields have restrictions on where they can be placed. You insert most fields in the body of a document, but you can also insert fields in headers and footers. You can even insert most fields inside other fields, which is called "nesting."

What does a field look like? A field has two appearances: field codes and field result, as shown on the next page. Field codes are the directions for how and from where to produce the field's result. For example, the basic field code for an index is {index}, which tells Word to collect an index and insert it at the field's location. A field's result can be text, numbers, or graphics. This result can be as large as an entire document. It can also produce no text, numbers, or graphics at all when the field's purpose is to provide information for other fields, such as index entry fields, which provide index entry information (text and page number) for the INDEX field.

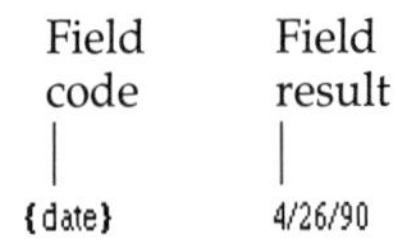

The View menu contains the Field Codes command, which you use to switch between the two views of all fields. You can use the TOGGLE FIELD key combination (Shift+F9) in normal editing view, Outline View, or Draft View (but not in Page View) to switch the view of individual fields. (Before you use Shift+F9, be sure that the insertion point is either immediately to the left of the field or inside the field.) In Page View, TOGGLE FIELD (Shift+F9) toggles all fields because it corresponds to the Include Field Codes option in the File Print dialog box.

Also, if you turn on the Show All option in the View Preferences dialog box, you always see field codes. The View Field Codes command and the TOGGLE FIELD key combination (Shift+F9) have no effect on the appearance of fields as long as the Show All option is turned on. To turn on the Show All option, do one of the following: Choose the Show All option in the View Preferences dialog box, press the SHOW ALL key combination (Ctrl+*), or click the SHOW ALL icon (*) on the ribbon.

What is a field made of? One part of a field is its enclosing field characters, which look like braces: { }. These are not, however, the brace characters you can insert using the keyboard. Word inserts the enclosing field characters for you. Inside those characters are the field type, the instructions, and the options. The field type is the name of the action that the field performs. Instructions make the field's action more specific; options refine the result of the field. The following shows a typical field:

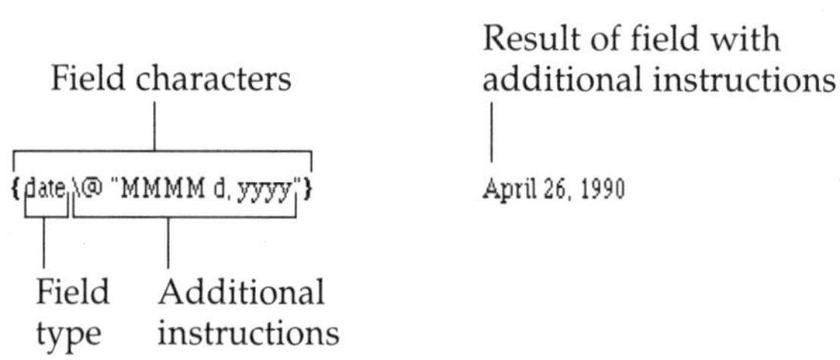

This field contains additional instructions or options for formatting the resulting date as April 26, 1990. You can insert additional instructions to format the date in various ways. More details about instructions and options appear in Chapter 8, "Fields: Facts and Functions."

How do you insert a field? To insert a field, position the insertion point where you want the result to appear, choose one of the special commands that insert a field (see below), press the Ctrl+F9 keys, and type the field codes, or choose the Insert Field command, and select the field type and instructions you want. To see the result of the field, press the UPDATE FIELD key (F9) to update the field. The following sections explain more about inserting fields.

Fields with Their Own Insert Commands

Word includes fields that you can insert quickly and easily either using the appropriate commands on the Insert menu or using icons. These fields insert the types of information you use most often in your documents, such as page numbers and dates. Inserting these fields is so effortless, you probably will not realize that you're using fields. The following topics show what information you can insert using these fields and how to use the appropriate commands or icons to insert the information:

Page numbers. To insert page numbers in your document, choose the Insert Page Numbers command (Alt,I,U). In the Insert Page Numbers dialog box, choose the Top option or the Bottom option; choose the Left option, the Center option, or the Right option; and then choose OK. You can also use this alternative method: First, be sure you are not in Page View. Then, choose the Edit Header/Footer command (Alt,E,H), select either Header or Footer in the Edit Header/Footer dialog box list, and then choose OK. To insert the PAGE field, either click the page icon (which is the leftmost of the three icons displayed) on the icon bar or press the Alt+Shift+P keys. Click the Close button on the icon bar or press the Alt+Shift+C keys to close the header/footer pane.

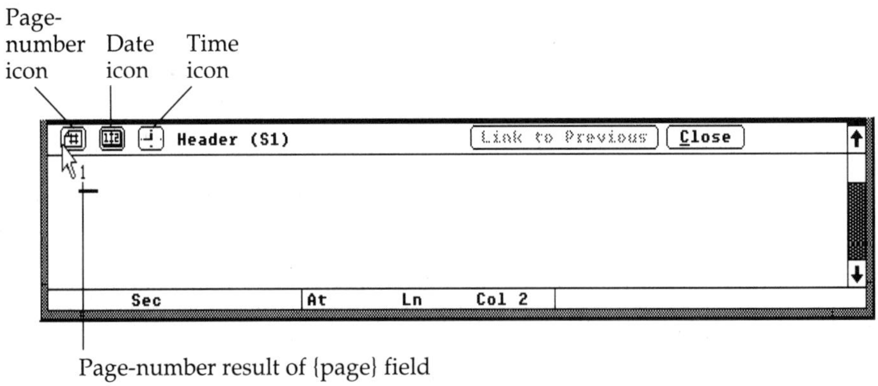

Date. To insert a date in a header or a footer, choose the Edit Header/Footer command (Alt,E,H), select either Header or Footer in the Edit Header/Footer dialog box list, and then choose OK. Click the date icon (the middle of the three icons) on the icon bar, or press the Alt+Shift+D keys. Click the Close button on the icon bar or press the Alt+Shift+C keys to close the header/footer pane. To insert the date elsewhere in a document, position the insertion point and then press the Alt+Shift+D keys.

Time. To insert a field in which Word displays the time in a header or a footer, choose the Edit Header/Footer command (Alt,E,H), select either Header or Footer in the Edit Header/Footer dialog box list, and then choose OK. To insert the TIME field, either click the time icon (the rightmost of the three icons) on the icon bar or press the Alt+Shift+T keys. Click the Close button on the icon bar or press the Alt+Shift+C keys to close the header/footer pane. To insert the time elsewhere in a document, position the insertion point and then press the Alt+Shift+T keys.

File. To insert the entire contents of another file in your document, choose the Insert File command (Alt,I,F), either select the name of the file from the list in the Insert File dialog box or type a file name (if necessary, change directories or type a pathname), and then choose OK.

Table of contents. To insert a table of contents, first be sure you have formatted all the paragraphs that you want to appear in the table of contents with one of the heading styles (heading 1 through heading 9). Then, position the insertion point where you want the table of contents to appear, choose the Insert Table of Contents command (Alt,I,C), and choose OK.

Index. Before you can insert an index, you must create your index entries by selecting a piece of text that you want in the index, choosing the Insert Index Entry command (Alt,I,E), and then choosing OK. Repeat this process for each of your index entries. Then, position the insertion point where you want the index to appear, choose the Insert Index command (Alt,I,I), and choose OK.

Inserting Other Fields Using the Insert Field Command

When you need to insert a field that's not included in the ready-made field commands that the preceding section describes, you can use the Insert Field command (Alt,I,D) to help you easily insert field codes correctly. Insert Field displays a dialog box that lists all the types of fields that you can insert and many of the available options that accompany those field types. You simply choose the field type and options, and Word inserts the field for you.

To try this approach, choose Insert Field (Alt,I,D). Word displays the Insert Field dialog box:

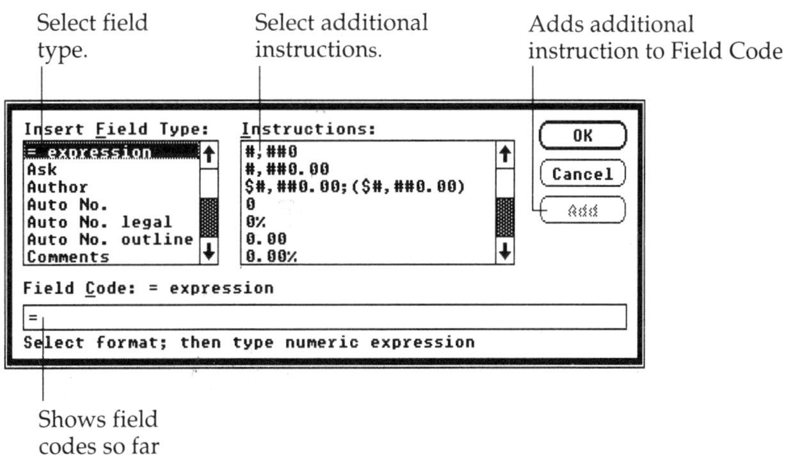

From the list in the Insert Field dialog box, select a Field Type. If any Instructions are available for that Field Type, select an Instruction. To add further Instructions, choose the Add button and select the next Instruction. Choose the Add button for each Instruction you want. Then, choose OK to insert the field at the insertion point. Word updates the field. The next section explains more about the different ways in which you can update fields.

Updating a Field

When you update a field, Word follows the instructions in the field and generates a new result. You update fields in several ways:

- By positioning the insertion point immediately to the left of the field or inside the field and pressing the UPDATE FIELD key (F9) to update a field on demand
- By printing and by switching to Print Preview or Page View to update only some fields in a document
- By turning on the Update Fields option in the File Print dialog box to update all fields in a document during printing

NOTE: *When you insert a field using one of the special Insert commands or the Insert Field command, Word updates the field for you. When you insert a field by pressing the INSERT FIELD key combination (Ctrl+F9), you must press the UPDATE FIELD key combination (F9) to update the field.*

To try updating a field on demand, select the field and then press the UPDATE FIELD key (F9). If the View Field Codes command is turned off, you see the result of the field when updating is complete, even if you used the TOGGLE FIELD key combination (Shift+F9) to switch a field temporarily to show its field code.

To update all fields during printing, choose the File Print command (Alt,F,P), choose the Options button (Alt+O) to open the dialog box to full size, and turn on the Update Fields option (Alt+U). Choose OK to start printing. Word updates the fields on each page before that page is printed.

Breaking the Field Codes

As mentioned earlier in this chapter, a field has two appearances: its codes and its result. You can switch between the two views of fields to see which codes produce which results. This ability to switch between views can be especially handy when you first learn about fields because you can easily insert one of the fields that have their own commands and then look at that field's codes. You can also use the Insert Field command to insert a field with additional instructions, and then look at the codes to see how Word sets up a field. The field's setup is called its "syntax."

Open the View menu (Alt,V) to see if Word displays a check mark next to the Field Codes command name. If a check mark is displayed, the field codes are turned on. If no check mark is displayed, choose the Field Codes command (press C) from the View menu to turn on field codes. To view the results in all fields, choose View Field Codes (Alt,V,C) to turn field codes off.

You can toggle between viewing field codes and viewing results for selected fields. To view temporarily the codes in selected fields when View Field Codes is off, select the fields you want and then press the TOGGLE FIELD key combination (Shift+F9).

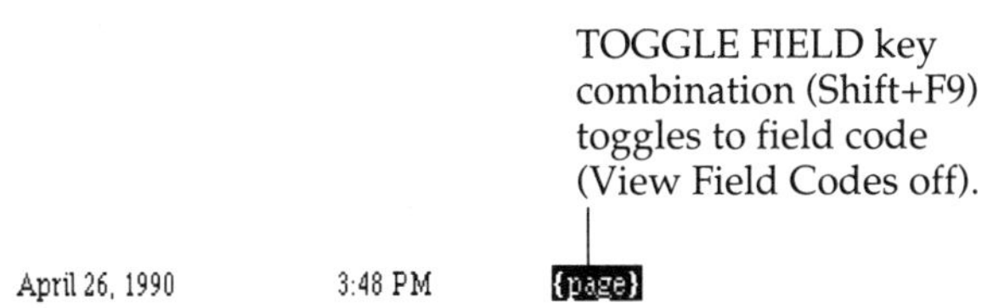

And, to view temporarily the results in selected fields when View Field Codes is on, select the fields you want and then press Shift+F9.

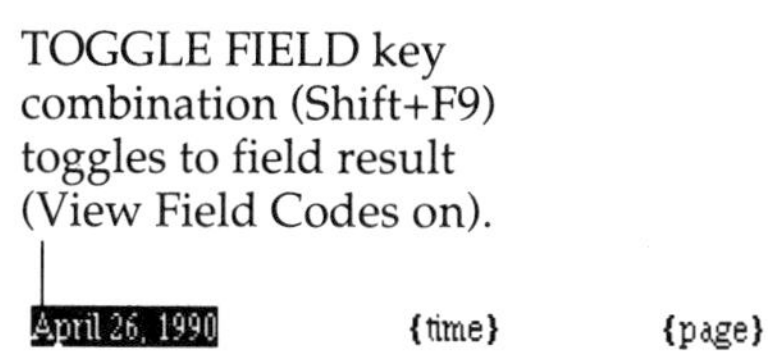

To toggle some fields and not others, use the NEXT FIELD key or key combination (F11 or Alt+F1) or the PREVIOUS FIELD key combination (Shift+F11 or Alt+Shift+F1) to jump to each field, toggling when you want.

Macros

A macro is a series of commands, keystrokes, and other actions—except mouse actions—that you put together to perform a task. For example, you could combine commands and keystrokes to create a macro that would find each field in a document.

Macros are like miniature programs. Although a feature that involves programming might intimidate some people, macros are actually easy to create and use—you need no programming experience. If you're familiar with Word's basics, you can turn over your more mechanical tasks to macros, saving your energy for more thoughtful tasks.

To use a macro, you first create it and then run it. You create macros either by using the Macro Record command to record your actions or by writing a series of macro statements. Chapter 10, "Macros," explains more about writing your own macros.

Recording a Macro

The easiest way to create a macro is to record a series of the actions you take while processing a document. First, be sure you have a document open, and then choose the Macro Record command (Alt,M,C).

Type macro name.

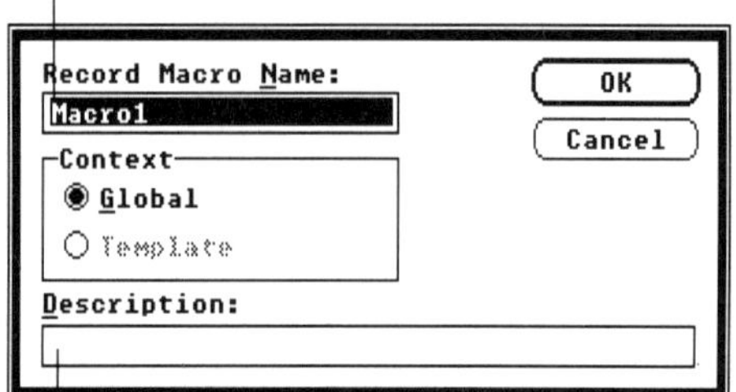

Type description of macro.

In the Macro Record dialog box, type a name for the macro, choose the macro's Context, type a short Description to remind you of what the macro does, and then choose OK. Word displays "REC" in the status bar to show that you're now recording, as illustrated on the next page.

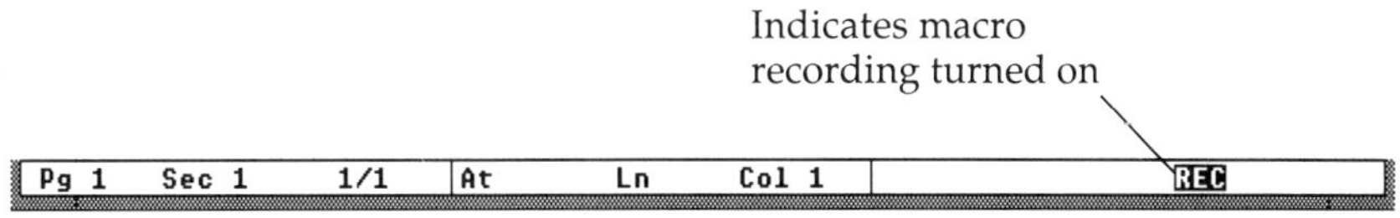

Next, perform all the actions you want to record. These actions affect the active document, so you can see the effects of your actions and check them as you go. As you record a macro, you might make errors. To start over, follow the same steps for recording and give the macro the same name. When Word asks if you want to replace the existing macro, choose Yes and then repeat the actions you want to record.

When you finish performing all the actions you want to record, choose the Macro Stop Recorder command (Alt,M,C). If your last action was to close all documents, choose the File Stop Recorder command (Alt,F,C).

Running a Macro

After you create a macro, it's ready to be used. To use a macro, you run it, much like you run an application program, by using the Macro Run command, by assigning the macro to a key combination and then pressing those keys, or by assigning the macro to a menu and then choosing that menu command.

Using the Macro Run command

To run a macro using a command, start by choosing the Macro Run command (Alt,M,R) if a document is open. (If no document is open, choose the File Run Macro command [Alt,F,R] instead.) In the Macro Run dialog box, select the macro you want from the Run Macro Name list, and then choose OK to run the macro.

Although running a macro by using the Macro Run command works fine, you might find it more efficient to run a macro by using the keyboard or by choosing the macro from a menu. The following sections explain these two alternatives.

Assigning a Macro to a Key Combination

Assigning a macro to a key combination gives you a convenient way to run a macro. When you press the key combination, Word runs the macro for you.

Assign a macro to a key combination if you'll use the macro often enough to remember which keys run it. After you assign macros to keys, you can save the assignments by choosing the File Save All command. If you do not save the assignments—for instance, because you want them only for a single work session—Word asks when you quit whether you want to save the changes. Either save all the assignments or discard them all. Of course, you can unassign macros from keys to eliminate the assignments that you do not want to save.

Word contains a built-in command for copying text and paragraph formatting; this command is not assigned to any keys or menu. Using the Macro Assign to Key command, practice using macros by assigning this useful built-in copying command to a key combination.

> **NOTE:** *Think of Word's built-in commands as macros. You use these commands in the same ways that you use macros; what applies to one applies to the other, with few exceptions. Chapter 10, "Macros," describes those exceptions.*

First, choose the Macro Assign to Key command (Alt,M,K). Then, in the Macro Assign to Key dialog box, select CopyFormat from the Assign Macro Name list (press the C key to step through the macros that start with "C" until CopyFormat is selected).

By showing any existing assignment in the Current Keys box, Word lets you know if the macro you select is already assigned to a key combination. You can assign a macro to as many key combinations as you want. It's best to assign it to only one combination because the number of unassigned key combinations available is limited. And limiting the total number of key assignments makes it easier to remember the combinations that you have assigned.

Press the combination of keys to which you want to assign this command. The available keys are the function keys; Ctrl+ any letter, number, or function key; and Ctrl+Shift+ any letter, number, or function key. For example, try the Ctrl+Shift+C keys. If the combination is already assigned to another command or macro, the current assignment appears in the Key box. Either choose another combination or remove the current assignment by choosing the Unassign button (Alt+U). If the combination has nothing assigned to it, you see "[currently unassigned]" in the Key box.

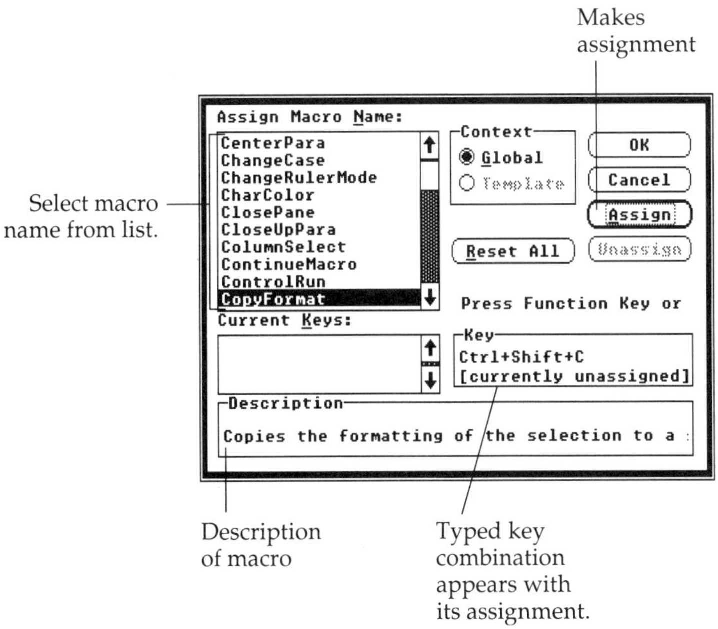

Choose the Assign button (Alt+A). If you're finished assigning keys, choose OK.

Assigning a Macro to a Menu

You can also assign a macro to a menu. By doing so, you can choose the macro from the menu as you would choose any other menu command. Assigning a macro to a menu makes the most sense if you plan to use the macro often enough to make having it on the menu worthwhile but not often enough to remember a key combination for it. You might also assign a macro to a menu if someone else will be using the macro and is less likely than you to remember a key combination or a macro name (displayed in the Macro Run dialog box). Having a macro on a menu also provides an occasional reminder that the macro is available.

After you assign macros to menus, you can save the assignments by choosing the File Save All command. If you do not save the assignments—for instance, because you want them for only one work session—Word asks when you quit if you want to save the changes. Either save or discard all the assignments. You can unassign macros from menus to eliminate the assignments that you do not want to save.

Word contains a built-in command, called ClosePane, that closes any type of window pane. Putting this command on a menu is more convenient, for example, than remembering and using the existing key combination for closing header/footer panes (Alt+Shift+C or Shift+F10,C).

Using the Macro Assign to Menu command, assign the built-in ClosePane command to a menu as a way to practice using macros. First, choose the Macro Assign to Menu command (Alt,M,M). Next, select ClosePane from the Assign Macro Name list. (Press the C key to step through the macros that start with "C" until ClosePane is selected.) Move to the Menu list (Alt+M), and select the menu on which you want the macro to appear—Window, in this case. The Window menu is short and also is a logical choice for a command that removes a window split.

Move to the Menu Text box (Alt+T), and edit the name as you want it to appear on the menu. You can include spaces. Note that an ampersand (&) must precede the letter that you want to use for choosing the command using the keyboard. The letter following the ampersand will be underlined in the menu. In this example, the text and the ampersand position that Word proposes for ClosePane are acceptable—you can leave them intact.

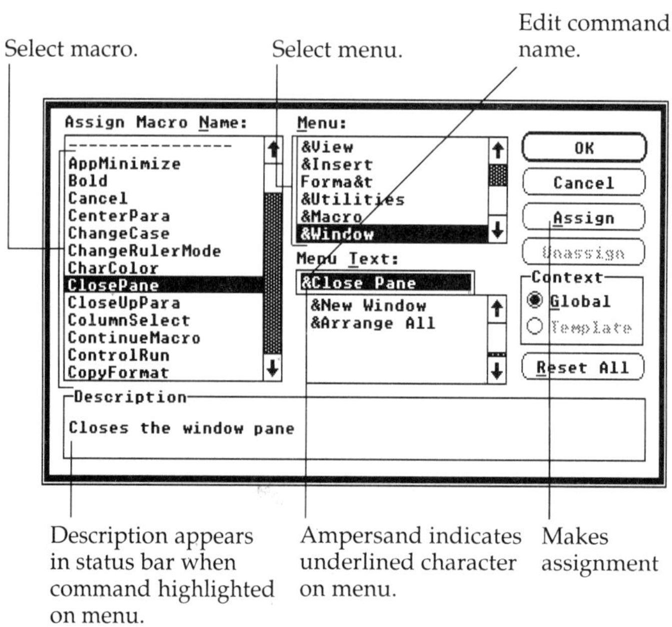

Choose the Assign button (Alt+A) to add ClosePane to the Window menu. If you're finished assigning macros, choose OK. From now on, you can choose the Window Close Pane command (Alt,W,C) when you want to close a window pane.

Deleting a Macro

When you no longer need a macro, you should delete it to save computer memory and to avoid confusion when you want to reuse a macro name. To delete a macro, choose the Macro Edit command (Alt,M,E). In the dialog box, be sure the Show All option is turned off so that you see only the macros that you created or that Microsoft provided and not the built-in commands. Select the macro that you want from the Edit Macro Name list. Then, choose the Delete button (Alt+D) to delete the macro. Note that after you choose Delete, the Cancel button changes to Close because you cannot cancel the delete action. Choose the Close button to close the dialog box.

Templates

A document template in Word is a model, or pattern, from which you create documents. All Word documents are based on document templates. If you do not specify a template, Word uses a template named NORMAL.DOT, which allows you to create a document without having to deal with templates.

A typical document template contains some boilerplate text and graphics and some formatting so that all documents created from that template contain the same text, formatted and positioned uniformly. More advanced document templates can contain styles, special glossary entries, macros, and menu and key assignments.

You use document templates to quickly create new documents that follow a standard layout. For example, by creating all your memos from a memo document template that follows your standard memo layout, you ensure that your memos will match the standard. Word also lets you switch the template that underlies a document by selecting the new template in the Format Document dialog box. You can use this capability to gain temporary access to template context features that the current template does not contain or to permanently change the underlying template and change a document to a different type. For example, if a memo grows too large, you might convert it to a report or a proposal and switch to a different template to make an easier task of changing the document.

You can create a document template in a number of ways:

- By saving an existing document as a template
- By modifying an existing template
- By creating a template from scratch as you would create a document

Here you see how to use a template to create a document and how to create a template by saving an existing document as a template. Chapter 11, "Templates," explains how to create templates from scratch and how to modify templates.

Using a Template to Create a Document

Word comes to you with document templates on the Setup disk in your Word package. You can use many of these templates by making only slight modifications.

TIP

A Word About NORMAL.DOT, the Default Template

You can create a document without explicitly choosing a document template. If you choose no template in the File New dialog box, Word creates the document based on a global template named NORMAL.DOT. This template is not a document template in the same sense as other templates. NORMAL.DOT does behave much like any document template in terms of what you see when you create a document and what you can do with the document template file (that is, open it, edit it, and modify it). NORMAL.DOT is never listed in the File Open dialog box, so you have to remember this template's name and type it yourself when you want to edit NORMAL.DOT. For convenience, however, various commands in Word let you add changes directly to NORMAL.DOT without opening it and editing it directly. In Chapter 11, "The default template: NORMAL.DOT" explains how to edit NORMAL.DOT.

These sample document templates should have been copied to your hard disk during setup. If they were not, you need to copy all the Setup disk files that have a DOT file-name extension into the directory in which you keep your Word program file (WINWORD.EXE) or to the directory specified for the DOT-PATH= entry in your WIN.INI file. After you copy the document template files to your hard disk, the templates are ready to be used for creating documents.

To use a template to create a document, choose the File New command. In the File New dialog box, select a document template in the Use Template box. For this example, select MEMO, which is one of the sample document templates from the Setup disk.

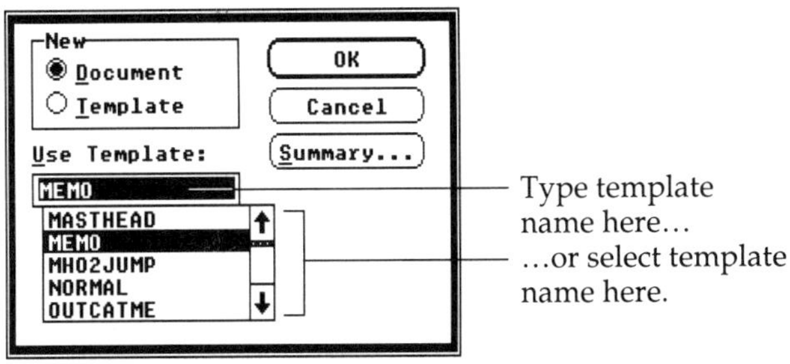

Then, choose OK to create a document that's based on the MEMO template. The new document contains the name and address of Trey Research, but you can change the name and address and anything else in the document by using the same methods you use to edit any document. The text and formatting Word copied from the document template are not locked—you still have full control over the document.

Eventually, you'll want to modify the sample document templates as well as create your own templates. By using your own templates, you will no longer have to repeatedly change the parts of the document that come from the template.

Creating a Template by Saving an Existing Document as a Template

The easiest way to create a document template is by saving an existing document as a template. The document you use should match the look you want for all documents of a particular type. For example, if you're working on a memo document, your company name and address should be positioned at the top (or with enough blank space included so that you can print your memos on letterhead paper). And the lines for To, From, Date, and Subject should be positioned correctly. If you have special memo paper with this address information and the To and From text already printed on it, you can also set up a document that aligns the memo text with the labels. Then the next time you create a memo, you simply type the body of the memo and print. You never have to worry about positioning because the document template takes care of positioning for you.

You can either create a new document on which to base the template or use a document you already have. If you're creating a new document, insert in it only the text and formatting that you want to include in your document template. If you're using a completed document, be sure to delete any unneeded text. Deleting the text will save you time and effort later, when you start creating documents from the template.

When the document is ready to serve as a template, choose the File Save As command (Alt,F,A). In the File Save As dialog box, type a name for the template. You can omit the DOT file-name extension because Word adds it for you. Next, choose the Options button (Alt+O) to open the full dialog box. Move to the File Format box (Alt+F), and select Document Template from the list.

Type new template name.

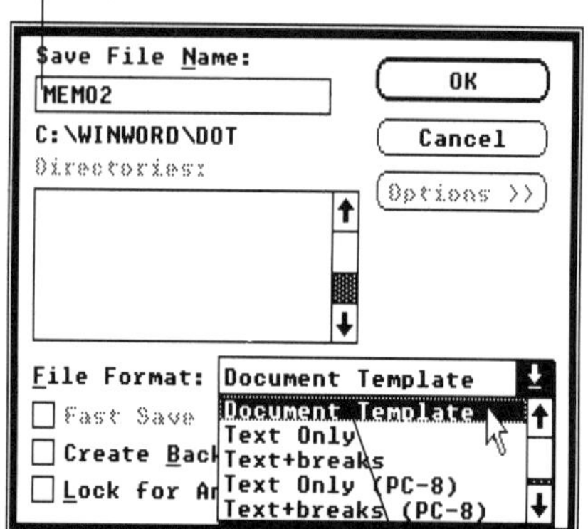

Select Document Template file format.

Then, choose OK. If the Summary Info dialog box appears, supply any information you want and then choose OK. Word saves the document as a document template, and the original document is unchanged. From now on, you can create documents based on this new document template.

Changing the Template That Underlies a Document

After you create a document, you might find that you want the document to be based on a different document template. For example, another template might include glossary entries, styles, or macros that would be useful in the current document.

When you change the template that underlies a document, the new template's glossary entries and macros become available. You can combine styles from the new template with styles already in the document. Or you can leave the document styles as they are. The boilerplate text and graphics do not merge from the template to the document, but you can copy any needed text from the template. This arrangement of changes protects the integrity of your document while giving you the new tools you want from another template.

To change the document template that underlies an open document, choose the Format Document command (Alt,T,D). In the Format Document dialog box, move to the Template box (Alt+M), select the template you want to use, and then choose OK.

Chapter 7

Styles

A style is a collection of paragraph and text formatting that you can reuse. After you create a style, you apply the style name to a paragraph instead of having to choose individual formatting commands. The style name remains with that paragraph as long as you want. To change the format of the paragraph at any time, you apply a different style. And to change the format of all paragraphs to which you applied the same style, change the formatting of the style so that Word for Windows will apply those formatting changes to all the paragraphs that are formatted in that style.

Use styles when you want the following:

- Consistent formatting within and among documents
- Easy-to-change formatting for many paragraphs
- The ability to apply many formats at one time
- Structured documents (documents built on outline headings)
- Headings that make creating a table of contents fast and easy

You can apply a style to any paragraph in any part of a document. In addition to a document's body text, you can use styles for headers, footers, footnote reference marks and footnote text, annotation reference marks and annotation text, the table of contents (all levels), the index (all levels) and index headings, and line numbers.

Each document can have as many as 220 styles. If you reach the limit of possible styles but need to define another style, you have to delete one of the existing styles before you can add another. Of the possible 220 styles, 35 are automatic styles that are already created for you in Word. Word applies the automatic styles to the text elements to which they belong. For example, if you add a header, Word applies the header style to it. For descriptions and information about using these automatic styles, see "Modifying and Refining the Automatic Styles" later in this chapter.

Styles: The Foundation of Formatting

You always use a style in Word, even if you're not aware of it. Whenever you create a document, Word assigns it the Normal style, which looks like the following:

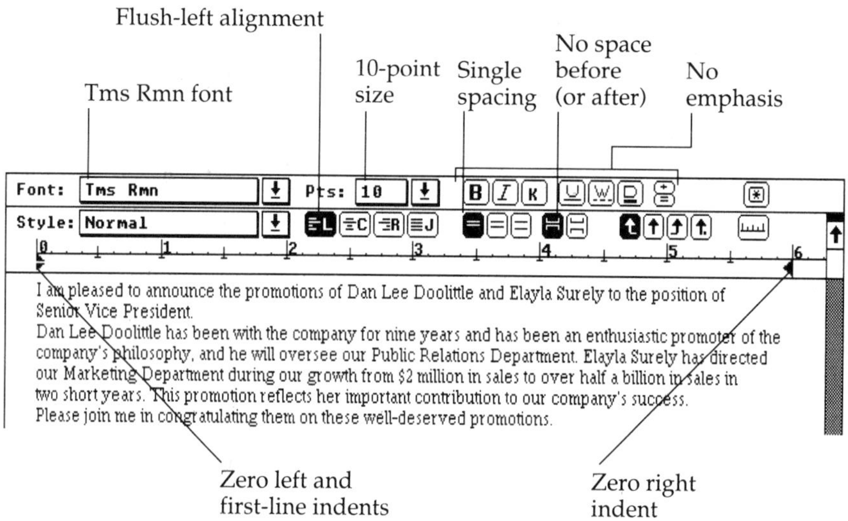

Normal style applies the following paragraph formatting: flush-left alignment, all indents at the margins (zero), no space before or after the paragraph, line spacing single-space automatic (as tall as the tallest character in each line), no border, no "keep" options, no page break before, line numbering turned on (if turned on in the Format Section dialog box), and default tab stops every one-half inch. The default font is Tms Rmn, and the default point size is 10 points.

By default, Word applies the Normal style to every paragraph for which you do not specify a style. And more important, Normal is the basis for all other styles. Every style you define or modify is based on the Normal style, even if you create a style that's based on a different style. That base style, somewhere down the line, is also based on Normal. A style can actually have as many as seven layers of styles between it and Normal, but in the end, as in a tree, the branches all connect at the base to a single trunk.

Because you start every document with the Normal style, any formatting you apply to a paragraph is actually changing the formatting applied by Normal. When you center a Normal paragraph, you're overriding Normal's left alignment with centered alignment. In the same way, when you apply boldface to text in a Normal paragraph, you're overriding Normal's nonboldface text format with boldface text format. When you collect these additions to Normal and give the whole bundle of formatting a name, you create a style.

By applying formatting directly to a paragraph, you can modify the effect of a style on an individual paragraph. You can also collect your modifications either to create a new style or to modify the paragraph's existing style.

You might find that styles take some getting used to. But after you're accustomed to them and after you create styles that make your formatting work less complex, you'll find that styles are easier to use than direct formatting. Some writers even find themselves unwilling to begin working on a document until they've set up their styles. You can certainly create and format text for a Word document without creating any styles. But if you use direct formatting instead of styles, refining the formatting later is more difficult.

The rest of this chapter describes how to create and modify styles by capturing existing paragraph formatting or by changing the style definitions directly in the Format Define Styles dialog box to create a style from scratch. At the end of the chapter, you'll find information about how to use two of the most powerful features of styles—chaining styles together and basing one style on another. You'll also find descriptions of other actions that you can take with styles: renaming, merging, and deleting.

Creating and Modifying Styles by Capturing Existing Paragraph Formatting

In Chapter 6, "Using Word's Four Pillars: Styles, Fields, Macros, and Templates," you tried creating and modifying a style that was based on an existing paragraph's formatting. To refresh your memory about that process, you create a title style here that you could use for the titles of either the major sections of a report or the chapters of a book. Then you modify the style.

Creating a Title Style

In this example, you create a style that centers a title and formats the characters in Helv font, 14-point size, boldface, and underlined.

TIP

Style Definitions

When you choose the Format Styles command or the Format Define Styles command, you see a description of the formatting defined for the selected style. The definition starts with the style that forms the basis of the selected style followed by a plus sign and the changes from the base style. The following two examples show you the basic parts of a style definition.

```
Normal + Font: Helv 12 Point, Bold
Underline, Space Before 12pt
```

Note the colon following "Font." The colon gives you a visual clue about where a new part of the definition begins. The next example shows a definition that has two parts: "Indent" and "Tab Stops."

```
Normal + Indent:  Left  1" Right
0.5", Tab stops: 5.75" ...; 6"
Right Flush
```

In the definition above, the text formatting is the same as it is for its base style, Normal. The paragraph formatting indents lines from both the left and the right. After the paragraph formatting comes the tab stop formatting: one at 5¾" that has dot leaders and one at 6" that has right alignment. If you define a position for a style, the position formatting appears before the tab stop formatting.

```
Normal + Position:  Center Horiz.
Relative To Column, Tab stops: 1"
```

Before you start this example, open the style name area so that you can see what styles are applied to the paragraphs. To open the style name area, choose the View Preferences command (Alt,V,E), move to the Style Area Width box (Alt+W), type *0.7"*, and then choose OK. You see a vertical band along the left side of the window that shows style names, as follows:

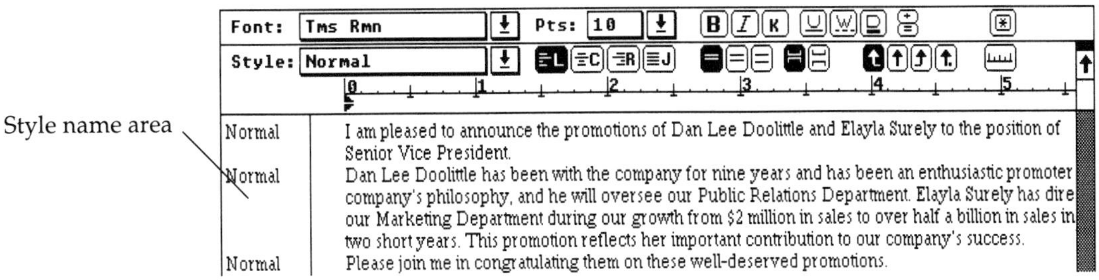

First, type the title text, as shown below:

History of the Project

Then, select the entire paragraph. Press the Ctrl+F keys, type *Helv,* and then press the Enter key to assign the Helv font to the paragraph. Next, press the Ctrl+P keys, type *14*, and then press Enter to assign 14-point size to the paragraph's text. Press the Ctrl+B keys for boldface. Then, press the Ctrl+U keys for underlining. To center the paragraph, press the Ctrl+C keys.

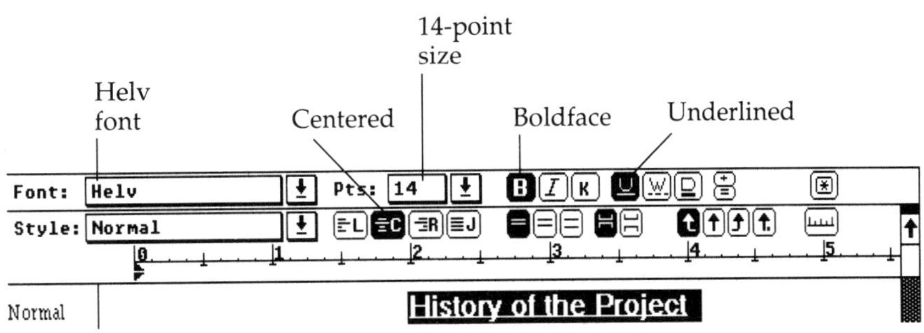

To define this style, press the Ctrl+S keys, type *Title*, and then press the Enter key. Choose Yes when Word asks if you want to define the style "Title" based on the selection. You just created a title style. When you save the document, Word saves the style along with the document.

Modifying the Normal Style

Because the Normal style is a block style—the first line is not indented—it's sometimes hard to tell where one paragraph ends and the next begins in text that's formatted as Normal style. One way to make the paragraphs more distinguishable is to leave a blank line between them. Word has a paragraph format—called spacing before—that leaves a blank line when you start a new paragraph. Try adding this spacing format to the Normal style.

First, insert a paragraph that has the Normal style, such as the following:

They completed the project in seven phases.

(If the paragraph has another style applied to it, press the Alt+Shift+5 keys, using the 5 on the numeric keypad, to apply the Normal style.) With the insertion point anywhere in the Normal paragraph, press the Ctrl+O keys to open a blank line above the paragraph. To define this style, press the Ctrl+S keys, type *Normal,* and then press the Enter key. Choose Yes when Word asks if you want to redefine Normal based on the selection. You just modified the definition of the Normal style. All Normal style paragraphs throughout the document now have a blank line above them. Also, all styles based on Normal that do not have their own Space Before setting now have a blank line above them—including the Title style that you created earlier in this chapter. When you save the document, Word saves the new definition of the style along with the document.

TIP

Style Names and the Unique String

A style name must be different from every other style name. Any group of characters, whether or not the characters form a word, is called a string. When the string is different from all other strings, it is called a unique string. When you name styles, remember to use short, unique names so that you have fewer characters to type. Try to avoid names like heading 1 through heading 9, which require you to type many characters before you have a unique string.

Creating Styles from Scratch

To create and modify a style, you most often rely on the method explained in the preceding sections: formatting a paragraph and then defining or redefining a style based on the paragraph's formatting. That method is the quickest, particularly if you're new to styles and you need a style or style change on the fly as you work on a document. It's quicker yet if you use the formatting keys to set the formatting changes so that you don't need to open any dialog boxes.

But if you're simply creating or refining styles and you do not need text to base them on, you can create styles from scratch instead, without having to first insert and format text. And you create these styles without having to apply them to selected text. You choose the Format Define Styles command only one time to create and modify as many styles as you need, and then close the dialog box when you finish. This method takes more planning and an ability to visualize the styles that you want from abstract dialog box settings, but the benefits in speed and efficiency are great. You might find that the most effective time to use this method of creating styles from scratch is when you add styles to a template because a template might have little or no text and you will not want to add text to the template merely to create styles. Chapter 11, "Templates," explains how to add styles to a template.

Using the Format Define Styles Command

When you first choose the Format Define Styles command to create styles from scratch or to modify styles, you see the following compact version of the dialog box:

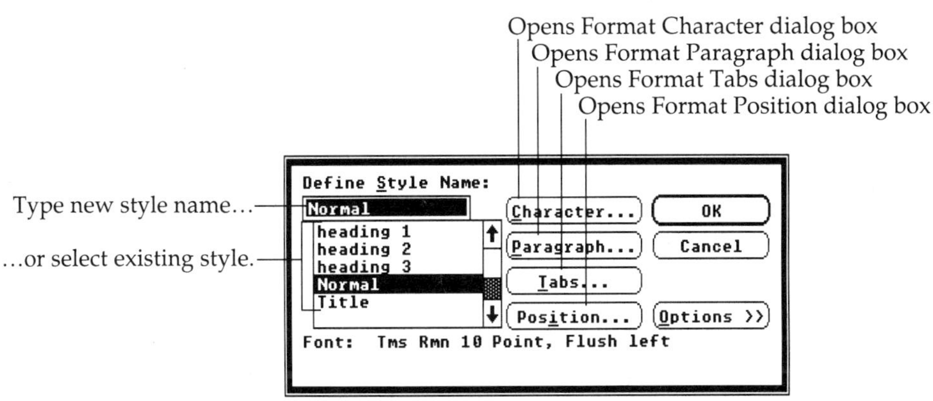

For every style, you can add settings using the four formatting commands whose names appear in the Format Define Styles dialog box: Character, Paragraph, Tabs, and Position. To avoid an overwhelming and large dialog box, Word uses these special buttons. Each button opens another dialog box while leaving the Format Define Styles dialog box open underneath:

Format Define Styles dialog box is still open underneath.

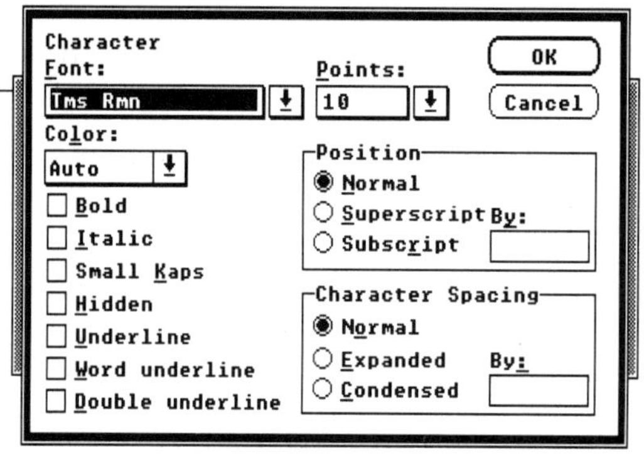

When you close the second dialog box, Word uncovers the Format Define Styles dialog box so that you can either choose other actions or finish that style. The following sections explain how you use the dialog boxes that are displayed when you choose the four formatting buttons. Following the explanations of the Format Define Styles dialog box, you'll find several examples that you can use to practice creating styles.

But first, the following is the basic process of defining a single style from scratch: Start by choosing the Format Define Styles command (Alt,T,F). In the Format Define Styles dialog box, type or select a style name and choose one of the four formatting buttons. Then, set the formatting in the dialog box that appears and choose OK. Continue choosing from among the four formatting buttons and setting the formatting in each of the dialog boxes. When you finish and are back in the Format Define Styles dialog box, choose OK.

Character Button

Choosing the Character button in the Format Define Styles dialog box opens the Format Character dialog box:

Character button
opens this dialog box.

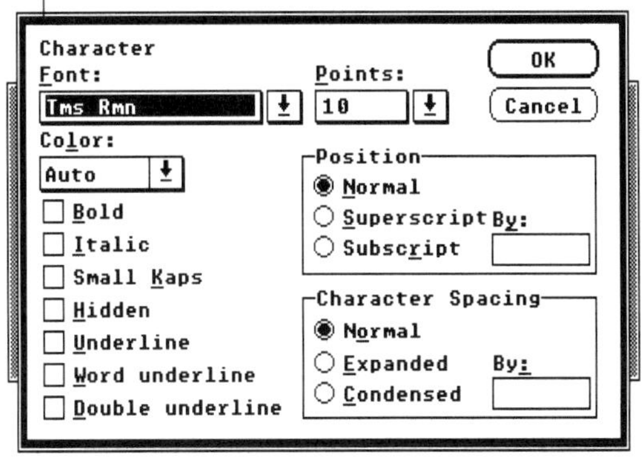

You adjust the settings in the dialog box and then choose OK to add them to the style definition. Instead of using the Character button, you can use the text-formatting keys while the Format Define Styles dialog box is open. After you press the text-formatting keys, Word adds the format to the selected style's definition and adds a description of the format to the style's description. Some keys perform a different action in the Format Define Styles dialog box than they do in a document—in particular, the Ctrl+F keys for font, the Ctrl+P keys for point size, and the Ctrl+V keys for color. See a summary of what the text-formatting keys do in the Format Define Styles dialog box in Figure 7-1 later in this chapter. Using the dialog box instead of the text-formatting keys in the Format Define Styles dialog box lets you see all the text formatting that has been applied to the style and what additional settings are available, adjust all aspects of text formatting in one place at one time, fine-tune the superscript and subscript measurements, and adjust character spacing.

Paragraph Button

Choosing the Paragraph button in the Format Define Styles dialog box opens the Format Paragraph dialog box:

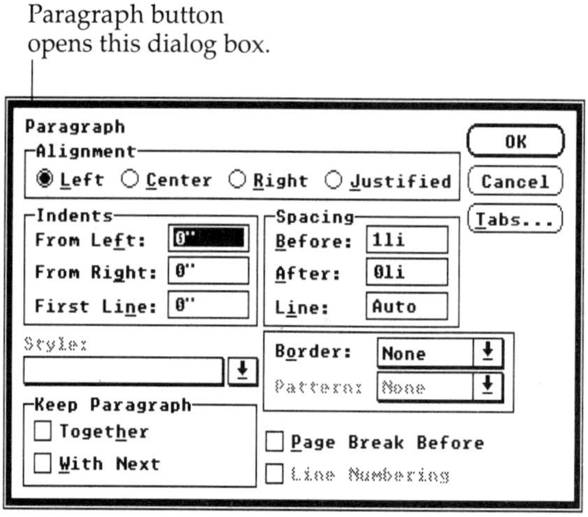

You adjust the settings in the dialog box and then choose OK to add them to the style definition. Instead of using the Format Paragraph dialog box, you can use the paragraph-formatting keys while the Format Define Styles dialog box is open. After you press the paragraph-formatting keys, Word adds the format to the selected style's definition and adds a description of the format to the style's description. All the paragraph-formatting keys perform the same action in the Format Define Styles dialog box as they do in a document. See a summary of what the paragraph-formatting keys do in Figure 7-2 later in this chapter. Using the Format Paragraph dialog box instead of the paragraph-formatting keys in the Format Define Styles dialog box lets you see all the paragraph formatting that has been applied to the style; adjust all aspects of paragraph formatting in one place at one time; and fine-tune the left indent, first-line indent, space before, and line-spacing measurements. The Format Paragraph dialog box also lets you adjust the right indent and the space after the paragraph, add borders or a page break before the paragraph, set the Keep Paragraph Together and the Keep Paragraph With Next options, and turn off line numbering.

Tabs Button

To set tab stops as part of a style's definition, choose the Tabs button in the Format Define Styles dialog box:

Tabs button opens this dialog box.

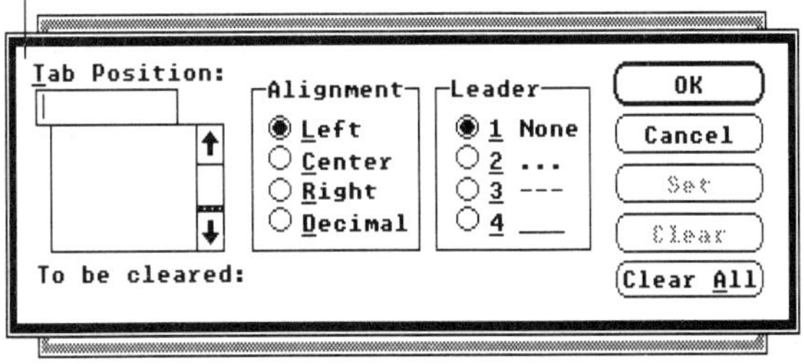

The Tabs button opens the Format Tabs dialog box. If you choose the Paragraph button in the Format Define Styles dialog box, you can choose the Tabs button in the Paragraph dialog box to switch to the Tabs dialog box. You set tab stops in this dialog box and then choose OK to add the tab stops to the style's definition. Using the Format Tabs dialog box is the only way to add tab stops to a style when the Format Define Styles dialog box is displayed; you cannot use the ruler.

Position Button

You can also set the position of a paragraph as part of a style's definition. First, choose the Position button in the Format Define Styles dialog box, which opens the Format Position dialog box:

Position button opens this dialog box.

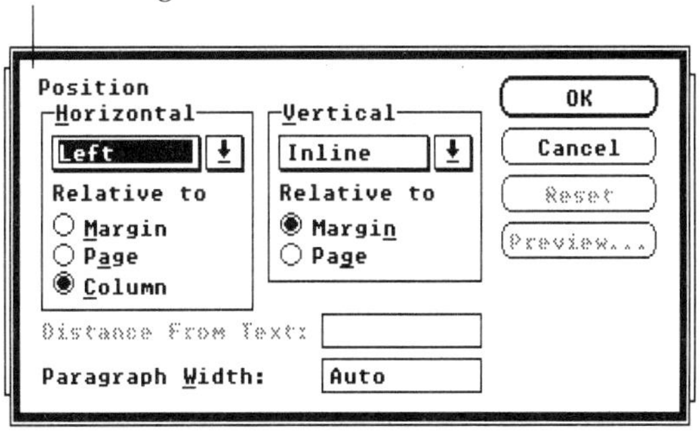

You set the paragraph position in this dialog box and then choose OK to add the position to the style's definition.

Options Button

You use the Options button in the Format Define Styles dialog box to set the Next Style and Based On Style names and to rename, delete, and merge styles. You'll read more about these topics in the upcoming sections "Next Style Chaining," "Basing One Style on Another," and "Doing Your Styles Housekeeping."

Summary of Text-formatting Keys

Inside the Format Define Styles dialog box, you can also press the text-formatting keys to add and remove text formatting in a style's definition. You select the style you want to change and then press the key combination for the format you want to add or remove. For example, to add italic to the heading 1 style, select the style in the Format Define Styles dialog box and then press the Ctrl+I keys. Or, to remove underlining from the heading 1 style, select the style and then press the Ctrl+U keys. Figure 7-1 shows what the text-formatting keys do in the Format Define Styles dialog box. Some keys perform differently than they do when you work in document text.

Keys	*Action*
Ctrl+F	For the printer you're connected to, changes to the next font in the list
Ctrl+Shift+F	For the printer you're connected to, changes to the previous font in the list
Ctrl+P	Increases point size by one-half point, up to 127 points, and then starts over at 4 points
Ctrl+Shift+P	Decreases point size by one-half point, down to 4 points, and then starts over at 127 points
Ctrl+B	Turns boldface on or off
Ctrl+I	Turns italic on or off
Ctrl+K	Turns small capitals on or off
Ctrl+H	Turns hidden text on or off
Ctrl+U	Turns continuous underlining on or off

Figure 7-1. *(continued)*
Text-formatting keys in the Format Define Styles dialog box.

Figure 7-1. *continued*

Keys	*Action*
Ctrl+W	Turns word underlining on or off
Ctrl+D	Turns double, continuous underlining on or off
Ctrl+equal sign	Turns 3-point subscript on or off
Ctrl+Shift+ equal sign	Turns 3-point superscript on or off
Ctrl+V	Changes to next color in the list of available colors: Black, Blue, Cyan, Green, Magenta, Red, Yellow, White, and Auto (the default text color set in Windows)
Ctrl+Shift+V	Changes to previous color in the list of available colors
Ctrl+spacebar	Removes all text formatting that differs from the style's base style (Based On)

Summary of Paragraph-formatting Keys

In the Format Define Styles dialog box, you can press the paragraph-formatting key combinations to add to and remove paragraph formatting from the definition of a style. You select the style you want to change and then press the key combination for the format you want to add or remove. For example, to add centered alignment to a style, select the style in the dialog box and then press the Ctrl+C keys. Or, to remove open space above a paragraph from a style, select the style and then press the Ctrl+E keys. Figure 7-2 shows what the paragraph-formatting keys do in the Format Define Styles dialog box. These keys perform the same way they do when you work in document text.

Keys	*Action*
Ctrl+L	Applies left alignment
Ctrl+C	Applies centered alignment
Ctrl+R	Applies right alignment
Ctrl+J	Applies justified alignment

Figure 7-2. *(continued)*
Paragraph-formatting keys in the Format Define Styles dialog box.

Figure 7-2. *continued*

Keys	*Action*
Ctrl+N	Increases the left indent to the next tab stop; leaves the first-line indent at its current measurement (the first line moves to the right the same distance as the left indent moves)
Ctrl+M	Decreases the left indent to the previous tab stop; leaves the first-line indent at its current measurement (the first line moves to the left the same distance as the left indent moves)
Ctrl+T	Increases the left indent to the next tab stop; adjusts the first-line indent measurement so that the first line remains indented the same distance from the left margin
Ctrl+G	Decreases the left indent to the previous tab stop; adjusts the first-line indent measurement so that the first line remains indented the same distance from the left margin
Ctrl+1	Sets the line spacing to single-space automatic, with a minimum of 12 points, or as tall as the tallest character in each line
Ctrl+2	Sets the line spacing to double-space automatic, with a minimum of 24 points, or as tall as the tallest character in each line
Ctrl+5	Sets the line spacing to one-and-one-half-space automatic, with a minimum of 18 points, or as tall as the tallest character in each line
Ctrl+O	Sets Spacing Before to 1 line
Ctrl+E	Sets Spacing Before to 0 lines
Ctrl+X	Removes all paragraph formatting that differs from the style's base style (Based On)

Example 1: Creating a Numbered List Style

A numbered list is usually made up of paragraphs whose first lines extend to the left of the rest of the text, providing greater readability. This arrangement, which is called a "hanging indent," is shown in the example on the next page.

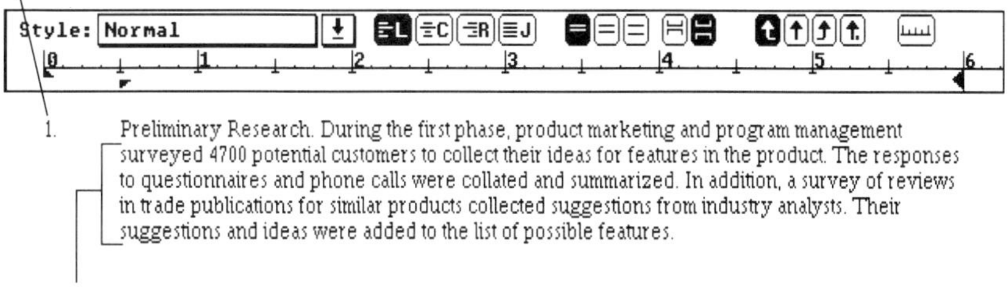

To create a numbered list style, set the left indent in, set the first-line indent out by giving it a negative measurement, and set two tab stops.

To practice creating a numbered list style from scratch, choose the Format Define Styles command (Alt,T,F). Type *Number List* in the Format Define Styles dialog box for the style's name. (You can type the style name using any combination of uppercase and lowercase characters.) Next, choose the Paragraph button (Alt+P) to open the Format Paragraph dialog box.

Type *0.5"* in the Indents From Left box to set the left indent in by one-half inch. Then, move to the Indents First Line box (Alt+N) and type *-0.5"* to set the first-line indent at the left margin.

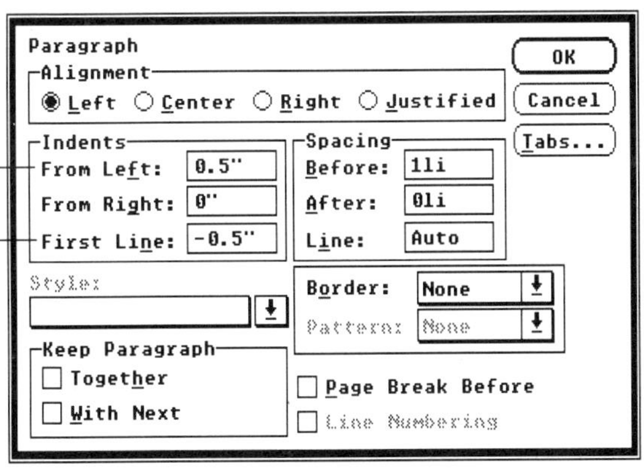

Choose OK to set the two indents and to return to the Format Define Styles dialog box. To open the Format Tabs dialog box, choose the Tabs button (Alt+T). Type *0.25"* in the Tab Position box, choose the Right Alignment option (Alt+R), and then choose the Set button (Alt+S). You set a right-aligned tab stop for the number so that if the numbering goes beyond 9, the numbers expand to the left and the periods following the numbers remain aligned. To specify a second tab stop setting, type *0.5"* in the Tab Position box and choose the Left Alignment option (Alt+L).

Alignment of position in edit box under Tab Position (0.5")

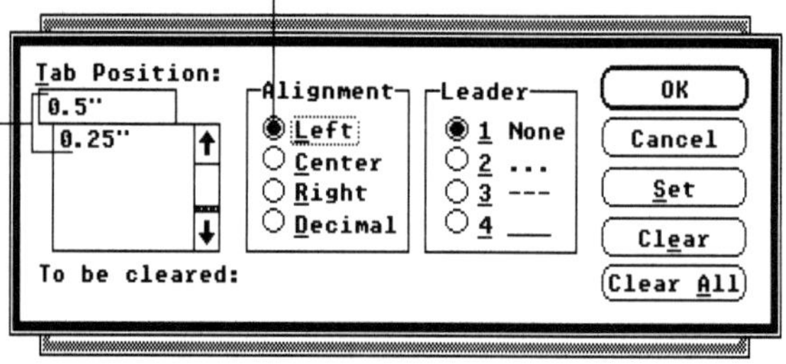

Set tab stop positions.

Choose OK to set the two tab stops and to return to the Format Define Styles dialog box. Then, choose OK to define the style.

To use the Number List style, choose the Format Styles command, select Number List from the list of style names, and choose OK. Press the Tab key, type the number for the paragraph (or insert a field that gives you the number automatically), press Tab again, and then type the text for the numbered item.

First tab aligns number.

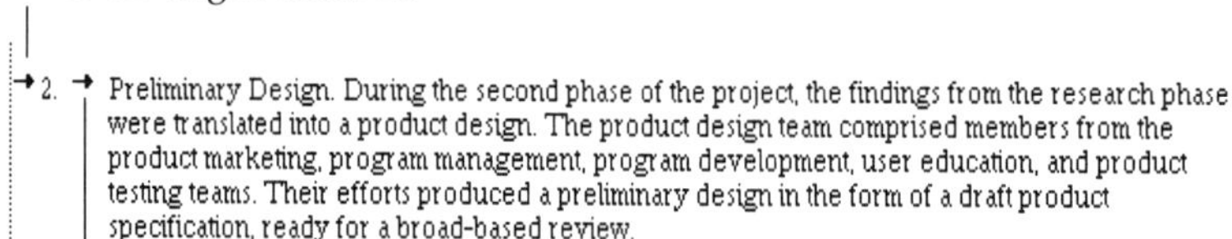

Second tab aligns text.

Example 2: Creating a Sidebar Style

A sidebar is an article within an article. In magazines you sometimes see a sidebar—in a box at the top, bottom, or edge of a page—that contains a short description of the article or some related information. Figure 7-3 shows an example of a sidebar.

To set up a style that adds a sidebar to a page, you position a paragraph and add a border around it. This example shows you how to

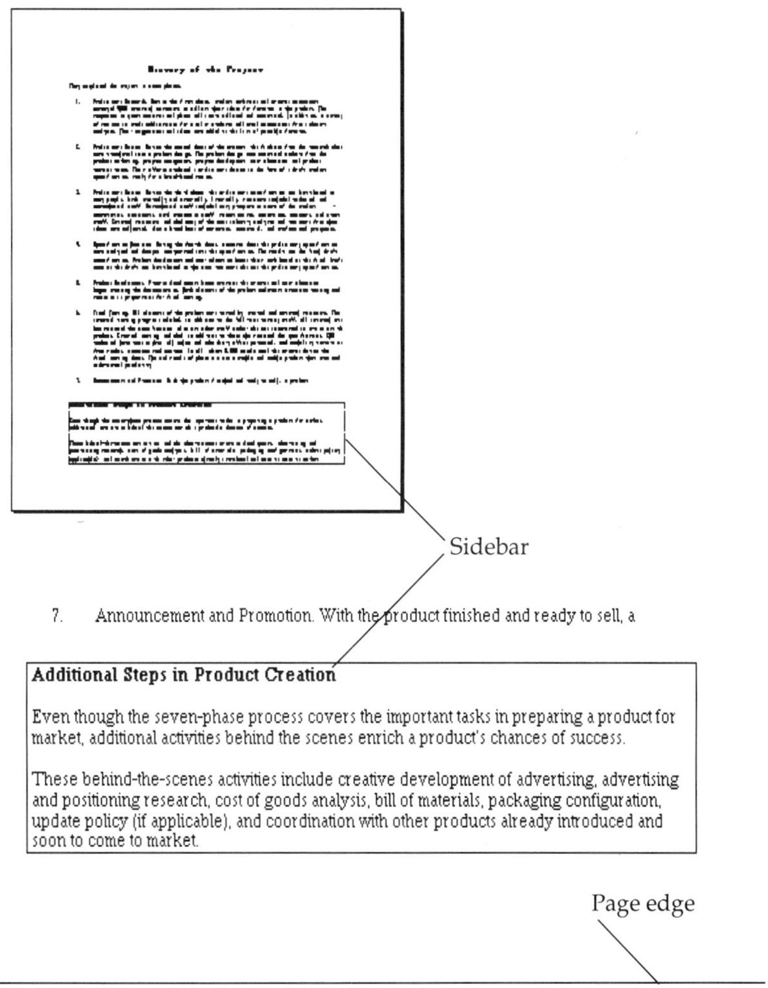

Figure 7-3.
Sidebar.

create a sidebar style that puts the sidebar text at the bottom of the page, with a box around it. First, position the insertion point in a paragraph that has Normal style applied to it (or apply Normal style to the paragraph that contains the insertion point). Then, choose the Format Define Styles command (Alt,T,F) and type *Sidebar* in the Format Define Styles dialog box. Later you might want to create several sidebar styles—for example, for the top, bottom, left, and right sides of the page. If so, you should give the style a name that tells you which type of sidebar it formats. You might use "BSidebar," for example, for a sidebar that's positioned at the bottom of the page.

Choose the Position button (Alt+I) to open the Format Position dialog box.

For Horizontal Position, leave the settings at Left and at Relative to Column. The Left setting positions the sidebar at the left edge of its column. The left edge of the column is the same as the left margin when the document has only one column. Move to the Vertical Position list (Alt+V), and select Bottom (Relative to Margin is selected for you) to position the sidebar just above the bottom margin of the page.

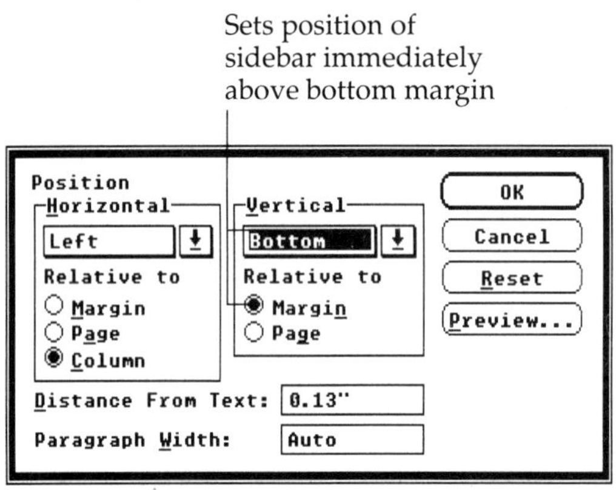

Choose OK to add the position to the style definition and to return to the Format Define Styles dialog box. To open the Format Paragraph dialog box, choose the Paragraph button (Alt+P). Move to the Border list (Alt+O), and select Box to put a box around the sidebar text. Next, move to the Pattern list (Alt+E), and select Single to make the box from a single line.

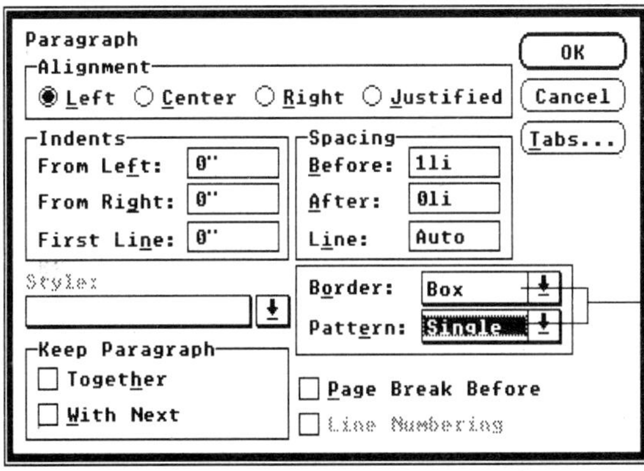

Adds single-box border to sidebar style

Then, choose OK to add the border to the style definition and to return to the Format Define Styles dialog box.

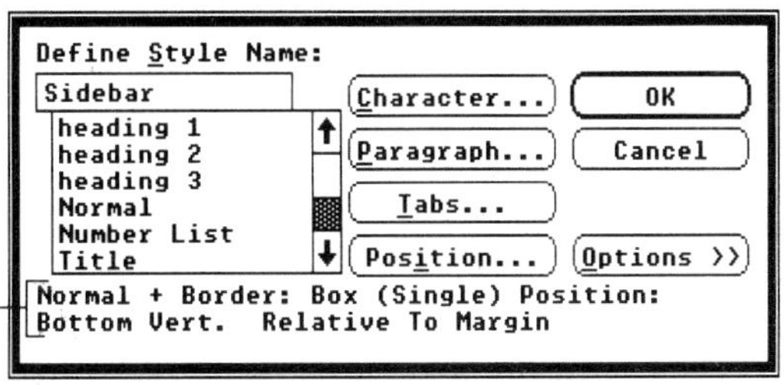

Sidebar style definition

Choose OK to define the style. To use the sidebar style, choose the Format Styles command, select Sidebar from the list of style names, and choose OK. As an alternative method, you can also press the Ctrl+S keys, type *Sidebar*, and then press the Enter key. When you start typing the sidebar text, Word creates a boxed set of paragraphs that will print immediately above the bottom margin of the page. In normal editing view, the paragraphs appear on the screen where you type them in the document text. In Print Preview and Page View, the sidebar paragraphs appear immediately above the bottom of the page. The box grows as large as necessary to hold all the sidebar text that you type, both in normal editing view and in Page View. Note in Figure 7-3 that Word places only one box around all the paragraphs so that successive paragraphs within a box border will not have a border between them if they're formatted in exactly the same way. If you want lines between the paragraphs, either alter the formatting of each of the other paragraphs slightly or place a short paragraph that has a different style between the paragraphs. "Creating Spacing Styles," later in this chapter, explains how to make style changes such as these. You can also choose to put the paragraphs into a table that has border lines around its cells. For more information about using tables in this way, see Chapter 13, "Tables the New, Easy Way."

Example 3: Creating a Sidehead Style

A sidehead is a heading that appears in the margin next to a topic's first paragraph. Sideheads appear frequently in materials such as annual reports, employee handbooks, and technical manuals. Figure 7-4 shows an example of a sidehead.

To create a sidehead, you position the sidehead paragraph, set its width and its distance from the text with which it's associated, and give it some appropriate text formatting, such as boldface. In addition to creating the style, you also need to adjust the page margins to accommodate the sidehead. First, position the insertion point in a paragraph to which you've applied Normal style (or apply Normal style to the paragraph that contains the insertion point). Choose the Format Define Styles command (Alt,T,F), and type *Sidehead* in the Format Define Styles dialog box. Later you might want to create several sidehead styles for

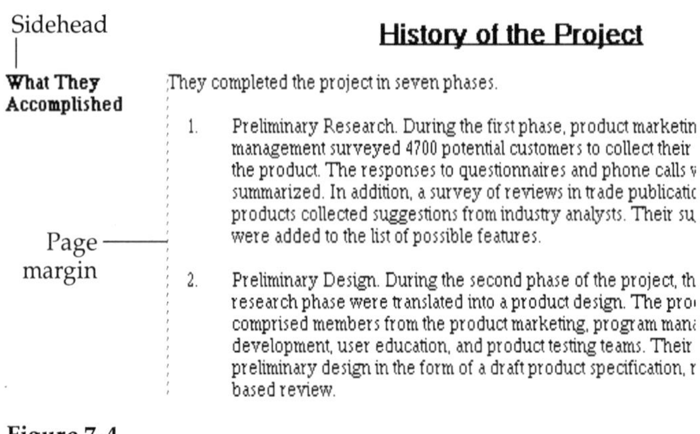

Figure 7-4.
Sidehead.

the various positions you can assign to sideheads. For example, you might create a sidehead in the right margin and give the style a name that tells you which type of sidehead it formats, such as "RSidehead."

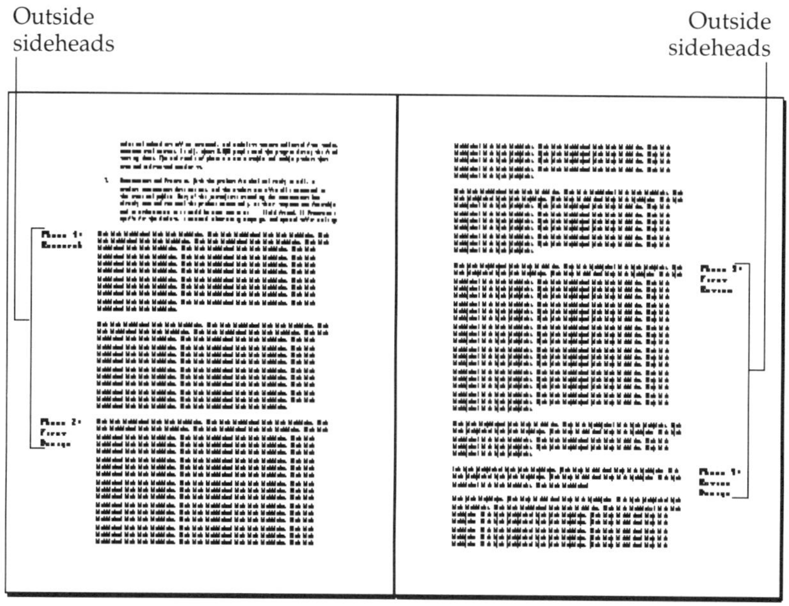

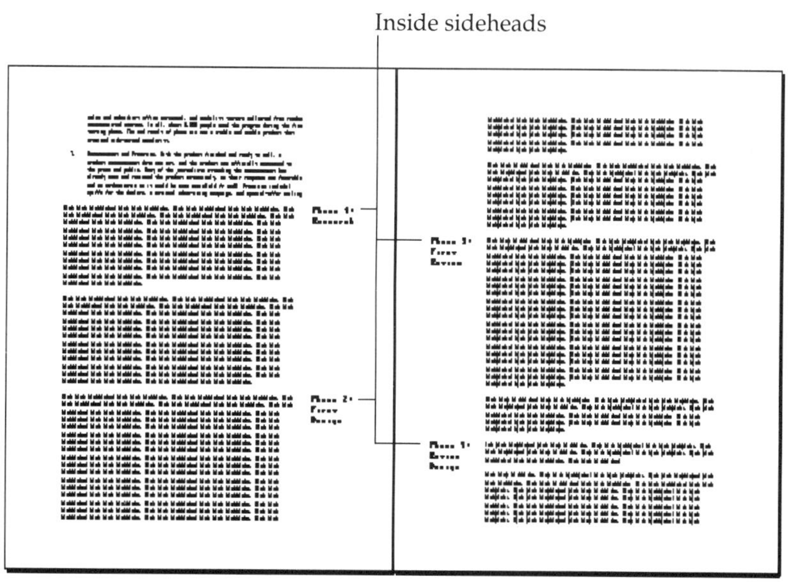

Press the Ctrl+B keys to apply boldface text format to the definition. To open the Format Position dialog box, choose the Position button (Alt+I). For Horizontal Position, leave the setting at the Left option and select the Relative to Page option (Alt+A). The Left setting positions the sidehead in the left margin of all pages. Choosing a Right setting positions the sidehead in the right margin of all pages. The Outside and Inside positions are designed for documents that you plan to print on both sides of the paper, as illustrated on the preceding page. Outside means the right side of odd-numbered pages and the left side of even-numbered pages. Inside means the left side of odd-numbered pages and the right side of even-numbered pages.

For Vertical Position, leave the setting at Inline so that the sidehead paragraph will appear beside its related text. Move to the Distance From Text box (Alt+D) and type *0.25″*. This measurement leaves horizontal blank space between the sidehead and the text it heads. One-quarter inch of space prevents a crowded look on the page. Next, move to the Paragraph Width box (Alt+W) and type *1″* to replace Auto. You'll often find that one inch is a good width for a sidehead. If you leave Auto in the Paragraph Width box, however, the sidehead will be as wide as the margins.

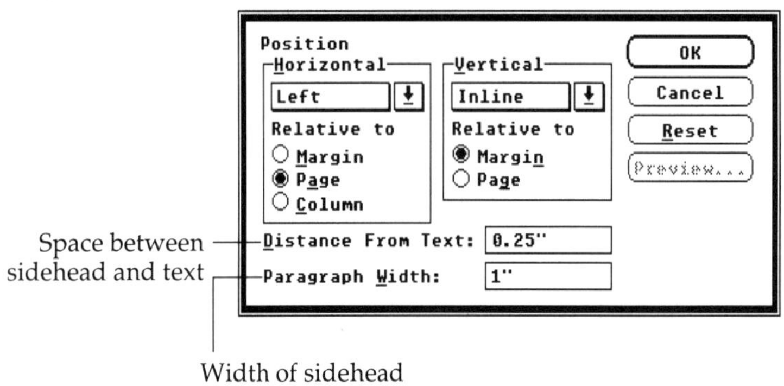

Choose OK to add the position settings to the style definition and to return to the Format Define Styles dialog box. Then, choose OK to define the style.

To adjust the page margins, choose the Format Document command (Alt,T,D). In the Format Document dialog box, move to the Left Margin box (Alt+L) and type 2″. A two-inch setting leaves plenty of room for the one-inch-wide sidehead text, the one-quarter-inch blank space, and the three-quarter-inch left margin between the edge of the paper and the sidehead.

Type a two-inch setting for the sidehead space.

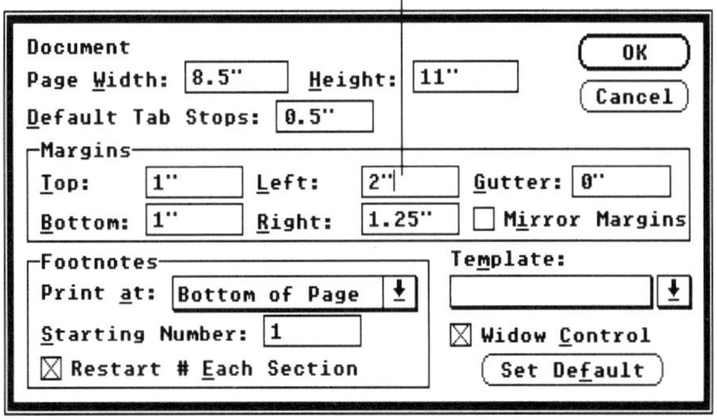

Now, choose OK. Because you're using the Left Margin position for sideheads in this example, adjust the Left Margin setting in the Format Document dialog box. If you were using other positions for sideheads, you would adjust the appropriate margin, as shown in the following table:

Sidehead Position	*Adjust Margin*
Left	Left
Right	Right
Outside	(Turn on Mirror Margins) Outside
Inside	(Turn on Mirror Margins) Inside

When you turn on Mirror Margins in the Format Document dialog box, Left changes to Inside and Right changes to Outside.

Modifying and Refining the Automatic Styles

As mentioned earlier in this chapter, Word contains 35 automatic styles. Word applies these styles when you insert the text elements they belong to. For example, when you insert a footnote, Word applies the footnote text style to the footnote text. After you apply an automatic style in a document, that style appears in the list of styles that Word displays in the ruler and in the Format Styles and Format Define Styles dialog boxes. To streamline these lists, Word does not show the automatic styles (except Normal, heading 1, heading 2, and heading 3) until you apply them. For the names and definitions of Word's automatic styles, see "Summary of the Automatic Styles" later in this chapter.

After you insert a text element that has an automatic style, you can apply any style you want in place of the automatic style. Doing so, however, defeats the convenience that using an automatic style offers. Instead, you can modify the automatic style if you do not like the way Word defined it.

The process of modifying and refining the automatic styles is the same as it is for any style. You modify a style either by copying an existing paragraph's formatting or by using the Format Define Styles dialog box to change the option settings. In the following three examples, you'll change the formatting definition of three of the automatic styles, using three interchangeable methods.

These examples show you how to modify automatic styles within a single document only. To change the definition of an automatic style for all documents, change the style's definition in all the templates you use. In particular, you'll want to change the style's definition in the NORMAL.DOT template, which will share the change with many documents.

NOTE: *You cannot change the names of the automatic styles.*

TIP

Using SHOW ALL STYLES to Display Style Names

Automatic styles do not appear in the list of names in the Format Define Styles dialog box until you apply them in your document. When you want to modify an automatic style before applying it, you need to select or type its name. You can also use the SHOW ALL STYLES key combination (Ctrl+A) to display the entire list of names—all of the automatic styles along with any styles you've created. You press the Ctrl+A keys when you're in the Format Styles or Format Define Styles dialog box.

Heading 1: Getting Rid of the Underline and Adding Italic

Word defines the automatic style called heading 1 as shown below:

`Normal + Font: Helv 12 Point, Bold Underline` — Word's definition of heading 1 style

Heading 1 produces boldface and underlined text, as in the following example:

The Year in Review — Result of heading 1 style

As Word defines it, heading 1 gives you a highly distinguishable format. Some users, however, might prefer using a heading that achieves its emphasis from a different typeface rather than from underlining. The following explanation shows one way to remove the underlining and to add italic to the style's definition.

First, if you do not have a heading 1 paragraph in your document, apply the heading 1 style to a paragraph by selecting an entire Normal paragraph and pressing the Alt+Shift+left arrow keys. Be sure to select the entire paragraph so that the following changes affect all the text in the paragraph. Press the Ctrl+U keys to remove underlining, and then press the Ctrl+I keys to add italic. The selected heading now looks like the following:

The Year in Review — New format for heading 1 style

Next, to redefine the heading 1 style, press the Ctrl+S keys, type *heading 1*, press the Enter key, and then choose Yes when Word asks if you want to redefine the heading 1 style. From now on, all heading 1 paragraphs in this document will have the new format.

Footnote Text: Setting a Hanging Indent

Word defines the automatic style called "footnote text" as shown below:

Normal +

This definition shows that the paragraph format for the footnote text style is flush left, which is one part of the Normal style's definition.

For any footnote that's longer than one line, the second and following lines wrap back under the footnote reference mark, as in the following example:

[1]The year in review is 1988. This is the thirteenth annual review. Annual reviews are conducted in the month following the end of the fiscal year, June 30.

Automatic footnote text style hides reference mark.

This arrangement makes the reference mark hard to see. Try changing the footnote text style so that it has a hanging indent, making reference marks more visible. First, choose the Format Define Styles command (Alt,T,F). If the footnote text style is not listed in the Format Define Styles dialog box, press the Ctrl+A keys to show all the automatic styles. Next, select the footnote text style from the list. Then, choose the Paragraph button (Alt+P) to open the Format Paragraph dialog box. In the From Left box under Indents, type *1pi,* which stands for 1 pica. (A pica is a typesetter's unit of measurement that's about the width of the letter "m" in the typeface you're currently using.) Later, when you see the definition for this style in the Define Styles dialog box, Word will have converted this 1-pica measurement to the default unit of measurement that's set in the Utilities Customize dialog box. If you have the default unit of measurement set to inches, for example, the 1 pica will be converted to 0.17".

Move to the First Line box under Indents (Alt+N), type *-1pi,* and then choose OK to set the two indents and to return to the Format Define Styles dialog box. Choose OK, and then choose Yes when Word asks if you want to change the properties of the standard style. From now on, your footnote text paragraphs will look like the following:

[1]The year in review is 1988. This is the thirteenth annual review. Annual reviews are conducted in the month following the end of the fiscal year, June 30.

Hanging indent set to 1 pica (0.17")

If you use the Tab key before you start typing the footnote text, the first word lines up with the rest of the lines, as shown on the following page.

Tab makes first line of text align with rest of paragraph.

1→The year in review is 1988. This is the thirteenth annual review. Annual reviews are conducted in the month following the end of the fiscal year, June 30.

You might find this last footnote format preferable because it's the easiest to read.

Annotation Reference and Text: Adding Your Color

If you want your annotations in a document to be easily distinguishable from others', you can display them in a different color. You add your color to the definition for both the annotation reference style and the annotation text style. If you have at least an EGA display with more than 64 KB of memory on the display adapter, you can see that color on your screen. And, if you have a color printer, Word can print the colors through Windows.

To add your annotation color, first choose the Format Define Styles command (Alt,T,F). Press the Ctrl+A keys if all the automatic styles are not displayed, and then select the annotation reference style from the list. Next, press the Ctrl+V keys until the color you want to use for annotation references appears in the style definition.

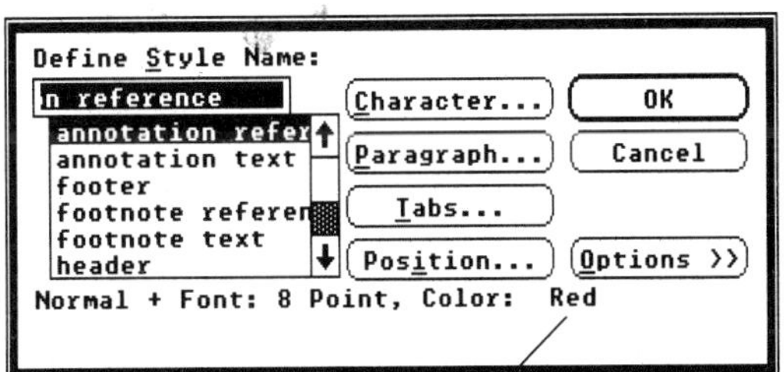

Red is added to annotation reference style.

Choose the Options button (Alt+O) to show the full dialog box. Then, choose the Define button, and choose Yes when Word asks if you want to change the properties of the standard style. By choosing the Define button instead of OK, you leave the dialog box open so that you can go on to change the annotation text style without having to choose the Format Define Styles command again.

Select the annotation text style from the list, and then press the Ctrl+V keys until the color you want to use for annotation text appears in the style definition. Choose OK to change the style's definition and to close the dialog box. (Again, to continue changing styles, choose the Define button instead of OK.) Choose Yes when Word asks if you want to change the properties of the standard style.

Summary of the Automatic Styles

The table that begins on the following page lists the 35 automatic styles and their definitions. In addition, 28 of the 35 automatic styles show a NextStyle name. Styles that do not show a next style have themselves as their next style. For an explanation of Next Style and of how you see each style's next style, see the following section, "Next Style Chaining."

TIP

Coloring Reviewers' Annotations

Because the annotation reference style applies only to text formatting, an annotation reference mark retains the color it had at the time you inserted it, even if you later change the color defined for the style. Word displays any new annotation reference mark with whatever color is currently defined for its style. The annotation text style, however, works in the same way as other styles—if you change the color in the style's definition, the color changes for all annotations. You can use this quirk in annotation reference marks to your advantage: Each person who inserts annotations can define a different color for his or her own annotation reference marks, and the color holds even if subsequent reviewers define the annotation reference style with other colors. For annotation text, though, each reviewer must apply a color directly to make reviewers' remarks appear in different colors. To apply a color to annotation text, select all your annotations in the annotation pane and then use either the Format Character command or the Ctrl+V keys to apply the color.

annotation reference

NextStyle: Normal
Normal + Font: 8 Point

annotation text
Normal +

footer
Normal + Tab stops: 3" Centered; 6" Right Flush

footnote reference

NextStyle: Normal
Normal + Font: 8 Point, Superscript 3 Point

footnote text
Normal +

header
Normal + Tab stops: 3" Centered; 6" Right Flush

heading 1

NextStyle: Normal
Normal + Font: Helv 12 Point, Bold Underline, Space Before 12pt

heading 2

NextStyle: Normal
Normal + Font: Helv 12 Point, Bold, Space Before 6pt

heading 3

NextStyle: Normal Indent
Normal + Font: 12 Point, Bold, Indent: Left 0.25"

(continued)

continued

heading 4

NextStyle: Normal Indent
Normal + Font: 12 Point, Underline, Indent: Left 0.25"

heading 5

NextStyle: Normal Indent
Normal + Bold, Indent: Left 0.5"

heading 6

NextStyle: Normal Indent
Normal + Underline, Indent: Left 0.5"

heading 7

NextStyle: Normal Indent
Normal + Italic, Indent: Left 0.5"

heading 8

NextStyle: Normal Indent
Normal + Italic, Indent: Left 0.5"

heading 9

NextStyle: Normal Indent
Normal + Italic, Indent: Left 0.5"

index 1

NextStyle: Normal
Normal +

index 2

NextStyle: Normal
Normal + Indent: Left 0.25"

(continued)

continued

index 3

NextStyle: Normal
Normal + Indent: Left 0.5"

index 4

NextStyle: Normal
Normal + Indent: Left 0.75"

index 5

NextStyle: Normal
Normal + Indent: Left 1"

index 6

NextStyle: Normal
Normal + Indent: Left 1.25"

index 7

NextStyle: Normal
Normal + Indent: Left 1.5"

index heading

NextStyle: index 1
Normal +

line number

NextStyle: Normal
Normal +

Normal
Font: Tms Rmn 10 Point, Flush left

(continued)

continued

Normal Indent

NextStyle: Normal
Normal + Indent: Left 0.5"

toc 1

NextStyle: Normal
Normal + Indent: Right 0.5", Tab stops: 5.75" ...;
6" Right Flush

toc 2

NextStyle: Normal
Normal + Indent: Left 0.5" Right 0.5", Tab stops: 5.75" ...;
6" Right Flush

toc 3

NextStyle: Normal
Normal + Indent: Left 1" Right 0.5", Tab stops: 5.75" ...;
6" Right Flush

toc 4

NextStyle: Normal
Normal + Indent: Left 1.5" Right 0.5", Tab stops: 5.75" ...;
6" Right Flush

toc 5

NextStyle: Normal
Normal + Indent: Left 2" Right 0.5", Tab stops: 5.75" ...;
6" Right Flush

toc 6

NextStyle: Normal
Normal + Indent: Left 2.5" Right 0.5", Tab stops: 5.75" ...;
6" Right Flush

(continued)

continued

toc 7

NextStyle: Normal
Normal + Indent: Left 3" Right 0.5", Tab stops: 5.75" ...;
6" Right Flush

toc 8

NextStyle: Normal
Normal + Indent: Left 3.5" Right 0.5", Tab stops: 5.75" ...;
6" Right Flush

Next Style Chaining

Next style chaining is a way to set up a style so that when you finish a paragraph in that style and then start another paragraph, the new paragraph has a different style. For example, after you insert a heading paragraph, you might want the next paragraph to have a normal paragraph format.

You change styles most often around headings, lists, and other such elements that are made up of short pieces of text. In many of these situations, the sequence of formatting is predictable: First comes a heading, followed by some regular text; or first come the column headings and then a table or list in two columns. When two such styles always—or almost always—appear in the same sequence, you can save yourself time and effort by using next style chaining to automate the application of the next appropriate style.

Word takes advantage of next style chaining for some automatic styles. Heading 1 and heading 2, toc 1 through toc 9, and index 1 through index 7 have Normal as their next style. Index heading has index 1 as its next style. Heading 3 through heading 9 have Normal Indent as their next style. All other automatic styles have themselves as their next style. When you create a new style, Word sets that style as its own next style so that you can type a series of paragraphs that have the same style. But when you know that the next paragraph should look different, you can set up a different next style.

Here you'll look at a number of ways in which you can use next style chaining: changing the next style for heading 3 through heading 9, creating a column heading style and a two-column hanging indent as the style's next style, and creating spacing styles. Spacing styles are empty paragraphs that are formatted to a specific line height and used to provide additional space between two other paragraphs.

Using the Options Button and the Options

Pressing the Options button in the Format Define Styles dialog box opens the dialog box to its full size, providing you with the following additional options: Based On, Next Style, Define, Delete, Rename, Merge, and Add to Template.

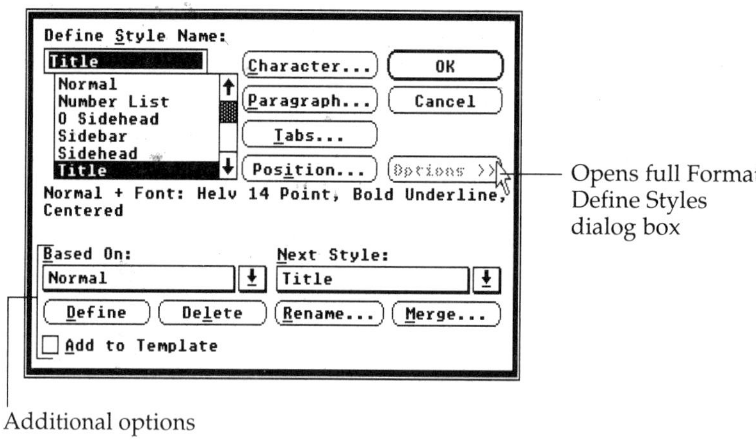

Heading 3 Through Heading 9: Modifying the Next Style

The next style for heading 3 through heading 9 is Normal Indent. The Normal Indent style indents by one-half inch the first paragraph following one of these headings. Subsequent paragraphs are not indented because Normal Indent's next style is Normal. Some documents use this indentation scheme, but it is not universally accepted. To change this formatting, you have two choices: Either redefine the Normal Indent style or change the heading's next style from Normal Indent to Normal. In the following example, you leave the Normal Indent style as is and change the heading's next style to Normal.

First, choose the Format Define Styles command (Alt,T,F). Then, choose the Options button (Alt+O) to display the full dialog box, and press the Ctrl+A keys if the automatic styles are not displayed in the list. Select the heading 3 style, move to the Next Style list (Alt+N), select Normal, and then choose the Define button (Alt+D). Word displays a message that asks if you want to change the properties (i.e., definition) of a standard style. Choose Yes (Alt+Y). For each of the heading 4 through heading 9 styles, repeat the process by selecting the style name, selecting Normal for the next style, choosing the Define button (Alt+D), and then choosing Yes (Alt+Y). Then, when you finish changing all the styles, choose OK.

From now on, when you insert a paragraph in this same document and apply one of the heading 3 through heading 9 styles, the next paragraph following the heading will have the Normal style instead of the Normal Indent style.

Two Columns: Column Heading Style Followed by Hanging Indent Style

Some information is easiest to understand when you present it in a two-column arrangement. For example, you can put a title or a short description in the left column and an explanation in the right column. Headings at the top of each column tell readers what type of information each column contains, as the example in Figure 7-5 shows.

Feature	**Benefit**
Low-tech methods	Personal touch and easy to understand and use
High-quality standards	Best results and your money's worth from every purchase

Figure 7-5.
Candidate for next style feature.

In the following example, you create two styles that produce a two-column format. You start by creating the hanging indent style so that it exists when you're ready to assign it as the column heading style's next style.

Choose the Format Define Styles command (Alt,T,F). For the style name, type *2 col hang* and then press the HANGING INDENT key combination (Ctrl+T) four times, until the style definition shows "Left 2" First –2"." When you set a hanging indent, Word removes all default tab stops to the left of the left indent. Choose the Options button (Alt+O) to display the full dialog box. Choose the Define button (Alt+D) to define the style and to get ready for defining the column heading style.

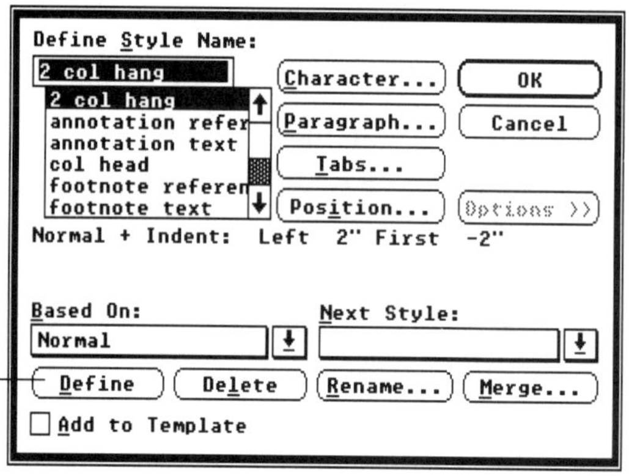

Sets style definition and prepares to define another style

For the column heading style name, type *col head,* and press the Ctrl+B keys to add boldface to the definition. Choose the Tabs button (Alt+T) to display the Format Tabs dialog box. In the Tab Position box, type 2″ to add a tab stop at 2 inches to the definition, and then choose OK to return to the Format Define Styles dialog box.

To display the Format Paragraph dialog box, choose the Paragraph button (Alt+P). Move to the Border list (Alt+O), and select Below to add a border line under the column headings. The Pattern list shows Single, which creates the border from a single line. Then, choose OK to add the border to the definition and to return to the Format Define Styles dialog box. Move to the Next Style list (Alt+N), and select "2 col hang."

TIP

Two Important Details About Next Style

Keep in mind that you cannot assign a next style unless that style already exists. For example, if you have a style named Title and you want its next style to be Author (for the author's name), you must first create the Author style.

Also keep in mind that the next style is applied only if you're creating a new empty paragraph. If you break an existing paragraph in two, both paragraphs retain the same style and formatting; the next style is not applied. And, if you apply a style to an existing paragraph, its next style is not applied to any following paragraph; you must start a new, empty paragraph to apply the next style.

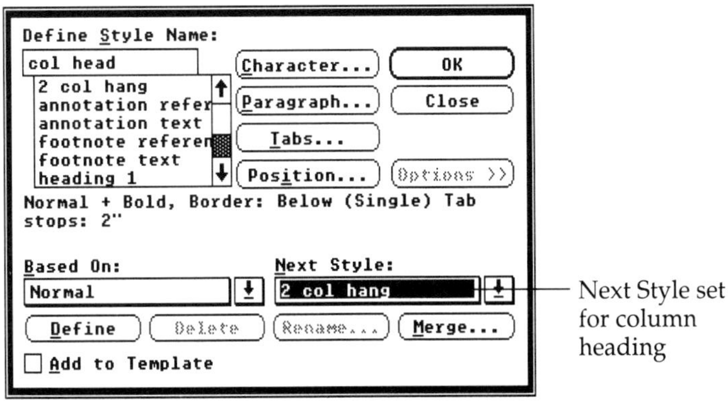

Choose OK to define the style.

Now that you've defined these two styles, you're ready to create a two-column list with a hanging indent. First, press the Enter key to start a new paragraph and then apply the col head style to it. Type *Feature* as the column heading for the first column, press the Tab key, type *Benefit* as the column heading for the second column, and press Enter. Then, type *Low-tech methods* as the text for the first column, press the Tab key, and type *Personal touch and easy to understand and use* as the text for the second column.

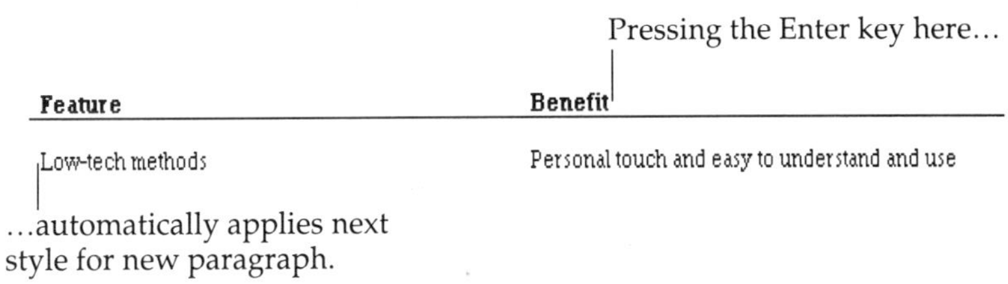

When you press Enter again, the next paragraph also has the 2 col hang style so that you can add more text to the list.

Creating Spacing Styles

When working to refine a document, a document designer takes special care to place enough space between paragraphs and between different text elements. For example, a document designer usually adds extra space at the top of a list to separate the list from the paragraph above it. Likewise, when you insert a graphic in a document, you might want additional space before and after it so that the page does not look crowded.

To create such spacing, you could use the Spacing Before and Spacing After settings in the Format Paragraph dialog box. Those settings, however, provide a consistent but somewhat rigid technique. The spacing is exactly the same each time it's used, which can produce an awkward appearance. Should the before and after spacing come together, for example, you'll find yourself with a gap in your document that's larger than you wanted.

One way to better control spacing is to create a collection of spacing styles that are intended to act only as different types of spaces between text elements. For example, you might insert an empty paragraph (only the paragraph mark), format the paragraph with the height you want, and define the paragraph as a style that you can then use to create that extra spacing. The following example gives you practice creating a spacing style that inserts an extra four points of space.

Start by choosing the Format Define Styles command (Alt,T,F). In the Define Style Name box, type *sp4pt list* to clarify that this is a style that will give you 4 points of space at the front of a list. Then, choose the Options button (Alt+O) to open the full dialog box.

Move to the Next Style box (Alt+N), and select the style that will always—or nearly always—follow the one you chose or typed in the Define Style Name box. For this example, select the Number List style you created earlier in this chapter, as illustrated below.

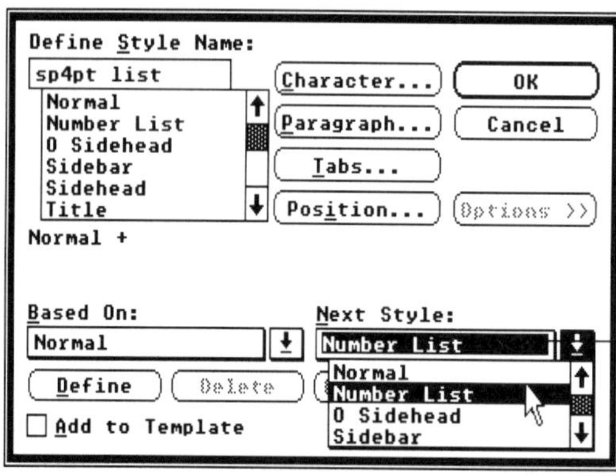

Sets next style for sp4pt list

To open the Format Paragraph dialog box, choose the Paragraph button (Alt+P). Move to the Line box under Spacing (Alt+I), type *-4pt*, and then choose OK to add this line spacing to the style definition and return to the Format Define Styles dialog box. The minus sign (-) in front of the line spacing measurement tells Word to fix the line spacing at 4 points, no matter how tall the characters are. Recall that setting Auto as the line spacing tells Word to adjust up or down to the tallest character in the line. A specific measurement, such as 4pt, however, ensures that the line spacing will be no smaller than that measurement, although spacing can still adjust to accommodate the tallest character in the line.

Next, choose the Define button (Alt+D) to define the style. For any other spacing styles you need, repeat the process by typing a style name, setting the paragraph spacing, and selecting a next style. Then, when you finish the spacing style, choose OK.

After you define a spacing style, you can apply it whenever you're ready to insert the text element that follows it. For example, when you want a numbered list with 4 points of space above it, you can insert a paragraph that has the sp4pt list style that you just defined and then press the Enter key. The next style of the paragraph that follows will be Number List.

Basing One Style on Another

In the full Format Define Styles dialog box, you see a box called Based On, in which Word shows you on what style the style that you're defining is based. Basing one style on another means starting with one style and then changing its definition to create a new style. This method offers an efficient way to create new styles that are variations of a common source style. All the automatic styles in Word are based on the Normal style. And most styles you create will probably also be based on Normal. But it is possible to create groups of styles that are based on a single base style (which is itself based on Normal), or on a chain of styles, as shown in Figure 7-6 on the following page.

Three sets of Word styles in particular can profit from being based on a common style: heading 1 through heading 9, toc 1 through toc 8, and index 1 through index 7, all of which are based on Normal when Word is shipped. In any document that uses multiple heading levels, the similarities from one level to the next are strong. The advantage of basing the styles in each of these groups on a common style is that if you want to change the formatting that the group has in common, you

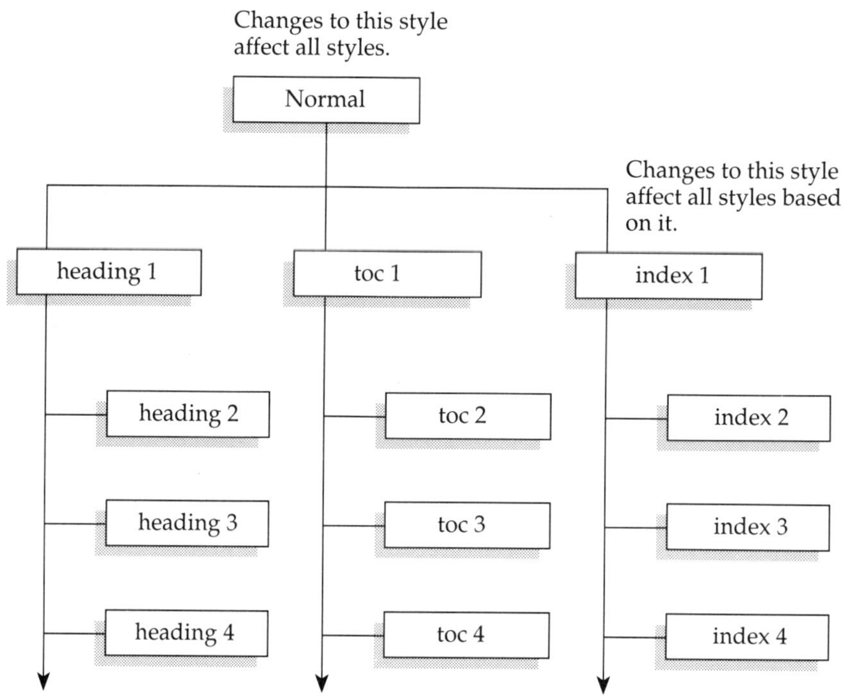

Figure 7-6.
Relationship of styles based on other styles.

change only the base style in the group. Word then passes the new formatting to other members of the group.

To practice setting up a group of styles that are based on a common style, change the base style of heading 2 through heading 9 to heading 1 instead of Normal. Start by choosing the Format Define Styles command (Alt,T,F), and press the Ctrl+A keys if the automatic styles are not displayed. Select the heading 2 style, and then choose the Options button (Alt+O) to open the full dialog box. Move to the Based On list (Alt+B), select the heading 1 style, and then choose the Define button. When Word asks if you want to change the standard style, choose Yes. You see this message for each style as you redefine its Based On style. For each of the heading 3 through heading 9 styles, repeat the process by selecting the heading style name and heading 1 for Based On and then choosing the Define button. For the toc 2 through toc 8 styles, repeat the process, basing those styles on toc 1.

Also repeat the process for the index 2 through index 7 styles, basing them on index 1. When you finish changing the Based On styles, choose OK.

Now, to change all your heading styles to Helv bold, you need change only the heading 1 style. You can still add or remove formatting from the other heading styles to distinguish them from each other.

Doing Your Styles Housekeeping

Occasionally, you need to do some styles housekeeping. Word gives you the tools to rename styles, share styles by merging them between documents and templates, print all of a document's style names and definitions, and delete unneeded styles.

Renaming Styles

After you create a style of your own, you might discover that the name you gave it causes confusion because it is hard to remember or is not different enough from other style names. To rename a style, choose the Format Define Styles command (Alt,T,F). In the Format Define Styles dialog box, select the style that you want to rename from the list of style names. Do not select the name of an automatic style because you cannot rename automatic styles. Then, choose the Options button (Alt+O) to open the full dialog box, and choose the Rename button. Type the style's new name, and then choose OK. For each style you want to rename, repeat the process by selecting the style name, typing the new name, and choosing OK. When you finish renaming styles, choose the Close button (Esc).

Sharing Styles by Merging Them

After you define styles, you get the most benefit from them if you can share them among many documents. The easiest way to share styles is to add the styles to document templates as you define the styles. Then, when you create new documents, the styles become a part of the new documents.

You can add to and change the styles in a template. To protect your document formatting, Word does not pass these changes, however, to documents that were created previously. To add template style changes to an existing document, merge the template's styles with the document's styles. Likewise, if you define additional styles in a document but do not add those styles to the template, you can merge the document's styles with the document template's styles. For broader-based sharing, share styles by merging those of any document or template with those in the current document (not only those of the template from which the document was created). Two procedures in the following sections show you how to quickly merge a document's styles with its template's styles and the current template's styles with the current document's styles. You can also share styles from other documents and templates. The Merge dialog box includes a list of template files and a box in which you can type a Merge File Name if the file you want is not in the list. You can change *.DOT to *.DOC to see a list of document files instead of a list of template files.

Merging document style changes with the template's styles

After you create a document and add to or change its styles, you might want to merge your changes with the template's styles. After you do, those style changes will be part of any new documents that are created from the template. The Style changes can be easily merged with existing documents created from the template.

Try merging a document's styles with its template's styles. First, choose the Format Define Styles command (Alt,T,F). Then, choose the Options button (Alt+O) to display the full dialog box. Choose the Merge button (Alt+M). In the Merge File Name dialog box, choose the button for the direction in which you want the styles to merge:

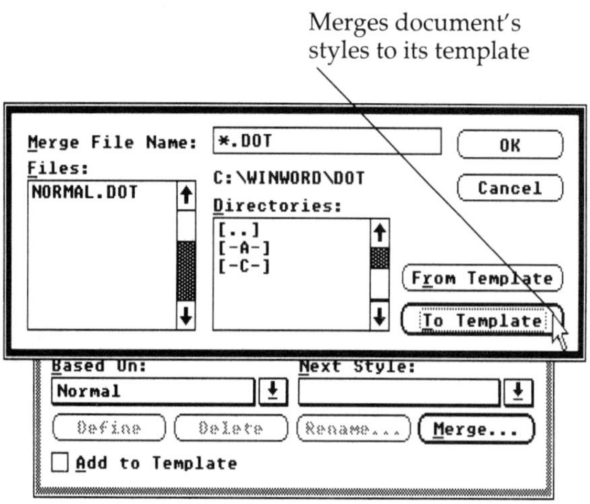

For this example, choose the To Template button (Alt+T). If duplicate style names exist, a message informs you that merging replaces styles that have the same name and asks if you want to continue. Choose Yes. (Choosing No stops the merge.) You see this message even if only one style shares the same name in both the document and its template. Choose the Close button (Esc) to close the Format Define Styles dialog box.

Merging template style changes with the document's styles

In the same way that you merge a document's styles with its template's, you can merge styles that you defined and changed in a template with those in any document that's based on the template. This method allows you to update styles that you defined or changed in the template after you created the document.

Practice merging a template's styles with a document that's based on the template. Start by choosing the Format Define Styles command (Alt,T,F). Next, choose the Options button (Alt+O) to display the full Format Define Styles dialog box. Then, choose the Merge button (Alt+M).

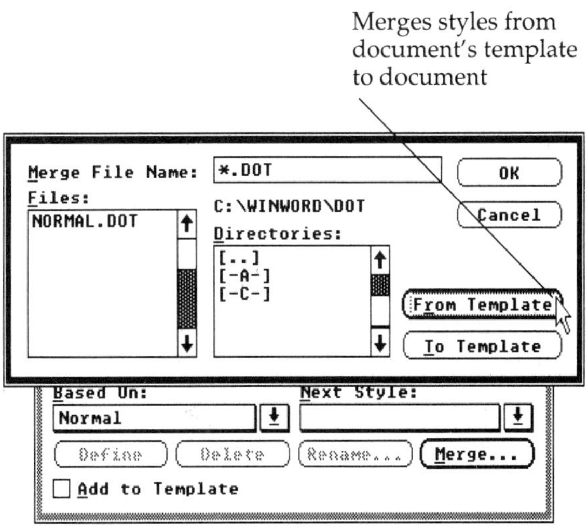

In the Merge File Name dialog box, choose the From Template button (Alt+R) to merge the template's style changes with your document's styles. If duplicate names exist, a message informs you that merging replaces styles that have the same name and asks if you want to continue. Choose Yes. (Choosing No stops the merge.) You see this message even if only one style shares the same name in both the document and its template. Choose the Close button (Esc) to close the Format Define Styles dialog box.

Merging the styles of another template or document

You can merge any document's or template's styles with the document that's currently open. Here you practice merging another document's or template's styles with the current document's styles. Choose the Format Define Styles command (Alt,T,F), and then choose the Options button (Alt+O) to display the full Format Define Styles dialog box. Choose the Merge button (Alt+M). In the Merge File Name dialog box, select the name of the document or template whose styles you want to merge with the current document's styles. Next, choose OK to start merging. If duplicate names exist, a message informs you that merging replaces styles that have the same name and asks if you want to continue. Choose Yes. (Choosing No stops the merge.) You see this message even if only one style shares the same name in both the document and its template. Choose the Close button (Esc) to close the Format Define Styles dialog box.

Printing Style Names and Their Definitions

Reviewing style definitions in the Format Define Styles and Format Styles dialog boxes can be limiting. Although the style definitions that appear in the dialog boxes are often complete, longer definitions might not show in their entirety. Also, you can see only one style at a time in the dialog box, so comparing two similar style definitions to determine the difference between the styles can be difficult. If the styles are not next to each other in the list, switching between them is slow.

To overcome this limited presentation, you can print all the style names and their complete definitions and then study them at your leisure. Choose the File Print command (Alt,F,P), move to the Print list (Alt+P), select Styles (press the S key to step through the options until Styles is selected), and then choose OK to start printing.

Deleting a Style

When you no longer need a style, delete it to save computer memory space and to avoid confusion. You can define a maximum of 220 styles for a document, so if you have reached that limit and you need an additional style, you must delete one before you can define a new style.

> **NOTE:** *If you delete a style on which another style is based, Word changes the remaining style's based on style back to Normal. Likewise, if you delete a style that's the next style for another style, Word changes the remaining style's next style to the style on which the deleted style was based.*

To practice deleting a style, choose the Format Define Styles command (Alt,T,F). From the list of style names, select the style that you want to delete, and then choose the Options button (Alt+O) to display the full Format Define Styles dialog box. Choose the Delete button (Alt+L). When Word asks if you want to delete the style, choose Yes. (No and Cancel stop the deletion process.) For each of the styles that you want to delete, repeat the process by selecting the style name and choosing the Delete button. When you finish deleting styles, choose the Close button (Esc) to close the Format Define Styles dialog box.

Chapter 8

Fields: Facts and Functions

A field in Word for Windows is a capsule of instructions that tells Word what type of contents to generate and insert at the field's position. When you use a field, Word keeps the information in that field updated for you. A date field, for example, looks like the following: {date}. It inserts the current date in your document and will update when you tell Word to update the field. This chapter plus Chapter 9, "Fields II: Creating Special Effects," and the Appendix, "Field Types and Their Instructions," describe all you need to know to use fields in Word.

This chapter starts with an overview of how fields work and how you use them. It continues with an explanation of the special commands that insert commonly used fields for you. The chapter ends with hints about editing, modifying, and refining fields, and with a summary list of the keys that you can use for fields.

Chapter 9 describes some sophisticated approaches to formatting field results and how to combine fields to generate more elaborate results. The Appendix explains how you use all the different types of fields.

How Fields Work

Before the arrival of Word, assembling, reusing, and formatting text were mostly handwork—typing, selecting text, choosing commands, applying formatting, and so on. Tasks such as generating tables of contents, indexes, and form letters were automated, but in a confusing variety of ways. Each task required a different procedure. Word now unifies the elements of a document that the computer can generate for you under one umbrella, called fields.

Turn over to fields whatever document contents you want Word to generate for you. For example, suppose you want to print across the top of a page the title of a topic that appears on that page. Suppose also that the text on the page keeps changing, and that you are not using fields. When you think all the changes are complete, you type the proper topic title in the header and then print the document—only to discover that the pagination changed during printing and that your header is now wrong. In Word, to keep the header information current you simply insert a field that refers to the first or last topic heading on the page. Then, when you print the document, Word finds the correct text and prints it in the header. Fields streamline the process of generating document contents because you always use the same method to produce any kind of contents: You insert a field with the appropriate instructions and then direct it to produce the text or graphics.

A field has two forms—the field instructions, like {date}, and the field result, which in the following example is the current date that Word calculates and inserts:

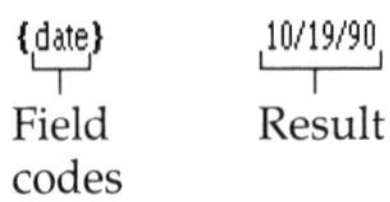

The field instructions, called field codes, are the programming instructions. Each part of an instruction directs Word to perform a particular action, either outside the field—like collecting text—or inside the field—like calculating a numeric result. The actions that these instructions produce resemble some Word commands. For example, one type of field produces a textual cross-reference by looking for and inserting text from another part of the document. The field's action resembles those of the Copy and Paste commands that you might use during editing.

Later in this chapter, "A Closer Look at What's in a Field" explains in more detail the components of a field.

Learning to Use Fields

To use fields effectively, start by learning four basic skills: how to insert fields, how to get fields to produce results, how to get from one field to another quickly, and what the relationship is between fields and bookmarks. (Bookmarks are marks you can use to identify specific chunks of text and graphics.)

Inserting Fields

To insert a field, you can choose from the Insert menu one of the six special commands that insert fields, such as Insert File. You can choose among a number of other commands that insert fields (for example, the Utilities Renumber command, the Edit Header/Footer command, or the Edit Paste Link command). Or you can choose a general command for inserting all fields (Insert Field), as shown on the following page.

TIP

Combining Documents Using the Print Merge Fields Feature

Word gives you the tools to combine a standard document (for example, a form letter) with many individual pieces of information (for example, customer names and addresses) to create individualized letters. To merge this information, you use Word's print merge fields feature. Form letters are only one use for Word's print merge fields. Address labels, rosters, league standings, contest results, and phone lists are other examples, and you can probably think of many more. Any time you need to combine two documents, you can use the print merge fields feature.

Some fields—DATA, NEXT, NEXTIF, SKIPIF, and MERGEREC—work only when you use the File Print Merge command. You also cannot nest the print merge fields or use them in headers, footers, footnotes, or annotations. In this section of the chapter, the descriptions of the other fields suggest additional ways to improve your control of print merge.

See Chapter 15, "Merge Printing," for details and examples of how to print merge documents.

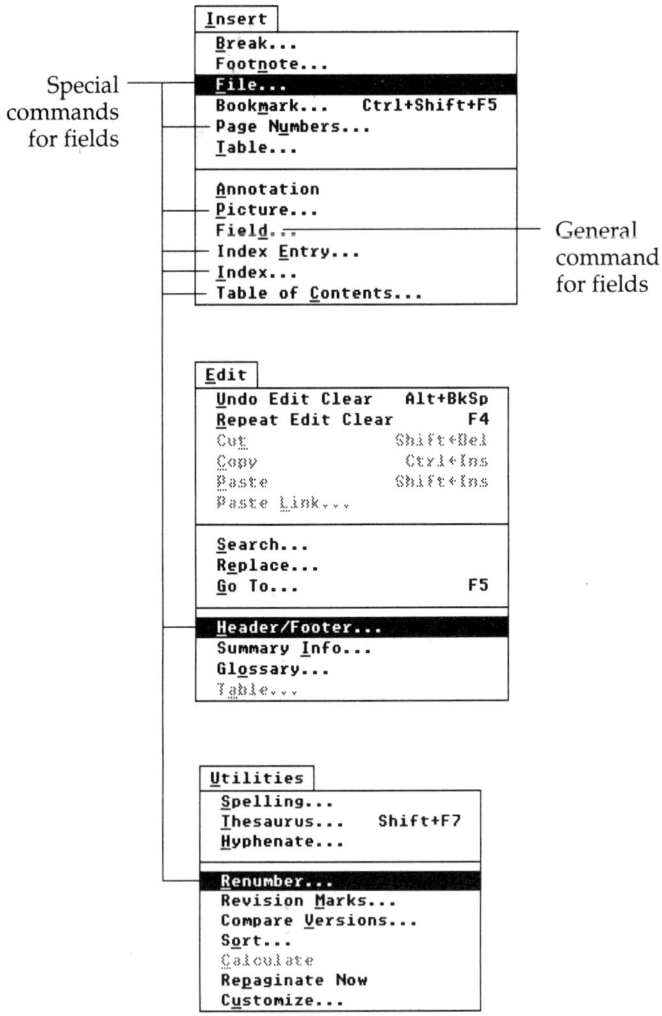

You can also insert a field by using a shortcut key combination and then building the instructions from scratch.

Use any of the eight field commands when you want to insert fields easily, without having to be concerned about the intricacies of using and formatting fields. These eight commands insert document-specific elements that are well known and often used, like Insert Page

Numbers. Later in this chapter, "Fields the Easy Way" explains how to use these eight field commands. "Do It Yourself Using the Insert Field Command," also later in this chapter, explains how to use the Insert Field command to insert any kind of field.

You use the INSERT FIELD key combination (Ctrl+F9) to insert an empty field.

Then you type the instructions in the empty field yourself. This method is designed for people with an interest in programming who want to delve into the more advanced aspects of fields and who prefer to build fields from scratch rather than by using dialog boxes.

Updating Fields to Produce Your Results

After you insert a field in your document, you're ready for the field to produce the text, numbers, or graphics that you want. To make a field produce its result, you update the field. Some fields update automatically. Other fields update only when you press the UPDATE FIELD key (F9).

Several other actions update fields. Printing a document updates some but not all fields. To update all fields when you print, choose the Update Fields option in the File Print dialog box, as shown on the next page.

Updates all fields during printing

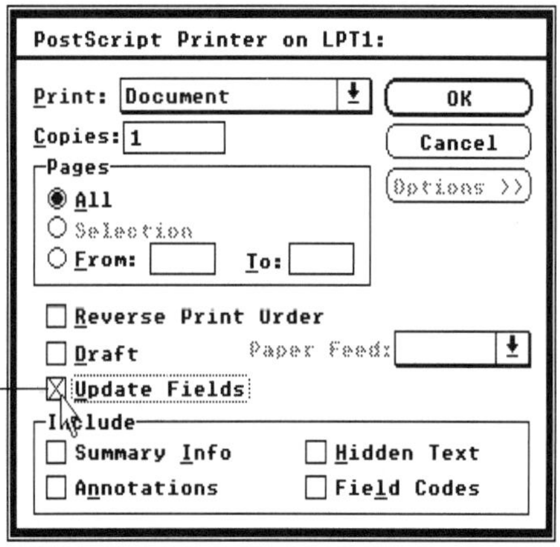

Jumping from One Field to Another

To update, edit, modify, move, copy, or delete fields, you need to first get to those fields. You can turn on the View Field Codes command and then scroll through the document looking for fields. If many of the fields are close together, this approach is acceptable. But if fields are scattered throughout a document, you need a more direct method of moving between fields. The easiest way to move from one field to another is to press the NEXT FIELD key combination (F11 or Alt+F1) and the PREVIOUS FIELD key combination (Shift+F11 or Alt+Shift+F1). Press these key combinations to jump from the insertion point to the next or previous field; Word selects the field.

Using Bookmarks in Fields

Perhaps the single most useful tool you'll use with fields is the bookmark. A bookmark in Word is a mark you set on a piece of text or a graphic. It works as a bookmark that you insert in a book does, as a marker for the page that you want to find again. But a Word bookmark can be more inclusive in what it marks. It can mark an entire selection, including a range of pages, so that you can jump to and select a particular passage instantly. Because a bookmark marks a passage, you can use a field to refer to that passage and to display its text, graphics, or page number elsewhere in your document.

For example, you can insert a field that contains a bookmark, as shown on the following page.

The REF field type
uses a bookmark.

See {ref Go_To_Section_Name} for more information.

Bookmark name

That bookmark, "Go_To_Section_Name," refers to the section title "Go To and the Destinations." After you update the field, your text looks like the following when field results are displayed:

See **Go To and the Destinations** for more information.

Field result

Using a field as shown above allows you to change the title later (for example, to "Using the Go To Command"), update the field, and still be assured that your cross-reference will be accurate. You can set up page cross-references to text in the same way. For example, you can insert a field that contains a bookmark for information that's on a particular page:

See page {pageref Go_To_Section_Name} for an illustration of the new office layout.

Bookmark name

After you paginate the document and update this field, your sentence always gives the correct page number when field results are displayed:

See page 7 for an illustration of the new office layout.

Field result

If the text or graphic ends up on a different page because of editing or formatting changes, Word still prints the correct page number when you update the field. Because a bookmark marks a block of text, even across many pages, you can use a bookmark to indicate a range of pages either to limit the actions of some fields—so that they act only on the text marked by the bookmark—or to indicate that an action should refer to more than one page.

To mark a selection with a bookmark, select the text and graphics you want. Then, choose the Insert Bookmark command (Alt,I,M). Word displays the Insert Bookmark dialog box, which is shown on the next page.

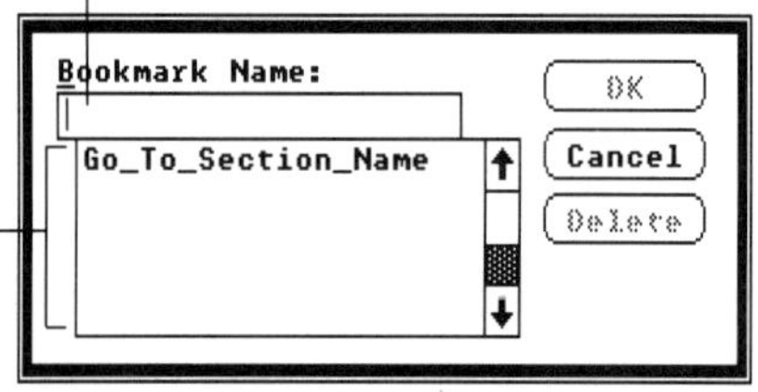

Type a one-word name for the bookmark, beginning with a letter. (The bookmark name can consist of any letters, any numbers, and underscores, but of no other characters.) Then, choose OK. You can also simply press the INSERT BOOKMARK key combination (Ctrl+Shift+F5). The message "Insert Bookmark:" appears in the status bar. Type a bookmark name and press the Enter key to set the bookmark. Note that if you press Ctrl+Shift+F5 while the "Insert Bookmark:" message is visible in the status bar, Word displays the Insert Bookmark dialog box and displays the name you typed in the Bookmark Name box. You can continue to edit the proposed bookmark name in the dialog box before you choose OK. If you type the name of an existing bookmark in either the Insert Bookmark dialog box or the status bar, Word redefines the bookmark to mark the new selection. Word does not ask you to confirm when you redefine a bookmark.

You can also use bookmarks outside of fields, in particular with the Edit Go To command and the GOTO key (F5). For more information about using bookmarks with go-to actions, see "Moving Around in a Document" in Chapter 2. That information is also useful when you use the GOTOBUTTON field, which is explained in Chapter 9, "Fields II: Creating Special Effects."

Fields the Easy Way

If you do not want to concern yourself with the concepts, structure, and intricacies of fields, you can use the Word commands that insert fields for you. These fields insert the more common elements that you include in a document: a file, page numbers, the date and time, a graphic, an index entry, a full index, a table of contents, and contents from another application. This section explains each of these commands.

When you use one of these commands to insert a field, a dialog box presents the options you can choose from in a readily readable format. And Word updates the fields for you. These field commands, however, offer more than a simple way to insert and update fields. By using these commands to insert fields and then looking at the field codes, you can learn how various fields are constructed, making learning to edit fields an easier task.

Insert File

When you want to insert another file in a document, choose the Insert File command (Alt,I,F). Word displays the Insert File dialog box:

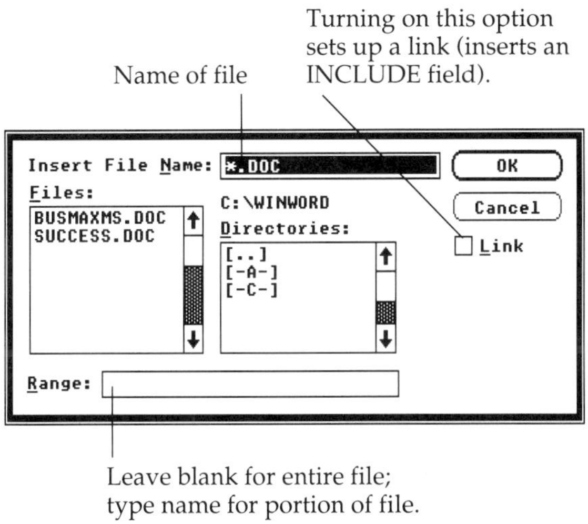

In the Insert File dialog box, either type in the Insert File Name box the name of the file that you want to insert or select a name from the Files list. Change directories, if necessary.

You can insert an entire file, or you can insert only a portion of a file. To insert an entire file, leave the Range box blank. To insert only part of a file, type a name in the Range box: Type either the name of a bookmark that's in a Word document or the name of a named range that's in a spreadsheet. (A named range is a named block of spreadsheet cells.) The Link option in the Insert File dialog box lets you set up a link between the file you insert (the source file) and the document into which you insert the source file. A link tells Word to keep track of the source file and to pull in new contents from it on your command. This link makes it possible to update both the document and the source file. Turn on the Link option (Alt+L) if you want to update your document whenever the source file changes.

When you turn on the Link option, Word inserts in your document an INCLUDE field that contains the file name you specify. You see this field when you view the field codes:

{include C:\\WINWORD\\SUCCESS.DOC} — INCLUDE field for entire file

File name

Bookmark name for range

{include C:\\WINWORD\\SUCCESS.DOC PR_YAWL} — INCLUDE field for portion of file

You see the contents from the file when you view the field's result:

{include C:\\WINWORD\\SUCCESS.DOC PR_YAWL}

Public relations means making converts.

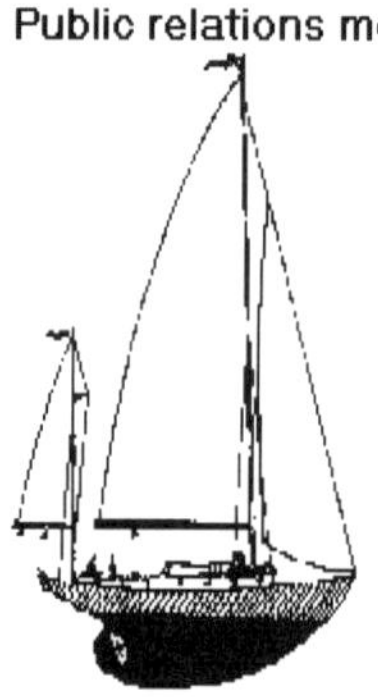

You do not see both the field codes and the result at the same time; you see one or the other. "Splitting the Window—Two Views at Once" later in this chapter, however, explains how to see the field codes and the result at the same time.

To update the contents from the inserted source file, position the insertion point anywhere in the INCLUDE field codes or the result and press the UPDATE FIELD key (F9). To update the source file itself, position the insertion point anywhere in the INCLUDE field codes or the result and press the UPDATE SOURCE key combination (Ctrl+Shift+F7).

This source updating tool can be especially handy when you compile a number of files to form a complete document because when you see something that needs changing in the inserted text, you can easily make the same change to the source file. When the Link option in the Insert File dialog box is turned off, however, Word inserts the contents of the source file at the insertion point but does not insert a field. To update the contents, you must delete them, update the source file text or graphic, and then insert the file again. And with the Link option turned off, you cannot use the Ctrl+Shift+F7 keys to update the source file.

TIP

Inserting Files in Other File Formats

You can insert any file that's in one of the file formats that Word understands (such as Windows Write and text-only files) or for which you have a file format conversion program. (A conversion program converts a file from such formats as Word for MS-DOS, RTF, DCA, and a number of popular word processors, to Word's file format.) To see the list of available file formats that Word understands, choose the File Save As command (Alt,F,A). In the File Save As dialog box, choose the Options button (Alt+O) and then open the File Format list (Alt+F,F4). To convert a file in another file format, you must add an additional instruction manually. This instruction is called a switch. This switch takes the form \c, followed by the name of the conversion program as it appears in the File Save As dialog box. For example, to convert a document stored in Microsoft Word for the PC format, type *\c "PC Word"* in the INCLUDE field. Because the Insert File command does not insert this switch, you must insert it manually by switching to the field codes view and then typing the switch and the name of the conversion program. Enclose the name of the conversion program in quotation marks.

You can also insert Microsoft Excel spreadsheet files and chart files, Lotus 1-2-3 spreadsheet files, and Microsoft Multiplan files. Word contains built-in conversion functions to read these file formats but none to save in them, so they are not listed in the File Save As dialog box.

Inserting Page Numbers Using the Insert Page Numbers Command

If you want Word to print page numbers on every page, you can use the Insert Page Numbers command (Alt,I,U). Insert Page Numbers inserts a PAGE field in a header or footer. Word lets you print page numbers at the top or bottom of every page, and at the left, center, or right of the header or footer. By using this command a number of times, you can print page numbers at both the top and the bottom and at any or all of the three horizontal positions.

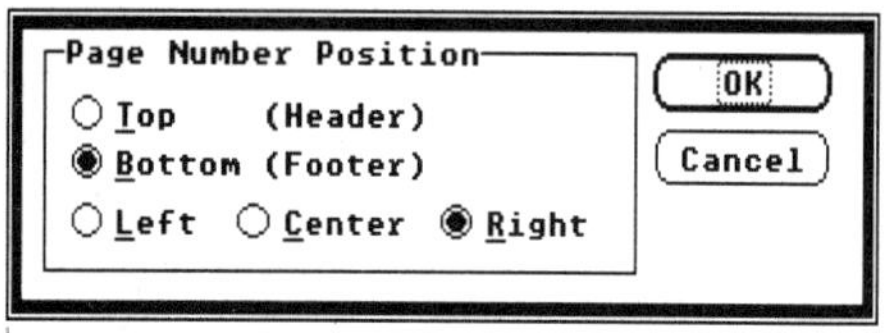

If your document already has a header or footer when you use Insert Page Numbers, Word asks if you want to replace the existing header or footer:

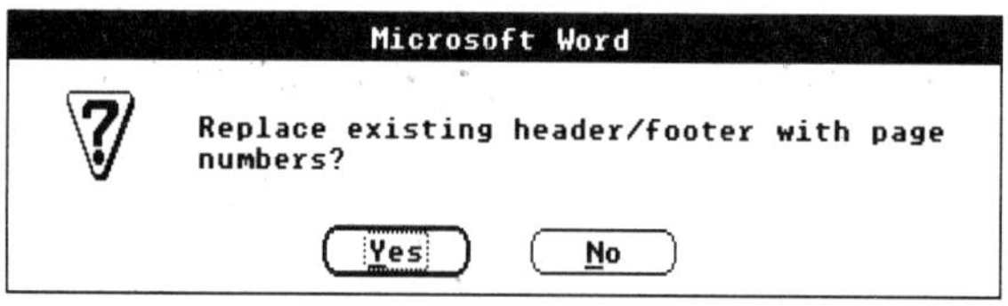

If you choose Yes, your header or footer will contain only the page number. If you choose No, the existing header or footer will be left as is, and unless it already has a page number field, page numbers will not be added to the header or footer. As a result, if your document has headers or footers without page numbers and you want to add page numbers to them, use the Edit Header/Footer command instead of Insert Page Numbers, as the next section explains.

TIP

Inserting Several Portions of a File

To insert several disconnected portions of a file, use the Insert File command for each portion. For documents that are in file formats other than Word's or for a spreadsheet that has named ranges, insert the entire file and then delete what you do not need.

Inserting Page Numbers Using the Edit Header/Footer Command

In addition to the Insert Page Numbers command, you can use the Edit Header/Footer command (Alt,E,H) to insert your page numbers. Edit Header/Footer can also insert the date and time in headers and footers.

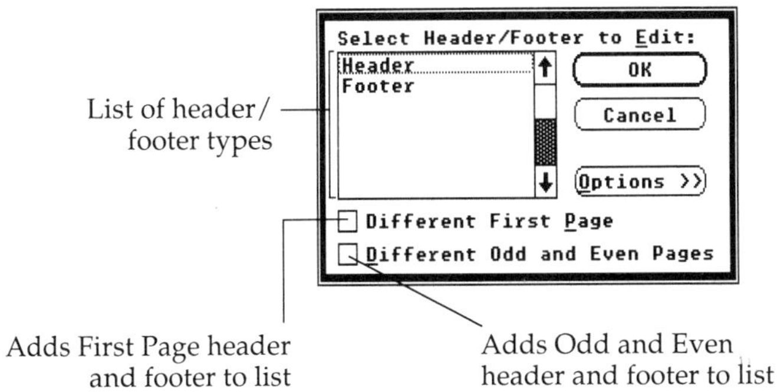

After you select Header or Footer in the Edit Header/Footer dialog box and then choose OK, the header/footer pane opens at the bottom of the document window. Across the top of the header/footer pane, you see the header/footer icon bar. You use the header/footer icon bar to insert the page number, the date, or the time in the header or footer. Word inserts the PAGE field for the page number, the DATE field for the date, and the TIME field for the time.

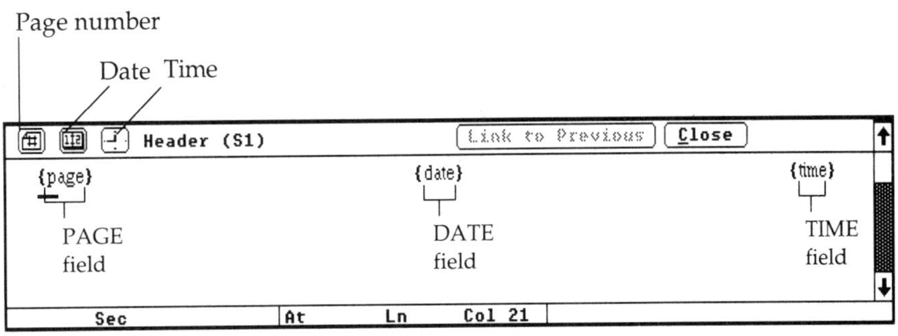

Inserting Graphics Using the Insert Picture Command

The Insert Picture command (Alt,I,P) inserts any of the following: a Tagged Image File Format (TIFF) file, a Windows metafile (such as Windows Paint produces), file formats from some drawing and CAD programs, or an empty picture frame. (An empty picture frame reserves space so that you can later glue graphics onto the printed pages.)

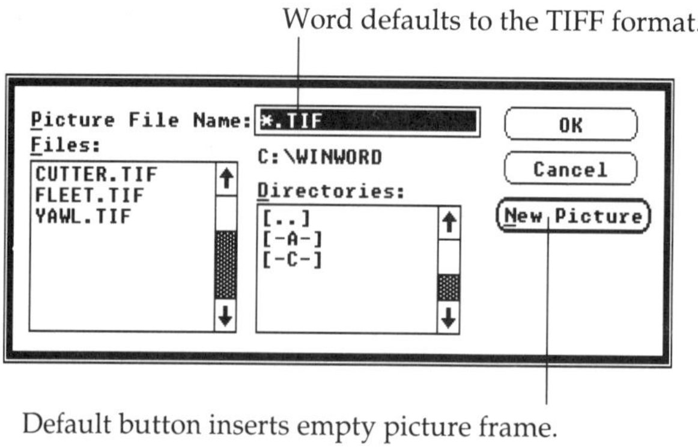

Type * plus the file-name extension and choose OK for a list of files in another format. A TIFF file contains a description of a graphic rather than only a bit-map image. Most scanners create TIFF files. See "Creating Document Contents" in Chapter 4 for a list of the supported graphics file formats. When you insert the contents from any of the supported graphics file formats, Word inserts an IMPORT field. Word does not use a field for an empty picture frame.

TIP

Date, Time, and Page Numbers in the Document Text

Word provides shortcut keys for instantly inserting the date, the time, and page numbers anywhere in a document, including in headers or footers. These shortcut keys are related to the header/footer icon bar. Thus, you can press the Alt+Shift+P key combination in the header/footer pane to use the keyboard to "click" the page number icon. But the icon bar need not be visible to use the shortcut keys. You can press this key combination while the insertion point is positioned anywhere in the document to insert the page number field, {page}, at the insertion point.

To insert the date, the time, or the page number anywhere in document, position the insertion point and then press the appropriate key combination, as follows:

Field Type	*Key Combination*
Date	Alt+Shift+D
Time	Alt+Shift+T
Page number	Alt+Shift+P

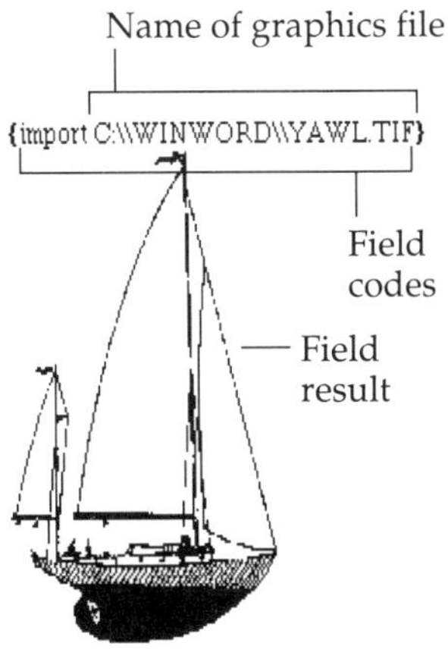

After you insert either a graphics file or an empty picture frame in your document, you can change its size in two ways: by cropping or by scaling. Cropping means cutting off part of the image. If you want only a portion of the graphic, you crop it so that only that portion is visible. The cropped portions are not lost, however, because Word keeps the whole graphic in the document file. Scaling means changing the size of the image's parts. Scaling is the same as enlarging or reducing a photograph, except that the image is not changed permanently. Cropping and scaling affect only how the graphic appears on your screen and how it prints. You can always adjust the graphic to any size or return it to its original size. To crop or scale a graphic, use either the Format Picture command or the mouse. See Chapter 5, "Refining Documents," for information about cropping and scaling pictures.

Preparing an Index Using the Insert Index Entry Command

Before you can create an index, you must insert index entry (XE) fields to identify the specific pieces of text that you want in the index. This text can be text that you select in the document or text that you type in the Insert Index Entry dialog box. These index entry fields also tell Word where the entries are in the document so that Word can assign a page number to each index entry. Then, when you use the Insert Index command, Word gathers these index entries into a full index. The next section describes the Insert Index command.

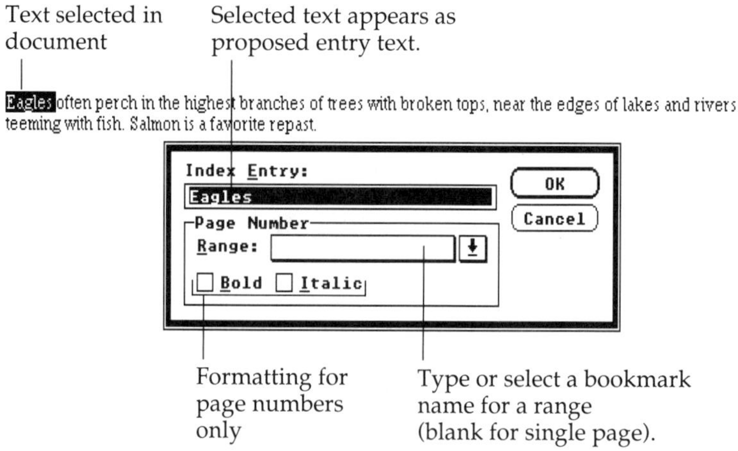

To include an index entry that is not in your document text, choose the Insert Index Entry command (Alt,I,E). In the Insert Index Entry dialog box, type the entry in the Index Entry box. If the document already contains text that you want to put in the index, select the text and choose Insert Index Entry (Alt,I,E). Word uses up to the first 64 characters as the index entry text; before you tell Word to insert the entry, you can edit the text in the dialog box.

To create a multiple-level index entry, type a colon between the levels. For example, to create the bald eagle entry in Figure 8-1 on the next page, type *Birds:eagles:bald* in the Index Entry box. You can include up to seven levels in an index entry. If you select document text that contains colons, quotation marks, or backslashes and then choose the Insert Index Entry command, Word inserts a backslash in front of each entry. The backslashes that Word inserts are included in the maximum of 64 characters permitted. If you want the colon in the selected text to create subentry text, delete the backslash that Word inserted. If you want an index entry to show a range of pages (such as 34–42), type or select the bookmark name that you set for those pages in the Page Number Range box.

The Insert Index Entry command inserts an XE field, which keeps the index entry text separate from the text you want to print. If you select document text and then choose Insert Index Entry, Word copies that text to the index entry field, which has no visible result, so it does not change your document's pagination. To see the XE fields, turn on the Hidden Text or Show All option in the View Preferences dialog box.

Inserting an Index Using the Insert Index Command

Use the Insert Index command after you finish marking all your index entries. This command inserts an INDEX field and collects text from all the index entry fields to generate an index. You control how the index is formatted by choosing options in the Insert Index dialog box:

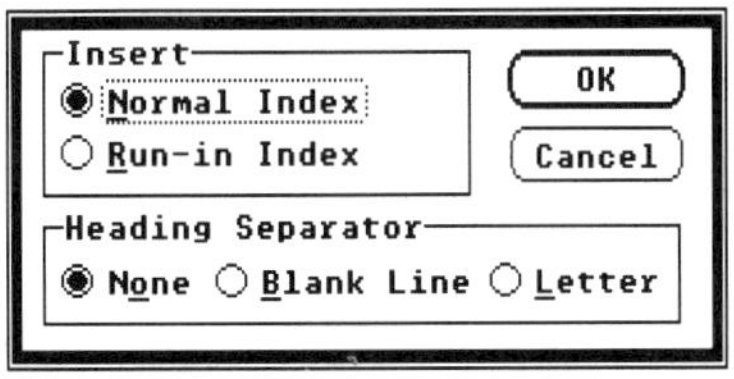

A normal index looks like the following:

Birds
    eagles
        bald, 1
        golden, 2
    hawks
        black, 3
        red-tailed, 4
    owls, 5
Cats
    feral, 8
    house, 6
    show, 6
Dogs
    herding, 9
    sporting, 11
    working, 11
Eagles, 1, 2, 4

Figure 8-1.
Normal index with multiple levels.

And a run-in index looks like the following:

Birds: eagles, 6; hawks, 11; owls, 15

Subentries

A run-in index loses its effectiveness if it includes more than two index levels because it's difficult for the reader to distinguish among the sublevels. The following example shows how difficult a reader will likely find it to read an index that has too many levels; the reader will have a hard time seeing where the subentries for hawks end and the next subentry for Birds begins:

Birds: eagles; bald, 1; golden, 2; hawks; black, 3; red-tailed, 4; owls, 5

TIP

Inserting Blank Lines and Letters Between an Index's Letter Sections

In the Insert Index dialog box, you can choose only one of the Heading Separator options: a blank line, a letter, or no separator. You can have both a blank line and a letter to separate your index sections, however, if you edit the INDEX field that the Insert Index command inserts in your document. Choose Insert Index (Alt,I,I), and choose the Letter option (Alt+L) for Heading Separator in the Insert Index dialog box. After Word inserts the index, position the insertion point anywhere in the index and press the TOGGLE FIELD key combination (Shift+F9). Shift+F9 toggles between displaying the field codes and displaying the field result. With the field codes displayed, look for the following characters in the field:

```
{index \h "A"}
```

Position the insertion point after the first quotation mark.

Position the insertion point between the first quotation mark and the letter A, and press the Enter key. The field looks like the following:

```
{index \h "
A"}
```

Now, press the UPDATE FIELD key (F9) to generate the index again, this time with a blank line and a letter in front of each letter section.

```
B
Birds
    eagles
        bald, 1
        golden, 2
    hawks
        black, 3
        red-tailed, 4
    owls, 5

C
Cats
    feral, 8
    house, 6
    show, 6

D
Dogs
    herding, 9
    sporting, 14
    working, 11

E
Eagles, 1, 2, 4
```

After you insert the INDEX field, you can update the index by positioning the insertion point anywhere in the index and pressing the UPDATE FIELD key (F9).

Inserting a Table of Contents Using the Insert Table of Contents Command

The Insert Table of Contents command collects specific pieces of text and generates a table of contents. The text that Word collects can be assigned heading 1 through heading 9 styles. It can also be text that you marked with table of contents entry fields, similar to the way you mark index entries. Insert Table of Contents inserts a TOC field.

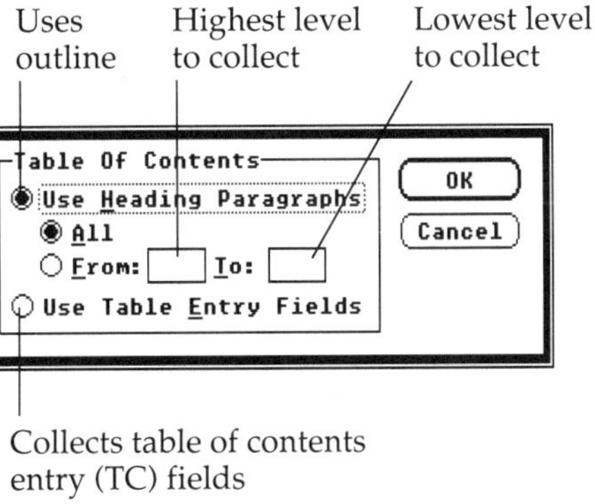

Generating a table of contents from heading paragraphs is the easier of the two methods. (You tried this method in Chapter 5, "Refining Documents.") To insert table of contents entries, you insert table of contents entry fields, using either the Insert Field command or the INSERT FIELD key combination (Ctrl+F9). Chapter 9, "Fields II: Creating Special Effects," describes how to insert table of contents entry (TC) fields and how to use those fields to generate a table of contents and other lists of contents, such as lists of illustrations or charts. Chapter 13, "Tables the New, Easy Way," describes how to create a list of tables.

Using the Edit Paste Link Command to Link Applications

To link your document with other applications that can place linkable file contents on the Clipboard, you can use the Edit Paste Link command to set up a Dynamic Data Exchange (DDE) link between Word and a source application. You must have a full version of Windows (not only the special run-time version that came with Word), and you must have enough memory to run both applications at the same time. Currently, Microsoft Excel is the only Windows application that Microsoft can guarantee will link with Word for Windows.

To use the Edit Paste Link command, you must first copy linkable contents—for example, a Microsoft Excel spreadsheet or chart—to the Clipboard. When Word detects linkable contents on the Clipboard, Edit Paste Link becomes available and is no longer grayed on the Edit menu. When you choose Edit Paste Link (Alt,E,L), the Edit Paste Link dialog box appears.

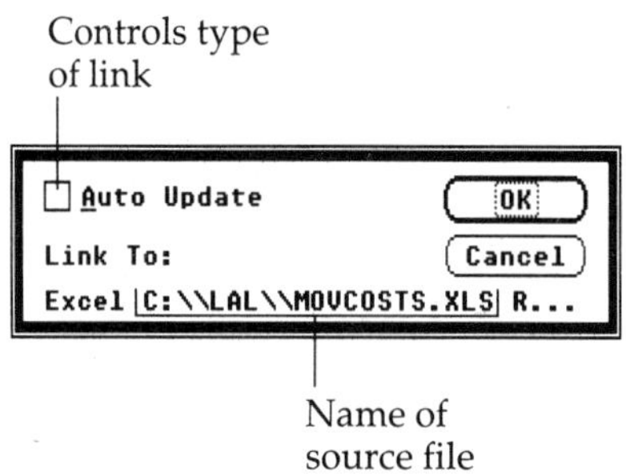

The Edit Paste Link dialog box displays the name of the source file and allows you to create a regular link or an automatically updated link. A regular link (the default) gives you the latest result from the source application whenever you update the field. This link gives you control over when the field result is updated because you update the field yourself. When you use a regular link, Word inserts a DDE field.

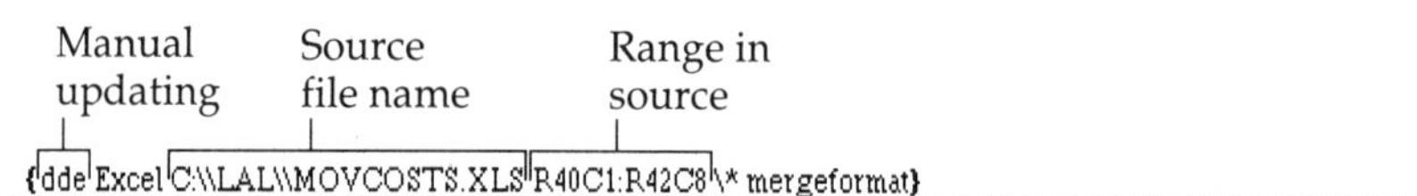

Least Expensive						
Method\Costs	Goods Tariff	Surely	LAL Airfare	RE Carfare	Meals	Rc
NA Ship + LAL fly	$1,386.20	$0.00	$159.00	$0.00	$0.00	

An automatically updated link, however, updates its result whenever the source application notifies Word that it has a new result to pass along. This link is useful when you need the latest result quickly or on an ongoing basis. When you choose an automatic link, Word inserts a DDEAUTO field, as shown on the following page.

Note that when you or Word updates these fields, the application that created the source file must be running. If you have less than two

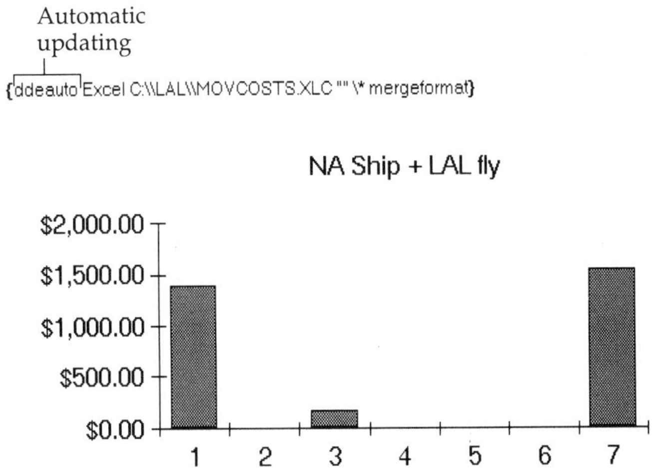

megabytes of memory, you should stick with regular links until you have enough memory to run another application with Word.

Do It Yourself Using the Insert Field Command

You can insert any type of field in Word using the Insert Field command. You choose Insert Field (Alt,I,D), and a dialog box assists you with lists of field types that you can choose from, additional instructions for some fields, and descriptive text that guides you in building fields. This dialog box makes it possible to insert any field and choose from a variety of options without having to remember all the different field types and what they do.

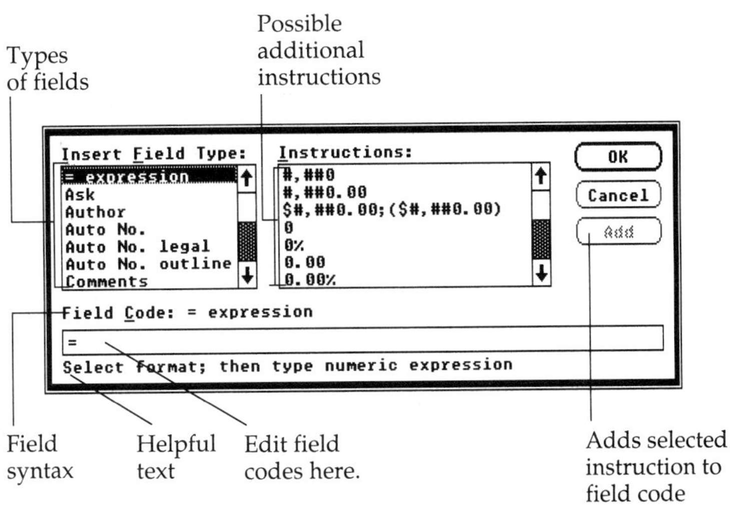

Selecting a Field Type

In the Insert Field dialog box, the Insert Field Type list contains the names of all the possible types of Word fields. The names are shown as words rather than as their field type code names to make them more readily understandable. Below the list is the Field Code display. This display shows you how the field type looks inside a field and what the syntax of the field is. (Syntax is the arrangement of the codes in a field.) The field type is shown in capital letters. Any words following the field type are descriptions of additional instructions that you can add to the field code. If you want to include additional instructions but none are listed in the Instructions list for a field type, you must type the additional instructions yourself in the box below the display of the field code. You use that box to edit the field code by either deleting or inserting field code parts. The text below the Field Code box is a message that explains what you should put in the field.

Adding Instructions

As mentioned, some of the fields in the Insert Field dialog box provide in the Instructions list additional instructions that you can add to the field code. These instructions are listed in the dialog box in an easy-to-understand form and not in the code form in which they actually appear in the field. For example, you see an entry called "Heading letters" in the Instructions list for the Index field type. If you select "Heading letters" and choose the Add button, Word adds \h "A" to the Field Code box:

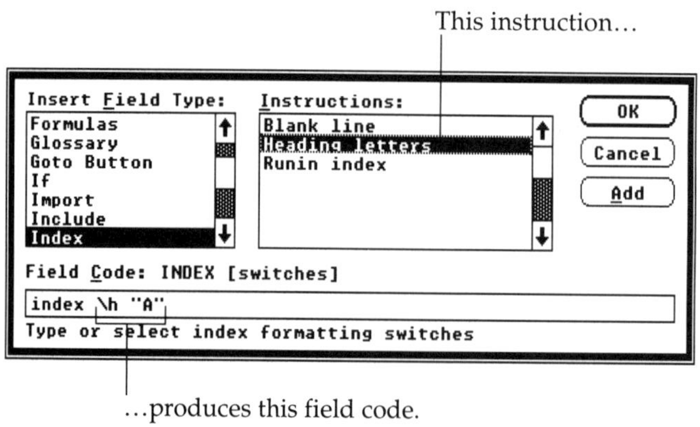

To add an instruction to a field code, select the instruction and then choose the Add button (Alt+A). (If you want to add only one instruction, select the instruction and choose OK. Using this method, you add the instruction and insert the field at the same time, without having to choose the Add button.) After you choose the Add button in the dialog box, the instruction is added to the Field Code box in the code form in which it will appear in the field. By comparing how the instruction looks in the Instructions list with how it looks as coding in a field, you can learn more about the additional instructions you can add to a field code. And you can also learn how to decipher field codes.

If you decide not to keep an instruction after you add it, you can select the instruction in the Field Code box and delete it. You can edit any part of a field's instructions to modify and refine the field code. To edit an instruction, select the parts you want to edit, and then type, press the Backspace key, or press the Delete key to add to, modify, or delete the additional instructions. The descriptions in the Appendix, "Field Types and Their Instructions," explain which instructions are available for each type of field.

Viewing Field Codes or Results

As you've seen, you can display a field in two different ways: as field codes or as a field result. When you display field codes, you see the instructions that tell Word how to generate the result of a field, as shown in the following example:

```
{date \@ "MMMM d, yyyy"}
```

When you display field results, you see the contents that Word generates as a result of carrying out the field codes—for example, "October 19, 1990". Under what circumstances would you choose one view over the other? And how do you see both views at the same time? The following sections explain.

Using the View Field Codes Command

The View Field Codes command displays all fields either as their field codes or as their field results.

Check means Word shows codes.

To display all fields as their codes, turn on View Field Codes (Alt,V,C). To display all fields as their results instead, turn off View Field Codes (Alt,V,C). View Field Codes is grayed in the View menu if the Show All option is turned on in the View Preferences dialog box. The Show All option overrides your ability to switch the view of a field by causing fields to always show their codes. After you turn off the Show All option, you can use the View Field Codes command as usual.

Toggling a Field's Display

You can switch between viewing an individual field's codes and viewing its result by positioning the insertion point in the field and pressing the TOGGLE FIELD key combination (Shift+F9). Even when the View Field Codes command is turned off, you can press Shift+F9 to see the codes; likewise, when View Field Codes is turned on, pressing Shift+F9 displays the result. You'll most often toggle a field's display when you want to either edit the field codes or check the new results after updating a field.

> **NOTE:** *The TOGGLE FIELD key combination will not switch a field's display if the Show All option is turned on in the View Preferences dialog box.*

Neither the View Field Codes command nor the TOGGLE FIELD key combination displays a field's hidden text (text that's hidden within a field because it has the Hidden Text format). To see hidden text in a field, turn on either the Hidden Text option or the Show All option in the View Preferences dialog box. You can also press the SHOW ALL key combination (Ctrl+*), which toggles hidden text on and off.

Splitting the Window—Two Views at Once

It's easier to correct errors in a field if you can see the field codes and the field result at the same time. That way, you see the result of your change without losing sight of the field codes. Although you can view the field codes or the field result for individual fields by using the TOGGLE FIELD key combination (Shift+F9), you cannot see both views of a single field simultaneously within one window. Word's split-window feature, however, lets you see the codes and the result at the same time.

To split a window into two viewing panes, choose the Control Split command from the Document Control menu (Alt,hyphen,T) and press the Enter key. Or, using the mouse, double-click the split box at the top of the vertical scroll bar. Turn on the View Field Codes command (Alt,V,C) in one pane, and turn off View Field Codes in the other. Press the NEXT PANE key (F6) to switch between panes. View Field Codes affects only a single pane at a time. After the window is split, scroll the contents in each pane to see the field codes and the field result at the same time.

View Field Codes turned on

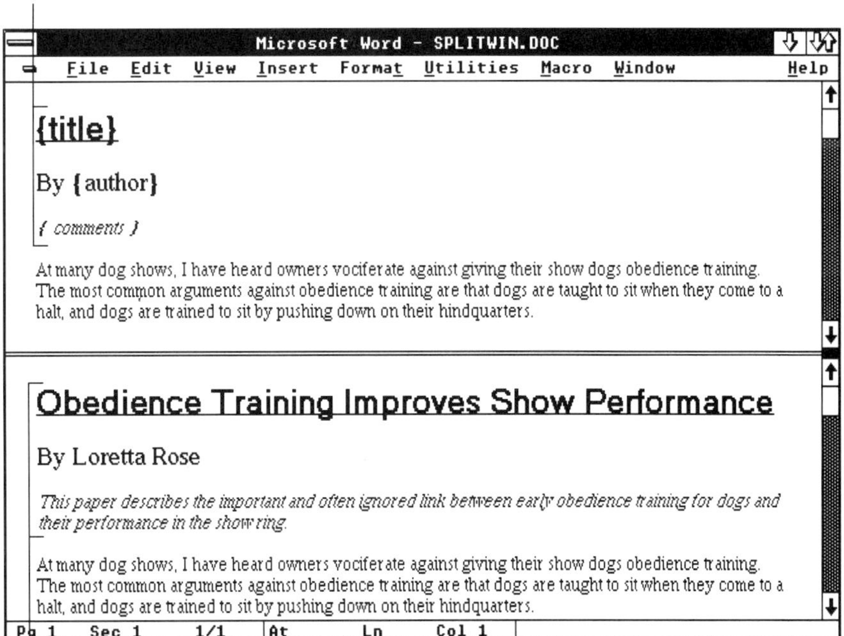

View Field Codes turned off; shows results

To show the same view of a field in both panes, turn on or off the View Field Codes command in both panes.

This split-window feature is especially effective when you use the Formula (EQ) field and the button action fields MACROBUTTON and GOTOBUTTON. See the descriptions of these fields in Chapter 9, "Fields II: Creating Special Effects," in Chapter 16, "Mathematical Typesetting," and in the Appendix, "Field Types and Their Instructions."

Updating Fields' Results

In addition to generating new results for most fields, the UPDATE FIELD key (F9) sets a field's display to match the setting of the View Field Codes command. If View Field Codes is turned off, therefore, updating a field displays the field's result, even if the field was showing its codes when you updated it. If View Field Codes is turned on, updating a field displays the field's codes, even if the field was showing its result when you updated it.

Because updating a field generates a new result, be aware that if you edited the field's result, updating the field replaces your edit changes with the new result. Your edit changes are lost. Any formatting changes are also lost if you formatted the result. For information about preventing field updating, see "More Field Actions" later in this chapter. You can use a special instruction called the * MERGEFORMAT switch to save your formatting even when you update a field. See Chapter 9, "Fields II: Creating Special Effects," for an explanation of this instruction.

Printing Field Codes

Studying field codes on paper can help you set up fields correctly. Also, when a field gets its result from several pages later or earlier in a document, it might be easier to see the field codes side by side and in a larger context than you can view in two panes on the screen.

To see field codes in printed form, print your document showing the field codes rather than the results. What you get is the printed equivalent of turning on the View Field Codes command. Note, however, that simply turning on View Field Codes before you print your document does not cause Word to print field codes, even though you do see field codes on the screen.

To print field codes, choose the File Print (Alt,F,P) command. In the File Print dialog box, choose the Options button (Alt+O) to display the full File Print dialog box. Then, turn on the Include Field Codes option (Alt+L) as shown below, and choose OK to start printing.

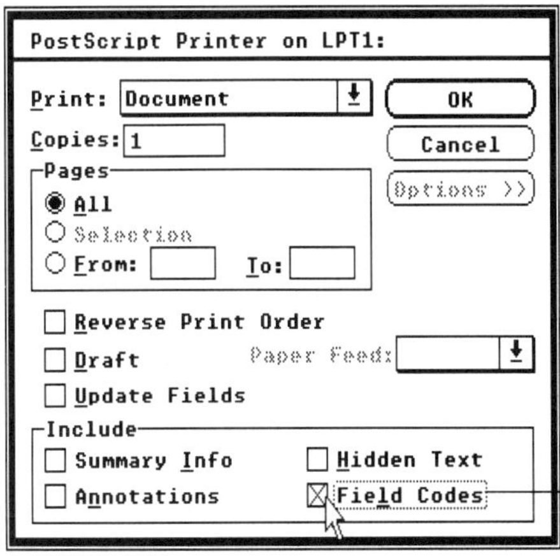

Prints field codes instead of results

Selecting Inside a Field

Selecting inside a field is the same as selecting text and graphics outside a field. You need to remember one point, however, when you select inside a field: If the selection includes one of the field characters ({ or }), Word extends the selection to include the whole field. So, if you want to select inside a field only and you accidentally extend the selection to the whole field, you need to select over again. But if you want to quickly select the whole field, you select one of the field characters and Word extends the selection.

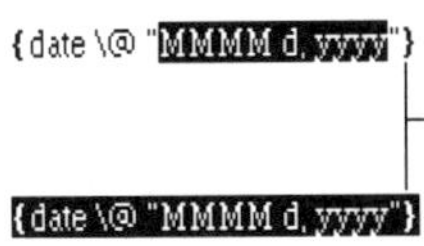

When the selection includes a field character, the whole field is selected.

The EXTEND key (F8) recognizes field characters as the boundaries of a field. If the insertion point or selection is inside a field, pressing EXTEND (F8) more than one time extends the selection in the same manner as it does in text outside a field—from character to word to sentence to paragraph. But F8 selects the whole field wherever it occurs in the sequence of text selection sizes. If fields are nested, F8 extends the selection until the first field is selected; when you press F8 again, Word selects the field that encloses it.

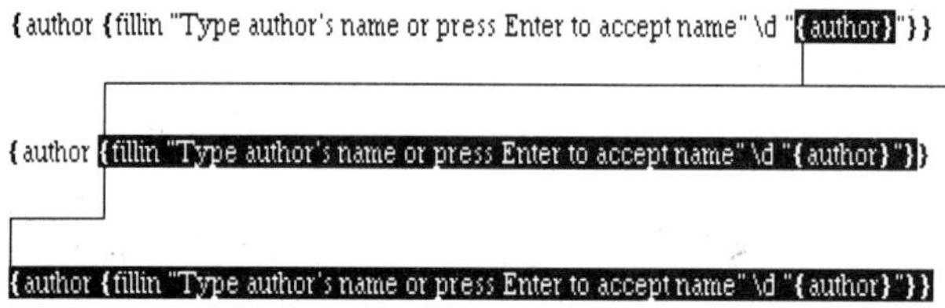

Each time you press F8, Word selects the next enclosing field.

After the selection contains the full nest of fields, pressing F8 again extends the selection as usual to include text outside the fields.

When you select inside a field, remember these two additional points: A graphic is treated as a character in terms of selection. And, if the result of a field is text, the entire result is selected if your selection crosses one end of the result into text outside the field. This occurrence might surprise you if the field's result is lengthy text from another file.

Crossing the field boundary selects the whole field result.

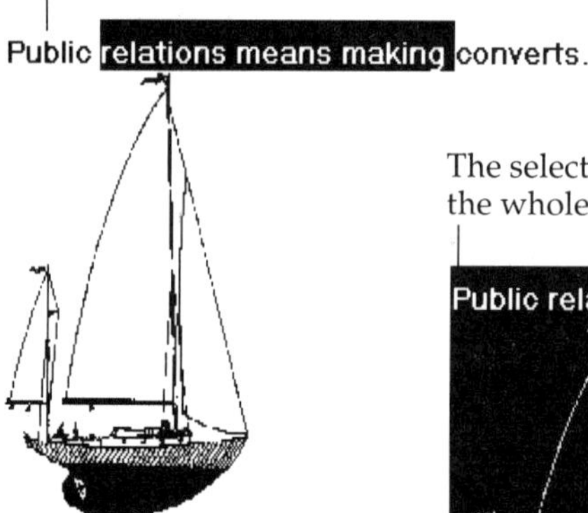

The selection includes the whole result.

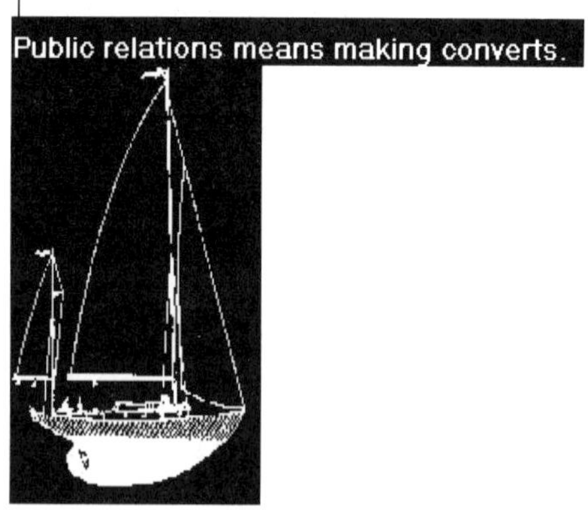

Editing Inside a Field

You will want to edit codes inside a field when you want to correct or improve the field's result. For most fields that display a result, however, you can also edit the result itself. If a field's result is not satisfactory, you can work with it by typing additional text, deleting or editing text, inserting graphics, or moving elements. You can also move part of a result from within a field to outside the field.

You treat the result of a field in the same way that you treat text that's outside the field. To edit a field's contents, you can use all the editing techniques that you use for regular text and graphics outside fields. But remember the following two editing points when you edit inside a field: You cannot delete only one of the field characters ({ }), and you cannot edit the results of the EQ, GOTOBUTTON, and MACROBUTTON fields.

To prevent you from deleting one of the field characters, Word does not let you backspace over them. And, if you position the insertion point in front of a field character and then press the Delete key, Word beeps instead of deleting. You must select a field character when you want to delete it, which also selects the entire field. Then, delete the entire field. To save the contents of a field but take them out of the field, move the contents first, and then select and delete the two field characters.

The GOTOBUTTON and MACROBUTTON fields' results are text and graphics that you insert as part of the field codes. To edit those results, switch to displaying the field codes and then edit the text and graphics that you encoded as the result. The EQ field sets up a mathematical formula. You cannot edit its result, either. To change the field result, switch to displaying the field codes and then edit those. Splitting the window into two panes—with the field codes in one pane and the field result in the other—is particularly helpful when you edit an EQ field. As you edit the field, the result changes, so you can see immediately if your changes are correct.

More Field Actions

You might not want Word to update a field in some situations. Or you might want to permanently replace a field with its result. For example, if you sent a letter that used the DATE field and then at a later date needed to print a copy of the letter, you'd want the letter to retain its original date. In this and similar situations, you need to tell Word not to update fields. If you do not alert Word, you might see unexpected or unwanted results.

To prevent a field from being updated, you have two choices. You can lock the field temporarily and then unlock it later when you do want to update. Or, if you'll never need to update the field, you can also unlink it, which means to convert it permanently to its result.

Locking and Unlocking a Field

Locking means preventing updating, either manual or automatic. After you lock a field, Word cannot update it. You lock a field when you might want to unlock and update its result later. Locking does not prevent you from editing the field codes or the field result. Nor does it affect switching a field between its field codes and its result. If you will never want to update the field, you should unlink it instead of locking it. The next section explains unlinking.

To lock a field, position the insertion point in the field and press the LOCK FIELD key combination (Ctrl+F11 or Alt+Ctrl+F1). It does not matter whether the field code or the field result is currently displayed in the field.

To unlock a field, position the insertion point in the field and then press the UNLOCK FIELD key combination (Ctrl+Shift+F11 or Alt+Ctrl+Shift+F1).

Word gives no visual indication that a field is locked. But Word beeps if you try to update the field using the UPDATE FIELD key (F9).

Unlinking a Field

Unlinking a field means permanently replacing the field with its result. When you unlink a field, Word converts the result to regular text and removes the field codes from the document. You can undo this conversion by choosing the Edit Undo command or pressing the UNDO key combination (Alt+Backspace) right away. Before you unlink a field, therefore, you'll want to carefully consider whether you really want only the current result. If even a remote chance exists that you'll want to update the field, lock it instead of unlinking it.

To unlink a field, position the insertion point in the field and then press the UNLINK FIELD key combination (Ctrl+Shift+F9). It does not matter whether the field codes or the field result is currently displayed in the field. The result is then displayed, even if the field codes were displayed when you pressed the UNLINK FIELD key combination. You see no result when you unlink the following fields: Formula (EQ), IMPORT, GOTOBUTTON, MACROBUTTON, ASK, SET, TC, and XE.

A Closer Look at What's in a Field

A field contains words, letters, and symbols in forms that Word understands. The form and order inside a field constitute its syntax, and a field's syntax is made up of three main parts, which can contain many levels of subparts. These three main parts are the field characters ({}), the field type, and additional instructions.

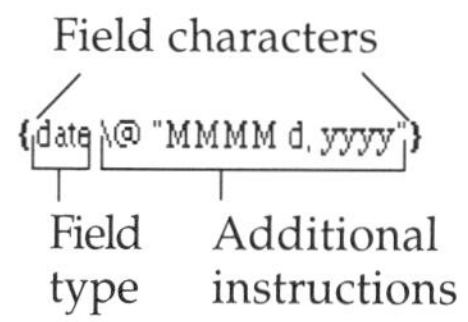

The field characters enclose the field and tell Word where the field begins and ends. The field type identifies a field's basic action. (The field type DATE inserts a date in a document.) The additional instructions further define what a field should do and how it should do it. For examples, see Chapter 9, "Fields II: Creating Special Effects" and the Appendix, "Field Types and Their Instructions."

Field Characters

Every field is enclosed between two field characters: an opening or beginning field character, which looks like a left brace ({), and a closing or ending field character, which looks like a right brace (}). You cannot insert or delete these characters individually, nor can you insert them by typing the brace keys on the keyboard. When you insert a field, Word inserts the field characters for you. For information about the three ways you can insert fields, see "Inserting Fields" earlier in this chapter.

Field Type

A field type is a special word or symbol that identifies what a field does; for example, the TIME field type inserts the time in a document. The field type is usually the first item in a field and can be preceded only by spaces and a backslash (\), which you probably will not see often. Spaces and backslashes are unnecessary; they have no effect on a field. But people with an interest in programming might prefer a backslash, or you might want a space for aesthetic reasons. The Appendix, "Field Types and Their Instructions," explains all the field types.

Additional Instructions

Everything else in a field other than the field characters and the field type is called the field's additional instructions. These instructions refine the actions of the field type and supply additional information, in much the same way that choosing options in a dialog box refines and defines a command's actions. Instructions can consist of text that you want to include as part of a field's result, descriptions of text that appears elsewhere in the document that you want to appear in the result, directions for combining text or numbers in a result, or directions for the field type about how to calculate a result. All these different elements can be given names and precise definitions, but rather than trying to remember all that information, it's probably more useful to take a look at the description of each field in the Appendix, "Field Types and Their Instructions." Those descriptions tell you what parts a field can contain.

Introduction to Switch Instructions in Fields

Fields produce their results in a default format. For fields that pull their results from another place in the document or from another document, the default format is the character formatting of the source text or graphic. For fields that generate a result immediately—such as a date or a numeric calculation—the default formatting is taken from the character formatting of the field codes. In addition to character formatting, some fields—such as the fields for the date, time, and page number—produce their results in the default format you have set in Windows or in Word. To alter the default formatting of a field's result, you can add special instructions, called switch instructions, to a field. Below, a switch instruction is added to a DATE field to format the date:

{date} — Date field code for default date

10/19/90 — Date field result in default format

{date \@ "MMMM d, yyyy"} — Date field codes with switch instruction

October 19, 1990 — Date field result from switch instruction

Word provides switch instructions for character formatting, for numeric formatting, and for date and time formatting, as the examples below show:

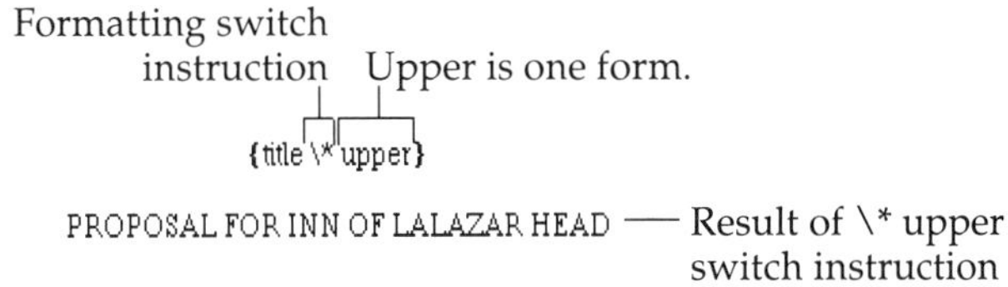

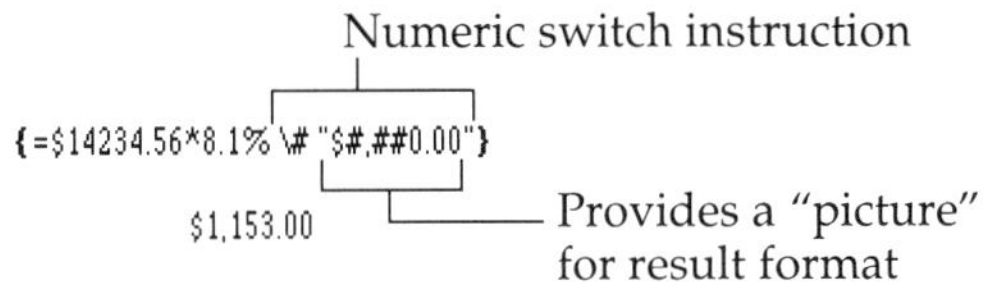

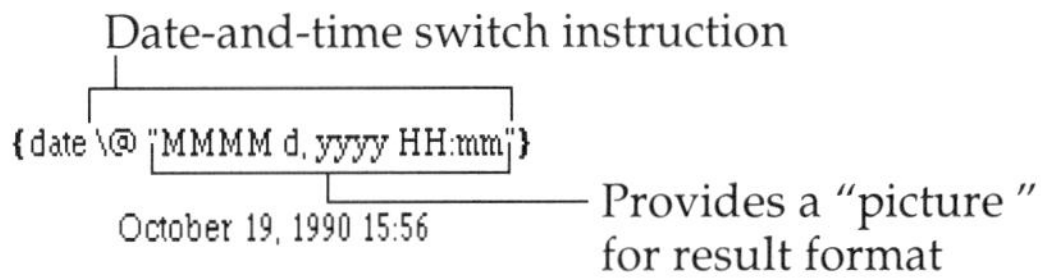

These switch instructions—character, numeric, and date and time—are general switch instructions; you can use them in most fields. Many fields also have specific switch instructions that apply only to that specific field. See the Appendix, "Field Types and Their Instructions," for a list of all the general switch instructions; the field-specific switch instructions are included with the description of each field.

Summary of Field Keys

Word provides keyboard shortcuts for inserting, updating, locking, unlocking, and unlinking fields; for moving from field to field; for toggling the view of a field; and for other field actions you can take, as shown in the table on the following page.

Key Combination	*Action*
UPDATE FIELD (F9)	Generates new result for field
INSERT FIELD (Crtl+F9)	Inserts field characters ({}) and positions insertion point between them; anything that's selected when this key is pressed is placed inside field characters
TOGGLE FIELD (Shift+F9)	Switches field of view from result to codes or from codes to result; does not work if Show All option is turned on in View Preferences dialog box
UNLINK FIELD (Ctrl+Shift+F9)	Permanently converts field to its result; removes field structure
NEXT FIELD (F11 or Alt+F1)	Jumps to next field after insertion point and selects field
PREVIOUS FIELD (Shift+F11 or Alt+Shift+F1)	Jumps to previous field before insertion point and selects field
LOCK FIELD (Ctrl+F11 or Alt+Ctrl+F1)	Locks field result so that updating will not affect field
UNLOCK FIELD (Ctrl+Shift+F11 or Alt+Ctrl+Shift+F1)	Unlocks field so that it can be updated
UPDATE SOURCE (Ctrl+Shift+F7)	Copies changes made in result of INCLUDE field to field's source file; for INCLUDE fields only
DO FIELD CLICK (Alt+Shift+F9)	Makes GOTOBUTTON and MACROBUTTON fields carry out their actions (Go To jump or run a macro)

For descriptions of the GOTOBUTTON and MACROBUTTON fields, see Chapter 9, "Fields II: Creating Special Effects." For examples of those fields, see the Appendix, "Field Types and Their Instructions."

Chapter 9

Fields II: Creating Special Effects

Fields in Word for Windows are designed to provide an easy method of producing text and graphics in a document. Chapter 8, "Fields: Facts and Functions," showed how to work with fields and included examples of the kinds of information that fields can produce. This chapter takes you a step further by showing you how to insert two classes of fields: fields that create text that's often difficult to create manually and fields that perform special actions not available in other word processors. You learn to create compound cross-references, dictionary-style headers, multiple references to a single footnote, document self-references, nested fields, simple hypertext jumps, and fields that run macros. The chapter ends with references to other chapters in this book that provide examples of fields in documents.

Word contains many more fields than are described in Chapter 8 and in this chapter. For a description of all the fields in Word, see the Appendix, "Field Types and Their Instructions."

Building Compound Cross-References

A cross-reference is a direction given to a reader to look in another part of a document for more information. Usually, a cross-reference looks like the one shown in Figure 9-1 on the next page.

Refer to "Go To and the Destinations" on page 27 in Chapter 2, "Essentials," for a list of possible go-to destinations.

Figure 9-1.
Compound cross-references.

The example above shows two textual cross-references (titles) and two numeric cross-references (page number and chapter number). In Chapter 8, "Fields: Facts and Functions," you saw individual examples of textual (REF) and page number (PAGEREF) cross-references. Chapter 13, "Tables the New, Easy Way," contains an example of the SEQ field, which you use to produce sequential numbers. And the Appendix, "Field Types and Their Instructions," contains information about the REF, PAGEREF, and SEQ fields, which are used in the example in Figure 9-1. Here you put that information together to produce a compound cross-reference, as shown in Figure 9-1. The following is how the text looks with the field codes in place:

Refer to "{ref go_to_dests}" on page {pageref go_to_dests} in Chapter {seq chapter n_essents}. "{ref essents}." for a list of possible go-to destinations.

Those field codes depend on the following bookmarks and sequences:

Bookmark or Sequence	*Description*
go_to_dests	This is the name of a bookmark that's set on the topic "Go To and the Destinations." To insert this bookmark, select the topic text, press the INSERT BOOKMARK key combination (Ctrl+Shift+F5), type *go_to_dests,* and then press Enter.
chapter	This is the sequence name for chapter numbers. In the chapter title, a sequence field gives a chapter number as its result. Insert a chapter title as shown below: Field generates chapter number Chapter {seq chapter}. Essentials The SEQ field looks the same for each chapter, but you change each chapter's title.

(continued)

continued

Bookmark or Sequence	***Description***
n_essents	This is the name of a bookmark that's set on the title paragraph for the "Essentials" chapter. Select the entire chapter title paragraph, and insert the bookmark as described above for the go_to_dests bookmark. The bookmark must include the SEQ field if the cross-reference is to show the chapter number as its result.
essents	This is the name of a bookmark that's set on only the title text for the "Essentials" chapter. Select only the text of the title, and not the chapter number, when you insert the bookmark. By using a separate bookmark for the title text, you can control the punctuation between and around the chapter number and the title.

You use the SEQ field with a bookmark name to tell Word that you want the number of the SEQ field to be included in the bookmark. If you use only a REF field, the SEQ field that's part of the REF field's result affects chapter numbering. By using the SEQ field with a bookmark, you do not affect chapter numbering.

If your document's pages are numbered by chapter (for example, 4-1), you can combine a SEQ field with a REF field to produce a page number cross-reference, such as the following:

```
See page 4-14 for a chart of the results.
```

The example below shows the field codes used in those two fields:

```
See page {seq chapter n_essents}-{pageref go_to_dests} for a chart of the results.
```

To set up chapter page numbering that starts over at the beginning of every chapter, place each chapter in a separate section or file. Position the insertion point in the second chapter's text, and then choose the Edit Header/Footer command (Alt,E,H). In the Edit Header/Footer dialog box, select the header or footer that contains the page numbers. Then, choose the Options button (Alt+O) to display the full dialog box, as shown on the next page.

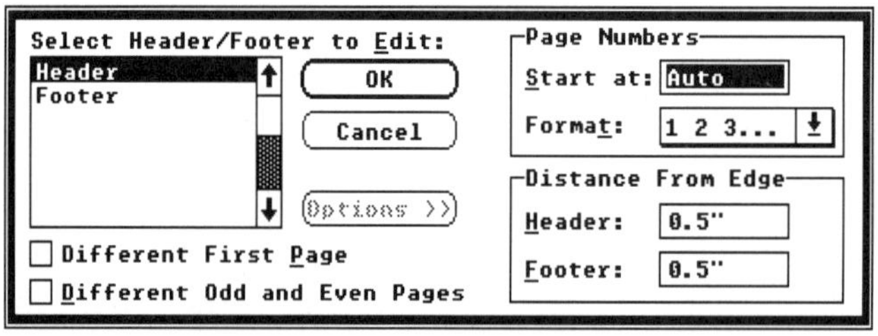

In the Start at box under Page Numbers, type *1*. Choose OK, and insert the following fields at the appropriate position in the header or footer:

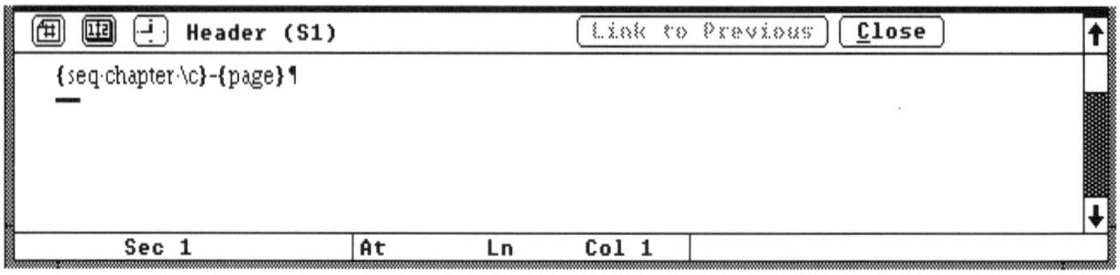

The SEQ field's result is the current sequence number that's created by a {seq chapter} field. The \c part of the field specifies the current number rather than the next one in the sequence. Press the Alt+Shift+C keys to close the header/footer pane. Then, move the insertion point to the text for the third chapter and repeat the process by choosing Edit Header/Footer, selecting the header or footer you want, choosing the Options button (Alt+O), typing *1* in the Start at box, pressing Enter, and pressing Alt+Shift+C to close the header/footer pane. Repeat the steps for every chapter in the document.

Setting Up Dictionary-Style Headers

When you look at the top of a page in a dictionary, you see two words; the first refers to the first word on the page, and the second refers to the last word on the page. These two words form a dictionary-style header. In reports and books that use this type of header, the header usually represents the first major topic on the page or the first and last major topics on the page.

Adding this type of header to a document can be difficult because page breaks can change, affecting the first and last elements on a page. And if you edit or format after you set up the headers, you might have to redo your headers. In addition, putting different headers on every page or on every two pages requires special page formatting so that the word processor knows where to stop one set of headers and start another, a task that some word processors cannot perform.

Word contains a field called STYLEREF that's designed to give you dictionary-style headers on every page. You insert this field in your headers, and Word finds the specified text and creates the correct header. Word can create the correct header regardless of how much editing or formatting you've done since you inserted the STYLEREF field, even if your modifications have changed the page breaks. The syntax for the STYLEREF field is as follows:

```
{styleref style-name }
```

This field directs Word to look for the first paragraph on the page to which the specified style has been applied. The *style-name* can be the name of any style that you created or any of the automatic styles. As a shorthand for the heading 1 through heading 9 styles, you can simply type the heading number. For example, {styleref 1} finds the first paragraph on the page to which the heading 1 style has been applied.

When Word finds a paragraph that has the specified style, Word copies the first 255 characters of the paragraph up to the paragraph mark as the STYLEREF field's result. The field syntax shown above finds the first paragraph that has the specified style on the page. To create a dictionary-style header, you also need Word to copy the text of the last paragraph that has the specified style on the page. For this second half of a dictionary-style header, the field syntax is:

```
{styleref style-name \l}
```

The \l switch directs Word to find the last paragraph on the page to which the specified style has been applied and to copy the first 255 characters of that paragraph up to the paragraph mark as the field's result. If you then put the two fields together into a header, as shown below, you create a complete dictionary-style header that is on every page each time you print your document:

```
{styleref style-name }—{styleref style-name \l}
```

The example on the following page shows how this header looks on a page on which the topics are formatted using heading 1 style.

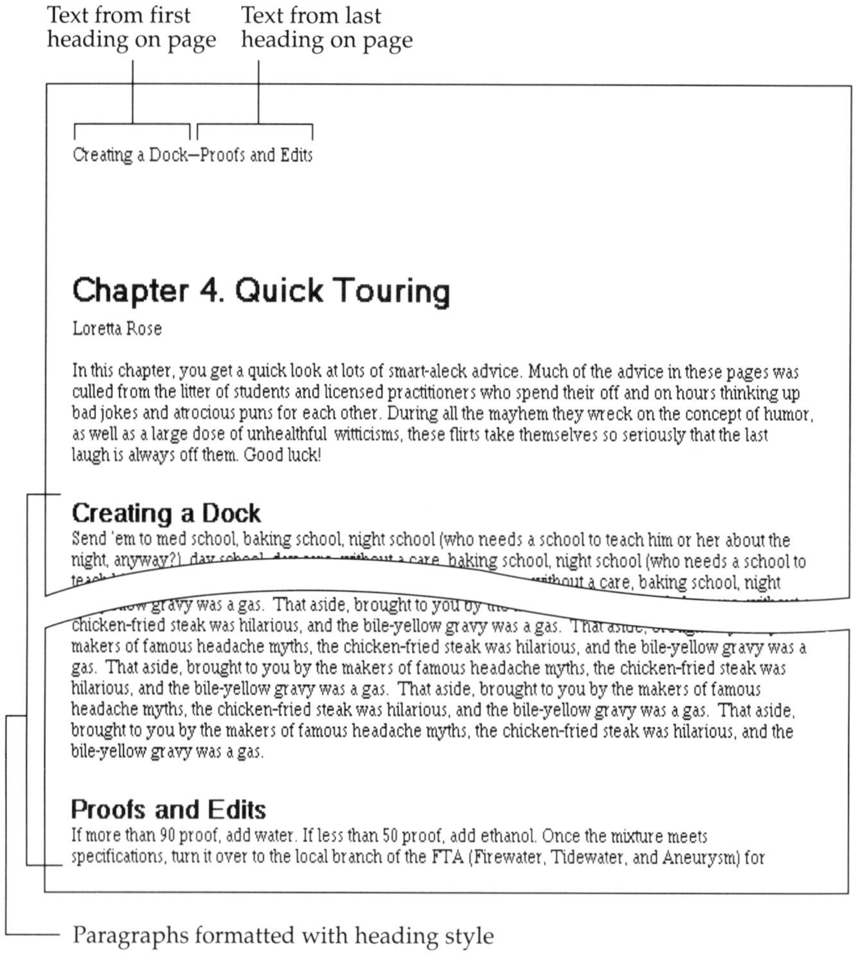

TIP

Dictionary-Style Headers on Every Other Page

If you'd rather the dictionary-style headers appeared on only every other page instead of on every page, turn on the Different Odd and Even Pages option in the Edit Header/Footer dialog box. Then, select either Even Header or Odd Header from the list, depending on whether you want the header to appear on even-numbered pages or odd-numbered pages, and insert the STYLEREF fields in that header. The topics in the header will show the page range for only the single page on which they appear.

Inserting Multiple References to a Single Footnote

In a document that contains footnotes, you might want to be able to insert a second footnote referring to a previous footnote. In Word, you can do so manually. A manual footnote reference does not renumber when you add or delete footnotes. If the original footnote reference number changes, you have to manually edit the subsequent references. By using the FTNREF field for the subsequent references to a single footnote, you can be sure that the reference number for the subsequent references will update when you print the document or update the field. The syntax for the FTNREF field is as follows:

{ftnref *bookmark*}

You insert a FTNREF field in place of a footnote reference for subsequent references to a single footnote. That is, you use the Insert Field command or the INSERT FIELD key combination (Ctrl+F9) instead of the Insert Footnote command (Alt,I,N). (FTNREF is the only field type not listed in the Insert Field dialog box.) The bookmark name in the FTNREF field is the name of the bookmark that you set on the original footnote reference, as the following shows:

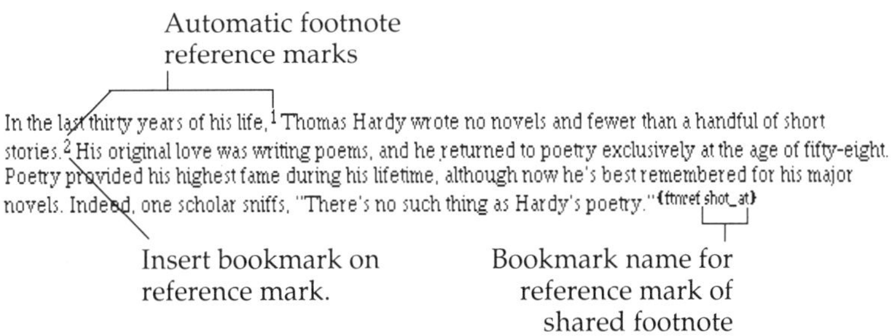

To create this example, type the text as shown above. Position the insertion point at the end of the first phrase, choose the Insert Footnote command (Alt,I,N), choose OK, and then type the text of the first footnote. Next, press the NEXT PANE key (F6) and position the insertion point at the end of the first sentence. Choose the Insert Footnote command (Alt,I,N), choose OK, and then type the text of the second footnote. Switch back to the document pane by pressing F6 again, and select the footnote reference mark, 2. Choose the Insert Bookmark command (Alt, I,M), type the bookmark name *shot_at*, and then choose OK.

Now, position the insertion point at the end of the passage. Press the INSERT FIELD key combination (Ctrl+F9), and type *ftnref shot_at*. Press the UPDATE FIELD key (F9). The result of the FTNREF field is the footnote reference mark, 2. To format the result of the FTNREF field as you would a footnote reference mark, select the result, press the SUPERSCRIPT key combination (Ctrl+Shift+equal sign key) to apply superscript format, and then press the SHRINK FONT key combination (Ctrl+Shift+F2) to reduce the result's point size. This formatting remains even when you update the field.

To see the benefit of using the FTNREF field instead of manually inserting a footnote reference number, select the first footnote reference mark, 1, and move it to the end of the second sentence; the two footnote reference marks swap numbers. Position the insertion point on the FTNREF fields result and press the UPDATE FIELD key (F9); the number changes to 1.

Moved footnote reference mark becomes 2.

In the last thirty years of his life, Thomas Hardy wrote no novels and fewer than a handful of short stories.[1] His original love was writing poems, and he returned to poetry exclusively at the age of fifty-eight.[2] Poetry provided his highest fame during his lifetime, although now he's best remembered for his major novels. Indeed, one scholar sniffs, "There's no such thing as Hardy's poetry."[1]

Updated field shows
new number, 1.

You can, of course, let Word update this field during printing, rather than manually updating the FTNREF field.

Creating Document Self-References

Within a document, you can use fields to print many different kinds of document information. For example, you can print the document's title, author, number of pages, number of words, file name, and revision number. All the fields you use to insert this information in a document get their results from the Edit Summary Info dialog box and its subordinate dialog box, Statistics. To review the summary information, choose the Edit Summary Info command (Alt,E,I).

You'll usually make use of this self-referencing feature when your document is in the draft stage, but you can also include this information in the final printed document.

Using a Field to Produce a Title

The result of the TITLE field is the text that appears in the Title box in the Edit Summary Info dialog box. Using the TITLE field to insert the title rather than typing it in the document allows you to use the TITLE field in a document template, thus saving yourself the time of typing and updating the title for each document created from that template.

Placing a title field in the document. . .

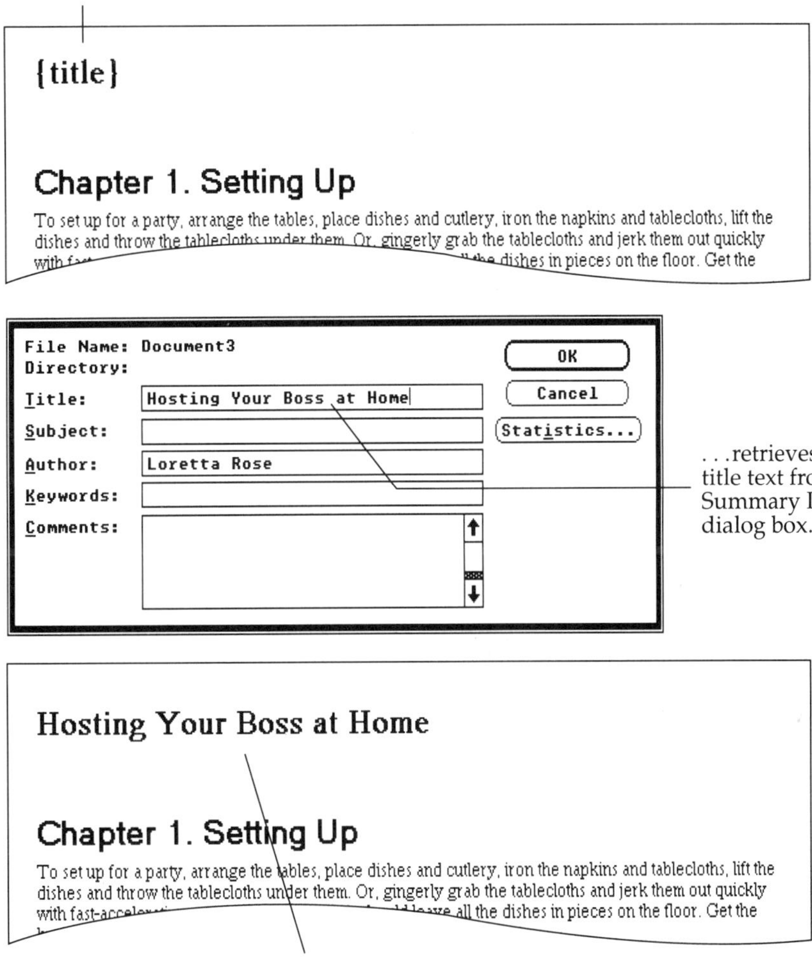

. . .retrieves the title text from the Summary Info dialog box. . .

. . .and places the title text in the document.

See Chapter 11, "Templates," for information about how a document template contributes contents to a document.

You can also reverse the process and use the TITLE field to fill in the Title box in the Edit Summary Info dialog box. The result of the following field is the text you insert in the field; Word also inserts this same text in the Title box:

{title "*text*"}

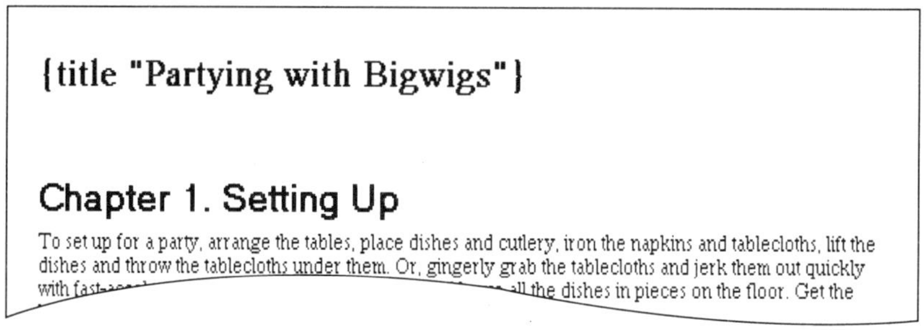

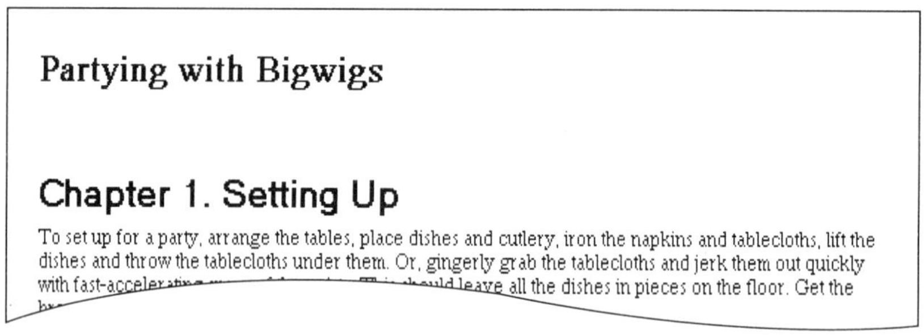

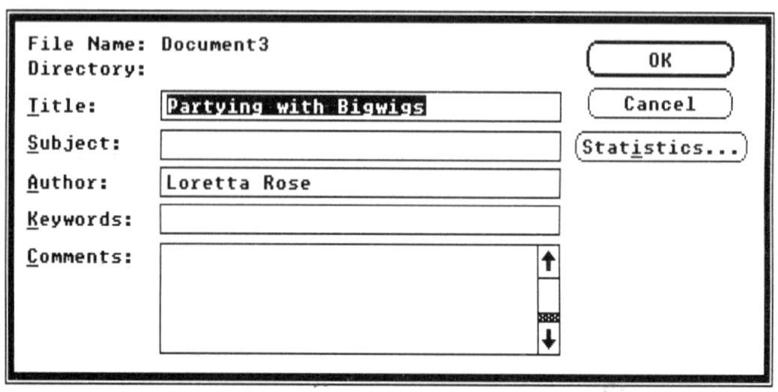

Using the TITLE field in this way allows you to type the document's title once only and keep the Edit Summary Info dialog box up to date at the same time. See "Example 1: Nested Prompting" later in this chapter for information about setting up a TITLE field that prompts you for the document's title text.

Using a Field to Produce an Author's Name

The AUTHOR field's result is the name that appears in the Author box in Word's Edit Summary Info dialog box. By using the AUTHOR field to insert the author's name, you can fill in the name more quickly than if you type it. The Author box in the Edit Summary Info dialog box receives the name that Word finds in the Utilities Customize dialog box.

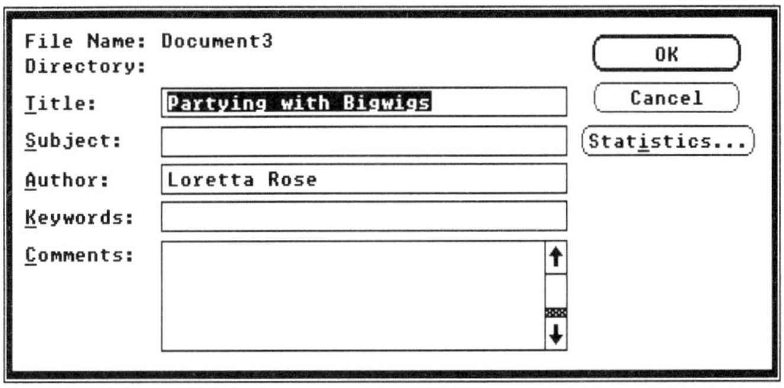

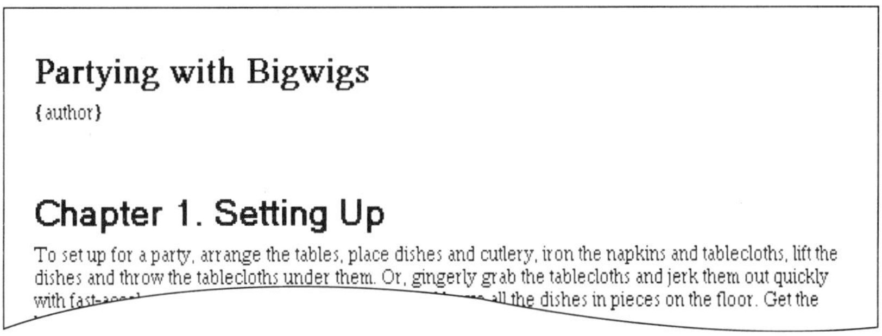

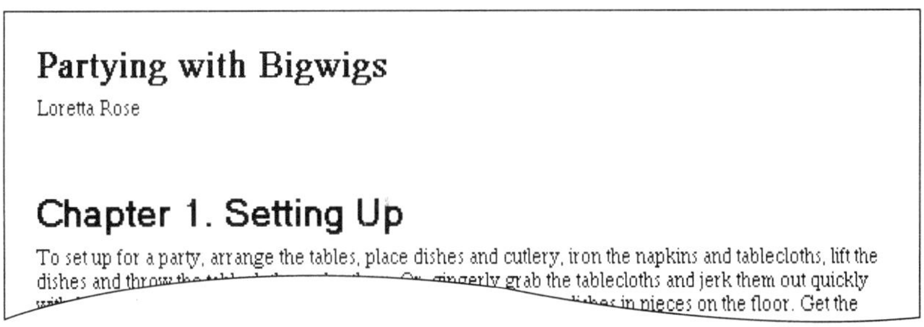

You can also use the AUTHOR field to fill in the Author box in the Edit Summary Info dialog box. The result of the following field is the name you insert in the field; Word also inserts this name in the Author box:

{author "*name*"}

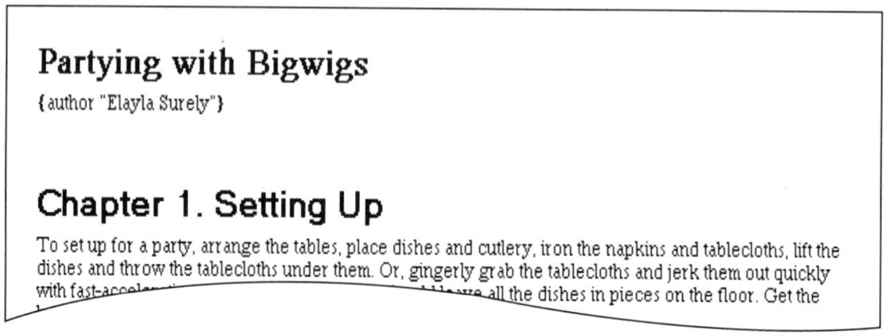

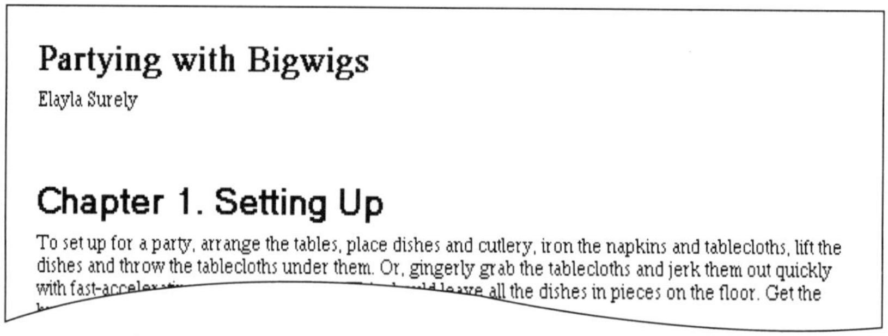

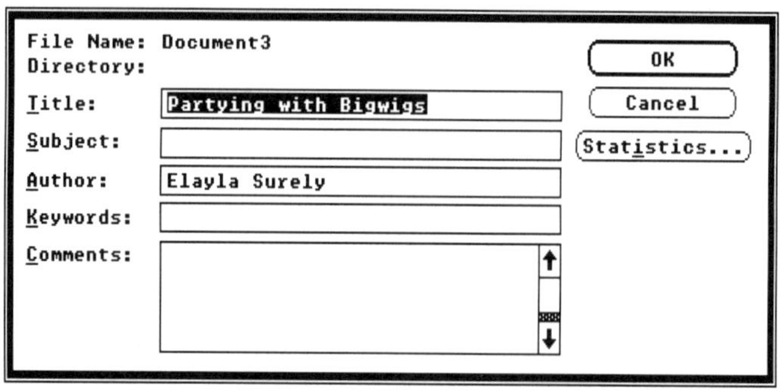

Using the AUTHOR field in this way allows you to update the Edit Summary Info dialog box easily. For example, it's a quick way to change the author information when you need to replace your name with the author's name in the Edit Summary Info dialog box. See "Example 1: Nested Prompting" later in this chapter for information about how to set up an AUTHOR field that prompts you for the author's name.

Using a Field to Produce the Number of Pages

The result of the NUMPAGES field is the number of pages in the document, as last updated in the Statistics subdialog box. To update the number in that dialog box, either print the document or choose the Update button (Alt+U) in the Statistics subdialog box of the Edit Summary Info dialog box.

One useful application of this field is in documents that include the word "Page" and the page count in the page numbers, as in "Page 1 of 22." To set up such a page numbering system, choose the Edit Header/Footer command (Alt,E,H), select a header or footer (whichever you want to contain the page numbers), and then choose OK. In the header/footer pane, position the insertion point where you want the page numbers to appear, type *Page* followed by a space, insert a PAGE field by pressing the Alt+Shift+P keys, and type a space followed by *of* and then by another space. Now, press the INSERT FIELD key combination (Ctrl+F9) and type *numpages*. The header or footer text looks like the following:

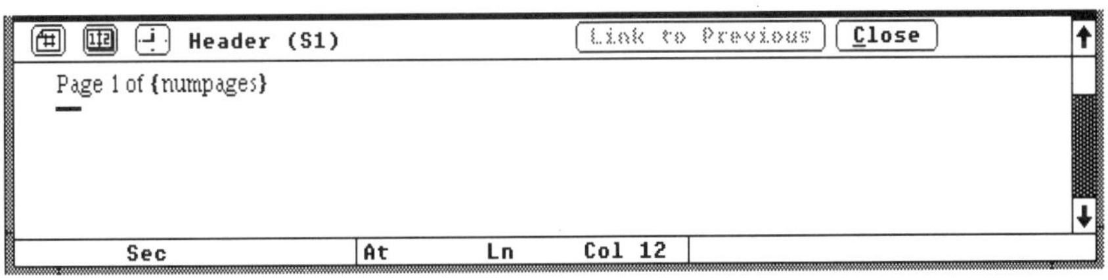

When you print the document, the header or footer will display the page numbers in the format "Page X of XX."

Using a Field to Produce the Number of Words

Magazines often impose a word limit on their articles. In many cases, the magazine's editors want to receive a word count along with the article. To include the number of words in a document, you can use the NUMWORDS field. The NUMWORDS field's result is the number of words in the document, as last updated in the Statistics subdialog box.

To update the number in that subdialog box, either print the document or choose the Update button (Alt+U) in the Statistics subdialog box of the Edit Summary Info dialog box. Until you use the Update button, Word estimates the number of words in the document by dividing the number of characters by 5.5. When you print the document or choose the Update button, however, the number Word provides is the actual number of words in the document.

To use this field in a document for which you must report the number of words, insert the NUMWORDS field where the number should be printed—for example, at the top of the first page. Choose the Edit Header/Footer command (Alt,E,H), turn on the Different First Page option (Alt+P), select First Header from the list, and then choose OK. In the header/footer pane, type *Number of words:* followed by a space. Then, press the INSERT FIELD key combination (Ctrl+F9) and type *numwords*. The first page header looks like the following:

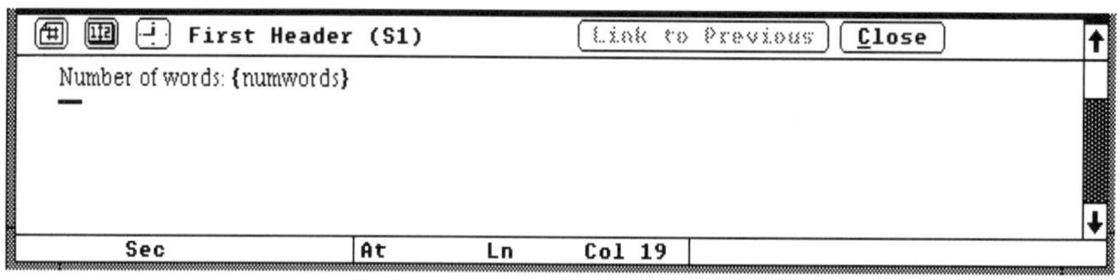

When you print the document, "Number of words: XXXX" prints at the top of the first page only. Subsequent pages can have any header that you want.

Using a Field to Produce the File Name

Occasionally you might want a document's file name printed at least once in the document. The result of the FILENAME field is the MS-DOS file name, which is shown in the Edit Summary Info dialog box. If you want the file name to print on every page, insert the FILENAME field in a header or footer. To print the file name at the bottom of the last page only, insert the FILENAME field at the end of the document.

Using a Field to Produce the Revision Number

Documents that are created as official versions for release to customers should include a version number. The result of the REVNUM field is the number of times that the document has been saved since it was created plus 1, as shown in the Statistics subdialog box of the Edit Summary Info dialog box.

Nesting Fields

Nesting means inserting a field inside another field. Each field, whether it's an inside field or an enclosing field, can appear independently as either its result or its codes. A nested field generates part of another field's instructions. For example, to combine the results of two fields to create the result for another field, nest the two fields inside the third, as in the following example:

```
{={sales-{costs}}}
```

The *sales* name is a bookmark name for the amount of sales. The *costs* name is a bookmark name for the amount of costs. The third field subtracts the result of *costs* from the result of *sales* to produce the field's result. You can nest a field inside an existing field, or you can nest an existing field inside a new field. And you can unnest fields. To nest a new field inside an existing field, position the insertion point inside the existing field and then insert the new field, using any of the methods for inserting explained in Chapter 8, "Fields: Facts and Functions."

You can also nest an existing field inside a new field by selecting the existing field and then pressing the INSERT FIELD key combination (Ctrl+F9). Word inserts the selected field inside a new field. You can use this technique to enclose any text or graphic that you want as part of a field; however, you can use it only with Ctrl+F9.

When you want to remove field nesting—that is, take a field out of another field—you move the nested field outside of its enclosing field. First, select the inside field that you want to unnest. Then, press the MOVE key (F2), position the insertion point where you want to move the nested field, and press the Enter key.

Note that you cannot simply remove the enclosing field characters from around inner fields; if you try to do so, you delete the nested field too. Instead, first move out the contents of the nested fields and then delete the field characters from the empty field.

The examples on the following pages demonstrate how nesting looks and how it works, and they show you how to build nested fields easily.

Example 1: Nested Prompting

In this example, two fields are nested inside the AUTHOR field. You can specify a name after the AUTHOR field type as the result of the field. The syntax of this field is as follows:

```
{author}        or        {author new-name}
```

A *new-name* is optional. If you do not include a *new-name*, the result of the AUTHOR field is the author's name as it appears in the Edit Summary Info dialog box. If you do include a *new-name*, however, Word changes the author's name in the Edit Summary Info dialog box, and *new-name* is the result of the field. This is a handy way to change the author information in the Edit Summary Info dialog box when the document's author is not the person processing the document. You can also use the FILLIN field, which requests information, for the optional *new-name*. If you substitute with the FILLIN field, you can have Word prompt for the name of the author. The nested example is shown in Figure 9-2:

```
{author {fillin "Who's writing this?" \d {author}}}
```

Figure 9-2.
Author field that contains two nested fields.

The FILLIN field presents a dialog box in which you can type information:

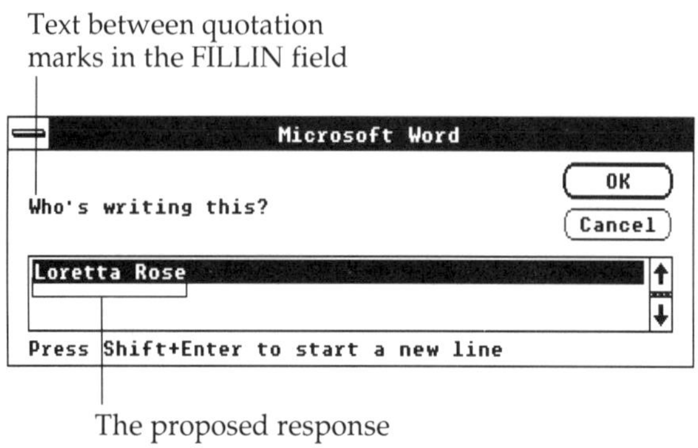

The proposed response is either the last result of the field, if any, or the default response if a default is set up, as in the \d switch in this example.

The \d switch instructs Word to display the text or graphic following the \d switch as the default response in the FILLIN field dialog box. If you do not use the \d switch, Word displays the field's last result as the proposed response. If the response shown in the dialog box is correct, choose OK in the FILLIN field dialog box. If the response is not correct, type the correct response and then choose OK. The information following the \d switch can be text, a graphic, or another field. In the example in Figure 9-2, the AUTHOR field was chosen as the text following the \d switch to make the author name already in the Edit Summary Info dialog box the default response. If you're working on a document that includes an AUTHOR field such as the one in Figure 9-2, your name will be proposed. If you're the author of the document, choose OK. If you're not the author, type the author's name and then choose OK.

Finally, you should note that if you delete the response in the FILLIN field dialog box and then choose OK, the AUTHOR field will have no result. Also, the Author box in the Edit Summary Info dialog box will be blank, which can be useful when you do not want the author's name to appear in a particular document in which it otherwise would.

Example 2: Nested Calculations

Nested fields can provide sophisticated results. In particular, nested Expression (=) fields can perform multiple layers of calculations that produce a single result. For example, you can construct a series of nested fields to calculate the percentage increase or decrease in sales from one year to the next, as shown in Figure 9-3 on the following page.

Before looking at this field's structure, take a look at what the Expression (=) field does in the above example. The field adds the total sales from three international sales areas for 1987 and then for 1988. It then subtracts the 1987 sales total from the 1988 sales total to get the increase or decrease in sales from 1987 to 1988. The field divides the difference by the total of the 1987 sales to produce a decimal fraction of the change from the 1987 sales total. Finally, the field multiplies the fraction by 100 to produce a percentage. Using a numeric switch, the field displays the result as a positive or negative percentage. (For a description of the numeric switch, see the Appendix, "Field Types and Their Instructions.") In the unlikely event that sales stayed the same for 1988, the field displays a text message that expresses surprise and dismay. At the

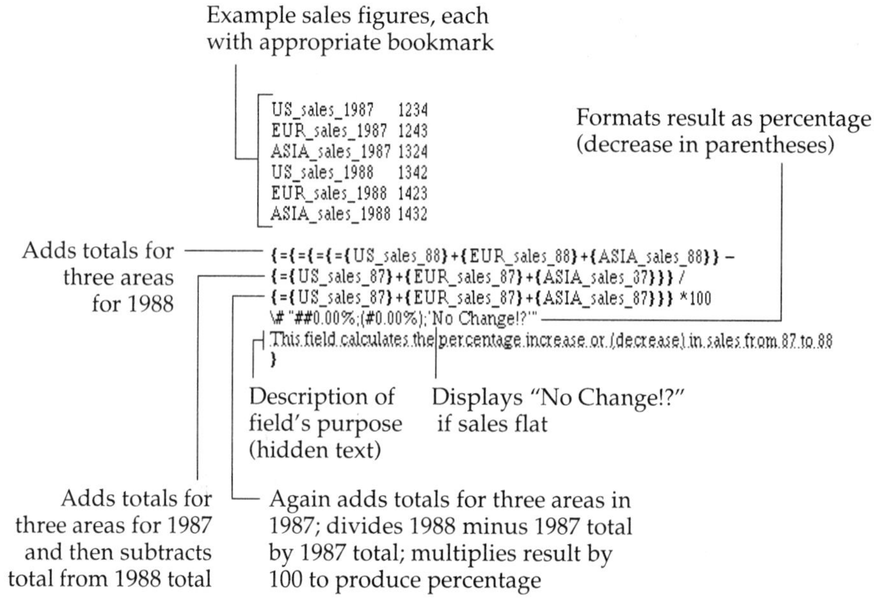

Figure 9-3.
Nested Expression (=) fields for calculations.

end of the field is a brief description of what the field does. The description is formatted with hidden text character formatting so that the description will not appear in the field's result.

An easy way to see what this example field does is to select the whole field and then press the TOGGLE FIELD key combination (Shift+F9) to show all the codes. Select one at a time and press the UPDATE FIELD key (F9) to see the result.

```
{={={={=1342+1423+1432} –
{=1234+1243+1324}} /
{=1234+1243+1324}} *100
\# "##0.00%;(#0.00%);'No Change!?'"
This field calculates the percentage increase or (decrease) in sales from 87 to 88
}
```

After you update the sales fields, for each line that contains numbers position the insertion point between the equal sign and the first number and press F9 in turn. You see the following:

```
{={={=4197 –
3801} /
3801} *100
\# "##0.00%;(#0.00%);'No Change!?'"
This field calculates the percentage increase or (decrease) in sales from 87 to 88
}
```

Position the insertion point between the equal sign and the number in the first line and press the UPDATE FIELD key (F9). You see one number divided by another number. If you repeat this step, positioning the insertion point between the equal sign and the number in the first line and then updating, you see a number multiplied by 100. The insertion point should still be between the equal sign and the number in the first line, so update to see the field's final result, 10.00%. The result is a positive percentage, a negative percentage inside parentheses, or the text "No Change!?" The result's final formatting originates from the numeric switch, which uses a positive;negative;zero picture for formatting.

Looking at the field now from the outside in reveals how the nesting is built into an Expression (=) field. The syntax of the field is as follows:

```
{=expression}
```

When you reduce the example to the simplest description of its parts, it's an expression with a numeric-switch added to format the result:

```
{=expression numeric-switch}
```

The expression consists of a nested expression that's multiplied by 100:

```
{=expression*100 numeric-switch}
```

The following expression consists of two nested expressions, one divided by the other:

```
{={=expression/expression}*100 numeric-switch}
```

The first of these two inner expressions consists of two expressions, one subtracted from the other:

```
{={={=expression-expression}/expression}*100 numeric-switch}
```

Each of these three expressions consists of a REF field with a bookmark. Note that in a REF field, the field type, REF, is optional. You can simply type a bookmark name.

```
{={={={={bookmark}={bookmark} + {bookmark}} - {={bookmark} + {bookmark} +
{bookmark}}}/{={bookmark} + {bookmark} + {bookmark}}}*100 numeric-switch}
```

At the end of the field, hidden text describes what the field does. You use hidden text to insert comments about a field—what it does, how it's supposed to perform, how to use it—within the field itself. Hidden text within a field has no effect on the field's result or performance. To format text using hidden text character formatting, select the text and then press the Ctrl+H keys. You can also press Ctrl+H to format as hidden text what you type before you start typing the text. Press Ctrl+H again to turn off hidden text formatting when you finish typing the comment.

TIP

Using Tabs and Paragraphs to See Field Nesting More Clearly

Notice that in this structural picture of the field and in Figure 9-3, the fields are typed without carriage returns or tab characters. In a field, you have the option of including spaces, paragraph marks, new lines, and tab characters. The example in Figure 9-3 could be typed like Figure 9-4:

```
{=¶
→   {=¶
→   →   {=¶
→   →   →   {=¶
→   →   →   →   {US_sales_88}+{EUR_sales_88}+{ASIA_sales_88}¶
→   →   →   }¶
→   →   →   -¶
→   →   →   {=¶
→   →   →   →   {US_sales_87}+{EUR_sales_87}+{ASIA_sales_87}¶
→   →   →   }¶
→   →   }¶
→   →   /¶
→   →   {=¶
→   →   →   {US_sales_87}+{EUR_sales_87}+{ASIA_sales_87}¶
→   →   }¶
→   }¶
→   *100¶
\#·"##0.00%;(#0.00%);'No·Change!?'"¶
This·field·calculates·the·percentage·increase·or·(decrease)·in·sales·from·87·to·88¶
}¶
```

Figure 9-4.
Nested fields formatted using tabs and paragraph marks.

These characters have no effect on the result unless you include them as part of the result's formatting. You include line breaks and indentations to format the appearance of the field codes so that when you use nested fields, you can more readily see what actions take place at each nesting level. You can then correctly select and edit any erroneous field codes.

TIP

Using Nesting Format Instead of Tabs

If you're nesting fields and you want to structure the nesting like that in the example shown earlier in Figure 9-4, you can use the NEST key combination (Ctrl+N) to indent each paragraph in the field, rather than using tab characters. This approach gives you a cleaner-looking field structure when you turn on the Show All option (Ctrl+*) in the View Preferences dialog box because you will not see multiple lines of multiple tab characters.

The example field in Figure 9-4 shows that you can do the following:

- Use a REF field without the REF field type; a bookmark name by itself in a field is a REF field.
- Insert spaces, paragraph marks, tab characters, and newline characters within a field to make its structure clearer.
- Insert comments inside a field to document the field, as long as you format the comments as hidden text.
- Nest fields in order to group mathematical operations because updating a field causes Word to update the innermost fields first.

Using Fields to Jump Around in a Document

The GOTOBUTTON field lets you jump around a document to specific places. Using the GOTOBUTTON field, you can insert various pieces of text anywhere in the document and then connect those pieces. By using the GOTOBUTTON field, you can create documents that provide explanations as Help does or a list of choices similar to a table of contents, index, or menu.

Because you can use the GOTOBUTTON field to jump to any point in a document, the GOTOBUTTON field can provide a simple approximation of hypertext. Hypertext is the ability to connect text and graphics in multiple dimensions. You could, for example, insert GOTOBUTTON fields throughout a document to lead the reader to additional information about specific points and topics. The information could be placed anywhere in the document, connected by an extensive chain of go-to destinations that take you from one field to the next. The syntax of the GOTOBUTTON field and its result are shown below:

```
{gotobutton destination display}     display
```

The go-to destination is any destination that you can use in the Edit Go To dialog box or with the GOTO key (F5). For a list of possible go-to destinations, see "Moving Around in a Document" in Chapter 2.

The result of the GOTOBUTTON field is always the text or graphic that you provide, which is not enclosed in quotation marks unless you want the quotation marks to appear in the result. The result must fit on one line, regardless of the line's length. You can apply any character formatting to the result. And by putting this field in a paragraph by itself, you can apply any paragraph formatting. For example, you can add a border around the field, creating a buttonlike appearance. If you do not add any special formatting to the field's result, the result appears in the document as regular text or as a graphic.

When you activate the GOTOBUTTON field, Word jumps to the destination that you've specified in the field. You can choose either of two ways to activate a GOTOBUTTON field:

- With the left mouse button, double-click the field.
- Position the insertion point immediately in front of the field (or select the field), and press the DO FIELD CLICK key combination (Alt+Shift+F9).

The following example demonstrates one simple use of the GOTOBUTTON field.

GOTOBUTTON Example: A Definition and Additional Information

This example uses a document that explains a specific topic. Within the document, additional information that does not fit well within the flow of information is available at certain places. The additional information is placed at the end of the document, and the first character of each piece of information is assigned a bookmark. By assigning the bookmark to only the first character, you prevent Word from highlighting all the text at the destination.

The following text segments represent main text from the document, with a couple of GOTOBUTTON fields and the additional information. The double-underlined phrase is the result of a GOTOBUTTON field.

During the course of our meetings with the engineering staff, we discovered some fundamental disagreement about the nature of the product we are producing. Engineering believes we are creating a technological tool. Marketing believes we are creating an automation tool. Usability believes we are creating a methodological tool. All of these views have some merit, but each implies fundamentally very different approaches to marketing and documentation. The current action item is for each group to write a full description of its viewpoint, as well as proposed guidelines for product development, marketing, and documentation. The results of this action item will be the subject of a future memo and report.
The remainder of the meeting was devoted to resolving specific issues related to staffing, implementation, and scheduling....

The GOTOBUTTON field codes looks like the following:

{gotobutton mktg_def approaches to marketing and documentation}

The bookmark named "mktg_def" marks the beginning of the text that's shown below:

If the product is a technological tool, the implied marketing approach is to promote the power and advanced features of the product. "Leading edge" is a common label. If the product is an automation tool, the implied marketing approach is to promote speed and ease of completion. Productivity is a common description. If the product is a methodological tool, the implied marketing approach is to promote effectiveness and efficiency. Getting better results is a common description.
The documentation for a technological tool emphasizes features and technical details. The documentation for an automation tool emphasizes procedures for converting current paperwork tasks to on-line tasks. The documentation for a methodological tool emphasizes procedures for accomplishing common tasks and new tasks in ways that produce superior results.

Click here to return to the report

The box at the end of the text is the result of another GOTOBUTTON field:

{gotobutton rpt4 Click here to return to the report}

The field is in a separate paragraph, bordered by a shadow box. The right indent has been moved in to make the box fit tightly around the text that's the GOTOBUTTON field's result. The bookmark named "rpt4" marks the GOTOBUTTON field that points to this explanatory text.

Launching Macros from a Field

The MACROBUTTON field lets you run a macro from within a document. When you activate the MACROBUTTON field, the macro you specify runs in the same way that all macros run, just as if you chose the Macro Run command and then ran the macro.

The syntax for the MACROBUTTON field and its result are shown in the following example:

{macrobutton *macro-name* display}   display

The result of the MACROBUTTON field, like the result of a GOTOBUTTON field, is always the text or graphic that you provide—it's not enclosed in quotation marks unless you want the quotation marks to appear in the result. The result must fit on one line, regardless of the line's length. You can apply any character formatting to the result. And, by putting this field in a paragraph by itself, you can apply to it any paragraph formatting. If you do not add any special formatting to the field's result, the result will appear in the document as regular text or as a regular graphic. When you activate the field, Word runs the macro that you've named in that field. You activate a MACROBUTTON field in the same ways that you activate a GOTOBUTTON field:

- With the left mouse button, double-click the field.
- Position the insertion point immediately in front of the field (or select the field), and press the DO FIELD CLICK key combination (Alt+Shift+F9).

The MACROBUTTON field can run any macro or any built-in command, making it possible to create some exciting actions and results. You can also use macro buttons to provide help information. By creating a help macro, you can provide context-sensitive help anywhere in a document.

MACROBUTTON Example: KEYCAPS.DOC

One sample document that Microsoft provides with Word is named KEYCAPS.DOC. The Setup program copies this document to your hard disk. The entire contents of KEYCAPS.DOC are MACROBUTTON fields that are placed in a table designed to represent a keyboard. The top part of the document looks like Figure 9-5 on the following page.

If you choose the View Field Codes command (Alt,V,C), you see the field codes behind each character that appears in the window. In Figure 9-6 on the following page, the MACROBUTTON field type and the macro name are formatted in the Symbol font. The KEYCAPS.DOC document was locked for annotations by Microsoft, so you cannot change the document.

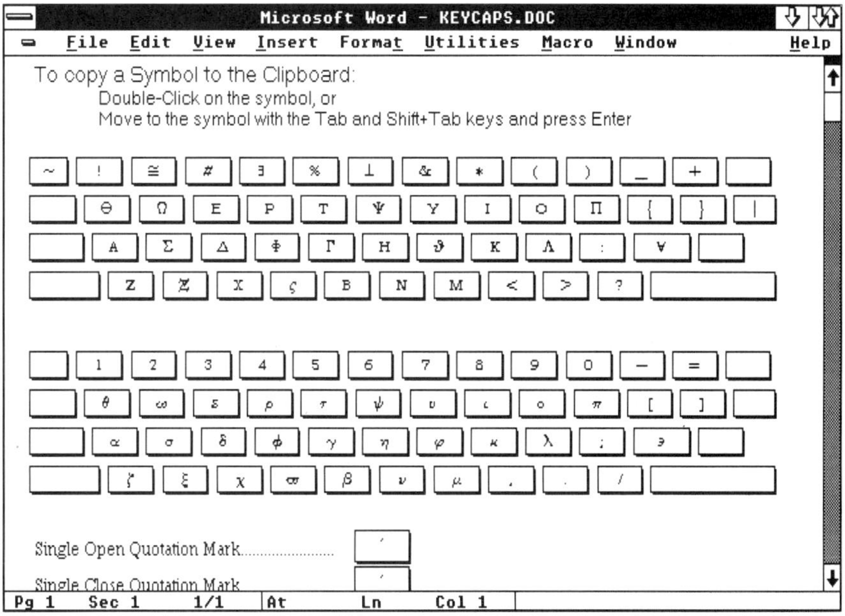

Figure 9-5.
MACROBUTTON fields in a table designed to look like a keyboard.

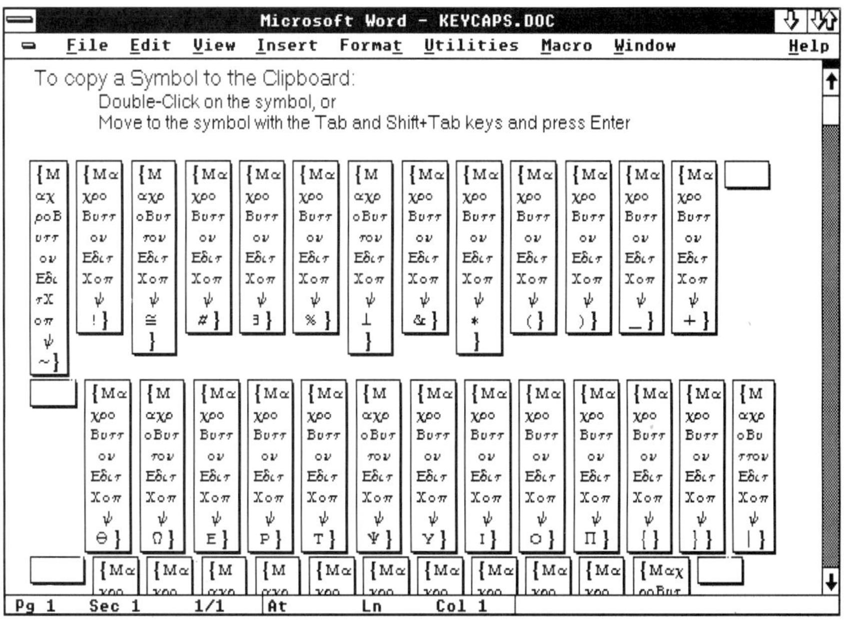

Figure 9-6.
The field codes behind the table.

Each field in the table is basically the same. By copying one of the fields to a new document and formatting the MACROBUTTON field type and the macro name as Tms Rmn font in 10-point size, you can see the field codes in a single line, such as the following:

```
{MacroButton EditCopy ϑ }
```

The "macro" in this example is the built-in EditCopy command. When you activate one of the MACROBUTTON fields in KEYCAPS.DOC, Word places the character that is the result on the Clipboard. You can then paste that character to a document. The KEYCAPS.DOC document is designed to help you insert in your documents characters from the symbol font. The border that's under each key box in KEYCAPS.DOC is a table cell border.

A List of Additional Field Examples in This Book

Elsewhere in this book, you can find examples of fields that produce special results. The following table lists the results, the fields, and the chapters that contain examples:

Result	*Field*	*Chapter*
Date	DATE	8
Time	TIME	8
Page number	PAGE	8
Imported contents	INCLUDE, IMPORT	8, 13
Sequences and automatic numbering	SEQ, AUTONUM	13
Calculations, equations	=	13
Mathematical typesetting	EQ	16
Table of contents	TC, TOC	5, 8
List of tables	TC, TOC	13
Index	INDEX	5, 8
Formatting results with switch instructions	*upper, \# "$#,##0.00", \@ "MMMM d, yyyy HHmm"	8

The Appendix, "Field Types and Their Instructions," describes the fields and the switch instructions.

Chapter 10

Macros

A macro is a group of instructions and commands that are collected under a single name as a way to automate a series of actions. You can choose the macro, which chooses those commands for you so that you do not have to choose or type each command manually. Macros can make the mechanical parts of your work flow easier and faster, leaving you more energy for creativity and thought. You can create your own macros as well as run (and modify) the macros that come with Word for Windows.

Using Macros to Customize Word

You can use Word's macros to reprogram the Word program. That is, you can change Word's commands by changing their names, the actions they perform, their locations on menus, or the keys they're assigned to.

Using macros also provides a way to build additional commands and features into Word, making macros the basis for customizing Word. Because you can change menus, commands, and key assignments, you can create your own personal word processor or several different word processors for each of the different types of documents that you create. And, if you decide you want to use the original Word setup, you can quickly reset the menus and key assignments.

Along with macros, Word gives you a built-in BASIC programming language that you can use to create macros that are like BASIC programs. You can even create your own dialog boxes for advanced macro programs. To make good use of these programming features, you need to understand programming concepts and how to program in BASIC. See the *Microsoft Word for Windows Technical Reference* for descriptions of Word's advanced programming features. You can get a copy of this reference from Microsoft by filling out the order form that comes in your Word product package. For everyday Word use, however, you do not need to know programming concepts or BASIC. To use macros in Word, you need only know how to use the keyboard to choose commands, how to position the insertion point, and how to select text.

If you've been using Word or another word processor for any length of time, you probably already know some tasks that you'd like to automate. Whenever you find yourself using the same series of commands and keystrokes to complete a repetitive task, you have a candidate for a macro.

Word gives you three ways to create a macro. The easiest method—and the one you spend the most time with in this chapter—is to record commands and keystrokes, which is simply a matter of performing the actions you have performed many times before, but with Word's built-in recording feature (the macro recorder) turned on. Another way to create a macro is to borrow parts from the macros that come with Word or to modify these packaged macros. Later in the chapter, the section called "Packaged macros" explains more about the macros Word includes. At the end of the chapter, you try your hand at modifying a macro. The third way to create a macro is to write a macro as you would write a program in a programming language.

After you create a macro, you can use it in three ways: by running it with the Macro Run command, by putting it on a menu and then choosing the macro name as you choose any command from a menu, or by assigning it to a key combination and pressing the keys. Using the menu and key methods, you change the setup that comes with Word, including removing a command or macro from any menu or key.

The Parts of the Macro Universe

A macro can contain all the Word menu commands, dialog box options, commands that are assigned to keys, and typing and cursor keys. After you create a macro, you can also use its name inside other macros as an instruction. But before you begin creating macros, you need to know about the commands that you use to create, assign, and run macros. You'll also want to know about Word's built-in commands and the macros that are included in the Word program.

The Macro menu

Emphasizing the importance of macros, Word has a separate Macro menu that contains all the macro commands:

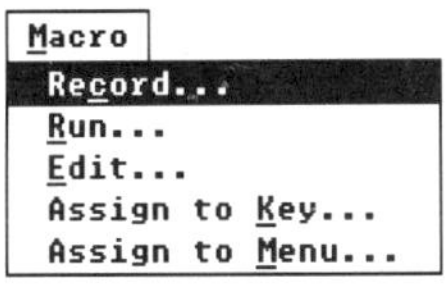

Later in the chapter, you'll see the dialog boxes for macro commands as you practice working with macros. For now, the descriptions in the following sections give you a sense of what each command does.

The Macro menu also provides a way to isolate macros. If you switch from Full Menus to Short Menus, the Macro menu disappears because the Short Menus include commands only for the most basic Word tasks.

TIP

Putting Macro Commands on the File Menu

To record actions that affect a document, you must have a document open while you record a macro. You might also want to record or run a macro that opens or creates a document. To make doing so possible, Word places Record Macro and Run Macro commands on the File menu when no documents are open. Similarly, you might want to record closing a document as the last action in a macro. After you close all document windows, while recording a macro, Word places the Stop Recorder command on the File menu.

Using the Macro Record command. When you choose the Macro Record command, Word prepares to record every action you take until you choose the Macro Stop Recorder command, including every keystroke, command choice, and dialog box setting. Choosing Macro Record displays a dialog box that asks for a name for the macro:

After you type a macro name and choose OK, Word displays "REC" in the status bar to let you know that the macro recorder is recording. Be aware that Word does not record any mouse actions other than choosing a command from a menu and selecting options in a dialog box, the ribbon, and the ruler. In particular, Word does not record positioning the insertion point, selecting text, or scrolling using the mouse. To record these actions, use the keyboard instead of the mouse. To let you know that only certain mouse actions are recorded when the macro recorder is on, the pointer appears on the screen as a transparent arrow.

Using the Macro Stop Recorder command. The Macro Stop Recorder command replaces the Macro Record command on the Macro menu while Word records. When you choose Macro Stop Recorder, Word stops recording your actions and removes "REC" from the status bar. The macro you recorded is now ready for you to run, edit, or assign to keys or to a menu.

Using the Macro Run command. When you choose the Macro Run command, Word displays a dialog box, as shown on the following page, that lists both the macros you created and the MoreExamples macro that opens the EXAMPLE.DOC document, which contains many sample macros.

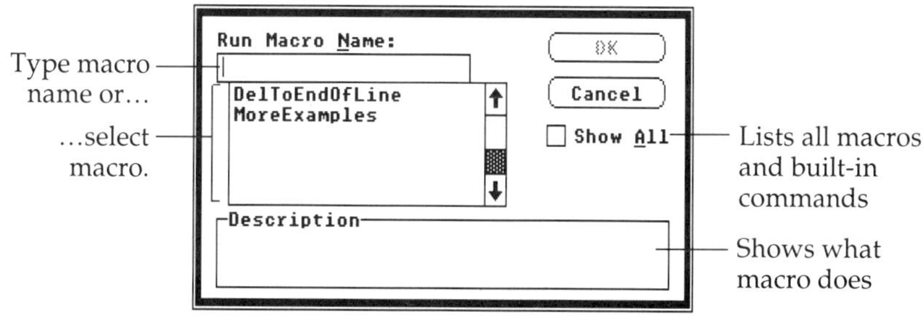

By turning on the Show All option in the Macro Run dialog box, you can add to the list the names of all of the macros that run all of Word's built-in commands. These built-in commands form the basic structure of Word. They underlie the commands that you can access using the Word menus, using macros, and using key combinations. Adding the names allows you to run the commands as you do macros and to run built-in commands, which neither appear on any menu nor are assigned to any key. Later in the chapter, "Built-in commands" explains these commands further.

To run a macro, select the macro name from the list and then choose OK. Word runs the macro, beginning at the insertion point or selection and continuing to the end of the document. If a macro includes built-in commands, the prompt text that usually appears in the status bar when you highlight a command on a menu still appears in the status bar as the macro chooses the command.

Using the Macro Edit command. Choosing the Macro Edit command displays a dialog box that lists both the macros you have created and the MoreExamples macro:

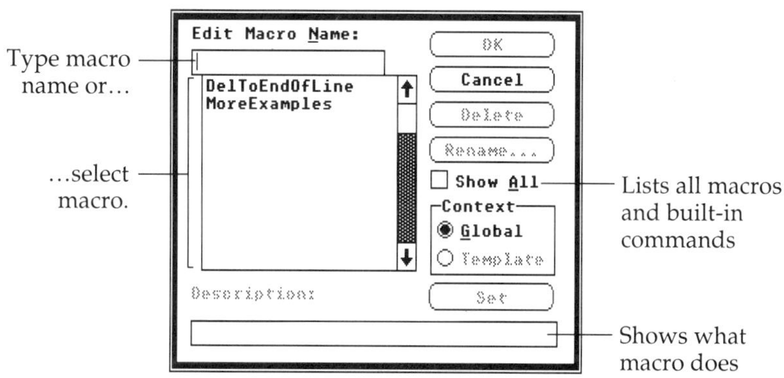

Turn on the Show All option in the Macro Edit dialog box. This option adds to the list the names of all of the macros that run all of Word's built-in commands. By adding the built-in commands to the list, you can run the commands as you do macros, and you can run built-in commands, which neither appear on any menu nor are assigned to any key. To edit a macro (in other words, add, remove, or modify instructions), select the macro name from the list and then choose OK, which opens the macro editing window. To close the macro editing window, press the Alt,hyphen,C keys. In the Macro Edit dialog box, you can also change the macro's summary description, which is displayed at the bottom of the dialog box, or rename the macro using the Rename button.

Using the Macro Assign to Key command. Choosing the Macro Assign to Key command displays a dialog box that lists macros that you created, macros that come with Word, and names that match all of Word's built-in commands:

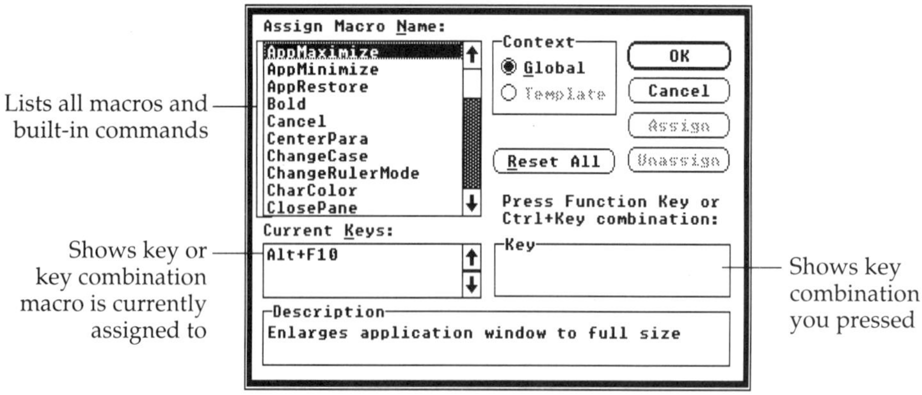

To assign a macro to a function key or to a key combination, select the macro name, press the function key or the key combination you want to assign the macro to, and choose the Assign button. To remove assignments from keys, press the keys and choose the Unassign button.

Using the Macro Assign to Menu command. When you choose the Macro Assign to Menu command, Word displays a dialog box, as shown on the following page, that lists macros you created, macros that come with Word, and the names of all of the macros that run all of Word's built-in commands.

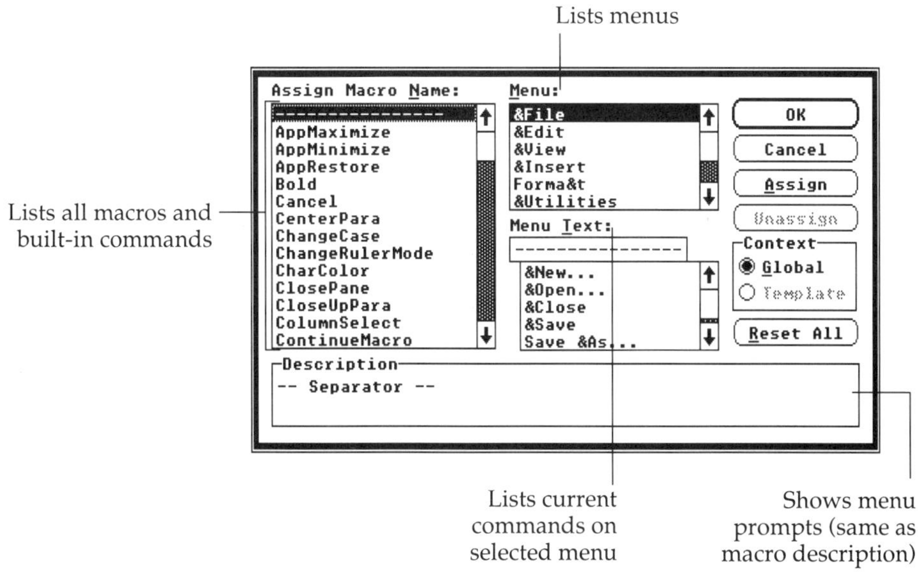

To assign a macro to a menu, select the macro name from the list, select the name of the menu you want to assign the macro to, type or edit the name as you want it to appear on the menu, and choose the Assign button. You can also remove a macro from a menu by selecting the macro name and the menu name from the lists in the Macro Assign to Menu dialog box and then choosing the Unassign button. If you assign a macro to a menu and then highlight the macro on the menu, the summary description appears in the status bar as it does when you highlight any menu command.

Packaged macros

The Word product package includes a group of sample macros. The sample macros are contained in the EXAMPLE.DOC document, which should have been copied onto your hard disk when you set up the Word program. To see a list of these macros, choose the Macro Run command (Alt,M,R), select MoreExamples from the Run Macro Name list, and then choose OK. When the EXAMPLE.DOC document appears, choose Macro Run (Alt,M,R) again. The Macro Run dialog box lists all the packaged macros, along with any macros that you created (or that someone else created for you). Each macro contains a special help macro that describes what the macro does and what you should use it for.

Each macro also contains a summary description that appears in the Description box in the Macro Run dialog box. This description explains the macro's purpose.

Built-in commands

As mentioned earlier in this chapter, Word's built-in commands form the basic structure of Word. The names of all the Word commands are available in the Macro Run, Macro Edit, Macro Assign to Key, and Macro Assign to Menu dialog boxes. These commands are those that are on menus, are assigned to keys, appear as options in dialog boxes, and are mouse actions. You can run, edit, and assign the names of the built-in commands as you do your own macros or Word's packaged macros. In a dialog box, when you select the name that matches a built-in command, Word creates a macro by that name. You cannot edit a built-in command directly. By selecting a name that matches a built-in command, you can run a built-in command that is not assigned to any key or menu. You can change the action associated with the name of a built-in command by creating a macro with the name of a built-in command and adding the instructions you want to it. For example, you can modify the action of the File Print command so that it prints the active document without displaying the File Print dialog box. To do so, you would create a macro named FilePrint to replace the built-in command named FilePrint that normally underlies the File Print menu command.

The Macro Assign to Key and Macro Assign to Menu dialog boxes always show all the macros and built-in commands, so these dialog boxes do not need a Show All option. These two dialog boxes do have Reset All buttons so that you can quickly return all menus and keys to the original setup that comes with the Word program.

Recording Macros: Some Examples

The next few sections contain examples that lead you step by step through recording macros and then running them to see that they perform correctly. These examples give you a base to work from when you learn how to modify macros later in this chapter. The macros you'll record perform the following actions:

- Delete from the insertion point to the end or beginning of the line.

- Move the insertion point forward and backward a sentence at a time, using the keyboard. Also, they delete a sentence.
- Strip extraneous paragraph marks at the ends of lines, leaving a single paragraph mark at the end of each paragraph.
- Indent the first line of the first paragraph after any paragraph that has the style named heading 1.

Some of these example macros are good candidates for being assigned to keys because it's more efficient to position the insertion point and then press keys than it is to choose the macro from a dialog box. For information about how to assign a macro to keys, see "Assigning a Macro to a Key Combination" later in this chapter.

NOTE: *For the following examples, be sure to use a document that has at least a couple of paragraphs of text. If a macro does not correctly perform the action you tried to record, try the steps again, recording the corrected macro over the incorrect one. If you make a mistake while recording a macro, start recording again from the beginning.*

Example 1: Delete to the End of the Line

In this example, you record a macro that you can use to delete text from the insertion point to the end of the line that contains the insertion point. Be sure to use a document that has at least six lines of text.

Position the insertion point anywhere in any line, except at the end of a line. Choose the Macro Record command (Alt,M,C), type a name for the macro (for example, *DelToEndOfLine*), move to the Description box (Alt,D), type *Deletes to end of line*, and then choose OK. "REC" appears in the status bar to indicate that Word's macro recorder is running. Press the Shift+End keys to select from the insertion point to the end of the line, and then press the Delete key to delete the text. Choose the Macro Stop Recorder command (Alt,M,C) to stop recording.

Now, to run the macro, position the insertion point anywhere in any line, except at the end of a line. Choose the Macro Run command (Alt,M,R), select DelToEndOfLine from the list of macro names, and then choose OK.

This macro is a good candidate for assignment to a key combination, which would allow you to position the insertion point and then simply press the key combination to quickly delete to the line's end. For information about how to assign a macro to keys, see "Assigning a Macro to a Key Combination" later in this chapter.

As a variation, record a macro that deletes from the insertion point to the beginning of a line. The steps are the same as those listed above, except that you press the Shift+Home keys instead of Shift+End. And, of course, you would give the macro a name that indicates that it deletes to the beginning of a line (for example, *DelToBegOfLine*).

Example 2: Move to Next or Previous Sentence and Delete a Sentence

Many word processors have key assignments that move the insertion point forward or backward a sentence at a time. These assignments can be combined with selecting so that you can easily delete a sentence. Word does not have that kind of keyboard action, although you can use the mouse to select and then delete a sentence. To be able to use the keyboard to move forward and backward by sentences and to delete sentences, record the following three macros.

Move to the beginning of the next sentence

In a document that has at least six sentences, be sure that the insertion point is somewhere in the sentence that precedes the sentence to which you want to move the insertion point.

Choose the Macro Record command (Alt,M,C) to start recording, type a name for the macro (for example, *NextSentence*), move to the Description box (Alt+D), type *Move to next sentence beginning*, and then choose OK. Next, choose the Edit Search command (Alt,E,S), type a period in the Search For box, choose the Down Direction option (Alt+D), and then choose OK. Edit Search moves the insertion point to the end of the current sentence. To move to the first word of the next sentence, press the Ctrl+right arrow keys. Choose the Macro Stop Recorder command (Alt,M,C) to stop recording.

To run the macro, position the insertion point anywhere in the sentence that precedes the sentence you want to move to, choose the Macro Run command (Alt,M,R), select NextSentence from the list of macro names, and then choose OK.

Move to the beginning of the preceding sentence

In a document that includes six or more sentences, be sure that the insertion point is somewhere in the sentence that follows the sentence to which you want to move the insertion point.

Choose the Macro Record command (Alt,M,C) to start recording, type a name for the macro (for example, *PrevSentence*), move to the Description box (Alt+D), type *Move to begin preceding sentence*, and then choose OK. Then, choose the Edit Search command (Alt,E,S), type a period in the Search For box, choose the Up Direction option (Alt+U), and choose OK. Edit Search moves the insertion point to the end of the preceding sentence. Press the Shift+F4 keys to repeat the search and to move the insertion point back one more sentence. Next, press the key combination (the Ctrl+right arrow keys) to move to the first word of the sentence that's before the sentence in which the insertion point started. To stop recording, choose the Macro Stop Recorder command (Alt,M,C).

To try running the new PrevSentence macro, position the insertion point anywhere in the sentence that follows the sentence you want to move to, choose the Macro Run command (Alt,M,R), select PrevSentence from the list of macro names, and then choose OK.

Delete the sentence that contains the insertion point

Position the insertion point somewhere in the sentence that you want to delete, in a document that has at least six sentences.

Choose the Macro Record command (Alt,M,C) to start recording, type a name for the macro (for example, *DelSentence*), move to the Description box (Alt+D), type *Deletes current sentence*, and then choose OK. Next, choose the Edit Search command (Alt,E,S), type a period in the Search For box, choose the Up Direction option (Alt+U), and then choose OK. Edit Search moves the insertion point to the end of the preceding sentence. To move to the first word of the current sentence, press the Ctrl+right arrow keys. Press the EXTEND key (F8) to turn on the extend selection mode so that when you move the insertion point Word selects from the insertion point to the position to which the insertion point moves. F8 works with the cursor keys and with the Edit Search command. Now, choose Edit Search (Alt,E,S), type a period in the Search For box, choose the Down Direction option (Alt+D), and then choose OK to select the current sentence. Either press the Delete key to delete the selected sentence or press the Shift+Delete keys to delete the sentence and place it on the Clipboard. Choose the Macro Stop Recorder command (Alt,M,C) to stop recording.

To run the macro, position the insertion point anywhere in the sentence that you want to delete, choose the Macro Run command (Alt,M,R), select DelSentence from the list of macro names, and then choose OK.

Example 3: Strip Paragraph Marks

Because much of Word's formatting focuses on paragraphs, having an extraneous paragraph mark at the end of every line of text can cause formatting problems. Plain text files from word processors or text editors typically contain a paragraph mark at the end of every line. Also, when you delete or insert text, a paragraph mark at the end of every line defeats word wrap, which would otherwise reformat the lines within a paragraph as you insert or delete. Deleting these extraneous paragraph marks can be time-consuming because you must select each mark and then delete it. In Word, you can record a macro that will remove the extraneous paragraph mark at the end of each line and the second paragraph mark at the end of each paragraph.

The following procedure builds a macro for a document that has a single paragraph mark at the end of every line and two paragraph marks in a row at the end of every paragraph. This macro works on one paragraph at a time because you might want to keep the paragraph

TIP

Modifying Sentence Macros for Other Punctuation

The preceding Example 2 described how to create a macro that would move to the next or previous sentence and delete a sentence. Not every sentence, however, ends with a period. A question mark or exclamation point, for example, can also end a sentence. Some sentences also appear inside quotation marks. To account for these different types of sentences, you might want to record macros that recognize a question mark, an exclamation point, and quotation marks instead of a period. For questions, type a question mark (?) instead of a period when you use the Edit Search command. For exclamations, type an exclamation point (!). And for quotations, type a quotation mark (") in addition to a period, question mark, or exclamation point.

mark at the end of every line in some paragraphs—for example, in lists and tables. Before you start recording this macro, open or create a document that has at least three paragraphs of text, with a paragraph mark at the end of each line and two paragraph marks at the end of each paragraph. Then, choose the View Preferences command (Alt,V,E), turn on the Paragraph Marks option (Alt+P), and choose OK. Turning on this option makes it easier to see where paragraphs end.

Position the insertion point at the beginning of a paragraph. Then, choose the Macro Record command (Alt,M,C), type a name for the macro (for example, *StripParaMarx*), move to the Description box (Alt+D), type *Strips paragraph marks*, and choose OK. Press the EXTEND key (F8) to turn on the extend selection mode so that you can select a whole paragraph using the keyboard. Even though you can press F8 several times to select a paragraph, you need to select all the lines down to the next pair of paragraph marks because each line is a paragraph. Choose the Edit Search (Alt,E,S) command, type *^p^p* in the Search For box to direct Word to find two consecutive paragraph marks, and then choose OK. The ^p character combination tells Word to search for a paragraph mark. Word selects all the lines from the insertion point to the next pair of paragraph marks.

Next, press the left arrow key to shrink the selection by one character so that the second of the two neighboring paragraph marks is no longer selected. Shrinking the selection keeps the second paragraph mark from being deleted so that you keep a single paragraph mark at the end of the paragraph. You leave the rest of the selection as is, however, so that Word limits the replacements you make in the next step to only the selected text.

Now, choose the Edit Replace command (Alt,E,E), and type *^p* in the Search For box to direct Word to find single paragraph marks within the selection. Press the Tab key to move to the Replace With box, press the spacebar so that Word will replace each paragraph mark with a single space, and press Alt+C to turn off the Confirm Changes option. Turning off this option tells Word to make all changes at once, instead of asking you to approve each one. Choose OK to direct Word to replace with spaces all the single paragraph marks in the selection.

Press the Ctrl+down arrow keys to position the insertion point at the beginning of the next paragraph so that it's in position for stripping extra paragraph marks from the next paragraph if needed. Choose the Macro Stop Recorder command (Alt,M,C) to stop recording.

Now, to run the macro, position the insertion point in the line that you want to begin a paragraph, choose the Macro Run command (Alt,M,R), select StripParaMarx from the list of macro names, and then choose OK.

Example 4: Indent First Lines After Headings

In some documents, the first paragraph that follows each heading is in indented style, with the first line indented, while the rest of the paragraphs are in block style, with all lines flush with the left margin:

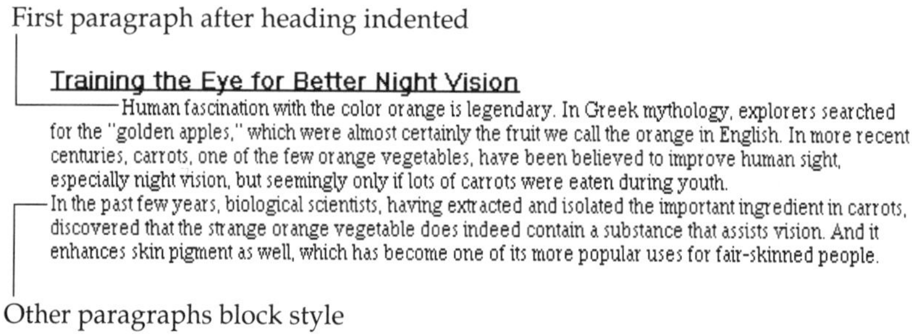

Other documents might have the opposite style, with the first paragraph following a heading in block style and the rest of the paragraphs in indented style:

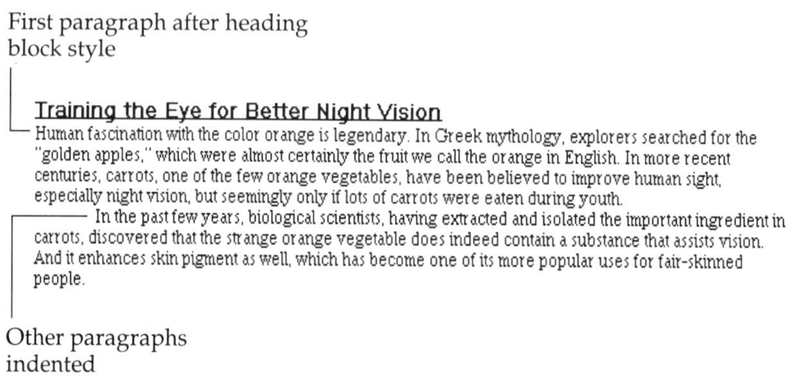

The easiest way to create these formats in Word is to create three styles: one style for the heading, one for the first paragraph following a heading, and another for the rest of the paragraphs. If you create these three styles and then connect them using the Next Style option that's available when you work with styles, you can format a document as you type it. This arrangement is great if you think of it ahead of time and set up the styles you need. But if you do not remember to plan ahead, you must work through the document and apply the appropriate formatting to each paragraph. Such a repetitive, mechanical task cries out for a recorded macro that will format for you.

This example shows you how to record a macro that indents the first line of the first paragraph that follows a heading (in other words, a heading 1 style paragraph). For information about recording macros for headings that have other heading styles and about alternate ways to approach this task, see the "Tip" that follows this example.

Before you start recording this macro, open or create a document that has at least three paragraphs in heading 1 style and three paragraphs in block style following each heading.

Start by positioning the insertion point at the beginning of the document. Choose the Macro Record command (Alt,M,C), type a name for the macro (for example, *FixIndents*), move to the Description box (Alt+D), type *Indents the first paragraph after level 1 headings*, and then choose OK. Choose the Edit Search command (Alt,E,S), type *^yheading 1* in the Search For box, and then choose OK. Word finds and selects the next paragraph that has heading 1 style. Next, press the Ctrl+down arrow keys to position the insertion point at the beginning of the first paragraph that follows the heading. Press the Tab key to indent the first line. Then, choose the Macro Stop Recorder command (Alt,M,C) to stop recording. To try running your new macro, choose the Macro Run command (Alt,M,R), select FixIndents from the list of macro names, and then choose OK.

Because it's unlikely that you'll use the FixIndents macro often, you can use the Macro Run command to run it whenever you need to indent the first paragraph that follows a heading. You can also assign the FixIndents macro to a menu. If you do so, you can choose it for the first paragraph at which you need it and then press the REPEAT key (F4) to indent the paragraph that follows. For information about how to assign this macro to a menu, see "Assigning a Macro to a Menu" later in this chapter.

TIP

Alternative Methods for Paragraphs That Follow Headings

You might want macros that handle the indentation of paragraphs that follow other heading levels in a document. You can also use styles instead of the Tab key to indent the first line. In other cases, you might want the first line of indented paragraphs that follow a heading to be block style (not indented). This tip describes the macros you use in these three situations. For paragraphs to which the heading 2 through heading 9 styles have been applied, you can record macros that search for those styles instead of for heading 1.

Rather than pressing Tab to indent the first line of a paragraph, you can create a style that indents the first line one-half inch, and then record a step that applies that style to the first paragraph following a heading. By taking this approach, you increase your control over changes made by the macro. And you avoid accidentally inserting two tab characters at the beginning of a paragraph.

To create a style that has a one-half-inch indent for the first line, position the insertion point in a paragraph to which Normal style has been applied (or press the Alt+Shift+5 keys [5 on the numeric keypad] to apply Normal style to the current paragraph). Choose the Format Paragraph command (Alt,T,P), move to the First Line box (Alt+N), type *0.5"*, and then choose OK. Press the Ctrl+S keys, type a new style name (for example, *First Indent*), press the Enter key, and then choose Yes (Alt+Y) in the message box that appears. These steps define a new style from the paragraph formatting you just applied. For example, record these steps: Use the Edit Search command (Alt,E,S) to find the heading paragraph. Then, move the insertion point to the paragraph that follows the heading, press Ctrl+S, type the name of the style you created to indent the first line—for example, *First Indent*—and then press Enter.

If you want the first paragraph that follows a heading to be block style while the other paragraphs are indented, record a macro that removes the first-line indentation. If the indentation comes from a tab character, move the insertion point to the beginning of the paragraph and press the Delete key. If the indentation comes from paragraph formatting, you can either apply another style (such as Normal) that formats paragraphs without an indentation or, while you record the macro, include a step that chooses the Format Paragraph command and changes the First Line Indent measurement to zero.

There's More to Macros Than Recording

The macros that you recorded in the preceding examples show that you can record many actions, even some sophisticated procedures. Correcting mistakes in a macro is much easier, however, if you know how to edit the incorrect steps. Moreover, using only recording to create all your macros means you can include in your macros only those actions that you can record, and Word offers much more functionality in the form of BASIC language statements that are not part of Word's commands. For example, if you want a macro to repeat a particular task throughout your document, you have to record each repetition of the steps. The macro will only perform the steps the number of times that you record them. You can, however, record one version of the steps that you need and then edit that macro to add alternative steps. For instance, the "Tip" called "Modifying Sentence Macros for Other Punctuation," earlier in this chapter, discusses recording three macros for various types of sentences. Instead of recording three macros, you can record only one and then edit that original macro.

When you edit a macro, you can tell Word to repeat the macro's steps until the task is complete, no matter how many times the steps need to be performed. You can also add instructions to the macro that tell Word to check whether any more steps remain. The instructions can tell Word to complete the steps if any remain or to stop if the steps are finished. Knowing how to edit a macro allows you to adapt existing macros and to write macros from scratch without recording. The section called "Editing Macros," later in this chapter, describes how to edit macros to customize them to your needs.

Using Macros to Customize Word's Interface

Word gives you the ability to customize many elements in its user interface, including the highly visible menu and keyboard assignments. You can set up different arrangements of menus, commands, and keys for each type of document on which you work. Word lets you build custom interfaces so that, for example, you have a memo processor, a letter processor, a report processor, an article processor, and a legal processor. Each different processor contains only the commands and keys you need, eliminating all others to avoid confusion and clutter.

To customize the interface, you assign macros to key combinations and to menus. The macros you assign can come from any source—your own recording and editing, the macros that come with Word, or macros someone else created for you. You can also remove or reassign existing macro assignments so that you're not stuck with someone else's interface.

You make all macro assignments using the Macro Assign to Key and Macro Assign to Menu commands. Both commands can assign any available macros, including Word's built-in commands. And, when you want the macro to be more convenient to use than it is via the Macro Run command, you can assign a macro to a key combination or a menu or to both. In general, assign the macro to keys when you use the macro frequently and you can readily remember the key combination. Assign the macro to a menu when you use a macro less frequently and need a reminder that the macro exists.

Assigning a Macro to a Key Combination

To assign a macro to a key combination, you select the macro name, press the key combination, and tell Word to make the assignment. You can also remove a macro assignment from a key combination, as well as move a macro assignment to a new key combination. All macros and key assignments can be changed, including Word's packaged macros and the macros you create.

You can assign a single macro to multiple key combinations (but you cannot assign more than one macro to a key combination). Doing so, however, wastes key assignments and creates unnecessary program overhead. Included in program overhead are the lists of key assignments and macro names, which Word must keep in memory while you work with Word. That overhead can waste system memory and slow down program performance.

When you assign a macro to a key, you can choose whether you want the key assignment to work in all documents or only in a certain type of document. Keys that work in all documents have a global assignment. Keys that work only in a specific type of document have a template assignment. In the following example, you practice making a global key assignment. For information about making template assignments, see Chapter 11, "Templates."

To add to, remove, or change keyboard assignments, choose the Macro Assign to Key command. For example, to assign the macro called DelToEndOfLine that you recorded earlier in this chapter to a key combination, first choose the Macro Assign to Key command (Alt,M,K). Select DelToEndOfLine from the Assign Macro Name list. The quickest way to select the name is to press the D key until you select DelToEndOfLine. To tell Word which key combination you want the macro assigned to, press the Ctrl+Shift+L keys. The key combination appears in the Key box. Word displays the following dialog box:

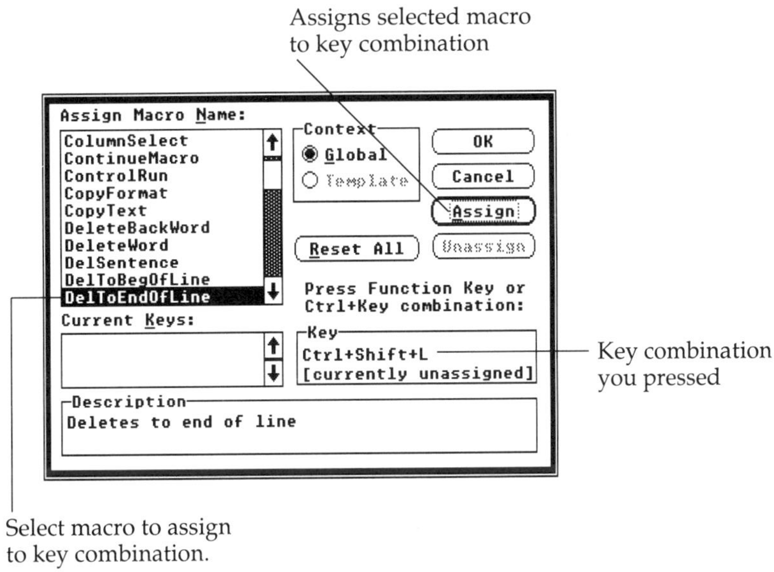

If a macro is already assigned to that key, the name of the macro also appears in the box and you have to choose the Unassign button (Alt+U) before you can make your own assignment. Choose the Assign button (Alt+A), and then choose OK to close the dialog box.

To test the key assignment and the macro, position the insertion point in a line and press the Ctrl+Shift+L keys.

Assigning a Macro to a Menu

Assigning a macro to a menu involves selecting a macro, selecting the menu name, specifying the macro name you want to appear on the menu, and telling Word to make the assignment. In addition, Word lets you remove a macro from a menu or move a macro to a new menu. You can change all macros and menus, including Word's packaged macros and the macros you create.

Word lets you assign a macro to more than one menu, but doing so wastes menu space, creates confusion, and creates unnecessary program overhead, which wastes system memory and can slow down program performance.

When you assign a macro to a menu, you can choose whether you want the menu assignment to be available in all documents (global) or in only a certain type of document (template). Here you practice making a global menu assignment. For information about making template assignments, see Chapter 11, "Templates."

To add, remove, or change menu assignments, choose the Macro Assign to Menu command. For example, to assign the FixIndents macro that you recorded earlier in this chapter, start by choosing Macro Assign to Menu (Alt,M,M). Select FixIndents from the Assign Macro Name list. The quickest way to select the macro name is to press the F key until you select FixIndents. Or, after the first time you press the F key, click the list's scroll bar to jump down to the middle of the macro names that begin with the letter "F," and then select FixIndents.

Next, move to the Menu list (Alt+M) and select Forma&t for the Format menu. The ampersand (&) precedes the letter of the menu name that you press after the Alt key to open the menu. The letter appears with an underline in the menu bar. For the Format menu, the letter is "t." Move to the Menu Text box (Alt+T), and edit the macro name so that it looks the way you want it to appear on the menu. (If you want, you can type a different name.) Note that Word puts a space in front of each capital letter in the macro name. And Word puts the ampersand in front of the first letter. If that letter is not already in use on the Format menu for an Alt key combination, you can leave it as is. If the letter is already in use, delete the ampersand and insert it in front of the letter you want to use. In the standard Full Menu setup, the F key already chooses the Define Styles command. So, in the FixIndents macro name, you can choose any of the following unassigned letters: i, x, n, or e. Because the letter x is rarely used in command names, insert an ampersand in front of "x" so that the command name looks like this: Fi&x Indents. The dialog box that you see is shown on the following page.

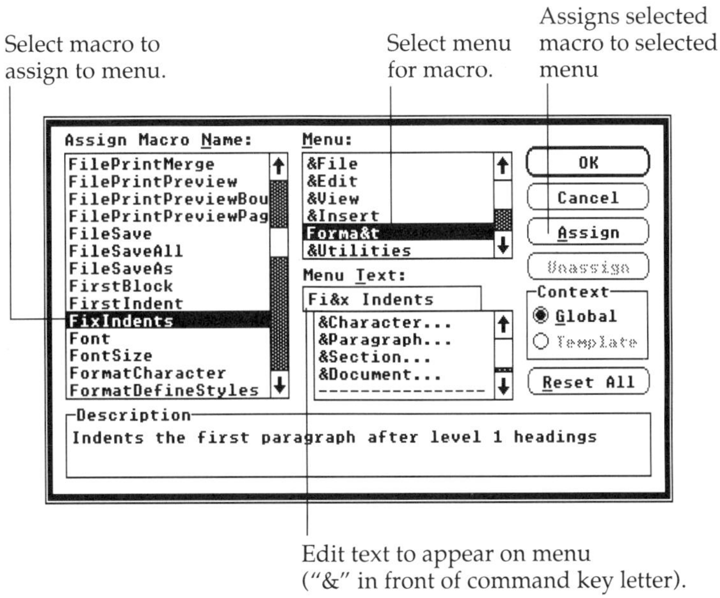

Choose the Assign button (Alt+A). To close the dialog box, choose OK.

To test the menu assignment and the macro, position the insertion point in a heading that has the heading 1 style, open the Format menu (Alt,T), and check the command name and letter assignment. Note that "x" is underlined. To test the macro, choose the Fix Indents command by pressing the X key.

To remove a command from a menu, choose Macro Assign to Menu (Alt,M,M), select the menu name, select the command name, choose the Unassign button (Alt+U), and then choose the Close button (Alt+C). Take care when you remove commands that you do not eliminate the possibility of restoring menus to their default arrangement or to some alternative menu arrangement. For example, if you remove all the Macro commands, you cannot use macros to alter the interface. If you remove all the commands from the Macro menu, you have to delete the file named NORMAL.DOT, which stores your macro assignments, to return the Macro menu to its default arrangement. See Chapter 11, "Templates," for a description of NORMAL.DOT.

Editing Macros

After you create a macro, you might want to change it. For example, the macro might not perform the actions you want it to, it might perform actions incorrectly or incompletely, or you might want to add more actions to the ones it already performs. Perhaps you want to change some of the macros that come with Word. Or you might want to change a macro you got from someone else.

One way to change a macro is by brute force: Replace your original macro by recording a macro that has the same name. But, as was mentioned earlier in this chapter, recording is a limited and time-consuming solution. Learning to edit a macro, however, gives you a direct way to correct any mistakes and to learn to write your own macros from scratch should you decide to go on to Word's more advanced levels.

The gateway you pass through to change macros is the Macro Edit command. Before taking a look at this command, however, you need to get your example macro ready for editing. Suppose that instead of using a tab character to create the first-line indentation, you change the FixIndents macro to use a style that indents the first line of the first paragraph following a level 1 heading. First, record the macro so that it applies a style that indents the first line of a paragraph (as in the second part of the "Tip" that follows Example 4 earlier in this chapter). Assume that you created a style named First Indent that sets a first-line indent of one-half inch. Also assume that you created a style named Large Indent that sets a first-line indent of one inch. The following steps record this variation of the FixIndents macro. Before you begin recording, open or create a document that has at least one paragraph of text with heading 1 style and at least one paragraph following it with a different style (for example, Normal).

Position the insertion point at the beginning of the document. Choose the Macro Record command (Alt,M,C), type a name for the macro (for example, *FixIndents*), and then choose OK. Because you already have a FixIndents macro, choose Yes when Word asks if you want to replace the existing FixIndents macro. (To keep the original macro, choose No and enter a different macro name.) Now, choose the Edit Search command (Alt,E,S), type *^yheading 1* in the Search For box, and choose OK. Word finds and selects the next paragraph that has the heading 1 style. Press the Ctrl+down arrow keys to position the insertion point at the beginning of the paragraph that follows the heading, press the Ctrl+S keys, type the name of the style you created to indent the first line of a paragraph, and then press the Enter key. Then, choose the Macro Stop Recorder command (Alt,M,C).

Your next step is to edit the macro to change the style name that the FixIndents macro applies. You change it from First Indent, which has a one-half-inch first-line indent, to Large Indent, which has a one-inch first-line indent.

Macro Edit

To edit a macro, choose the Macro Edit command (Alt,M,E). You see the Macro Edit dialog box:

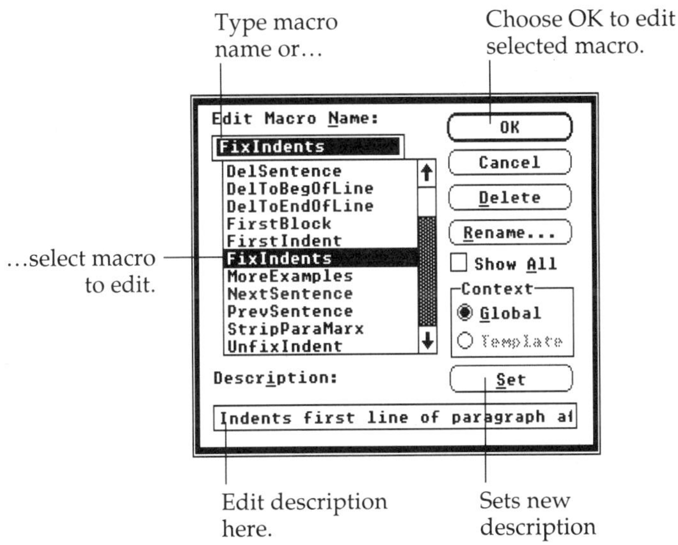

Select FixIndents from the Edit Macro Name list, and then choose OK. The macro editing window displays the macro's contents, as shown on the following page.

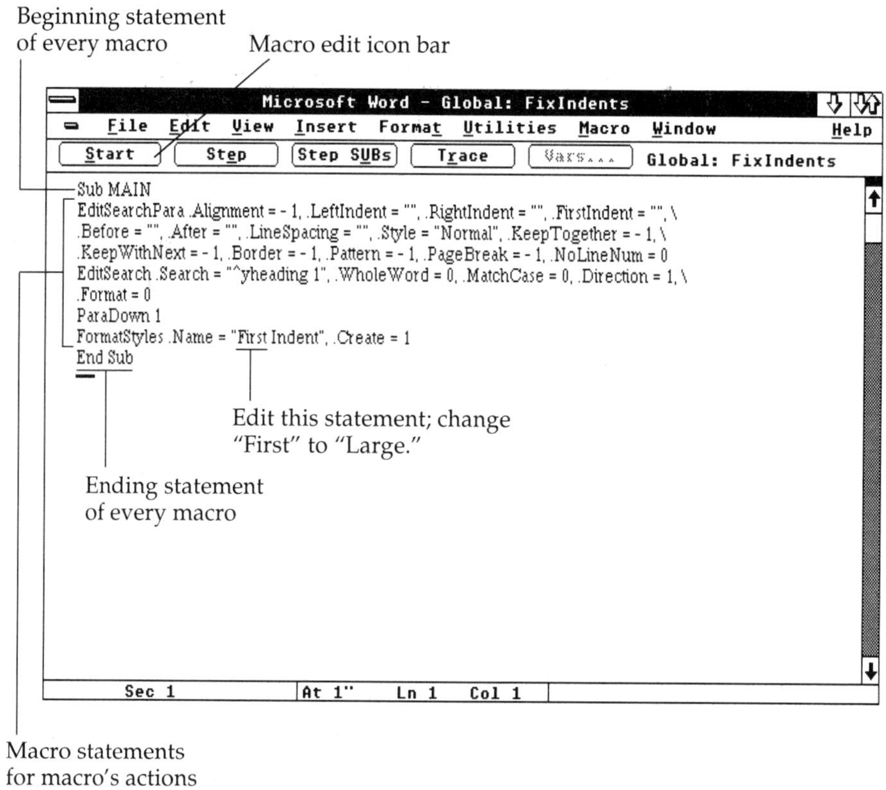

Across the top of the macro editing window is the macro editing icon bar. After you make the changes you want, you use the buttons on this icon bar to run the macro. Four of the buttons run the macro, each in a different way. The fifth button shows you information about the macro. Unless you're writing sophisticated macros or you have a strong programming bent, however, you'll most likely use only the Start button to test your macros.

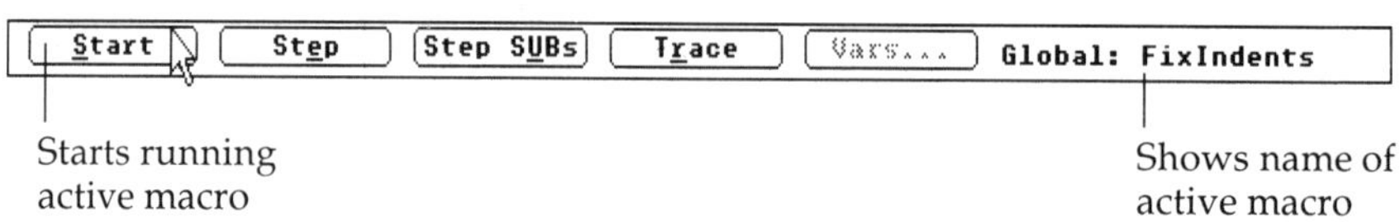

Editing Your FixIndents Macro

Now you're ready to edit your macro by changing the style name that the macro applies. In the line that begins with "FormatStyles," select "First" and the space following it in "First Indent." Delete "First," and type *Large* followed by a space. Then, press the NEXT WINDOW key combination (Ctrl+F6) to switch to the document window. Note that the macro editing icon bar is still visible at the top of the window, where it stays as long as a macro editing window is open.

To test the change you made to the FixIndents macro, choose the Start button (Alt+Shift+S) on the macro editing icon bar. Watch the actions in the document, noting any actions that are incorrect. If you see a problem and you want to stop the macro before it finishes, press the Esc key. When you press Esc the first time, Word suspends the macro and changes the Start button to the Continue button. If you choose Continue, Word continues running the macro from the point at which it suspended. If you press Esc a second time, however, Word stops running the macro altogether and changes Continue back to Start. At this point, you can choose Start again to start running the macro from the beginning.

If Word finds an error in a macro statement, Word stops running the macro and displays a message about the error. The message displayed depends on the type of error; most messages are written in programmer's language. The messages you probably see most often are "Undefined SUB or FUNCTION" and "Syntax Error." "Undefined SUB or FUNCTION" means that a statement contains a command name that either does not exist in Word or is not a macro. "Syntax Error" probably means that one of the statements is not typed correctly. If you need to correct an error, press the NEXT WINDOW key combination (Ctrl+F6) to activate the macro editing window, and edit the macro as necessary. The statement that contains the error appears in red (or highlighted on monochrome monitors); study the statement, and edit it to correct the error. When you finish editing the macro and want to close the macro editing window, choose the Control Close command (Alt,hyphen,C). Choose the File Save All command (Alt,F,E) to save the changes you made to the FixIndents macro.

Summary of Keys for the Macro Editing Icon Bar

To use keys to choose the buttons on the macro editing icon bar, press the Alt+Shift keys along with the underlined letter of the button's name. The following is a summary of the key combinations you press:

For This Button	*Press These Keys*
Start	Alt+Shift+S
Continue	Alt+Shift+C
Step	Alt+Shift+E
Step SUBs	Alt+Shift+U
Trace	Alt+Shift+R
Vars	Alt+Shift+V

More Practice Editing Macros

By editing macros, you can add functions to them that you cannot record. Also, it can be easier to edit an existing macro than to record a complete new macro. To get more of the flavor of how useful it is to edit macros, try the following two examples. The first example shows you how to quickly build variations of a macro using copying, pasting, and other editing commands. The second example shows you how to make a macro repeat its actions throughout a document and stop only after making all its changes.

TIP

Seeing a Macro and a Document at the Same Time

When you edit and test a macro, it's often convenient to see both the macro's steps as Word executes them and their effect on a document. To set up this arrangement, choose the Windows Arrange All command (Alt,W,A), which makes all the open windows into tiles. (Tiles do not overlap.) If you have only one document window and one macro window open at the same time, for example, the two windows share the screen equally. Then, if you choose the Trace button (Alt+Shift+R) or the Step button (Alt+Shift+E) on the macro editing icon bar to test the macro, you see Word highlight each macro statement and, at the same time, you see the effect on the document.

Example 5: Copying and Modifying Existing Macros

You can record nine individual macros that indent the first paragraph that follows each of Word's nine heading styles. But it's faster to create those macros by copying the statements from the existing FixIndents macro and then editing only one statement. Copying is sure to be accurate, helping you to prevent mistakes that might creep into a new recording. To begin this example, choose the Macro Edit command (Alt,M,E), select FixIndents from the Edit Macro Name list, and then choose OK. You see the following macro statements:

Select these statements and copy to Clipboard.

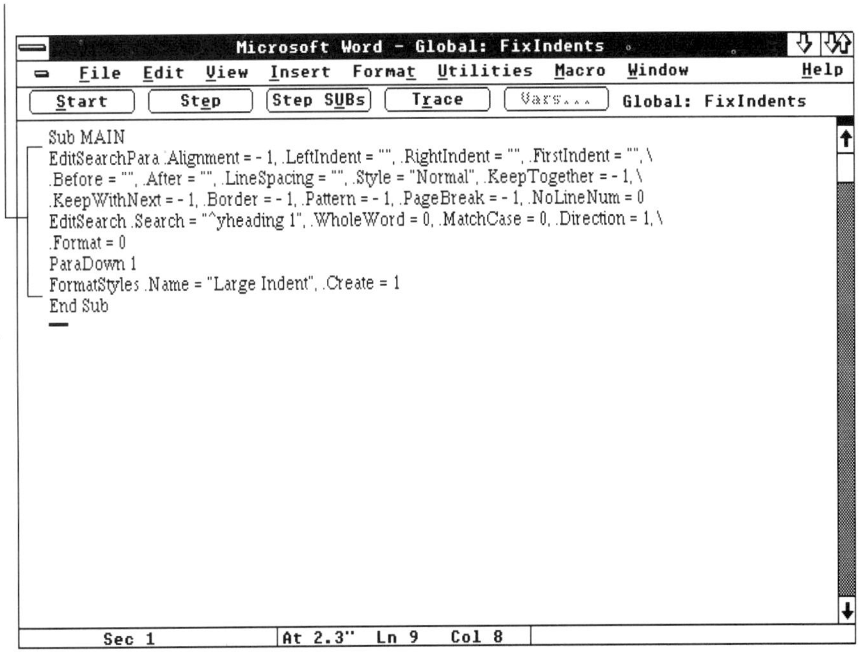

Select all the statements between "Sub MAIN" and "End Sub," press the COPY key combination (Ctrl+Insert) to copy all the statements to the Clipboard, and then choose the Control Close command (Alt,hyphen,C) to close the macro editing window. Next, choose Macro Edit (Alt,M,E), type the name for a new macro (for example, *FixIndents2*), type a description (for example, *Indents first paragraph after*

heading 2), and then choose OK. Press the PASTE key combination (Shift+Insert) to paste the statements from the Clipboard to the macro editing window, between "Sub MAIN" and "End Sub," and then press the Delete key to delete the extra blank line. In the statement that begins with "EditSearch," change *"^yheading 1"* to *"^yheading 2."* Choose the Control Close command (Alt,hyphen,C) to close the macro window, and choose Yes to save the changes to the macro.

For each additional macro variation that you want to create, create another macro, pasting to it the statements from the Clipboard. Be sure to change the heading style number in each macro's EditSearch statement. If you named the variations FixIndents2, FixIndents3, and so on, you might want to rename the original FixIndents macro FixIndents1. That name makes it clearer that the macro fixes the indentation of the paragraphs that follow the heading 1 style. To rename a macro, choose Macro Edit (Alt,M,E) and select FixIndents from the Edit Macro Name list. Choose the Rename button (Alt+R), and type the new name for the macro. Choose OK in the New Macro Name dialog box, and choose Close in the Macro Edit dialog box.

Example 6: Repeating Actions Throughout the Whole Document

Wouldn't it be nice to be able to run a macro one time and have it make all its changes, instead of having to run it over and over again through the entire document? Get macros to do the work while you take a coffee break. Earlier in this chapter, in Example 3, you recorded a macro that stripped the paragraph marks from one paragraph at a time. The following steps show you how to change that macro so that it strips extraneous paragraph marks from all paragraphs in a document, no matter how long the document is.

First, choose the Macro Edit command (Alt,M,E), select the StripParaMarx macro from the Edit Macro Name box, and choose OK. You see the following macro statements:

Insert new statement here… (points to the line after Sub MAIN)

```
Sub MAIN¶
ExtendSelection¶
EditSearch .Search = "^p^p", .WholeWord = 0, .MatchCase = 0, .Direction = 1, .Format = 0¶
CharLeft 1, 1¶
EditReplace .Search = "^p", .Replace = " ", .WholeWord = 0, .MatchCase = 0, .Confirm = 0, \¶
.Format = 0¶
ParaDown 1¶
End Sub¶
```

…and here. (points to the line after ParaDown 1)

Position the insertion point in front of "ExtendSelection," and type the following:

```
While CmpBookmarks("\sel", "\endofdoc") <> 0
```

Press the Enter key. That statement tells Word to check whether the insertion point is at the end of the document.

The parts of the statement do the following:

- CmpBookmarks literally compares the two bookmarks listed.
- "\sel" is a special bookmark name for the current selection or the position of the insertion point.
- "\endofdoc" is a special bookmark name for the end of the document.

If the insertion point is not at the end of the document, Word goes through the instructions listed. If the insertion point is at the end of the document, Word stops running the macro. Next, position the insertion point in front of "End Sub," type *Wend*, and then press Enter. This statement tells Word to go back to the While statement and check again. If the insertion point is at the end of the document, Word goes to the next statement after the Wend statement, which in this case tells Word that the macro finished its work.

Now, go back to the document window (Ctrl+F6) and open or create a document that's several paragraphs long and that has a paragraph mark at the end of every line and two paragraph marks at the end of every paragraph. Choose the Start button (Alt+Shift+S) on the macro editing icon bar to test the changes. If the macro does not perform correctly, check your typing to be sure that the two statements you typed are correct. Make any needed changes to eliminate errors that Word reports. When the macro works correctly, choose the Control Close command (Alt,hyphen,C), and then choose Yes to save the changed macro.

Example 7: Renaming Menus

If you would like to change the names of the menus, you can create a macro from scratch that changes the names. Choose the Macro Edit

TIP

Five Automatic Macros

You can create five automatic startup macros that Word will run at specific times. By using these macros, you can automate those tasks that you must do when you start Word; create, open, or close a document; or quit Word.

You create each automatic macro as you create any macro, but you give it one of the five special names that Word recognizes as automatic macros: AutoExec, AutoNew, AutoOpen, AutoClose, and AutoExit. The "Auto" part of each name indicates that Word runs these macros automatically. The second part of each name tells you when Word runs the macro. AutoExec runs when you start Word. AutoNew runs when you create a new document. AutoOpen runs when you open a document. AutoClose runs when you close a document. And AutoExit runs when you quit Word.

The AutoNew, AutoOpen, and AutoClose macros are available in both the global and template contexts. In the global context, these automatic macros run every time that you create, open, or close a document. In the template context, the macros run when you create a document based on that template or when you open or close a document created from the template. The AutoExec and AutoExit macros are available only in the global context. To prevent AutoExec from running, start Word by typing *winword /m*. Also, when you start Word with any other macro, Word does not run the AutoExec macro. For example, if you type *winword /mfile1*, Word runs the "file1" macro but not AutoExec. To run AutoExec in this case, add it to the command line that you type to start Word. For example, you would type *winword /mfile1 /mAutoExec* to start Word and run the file1 and AutoExec macros.

A slick way to use the AutoNew macro is to have it update all the fields in the new document that are part of a template. For example, you can insert a field that asks you for the name and address for a letter. By having the AutoNew macro update the fields, it can guide you through inserting specific text in a document and can place the text at the field's position. You can also set up an AutoOpen macro to update fields so that the document is up to date each time you work on it or print it.

For information about how to associate macros with document templates, see Chapter 11, "Templates."

command (Alt,M,E), type a name for the macro, move to the Description box (Alt+I), type a short description that tells you which menu names the macro changes, and then choose OK. In the macro editing window, move the insertion point to the blank line between "Sub MAIN" and "End Sub," and then type the statement *RenameMenu*, followed by the number of the menu (see the list below) and a comma, and then the new name for the menu surrounded by quotation marks. Be sure to insert an ampersand (&) in front of the letter you want to use as the keyboard letter for choosing the menu. For example, the following macro changes the name of the File menu to Document, the Format menu to Looks, and the Utilities menu to Tools.

```
Sub MAIN
RenameMenu 0, "&Document"
RenameMenu 4, "&Looks"
RenameMenu 5, "&Tools"
End Sub
```

After you type the macro statements, close the macro window (Ctrl+F4), choose Yes to save the macro, choose the Macro Run command (Alt,M,R), select the name of the macro, and then choose OK. After the macro runs, the menus look as follows:

The menus are numbered as follows:

Number	*Original Menu Title*	*Number*	*Original Menu Title*
0	File	4	Format
1	Edit	5	Utilities
2	View	6	Macro
3	Insert	7	Window

TIP

Changing Menus Automatically When You Start Word

If you want the menus to change automatically when you start Word, name the macro that changes the menus AutoExec. (On the preceding page, see the tip called "Five Automatic Macros.")

Chapter 11

Templates

A template is an existing pattern or model from which you create a new product. A pattern used by a tailor for an article of clothing is a template. At the simplest level, tracing around the end of a soup can to draw a circle is using a template. In Word for Windows, a template is a pattern for a document; every Word document is based on a document template. To emphasize the importance and power of document templates, Microsoft ships a variety of templates in the Word package.

Document templates are tools for creating standard documents. Think of a document template as a special document that sets up the margins, formatting, and standard pieces of text for a new document. The beauty of document templates lies in their ability to pull together the elements and methods of creating, editing, and formatting documents in a way that simplifies word processing. When you work with document templates, you use the same features as when you create and format documents: styles, fields, macros, and glossary entries.

By concentrating the means by which you create documents in a single unit, a template becomes a default setup mechanism for a document. A document template is like a document-generation program: You tell Word to create a new document using a document generator, and the template inserts text and formatting for standard documents that you create routinely.

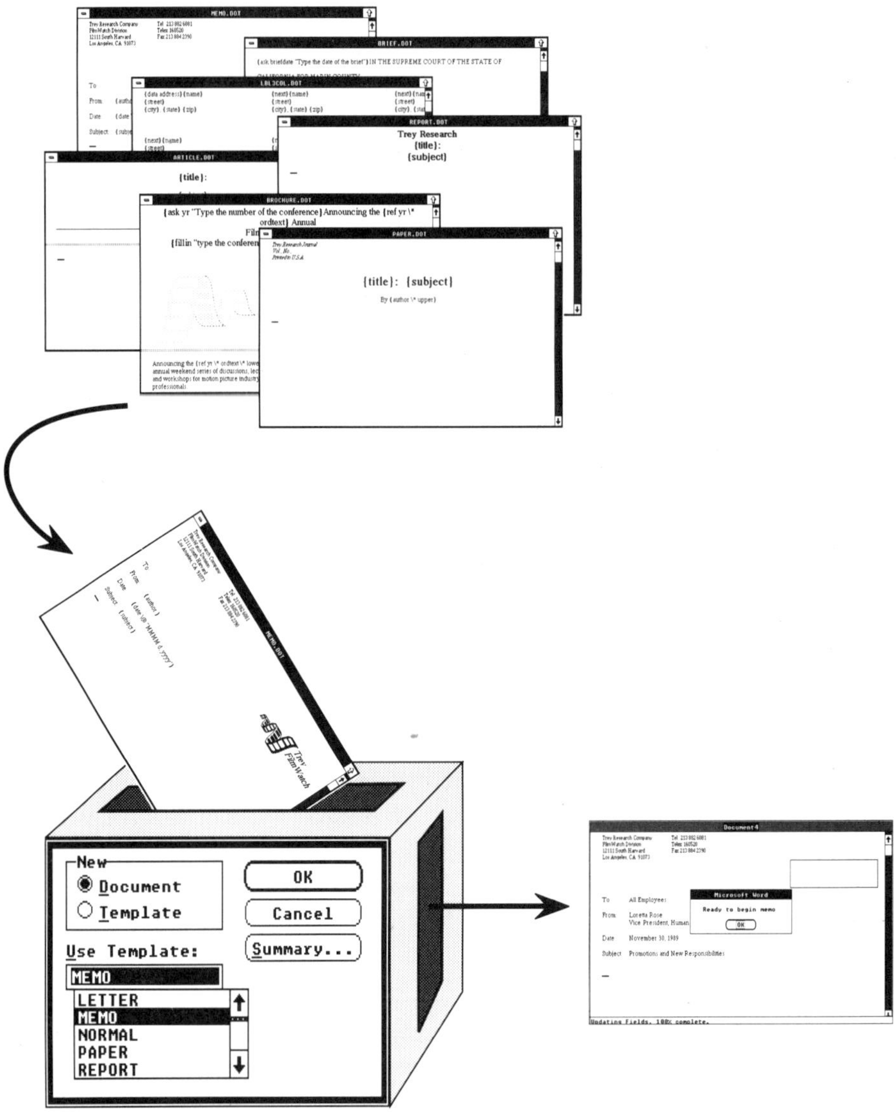

In Chapter 6, "Using Word's Four Pillars: Styles, Fields, Macros, and Templates," the section called "First, It's a Matter of Context" describes context and its importance in processing documents. A context determines the availability of Word's features for working on a particular document. Word contains three contexts—document, template, and global.

- Document context limits text, formatting, and styles to a document itself.
- Template context limits text, styles, glossary entries, macros, menus, and keyboard assignments to a model for a particular type of document.
- Global context provides text, glossary entries, macros, menus, and keyboard assignments for all documents.

Context allows Word to recognize different types of documents and to adjust menus, key assignments, styles, glossary entries, and macros accordingly.

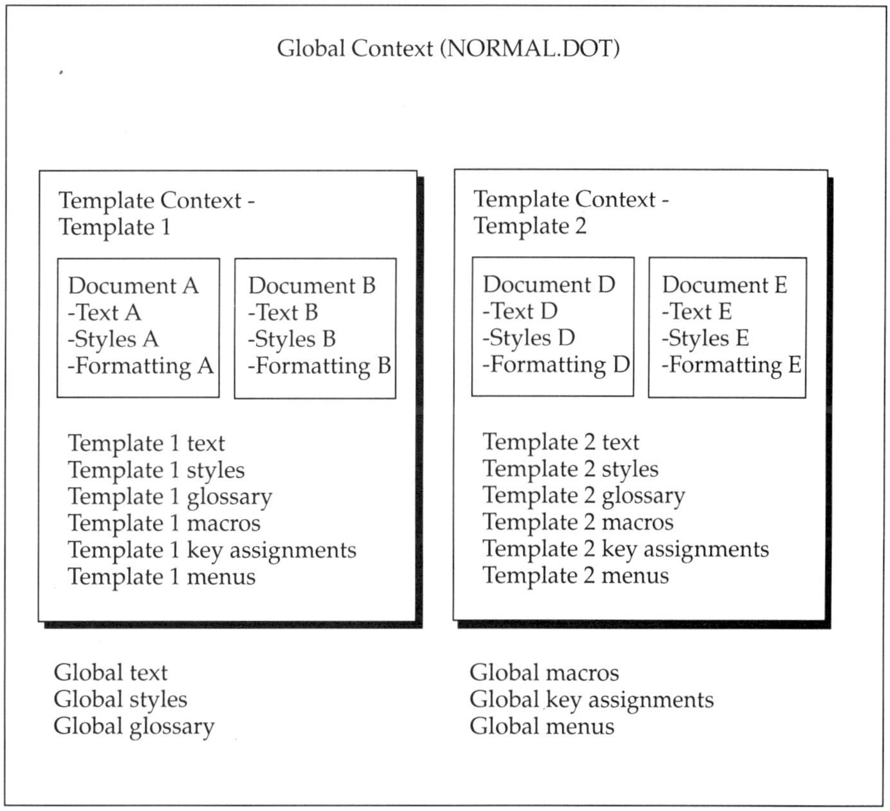

Word bases all documents on document templates. When you create a document, you can select a template as the basis for it. If you do not choose a template, Word bases the new document on a special file named NORMAL.DOT. NORMAL.DOT contains all global glossary entries, all global macros, all global menu and keyboard assignments, default definitions for the automatic styles, and default global contents. Initially, NORMAL.DOT includes no glossary entries. The global macros included are the MoreExamples macro, which comes with Word, and all the built-in commands. The menu and keyboard assignments are those defaults that Microsoft includes in the product for the keyboard and the full menus. NORMAL.DOT at first includes no default global contents.

NORMAL.DOT defines the global context. When you create a style, a glossary entry, or a macro for the global context, Word stores it in NORMAL.DOT. Likewise, any global key or menu assignments you make are stored in NORMAL.DOT.

It's the template context, embodied in document templates other than the default template named NORMAL.DOT, that gives Word its unique ability to adapt to your document task. A template can set up the menus and keys so that Word becomes a special word processor for a particular type of document. A template can also make available a specific list of styles, glossary entries, and macros as well as run any macros you want before you start typing.

Templates can guide you through the process of creating documents, which is especially helpful for documents that you create seldom and for which it is unlikely you will remember what formats are required. A template's true power becomes obvious when you work on a number of documents. For example, suppose you're working on a letter in one window, a memo in another, and a report in a third. As you activate each window in turn, the sets of glossary entries, styles, menu commands, keyboard commands, and macros change according to the template that underlies each document. The document template is what makes each window a document task arena, specially set up for processing the active document.

What Templates Contain

A document template can contain any text and graphics you want to include in the documents you create from that template. These contents can be formatted in any way you like. You can also define styles in a template so that you can easily and uniformly format additional text and graphics that you insert. To make editing, formatting, and other tasks easier, and to customize the menus and keyboards for the specific type of document you're working on, you can create macros in the template. Chapter 10, "Macros," explains how to use macros for customizing and how to assign macros to menus and keys.

Using Text and Graphics in Templates

Templates contain two elements that provide text and graphics for documents: boilerplate and glossary entries.

Boilerplate is text and graphics that are used repeatedly in the same place in every document of a particular type. For example, every memo of a certain type can have, at a specific place on the page, the same "To," "From," "Date," and "Subject" text plus a company logo graphic.

When you create a document from a template, boilerplate contents are inserted and positioned for you; you include boilerplate in the template when the text position does not vary. But boilerplate can also include fields, which are special instructions that generate text or a graphic and insert it in a document. By including fields in your boilerplate, you can have Word alter your document's boilerplate text. For example, you can include a field that inserts the date as part of the boilerplate. The field will insert the date on which you create the document, rather than the date on which you created the template.

Glossary entries are standard pieces of text or graphics that you store with a name so that you can easily reuse the pieces. You create glossary entries for contents that appear often in documents of the same type but that do not necessarily appear in every document or in any particular order or place in every document. See Chapter 12, "Glossaries," for information about creating and using glossary entries in the template context.

Formatting for Document Contents

You can format boilerplate and glossary entries any way you like, and Word transmits that formatting to documents you create from the template. For example, Figure 11-1 on the following page shows a variety of formatting applied to the boilerplate. The formatting can be direct, applied using the formatting commands and keys; or styles, the

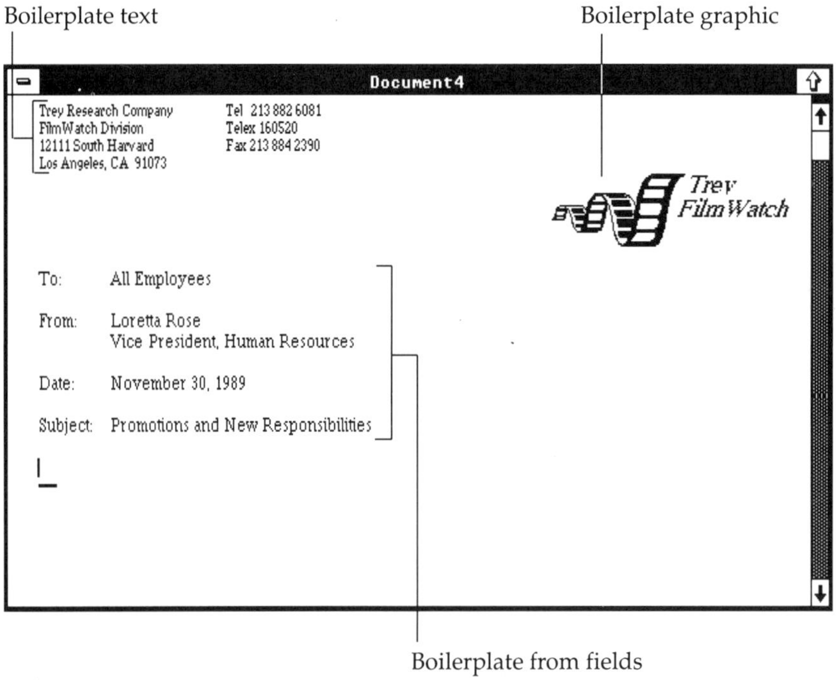

Figure 11-1.
Document created from MEMO.DOT.

named paragraph formatting. For example, if you apply page formatting (for example, margin settings) and section formatting (for example, number of columns) to the template, the documents you create from that template will have the same margin settings, number of columns, and other page and section formatting as does the template.

Command Tools for Document-specific Processing

Word has a programmable interface, which means that you can assign and reassign macros and commands to change Word's menus and keyboard assignments (as shown on the following page), making your document tasks easier.

A macro is a series of keystrokes and commands that you can carry out by choosing the macro's name. You can create macros that perform a series of commands and editing and formatting actions and then assign these macros to menus and keys. Or you can remove macros from menus and keys. Word also lets you change the macro or command that's assigned to a function key or to a key combination and thereby change the action the keys perform. By creating macros and changing menu and key assignments in a template, you create a specialized word processor for the whole group of documents that you create from that template.

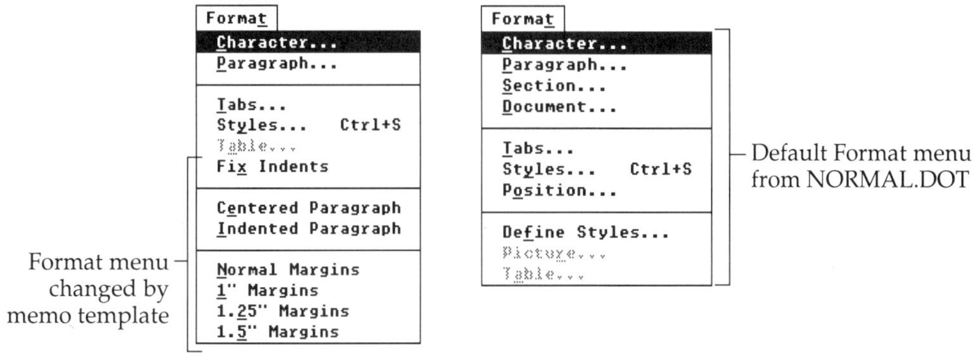

Creating and Modifying Document Templates

As the illustration on the following page shows, Word provides you with three methods for creating document templates:

- Creating or modifying a document and saving it as a template
- Modifying and refining an existing template and saving it as a new template
- Creating a template from scratch

Typically, you use the first method—creating or modifying a document and saving it as a template—when you've created or modified a document and want to save its setup (that is, styles and other formatting, glossary entries, macros, and text and graphics) so that you can use that setup to create more documents.

You use the second method—modifying an existing template and saving it as a new template—when the existing template's setup is similar to what you need, requiring few alterations.

And you use the third method—creating a template from scratch—when you do not have a document or a template that includes

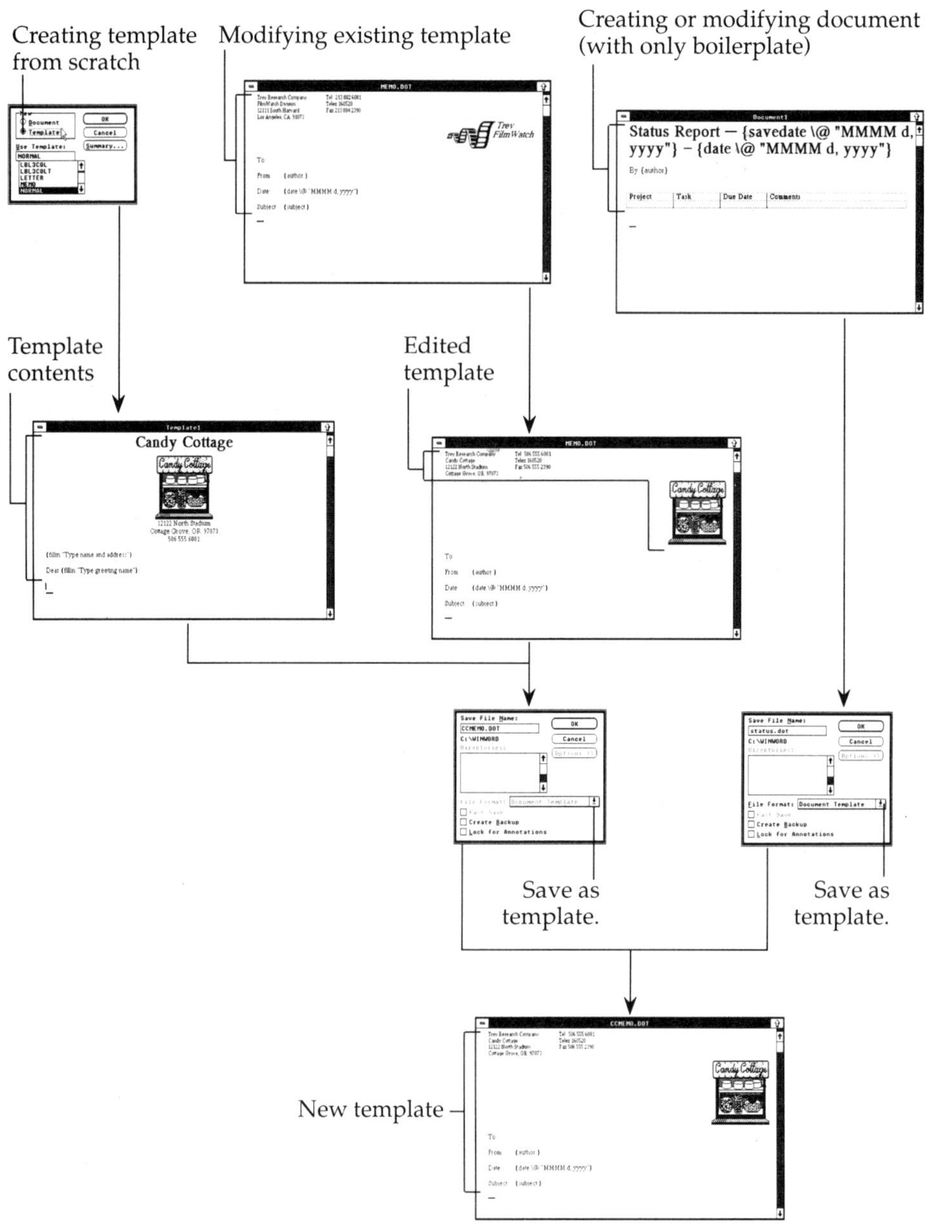

Three methods for creating document templates.

the setup that you want in your template. The following sections explain how to use the first and easiest of these methods. Later in the chapter, the section called "Advanced Technique: Creating a Template from Scratch" explains how to create a template from the ground up.

Creating a Template from a Document

One of the easiest ways to create a template is to create a document and save it as a document template. Before you create a template from a document, be sure that the document provides the formatting and contents placement that you need for creating similar documents. Remember that whatever you include in the template will be included in the documents that you create from it. For example, if you create a memo and then save it as a document template, all the text you type for the memo becomes part of the template and is inserted in all documents you create from that template. Similarly, any styles that you create for the document and any automatic styles that you use become part of the template and are also passed on to documents that you create from that template.

Glossary entries and macros are exceptions. You cannot create a glossary entry or a macro in a document that has no template and then save the glossary entry or macro as part of a template. Only the parts of a document that are in the document context are transferred when you use the File Save As command to save the document as a new template. Thus, glossary entries and macros, whose context is either global or template, cannot be transferred from a document to a template when you use File Save As. You first have to save the document as a template and then create your template glossary entry or macro there. Or you can create a document based on the template, and then in the document create a glossary entry or macro for the template context.

The next section summarizes the steps you take to create a template from a document, with an example for you to follow.

Summary of steps for creating a template from a document

To create a template from a document, you prepare the contents by deleting some contents from the document and then using the File Save

As command to convert the document to a template. Then you define other contents as glossary entries, convert paragraph formatting to styles, and set up macros.

First, open a document that's a good example of the kind of document you would want to create from the template. Then, convert to styles any direct paragraph formatting (that is, formatting you applied using the Format Paragraph command, the ruler, or the paragraph formatting keys). By converting the formatting to styles, you can reuse the formatting without having to retain the text in the document or having to copy the formatting, which is difficult and tedious. To convert paragraph formatting to styles, select the paragraph, press the Ctrl+S keys, type a style name, press the Enter key, and answer Yes when Word asks if you want to define a style using the name you typed. Define styles from all the different paragraph formats your document contains.

Convert to a field any contents of a particular type that are unique to the document in which they appear. For example, each document might include a date, but in every document you want the current date, and not the original document's date. Thus, you should replace the date with a DATE field. To convert contents to a field, analyze the contents to discern what type of information they represent. Look in the list of fields in the Appendix, "Field Types and Their Instructions," for a field that inserts the type of contents you need. Press the INSERT FIELD key combination (Ctrl+F9) to insert a field, and then type the appropriate field type and instructions inside the field. Or choose the Insert Field command (Alt,I,D), select the appropriate items from the lists of field types and instructions, and then choose OK. For more information about fields in general, see Chapter 8, "Fields: Facts and Functions."

Delete any unneeded text and graphics so that the document contains only the text and graphics you will want in the same position in every document. For now, leave in the document the text and graphics you want to store as glossary entries. Choose the File Save As command (Alt,F,A). In the File Save As dialog box, type a name for the template, choose the Options button (Alt+O), and select Document Template in the File Format list box.

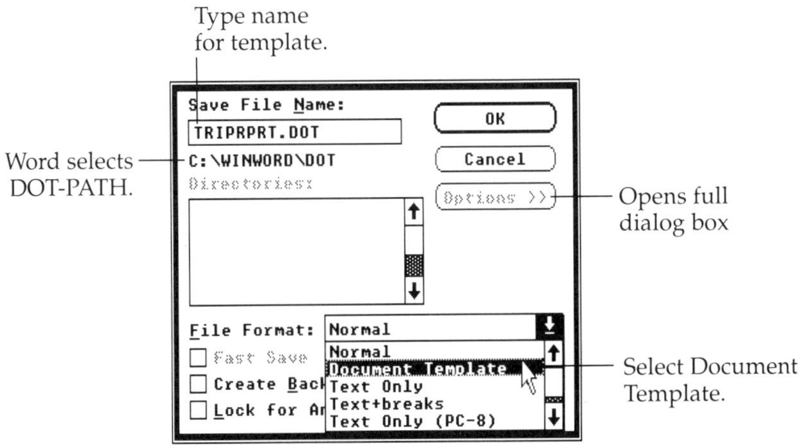

Choose OK. The Edit Summary Info dialog box appears. Fill it in, and then choose OK. You just created the template. Now you're ready to add two final touches to your new template: glossary entries and macros.

Create glossary entries from any text or graphics you might use regularly in the document but not necessarily in every document. Also create glossary entries for the text or graphics that you will use in every document but that you will not necessarily use in the same place in every document. You create glossary entries after you save the document as a template so that the context of the glossary entries will be template rather than global. To create a glossary entry, select the text or graphic you want (insert the text or the graphic if it's not already part of the template). Then, choose the Edit Glossary command (Alt,E,O). In the Edit Glossary dialog box, type a glossary entry name, and then choose the Define button (Alt+D). After you create each glossary entry, delete the text or graphic from the template.

Record macros for any sequence of commands that you used repeatedly when you created, edited, and formatted the document. See Chapter 10, "Macros," for information about recording macros. Be sure to define the macros for the template context.

Choose the File Save All command (Alt,F,E) to save the glossary and macro additions to the template.

Example 1: Creating a template from a document

This example reviews the process of producing a template by creating a document and then saving it as a template. You use the following social business letter in this example:

The Trey Juice Company
111 Apple Orchard Ave.
Bellevue, WA 98008

November 13, 1989

Mr. James Walker
Sales Manager
Sun Fruit, Inc.
223 Ivy St.
Los Angeles, CA 91009

Dear James,

Congratulations on your new position as Sales Manager for Sun Fruit. I'm sorry to see you leave us, and wish you good luck in your new career.

You did an excellent job distributing our products, and have been a pleasure to work with. If you're ever in town, let's have lunch.

Yours,

Hugh Sampson

Figure 11-2.
Social business letter used in this example.

Choose the File New command (Alt,F,N), choose OK in the File New dialog box, and then type and format the letter in Figure 11-2. Apply styles if you want to. In the following steps, you change the document to prepare for saving it as a template.

Choose the View Preferences command (Alt,V,E). In the View Preferences dialog box, turn on the Paragraph Marks option (Alt+P), be sure the Show All option is turned off (if it's on, press Alt+*), and then choose OK. These settings make the paragraph marks visible yet allow the fields you insert to show their result rather than their codes. Choose the Utilities Customize command (Alt,U,U). In the Utilities Customize dialog box, turn on the Typing Replaces Selection option (Alt+R), and then choose OK. This option lets you replace a selection by typing or by using other methods of inserting (such as pasting from the Clipboard), without having to press the Delete key first.

Select all the text in the letter between (but not including) the salutation ("Dear James,") and the complimentary closing ("Yours,"), and press the Enter key to replace the text with a paragraph mark, which holds a place for the letter's text. You delete the text because you do not want to include this text in other letters. Note that even though you delete text to which styles have been applied, Word does not delete the styles. They remain part of the template you're creating.

Replace the date with a DATE field. To do so, select the date (but not the following paragraph mark) and then choose the Insert Field command (Alt,I,D). In the Insert Field dialog box, select Date in the Insert Field Type list box. Move to the Instructions list box (Alt+I), and select MMMM d, yyyy. Choose OK to insert the DATE field in the template, where Word displays it as the current date.

Replace the inside address with a field that prompts you for an inside address. First, select the inside address but not the last paragraph mark after the ZIP code, and then choose Insert Field (Alt,I,D). In the Insert Field dialog box, select Fill-in from the Insert Field Type list box. Next, move to the Field Code text box (Alt+C), press the End key, and then type *"Type the name and address of the recipient"*, being sure to include the quotation marks. Choose OK to replace the inside address with the FILLIN field. When you choose OK in the Insert Field dialog box, Word updates the field, which displays a dialog box that asks for a name and an address. Leave the box blank and choose OK so that when you create a new document from this template, a name will not already be inserted in the document.

Replace the name in the salutation with a field that prompts you for a name. To do so, select "James" in the salutation and choose Insert Field (Alt,I,D). In the Insert Field dialog box, again select Fill-in in the Insert Field Type list box. Move to the Field Code text box (Alt+C), press the End key, and then type *"Type the name for the salutation"*, being sure to include the quotation marks. Choose OK to replace "James" with the FILLIN field. As you did for the inside address, leave the FILLIN dialog box blank.

Replace the author's name with a field that inserts the author's name at the end of the letter. Start by selecting "Hugh Sampson." Then, choose Insert Field (Alt,I,D), and select Author from the Insert Field Type list box. Choose OK to insert the AUTHOR field. When you create a document from this template, the field displays your name for you. If other people use this template, however, you'll want to choose the Edit Summary Info command (Alt,E,I), delete the name in the Author text box, and then choose OK before you insert the AUTHOR field. This change makes the initial result of the AUTHOR field you insert blank. The template now looks as shown on the following page.

TIP

Inserting a Name for Different Authors

You can use a special instruction in the AUTHOR field to prompt you for the author's name and to insert the name you type in both the letter and the document's summary information, which you can view in the Edit Summary Info dialog box. This special instruction makes it convenient to use one template for any number of authors.

The AUTHOR field can also contain a name as an additional instruction. The basic field codes look like the following:

```
{author}
```

The result of the above field is the author's name as entered in the Edit Summary Info dialog box. If you type a name, you change the field's result and the name in the Edit Summary Info dialog box. For example, take a look at the following field:

```
{author "Rita Rose"}
```

Inserts name typed here

Rita Rose is its result, and the Author box in the Edit Summary Info dialog box changes to Rita Rose.

Now, to make the AUTHOR field prompt for the new name, replace the name in the AUTHOR field with a FILLIN field, as follows:

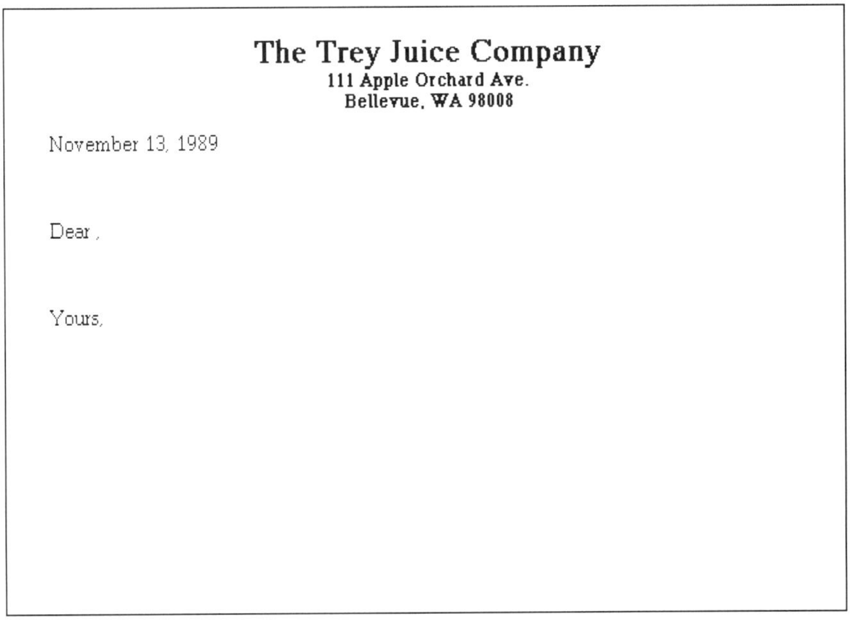
The Trey Juice Company
111 Apple Orchard Ave.
Bellevue, WA 98008

November 13, 1989

Dear ,

Yours,

```
{author {fillin "Type the author's name"}}
```

Prompts for author's name

Each time you create a document from the template, the FILLIN field inside the AUTHOR field prompts you for the name of the author. After you type a name, both the result of the AUTHOR field and the name in the document's summary information as shown in the Edit Summary Info dialog box are the name you type.

If you are sometimes an author, you can add one more instruction to the AUTHOR field to tell it to propose your name as the default author name. This additional instruction is \d:

```
{author {fillin "Type the author's name" \d {author}}}
```

Proposes your name
in response to prompt

With the \d instruction in place, the FILLIN field uses the current name for the author shown in the Edit Summary Info dialog box. If someone else is the usual author, you can substitute that person's name for the AUTHOR field that follows the \d instruction:

```
{author {fillin "Type the author's name" \d {author "Rita Rose"}}}
```

Proposes this name
in response to prompt

Now, before recording macros or creating glossary entries, you need to save the modified document as a document template. Choose the File Save As command (Alt,F,A). In the File Save As dialog box, type a name for the template (such as *BUSFREND*), choose the Options button (Alt+O), select Document Template from the File Format list, and then choose OK. If the Edit Summary Info dialog box appears, fill in or delete information as appropriate, and then choose OK to create a document template.

You can create a special macro to have Word update the fields for you. First, move the insertion point to the beginning of the document. Then, choose the Macro Record command (Alt,M,C). In the Macro Record dialog box, type *AutoNew* in the Record Macro Name text box, select the Template option for Context (Alt+T), and then choose OK. Select the whole document by pressing Ctrl+5 (5 on the numeric keypad). Then, press the UPDATE FIELD key (F9). Do not change the dialog boxes that appear; only press the Enter key when they appear. When Word finishes updating fields, move the insertion point to the empty paragraph between the salutation and the closing, and then choose the Macro Stop Recorder command (Alt,M,C). Now when you create a document from this template, Word updates the fields for you.

Choose the File Save command (Alt,F,S). The template is now ready to use. To create a document from this template, choose the File New command (Alt,F,N). In the File New dialog box, select the name of the template you just created from the Use Template list (Alt+U), and then choose OK. You see the document highlighted, and then you see in succession dialog boxes that prompt you for the inside address and the salutation name. After you fill in these dialog boxes and press the Enter key for each, you see the date, inside address, complimentary closing, and author's name in place. Now, you simply type the letter.

Creating a Template by Modifying Another Template

After you've worked with Word for a while, you might have created several document templates. And you might at some point need a template that's similar to an existing one. You can create a new document template by changing an existing template and then saving it with a new name.

Microsoft has included a number of document templates in your Word for Windows product package. (See Figure 11-3 for a list of template types and file names.) The *Microsoft Word for Windows Sampler* that's also included in your package describes some of these templates. The rest of the templates are documented by help macros that are in the templates themselves. Word provides useful templates for many different types of documents, but these templates probably will not suit your needs exactly, and you'll probably want to change them to suit your specific tasks. These changes can be as simple as changing the company name in a logo or letter or as complex as altering the menus or modifying the way a macro functions. In some cases, you'll want to create a new template based on an existing template and keep the original. In other cases, you'll refine an existing template without keeping its original version.

Template File Name	Purpose of Template
ARTICLE.DOT	Magazine articles
BASIC.DOT	Executive word processor
BRIEF.DOT	Legal briefs
BROCHDAT.DOT	Supports BROCHURE.DOT
BROCHMRG.DOT	Supports BROCHURE.DOT
BROCHURE.DOT	Conference brochure
CONTRACT.DOT	Legal contract—license agreement
DATADOC.DOT	Data document for FRMLTR.DOT
ENVELOPE.DOT	Print envelopes
FRMLTR.DOT	Form letter
LBL15COT.DOT	1.5-inch mailing labels in a continuous strip
LBL1COLT.DOT	One-column mailing labels in a continuous strip
LBL2COL.DOT	Two-column mailing labels on a sheet
LBL2COLT.DOT	Two-column mailing labels in a continuous strip
LBL3COL.DOT	Three-column mailing labels on a sheet
LBL3COLT.DOT	Three-column mailing labels in a continuous strip
LETTER.DOT	Letter
MEMO.DOT	Memorandum
PAPER.DOT	Academic, research, or scientific paper
PCWORD.DOT	Converts PC Word glossaries
REPORT.DOT	Business report

Figure 11-3.
List of shipped templates.

You can choose from a variety of methods to modify templates; this can simplify the process and permit you to take advantage of modifications you've already made to a document on which you based your template. For example, you can modify a template by opening a document that's based on the template and making changes through that document. Or you can modify a template directly by opening it as you would a document. You'll probably modify a template through a document when you discover, as you create or edit a document, that some modifications would make creating future documents easier. And you'll probably modify a template directly if any of the following happen:

- You think of a change when a document that's based on the template is not open.
- You want to add, change, or delete a field from a template.
- You want to change the boilerplate contents.

The following sections explain how to modify a template either through a document or directly.

Modifying a template through a document

To modify a template through a document, you usually choose the Template Context button in a dialog box. The Template Context button adds the settings and results in the dialog box to the document's template, which also makes the settings and results available for your use in the document. The commands that have Template Context buttons in their dialog boxes are Edit Glossary, Macro Record, Macro Edit, Macro Assign to Key, and Macro Assign to Menu. The Format Document dialog box contains a Set Default button, which acts like a Template Context button. In the Format Define Styles dialog box, the Template Context button is labeled "Add to Template."

Styles. When you use the Format Define Styles command (Alt,T,F) to create or modify a style, turn on the Add to Template option (Alt+A) in the Format Define Styles dialog box.

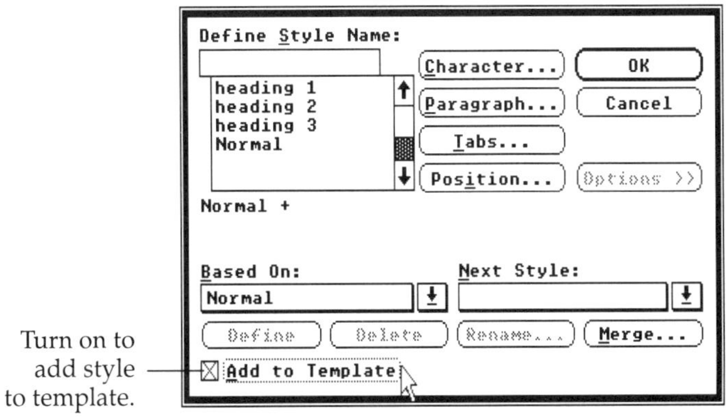

Figure 11-4.
Format Define Styles dialog box.

This method works well for individual styles. To add all the styles in a document to its template, choose Format Define Styles (Alt,T,F). In the Format Define Styles dialog box, choose the Options button (Alt+O) to display the full dialog box, and then choose the Merge button (Alt+M). Then, choose the To Template button (Alt+T) in the Merge Styles dialog box.

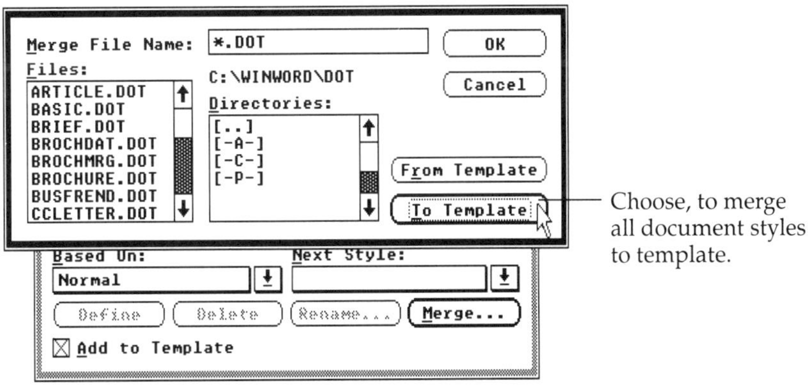

Figure 11-5.
Merge Styles dialog box.

Page formatting. As shown in Figure 11-6 on the following page, the Format Document dialog box contains a Set Default button. When you choose this button (Alt+F), Word applies all the settings in the Format Document dialog box to the document's template.

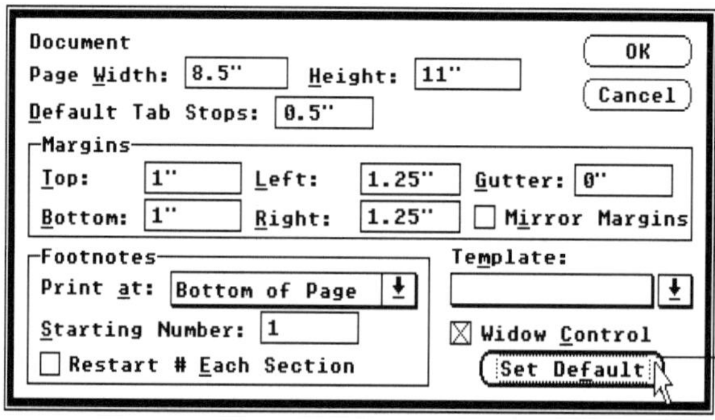

Figure 11-6.
Format Document dialog box.

Glossary entries. In the Edit Glossary dialog box, shown in Figure 11-7, choose the Template Context option (Alt+T) when you define a new glossary entry. To change a global context glossary entry to template context, insert the contents in the document, delete the existing glossary entry, and then define the glossary entry again, this time using the template context.

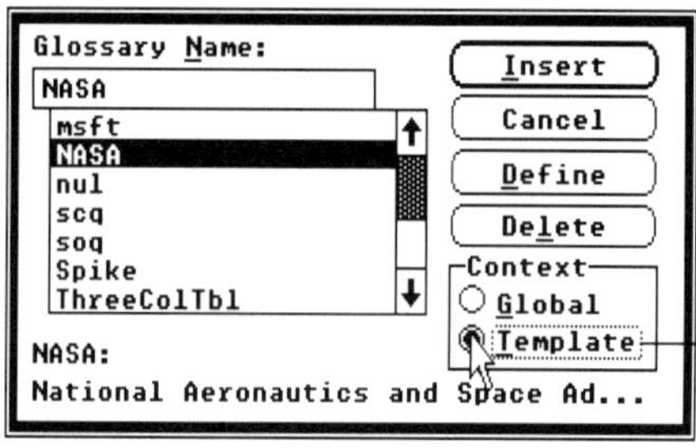

Figure 11-7.
Edit Glossary dialog box.

Macros, key assignments, and menu assignments. The dialog boxes for the Macro Record, Macro Edit, Macro Assign to Key, and Macro Assign to Menu commands contain a Template Context option, as shown in Figure 11-8 on the following page. Choose this option to make the macro or the assignment part of the document template. Save the changes to the template by choosing the File Save All command (Alt,F,E).

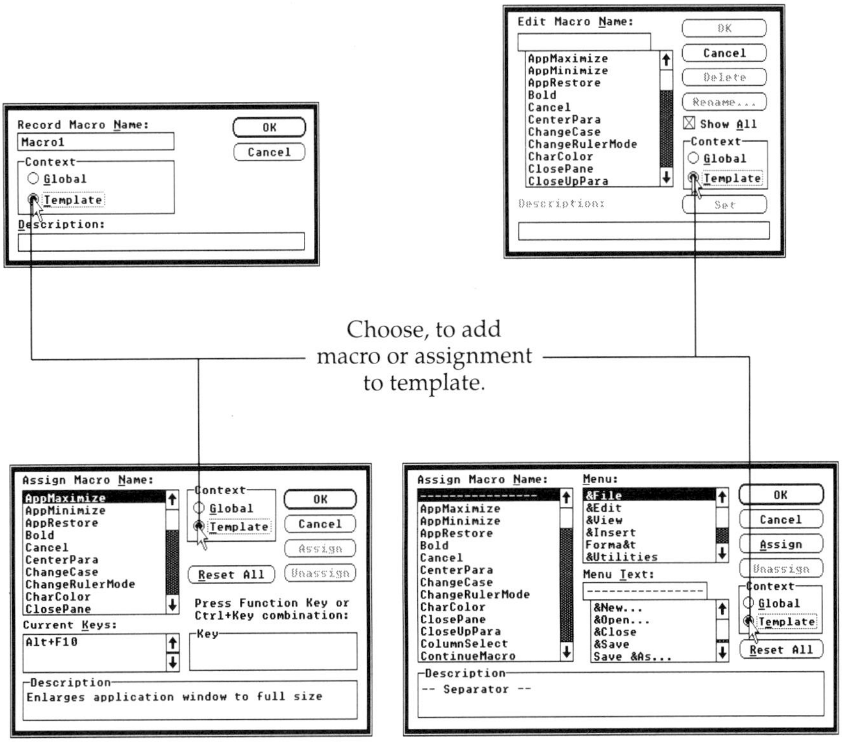

Figure 11-8.
Macro Record, Macro Edit, Macro Assign to Key, and Macro Assign to Menu dialog boxes contain Template Context options.

Modifying a template directly

When you modify a template directly, you can change its contents, formatting and styles, and menus and key assignments. You can also add and delete glossary entries and macros. As you modify a template, be sure to choose the Template Context option in the dialog boxes. This requirement does not apply to styles because styles are in either document or template context; while you work in a template, the two contexts are the same.

Styles. When you define or modify a style for a template by using the Format Define Styles command, you use the same methods you use to define or modify styles for a document. You do not need to turn on the Add to Template option. Figure 11-4 shows the Format Define Styles dialog box.

Page formatting. To set up margins and other page format elements that are available in the Format Document dialog box, you use the same methods you use to set page formatting in a document. You do not use the Set Default button because it is connected to NORMAL.DOT when you work on a template. NORMAL.DOT stores the global context page formatting. See Figure 11-6 for an illustration of the Format Document dialog box.

Glossary entries. When you create glossary entries, define them for the template context. Doing so limits the availability of the glossary entries to documents that are based on the template for which the glossary entries are defined. Within the documents based on the template, you will notice no difference between glossary entries that are in template context and those that are in global context. Figure 11-7 shows the Edit Glossary dialog box.

After you define a glossary entry for a particular context, you cannot move it directly to another context. Within a particular document, not being able to change a glossary entry's context does not matter because the glossary entry is available in that document no matter which context the entry is defined for. If you want to change the context, however, choose the Edit Glossary command (Alt,E,O). In the Edit Glossary dialog box, select the glossary entry, and then choose the Insert button (Alt+I) to insert the contents of the glossary entry in the document. Select the contents you just inserted, choose Edit Glossary (Alt,E,O) again, select the existing glossary entry, and then choose the Delete button (Alt+D) to delete it. Now, type the glossary entry name again, select the new context, and then choose the Define button (Alt+D) to define a new glossary entry for a different context. See Chapter 12, "Glossaries," for more information about working with glossary entries.

Macros. When you create new macros, assign them to the template context. After you create a macro, you can change its context to global by choosing the Macro Edit command (Alt,M,E), selecting the macro name from the list, choosing the Global Context button (Alt+G), and then choosing OK. You can add, remove, move, or rename menu commands and key assignments for the template context.

For menu commands, choose the Macro Assign to Menu command (Alt,M,M). In the Macro Assign to Menu dialog box, select the macro, select the menu, type a command name, choose the Template Context option (Alt+E), and then choose OK. For key assignments, choose the Macro Assign to Key command (Alt,M,K). In the Macro Assign to Key dialog box, select a macro, press the key combination you want (if the key combination is currently assigned, choose the Unassign button [Alt+U]), choose the Template Context option (Alt+T), and then choose OK. See Figure 11-8 for illustrations of the dialog boxes for the various Macro menu commands.

Example 2: Modifying the MEMO template

Using the MEMO.DOT template that came in your Word package, you can look at the ways in which you can modify a document template. The following illustrates what a memo based on that template might look like:

Trey Research Company
FilmWatch Division
12111 South Harvard
Los Angeles, CA 91073

Tel 213 882 6081
Telex 160520
Fax 213 884 2390

Trey FilmWatch

To: Acquisitions and Marketing

From: Rita Rose
Director of Acquisitions

Date: October 1, 1989

Subject: Spring Releases

At our semi-annual meeting we'll establish the list of films to be released in the next six months. The meeting will be held promptly at 11 A.M. on Wednesday, November 15, at the Deep Woods Off-site Conference Center.

Attached is a list of proposed releases, including a synopsis of each. Please be prepared to discuss and vote to release, postpone, or cancel each title.

To fit the template to your needs, change the company name, address, telephone, telex, and fax numbers. This example also shows you how to align the banner paragraphs ("To," "From," "Date," and

"Subject") along the center line, add a "Cc" line to the banner, record a macro that inserts a "Cc" line and prompts you for the recipients' names, and assign the macro to the Insert menu.

Choose the File Open command (Alt,F,O). In the File Open dialog box, press the End key, press the Backspace key, type a *T* so that the Open File Name box shows *.DOT, and then press the Enter key. Move to the Files list (Alt+F), select MEMO.DOT, and then choose OK. If Word cannot find any templates, type the pathname and the template name, *MEMO.DOT*. Choose OK to open the document template. The following shows what you see when the View Field Codes command is turned on (Alt,V,C) and the Show All option is turned on in the View Preferences dialog box (Alt,V,E,Alt+*):

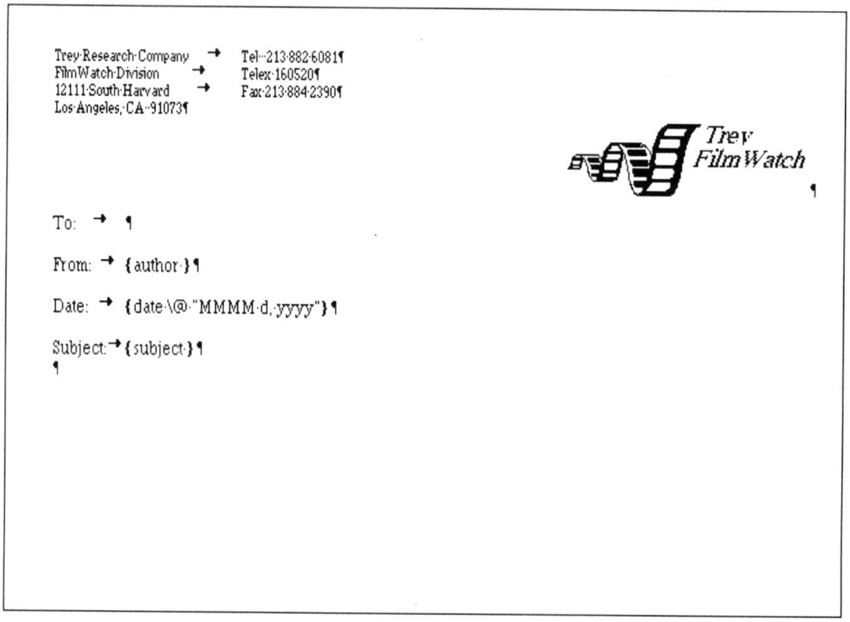

Trey·Research·Company → Tel··213·882·6081¶
FilmWatch·Division → Telex·160520¶
12111·South·Harvard → Fax·213·884·2390¶
Los·Angeles,·CA··91073¶

¶

To: → ¶

From: → {author·}¶

Date: → {date·\@·"MMMM·d,·yyyy"}¶

Subject:→{subject·}¶
¶

Start by replacing the company name, address, and numbers with your company's name, address, and numbers. Choose the Utilities Customize command (Alt,U,U). In the Utilities Customize dialog box, turn on the Typing Replaces Selection option (Alt+R), and then choose OK. Select "Trey Research Company," but do not select the tab character after it. Type your company's name. Then, in turn, select each line of the address (but not the tab character) and type over it with a line of your company's address. Also, select in turn the telephone, telex, and fax numbers (but not the paragraph marks) and type yours in place of those in the document template. Delete numbers you do not have. You just modified some of the template boilerplate text.

Next, change the format of the banner paragraphs and then convert the new format to a style. Select all the banner paragraphs ("To," "From," "Date," and "Subject"). Press the Ctrl+N keys six times to move the paragraphs to the middle of the page while maintaining the hanging indent. Next, to define a style from this new format, press the Ctrl+S keys, type *Banner* as the style name, and then press the Enter key. When a dialog box appears to ask if you want to redefine the Banner style based on the selection, choose Yes. You have now modified a template style. The template looks like the following:

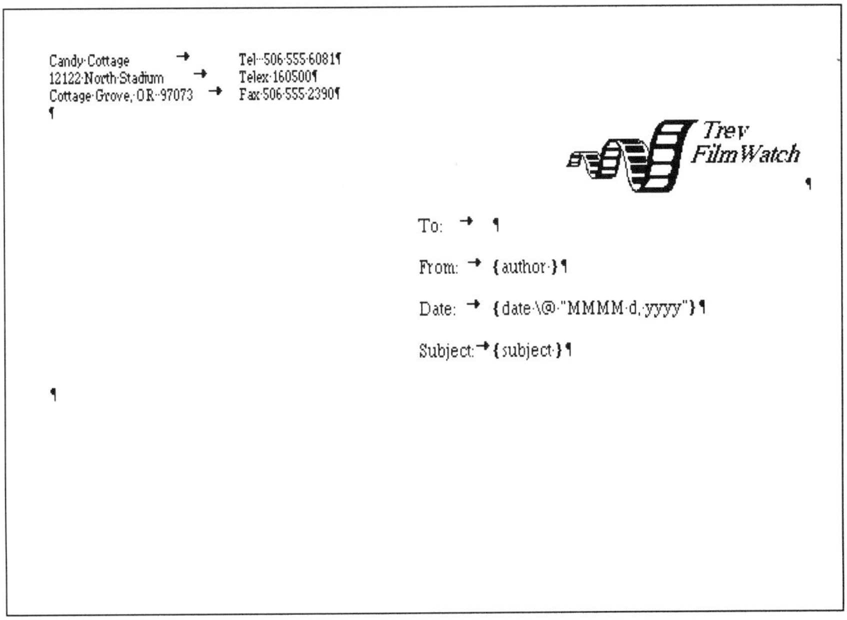
Candy Cottage → Tel 506 555 6081¶
12122 North Stadium → Telex 160500¶
Cottage Grove, OR 97073 → Fax 506 555 2390¶
¶

Trey FilmWatch
¶

To: → ¶

From: → {author }¶

Date: → {date \@ "MMMM d, yyyy"}¶

Subject: → {subject }¶

¶

Now, insert a "Cc" line immediately below the "Subject" line. Move the insertion point to the end of the "Subject" line, and press the Enter key to start a new paragraph. Type *Cc:* and press the Tab key. To add a field that asks for the "Cc" list names, press the INSERT FIELD key combination (Ctrl+F9), and type *fillin "Type the names for the Cc line."* The template now looks like the one shown on the following page.

Candy·Cottage → Tel··506·555·6081¶
12122·North·Stadium → Telex·160500¶
Cottage·Grove,·OR··97073 → Fax·506·555·2390¶
¶

Trey FilmWatch
¶

To: → ¶

From: → {author·}¶

Date: → {date·\@·"MMMM·d,·yyyy"}¶

Subject:→{subject·}¶

Cc: → {fillin·"Type·the·names·for·the·Cc·line."}¶

¶

You have to remember to update the FILLIN field for the "Cc" line yourself. Note that you might want to change or delete the Trey Film Watch graphic. Copy the graphic to Windows Paint or another graphics program to modify the graphic, and then paste the modified graphic over the existing one, insert a different graphic, or select and delete the graphic.

The template now contains a "Cc" line that will be part of every document that's created from this template. Leave the line as is if you want the "Cc" line to be part of the boilerplate text. If you want a "Cc" line to appear only when you send courtesy copies, however, delete the "Cc" line you inserted and create a macro that inserts a "Cc" line. You can then add the macro to a menu so that you can easily insert a "Cc" line when you need one.

NOTE: *The MEMO.DOT document template contains on the Insert menu a Copy List command that inserts a "Cc" line at the insertion point. The macro you create in this example inserts the "Cc" line below the Subject line and formats the "Cc" line in the same way as the other lines in the memo's banner.*

Now, record a macro that inserts a "Cc" line below the Subject line, formats the line the same as the other banner lines, and then prompts you for the recipients' names. First, choose the Macro Record command (Alt,M,C) to start recording. In the Macro Record dialog box, type a macro name (for example, *InsertCcLine*), choose the Template option (Alt+T) for Context, and type a description. The dialog box looks like the following:

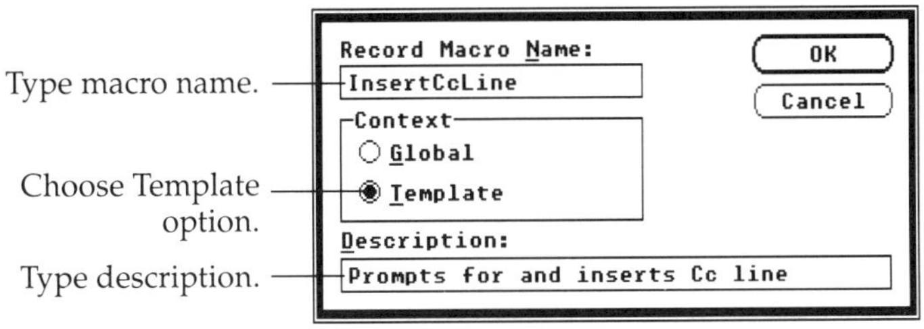

Choose OK to start recording. Press the Ctrl+End keys to move the insertion point to the end of the document. Press the PREVIOUS FIELD key combination (Shift+F11 or Alt+Shift+F1). The SUBJECT field following "Subject" is selected. (This step assumes that you have no fields following the "Subject" line in the template or in a document created from the template.) Press the End key, and then press the Enter key to start a new paragraph, type *Cc:*, and press the Tab key. Press the INSERT FIELD key combination (Ctrl+F9) to insert a field, and then type *fillin "Type the names for the Cc line."* Press the UPDATE FIELD key (F9). In the FILLIN field dialog box that appears, press OK without typing anything; the default response will be blank, avoiding confusing users when they see this dialog box. When Word finishes updating the field, press the Ctrl+End keys again to position the insertion point at the end of the document, ready to insert more memo contents. Choose the Macro Stop Recorder command (Alt,M,C). You just added a macro to the document template.

To add to the Insert menu the macro you just created, choose the Macro Assign to Menu command (Alt,M,M). In the Macro Assign to Menu dialog box, choose the Template Context option (Alt+E). Select your InsertCcLine macro, and then select the Insert menu. Either leave the proposed name as is (it's taken from the macro name) or type a new name, being sure to insert an ampersand (&) in front of the letter you want as the command letter; that letter appears underlined in the menu. Also, if you want the menu text to consist of more than one word, capitalize the first letter of each word. Word inserts a space in front of each capital letter in the name. Thus, InsertCcLine appears on a menu as "Insert Cc Line." Choose the Assign button (Alt+A). The dialog box now looks as follows:

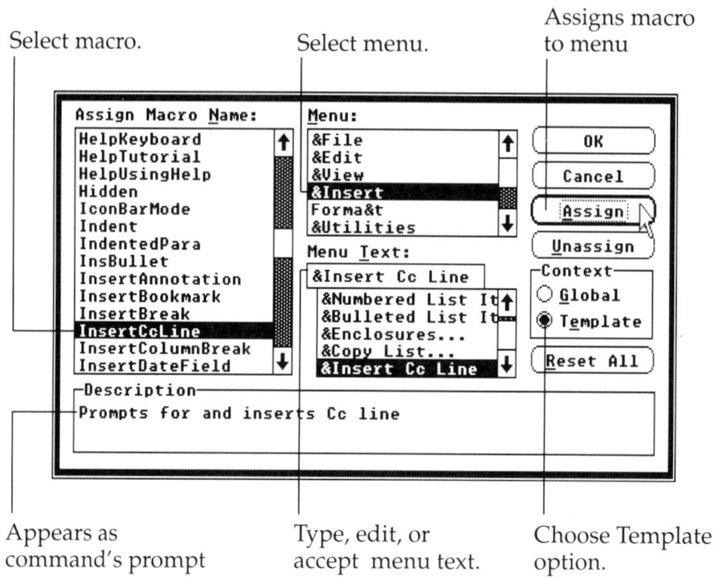

Choose OK or Close (Esc) to close the dialog box. You have just added an Insert Cc Line command to the Insert menu; open the menu to see it:

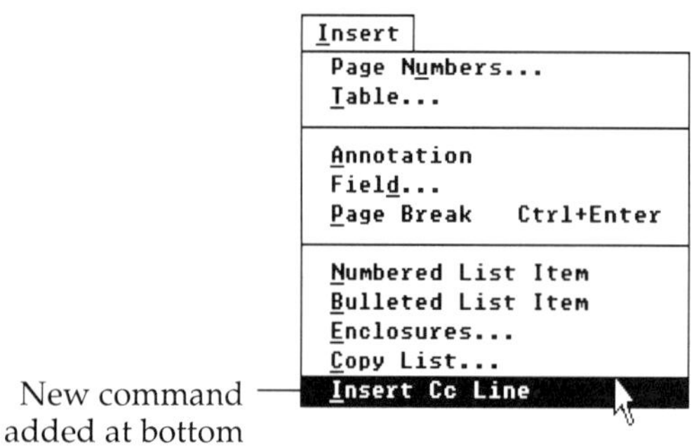

You might want to delete the "Cc" line from the template before you save it. Again, leave the line if you want the "Cc" line to be part of the boilerplate text. But if you want a "Cc" line to appear only when you want to send courtesy copies, remove it before saving the template.

To save the template, which includes your new macro and the new menu assignment, choose the File Save As command (Alt,F,A). In the File Save As dialog box, type a new name for the template, and then choose OK. If you want to save the modified template in place of the original template, however, choose the File Save command (Alt,F,S) instead of the File Save As command. If you prefer a different format for any of the boilerplate text or for any of the styles, particularly for the banner paragraphs, make the adjustments to the template and save it. You can now use the template to create memos for yourself.

Using a Document Template

Using a document template is usually as easy as creating a new document. To use a template, choose the File New command (Alt,F,N).

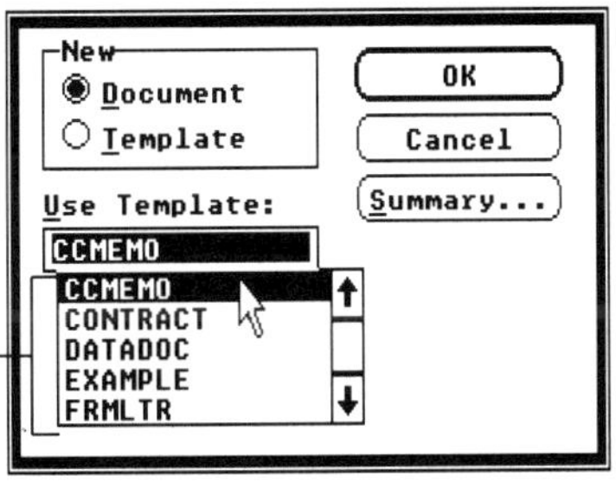

Select document template to use.

In the File New dialog box, which is shown above, select from the Use Template list the template you want to use as the basis for the new document, and then choose OK.

When you create a new document, the template you select (or NORMAL.DOT if you do not select a template) does the following:

- Inserts the boilerplate contents at the same position and with the same formatting as they have in the template.
- Loads the template glossary entries, styles, and macros into memory so that they're available for your use.
- Alters the command menus and sets up the keyboard assignments as assigned in the template.

- Runs a macro named AutoNew, if the template includes that macro, before you can start working on the document. AutoNew is a macro that runs automatically whenever you create a document using a template that has an AutoNew macro.

When you open a document or activate an open document's window, the template sets up Word to work on that document by doing the following:

- Loading the template glossary entries and macros into memory so that they're available for your use.
- Making the template styles available for application in the document.
- Making available for merging with the document's styles any changes that have been made to the template styles since the document was created. When styles are merged, the template styles' definitions replace the document styles' definitions. (To prevent making formatting changes without your explicit consent, Word does not merge style changes from a template to a document.)
- Altering the command menus and setting up the keyboard assignments as assigned in the template.
- Running the macro named AutoOpen, if the template includes that macro, before you can start working on the document. AutoOpen is a macro that runs whenever you open a document whose template contains an AutoOpen macro. AutoOpen does not run when you activate the window of a document that's already open.

As you work on a document, you might realize that a different document template contains macros, glossary entries, or styles that you need for the current document. You can use a different document template and its elements by changing the template that underlies a document.

To change the underlying template, choose the Format Document command (Alt,T,D). In the Format Document dialog box, which is

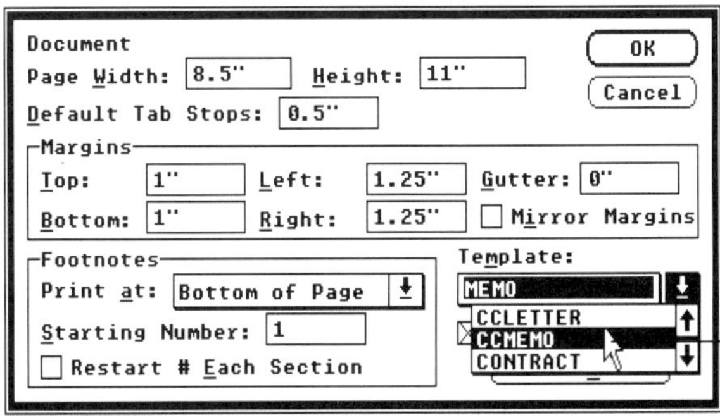

Select alternate template.

shown above, move to the Template list (Alt+M), select the new template, and then choose OK. You can also switch templates temporarily. For example, you might want to switch to another template temporarily to insert glossary entries, run macros, or merge style definitions. You can switch to any number of templates. The template that remains as the basis of a document is the one that's attached when you save the document.

When you change the template that underlies a document, the new template you attach to the document does the following:

- Loads the new template's glossary entries and macros into memory, replacing the previous template's glossary entries and macros.
- Makes the template styles available for merging with the document's styles. When styles are merged, the template styles' definitions replace the document styles' definitions. (To prevent making formatting changes without your explicit consent, Word does not merge styles from a template to a document.)
- Alters the command menus and sets up the keyboard assignments as assigned in the template.
- Runs no macros.

The main point to remember when you change a document's template is that nothing changes in the document itself. The only visible differences are on the menus. Actions change only because of the new template's different key assignments and macros.

Advanced Technique: Creating a Template from Scratch

Creating a template from scratch means creating the shell of a document and all styles, glossary entries, macros, keys assignments, and menu changes that go with that specific type of document. Although you can still use some of the techniques that you use when you create a document and save it as a template (for styles, for example), in many cases you will be programming a sort of document generator. Before you save the template, eliminate from the template any extraneous elements you created in the template so that extraneous elements are not passed from the template to documents. Creating from scratch is a method for people who want to program templates without having to create a document.

The following list of steps summarizes how you create a template from scratch. Following this summary is an example that you can work through.

Analyze. Analyze typical examples of the type of document you'll want to create from your template. Answer the following questions:

- What text is common to all the examples?
- Can any text of a similar type be generated profitably by using fields?
- What format do the documents have? Does a particular formatting sequence exist that's the same in most documents of this type? For example, you might have headings followed by normal text; tables followed by extra space; quotations followed by citations; and a title followed by a byline, an abstract paragraph, and normal text.
- Which commands will you use most often? Which commands will you never use? And which commands will you use occasionally?
- What macros would be useful? Would any of these macros be handier if assigned to a menu or to a key combination?

Plan. Plan the glossary entries, styles, and macros you need. Jot down their text, formatting, and actions.

Create. Create the new template using the File New command. Type the text that's the same in every document, insert fields for contents that are of a similar type but that are unique to each document (for example, the date), define the glossary entries, set up the formatting and define styles, and record or write macros. Link styles by selecting a Next Style in the Format Define Styles dialog box for segments in the document in which you can predict the sequence of formatting. Assign to menus and keys any macros that you'll use often.

Save. Save the template and give it a name that indicates the type of documents you'll be creating from it. If you do not specify a file name extension (it's recommended that you do not), the file name extension will be DOT by default.

Example 3: Creating a newsletter template from scratch

This example creates a newsletter template, illustrating the process of creating a template from scratch. You will insert boilerplate contents that include text, graphics, and fields. Then you will create glossary entries and styles and apply page formatting. To finish, you will create macros, assigning some to keys and others to menus. The finished template will look like the following:

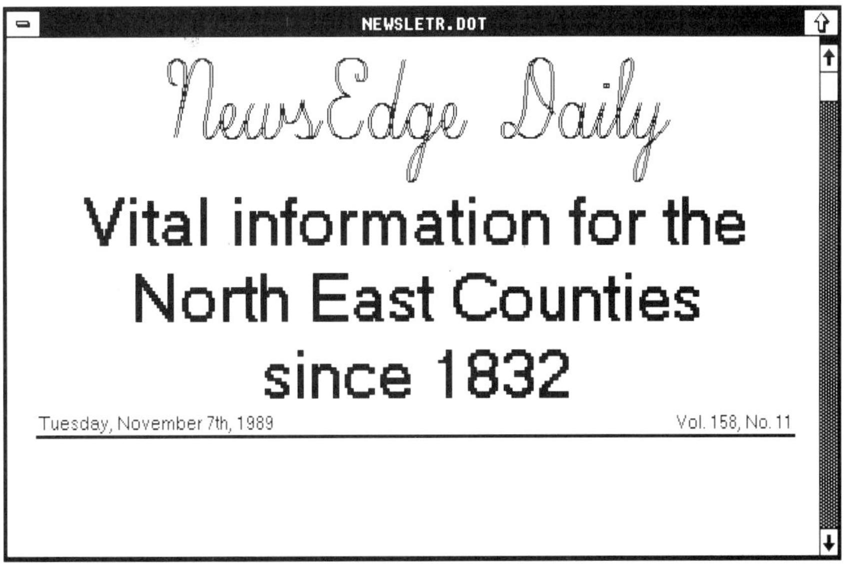

Figure 11-9.
Finished newsletter template.

An issue of a newsletter that you might create from the template would look like the one shown in Figure 11-10:

NewsEdge Daily

Vital information for the North East Counties since 1832

Tuesday, November 7th, 1989 Vol. 158, No. 11

Candidates Debate at Town Hall Meeting Tuesday

Candidates for County Council will face each other in public debate next Tuesday, November 14, at 7 PM in the Kamiakam Town Hall.

The debate will be the only agenda item for the November meeting of the regular Town Hall series.

Candidates scheduled to appear are Bernie Turncoat, Rita Main, Jessie Oakhurst, and Michael Green.

Moderators for the debate will be local reporters Julias Chaisar, Whitney Blossom, and Marie Angelica Juarez.

According to Ms. Juarez, the moderators will focus on major issues confronting the voters of the North East Counties.

Although admission is free, voters who want to witness the debate as part of the audience need to make reservations through the County Clerk's office or by calling 555-1234. Tickets can be mailed or picked up at the County Clerk's office, but will not be available at the door.

The candidates each issued a press release stating the most important issue facing voters.

For Bernie Turncoat, the major issue is property tax valuations, assessments, and rates. He wants the County Assessor's office to stop valuating all properties equally.

"Some properties are inherently more valuable—those with waterfront or views, for example. If we value these properties proportionally to their market value, we can increase the tax income without raising the rates for everyone."

Rita Main sees the major issue as greater involvement of all the inhabitants of the North East Counties in government and civic projects.

"We need to enable all men, women, youth, and ethnic groups to participate in all aspects of government and civic projects. This is more than saying, 'Come on, join us.' It's providing them the resources so that they have the time and energy to participate."

The major issue for Jessie Oakhurst is updating and improving the water supply sys-

Candy Cottage

12122 North Stadium
Cottage Grove, OR 97073
(506) 555 6081

Figure 11-10.
Newsletter that might be created from a newsletter template.

To start, choose the File New command (Alt,F,N) to create a new template. In the File New dialog box, choose the Template option

(Alt+T) and then choose OK. Add the text and formatting for the title as shown earlier in Figure 11-9.

> **NOTE:** *This example works correctly if you have an attached PostScript printer. For other printers, the font sizes or even the fonts themselves might not be available. To see the effect of the formatting on the screen, however, turn off the Display as Printed option (Alt+D) in the View Preferences dialog box (Alt,V,E).*

Creating boilerplate contents. Start by creating the masthead. When the template window appears (it looks like a document window), press Ctrl+F, type or select *Script* for the font, and press the Enter key to set it. Press Ctrl+P, type *72* for the point size, and press Enter to set it. Press Ctrl+B to turn on boldface formatting. To center the newsletter masthead, press Ctrl+C. Now, type *NewsEdge Daily* and press Enter.

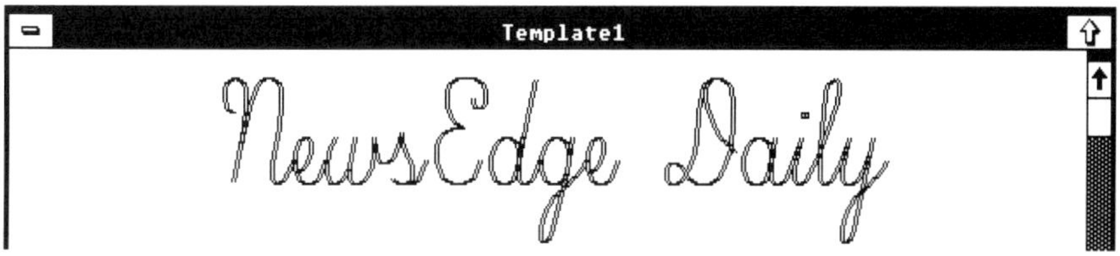

Change the font and point size, and add more text to the masthead. Press Ctrl+F, type or select *Helv* for the font, and press Enter to set it. Press Ctrl+P, type *36* for the point size, and press Enter to set it. Type *Vital information for the North East Counties since 1832* and press Enter.

Now, set up the formatting and fields for the issue date, volume number, and issue number. Press the Ctrl+Shift+F10 keys to display and activate the ruler, and press the End key to move the ruler cursor to the right-indent marker. Above the main typing area, press the 3 key to select a right-aligned tab stop, and then press the Insert key to insert it. Press the Enter key to set the tab stop and return to the document. Choose the Format Paragraph command (Alt,T,P), select the Below option for Border (Alt+O,B,B,B) and the Thick option for Pattern (Alt+E,T), and then choose OK. Press the Ctrl+P keys, type *10* for the point size, and press Enter to set it. Press the Ctrl+B keys to turn off boldface formatting. Press the Ctrl+L keys to left-align the paragraph.

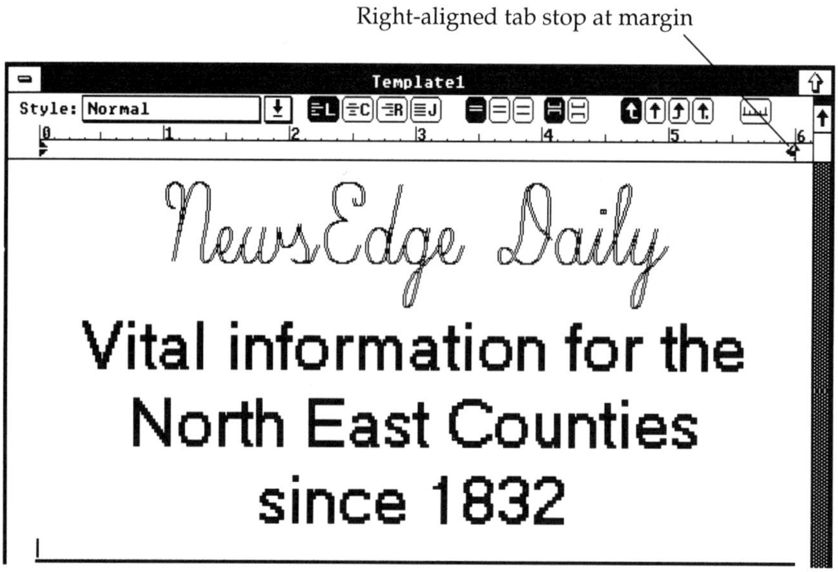

Now, insert fields that provide the day and month for the issue. To insert a field, press the INSERT FIELD key combination (Ctrl+F9) and then type the following between the field characters:

```
date \@ "dddd, MMMM '
```

With the insertion point still at the right end of the field, press the INSERT FIELD key combination (Ctrl+F9) to insert another field inside the one you just inserted, and then type the following between the new field characters:

```
{date \@ d \* ordinal}
```

This field inserts the date as an ordinal number (for example, 10th). Move the insertion point between the two closing field characters, and type *', yyyy"* to insert the year of the issue and finish the field:

```
{date \@ "dddd, MMMM '{date \@ d \* ordinal}', yyyy"}
```

Press the End key to move outside the fields, press the Tab key to place the insertion point at the right-aligned tab stop you set, and then type *Vol.* followed by a space. Press the INSERT FIELD key combination (Ctrl+F9) to insert a field to calculate the volume number. Inside the field, type an equal sign (=) followed by a space, press Ctrl+F9 again, and then type *date* \@ *yyyy* between the new field characters. Move the insertion point between the two closing field characters, and type *–1831* to set the starting date for the calculation. From the year information provided, this field calculates and inserts this issue's volume number. You use 1831 as the starting year because in 1832 the volume number was Vol I. Press the End key, and type a comma followed by a space and *No.* followed by a space. Press Ctrl+F9, and type the following:

```
fillin "Type the issue number and then choose OK"
```

This field prompts you for the issue number. If you're mathematically inclined, you might want to try to figure out how to set up fields that calculate the issue number from the date.

Press the End key to move to the end of the paragraph. Press the Enter key to start a new paragraph, and apply Normal style to the paragraph by pressing the Alt+Shift+5 keys (5 on the numeric keypad).

Now, create a lead headline format. Press the Ctrl+P keys, type *36* for the point size, and then press the Enter key to set the point size. Press the Ctrl+B keys to turn on boldface formatting. This paragraph will be the lead headline paragraph for the first page.

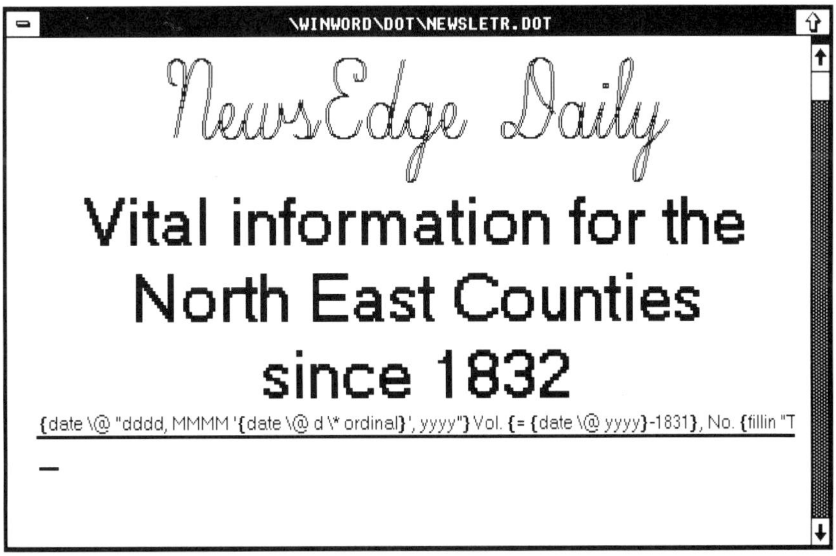

You now have the newsletter's boilerplate text and formatting in place. At this point, it's wise to save what you've created so far. Choose the File Save command (Alt,F,S). In the File Save dialog box, type a name for the template (such as *Newsletr*), choose OK, fill in any information you want to add to the summary, and then choose OK to save the template.

Creating glossary entries. The only way to create a glossary entry, regardless of which method you use to create a template, is to insert text or graphics you want for the glossary entry, select what you inserted, choose the Edit Glossary command (Alt,E,O), type a name for the glossary entry, choose the Template Context option (Alt+T), and then choose the Define button (Alt+D). In this newsletter example, the masthead is a candidate for a glossary entry because the newsletter might need to change its masthead later—for example, if the newsletter moves its offices. By storing the masthead in a glossary entry and using a GLOSSARY field for the masthead, you can update the masthead glossary entry in the document template when necessary, and the field will insert the current text and graphic in new newsletters. Also, when you store the masthead in a glossary entry, you make it available for use in other documents.

To create a masthead glossary entry, select the entire masthead, including any fields it contains. Choose the Edit Glossary command (Alt,E,O), type a glossary entry name (such as *newsletr_masthead*), and choose the Template Context option (Alt+T). In this case, brevity is not important because you'll type the name only one time, in the GLOSSARY field. Then, choose the Define button (Alt+D). To replace the masthead with the GLOSSARY field, press the Delete key with the entire masthead selected, press the INSERT FIELD key combination (Ctrl+F9) to insert a field, and then type *glossary newsletr_masthead* between the field characters. Press the UPDATE FIELD key (F9) to update the field and to display the contents of the "newsletr_masthead" glossary entry.

Creating styles and page formatting for the newsletter template. Now you're ready to turn the template's formatting into styles and set the formatting for the page.

After you format some paragraphs, you might find it useful to create styles from that formatting so that you can easily reuse the styles. In this newsletter example, the masthead text and formatting are inserted from the document template when you create a new document. It's unlikely that you'll need to reuse the formatting of these paragraphs for other newsletter text because the formatting does not fit into the columnar format that's typical in newsletters. You might want to reuse the lead headline's format in other parts of a single issue of the newsletter, however, so here's a look at how to create a style from the formatting. Also, you might want to create some additional styles to use for the newsletter's lower-level headlines; the following also describes that process.

Newsletters often have a more polished look if the text is printed in multiple columns. Here you make a three-column format part of the document template's page formatting.

To define a style from the lead headline's formatting, first position the insertion point in the template's last paragraph (the one immediately below the borderline). Choose the Format Define Styles command (Alt,T,F). In the Format Define Styles dialog box, type a name for the style (such as *Lead Headline*), remembering that style names can contain spaces. For the point size, press the Ctrl+P keys until "36 pt" appears. And for boldface, press the Ctrl+B keys. Choose the Options button (Alt+O), move to the Next Style box (Alt+N), and then type or select Normal as the Next Style (that is, the style of the following paragraph). Choose the Define button (Alt+D), and choose OK. To apply the style to the paragraph, press the Ctrl+S keys, type *Lead Headline,* and then press OK. With the insertion point still in the Lead Headline paragraph, press the Enter key to start a new paragraph, which will have the Normal style.

Currently the newsletter is one column wide. To set the number of columns to three, be sure the insertion point is at the beginning of the Normal paragraph you just inserted and choose the Insert Break command (Alt,I,B). In the dialog box, choose the Continuous Section Break option (Alt+T) and then choose OK. A double dotted line appears on the screen to represent the section break that you just inserted. Now, choose the Format Section command (Alt,T,S). In the dialog box, type *3* in the Number box for Columns, move to the Spacing box and type *0.25"*, turn on the Line Between option (Alt+L) so that the newsletter prints with a line between the columns, and then choose OK. The body of the newsletter below the lead headline is now in three columns. You see the text in three columns on the screen in Page View or in Print Preview. (See Chapter 14, "Previewing and Perfecting Page Layout," for descriptions of these two views.) You see text in three columns when you print the newsletter. Without text, you cannot see the effect of formatting the document template in three columns.

In Normal style, all lines are flush with the left margin. Most newsletters indent each paragraph's first line to better indicate where new paragraphs start. Many newsletters also justify paragraphs to make the three-column format look more polished. To achieve indented first lines and justified paragraph formats without intervention, modify the Normal style to include these formats. Choose the Format Define Styles command (Alt,T,F). In the Format Define Styles dialog box, select the Normal style. Choose the Options button (Alt+O), and then choose the Paragraph button (Alt+P). In the Paragraph dialog box, choose the Justified option (Alt+J) for Alignment, move to the First Line box (Alt+N) for Indents, type *9 pt* (9 points equal ⅛ inch, which appears as 0.13" in the style description), and then choose OK. When the Format Define Styles dialog box reappears, choose the Define button (Alt+D).

Now you need to make some corrections to the Lead Headline style and to the other paragraphs in the newsletter's masthead. Because all the styles are based on Normal, they now all have a 9-point first-line indent. You want this indent only for text paragraphs in articles, so you need to remove the indent from all other styles. While still in the Format Define Styles dialog box, select Lead Headline from the list of styles. Choose the Paragraph button (Alt+P). In the Paragraph dialog box, move to the First Line Indents box (Alt+N), type *0* (zero), and then choose OK. When the Format Define Styles dialog box reappears, choose the Define button (Alt+D). Repeat these corrective steps for the first-line indent for each of the heading styles listed (heading 1, heading 2, and heading 3), and then choose the Close button (Esc).

In the document, select all the masthead's paragraphs and press the Ctrl+Shift+F10 keys to activate the ruler. Note that the ruler cursor is at the ⅛-inch mark.

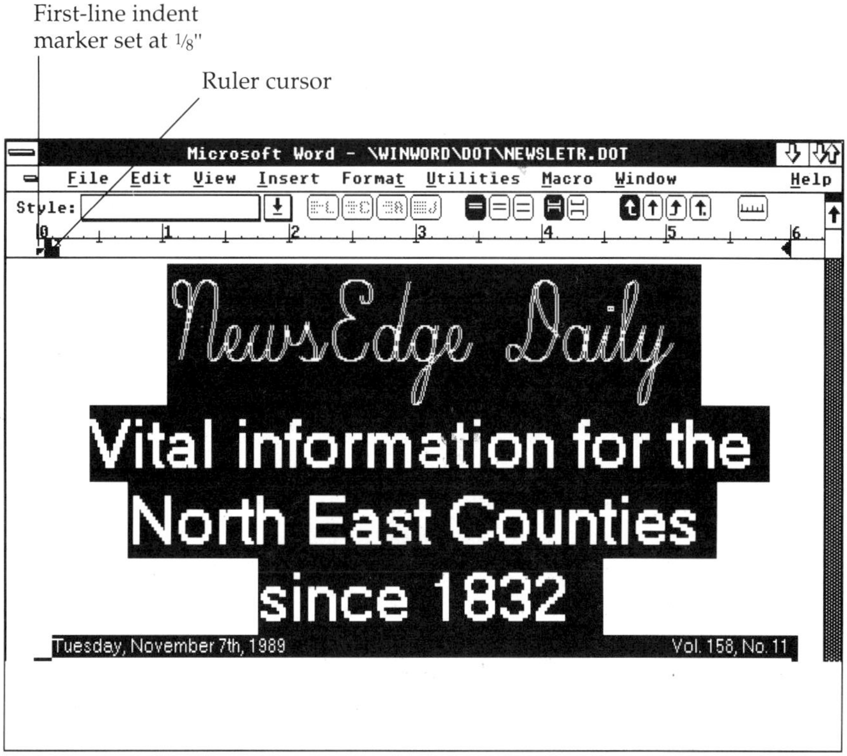

Press the Home key to move the ruler cursor to the 0 mark, and press the F key to move the first-line indent marker to the position of the ruler cursor.

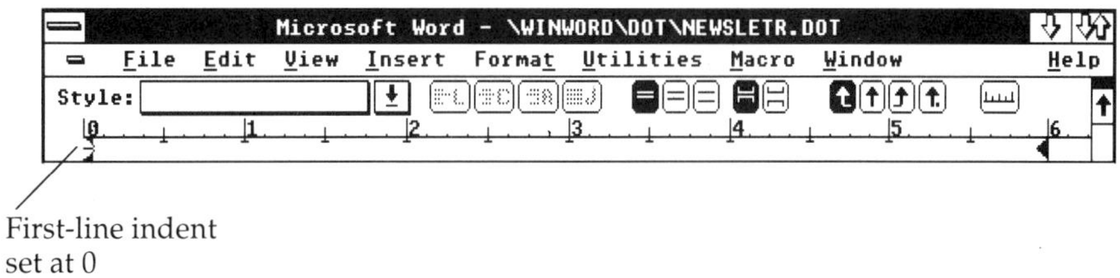

Now, press the Enter key to set the first-line indent to 0.

Now you need to create styles for two additional headline sizes. The easiest course is to modify the heading 1 and heading 2 styles. Choose the Format Define Styles command (Alt,T,F). In the Format Define Styles dialog box, select the heading 1 style. Remove Underline from the style's definition by pressing the Ctrl+U keys. Remove Space

Before by pressing the Ctrl+E keys. Set the alignment to Left by pressing the Ctrl+L keys. Leave the rest of the style definition as is. Choose the Options button (Alt+O), and then choose the Define button (Alt+D). Remove the Space Before measurement and set the alignment to Left for the heading 2 style, as you just did for the heading 1 style. Be sure to choose the Define button (Alt+D) after you make the change to the heading 2 style. If you need another headline size, set the heading 3 style to 10 points by pressing the Ctrl+Shift+P keys until the point size disappears from the style's definition. (The point size disappears because heading 3 now has the same point size as Normal—10 points.) Also press the Ctrl+L keys to set the alignment Left. Now, remove the Left Indent of 0.25" by pressing the UNNEST key combination (Ctrl+M). Choose the Define button (Alt+D) after you make the changes that you want to the heading 3 style. When you finish adjusting these heading styles, choose the Close button (Esc).

Creating macros for the newsletter template. For your newsletter template, you can create several macros that make formatting changes quickly. For example, you might want to balance columns (make them the same length) at the end of an article, or you might want to change

TIP

Avoiding the Normal Style Ripple Effect

As you saw earlier in this example, change ripples through all the styles that are based on Normal when you change the Normal style. The only time this ripple effect does not occur is when a style has an explicit definition that's different from Normal. For example, if a style's font is defined as Helv, changing the font for Normal from Tms Rmn (the default) to Script does not affect the style that uses Helv. But all styles that do not have an explicitly defined font change to Script.

To avoid this ripple effect, make only those changes to Normal that you want in every style. For changes that you do not want to ripple through every style, define a style (such as Standard) that includes the formatting you use for most text paragraphs. Then, change to Standard the definitions of all styles that have Normal as their Next Style. This method affects the document's format in the same way as changing the definition of Normal but without the negative ripple effect.

the number of columns on a page. Although Word contains commands for these tasks, creating a macro lets you automate the process and frees you from memorizing steps. The examples in the next two sections show you how to create these two macros.

As a bonus, creating macros for the template context means that you can limit the availability of template macros to documents that were created from that template. Template macros let you easily perform special actions that are unique to particular types of documents, without cluttering Word's macro facility with unneeded macros while you work on other types of documents.

In addition, because template macros override global macros, you can create template macros that have the same names as global macros. And you can have the macro that's assigned to the template context perform a special version of the global macro. For example, the Print command is a global macro (FilePrint) that's built into Word. If you create a template macro named FilePrint, you can have a specialized print command for the type of document you create from that template.

After you create macros, you can assign them to menus or to key combinations. To reduce menu and keyboard clutter, you can also remove unneeded existing assignments. After the examples in which you create template macros, you'll find explanations of how to make menu and key assignments that are specific to the newsletter template.

Creating a macro to insert a continuous section break. In a newsletter, you want to be able to print text evenly across multiple columns in the shape of a box; evening out columns is called column balancing. To set up column balancing, you insert a continuous section break. When you do so, Word prints the text in the following section on the same page, balancing the columns of the preceding section as closely as possible, usually within a couple of lines. The preceding section must be set up in multiple columns.

To insert a section break, you normally choose the Insert Break command (Alt,I,B), select the Continuous option (Alt+T) for Section Break in the Insert Break dialog box, and then choose OK. When you choose Insert Break, you normally see a dialog box. To make inserting a continuous section break faster, you might want to assign the task to a key and bypass the dialog box. The following steps show you how to create a macro that performs all the steps that you use to insert a continuous section break. You make the macro part of the newsletter template.

With the newsletter template open and active, choose the Macro Record command (Alt,M,C). In the Macro Record dialog box, type a macro name (for example, *BalanceCols*), and choose the Template Context option (Alt+T). Even though this macro is handiest when assigned to a key, move to the description box (Alt+D) and type a description (for example, *Inserts continous section break*). A description is primarily used for menu help text when you assign a macro to a menu. You can type a description, however, if you prefer to have on hand a more detailed explanation of the macro than its name gives you. You see the Description in the dialog boxes that Word displays when you choose the Macro Run, Macro Edit, Macro Assign to Menu, and Macro Assign to Key commands. Choose OK.

Choose the Insert Break command (Alt,I,B). In the Insert Break dialog box, choose the Continuous option (Alt+T) for Section Break and then choose OK.

Choose the Macro Stop Recorder command (Alt,M,C). You do not need to keep the section break that you inserted while recording the macro as part of the template, so select and delete it. To assign this macro to a key, see "Assigning a macro to a key combination for the newsletter template" later in this chapter.

Creating macros to set the number of columns. In documents that have multiple columns, such as newsletters, you want to be able to change the number of columns easily. Normally you must insert a continuous section break, choose the Format Section command, type the number of columns, and then choose OK. To make this process easier, create macros for the various numbers of columns you use commonly and then assign those macros to a menu or a key combination or to both. Here you record macros for inserting a continuous section break and setting one, two, and three columns. For more information about assigning macros to menus and keys, see the following section, "Changing the menus and key assignments for the newsletter template."

To create a macro that changes the number of columns to two, choose the Macro Record command (Alt,M,C), type a macro name (such as *TwoColumns*), choose the Template Context option (Alt+T), type a description (such as *"Sets two columns"*), and then choose OK. Choose the Insert Break command (Alt,I,B), select Continuous under Section Break (Alt+T), and choose OK. Next, choose the Format Section command (Alt,T,S), type *2* in the Number box for Columns, and choose OK. Choose the Macro Stop Recorder command (Alt,M,C).

In addition to a macro that sets the number of columns to two, you might want macros that set the number of columns to one and to three. To set the number of columns to one, record a macro as you did for the two-column macro. Give this new macro a name, such as OneColumn. And in the Format Section dialog box, type *1* in the Number box for Columns.

To set the number of columns to three, record another macro and give it a name, such as ThreeColumms. In the Format Section dialog box, Type *3* in the Number box for Columns.

Changing the menus and key assignments for the newsletter template. As described in Chapter 10, "Macros," you can change Word's menus and key assignments. If you make changes to a template, you can create a set of menus and key assignments specifically designed for the type of document you're working on. The following sections describe how to change the menus and key assignments for the newsletter template. First, you assign to the Format menu the three macros that you created to set the number of columns. Then, you remove some menu assignments to streamline several menus. Next, you assign to a key combination the macro that you created to insert a continuous section break for column balancing.

To assign to the Format menu the macros that set up different numbers of columns, choose the Macro Assign to Menu command (Alt,M,M). Choose the Template Context option (Alt+E). Move back to Assign Macro Name (Alt+N), and select the OneColumn macro from the list of macro names. From the Menu list, select the Format menu. The Format menu already contains a command name that uses the letter "o" as its command letter (Position), so you need to edit the Menu Text name by deleting the ampersand (&) in front of the "O" in

"One" and inserting an ampersand in front of the "n" in "One." (The "n" will be underlined on the menu.) Choose the Assign button (Alt+A). The dialog box remains open, and you can make the other two assignments without having to choose the Macro Assign to Menu command again. Select TwoColumn from the list of macros, choose the Format menu, edit the Menu Text name to put the ampersand in front of the "w" in "Two," and then choose the Assign button (Alt+A). Select ThreeColumn from the list of macros, choose the Format menu, edit the Menu Text to put the ampersand in front of the "h" in "three," and then choose OK. The OK button assigns the macro and closes the dialog box. Word adds the three commands to the bottom of the Format menu:

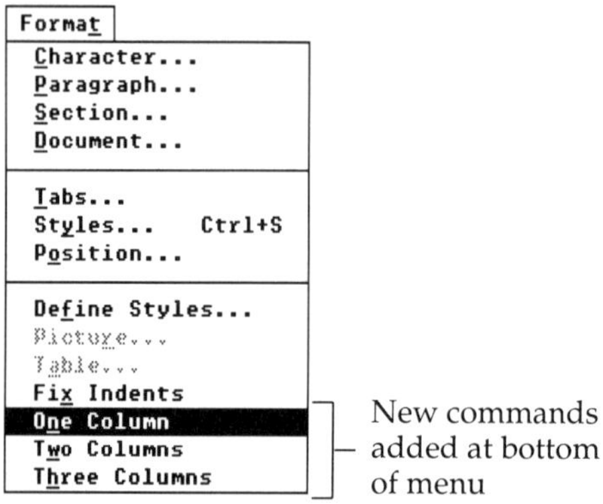

Removing commands from the newsletter template's menus. Not all documents need every Word command. In the newsletter example, for instance, you would seldom use the Utilities Calculate, Insert Footnote, and View Footnote commands, so you could remove those commands using the Macro Assign to Menu command.

To remove the three commands, choose Macro Assign to Menu (Alt,M,M). Select the Utilities menu from the Menu list. From the Menu Text list, select &Calculate. Word selects UtilCalculate from the list of macro names. Choose the Template Context option (Alt+E), and then choose the Unassign button (Alt+U). Repeat these steps for the Insert Footnote command by choosing the Insert menu and selecting Foot&note from the Menu Text list. Word chooses InsertFootnote from the list of macro names. Choose the Template Context option (Alt+E), and then choose the Unassign button (Alt+U). Remove the View

Footnotes command by choosing the View menu and selecting &Footnotes from the Menu Text list. Word chooses ViewFootnotes from the list of macro names. Choose the Template Context option (Alt+E) again, and then choose the Unassign button (Alt+U). When you finish removing the commands, choose the Close button (Esc). Now, open the View, Insert, and Utilities menus to see that the three commands have been removed:

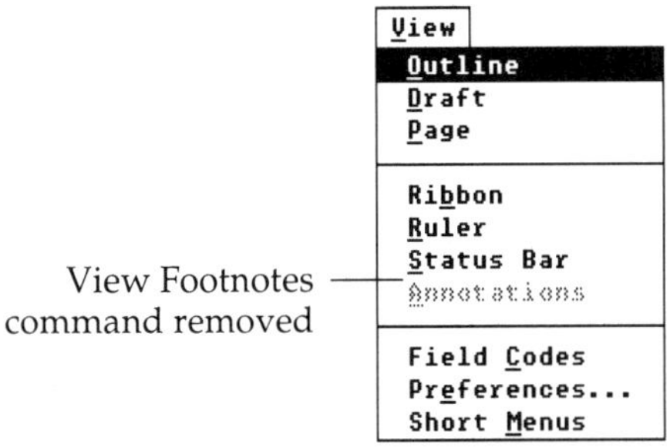

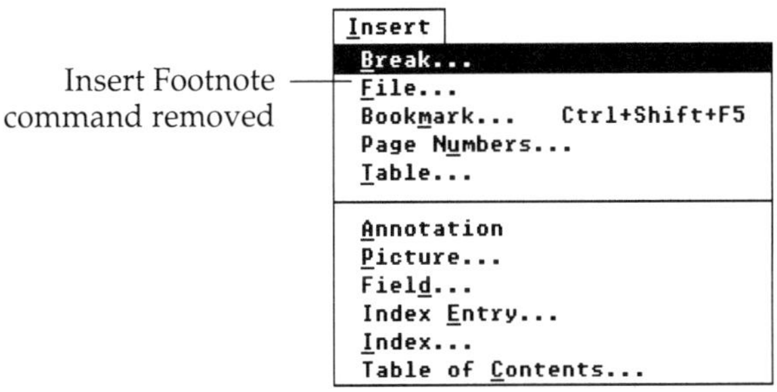

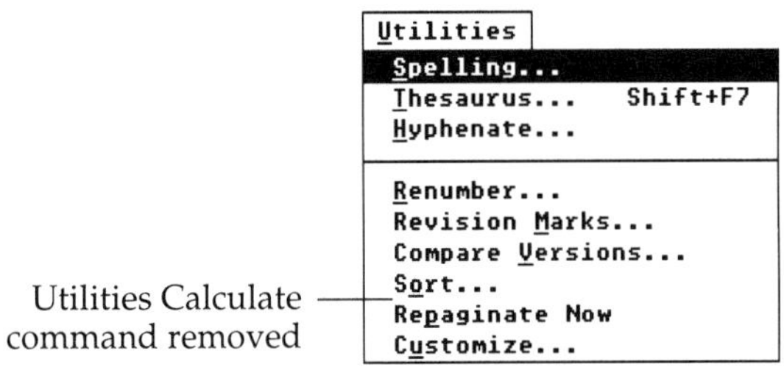

Assigning a macro to a key combination for the newsletter template. By assigning the macro that inserts a continuous section break to a key combination, you will be able to insert the section break quickly, which makes it easy to balance columns at the end of an article. First, choose the Macro Assign to Key command (Alt,M,K). Choose the Template Context option (Alt+T), move to Assign Macro Name (Alt+N), and select the BalanceCols macro from the list of macros. Then, specify the key combination you want. For this example, press the Ctrl+Shift+E keys. Choose OK to assign the macro to the key combination and to close the dialog box. To make several assignments at one time, choose the Assign button (Alt+A) instead.

Additional Special Tips for Templates

To make templates better fit your work situation and to make templates easier to store and use, employ as many of the following special tips as appropriate.

The default filename extension for templates. If you do not specify differently, the default file name extension for document templates is DOT. This extension is set in the WIN.INI file. You can change an individual template's file name extension to any one, two, or three characters when you name the file or change the name using the File Save As command. You can even omit an extension. If you change a template's extension and leave the default extension set to DOT, the template with the changed extension does not appear in the lists of templates in dialog boxes.

You can also change the default template file-name extension to any one, two, or three characters. To do so, edit the WIN.INI file: In the section labeled "Microsoft Word," add or change a line that begins with DOT-EXTENSION=. For example, if you want the default extension to be DTM instead of DOT, that line should read as shown below:

```
DOT-EXTENSION=DTM
```

After you change the default extension for document templates, Word assigns the new extension to newly created templates and displays only those files that have the new extension in lists of document templates in dialog boxes.

Default directory for templates. If you do not specify differently, document templates are stored in the same directory as the Word program file (WINWORD.EXE). If Word finds no templates in the program directory when you choose a command that lists available templates, Word looks in the current directory for templates. The commands that list templates are File New, File Open, Format Document, and Format Define Styles Merge.

You can change the default directory for storing document templates by editing the WIN.INI file: In the section labeled "Microsoft Word," add or change a line that begins with DOT-PATH=. To store templates in a directory that is named C:\WINWORD\TEMPLATES, for example, that line should read as shown below:

DOT-PATH=C:\WINWORD\TEMPLATES

You can also change the directory for an individual template by typing a pathname in front of the template's file name. If you store a template in a directory other than the default directory, you will not see that template in the lists of templates in dialog boxes unless you specify the directory explicitly.

Read-only templates. Within a company, it might be practical for one group or department—for example, a Management Information Systems (MIS) department or a graphic design group—to set up the document templates for standard documents. After the templates are set up to reflect the company's standards, it's useful to protect the templates from changes. To do so, change the file attributes of template files to read-only. In read-only form, users cannot alter the original file but must save changes in a different file instead. To change a file to read-only, type *ATTRIB +r file-name* at the MS-DOS prompt.

If you change a read-only template and then try to save it, Word displays a message to tell you that you cannot save the template using the same name; you must use a different name. Similarly, if you try to save a template and the directory is read-only, you must specify a different directory.

The default template: NORMAL.DOT. NORMAL.DOT can be a powerful ally when your work is limited to creating a few standard documents. To make NORMAL.DOT work for you, modify the NORMAL.DOT file that serves as a template for the type of document you create most often. Then, each time you create a new document, you need not worry about selecting the correct template upon which to base the document.

If you create several types of documents regularly (probably a maximum of four) but you create only one type of document for an extended period of time, create a NORMAL.DOT file for each type. Rename each file something other than NORMAL.DOT, although you might want to keep the DOT file-name extension as a handy way to identify these files quickly. Then, when you need a particular type of document, copy the applicable DOT file to NORMAL.DOT. Note, however, that you can as easily choose an alternative template when you create a document, without having to rename a template file. This renaming approach saves steps only if you plan to create numerous documents based on one particular template.

Merging styles. If your document contains styles that you want to merge into several templates, use the Format Document command (Alt,T,D) to change the template that's associated with the document. Then, use the Format Define Styles command (Alt,T,F) to merge the styles into the new template. Repeat this procedure for each template into which you want to merge the styles. When you finish merging, remember to change back to the template that you want underlying the document.

PART III

Simplifying Word Tasks

Word for Windows contains hundreds of features. In this part of the book, you'll learn about Word's most complex yet most useful tools that simplify creating documents.

Two of the features described in this part of the book are tables and page preview. Word's table feature allows you to quickly construct a table without having to bother with tab stops. The preview feature lets you preview a page before you print it and make last-minute changes to text and to the positions of graphics and text on a page.

You'll also find a chapter that explains how to use glossaries to store text, graphics, and formatting so that you can reuse them. Another chapter covers merge printing, including merging a form letter with an address file to create a bulk mailing. The final chapter in the book describes the instructions you can insert in a document to produce mathematical and scientific typesetting. Even if you do not work on documents that contain mathematical and scientific formulas, you can use the methods explained there to create unusual effects with text.

Chapter 12

Glossaries

A glossary is a collection of stored items, including graphics or text, each of which you give a name. Each named item is called a glossary entry, and you use the name to insert the contents of a glossary entry in as many documents as needed. Figure 12-1 on the next page shows how you define and insert glossary entries.

Later in this chapter, you work through six examples to practice what you've learned about how to create and use glossary entries.

What Can You Keep in a Glossary Entry?

You can keep text and graphics, along with their formatting, in glossary entries. The text can be any length, and the graphics can be any size.

Along with the letters, numbers, punctuation, and symbols that you type, paste, or otherwise make a part of a document's text, the text in a glossary entry can include any additional characters. So you'll see paragraph marks, section marks, page-break characters, and tab characters, as well as tables and pictures, in a glossary entry. In particular, paragraph marks and section marks—characters that can carry formatting—can be overlooked as contents for glossary entries. You can also store footnote and annotation reference marks in glossary entries. Although footnotes and annotations are often specific to the information in a particular document, you might occasionally reuse them in other documents. By storing a footnote reference mark or an annotation reference mark in a glossary entry, you can easily insert the footnote or annotation in another document. The text of a footnote or annotation

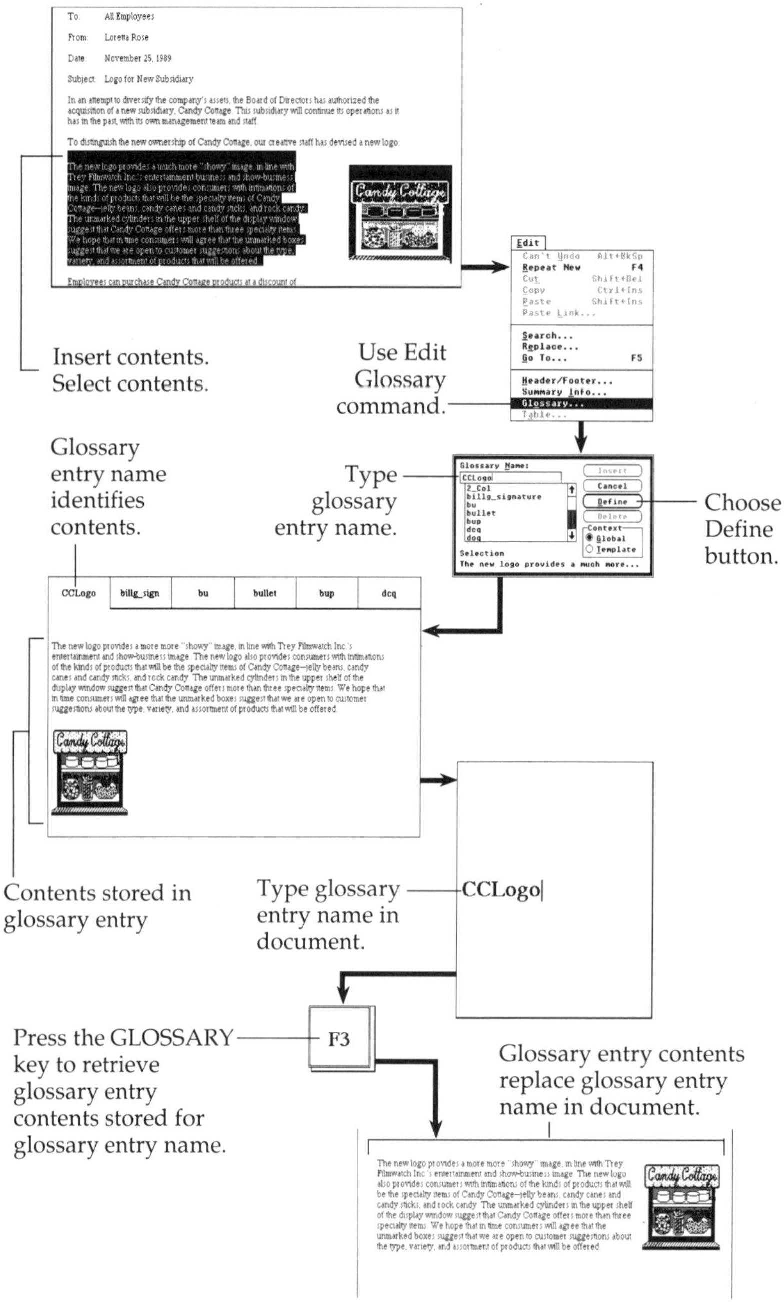

Figure 12-1.
Defining and inserting glossary entries.

travels with its reference mark, so you need store only the reference mark, and Word will store the full text. And, when you insert an automatically numbered footnote or annotation reference, Word adjusts the reference's number to correctly show the footnote or annotation's place in the document.

A glossary is also a good place to store special characters that are difficult or time-consuming to produce. For example, characters like bullets, open and close quotation marks, and dashes require several steps that can interrupt the flow of typing and are hard to remember. If you insert these special characters only one time in a document and then save the characters in glossary entries—giving the entries names that you can recognize and remember—you can insert the characters easily and quickly.

You can store in a glossary entry any graphic that you can insert in a Word document. See the description of the IMPORT field in the Appendix, "Field Types and Their Instructions," for a list of the graphic formats that Word lets you insert in a document. Because Word treats a graphic as a character, you use the same methods to store graphics in a glossary entry as you do to store text.

Creating and Using Glossary Entries

To create and use glossary entries, you use the Edit Glossary command. When you choose Edit Glossary (Alt,E,O), you see a dialog box, as shown on the next page, that contains all the controls you use to define a glossary entry, insert the contents of a glossary entry in a document, and delete an unneeded glossary entry. The following explains these controls.

Glossary Name. This box shows the names of the glossary entries that exist; to create a new glossary entry, type a new name.

Text at bottom left. This area of the dialog box displays the name of the selected glossary and the first few words of its contents, or it displays "Selection" and the first few words of the selection in the document. Word includes an ellipsis (...) if the text is longer than can be displayed in the dialog box; a character the dialog box cannot display (such as a graphic) appears as a period.

Insert. The Insert button inserts the selected glossary entry contents.

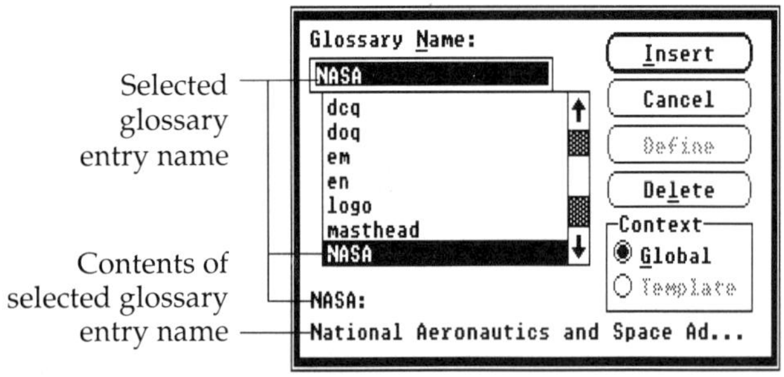

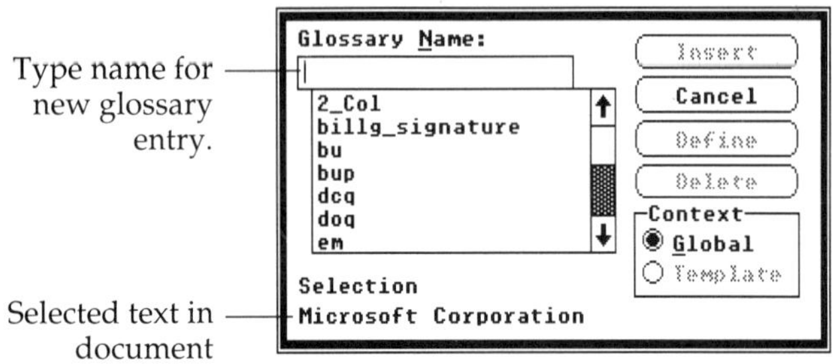

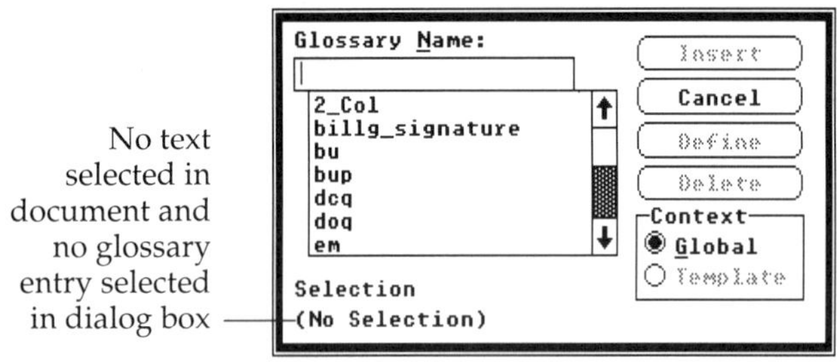

Define. The Define button creates a glossary entry from the selection, using the name you typed in the Glossary Name box.

Delete. The Delete button deletes the selected glossary entry, leaving the dialog box open.

Context Global. This option indicates that a glossary entry is available for all documents.

Context Template. This option indicates that a glossary entry is available only for documents that were created from the active document template. Word lets you choose a Context option only when you first create a glossary entry.

Creating a Glossary Entry

To create a glossary entry, you insert contents in a document, select the contents, choose the Edit Glossary command, and give the glossary entry a name.

Type or paste text or graphics, or both, to create contents for a glossary entry if you do not already have the contents you want. If your document is empty, with no glossary entries yet defined, the Edit Glossary command is unavailable until you type and select some text or bring in a graphic. To include a style or paragraph formatting in the contents, be sure to select the paragraph mark for the paragraph that contains that style or formatting.

Choose the Edit Glossary command (Alt,E,O). Note that part of the first line of text appears at the bottom of the Edit Glossary dialog box. A graphic appears as a period. If nothing was selected when you chose Edit Glossary, you see "(No Selection)"; cancel the dialog box, select text or graphics, and choose Edit Glossary (Alt,E,O) once more.

Type a name for the glossary entry. The name can be up to 31 characters long and can include spaces.

Accept (do not change) the Global Context setting—you cannot change it if the Template option is gray. Global is the default setting,

TIP

Giving Glossary Entries Convenient Names

The method you use to insert glossary entries influences the style of glossary entry name you assign. To insert the contents of a glossary entry, you can type the glossary entry name in a document and then press the GLOSSARY key (F3), or you can use the Edit Glossary command.

If you type the names in the document, you might consider using a short name to reduce the typing—for example, "bup" for bulleted paragraph, as used in Example 3 later in this chapter. Note, however, that "bup" might be difficult to remember, especially if you do not use its glossary entry often. For glossary entries you use infrequently and for entries that you insert using the Edit Glossary command, assign a longer name that describes the contents. For example, "Bulleted_Paragraph" and "Bulleted Paragraph" are both shorter than the 31-character limit, and yet these names do a good job of describing the glossary entry's contents.

which makes a glossary entry available in all documents. For more information about choosing a context, see "Selecting a Context for Your Glossary Entry" below. Now, choose the Define button (Alt+D) to create the glossary entry.

Inserting the Contents of a Glossary Entry

Type the glossary name in the document, and then replace the name with the contents by pressing the GLOSSARY key (F3). Or insert the glossary entry's contents by using the Edit Glossary command (Alt,E,O).

To try inserting the glossary entry you just created, position the insertion point where you want the entry. Type the name of the glossary entry, and press F3. Or you can position the insertion point, choose Edit Glossary (Alt,E,O), select the name of the glossary entry you want, and then choose the Insert button (Alt+I).

Glossary entry name — NASA

Glossary contents inserted — National Aeronautics and Space Administration

Selecting a Context for Your Glossary Entry

If you use your glossary entries in every document or in most documents, define all glossary entries for the global context. If you use a glossary entry in only one or two types of documents, however, define that glossary entry for the appropriate template context.

You must choose the context in the Edit Glossary dialog box when you create the glossary entry. When you create a document from a template, all the template's glossary entries plus all the global glossary entries are available to you. Because global glossary entries are available in all documents, you will seldom want to convert a global glossary entry to a template entry. You might want to convert a template entry to a global entry, however, so that you can use it in additional types of documents. After you define the context, the only way to change it is to delete and redefine the entry.

To change the context for a glossary entry, first insert the contents of the glossary entry in a document. Then, select the text or graphic that you just inserted. Choose the Edit Glossary command (Alt,E,O) and, in the Edit Glossary dialog box, select the glossary name. Then, choose the Delete button (Alt+L). Note that you cannot undo the deletion of a glossary entry. Now, type the glossary name, using the same name or a new one if you prefer. Then, change the Context setting and choose the Define button (Alt+D).

Examples of Using Glossary Entries

Following are six examples of practical glossary entries, including the steps you take to create them. The examples show you how to store text, graphics, styles, other formatting fields, and tables in glossary entries and then use those entries.

Example 1: Storing Text in a Glossary Entry

A glossary entry is often used to store a long company name or a long institutional name. When such a name has a common abbreviation, that abbreviation would also serve well as the glossary's name. For example, National Aeronautics and Space Administration is generally known as NASA, and NASA makes a good glossary name for the glossary entry that stores the full name for NASA.

You might also use glossary entries to store such text as contract clauses, closings and signatures for letters, return addresses for letters and envelopes, and special characters—for example, bullet characters (black dots or circles) or dashes. Here you see how to put one type of special character into a glossary: a bullet.

In publishing circles, open and close double quotation marks, open and close single quotation marks, bullet characters, and dashes replace the versions of those characters that you use when you create text using typewriters and most word processors. These characters give a document a more polished look, but in Word they are not assigned to the keyboard. You use the keys shown in the table on the next page with the NumLock key turned on to insert these special characters.

Character	*Keys (Requires NumLock On)*
Single open quotation mark (‘)	Alt+0145
Single close quotation mark (’)	Alt+0146
Double open quotation mark (“)	Alt+0147
Double close quotation mark (”)	Alt+0148
Bullet character (◦)	Alt+0149 (Character must be in Symbol font)
Em-dash (—)	Alt+0150
En-dash (–)	Alt+0151

Each time you want to insert one of these characters, you need not repeat the process of turning on the NumLock key and then holding down the Alt key while you type a four-digit number. Instead, you can place these characters in glossary entries. Give each glossary entry a two-character or three-character name that you can easily remember or recognize, and then you're ready to insert the entries easily.

For example, suppose you want to create a glossary entry that contains the bullet character. First, press Ctrl+F, type *Symbol,* and then press the Enter key. Next, turn on the NumLock key. Hold down the Alt key while you type 0149 on the numeric keypad. Turn off NumLock so that you can use the arrow keys to move the insertion point and to select text. Now, select the bullet character and choose the Edit Glossary command (Alt,E,O). The Edit Glossary dialog box is displayed below:

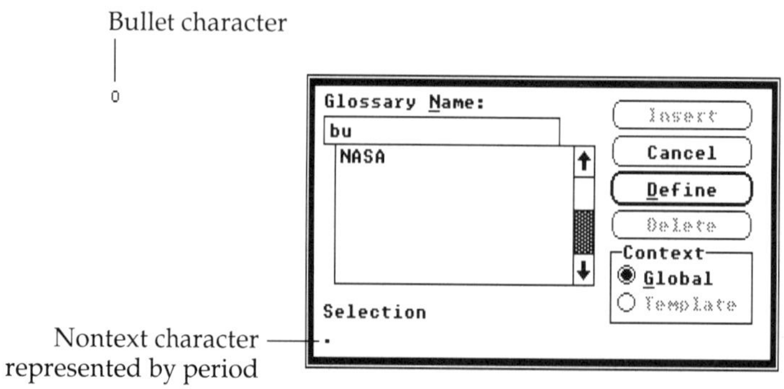

Type a glossary entry name, such as *bu,* and then choose the Define button (Alt+D). To insert a bullet character, position the insertion point where you want a bullet, type *bu,* and press the GLOSSARY key (F3).

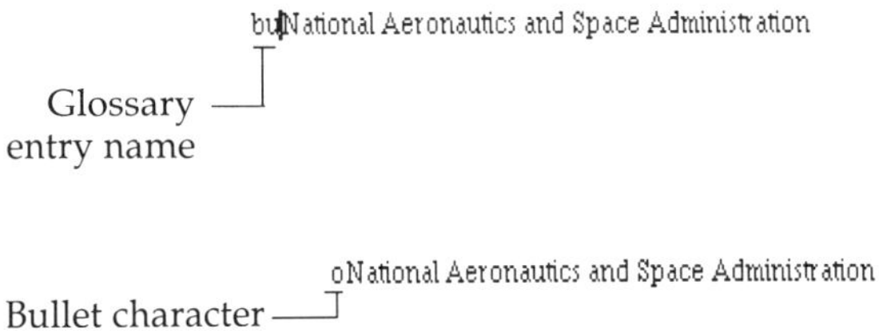

For information about creating and inserting glossary entries, see "Creating and Using Glossary Entries" earlier in this chapter.

Example 2: Storing Graphics in a Glossary Entry

Because creating complex graphics must be done outside Word, inserting graphics requires special procedures. One of these procedures is cutting and pasting from the graphics file, which can be tedious, especially when you use the same graphic repeatedly. The Insert Picture command inserts graphics by inserting a field (IMPORT), which requires choosing the command and finding and selecting the graphics file. You can store graphics that you will reuse in the glossary. The following are some candidates for graphic glossary entries:

- Logos. If you use a company logo on letterhead, memos, reports, or any other documents, putting the logo in a glossary entry can save you effort and expense. And when the company return address is part of the logo, you can position the return address correctly in relation to the graphic and then store the logo in a glossary entry. The logo will print correctly every time in every document.

TIP

Including a Tab Character with the Bullet Character

Often a bullet character is followed by a tab character to provide space between the bullet character and the beginning of the text. Consider storing a tab character with the bullet character in the glossary entry. First, insert a tab character following the bullet character, select both, and then create a glossary entry. You might name this entry *but* to distinguish it from a glossary entry that contains only a bullet character.

- Closing and signature for letters. Although the closing in a letter is text, the signature must be created using a graphics tool. You can produce a signature in a Word file by having the person sign on a sheet of paper and then by using an electronic scanner to transfer a copy of the signature to a file.
- Illustrations for a document. When a document contains many illustrations, putting them all in glossary entries cuts the copy-and-paste work between the graphics program and Word to a one-time process. After you complete the glossary entries, you can create your document and insert the illustrations easily, wherever they're needed.

For more information about how to create and insert glossary entries, see "Creating and Using Glossary Entries" earlier in this chapter.

TIP

Inserting Glossary Entry Contents Using a Field

You can use a field to insert the contents of a glossary entry. The GLOSSARY field uses a glossary entry name as its instruction. For example, to insert a signature for Bill Gish at the end of a letter, you insert the following field:

```
{glossary billg_signature}
```

Glossary entry name

The instruction "billg_signature" is the name of the glossary entry that contains Bill Gish's signature. You select the field and press the UPDATE FIELD key (F9) to insert the signature. To insert the signature without having to update the field, choose the Options button (Alt+O) in the File Print dialog box and, before you start to print, turn on the Update Fields option (Alt+U). For more information about using the GLOSSARY field, see the Appendix, "Field Types and Their Instructions." And, for more information about using fields in general, see Chapter 8, "Fields: Facts and Functions." Chapter 11, "Templates," contains an explanation of how the GLOSSARY field is used to insert a glossary entry. See the section named "Creating glossary entries" in Chapter 11.

Example 3: Storing Styles in a Glossary Entry

To store styles in glossary entries, you must store some text, even if it's only a paragraph mark. If you plan to use a style by itself for various graphics or text, you do not need to store the style in a glossary entry because Word lets you simply apply the style rather than using a glossary entry. But if you have particular graphics or text to which you have applied styles, you can profitably store the graphics or text in a glossary entry. When you create a glossary item to which you have applied a style, the style is also saved if you include a paragraph mark in the glossary entry.

The following steps show you how to store text in a glossary entry and also store the styles that format the text and paragraphs.

Storing list-item styles in a glossary entry

A list item is one part of a list. In a bulleted list, each list item begins with a bullet character; in a numbered list, each list item begins with a number. The bullet character or the number typically appears to the left of the item's text. Because inserting a bullet character or a field for a number can be time-consuming and awkward, bullet characters or number fields are good candidates for glossary entries. Also, by including a paragraph mark in the glossary entries, you can keep the indented paragraph formatting of bulleted and numbered list items.

In this part of the example, you see how to save time by creating a bulleted list item and putting it in a glossary entry. Each of these items contains a bullet character plus a tab character and a paragraph mark. To see the tab character and paragraph mark as you work, press the SHOW ALL key combination (Ctrl+*). To turn off the display of special characters, press the SHOW ALL key combination (Ctrl+*) again. For information about how to create a numbered list, see "Example 5: Storing a Field in a Glossary Entry" later in this chapter.

The unusual part of a bulleted list is the bullet character itself. Although you can type a bullet character in Word, it's not a speedy process. Inserting a glossary entry that contains the bullet character is much faster. To increase your efficiency even more, you might also include in the same glossary entry the tab character and the paragraph mark to which you've applied the bulleted list style.

First, start a new, blank paragraph. Then, in the paragraph, type a bullet character by pressing the Ctrl+F keys, typing *Symbol,* and then pressing the Enter key. Turn on the NumLock key and hold down the Alt key while you type *0149* on the numeric keypad. Turn off NumLock. Next, press the Ctrl+spacebar keys to return to the default font, press the Tab key, press Enter, and then press the Shift+Ctrl+up arrow keys to select the paragraph you just created:

Choose the Edit Glossary command (Alt,E,O), and type a name for the glossary—for example, *bup* for bulleted paragraph. Now, choose the Define button (Alt+D) to create the glossary entry.

To insert a bulleted paragraph, position the insertion point where you want the paragraph, type *bup,* and then press the GLOSSARY key (F3). To insert text in the bulleted paragraph, first position the insertion point between the tab character and the paragraph mark. (If these characters are not visible, press the SHOW ALL key combination, Ctrl+*.) Then, type the text.

Storing a glossary entry with its position style

If you want to position a graphic or a piece of text in a particular place on a page, store the graphic or text in a glossary entry along with its position style. For example, you might have a company logo that you want to appear at the top center of letters and reports.

The Format Position command lets you easily specify different fixed positions on a page for text and graphics. By assigning a paragraph or a table to a specific, fixed position on a page, you ensure that the element will appear in the position you want. For example, you can assign a title to the center of a page, or a paragraph that contains a graphic to the upper-right corner.

You specify a fixed position by combining a horizontal position (Left, Center, Right, Inside, or Outside) with a vertical position (Top, Center, Bottom, or Inline).

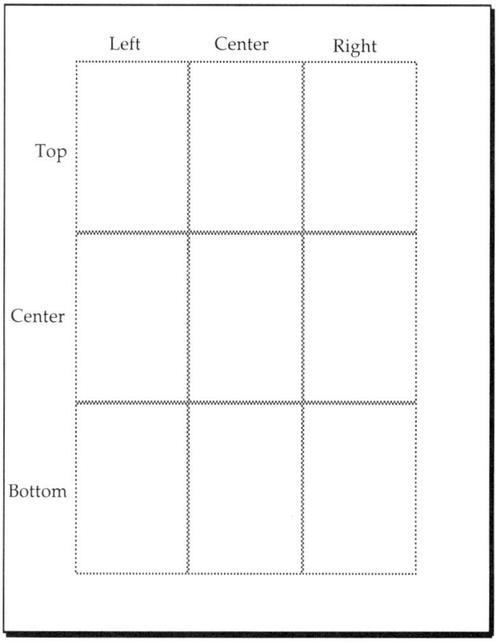

You can create styles for each of these page positions, which makes it easy to set the position of a paragraph or a table by applying the appropriate style. The styles can include a paragraph width measurement so that the object to appear in any of these positions will be only as wide as you want it—for example, a paragraph can be only 2 inches wide.

Suppose you want to create a glossary entry containing a logo that appears at the top center of a page. First, insert the logo graphic in a document, either cutting and pasting the logo in or inserting it from a glossary entry if it is in one. Or, if the graphic is in a graphic file for which Word has a graphic interpretation file, use the Insert Picture command to insert it. For information about file formats that Word can import, see the entry for IMPORT in the Appendix, "Field Types and Their Instructions."

Next, choose the Format Position command (Alt,T,O). In the Format Position dialog box, select the Center option in the Horizontal Position list, select the Top option in the Vertical Position list, move to the Paragraph Width box (Alt+W), and type the width of the logo—for example, 2".

Now, select the logo graphic, choose the Edit Glossary command (Alt,E,O), and type a glossary name—for example, *logo.* If your document is based on a template and if you will use the logo in that template only, choose the Template option for Context (Alt+T). If your document is not based on a template or if you want to be able to use the logo glossary entry in every document, leave Context set to Global. Then, choose the Define button (Alt+D) to create the glossary entry.

To insert the logo in a document, position the insertion point anywhere on the page on which you want the logo to appear. You can ensure that the logo will appear on the correct page by inserting it as the first element on that page. Type *logo,* and press the GLOSSARY key (F3). When you print the page or view the document in Page View (Alt,V,P) or in Print Preview (Alt,F,V), the logo will appear in its assigned position.

Storing a sidebar in a glossary entry

A sidebar is a self-contained article or note that appears in a larger article or report and that usually contains background or supplemental information related to the main article. A sidebar often appears in a box.

Like the logo graphic, you can use styles to format the position of a sidebar. You store a sidebar in a glossary entry only if the sidebar is standard text or a standard graphic that appears in many documents. For example, in a newsletter you might include the publishing and circulation information in a box that appears in every issue in the bottom-left corner of page 2. Or, in employee handbooks or press releases, an equal opportunity statement might be printed at the bottom of the last page. In both these instances, you would save time and effort by storing the sidebar's text and style in glossary entries. This example shows you how to create a sidebar in the bottom-left corner of a page in your document.

First, type the text for the sidebar, as shown below:

Text is centered (Ctrl+C).

reVision Aerie

Merle Rotti, *Editor*

Executive Editor
Brittany deSpain

Royal Leeds, *Art Director*

© Copyright 1989 reVisionary Publishers

Select all the text, and then choose the Format Paragraph command (Alt,T,P). In the Format Paragraph dialog box, choose the Box option for Border (Alt+O,B) and the Double option for Pattern (Alt+E,D), and then choose OK. With the text still selected, choose the Format Position command (Alt,T,O). In the Format Position dialog box, choose the Bottom option for the Vertical position (Alt+V,Bottom), move to the Paragraph Width box (Alt+W), and type *1.67"*. You can make the paragraph wider or narrower, depending on the width of your sidebar information. Choose OK to apply the position formatting to the paragraph.

To create a style based on the selection, press the Ctrl+S keys, type an appropriate name—for example, *masthead*—and then press the Enter key. Choose the Edit Glossary command (Alt,E,O), and type a glossary entry name—for example, *masthead*. Then, choose the Define button (Alt+D) to create the glossary entry. Giving a style and a glossary entry the same name is not a problem. In fact, it's a plus because the name can suggest that the style and the glossary entry work together.

Example 4: Storing Other Formatting in a Glossary Entry

Word does not have styles for sections. A section style would be a named, stored format for a section that you might use, for example, to format text in multiple columns. In place of section styles, however, you can format sections and then store the section marks in glossary entries. When you need a particular section format, you simply insert a section mark from the appropriate glossary entry. You can format section marks to create such section formatting as varied section beginnings and varied number of columns. This example shows you how to create a glossary entry that sets up a two-column format for a section mark. For the example you can use a blank document, or you can insert text so that you'll be able to see the effects of the formatting.

Start by choosing the Insert Break command (Alt,I,B). In the Insert Break dialog box, select the Section Break option that suits your document. The Next Page option (Alt+N) inserts a page break before starting to print the contents of the section. In the same way, the Odd Page (Alt+O) and Even Page (Alt+E) options insert a page break (or two, if needed) before printing the section's contents on an odd-numbered or an even-numbered page. The Continuous option (Alt+T) prints the section's contents at the end of the previous section without inserting a page break. This option lets you change the number of columns within a page. Then, choose OK to insert a section mark, which appears as a double dotted line.

Position the insertion point on the section mark, and choose the Format Section command (Alt,T,S). In the Format Section dialog box, type 2 in the Number box for Columns, and then choose OK. Now, select the section mark, choose the Edit Glossary command (Alt,E,O), and type an appropriate glossary name—for example, *2_Col*. Choose the Define button (Alt+D) to create the glossary entry.

To use this "2_Col" glossary entry, position the insertion point at the end of the text that you want to print in two columns, type *2_Col*, and then press the GLOSSARY key (F3). If the document contains no text, insert the "2_Col" glossary entry, press the Ctrl+Home keys to move the insertion point (in the section mark) to the beginning of the document, and then press the Enter key to insert a paragraph mark. Move the insertion point up to the empty paragraph above the section mark, and insert the contents.

A document might already contain text that's formatted in a different number of columns (for example, one column), and you might need to insert the two-column text following the existing text. To preserve the section formatting of the existing text, insert a section break at the end of the existing text. Then, position the insertion point after the text for the two-column section, and insert the "2_Col" glossary entry. If the two-column section does not yet contain any text, move the insertion point into the two-column section mark, press the Enter key, move the insertion point up to the new empty paragraph, and insert the contents. Note that to see the effect of the section you insert from the "2_Col" glossary entry, you must switch to either Page View (choose the View Page command—Alt,V,P) or Print Preview (choose the File Print Preview command—Alt,F,V).

The following list suggests other section formatting you might save in glossary entries, either separately or in any combination:

- Various numbers of columns, with a line between each
- The Top, Center, and Justify vertical alignment settings
- Line numbering turned on, with its various options for starting number, position, frequency, and range

Example 5: Storing a Field in a Glossary Entry

A glossary entry is a good place in which to store a field that you use often. A field that you insert only occasionally, however, is not worth the memory space the glossary entry would require. You can easily insert a field that you use infrequently by using either the INSERT FIELD key combination (Ctrl+F9) or the Insert Field command.

You might find the following three automatic-numbering fields the most useful to put into glossary entries: AUTONUM, AUTONUMLGL, and AUTONUMOUT. Storing these numbering fields in glossary entries is particularly useful when you also store tab characters and a paragraph mark with each field. Using a glossary entry reduces the amount of typing you need to do and eliminates the need to apply paragraph formatting and to set tab stops each time you use the field.

You can create a glossary entry that contains the elements of a numbered list item—numbers, tab characters, and paragraph formatting that indents the text to the right of the number. Word lets you use the AUTONUM field to insert and automatically update numbers in a list. To insert an AUTONUM field, create a new, blank paragraph and press the Tab key. Then, to insert an AUTONUM field, press the INSERT FIELD key combination (Ctrl+F9) and type *autonum*. For more information about the AUTONUM field, see the Appendix, "Field Types and Their Instructions."

Press the End key to move the insertion point outside the field, press the Tab key again, and then press the Enter key. To select the paragraph you just created, press the Shift+Ctrl+up arrow keys, and then press the TOGGLE FIELD key combination (Shift+F9) to see the number. Press the HANGING INDENT key combination (Ctrl+T) to apply a hanging indent of one-half inch. Choose the Format Tabs command (Alt,T,T). In the Format Tabs dialog box, type *0.17"* in the Tab Position box, choose the Right option for Alignment (Alt+R), choose the Set button (Alt+S), type *0.5"* in the Tab Position box, choose the Left option for Alignment (Alt+L), and then choose OK to set both tab stops.

To capture this formatting as a style, press the Ctrl+S keys, type a style name such as *Numbered List*, and then press the Enter key. Choose Yes when you see a message that asks whether you want to create the style. Word applies this style to the paragraph. Next, choose the Edit

Glossary command (Alt,E,O). In the Edit Glossary dialog box, type a brief name such as *nul* in the Glossary Name box, and choose the Define button (Alt+D) to create the glossary entry. To insert a paragraph that's a numbered list item, position the insertion point where you want to insert the paragraph, type *nul*, and then press the GLOSSARY key (F3). And to insert text in the paragraph that's a numbered list item, position the insertion point after the NUMBER field and tab character and immediately before the paragraph mark; if the field, tab character, and paragraph mark are not visible, press the SHOW ALL key combination (Ctrl+*). Then, type the text. Press Ctrl+* again to display the number instead of the field.

Example 6: Storing a Table in a Glossary Entry

You can create different kinds of table formats without text in them and then store these blank, formatted tables in glossary entries. Inserting such a table format in a document makes creating tables faster. You might want to store a frequently used table format. In this example, you see how to create a basic three-column table that has one-inch-wide columns. See Chapter 13, "Tables the New, Easy Way," for more information about creating tables and more examples of tables that you can store as glossary entries.

In any document, even if it's empty, position the insertion point at the beginning of a paragraph. Choose the Insert Table command (Alt,I,T), and Word displays the Insert Table dialog box:

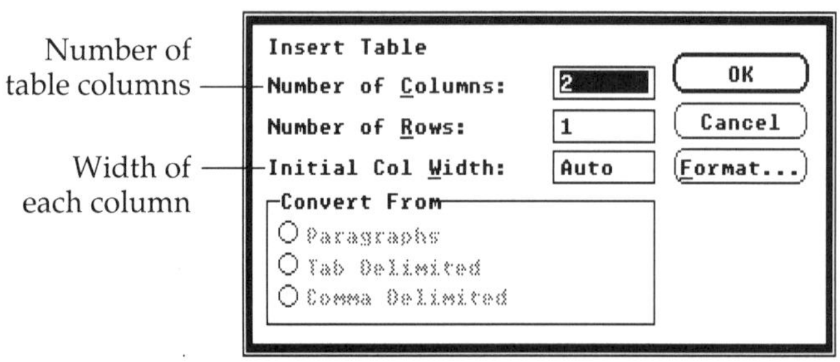

In the Number of Columns box, type 3 to set up a three-column table. Move to the Initial Col Width box (Alt+W), and type *1"* to set the width of the columns to one inch. Choose OK, and Word inserts the table. Press the Alt+5 keys (5 on the numeric keypad) to select the whole table.

Then, choose the Edit Glossary command (Alt,E,O). In the Edit Glossary dialog box, type a glossary entry name such as *ThreeColTbl* in the Glossary Name box, and then choose the Define button (Alt+D) to store the table format in a glossary entry.

To use the three-column table glossary entry, position the insertion point where you want the table, type *ThreeColTbl*, and press the GLOSSARY key (F3). Word inserts the table. Move the insertion point into the table's first column, and type the text or numbers or insert a graphic. Note that if the contents of a cell are wider than the column, Word wraps the contents to additional lines in the column. To move the insertion point to the next column, press the Tab key. To add another row to the table, move the insertion point to the third column and press Tab.

Special Glossary Entry: Spike

Word contains a special glossary entry named Spike. Spike is special because it can accumulate text and graphics rather than storing only one selection at a time, as other glossary entries do. Using Spike, you can collect text and graphics from various places in a document and then insert them all at one time at a new location in any document. Spike is an electronic version of a spindle file, which looks like a large pin mounted on a stand and is sometimes seen on an office desk. Word's version of the spindle lets you collect text or graphics and then insert the whole collection in your document.

Remember a couple of important points about Spike. First, if you try to store additional text or graphics in a regular glossary entry, the new text or graphics replace what's already in the entry. Not so for Spike. If you use the SPIKE key combination (Ctrl+F3), Spike accumulates all the text and graphics that you send to it. Second, when you insert the contents of a regular glossary entry, the contents stay in the glossary entry while a copy of the contents appears in the document. When you insert the contents of Spike using the UNSPIKE key combination (Ctrl+Shift+F3), however, Spike empties; its contents move permanently from the Spike glossary entry to the document.

To see how Spike works, open or create a document that contains at least six lines of text or several graphics. Select part of the text or a graphic, and press the SPIKE key combination (Ctrl+F3). The selection disappears from the document. Choose the Edit Glossary command (Alt,E,O), and you see "Spike" listed as a defined glossary entry. Now, choose the Cancel button (Esc) to close the dialog box. Select another piece of text or a graphic, or a combination of text and graphics, and then press Ctrl+F3 again. Then, position the insertion point at the end of the document so that you can see the contents of Spike being inserted, and press the UNSPIKE key combination (Ctrl+Shift+F3). Spike's contents appear in the document. To be sure that Spike is empty, press Ctrl+Shift+F3 again. This time nothing new appears in the document because Spike is now empty.

You can also create Spike by choosing the Edit Glossary command (Alt,E,O). First, select the text or graphics, and then, in the Edit Glossary dialog box, type *Spike* in the Glossary Name box and choose the Define button (Alt,D). This method does not delete the selection from the document. If you use the Edit Glossary command, Spike does not accumulate contents. New contents replace existing contents, in the same way as a regular glossary entry. If, however, you create Spike using the Edit Glossary command and then add contents to Spike using the SPIKE key combination (Ctrl+F3), Spike does accumulate contents. If you mix the standard glossary methods and the Spike key combination methods, Spike accumulates and empties its contents when you use the Spike key combinations but replaces and retains its contents when you use the Edit Glossary command.

The table on the following page summarizes the actions for each Spike method.

TIP

Reusing Spike's Contents

When you use the UNSPIKE key combination (Ctrl+Shift+F3) to insert Spike's contents, Spike empties. If you want to insert Spike's contents in several places, however, use one of the standard methods to insert glossary entries. Type *Spike* and press the GLOSSARY key (F3), or choose the Edit Glossary command (Alt,E,O), select Spike, and choose OK. When you use the standard methods, Spike works in the same way as a regular glossary entry and does not empty.

Method	*Actions*
SPIKE (Ctrl+F3)	Deletes selection from document and adds it to Spike glossary entry
UNSPIKE (Ctrl+Shift+F3)	Empties Spike's contents and inserts them in document at insertion point
Edit Glossary—Define (Alt+D)	Replaces Spike's contents with selection from document and does not delete selection from document
Edit Glossary—Insert (Alt+I) or GLOSSARY key (F3)	Inserts Spike's contents at insertion point in document and does not empty Spike

TIP

Converting Glossaries from PC Word

To convert a PC Word glossary for use in Word for Windows, start PC Word with a blank document. Choose the Transfer Glossary Merge command (Esc,T,G,M), type the glossary name and press Enter. (If you are converting NORMAL.GLY, skip this first step.) Choose Transfer Glossary Merge again, type *convert.gly*, and press Enter. In the blank PC Word document, type *Convert_Glossary* and press the GLOSSARY key (F3). Word runs the macro stored in CONVERT.GLY and stores the converted glossary entries in a file with the same name as your PC Word glossary file but with the extension CVT. When PC Word finishes converting glossary entries, a message tells you to press Enter to quit PC Word. Start Word for Windows. Choose the File New command (Alt,F,N), select PCWORD.DOT from the Use Template list, and choose OK. Choose the File Open command (Alt,F,O), and select the conversion glossary file. (Its extension is CVT.) Word for Windows runs a macro named PCWordGlossary, which asks if you want the glossary entries to belong to the global context or to a template context. Choose a context and choose OK. If you choose the template context, the macro asks for a template file name. Type a new name, or type or select an existing template name, and choose OK. The macro processes the glossary entries and saves the template. You can now use the converted glossary entries in your Word for Windows documents. This process converts all text and formatting in each glossary entry (including date and time formats) with these exceptions: Font color is changed to black, side-by-side paragraphs are reset to No, gutter margin is changed to zero, and PC Word macros are converted to text only—they will not run in Word for Windows.

Chapter 13

Tables the New, Easy Way

We've all seen and used tables in documents, even in handwritten letters and notes. A table is information arranged in columns and rows, as the following example of a simple table shows:

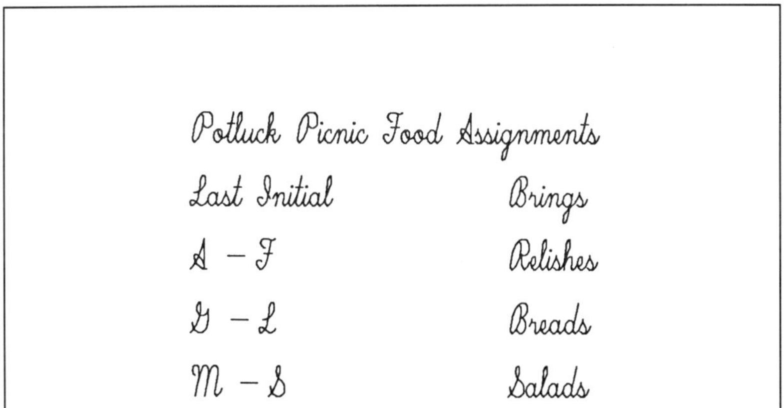

Potluck Picnic Food Assignments

Last Initial	Brings
A – F	Relishes
G – L	Breads
M – S	Salads
T – Z	Desserts

The old, tedious, and often frustrating way to set up a table was to set tab stops. Often this method was an exercise in guesswork. Word for

Windows contains a table feature that simplifies setting up a table; it replaces tab stops, formatting paragraphs side by side, and guesswork with an easy-to-use approach. You tell Word where you want the table and how many columns you want it to contain, and Word sets it up. Then you type the text and paste the graphics without worrying about the table's length or format. If a document contains text and graphics that you want to use in a table, Word can convert them to table format. Or, if you want to take text and graphics out of table format, Word can convert the table to regular text and graphics format.

Word's table feature lets you set a different width for each table column. You can also set the width of a column for each individual row, expand the table length by inserting more text and graphics, and add or delete rows and columns anywhere in a table. And Word provides a way to add a border around any individual part of a table, around all parts of a table, or around the entire table.

The first part of this chapter shows you how to set up a basic table of the sort that you formerly set up using tab stops. First you insert a table and fill in its contents. Then you type text, select it, and convert it to a table. After you create a table, you learn how to move around in a table and select cell contents for editing and formatting, for adjusting the table's structure, and for other special actions. Examples show you how to use tables for side-by-side paragraphs and for spreadsheet operations. You also learn how to combine tables and fields and how to store special table arrangements in glossary entries so that you can easily reuse them.

Chapter 15, "Merge Printing," explains how to use tables to set up documents more easily for merge printing.

Creating a Standard Table

To create a table, try the two following examples, which illustrate the two methods of creating tables. In the first example, you set up the number of rows and columns and then type, copy, move, or paste contents into the cells. In the second example, you type the text that you want in the table, insert graphics, select the text and graphics, and then insert a table to enclose the selected text and graphics. No matter which method you choose, you can convert a table or part of a table back to regular text or move a graphic out of a table, as explained in "Converting a Table or Individual Rows Back to Text" later in this chapter.

Example 1: Inserting a Table and Then Filling It In

The usual way to create a table in Word is to insert an empty table and then fill it in with your text. In this example, you create the table shown in Figure 13-1:

First Quarter	East	West	North	South
Jan	1234	1243	1324	1342
Feb	1423	1432	2134	2143
Mar	2314	2341	2413	2431

Figure 13-1.
First quarter regional results.

In any document, position the insertion point where you want to insert the table. Then, choose the Insert Table command (Alt,I,T). In the Insert Table dialog box, type 5 for this example in the Number of Columns box:

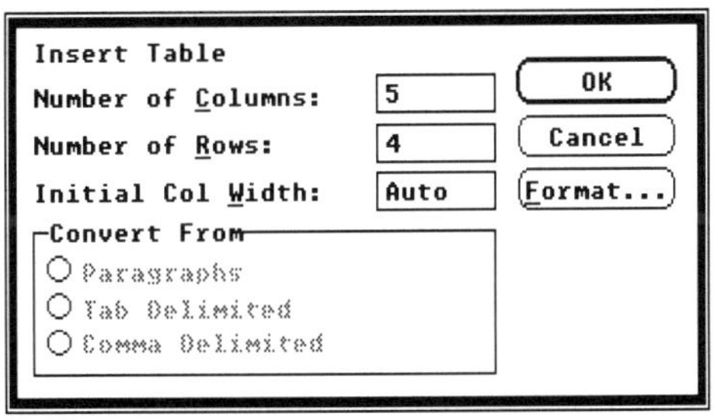

Word always proposes two columns. If you're not using two columns, type a number that's as close as possible to the number of columns you need, but remember that you can add or delete columns later. A table can contain a maximum of 31 columns.

In the Number of Rows box, type 4 for this example. In general, when you know how many rows the table will have, type that number. Word always proposes one row because it's easy to add more rows to the end of a table as you need them. You can also add and delete rows anywhere else in the table.

In the Initial Col Width box, leave the setting at Auto for this example. The Auto setting tells Word to divide the available width evenly among all the columns you insert. To make columns a specific width, type the measurement you want. Each column in the new table will be the width set in Initial Col Width. You can ignore the Convert From options in the dialog box, which are grayed because you selected an insertion point rather than text. You'll use these options in Example 2. For now, choose OK to insert the table. Note that the insertion point is in the table's first cell.

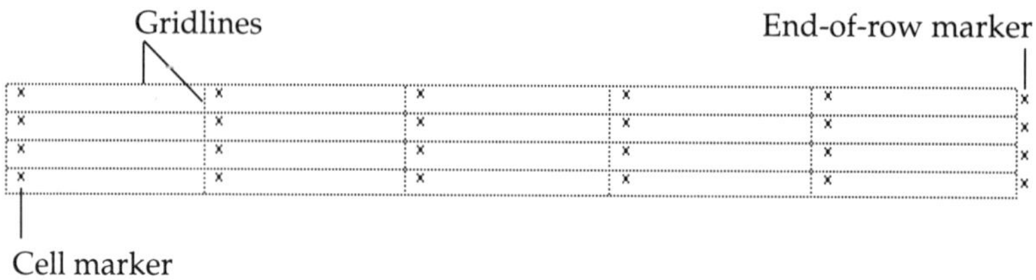

Each cell in a table contains a cell marker, which appears as a ¤ when the Paragraph Marks option or the Show All option is turned on in the View Preferences dialog box. (If the font size you are using is 10 points or smaller, the reduced size of the symbol might cause it to appear as an x rather than as the cell marker symbol, as in the above example.) Cell markers indicate the end of a cell's contents. At the end of each row, outside the last cell, is an end-of-row marker, which has the same appearance as a cell marker. The end-of-row marker is important when you insert additional columns at the right side of a table, as you'll see later in this chapter, in "Example 10: Inserting a Cell or Column at the Right Side of a Table."

In the first cell, type *First Quarter*. Press the Tab key to move to the second cell and then type *East*. Continue typing the text as shown in Figure 13-1, pressing Tab to move from cell to cell. To move back a cell, press the Shift+Tab keys.

Example 2: Inserting Text and Then Converting It to a Table

Sometimes you might prefer to type text first and put it in a table later. Or you might have a document containing text that's in columns, such as a table made using tab stops. To convert existing text to a Word table, select the text and then use the Insert Table command to insert a table that encompasses the selected text. For this example, create the table in Figure 13-2 below, which shows second-quarter sales figures for four geographic regions. The → characters indicate tab characters, and the ¶ characters indicate paragraphs. Note that the columns do not need to line up; the table will align columns for you. Be sure to insert only one tab character between each piece of text.

```
2nd Quarter → East → West → North → South¶
April → 2345 → 2354 → 2435 → 2453¶
May → 2534 → 2543 → 3245 → 3254¶
June → 3425 → 3452 → 3524 → 3542¶
```

Figure 13-2.
Table text typed with tab characters.

First, type the text for the table, pressing the Tab key between each column to separate the columns with tab characters. At the end of each row, press the Enter key.

Select the table's text, and then choose the Insert Table command (Alt,I,T).

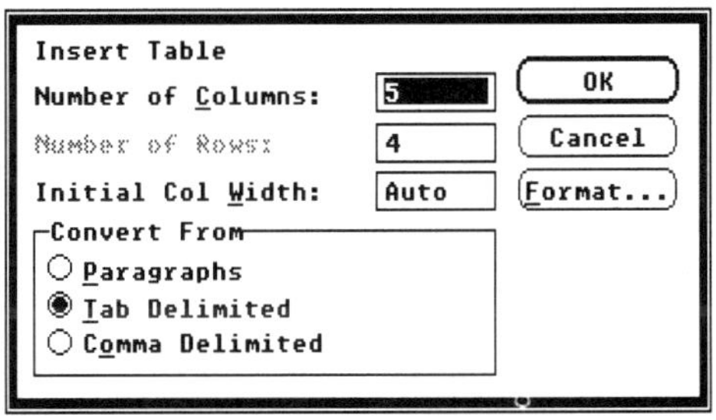

In the Insert Table dialog box, Word proposes a number of columns that's based on the number of columns of text you selected. Because you selected four paragraphs with five columns each for this example, Word proposes 5 columns and 4 rows. Also, because each row of text is separated by a paragraph mark, you can type a different number in the Number of Columns box and Word changes the number in the Number of Rows box, and vice versa. Retain 5 in Number of Columns and 4 in Number of Rows.

For this example, type *1″* over the default "Auto" in the Initial Col Width box. Type a measurement for Initial Col Width when you want the columns to be a specific width. Leave "Auto" for Initial Col Width when you want the table to be as wide as the document's margins. If it's not already chosen, choose the Tab Delimited option for the Convert

From setting. When you want the table setup to be based on a different type of conversion than that which Word proposes, choose that other option. The type of conversion you choose also affects the numbers of columns and rows that Word proposes. The Paragraphs option places in a cell all text and graphics that are between pairs of paragraph marks in the selection. The Comma Delimited option places in a cell all text and graphics that are between pairs of commas in the selection.

TIP

Getting Multiple Paragraphs into a Single Table Cell

If you select text that's separated by tabs or commas to convert to a table, Word proposes the number of columns and rows in the Insert Table dialog box. You can change the number of columns, and Word changes the number of rows. If you increase the number of columns, Word adds blank cells at the end of each row. You cannot, however, convert multiple paragraphs directly into a single cell.

One way to get around this limitation is to change some paragraph marks in the selection to tab characters or commas so that you can adjust the number of rows and columns you want in the table. But if you take this approach, you have to count paragraph marks, replacing them with commas or tab characters. And if you miscount, your table will not be formatted correctly.

As a way around this potential problem, select the text that's separated by paragraph marks, choose the Insert Table command (Alt,I,T), type the number of paragraphs in the Number of Columns box, and then choose OK. After the table is inserted, it remains selected. Now, choose the Insert Table to Text command (Alt,I,T). (This command replaces the Insert Table command on the menu when the selection contains only a whole table or whole rows of a table.) In the Insert Table to Text dialog box, turn on the Tab Delimited option (Alt+T) for Convert Table To, and choose OK. Word converts the table into one paragraph, all of it still selected. Choose Insert Table (Alt,I,T) again, and select the Paragraph option (Alt+P) for Convert From. Word sets Number of Columns and Number of Rows to 1. Type the number of columns and the number of rows you want. Choose OK. Choose the Edit Replace command (Alt,E,E), type *^t* for Search For, type *^p* for Replace With, turn off the Confirm Changes option (Alt+C), and then choose OK. The table will now have multiple paragraphs in one cell, and the table will be formatted in the number of rows and columns you want.

Comma list

Sporting, Working, Herding, Hounds, Non-Sporting, Terriers, Toys¶

Sporting	Working	Herding	Hounds	Non-Sporting	Terriers	Toys

Converted to table

If you change the type of conversion, Word adjusts the number of columns and rows to fit what's in the selection. Now, choose OK to insert the table structure as shown in Figure 13-3:

2nd Quarter	East	West	North	South
April	2345	2354	2435	2453
May	2534	2543	3245	3254
June	3425	3452	3524	3542

Figure 13-3.
Text of Figure 13-2 converted to a table.

Moving Around and Selecting in a Table

Before you start formatting a table or editing its contents, you need to know how to move around and select within a table using either the keyboard or the mouse. Within a cell, you move and select in the same way you do in text that's outside a table. You use a different approach, however, to select a whole cell (all the text and graphics and the cell marker), more than one cell, a row, or the whole table. To introduce selecting in tables, the following section describes the parts of a table structure.

Some Details About the Parts of a Table

A table consists of columns and rows. The space for one column in one row is called a cell. Thus, a table that is five columns by four rows contains twenty cells. Each cell can contain anything a Word document can contain except another table. The height of a row is set by the height of the tallest cell in that row. A row can be as short as 4 points or as tall as a page. If a row contains more text and graphics than can be printed on one page, Word prints only as much of that cell as fits on the current page. You can format the contents of cells in any of the ways you can format text or graphics outside of tables.

Think of a table as a collection of rows that can have independent formats. Because the rows are independent of one another, if you want to change the table formatting in a column, be sure to select all the cells in the column. Or select the whole table to format all the cells.

A table appears on the screen with dotted lines, called gridlines, which outline each cell. These gridlines are turned on so that you can see the outline of your table when you insert it. Word does not print these gridlines; they're only for display, and you can turn them off in the View Preferences dialog box. If you turn on borders around each cell using the Borders options in the Format Table dialog box, the borders replace the gridlines on the screen. Although Word does not print gridlines, Word does print these borders.

Using the Keyboard to Move and Select

The up, down, left, and right arrow keys; the Ctrl+left arrow keys; the Ctrl+right arrow keys; and the Home and End keys perform the same action within the text of a single cell that they perform in text outside a table. When the insertion point reaches the top edge, bottom edge, left edge, or right edge of a cell, however, the arrow keys work differently, as the following table shows:

Key	*Action*
Up arrow	When the insertion point is in the top line of a cell, pressing the up arrow key moves the insertion point up one cell in the same column.
Down arrow	When the insertion point is in the bottom line of a cell, pressing the down arrow key moves the insertion point down one cell in the same column.
Left arrow	When the insertion point is at the beginning of a cell, pressing the left arrow key moves the insertion point left one cell in the same row. If the cell is the first cell in the row, pressing the left arrow key moves the insertion point to the preceding row's end-of-row marker.
Right arrow	When the insertion point is at the end of a cell, pressing the right arrow key moves the insertion point right one cell in the same row. If the insertion point is at the end-of-row marker, pressing the right arrow key moves the insertion point to the first cell in the next row.

(continued)

continued

Key	*Action*
Tab	Pressing the Tab key selects the contents of the next cell. At the end of the row, pressing Tab selects the contents of the first cell of the next row. At the end of the last row, pressing Tab adds a new row to the bottom of the table.
Shift+Tab	Pressing the Shift+Tab keys selects the contents of the preceding cell. At the beginning of a row, pressing Shift+Tab selects the contents of the last cell of the preceding row. And if you press Shift+Tab in the first cell of the table, Word beeps to let you know that you cannot go backward any farther.
Home	Pressing the Home key moves the insertion point to the beginning of the current cell.
End	Pressing the End key moves the insertion point to the end of the current cell.
Alt+Home	Pressing the Alt+Home keys moves the insertion point to the first cell in the current row.
Alt+End	Pressing the Alt+End keys moves the insertion point to the last cell in the current row.
Alt+PgUp	Pressing the Alt+PgUp keys moves the insertion point to the top cell in the current column.
Alt+PgDn	Pressing the Alt+PgDn keys moves the insertion point to the bottom cell in the current column.
Alt+5 (5 on numeric keypad)	Pressing the Alt+5 keys selects the entire table.
Shift+arrow keys	Pressing the Shift+arrow keys selects within a cell; when the selection crosses a cell boundary, pressing the Shift+arrow keys selects whole cells.
F8	Pressing the F8 key selects within cell contents as it does in regular text, until the entire cell is selected; then F8 selects outside the table (for example, a section, and then the whole document).

If a table is wider than the screen, use the Alt+End keys to jump to the last column. Word scrolls the window to show the right end of the table. To scroll the window back to the left, press the Alt+Home keys. Of course, the Tab key and the Shift+Tab keys scroll the table horizontally after the selection jumps to a cell that is outside the window.

Using the Mouse to Move and Select

You can use the mouse to move the insertion point and to select text and graphics in the table as you do in text outside of tables. If you select by dragging, the selection grows by whole cells after you cross a cell boundary. The mouse also provides shortcuts for selecting cell contents, rows, and columns:

Mouse Action	*Effect*
Click in cell selection bar (along inner-left side of a cell).	Selects cell contents
Double-click in row selection bar (along left border of table), or double-click in any cell selection bar.	Selects entire row
Click in column selection bar (along top border of top cell in column), or click right button anywhere in column.	Selects entire column

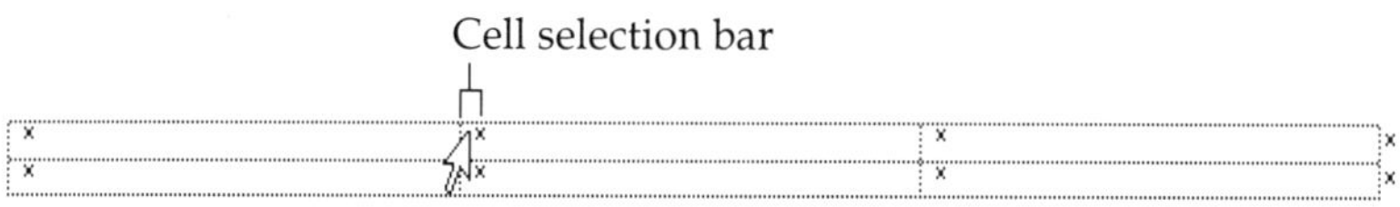

If a table is wider than the window, turn on the Horizontal Scroll Bar (Alt+H) in the View Preferences dialog box. Then you can scroll the table horizontally using the mouse by clicking or dragging in the horizontal scroll bar.

Editing in a Table

Within each cell, you can edit text and graphics in all the same ways you do outside a table. It's only when you cross cell boundaries that editing actions change. This section explains those changes in editing that occur when you delete cell contents, paste contents to cells, and copy and move cell contents.

Deleting Cell Contents

To delete the contents of cells, you use the same methods you use in regular text: Select the text, and either choose the Edit Cut command (Alt,E,T) or press the Delete key or the Shift+Delete keys. Deleting a selection that is completely enclosed within a table deletes the contents of its cells but does not delete the cells themselves; the empty cells remain in the table's structure. Note, however, that if a selection includes part or all of a table and part of the document outside the table, deleting does delete the cells from the table. For more information about how to delete or rearrange cells, see "Changing the Number of Cells in a Table" later in this chapter.

After you delete a selection that contains cells to the Clipboard, Word transfers both the cells and their contents to the Clipboard.

Pasting Cell Contents

When the Clipboard contains only text and graphics in cells, the Edit Paste command changes to the Edit Paste Cells command on the menu. You can paste cells from the Clipboard to an insertion point either outside or inside a table. If the insertion point is outside a table, choosing Edit Paste Cells inserts a table that's the same size and shape as the cells on the Clipboard. If the insertion point is inside a table cell, choosing Edit Paste Cells pastes the cells from the Clipboard to the existing table.

The contents of the cells you paste replace the contents of cells in a corresponding number and shape, starting at the insertion point. For rows of cells on the Clipboard that have more columns than the rows you paste into, Word adds columns of cells as needed from the Clipboard to the end of the row. If the Clipboard contains more rows than the existing table, Word adds new rows of cells from the Clipboard to the bottom of the table. In the following illustration, the insertion point is in the last cell in the last row:

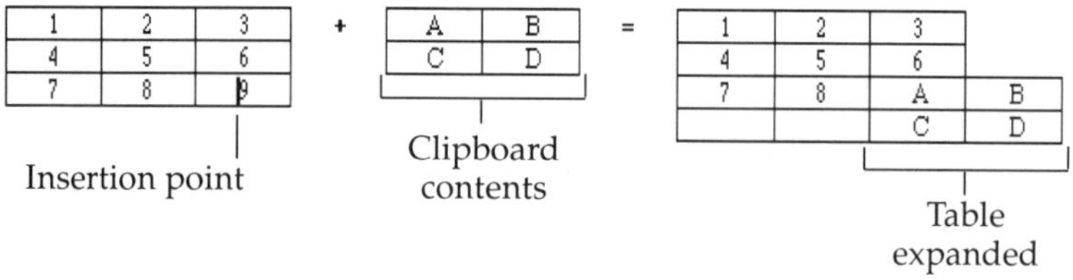

You can select cells in a table and then paste cells from the Clipboard, but be certain that the selection in the table is exactly the same size and shape as the cells on the Clipboard. If your selection is a different shape or size, you see the following message:

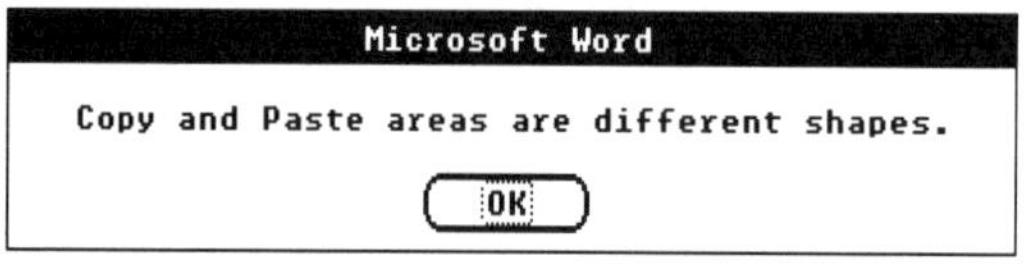

It's better to position the insertion point in the first cell in which you want the paste to start rather than to select a group of cells in the table. The insertion-point method always works because Word can determine the correct size and shape of the group of cells it needs. If you replace cell contents you want to keep, choose the Edit Undo command (Alt+backspace) immediately.

When the Clipboard contains a mixture of text that's from both inside and outside a table, you cannot paste the Clipboard's contents to a table. If you try, you see the following message:

TIP

What's on the Clipboard?

If you cannot remember what's on the Clipboard, how do you find out? Choose the Word Control Run command (Alt,spacebar,U), choose Clipboard in the dialog box, and then choose OK. Word opens the Clipboard window.

To paste cells to an existing table when the Clipboard contains a mixture, paste the contents of the Clipboard outside the table. Then, select only the table portion of the newly pasted text, choose the Edit Cut command (Alt,E,T) or press the Shift+Delete keys, and paste the cells to the table.

For a clue as to whether a paste to a table will work, open the Edit menu. When the menu shows the Paste Cells command, pasting to a table will work because the Clipboard contains only text that's in cells. When the menu shows only the Paste command, however, you need to look at what the Clipboard contains. (If the Clipboard contains only text outside a table, however, pasting to a single table cell will work.)

Copying and Moving Cell Contents

To copy text among cells, use the COPY key combination (Shift+F2) as well as the Edit Copy and Edit Paste commands and their shortcut keys. To move text among cells, use the MOVE key (F2) as well as the Edit Cut and Edit Paste commands and their shortcut keys. These commands and keys work as they do in regular text, with a few restrictions. For the COPY and MOVE keys, select within only one cell at a time. If you select a group of cells and try these keys, you see the message, "Not a valid selection." When you see this message, choose OK, select only one cell or part of one cell, and try the COPY key combination (Shift+F2) or the MOVE (F2) key again.

When you want to copy text from multiple cells, select the text, choose the Edit Copy command (Alt,E,C) or press the Ctrl+Insert keys, position the insertion point where you want to make the copy, and then choose the Edit Paste command (Alt,E,P) or press the Shift+Insert keys.

Word also lets you copy and move text and graphics from within a cell to outside a table, from outside a table into a cell, and from within a cell in one table to within a cell in another table.

Formatting Cells and Tables

When the insertion point or the entire selection is within a table, the Format Table command is available. The Format Table dialog box's options show you how you can format tables, as shown on the next page.

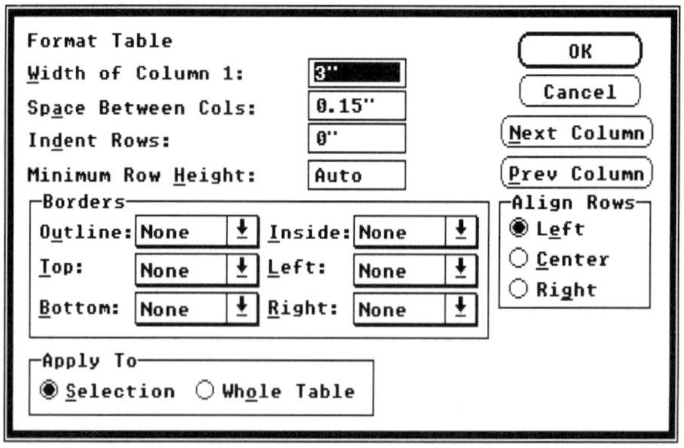

Width of Column shows the column number and the width of the cell that contains the insertion point. When more than one column is selected, the label shows the range of columns in the selection, as in "Width of Columns 2–4," and the figure in the box shows the common column width. If the selected columns are different widths, the box is blank.

Space Between Cols shows the minimum amount of blank space that Word leaves between the text in neighboring columns. Even though the table gridlines and cell borders do not show this space, Word leaves the space when you print the table to clearly separate columns. You'll seldom change this measurement—only when you have a special requirement for space between columns. This measurement affects all cells in the selected rows.

Indent Rows shows how far the selected rows are indented from the left margin.

Minimum Row Height shows the minimum height of all cells that are in the selected rows. If any cell in the row contains text or graphics that require more row height, the row expands vertically as necessary. But the tallest cell in a row determines the minimum row height. "Auto" and "0" (zero) tell Word to make the row one line tall or taller if needed. A line is as tall as the Line measurement under Spacing in the Format Paragraph dialog box. To set a row to a fixed height, type a negative height measurement in the Minimum Row Height box. For example, typing *–1"* fixes a row at 1", regardless of the height of the cell's contents.

Borders shows which cell borders have been added and what type each border is: single, thick, or double. "None" means no border. You'll learn more about borders in "Example 5: Adding and Removing Borders for a Group of Cells" and "Example 6: Adding a Border Around the Whole Table."

Align Rows shows the alignment between the margins of the selected rows. These row alignment options parallel the paragraph alignment options Word includes in the Format Paragraph dialog box. Examples later in this chapter help you learn more about row alignment.

Apply To tells Word how much of the table you want to format. Selection indicates that you want to format the selected cells only. Whole Table indicates that you want to format all the cells, even if not all the cells are selected. If any cells are selected when you choose the Format Table command, Word turns on the Selection option. If an entire table is selected when you choose Format Table, Word turns on the Whole Table option and makes the Selection option unavailable.

Next Column and **Prev Column** buttons apply your formatting selection and move the selection to a neighboring column so that you can format successive columns without having to close the dialog box. When a selection contains multiple cells in a column, these buttons direct Word to select the same number of cells in the neighboring column. When the selection is in the last column, the Next Column button jumps the selection to the first column. If cells are selected in more than one column, the Next Column button selects the first column to the right of the selection. The Prev Column button jumps to columns in the opposite direction from the Next Column button. You get practice using these two buttons later in this chapter.

In the following examples, you add cell borders to the Second Quarter table (see Figure 13-3 earlier in the chapter). You also align rows in another simple table that you create as you work through the example. At the end of the chapter, you'll find additional examples that apply what you learn here about adding borders and aligning rows.

Adding Borders to a Table

You can format a new table when you insert it or at any time. To format a table when you insert it, choose the Format button (Alt+F) instead of OK in the Insert Table dialog box. Word displays the Format Table dialog box, in which you can choose formatting options. To format a table at any time after you insert it, position the insertion point in the table or select entirely within a table, and then choose the Format Table command (Alt,T,A).

Word gives you the option of adding borders for a table—borders around individual cells, around a group of cells, and around the entire table. The following four examples give you practice adding borders to cells, to groups of cells, and to the whole table.

Example 3: Adding and Removing Borders for a Single Cell

To practice adding and removing borders for individual cells in a table, use the Second Quarter table that you created earlier in this chapter (see Figure 13-3).

First, position the insertion point in the top-left cell, where the text reads "2nd Quarter." Then, choose the Format Table command (Alt,T,A). In the Format Table dialog box, select Double for the Outline option (Alt+U,D) under Borders, which adds a double-line border around the cell. Note that Word selects the same border style in the Top, Bottom, Left, and Right border options. Outline is a shortcut for adding the four individual borders. Choose the Apply To Selection option (Alt+S) if it is not already turned on, and then choose OK. Your table now looks like the following:

2nd Quarter×	East×	West×	North×	South×	×
April×	2345×	2354×	2435×	2453×	×
May×	2534×	2543×	3245×	3254×	×
June×	3425×	3452×	3524×	3542×	×

Example 4: Formatting Cells from Column to Column

To format cells differently in each column, you select each column and apply the formatting in turn. As you saw earlier in this chapter, the Format Table dialog box contains Next Column and Prev Column buttons, which apply formatting to the selection and then select the next or previous column without closing the Format Table dialog box. These buttons provide a convenient way to format one column after another because they replace three actions: applying the formatting, selecting the next column, and choosing the Format Table command again.

To practice applying more borders and using these buttons, start by positioning the insertion point in the top row's second cell, where the text reads "East." Choose the Format Table command (Alt,T,A). In the Format Table dialog box, select the Thick option for Bottom (Alt+B,T) under Borders, which adds a thick-line border below the cell. Choose the Apply To Selection option (Alt+S) if it is not already turned on, and then choose the Next Column button (Alt+N) to add a thick bottom border to the cell containing "East" and to move to the third cell in the top row, where the text reads "West." Select the Thick option for Bottom (Alt+B,T) under Borders, and then choose the Next Column button (Alt+N) to move to the cell that contains "North." Select the Thick option for Bottom (Alt+B,T) under Borders, and then choose the Next Column button (Alt+N) to move to the cell that contains "South." Select the Thick option for Bottom (Alt+B,T) under Borders, and choose OK to apply the border to the cell and to close the dialog box. The borders in the table look like the following:

2nd Quarter×	East×	West×	North×	South×
April×	2345×	2354×	2435×	2453×
May×	2534×	2543×	3245×	3254×
June×	3425×	3452×	3524×	3542×

Example 5: Adding and Removing Borders for a Group of Cells

Although you can add and remove borders for individual cells, it's often more convenient to add borders to a group of cells all at one time when you want that group to have the same border style. For practice, select the group of cells in the Second Quarter table shown above that contains the names of the months April, May, and June. Then, choose the Format Table command (Alt,T,A). In the Format Table dialog box, select the Thick option for Right (Alt+R,T) under Borders to add a thick-line border along the right border of the group of cells. Choose the Apply To Selection option (Alt+S) if it is not already turned on, and then choose OK to format the table like the following:

2nd Quarter×	East×	West×	North×	South×
April×	2345×	2354×	2435×	2453×
May×	2534×	2543×	3245×	3254×
June×	3425×	3452×	3524×	3542×

Now, select the cells that contain the numbers, and choose the Format Table command (Alt,T,A). In the Format Table dialog box, select the Single option for Inside (Alt+I,S) under Borders. This option adds single-line borders between all the cells in the selection, but not around the outside of them. Choose the Apply To Selection option (Alt+S) if it is not already turned on, and then choose OK to see the table formatted:

2nd Quarter×	East×	West×	North×	South×	×
April×	2345×	2354×	2435×	2453×	×
May×	2534×	2543×	3245×	3254×	×
June×	3425×	3452×	3524×	3542×	×

To add single-line borders between the months, select the cells that contain the names of the months, choose the Format Table command (Alt,T,A), select the Single option for Inside (Alt+I,S) under Borders, choose the Apply To Selection option (Alt+S) if it is not already turned on, and then choose OK. Repeat this last step for the names of the regions to produce a table that now looks like the following:

2nd Quarter×	East×	West×	North×	South×	×
April×	2345×	2354×	2435×	2453×	×
May×	2534×	2543×	3245×	3254×	×
June×	3425×	3452×	3524×	3542×	×

Example 6: Adding a Border Around the Whole Table

Word provides a shortcut for adding a border around a whole table, rather than having to add each of the four borders separately. The Outline Border option in the Format Table dialog box adds left, right, top, and bottom borders for the selection.

To add a border around the outside of the whole Second Quarter table, position the insertion point anywhere in the table and press the Alt+5 keys (5 on the numeric keypad) to select the whole table. If you do not select the whole table, Word removes the existing cell borders. Then, choose the Format Table command (Alt,T,A). In the Format Table dialog box, select the Shadow option for Outline (Alt+U,S,S) under Borders, to add a shadow border around the outside of the table. Next, choose OK. Your table looks like the one in Figure 13-4.

2nd Quarter×	East×	West×	North×	South×
April×	2345×	2354×	2435×	2453×
May×	2534×	2543×	3245×	3254×
June×	3425×	3452×	3524×	3542×

Figure 13-4.
Second Quarter table complete with borders.

Notice that the double-line border around the outside edge of the top-left cell changed to a single-line border as part of the shadow-border effect. If you prefer the double-line border around the outside as well as the inside of the cell, select the cell and change its top and left borders to double. Examples later in this chapter use this table, so be sure to save it.

Adjusting Column and Row Width

As you create tables, you can adjust column or row widths. When you initially insert a table, all its columns are equal in width. The width is either one that Word calculated or one that you typed in the Initial Col Width box in the Insert Table dialog box. To adjust the width of a cell, column, row, or table, you can use either the keyboard or the mouse.

Using the keyboard to adjust the width of a cell, column, row, or whole table

The ability to selectively adjust the width of a cell, column, row, or table allows you to set up a table with a variety of cell widths to suit your needs. To adjust the width of a cell, column, or row, first select the element whose width you want to adjust or select the whole table. Choose the Format Table command (Alt,T,A). In the Format Table dialog box, type the width you want for the selected columns. To adjust the width of the whole table, choose the Apply to Whole Table option (Alt+O). To adjust only the selected columns, choose the Apply to Selection option (Alt+S). Then, choose OK. For example, suppose that you inserted a two-column table that had terms in the left column and definitions in the right column, like the table shown in Figure 13-5:

Terms×	Definitions×
Plot×	The actions that make up the story line and the overall course of events in a story.×
Character×	The personality, values, and attitudes of a person in a story.×

Figure 13-5.
Two-column table with equal-width columns.

To create the table in Figure 13-5, position the insertion point anywhere in any document and choose the Insert Table command (Alt,I,T). Then, choose OK. Type *Terms*, press the Tab key, type *Definitions*, press Tab (to start a new row), and then type the text you see in Figure 13-5, pressing Tab to move the insertion point to the next cell.

The table's columns are equal in width, which leaves plenty of space between the terms and their definitions. The table might be easier to read if the "Terms" column were narrower, and the table might require less vertical space if the "Definitions" column were wider. To make these changes, start by selecting the "Terms" column, and then choose the Format Table command (Alt,T,A). In the Format Table dialog box, type *1"* in the Width of Column 1 box, and choose the Next Column button (Alt+N). Type *5"* in the Width of Column 2 box, and choose OK. The table now looks like the one shown in Figure 13-6:

Terms	Definitions
Plot	The actions that make up the story line and the overall course of events in a story.
Character	The personality, values, and attitudes of a person in a story.

Figure 13-6.
Two-column table adjusted to 1-inch and 5-inch columns.

Using the mouse to adjust the width of a cell, column, row, or whole table

The mouse gives you the power to adjust the widths of cells and columns visually rather than by typing a measurement in the Format Table dialog box. To adjust column widths using the mouse, select at least one cell in each of the rows that you want to adjust. Select an entire column if you want to adjust the whole table. (Note that it is not necessary to select whole rows or the whole table when you use the mouse, but you can if doing so makes the process of adjusting column widths clearer to you.) After you select, drag the column markers on the ruler. To practice adjusting columns using the mouse, select the first column in the table in Figure 13-6. Turn on the ruler (Alt,V,R) if it is not already turned on. Click the ruler view icon until the ruler shows column view.

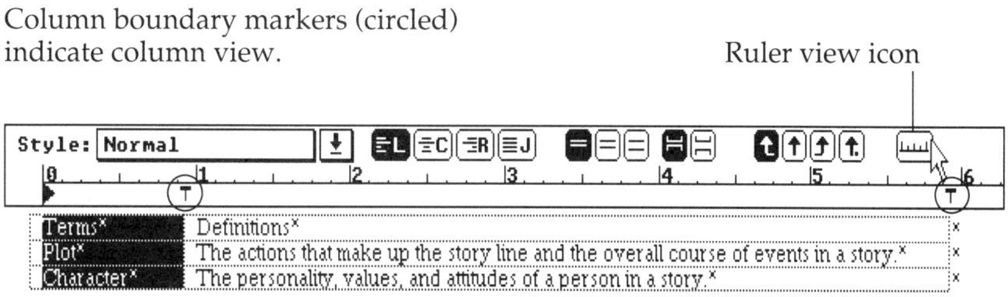

Drag the column marker T for the "Definitions" column, which is the marker near the 6-inch mark on the ruler, to the left to the 5-inch mark. Column boundary markers are associated with the boundaries on the right sides of the columns you want to adjust. Note that the "Terms" column retains its current width. To adjust the "Terms" column, drag its column marker to the 2-inch mark on the ruler. After the two adjustments, the table looks like the following:

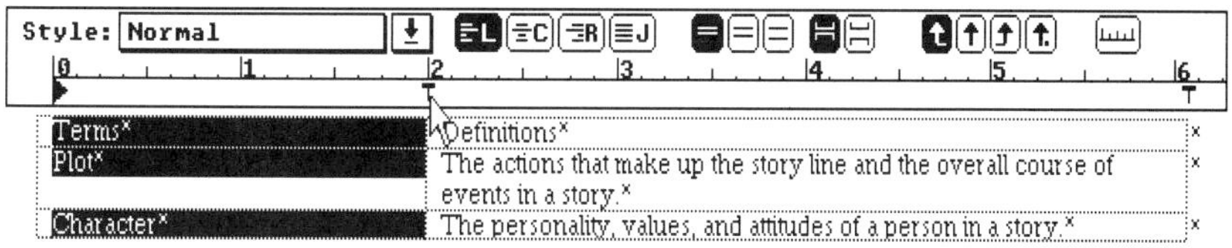

Note that when using the mouse, you adjusted the right column first. This order is not required, but adjusting the right end of a table first often makes the process easier. If you adjust the left end of a table first, the right end might extend beyond the right edge of the screen, making adjustments at the right end more difficult.

Adjusting Cell Height

Each row in a table adjusts its height for the tallest cell in the row. A cell adjusts its height to fit all the text and graphics you insert in it. In some cases, you might want to set a minimum row height, which makes the height of the row no less than the measurement you specify, even if the text or graphics in the row are not as tall as the minimum row height measurement. For example, suppose you have a table that has its title in the first row and you want to provide extra space above and below the cell contents, as shown on the following page.

January Region Rankings×

To create this cell, choose the Insert Table command (Alt,I,T), type *1* in the Number of Columns box, type *2"* in the Initial Col Width box, and choose the Format button (Alt+F). In the Format Table dialog box, type *3li* in the Minimum Row Height box, and then choose OK. Press the Ctrl+B keys to turn on boldface, and type *January Region Rankings*. Press the Ctrl+O keys to open space above the text and center the title vertically.

Even after you set a minimum row height, Word adjusts the height of a row if the contents of any cell in the row are taller than the minimum height you set.

TIP

Making a Table Fit the Document Margins

If you insert a table and specify a column width other than Auto, the table might be narrower or wider than the width between the document margins. Or, if you insert or delete cells or columns in a table that already fits between the margins, the table becomes wider or narrower than the width between the margins. To adjust a table so that it is flush with the margins, you use the Format Table command (Alt,T,A) and type *Auto* in the Width of Columns box. For example, if you have a table with four 1-inch columns, the table might be narrower than the space between the margins, as shown in Figure 13-7:

Sales×	Costs×	Taxes×	Net Profit×
$123,456.00×	$98,764.80×	$12,345.60×	$12,345.60×

Figure 13-7.
Table with four 1-inch columns.

To make the table fit between the margins, first select the whole table by pressing the Alt+5 keys (5 on the numeric keypad). Then, choose the Format Table command (Alt,T,A). In the Format Table dialog box, type *Auto* in the Width of Columns box. Word divides the width between the margins evenly among all the columns you selected so that the width of the table matches the width of the space between the margins. Choose the Apply To Whole Table option (Alt+O) if it is not already turned on, and then choose OK to make the table fit the margins, as shown on the next page.

Indenting Rows in a Table

You might occasionally want to indent a single row or a group of rows differently from others in a table. Word provides a way that you can indent rows that's similar to the way you indent paragraphs. (Indenting rows does not affect the alignment of the text within the cells of the indented rows. The text in the cells is assigned its indentation by the Format Paragraph command.) For example, suppose you want to create and set up a monthly table that has an indented second row that aligns the numbers with their regions, as in Figure 13-8:

January×	East×	West×	North×	South×
	1234×	1243×	1324×	1342×

Figure 13-8.
Monthly table, finished, with borders.

Sales×	Costs×	Taxes×	Net Profit×
$123,456.00×	$98,764.80×	$12,345.60×	$12,345.60×

Note that the table's columns are equal in width.

If you chose Apply to Selection (Alt+S) and you did not select all the columns in a table, those columns you did not select keep their current width; Word then allocates the remaining width among the selected columns. For example, suppose you selected only the first two columns in the table in Figure 13-7 and then typed *Auto* in the Width of Columns 1–2 box in the Format Table dialog box. The result would look like the following:

Auto-width columns

Sales×	Costs×	Taxes×	Net Profit×
$123,456.00×	$98,764.80×	$12,345.60×	$12,345.60×

1-inch columns

The third and fourth columns retain their original width, and the first and second columns expand equally to make the table fit the margins. You might find this method handier than the one you practiced earlier in the section called "Using the keyboard to adjust the width of a cell, column, row, or whole table."

Start by inserting a table that has five columns and two rows, with a column width of one inch. Fill in the table so that it looks like the following:

January	East	West	North	South
1234	1243	1324	1342	

Position the insertion point anywhere in the table's second row. Then, choose the Format Table command (Alt,T,A). In the Format Table dialog box, move to the Indent Rows box (Alt+D) and type *1"* to indent the second row 1 inch from the left margin. Next, choose the Apply To Selection option (Alt+S) if it is not already turned on, and then choose OK to see a table like the one shown in Figure 13-9:

January	East	West	North	South	
	1234	1243	1324	1342	

Figure 13-9.
Monthly table with second row indented 1 inch.

The second row in the table now has an extra cell that sticks out to the right. You'll learn how to get rid of this cell later in this chapter in "Example 11: Deleting One Cell," so save this table for that example. Earlier in this chapter you learned how to add cell borders like the ones in Figure 13-8. If you want to add borders to the table you just created, use those same methods.

Aligning a Table or Its Rows

Another element of table formatting is row alignment. Row alignment, like paragraph alignment, sets the alignment position of a table or its

TIP

Setting a Maximum Row Height

In forms and other special tables, you might want to set a table's row to a specific nonadjusting height so that no matter how much text and graphics the cells in the row contain, the row height remains unchanged. To set a row to a nonadjusting height, precede the measurement in the Minimum Row Height box in the Format Table dialog box with a minus sign. For example, typing *–1"* for Minimum Row Height sets the height of the selected row to 1 inch. If a cell contains text and graphics that are taller than the set row height, Word displays and prints only the top portion that fits in the height of the cell.

rows between the document's margins. Word provides three options for row alignment:

- Left alignment: The left edge of the table or rows is aligned with the left margin.
- Right alignment: The right edge of the table or rows is aligned with the right margin.
- Center alignment: The table or rows are centered between the margins.

Note that these options have an effect only if the table is narrower than the space between margins. You can adjust the alignment of the whole table, the alignment of a single row, or the alignment of a group of rows. The following two examples give you practice aligning tables between document margins. Note that row alignment does not affect the text within cells. Use the Format Paragraph command (Alt,T,P) to align text within cells.

Example 7: Aligning a Whole Table

Word gives you a shortcut for aligning a whole table between a document's margins. Assume that you want to center the Second Quarter table you created and formatted earlier in this chapter (see Figure 13-4). That table is aligned with the left margin. First, position the insertion point anywhere in the table. Then, choose the Format Table command (Alt,T,A). In the Format Table dialog box, choose the Center option (Alt+C) for Align Rows to center the table between the left and right margins. Choose the Apply To Whole Table option (Alt+O) if it is not already turned on, and then choose OK to center the table. Note the table's new position between the margins; the dotted lines in the following illustration show the margins:

2nd Quarter×	East×	West×	North×	South×	×
April×	2345×	2354×	2435×	2453×	×
May×	2534×	2543×	3245×	3254×	×
June×	3425×	3452×	3524×	3542×	×

Page margins

Be sure to save this table so that you can use it in Example 9 later in this chapter.

Example 8: Aligning a Row or Group of Rows in a Table

You can also select a single row or a group of rows and set the alignment. Suppose that you have a table with various alignments, such as the table shown in Figure 13-10:

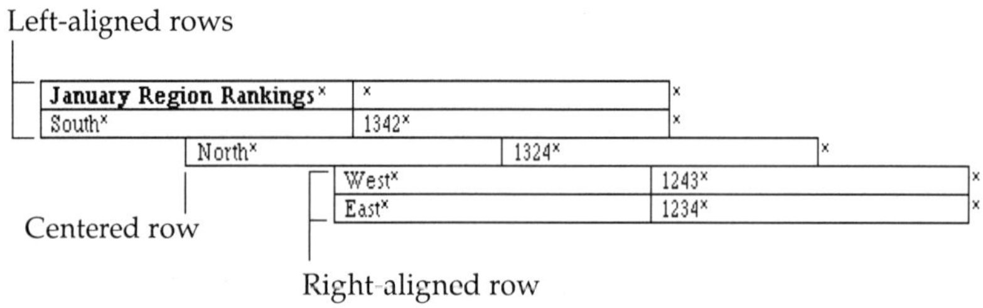

Figure 13-10.
Table with left, center, and right row alignment.

To create this table, choose the Insert Table command (Alt,I,T). In the Insert Table dialog box, retain the 2 in the Number of Columns box, type 5 in the Number of Rows box, type 2" in the Initial Col Width box, and then choose the Format button (Alt+F). Select Single for both Outline (Alt+U,S) and Inside (Alt+I,S) under Borders, and then choose OK. Type the text that appears in the table in Figure 13-10. Select the row that contains "North," choose the Format Table command (Alt,T,A), choose the Center option (Alt+C) under Align Rows, and then choose OK. Select the two rows that contain "West" and "East," choose the Format Table command (Alt,T,A), choose the Right option (Alt+G) under Align Rows, and then choose OK. The table now looks like the one in Figure 13-10.

Now suppose that you want to align all the table's rows at the left margin. First, select the rows for "North," "West," and "East." Choose the Format Table command (Alt,T,A). In the Format Table dialog box, choose the Left option (Alt+E) under Align Rows to align the rows at the left margin. Choose the Apply To Selection option (Alt+S) if it's not already turned on, and then choose OK. All the rows now align at the left margin:

January Region Rankings	
South	1342
North	1324
West	1243
East	1234

Changing the Number of Cells in a Table

Word lets you make many changes to the number of cells in a table. You can insert or delete cells, rows, and columns. And you can merge the contents of cells in the same row and later split the cells again if you want to split the contents of a merged cell among multiple cells.

Inserting Rows and Columns

You can insert rows and columns anywhere in a table. Word inserts new rows above the row that contains the insertion point. New columns are inserted to the left of the column that contains the insertion point. Therefore, to add new rows to the bottom of a table or additional columns to the right side of the table requires special steps. New rows inserted in a table using the Edit Table command (Alt,E,A) have the same cell and text format as the cells in the row below them. A new row added at the bottom of the table, however, has the same cell and text format as the cells in the row above it. New columns inserted in the table using Edit Table have the same cell and text format as the cells in the column to the right of the new columns. A new column added to the right side of a table, however, has only the text format of the cells that are in the column to the left of the new column.

To illustrate the special steps for adding a new row to the bottom and a new column to the right side of a table, the following two examples describe how to insert a new row at the bottom of a table and a new column at the right side of a table. Two more sections describe how to insert a row above an existing row and a column to the left of an existing column. A fifth section shows you how to insert a cell or group of cells between the rows or columns of a table.

Example 9: Inserting a Row at the Bottom of a Table

When you need to make a table longer, it's a simple matter to add a row to the bottom of the table. In the Second Quarter table (see Figure 13-4), position the insertion point in the last row's last cell. Press the Alt+End keys to move to the end of a row, and then press the Alt+PgDn keys to move to the bottom of a column. Press the Tab key. Word adds a new row to the bottom of the table, as shown in Figure 13-11 on the following page.

2nd Quarter	East	West	North	South
April	2345	2354	2435	2453
May	2534	2543	3245	3254
June	3425	3452	3524	3542

Figure 13-11.
New row added to the bottom of the table.

Be sure to save this table so that you can use it in Example 10 below.

Inserting a row above an existing row

To insert a row anywhere in a table other than at its bottom, you use the Edit Table command (Alt,E,A). First, position the insertion point in the row that's immediately below where you want to insert the new row. Then, choose Edit Table (Alt,E,A). In the Edit Table dialog box, choose the Row option (Alt+R), and then choose the Insert button (Alt+I) to insert a new row. If more than one row is selected when you choose Edit Table, Word inserts that number of new rows above the top row of the selection. In the newly inserted rows, each cell has the same format as the cell immediately below it.

Inserting a column to the left of an existing column

To insert a column to the left of an existing column, position the insertion point in the column that's to the right of where you want to insert the new column. Then, choose the Edit Table command (Alt,E,A). In the Edit Table dialog box, choose the Column option (Alt+C), and then choose the Insert button (Alt+I). If more than one column is selected when you choose Edit Table, Word inserts that number of new columns to the left of the selection. In the newly inserted columns, each cell is the same width as the corresponding cell in the first column of the selection.

Example 10: Inserting a Cell or Column at the Right Side of a Table

Occasionally you might want to insert another cell or column at the right side of a table, a process that is similar to inserting a new cell or column at the left side of an existing cell or column. When you insert a cell or column at a table's right side, however, you must position the insertion point outside the last cell in a row.

To practice inserting a new column at the right side of a table, position the insertion point to the right of the last cell in the last column in the Second Quarter table, as shown in Figure 13-12:

Insertion point

2nd Quarter	East	West	North	South
April	2345	2354	2435	2453
May	2534	2543	3245	3254
June	3425	3452	3524	3542

Figure 13-12.
Insertion point positioned to the right of the last cell in a row.

To position the insertion point, click to the right of the table. (You can also press the Alt+End keys to move the insertion point to the last cell in the row, press the End key if the cell contains text, and then press the right arrow key one time.) The insertion point appears between the cell gridline (or border) and the end-of-row marker ¤. Choose the Edit Table command (Alt,E,A). In the Edit Table dialog box, choose the Column option (Alt+C), and then choose the Insert button (Alt+I) to insert a column. If you choose the Selection option (Alt+S) Word inserts as many cells as you have selected. (Using an insertion point acts the same as selecting one cell.) Note that each cell in the new column is the same width as the cell to its left. The Second Quarter table now looks like the table shown in Figure 13-13:

2nd Quarter	East	West	North	South	
April	2345	2354	2435	2453	
May	2534	2543	3245	3254	
June	3452	3452	3524	3542	

Figure 13-13.
New column inserted at the right side of the table.

You can add borders to the new column of cells by selecting the column, selecting the Format Table command (Alt,T,A), selecting Shadow for Outline (Alt+U,S,S) and Single for Inside (Alt+I,S) under Borders, and then choosing OK. Save this table so that you can use it in the section titled "Calculations that refer to other cells" later in this chapter.

Inserting a cell or group of cells in a table

To insert a single cell, start by selecting the cell to the right of where you want the new cell. To insert a new group of cells, however, start by selecting a group of cells below or to the right of where you want the cells:

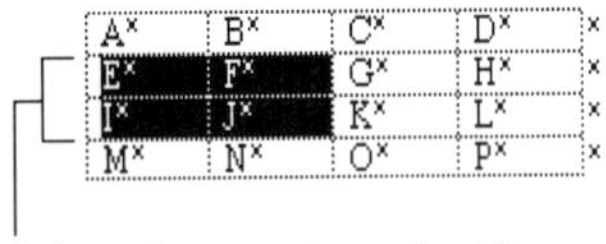

Select the number of cells you want to insert and the location.

Choose the Edit Table command (Alt,E,A). In the Edit Table dialog box, choose the Selection option (Alt+S) if it's not already turned on. Under Shift Cells, choose in which direction you want the existing cells to move to make way for the new cells. If you choose Horizontally (Alt+H), Word shifts the cells in the affected rows to the right when you choose the Insert button (Alt+I). Word inserts a new cell for each cell in the selection (but does not insert whole columns):

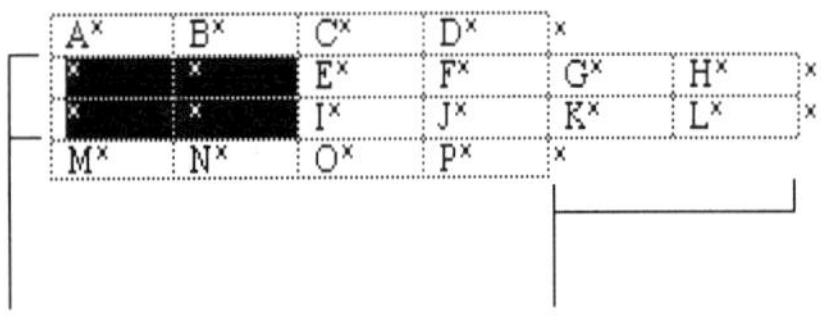

Word inserts the number of selected cells (horizontal shift).

If you choose Vertically (Alt+V), Word shifts the cells in the affected columns down when you choose the Insert button (Alt+I). Word inserts a new row of cells for each row in the selection:

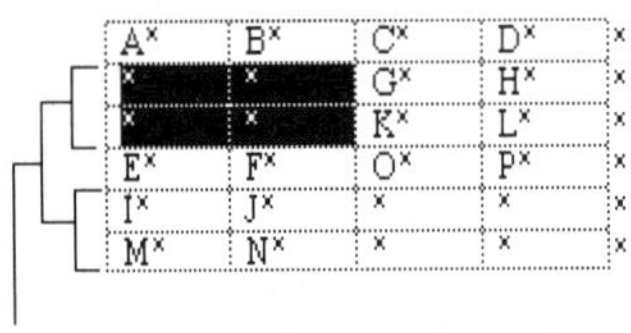

Word inserts the number of selected rows (vertical shift).

Whether you shift cells horizontally or vertically, each new, empty cell has the same format as the upper-leftmost cell in the selection.

Deleting Cells, Rows, and Columns in Tables

You use the Edit Table command to delete any number of cells, rows, and columns in a table. If you use the Edit Cut command, the Delete key, or the Shift+Delete keys instead, you will delete the contents of the cells but not the cells themselves.

Deleting cells has no effect on the formatting of the remaining cells or on the formatting of the contents within the remaining cells. After you delete cells, the remaining cells move either up or to the left to fill the gap, depending on whether you chose to shift cells horizontally or vertically in the Edit Table dialog box. If the Row option or the Column option is turned on in the Edit Table dialog box, the Shift Cells setting is unavailable, as indicated by the grayed labels for the Shift Cells options. When the Row option is turned on, the rows below the selection move up when you choose the Delete button. When the Column option is turned on, the columns to the right of the selection move to the left when you choose the Delete button. And when the Selection option is turned on, you can choose to shift cells either to the left (Horizontally) or up (Vertically).

Example 11: Deleting One Cell

Earlier in this chapter, the section called "Indenting Rows in a Table" showed you how to indent the second row in the monthly table shown in Figure 13-9. The table looked like the following:

January×	East×	West×	North×	South×	
	1234×	1243×	1324×	1342×	×

Here you find out how to delete the extra cell at the end of the table's second row. Start by positioning the insertion point in the last cell of the second row. Choose the Edit Table command (Alt,E,A). In the Edit Table dialog box, choose the Selection option (Alt+S) if it's not already turned on, and then choose the Delete button (Alt+D) to remove the extra cell from the table:

January×	East×	West×	North×	South×
	1234×	1243×	1324×	1342×

Because you deleted the last cell in its row, the rest of the table is not affected.

Deleting more than one cell

You can delete a group of cells that are in multiple rows and columns without having to select entire rows or columns. First, select the cells you want to delete. Choose the Edit Table command (Alt,E,A). In the Edit Table dialog box, choose the Selection option (Alt+S) if it's not already turned on. Under Shift Cells, choose the Horizontally option (Alt+H) if you want the cells to the right of the selected cells to close the gap by moving left. Choose the Vertically option (Alt+V) if you want the cells below the selected cells to close the gap by moving up. Then, choose the Delete button (Alt+D).

Deleting a row or a group of rows

Word gives you a shortcut for deleting a whole row or a group of rows; you do not have to select entire rows first. Begin by positioning the insertion point in the row that you want to delete. If you want to delete more than one row, select a cell in each of the rows that you want to delete. Choose the Edit Table command (Alt,E,A). In the Edit Table dialog box, choose the Row option (Alt+R) if it's not already turned on, and then choose the Delete button (Alt+D).

Deleting a column or a group of columns

Word also provides a shortcut for deleting a whole column or a group of columns without selecting entire columns. First, position the insertion point in the column you want to delete. If you want to delete more than one column, select a cell in each column that you want to delete. Choose the Edit Table command (Alt,E,A). In the Edit Table dialog box, choose the Column option (Alt+C) if it's not already turned on, and then choose the Delete button (Alt+D).

Merging Multiple Cells into a Single Cell

Word lets you use two methods to merge a group of cells within a row into a single cell and combine all the cells' contents into the resulting cell. After you merge the cells, you can split them again, as described in the next section.

Insert a table that has four columns, four rows, and a column width of 1 inch. Select the first row, and choose the Edit Table command (Alt,E,A). In the Edit Table dialog box, choose the Merge Cells button (Alt+M). Press the Delete key to delete the extra paragraph marks. Then, press the Ctrl+C keys to center the contents you will type, and press the Ctrl+B keys to make the contents boldface. Type *October Results*. Press the down arrow key to move the insertion point to the second row, and press the Alt+Home keys to move the insertion point to the first cell in the second row.

Next, press the Shift+right arrow keys twice to select the first two cells in the second row. Merge the cells (Alt,E,A,Alt+M), and delete the extra paragraph mark (press the Delete key while the contents of the merged cell are still selected). Press the Ctrl+C keys to center the contents, and then type *Revenues*. Merge the last two cells in the second row by selecting the cells, choosing the Edit Table command (Alt,E,A), choosing the Merge Cells button (Alt+M), and pressing the Delete key. Press the Ctrl+C keys to center the text you will type. Then, type *Profits*. Press the Tab key to move the insertion point to the first cell in the third row. Next, type the following text in the third row. (Press Tab to move from one cell to the next.)

October Results			
Revenues		Profits	
Amount	% Change	Amount	% Change

Type this text.

Now, merge the first two cells in the third and fourth rows so that "Amount" and "% Change" are stacked vertically. To do so, press the Alt+Home keys to move the insertion point to the first cell in its current row. If the insertion point is in the third row, press the Shift+down arrow keys and then the Shift+right arrow keys. If the insertion point is in the fourth row, press the Shift+up arrow keys and then the Shift+right arrow keys. Here's how the selection looks:

October Results			
Revenues		Profits	
Amount	% Change	Amount	% Change

Merge the cells (Alt,E,A,Alt+M). This time, do not delete the contents:

October Results		
Revenues	Profits	
Amount % Change	Amount	% Change

The cells merge horizontally in each row, but not vertically. Merge the third and fourth rows' last two cells without deleting their contents:

October Results	
Revenues	Profits
Amount¶ % Change	Amount¶ % Change
¶	¶

Now, to separate the numbers that you will type from the "Amount" and "% Change" labels, position the insertion point at the end of "Amount" in the third row's first cell (Alt+Home,End). Press the Ctrl+Tab keys to insert a tab character. Use Ctrl+Tab to insert tab characters after the other "Amount" label and the two "% Change" labels. To make the numbers align vertically, set left-align tab stops at 0.75" for both cells in row three. Select the entire third row, choose the Format Tabs command (Alt,T,T), type *.75"*, and then choose OK.

Now, copy the contents of the cells in the third row to the cells in the fourth row: Select the entire third row, press the Ctrl+Insert keys to copy the selection to the Clipboard, press the down arrow key to move the insertion point to the first cell in the fourth row, and then press the Shift+Insert keys to paste the Clipboard contents to the fourth row of cells. To see the alignment, type some numbers following the tab character after each label. The table now looks like Figure 13-15.

TIP

How Cell Contents Merge

When you merge cells, Word puts the contents of each cell into a paragraph. If a cell contains more than one paragraph, Word keeps each paragraph separate.

A	B¶ C	D¶ E	F

A¶ B¶ C¶ D¶ E¶ F

Result of merging cells

Figure 13-14.
Merged cells in paragraph form.

Press Ctrl+Tab to
insert tabs in cells.

October Results×		
Revenues×	Profits×	×
Amount → $123,456¶ % Change → 12%×	Amount → $12,345.60¶ % Change → 6%×	×
Amount → $110,228¶ % Change → 10%×	Amount → $11,646¶ % Change → 5%×	×

Figure 13-15.
Final table after merging cells and pasting.

Splitting Merged Cells

After you merge cells, you can split them again into the same number of cells you originally merged. Word lets you split only those cells that you previously merged at the same time.

First, select the cells you want to split. (If the selection contains cells that were never merged or cells that were merged at different times, a dimmed Merge Cells button is displayed in the Edit Table dialog box instead of the Split Cells button.)

For example, in the table you modified for Figure 13-15, select the first cells in the third and fourth rows. Choose the Edit Table command (Alt,E,A). In the Edit Table dialog box, choose the Split Cells button (Alt+P) to split the cells. You can repeat this procedure for the last cell in the third and fourth rows. The result of these cell splits looks like the following:

October Results×				
Revenues×		Profits×		×
Amount → $ 123,456×	% Change → 1 2%×	Amount → $ 12,345.60×	% Change → 6 %×	×
Amount → $ 110,228×	% Change → 1 0%×	Amount → $ 11,646×	% Change → 5 %×	×

To position the numbers better, replace the tab characters below the "Amount" and "% Change" labels with paragraph marks.

TIP

How Cell Contents Split

When you split a merged cell, Word divides the cell into the same number of cells it was merged from, and divides any text by putting one paragraph into each cell. If the merged cell contains more paragraphs than cells after splitting, all the split cells get one paragraph each, the last paragraph of the merged cell goes into the last cell after the split, the next-to-last paragraph goes into the next-to-last cell after the split, and so on. Word puts the remaining paragraphs into the first cell after the split.

Merged cell in Figure 13-14 after being split

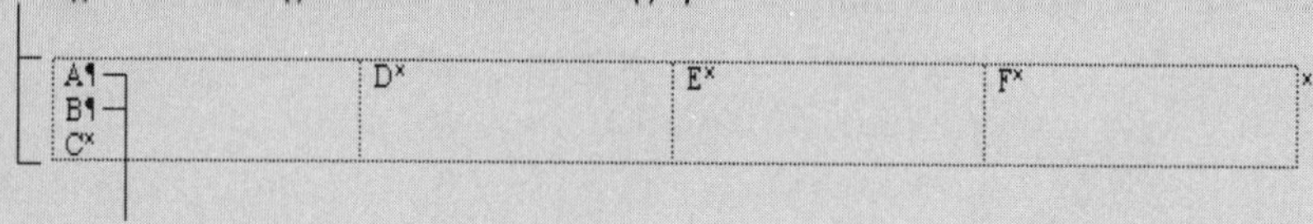

Extra paragraphs placed in first cell

If, after splitting, the merged cell contains fewer paragraphs than the number of cells, Word puts one paragraph in each cell, starting at the leftmost cell and leaving the remaining cells blank at the right.

Table before merging

Table after merging

Now, delete the empty paragraph in the merged cell, and split the cell (Alt,E,A,Alt+P). You see the following result:

Table after split

Doing More with Your Tables

Besides all the basic actions that you've learned so far for working with tables, you can perform the following special actions in tables:

- Add to a table a caption that identifies the table and explains its purpose.
- Number your tables, and then collect a List of Tables (similar to a table of contents), including the page numbers on which the tables appear in a document.
- Convert a table, a single row, or a group of rows back to regular text.
- Divide a table in two, between any two rows.
- Insert and control page breaks in a table that does not fit on one page.
- Set up tab stops within a cell to create columns.

The following sections explain how you can accomplish these tasks with tables.

Adding a Caption to a Table

A table often appears with a caption that identifies the table and explains what it represents. A caption can also include a number, as explained in the next two sections, "Numbering Tables" and "Producing a List of Tables." To add a caption to a table, insert a paragraph either before or after the table.

It's important to print a table and its caption together and on the same page. How you tell Word to keep the two together depends on whether you want to print the table wherever it falls in the document or print it at a specific position on the page. If you do not set a specific position for the table, select either the caption paragraph or the table—whichever is first—and choose the Keep Paragraph With Next option in the Format Paragraph dialog box. If you position a table on the page, be sure to select both the table and its caption together before applying the position format in the Format Position dialog box. As long as the table and the caption have been assigned the same position, Word will print them together as one item. You need not apply the Keep Paragraph With Next option if you position a table and its caption together.

Numbering Tables

If you want the tables throughout your document to be numbered consecutively, for each table insert a caption paragraph before or after the table, and then insert a SEQ field that includes an identifier used only to identify tables, as in the following example:

{seq table}

The caption paragraph can include caption text as well as the SEQ field. When you print the document or otherwise update these SEQ fields, Word numbers the tables. If you change the order of the tables in the document, Word renumbers the tables when you update the fields.

Producing a List of Tables

Word can collect a list of tables. The list includes each table's caption and the page number on which each table appears. To collect a list of tables, you need to identify each table's caption in either of two ways: using a heading style or using a TC field. Using a heading style is usually the easiest approach. Use TC fields if you plan to collect different types of lists of items in addition to a list of tables, like a list of figures and a table of contents. You'll also want to use TC fields if you're already using every available heading style in the document.

If you choose to use heading styles, apply to the captions one of the heading styles you are not currently using. For a list of tables, you can probably use the heading 7 style or heading 8 style because few documents contain that many heading levels. Then, in the Insert Table of Contents dialog box, type that heading number in the From and To boxes. The TOC field will collect only the paragraphs that have that heading.

To collect a list of tables by using fields, you must insert TC fields with special identification codes. A TC field consists of the field type TC, an identifier switch instruction, and the text for the list entry (enclosed in quotation marks), as shown in the following example:

{tc \f t "Sales Results for First Quarter 1988"}

The identifier switch instruction can appear either before or after the text for the list entry.

The easiest way to produce the text for the TC field is to make a copy of the table caption text and insert the copy in a TC field. You will see the duplicate text until you finish typing the TC code in the field. Then the field disappears, so it does not affect the display or pagination. Note that if either the Hidden Text or the Show All option in the View Preferences dialog box is turned on, you'll see the field codes until you turn off the option. Also, if you've chosen the View Field Codes command, you'll see the SEQ field codes (but not the TC field codes) until you choose the command again to turn it off.

To use a TC field to produce a list of tables, select a table caption and then insert a copy of the caption in front of the current caption by pressing the COPY key combination (Shift+F2), pressing the left arrow key one time, and then pressing the Enter key.

First Quarter	East	West	North	South
Jan	1234	1243	1324	1342
Feb	1423	1432	2134	2143
Mar	2314	2341	2413	2431

Sales Results for First Quarter 1988{seq table} Sales Results for First Quarter 1988¶

Next, select the copy of the caption and press the INSERT FIELD key combination (Ctrl+F9). Type *tc \f t* (with spaces between *tc* and *\f*, between *\f* and *t*, and between *t* and the text) in front of the copied caption text in the field, and enclose the copied caption text in quotation marks. If the TC field disappears after you type the *c* in *tc*, turn on the Show All or Hidden Text option in the View Preferences dialog box. The table, caption, and TC field look like the following:

First Quarter	East	West	North	South
Jan	1234	1243	1324	1342
Feb	1423	1432	2134	2143
Mar	2314	2341	2413	2431

{tc \f t "Sales Results for First Quarter 1988"}{seq table} Sales Results for First Quarter 1988¶

The \f switch tells Word that this TC field contains a special identification letter. The t is the letter that identifies this TC field as belonging to the list of tables.

To include the table sequence number in the list of tables, select the SEQ field too before copying the caption and inserting the TC field. The SEQ field should also be inside the quotation marks that surround the caption text. Be sure to alter the sequence identifier so that it will not interfere with the table numbering but will have the correct number.

For example, type an *l* at the front of the identifier *table*, as shown in the example below:

First Quarter	East	West	North	South
Jan	1234	1243	1324	1342
Feb	1423	1432	2134	2143
Mar	2314	2341	2413	2431

{tc \f t "{seq ltable} Sales Results for First Quarter 1988"}{seq table} Sales Results for First Quarter 1988¶

After you insert all the TC fields, insert a TOC field where you want the list of tables to appear in your document. Add an \f t switch to the TOC field to tell Word to collect only the TC fields that contain an \f switch with a t identifier. The TOC field should look like the following:

{toc \f t}

For more information about the SEQ, TC, and TOC fields, see the Appendix, "Field Types and Their Instructions." For more information about heading styles, see Chapter 7, "Styles."

Converting a Table or Individual Rows Back to Text

After you insert a table, you might realize that the information is better suited to standard paragraphs. Or you might need more than 31 columns, which is the limit for a table, and you might want to convert a table to tabular form using tab stops and tab characters. When you want to take information out of a table, use the command called Insert Table to Text. This command replaces the Insert Table command whenever you've selected either complete rows in a table or a whole table.

When you choose Insert Table to Text, a dialog box presents choices for how to divide the information that's now in cells:

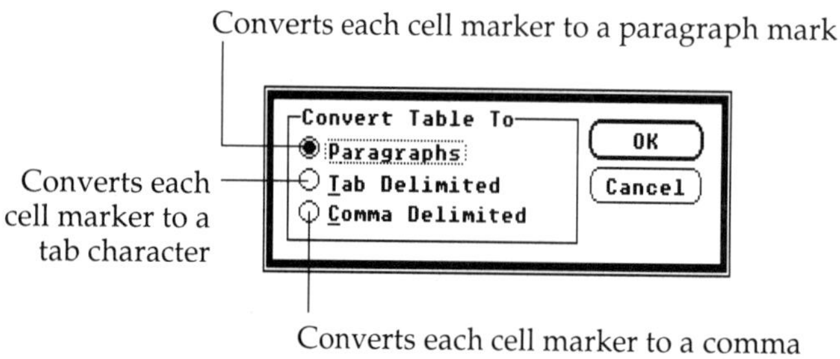

If each cell in your selection contains only one paragraph, Word separates the contents of the cells with the character you select in the Insert

Table to Text dialog box—paragraph, tab, or comma. If a cell contains more than one paragraph, the paragraph mark is kept intact after the conversion even if you did not choose the Paragraphs option in the Insert Table to Text dialog box. Because the paragraph mark is kept intact, a Tab Delimited or Comma Delimited conversion's result looks different from the arrangement in the table. For example, suppose a row in your table looks like the following:

Apple×	Banana¶ Cactus×	Dingo¶ Elephant¶ Fairy×	Giant×

To convert this row to text, select it and choose Insert Table to Text (Alt,I,T). In the Insert Table to Text dialog box, select the Tab Delimited option (Alt+T) and choose OK. Word replaces cell markers with tab characters, keeps the paragraph marks intact, and converts the last cell marker in each row to a paragraph mark. The resulting conversion looks like the example below:

Apple→Banana¶
Cactus→Dingo¶
Elephant¶
Fairy→Giant¶

Dividing a Table Between Rows

If you find that you need to divide a single table into a number of smaller tables, you can do so by dividing the table between rows. You can divide any table that has two or more rows.

First, position the insertion point in the row that's immediately below where you want the division to occur. Then, press the Ctrl+Shift+Enter keys. These keys divide the table above the row that contains the insertion point by inserting a paragraph mark between the two parts of the table. Word now sees the rows as parts of two tables rather than as parts of one table.

Inserting and Controlling Page Breaks in a Table

When you create a table, you often expect all of it to print on one page. Some tables, however, are longer than a page, and others begin near the bottom of a page and spill over to the next page. If you do nothing about a page break in a table, Word inserts a page break between rows. Word never splits a cell across a page break—a cell must print on a single page. If a cell's text is longer than the remaining space on a page, Word moves the row that contains the cell to a new page. If a cell's text is longer than a single page, Word prints only as much text as will fit on the current page. In this latter case, the cell's text prints to the bottom edge of the page rather than stopping at the bottom margin. The rest of the text is not printed, but it remains in the document.

If you do not like where Word breaks a table, you can insert a page break manually. To do so, you use either the Insert Break command (or, on Short Menus, the Insert Page Break command) or the PAGE BREAK key combination (Ctrl+Enter). First, position the insertion point in the row that's immediately below where you want to insert the page break. Choose Insert Break (or Insert Page Break) (Alt,I,B), and choose OK. Or press Ctrl+Enter. Word first inserts a paragraph mark above the row that contains the insertion point, and then inserts a page break above the paragraph mark. A manually inserted page break appears on the screen as a closely spaced dotted line across the width of the window:

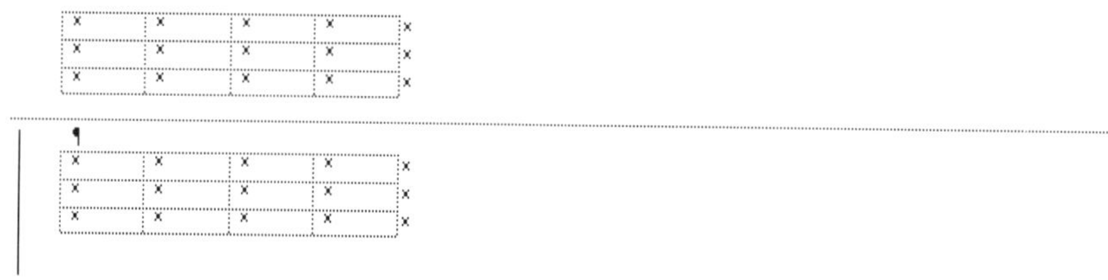

Manually inserted page break

TIP

Adding a Paragraph Above a Table at the Beginning of a Document

If you insert a table at the beginning of a document, you will not be able to insert a paragraph above the table, unless you know a special trick. The usual way to insert a paragraph is by pressing the Enter key, which in this case inserts a paragraph inside a table cell. To insert a separate paragraph above the table instead, use the same procedure you use when you divide a table between rows: Position the insertion point in the table's first row, and press the Ctrl+Shift+Enter keys. You can now insert paragraphs at the beginning of the document as you usually do—by pressing Enter. Note that if you press Ctrl+Shift+Enter outside a table, you insert a column break.

If the text in a cell is longer than a page, divide the text into two consecutive rows. Insert a new row by using the Edit Table command. (See "Inserting a row above an existing row" earlier in this chapter.)

Setting Tab Stops to Create Multiple Columns in a Cell

Table columns take the place of tab stops for aligning text and numbers in vertical columns. You might, however, want multiple columns inside a cell, where a table can't be used. Also, the only way to align numbers on a decimal point within a cell is by setting up decimal-aligned tab stops in the cell. But in most other cases, you'll find it preferable to create additional columns by inserting cells and making them narrow rather than by using tab stops.

Each cell in a table can contain more than one paragraph. Remember that every paragraph in Word can have its own tab stops. Thus, you can set different tab stops for each paragraph in every cell. With this flexibility in mind, before you start setting tab stops be sure to select all the paragraphs in all the cells in a column for which you want to set tab stops. If you do not set your own tab stops, paragraphs in a cell have only the default tab stops. Default tab stops are initially set to every one-half inch. (You can change the default tab stop setting in the Format Document dialog box.)

You use the same two approaches to set and clear tab stops inside a table as you use for tab stops outside a table. These two approaches are using the Format Tabs command or using the mouse or keyboard and the ruler. Note that when the insertion point is in a table cell, the paragraph indent markers show the width of the paragraph in the cell, as illustrated below.

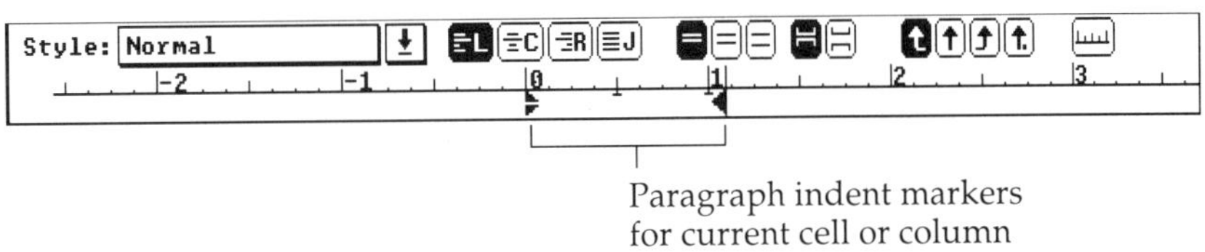

Set tab stops in a cell only between the paragraph indent markers on the ruler. Setting tab stops outside the indent markers makes the cell contents align incorrectly.

To set a decimal tab stop for a column in a table, first select the column and then choose the Format Tabs command (Alt,T,T). In the Format Tabs dialog box, type the tab stop measurement in the Tab Position box. This measurement is the distance from the left cell boundary. Select the Decimal option under Alignment (Alt+D), and then choose OK. Repeat these steps for each cell or column in which you want a decimal tab stop.

Word also lets you use the mouse to set a decimal tab stop on the ruler. To use the mouse to set a decimal tab stop for a cell, click the decimal tab stop icon on the ruler (choose the View Ruler command if the ruler is not already turned on). Then, click the ruler scale where you want to set the tab stop. Or you can use the keyboard in ruler mode. To use the keyboard, press the Ctrl+Shift+F10 keys to turn on ruler mode. Press the Ctrl+right arrow keys for a large jump (for example, 1 inch) or the right arrow key for a small jump (for example, one-quarter inch) to the position on the ruler at which you want a tab stop. Press the 4 key (above the letter keys) to select decimal tab stop alignment. Press the Insert key to insert the tab stop. Repeat these last three steps if you want to insert additional tab stops. Then, press the Enter key to turn off ruler mode and to set the tab stops. (The ruler is still visible. To take away the ruler, choose the View Ruler command—Alt,V,R.) Pressing the Esc key while in ruler mode turns off ruler mode without setting the tab stops you inserted.

Because Word uses the Tab key and the Shift+Tab keys to move back and forth between cells in a table, you cannot use Tab to insert tab characters. Instead, use the Ctrl+Tab keys.

TIP

Automatic Decimal Tab Alignment

After you set tab stops, you insert a tab character to push the text that follows it to the tab stop position. In a table cell with only one decimal tab stop, Word aligns the cell contents at the decimal tab stop for you. Do not insert a tab character or you will make the alignment incorrect. Automatic alignment of decimal tab stops makes it possible to enter a large table of numeric data quickly, without having to press the Ctrl+Tab keys. Note that if you insert more than one decimal tab stop or a tab stop that has any other alignment, you must use Ctrl+Tab to insert tab characters.

Advanced Table Tasks

Beyond using tables to display numbers, text, and graphics in columns, you can use Word's table feature for the following special tasks:

- Setting up and printing paragraphs side by side
- Setting up a simple spreadsheet
- Setting up complex table formats and saving them in a glossary for reuse in any document

The rest of this chapter describes how to use tables to accomplish these advanced tasks.

Using Tables to Set Up and Print Paragraphs Side By Side

Printing and displaying paragraphs side by side used to be a painful process. You had to either set tab stops and give up word wrap or apply mysterious formatting to alternate paragraphs. Yet side-by-side paragraphs have many uses, the most common of which are cost-and-benefit lists, question-and-answer lists, play scripts, and lists of terms and their definitions. Word's table feature makes setting up side-by-side paragraphs easy and viewing them on the screen clear. And, by using tables for side-by-side paragraphs, you see the paragraphs on the screen exactly as Word will print them. Figure 13-16 is an example of side-by-side paragraphs in a two-column table:

Features	Benefits
On schedule—a record of 100% on-time completion of every project undertaken, some under extremely adverse conditions	You get the research you need when you need it and when it's promised so that you can build your plans and schedules on solid data that's available in a timely manner.
Modern laboratories equipped with the most recent tools, many specially designed by our staff	In-depth research and a broader range of research capabilities allow you to tackle every aspect of each research problem you face.
Professional staff with master's and doctor's degrees and an average of 10 years of research experience in many disciplines	You can rely on our accurate and thorough research. Our experienced researchers know what they're doing, and they know how to find the answers to your questions. You get the right answers the first time.

Figure 13-16.
Features/benefits list in a two-column table.

To create these side-by-side paragraphs, start by choosing the Insert Table command (Alt,I,T). In the Insert Table dialog box, move to the Number of Rows box (Alt+R), type 2, and then choose OK to insert a two-column, two-row table. In the table's first cell, press the Ctrl+B keys to apply boldface. Type *Features*, press the Tab key, press Ctrl+B to apply boldface, and then type *Benefits*.

Now, press the Tab key to move to the second row, and type the following text under "Features":

> On schedule--a record of 100% on-time completion of every project undertaken, some under extremely adverse conditions

Press Tab, and type the benefit, as shown in Figure 13-16. Repeat this step for the features and benefits shown in the third and fourth rows. To provide the vertical space between the second, third, and fourth rows, press the OPEN SPACE key combination (Ctrl+O) before you type the paragraphs in the cells that are in the third row. The cells in the fourth row will have the same formatting as the cells above them in the third row. If you need more than one paragraph in a single cell, press the Enter key to start a new paragraph as you do in regular text, and press Tab to move to the next cell.

To give the table some visible boundaries, add the borders shown in Figure 13-16. Select the table's first column, choose the Format Table command (Alt,T,A), select the Single option for Right (Alt+R,S) under Borders, and then choose OK. Now, select the table's first row, choose the Format Table command (Alt,T,A), select the Single option for Bottom (Alt+B,S) and the Single option for Inside (Alt+I,S) under Borders, and then choose OK. The table now contains the border beneath the column headings and the border between the columns as shown in Figure 13-16.

Using Tables to Set Up a Simple Spreadsheet

One common use for tables in documents is to display numbers, calculate their sums, and display the totals. You might use tables in this way, for example, in letters that describe bids on jobs, in business activity reports, or in invoices. To satisfy the need for these sorts of calculations, Word provides a Utilities Calculate command.

To use Utilities Calculate, you type numbers and mathematical operators (+, –, *, /, %, ^) anywhere in a document and select the part of the document that contains the numbers. You can also select any table cells. Word ignores text in a selection, so you do not have to worry if your selection contains a mixture of text and numbers. Then, choose Utilities Calculate (Alt,U,C). Word displays the result in the status line and places the result on the Clipboard. When Word completes the calculation, you can paste the result anywhere in your document, including in a table cell.

Electronic spreadsheet programs such as Microsoft Excel and Lotus 1-2-3 were designed to calculate numbers for business reports and invoices—and to perform much more complicated calculations, too. Although you can easily import part or all of a Microsoft Excel, Microsoft Multiplan, or Lotus 1-2-3 spreadsheet into a Word document, it's a bonus to be able to perform some calculations right in Word. You do not have to run two programs at once, the results and the calculations are in one place (which makes it easy to change them quickly), and you can still perform calculations even if you do not own a spreadsheet program.

TIP

Numbering Paragraphs in a Table

To number paragraphs in a table, you must use manual paragraph numbers. Suppose, for example, you have a table that you want to look like the following:

Plan	Procure answers to a prescribed set of questions before starting project. Base start date and schedule on answers to prescribed questions.
Prescribed questions	1. Has the product specification been finished? 2. Has the specification been reviewed and approved? 3. Is the specification solid? 4. Is this a wholly new product or product area?

To number these paragraphs in a cell as shown above, select them, and then choose the Utilities Renumber command (Alt,U,R). In the Utilities Renumber dialog box, select Manual (Alt+M), select Sequence (Alt+F,S,F4) for Format, and then choose OK. Notice that the paragraph in the first column has a number and that the paragraphs in the second column begin at 2. To correct this problem, select and delete the number in the first column, and then select only the paragraphs in the second column. Choose Utilities Renumber (Alt,U,R) again. Select Numbered Only (Alt+N), select Manual (Alt+M), select Sequence (Alt+F,S,F4) for Format, and then choose OK.

In Word you can set up a table anywhere in your document and insert fields that will perform calculations and display the result. Using a field to perform a calculation can replace using the Utilities Calculate command. An Expression (=) field can calculate exactly the same expression that you would type, select, and apply the Utilities Calculate command to. Using a field rather than the Utilities Calculate command provides some benefits. You can see the result or the expression (which you can easily edit and update), you do not have to paste the result from the Clipboard and, most important, the field lets you set up spreadsheet operations.

The following sections show you how to do three types of calculations in a table: calculations that are limited to a single cell, calculations that refer to another cell in the same table, and calculations that refer to a cell in another table. Calculations that refer to another cell—either in the same table or in another table—resemble the calculations done by a simple spreadsheet.

Before you learn how to set up a table as a simple spreadsheet, you need to review the Expression (=) field, which is the backbone of spreadsheet operations in Word.

Expression fields can turn tables into spreadsheets

Calculations in tables that you want to set up as spreadsheets are performed by the Expression (=) field. Chapter 8, "Fields: Facts and Functions," and Chapter 9, "Fields II: Creating Special Effects," describe fields and how to insert them. And the Appendix, "Field Types and Their Instructions," contains an explanation of the Expression (=) field and its parts. Review those materials as the first step in learning how to set up calculations using a field.

As a quick review: An Expression (=) field contains an equal sign followed by a mathematical expression, which consists of numbers (called operands) and operators. Operators are the mathematical symbols for addition (+), subtraction (–), multiplication (*), division (/), percentage (%), exponents (^), and the functions. A function performs a mathematical operation. In an Expression (=) field, you can replace explicit operands with bookmark names that refer to numbers anywhere in the same document and with references to a table cell. Using bookmark names and references to table cells is the basis for spreadsheet operations, as explained below in the section called "Calculations that refer to other cells."

To review the Expression (=) field in practice, however, first take a brief look at how an Expression (=) field calculates without a cell reference.

Calculating within a single cell

To calculate numbers within a single cell, you can insert and update an Expression (=) field to perform the calculation you want. For example, to calculate the 8.1 percent sales tax for a purchase of $123.45, you insert an Expression (=) field that looks like the following:

```
{=$123.45*8.1%}
```

To insert the above field, press the INSERT FIELD key combination (Ctrl+F9), type *=$123.45*8.1%*, and then press the UPDATE FIELD key (F9) to see the result: $9.999. This example shows a simple calculation, but the Expression (=) field can perform much more complicated calculations, including calculations that use numbers from other cells.

Calculations that refer to other cells

Calculations that refer to other cells in a table are the rudiments of a spreadsheet. Within one table cell in Word, you can refer to one or more other cells as part of a mathematical expression that calculates numbers. Each cell in a table has an "address," which is counted from the top-left cell of the table. Each cell's address is the combination of its row and column information. As a result, the address of the top-left cell is R1C1, meaning Row 1, Column 1. (In fields you can use the lowercase form r1c1.) Figure 13-17 shows the cell addresses for a four-column, three-row table:

r1c1	r1c2	r1c3	r1c4
r2c1	r2c2	r2c3	r2c4
r3c1	r3c2	r3c3	r3c4

Figure 13-17.
Cell addresses in a table.

A cell reference consists of one or more cell addresses. You can use any of the forms of cell references in an Expression (=) field that are shown in the table on the following page. Note that you type a cell reference between brackets ([ ]).

Cell Reference	*Meaning*
[R*n*]	Refers to all cells in row *n*. The *n* represents the row number. For example, [r1] means all cells in the first row of the table. If a cell reference refers to its own row, the cell reference also refers to the cell that contains the reference.
[C*m*]	Refers to all cells in column *m*. The *m* represents the column number. For example, [c1] means all cells in the first column of the table. If a cell reference refers to its own column, the cell reference also refers to the cell that contains the reference.
[R*n*C*m*]	Refers to a cell in row *n* and column *m*. The *n* represents the number of the row, and the *m* represents the number of the column. For example, [r3c2] refers to the cell that's in the second column of the table's third row.
[R*n*C*m*:R*o*C*p*]	Refers to all the cells inside a square that has the two cell addresses at opposite corners. The *n* represents the row of the first corner cell, the *m* represents the column of the first corner cell, the *o* represents the row of the opposite corner cell, and the *p* represents the column number of the opposite corner cell. For example, [r1c1:r3c4] indicates all the cells in Figure 13-17.

To use a cell reference in an Expression (=) field, you must use one of the built-in mathematical functions listed on the next page. Remember that a function performs a mathematical operation. The explanation of the Expression (=) field in the Appendix, "Field Types and Their Instructions," includes a list and description of the functions available for the Expression (=) field. When you type the functions in an Expression (=) field and update the field, Word performs the mathematical operation associated with the functions. All these functions can work on a list of one or more operands inside parentheses. In a table, each operand can be a cell reference. Separate operands with commas.

Function Name	*Operation*
AVERAGE(,,...,)	AVERAGE calculates the average of the operands. If an operand is a cell reference, the values in every cell are added and counted in the calculation of the average.
COUNT(,,...,)	COUNT calculates the number of operands. If an operand is a cell reference, the COUNT function counts each cell referred to that contains a number as one operand.
MAX(,,...,)	MAX finds the highest value in the list of operands. If an operand is a cell reference, the result is the maximum value in the cells referred to.
MIN(,,...,)	MIN finds the lowest value in the list of operands. If an operand is a cell reference, the result is the minimum value in the cells referred to.
PRODUCT(,,...,)	PRODUCT calculates the product of the operands by multiplying them together, one after the other. If an operand is a cell reference, PRODUCT multiplies values in the cells referred to before using the next operand in the list. For example, {=PRODUCT([r1c1:r1c3],[r2c3],10%)} multiplies [r1c1]*[r1c2]*[r1c3]*[r2c3]*10% in that order.
SUM(,,...,)	SUM calculates the sum of the operands by adding them together. If an operand is a cell reference, SUM adds all the values in the cells referred to and counts them in the calculation of the sum.

To work through the following example, use the Second Quarter table (see Figure 13-13) that you've used throughout this chapter. Be sure that the table has an extra row and column so that it looks like Figure 13-18.

2nd Quarter×	East×	West×	North×	South×	×	×
April×	2345×	2354×	2435×	2453×	×	×
May×	2534×	2543×	3245×	3254×	×	×
June×	3425×	3452×	3524×	3542×	×	×
×	×	×	×	×	×	×

Figure 13-18.
Second Quarter table with extra row and column.

Now you can insert fields in the empty cells of the last column (C6) and the bottom row (R5) to calculate your totals. In column 6, you insert fields that will calculate the total for each month. In row 5, you insert fields that will calculate the total for each region. And in the bottom-right corner (R5C6), you insert a field that cross-checks the totals and shows you the total of all regions for the quarter. When you want the total of a group of cells, you insert an Expression (=) field that contains a cell reference to the group of cells inside a SUM function.

First, position the insertion point in the last cell of the first row, [R1C6], and type *Monthly Totals* as the column heading for the numbers that will appear below it. Next, press the down arrow key to move to the second row in the last column, [R2C6]. In this cell, which is at the end of the row for "April," you insert an Expression (=) field that calculates the sum of all regions for a month. Press the INSERT FIELD key combination (Ctrl+F9) to insert a field, and type the following between the field characters:

```
=sum([r2c2:r2c5])
```

The "April" row of the table now looks like the following:

April×	2345×	2354×	2435×	2453×	{=sum([r2c2:r2c5])}×

Do not be concerned if the text wraps to another line in the cell. The result will fit on one line, as you'll see shortly. Press the UPDATE FIELD key (F9) to update the field and to show the "April" result for all regions. If the result does not appear, check to be sure the View Field Codes command is turned off. If the View Field Codes command is turned off or is grayed and the result still does not appear, check to be sure that the Show All option is turned off in the View Preferences dialog box.

For the "May" and "June" rows, repeat this process of pressing the down arrow key, pressing the INSERT FIELD key combination (Ctrl+F9), typing an equal sign, typing the operator *sum* followed by the cell reference in parentheses and brackets, and then pressing the UPDATE FIELD key (F9). In the "May" row, the cell references are [r3c2:r3c5]; in the "June" row, they're [r4c2:r4c5]. The table now looks as shown on the next page.

2nd Quarter×	East×	West×	North×	South×	Monthly Totals×	×
April×	2345×	2354×	2435×	2453×	9587×	×
May×	2534×	2543×	3245×	3254×	11576×	×
June×	3425×	3452×	3524×	3542×	13943×	×
×	×	×	×	×	×	×

Turn on the View Field Codes command (Alt,V,C) to see the field codes as shown below:

2nd Quarter×	East×	West×	North×	South×	Monthly Totals×	×
April×	2345×	2354×	2435×	2453×	{=sum([r2c2:r2 c5])}×	×
May×	2534×	2543×	3245×	3254×	{=sum([r3c2:r3 c5])}×	×
June×	3425×	3452×	3524×	3542×	{=sum([r4c2:r4 c5])}×	×
×	×	×	×	×	×	×

Turn off the View Field Codes command (Alt,V,C). Position the insertion point in the last cell of the first column (R5C1), and type *Region Totals* as the row heading. Press the right arrow key to move to cell R5C2. In this cell, which is at the bottom of the column for "East," you insert an Expression (=) field that calculates the sum of the calendar quarter for each region. Press the INSERT FIELD key combination (Ctrl+F9) to insert a field, and type the following between the field characters:

```
=sum([r2c2:r4c2])
```

The "East" column of the table now looks like the following:

East×	×
2345×	×
2534×	×
3425×	×
{=sum([r2c2:r4 c2])}×	×

Press the UPDATE FIELD key (F9) to update the field and show the East region's second quarter result. For the "West," "North," and "South" columns, repeat this process of pressing the Tab key, pressing the INSERT FIELD key combination (Ctrl+F9), typing an equal sign, typing the operator *sum* followed by the cell reference in parentheses and brackets, and then pressing the UPDATE FILED key (F9). In the "West" column, the cell references are [r2c3:r4c3]; in the "North" column, they're [r2c4:r4c4]; and in the "South" column, they're [r2c5:r4c5]. The table on the next page shows the new results.

2nd Quarter	East	West	North	South	Monthly Totals
April	2345	2354	2435	2453	9587
May	2534	2543	3245	3254	11576
June	3425	3452	3524	3542	13943
Region Totals	8304	8349	9204	9249	

Turn on the View Field Codes command (Alt,V,C) to see the tables with the field codes visible:

2nd Quarter	East	West	North	South	Monthly Totals
April	2345	2354	2435	2453	{=sum([r2c2:r2 c5])}
May	2534	2543	3245	3254	{=sum([r3c2:r3 c5])}
June	3425	3452	3524	3542	{=sum([r4c2:r4 c5])}
Region Totals	{=sum([r2c2:r4 c2])}	{=sum([r2c3:r4 c3])}	{=sum([r2c4:r4 c4])}	{=sum([r2c5:r4 c5])}	

Turn off the View Field Codes command (Alt,V,C). Now it's time to insert Expression (=) fields in cell R5C6 to cross-check the totals of the quarter's regions and months and, if both sums are the same, to show the result as the quarter's total. If both sums are not the same, the result for the cell will be the message "Cross check error." Move the insertion point to the last cell in the last row, R5C6, and press the INSERT FIELD key combination (Ctrl+F9). Between the field characters, type *if* followed by a space (*if* tells Word to compare two operands). The field will compare the total of the monthly quarterly results with the total of the regions' quarterly results. Press Ctrl+F9 again, and type the following:

```
=sum([r2c6:r4c6])
```

Cell R5C6 now looks like the following:

{if {=sum([r2c6:r4 c6])}}

This field calculates the total of the monthly quarterly results in column 6. And this Expression (=) field acts as the first operand for the *if* comparison. Press the right arrow key, type a space, type <>, and type another space. These two symbols (<>) together make up an operator that means "not equal to." The not-equal-to operator compares the two operands to see if their values are unequal. Press the INSERT FIELD key combination (Ctrl+F9), and type the following:

```
=sum([r5c2:r5c5])
```

Cell R5C6 now looks as shown below:

```
{if
{=sum([r2c6:r4
c6])} <>
{=sum([r5c2:r5
c5])}}
```

The second Expression (=) field calculates the total of the regions' quarterly results in row 5. This field acts as the second operand for the *if* comparison. Press the right arrow key, type a space, type *"Cross check error"* (be sure to include the quotation marks), and type another space. This text will be the result that appears in the cell if the two operands in the *if* comparison are not the same. In this example, if the fields that calculate the totals in column 6 and in row 5 are inserted correctly, you will not see "Cross check error" as the result. Press the INSERT FIELD key (Ctrl+F9) again, and type the following:

```
=sum([r2c6:r4c6])
```

The third Expression (=) field also calculates the total of the monthly quarterly results in column 6. This field's result will be the result that appears in the cell if the two operands in the *if* comparison are the same. If the fields that calculate the totals for the months in column 6 and for the regions in row 5 are all inserted correctly, the result of the third Expression (=) field will be the result that appears in cell R5C6. The final formula should look like the following:

```
{if {=sum([r2c6:r4c6])} <> {=sum([r5c2:r5c5])} "Cross check error"
{=sum([r2c6:r4c6])}}
```

After you update the field to show the quarterly total result, the table looks as shown below:

2nd Quarter	East	West	North	South	Monthly Totals
April	2345	2354	2435	2453	9587
May	2534	2543	3245	3254	11576
June	3425	3452	3524	3542	13943
Region Totals	8304	8349	9204	9249	35106

Figure 13-19.
Final results for second quarter.

Save this table for use in "Calculations in text that refer to cells in a table" on the next page and in Example 15 later in the chapter.

If you select the whole table using the Alt+5 keys (5 on the numeric keypad) and press the TOGGLE FIELD key combination (Shift+F9), you see the table with field codes displayed, as shown on the next page.

2nd Quarter	East	West	North	South	Monthly Totals
April	2345	2354	2435	2453	{=sum([r2c2:r2c5])}
May	2534	2543	3245	3254	{=sum([r3c2:r3c5])}
June	3425	3452	3524	3542	{=sum([r4c2:r4c5])}
Region Totals	{=sum([r2c2:r4c2])}	{=sum([r2c3:r4c3])}	{=sum([r2c4:r4c4])}	{=sum([r2c5:r4c5])}	{if {=sum([r2c6:r4c6])} <> {=sum([r5c2:r5c5])} "Cross check error" {=sum([r2c6:r4c6])}}

If you need to edit any of the fields, you can do so now. To return to the display of the results, press the TOGGLE FIELD key combination (Shift+F9) again while the whole table is selected.

Calculations in text that refer to cells in a table

You can refer to a number in any cell in a table. The field that refers to a table cell can be inserted anywhere in a document, either outside or inside a table. You refer to a cell in a table by first inserting a bookmark anywhere in that table and then adding the bookmark name to the expression in the Expression (=) field, as in the following example:

{=sum(bookmark[cells])}

For a description of bookmarks, see Chapter 8, "Fields: Facts and Functions," and the Appendix, "Field Types and Their Instructions." For example, suppose that in text outside a table you want to use the quarterly results, the results for the best month, and the results for the best region from the Second Quarter table in Figure 13-19. Position the insertion point anywhere in the table. Choose the Insert Bookmark command (Alt,I,M), type *sq* as the bookmark name, and then choose OK to insert the bookmark in the table. (The bookmark name is not visible on the screen.) Outside the table, insert sentences like the following:

Our total for the second quarter was {=max(SQ[r5c6])}. Our best month total was {=max(SQ[r2c6:r4c6])}. Our best region total was {=max(SQ[r5c2:r5c5])}. Congratulations!

Update the fields to see the resulting sentences:

Our total for the second quarter was 35106. Our best month total was 13943. Our best regional total was 9249. Congratulations!

Imported values from spreadsheet files

For tasks that require extensive calculations, a spreadsheet program such as Microsoft Excel, Microsoft Multiplan, or Lotus 1-2-3 provides a more complete and powerful set of arithmetic and analytic tools. To help you take advantage of spreadsheet applications and still use their results in your Word documents, Word lets you import numbers from spreadsheet files. The following two examples describe two methods for importing: opening a spreadsheet file in Word and then copying the values to a Word document, or linking a Word document with a Microsoft Excel spreadsheet file. The first method works for all three spreadsheet programs' files—Microsoft Excel, Microsoft Multiplan, and Lotus 1-2-3. The second method works only for Microsoft Excel files. In addition, this linking method requires more than 640 KB of memory and a full version of Microsoft Windows.

Example 12: Opening a Spreadsheet File in Word and Copying Values

As you've seen, you can use either of two methods to copy information. You can use a copy command (Edit Copy or the Ctrl+Insert keys) and a paste command (Edit Paste or the Shift+Insert keys), both of which use the Clipboard. You can also use the COPY key combination (Shift+F2),

TIP

Adding Dollar Signs and Commas to the Results

The results of the Second Quarter fields discussed on the preceding page are dollar amounts larger than 1,000. But as the fields are set up currently, the numbers contain no commas and no dollar signs. You can add instructions to the fields to add any commas and dollar signs that are needed. For example, the field that results in the second-quarter total, {=max(sq[r5c6])}, shows its result as 35106. To add an instruction to format the result with a comma and a dollar sign, insert \# "$#,###" in front of the closing field character:

```
{=max(sq[r5c6]) \# "$#,###"}
```

When you update the field, the result appears as $35,106. The \# instruction is called a numeric switch. See the Appendix, "Field Types and Their Instructions," for information about switch instructions.

which does not use the Clipboard. Use either of these methods or their variations to copy values from spreadsheet files.

You can open a Microsoft Excel, Microsoft Multiplan, or Lotus 1-2-3 spreadsheet file from within Word, exactly as you open any Word document.

To copy values from a spreadsheet, first open the Word document into which you want to copy the spreadsheet values. Then, choose the File Open command (Alt,F,O). In the File Open dialog box, change to the directory in which you keep your spreadsheet files, type **.XLS* (or the proper file-name extension for your spreadsheets) in the Open File Name box, and then choose OK. Select the file from the Files list, and choose OK. If Word displays a dialog box asking you to confirm the spreadsheet's file format, select the proper format if it isn't already selected—BIFF for Microsoft Excel, Multiplan for Microsoft Multiplan, or WKS for Lotus 1-2-3. Choose OK to open the spreadsheet file. If Word displays a dialog box asking you to supply a password for the file, type the password and choose OK.

When you open a spreadsheet file in Word, the values in the spreadsheet are separated into columns by tab characters and into rows by paragraph marks:

```
Moving Costs for LAL from Ann Arbor to Seattle →   →   →   →   →   →   →   ¶
   →   →   →   →   →   →   →   ¶
Method\Costs → Goods Tariff → Surely→Airfare→2nd Carfare → Meals→Rooms→Totals¶
Rent TruckA (2dr)  →  $2007.00→$350.00→$199.03→$159.00→$150.00→$200.00→$2965.03¶
Rent TruckB (2dr)  →  $1914.00→$57.00→$186.56→$159.00→$150.00→$200.00→$2586.56¶
Rent TruckC (2dr)  →  $1354.00→$0.00 → $172.33→$159.00→$150.00→$200.00→$2035.33¶
   →   →   →   →   →   →   →   ¶
Rent TruckA (1 dr)  →  $2007.00→$350.00→$199.03→$0.00 → $75.00→$150.00→$2681.03¶
Rent TruckB (1dr)  →  $1914.00→$57.00→$186.56→$0.00 → $75.00→$150.00→$2302.56¶
Rent TruckC (1dr)  →  $1354.00→$0.00 → $172.33→$0.00 → $75.00→$150.00→$1751.33¶
   →   →   →   →   →   →   →   ¶
Rent TruckA (2dr)  →  $2007.00→$0.00 → $199.03→$159.00→$150.00→$200.00→$2615.03¶
Rent TruckB (2dr)  →  $1914.00→$0.00 → $186.56→$159.00→$150.00→$200.00→$2529.56¶
Rent TruckC (2dr)  →  $1188.27→$0.00 → $172.33→$159.00→$150.00→$200.00→$1869.61¶
   →   →   →   →   →   →   →   ¶
Rent TruckA (1 dr)  →  $2007.00→$0.00 → $199.03→$0.00 → $75.00→$150.00→$2331.03¶
Rent TruckB (1dr)  →  $1914.00→$0.00 → $186.56→$0.00 → $75.00→$150.00→$2245.56¶
Rent TruckC (1dr)  →  $1188.27→$0.00 → $172.33→$0.00 → $75.00→$150.00→$1585.61¶
   →   →   →   →   →   →   →   ¶
M Ship + LAL fly→$1978.08→$950.00→$159.00→$0.00 → $0.00 → $0.00 → $3087.08¶
M Ship + RT drive  →  $1978.08→$950.00→$129.25→$129.25→$135.00→$140.00→$3461.58¶
M Ship + 2-1W drive  →  $1978.08→$950.00→$172.33→$159.00→$120.00→$120.00→$3499.41¶
M Ship + 1-1W drive  →  $1978.08→$950.00→$172.33→$0.00 → $120.00→$120.00→$3340.41¶
   →   →   →   →   →   →   →   ¶
NA Ship + LAL fly  →  $1386.20→$950.00→$159.00→$0.00 → $0.00 → $0.00 → $2495.20¶
NA Ship + RT drive  →  $1386.20→$950.00→$129.25→$129.25→$135.00→$140.00→$2869.70¶
```

Choose the Window Arrange All command (Alt,W,A) so that you can see both windows at once. Next, select the values that you want to copy from the spreadsheet. To copy the values using copy and paste commands, choose the Edit Copy command (Alt,E,C or Ctrl+Insert). This step copies the values from the selected cells to the Clipboard.

Switch to the window that contains the Word document (Ctrl+F6), and position the insertion point where you want to insert the values from the spreadsheet file. Choose the Edit Paste command (Alt,E,P or Shift+Insert) to paste the numbers from the Clipboard to the Word document. Or, to use the COPY key method, press the COPY key combination (Shift+F2). If you use a mouse, select an insertion point in the document for the spreadsheet values and press the Enter key. If you do not use a mouse, press the NEXT WINDOW key combination (Ctrl+F6) to switch to the document window, use the arrow keys to select an insertion point in the document for the spreadsheet values, and then press Enter to copy the spreadsheet values to your Word document.

To put the spreadsheet values in a table, select the values, choose the Insert Table command (Alt,I,T), and choose OK. Then, adjust the table's formatting to suit you.

Example 13: Linking a Microsoft Excel Spreadsheet with a Word Document

You can link a Microsoft Excel spreadsheet file with a Word document file. A link is a direct connection that sends data from one file to another. When the two files are linked, Word will update the numbers for you in the Word document whenever they change in the spreadsheet file. You cannot link Microsoft Multiplan or Lotus 1-2-3 spreadsheet files to Word document files.

TIP

Converting a Spreadsheet File to a Word Document

You can easily convert an entire Microsoft Excel, Microsoft Multiplan, or Lotus 1-2-3 spreadsheet file to a Word document. To do so, open the spreadsheet file in Word, and Word converts the document. Then, save the file with a DOC file name extension. The spreadsheet is now stored in Word's file format. Note, however, that only the values are stored; spreadsheet formulas are neither converted nor stored.

Whether you can choose this method rather than pasting via the Clipboard or converting the spreadsheet file to a Word document depends on how much memory your computer has and whether you have a full version of Microsoft Windows. You must be able to run Word and Microsoft Excel together to use the link method. If your computer has no more than 640 KB of memory, you probably cannot run Word and Microsoft Excel together, so use the pasting method or the file conversion tip described earlier in this section. If you have 2 MB of expanded memory and are running Microsoft Windows/286 version 2.11 or later, or if you have 2 MB of extended memory and are running Microsoft Windows/386 version 2.11 or later, you can use the link method described in this section to insert values from a Microsoft Excel spreadsheet. If you want to link a Microsoft Excel spreadsheet with a Word document, you must use a full version of Microsoft Windows. The run-time version of Windows that comes with Word cannot set up links because it cannot run more than one application at a time.

To link a Microsoft Excel spreadsheet with a Word document, first start Microsoft Excel and open the spreadsheet with which you want to link the document. Next, select and copy to the Clipboard the spreadsheet cells that you want to copy to your Word document.

Start Word and open or create the document with which you want to link the spreadsheet. Choose the Edit Paste Link command (Alt,E,L). Edit Paste Link is available only if Microsoft Excel values are currently stored on the Clipboard. In the Edit Paste Link dialog box, turn on the Auto Update option (Alt+A) if you want the link to update itself. If you want the link to update only when you tell it to, leave the Auto Update option turned off. Choose OK to insert the field that links the two files and to see the values from the linked spreadsheet in your Word document.

Word inserts the values in a table that has the same number of rows and columns as were copied from the spreadsheet:

Least Expensive¤	¤	¤	¤	¤	¤	¤
Method\Costs¤	Goods Tariff¤	Car¤	Airfare¤	2nd Carfare¤	Meals¤	Rooms¤
NA Ship + 1 fly¤	$1,386.20	$0.00	$159.00	$0.00	$0.00	$0.00

If you see field codes instead of spreadsheet values, be sure that both the View Field Codes command and the Show All option in the View Preferences dialog box are turned off. If you'd like to see the field codes for a link with a Microsoft Excel spreadsheet file when the View Field Codes Command and Show All option are turned off, position the insertion point anywhere in the table and press the TOGGLE FIELD key combination (Shift+F9). The field for a manually updated link looks like the following:

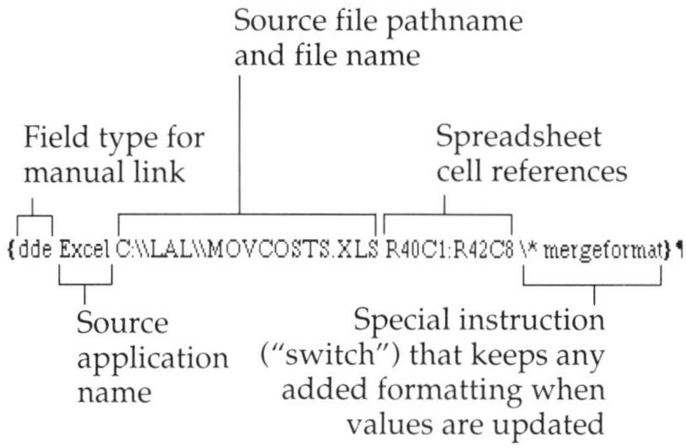

And here's how an automatically updated link looks:

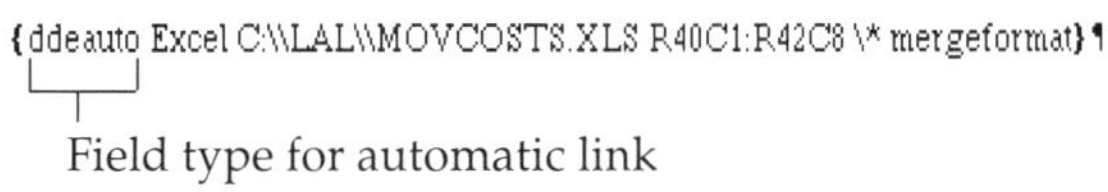

If you inserted a link that updates only when you tell it to, you update the values by positioning the insertion point anywhere in the values and pressing the UPDATE FIELD key (F9). If you inserted a link that updates automatically, the new values update in the Word document whenever the spreadsheet file changes, as long as Microsoft Excel is running. After the link is set up, Word asks if you want to run Microsoft Excel if it's not already running when you open the Word document:

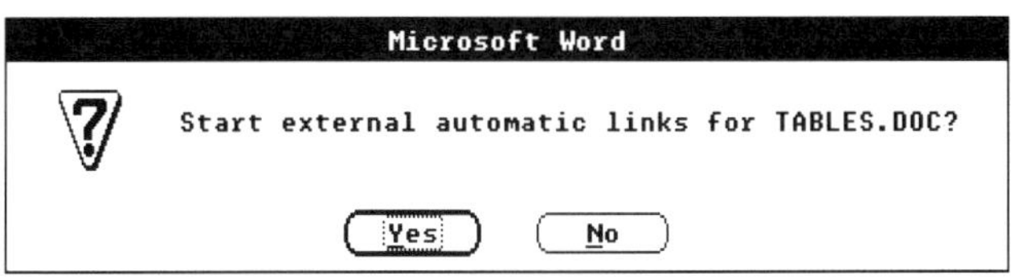

Choosing Yes in the message box starts Microsoft Excel and updates linked values. Choosing No means the linked fields cannot be updated either manually or automatically.

Reusing a Table: Save It as a Glossary Entry

Many of the tables you create are straightforward, containing several columns and several rows all the same width and height, with no special border formatting. But sometimes you might need to create an unusual table that you can save and reuse. For example, you might want a table whose column headings have special formatting or whose columns have different widths. A table might contain a simple spreadsheet that you want to reuse. Or you might want a particular type of table to appear in the same position on every page. If you create any kind of unusual or complex table, it's worth your while to store the table as a glossary entry so that you can easily reuse it. For more information about using glossaries, see Chapter 12, "Glossaries."

You use the same procedures to store all or part of a table as a glossary entry as you do to store text or graphics as a glossary entry. To store the table's structure only, delete the text using the Delete key, the Shift+Delete keys, or the Edit Cut command. To store text (such as headings or Expression (=) fields that set up a spreadsheet) in a table, leave intact the contents of the cells that contain the text and fields you want to store with the table. Start by selecting the whole table or the rows in the table that you want to store. Then, choose the Edit Glossary command (Alt,E,O), type a glossary name, and choose OK to create the glossary entry. If you see "(No Selection)" in the Edit Glossary dialog box and the Define button is dimmed even after you type a glossary entry name, cancel the dialog box and check your table selection to be sure you have selected complete rows.

When you quit Word, you see a dialog box that asks if you want to save global glossary and command changes. Choose Yes to save your table glossary entries. If you choose No, you lose the glossary entries when you quit Word.

The following four examples show special tables that you might want to keep as glossary entries. Word lets you store any table or any table rows as a glossary entry.

Example 14: A Table with Uneven Column Widths

When you insert a table, all its columns are the same width. You might find, however, that you occasionally need a table that has one narrow and one wide column, as shown in Figure 13-20.

x	x	x
x	x	x
x	x	x
x	x	x
x	x	x
x	x	x

Figure 13-20.
Table with uneven columns.

When you insert a table, it's as wide as the text area of the page, unless you set narrower column widths. Sometimes you'll want a table to be less than the full width of the text area. Although creating this table is easy, storing it in a glossary makes it faster to insert later and ensures consistency among other similar tables.

You create a table like the one in Figure 13-20 with only one row. Choose the Insert Table command (Alt,I,T). In the Insert Table dialog box, type 2 in the Initial Col Width box and choose OK. Turn on the ruler (Ctrl+Shift+F10) if it's not already on, and click the ruler view icon, if necessary, to switch to column view. Drag the middle column marker to the left or right to adjust the first column's width, and drag the right column marker to adjust the second column's width. For example, drag the first column marker in the table in Figure 13-20 to the 1-inch mark on the ruler, and drag the second column marker to the 4-inch mark. If you do not have a mouse, select the first column and choose the Format Table command (Alt,T,A). In the Format Table dialog box, type *1"* in the Width of Column 1 box and then choose the Next Column button (Alt+N). Move back to the Width of Column 2 box (Alt+W), type *3"*, and then choose OK.

To store the table as a glossary entry, select the table, choose the Edit Glossary command (Alt,E,O), type a glossary entry name (such as *Uneven_Tbl*), and choose OK.

Example 15: A Table with Special Borders and Contents

Throughout this chapter, you used the Second Quarter table as your working example. If you remove the individual numbers for each region and month in the table, keep the Expression (=) fields, and then store the table as a glossary entry, you'll have a ready-made table for the latest quarterly results.

The Second Quarter table is shown again below with its field codes displayed. To see the field codes, turn on the View Field Codes command (Alt,V,C).

2nd Quarter×	East×	West×	North×	South×	Monthly Totals×
April×	2345×	2354×	2435×	2453×	{=sum([r2c2:r2c5])}×
May×	2534×	2543×	3245×	3254×	{=sum([r3c2:r3c5])}×
June×	3425×	3452×	3524×	3542×	{=sum([r4c2:r4c5])}×
Region Totals×	{=sum([r2c2:r4c2])}×	{=sum([r2c3:r4c3])}×	{=sum([r2c4:r4c4])}×	{=sum([r2c5:r4c5])}×	{if {=sum([r2c6:r4c6])} <> {=sum([r5c2:r5c5])} "Cross check error" {=sum([r2c6:r4c6])}}×

If you delete the number of the quarter ("2nd"), the names of the months, and the numbers for each month and region, the table you store looks like the following:

Quarter×	East×	West×	North×	South×	Monthly Totals×
×	×	×	×	×	{=sum([r2c2:r2c5])}×
×	×	×	×	×	{=sum([r3c2:r3c5])}×
×	×	×	×	×	{=sum([r4c2:r4c5])}×
Region Totals×	{=sum([r2c2:r4c2])}×	{=sum([r2c3:r4c3])}×	{=sum([r2c4:r4c4])}×	{=sum([r2c5:r4c5])}×	{if {=sum([r2c6:r4c6])} <> {=sum([r5c2:r5c5])} "Cross check error" {=sum([r2c6:r4c6])}}×

Now, to store this table as a glossary entry, select the whole table, choose the Edit Glossary command (Alt,E,O), type a glossary entry name (such as *Qtrly_Tbl*), and choose OK.

Example 16: A Table with a Special Column Arrangement

Creating a table that includes merged cells can require a lot of your time. For example, take a look at the table in Figure 13-21:

Merged cells in columns 1 and 2

Border set to None

Terms		Meaning
Formatting codes		None — formatting effects displayed on screen
Formatting methods		Mouse with ribbon and ruler Ctrl-key combinations Menu commands and dialog boxes with Alt-key combinations Copy formatting with mouse or key combinations
Variations in display		Display as printed or display as formatted
Icons	Ruler	Style, paragraph alignment, tab stops and tab stop alignment, line spacing, paragraph spacing, ruler view: indents, columns, margins
	Ribbon	Font, point size, boldface, italic, small capitals, underline continuously, word underline, double underline, superscript, subscript, show all

Figure 13-21.
Table with merged cells and special borders.

To create a table structure like the one above, you insert a three-column, six-row table. First, choose the Insert Table command (Alt,I,T). In the Insert Table dialog box type *3* in the Number of Columns box, type *6* in the Number of Rows box, and then choose the Format button (Alt+F) to add borders. In the Format Table dialog box, select the Single option for Outline (Alt+U,S) under Borders and the Single option for Inside (Alt+I,S) under Borders, and then choose OK. This step adds a border around the outside of the whole table and adds borders between all the cells.

Then, to make the bottom border of the first row thick instead of single, select the table's first row, choose the Format Table command (Alt,T,A), select the Thick option for Bottom (Alt+B,T) under Borders, and then choose OK. To give the bottom-left cells the appearance of one cell that is two rows tall, remove the border by selecting the last two cells in the first column, R5C1:R6C1, choosing the Format Table command(Alt,T,A), selecting the None option for Inside (Alt+I,N) under Borders, and then choosing OK. The table now looks as shown on the next page.

Gridline does not print.

To adjust the first column to 0.4" wide, select the first column, choose the Format Table command (Alt,T,A), type *0.4"* in the Width of Column 1 box, and then choose the Next Column button (Alt+N). Adjust the second column to 1 inch wide by typing *1"* in the Width of Column 2 box, and then choose the Next Column button (Alt+N). To adjust the third column to 2.6 inches wide, type *2.6"* in the Width of Column 3 box, and then choose OK. With these column width adjustments, the table now looks like the following:

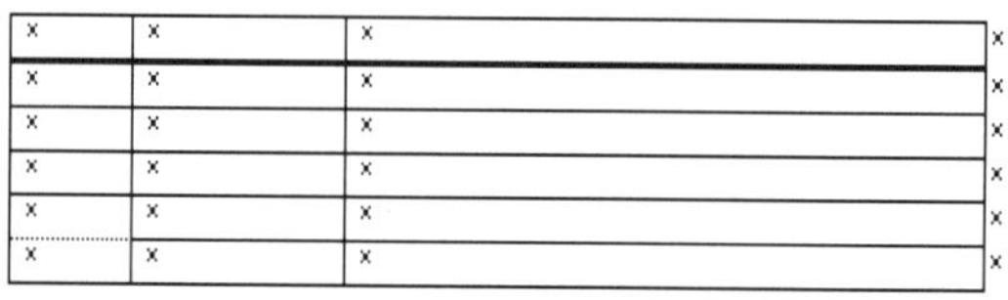

Next, merge the cells in the first and second columns of the first four rows (R1C1:R4C2) by selecting the cells. Choose the Edit Table command (Alt,E,A), and choose the Merge Cells button (Alt+M). Press the Delete key to delete the extra paragraph marks. The table is now ready to store as a glossary entry. The rows are not as high as the rows in Figure 13-19 because here the rows contain no text. By not setting minimum row heights, you ensure that the table will be as compact as possible but will still fit any text or graphics you insert in it. If you want rows to have a specific minimum height, however, you can always set minimum row heights and store the table with that format. Here's how the final table structure looks:

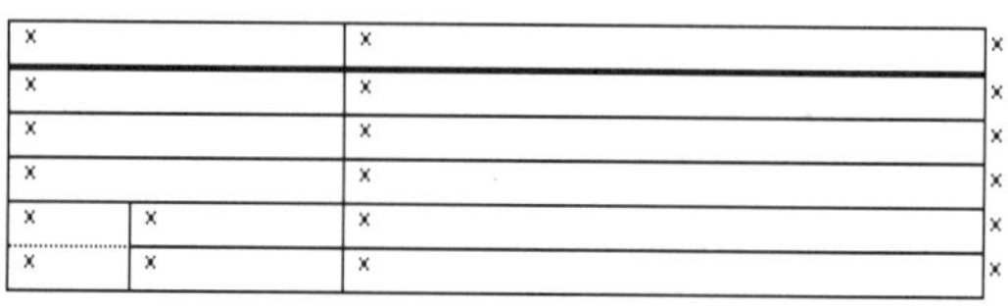

Note that the cell at the bottom of column one appears to be two rows high, but it's not. It has no border between two cells, which gives it this appearance. You cannot merge cells vertically across rows, only within a row. If you insert text or graphics in the top of this two-cell space, you see that the height of the top cell grows. To keep the cell height from growing taller than you want, continue the text in the lower cell by manually moving some of the text down.

Now, to store the table as a glossary entry, select the table, choose the Edit Glossary command (Alt,E,O), type a glossary entry name (such as *Terms_Tbl*), and then choose OK.

Example 17: Sidebars

Sidebars are miniature articles within larger articles. You often see sidebars in boxes that run either across the bottom or along one side of a page in a magazine. It's not necessary to use tables for sidebars. You can as easily type the sidebar paragraphs and then select them and give them positions and borders. You can even specify the sidebar's width using this method. And if you need to include a table within the sidebar, you cannot use a table to create the sidebar itself because a table cannot contain another table. Also remember that if you want to insert a tab character in a sidebar table, you must press the Ctrl+Tab keys instead of the Tab key (which will add another row).

Using a table for a sidebar, however, gives you the advantage of not having to worry about selecting all the sidebar text when you want

TIP

Figuring Out How Many Rows to Store

Before you store a table as a glossary entry, decide how many rows to store. If the table has the same cell and text format in every row, save only one row as a glossary entry. You can add rows to the table later by pressing the Tab key at the end of the last row. The added row has the cell and text formatting of the row above it. If the table has column headers that are different from the rest of the table's rows, however, save the header row plus one regular row. Save the whole table when the table has any unique rows, particularly if one of the unique rows is below the table's first row. Otherwise, you have to manually format them after you insert the table, which defeats the purpose of saving the table structure as a glossary entry.

to position the sidebar. You also have more control over the types of borders for each side of the sidebar, and you can more easily change the sidebar's width. For example, suppose you want to set up a table to use as a sidebar that appears at the bottom of a page, like the following:

Sidebar table

5. Product Development. Program development began creating the program and user education began creating the documentation. Both elements of the product underwent extensive testing and revision in preparation for final testing.

Additional Steps in Product Creation Even though the seven-phase process covers the important tasks in preparing a product for market, additional activities behind the scenes enrich a product's chances of success. These behind-the-scenes activities include creative development of advertising, advertising and positioning research, cost of goods analysis, bill of materials, packaging configuration, update policy (if applicable), and coordination with other products already introduced and soon to come to market.

Footer — **Tablet History** **Confidential** **November 17, 1989**

Bottom page edge

To create this sidebar table, choose the Insert Table command (Alt,I,T), type *1* in the Number of Columns box, and then choose the Format button (Alt+F). Select the Single option for Outline (Alt+U,S) under Borders, and choose OK. With the insertion point still in the table, choose the Format Position command (Alt,T,O). Select the Bottom option under Vertical (Alt+V,B,F4), and then choose OK. Now, select the table, choose the Edit Glossary command (Alt,E,O), type a glossary entry name (such as *Bottom_Sbar_Tbl*), and then choose OK.

Chapter 14

Previewing and Perfecting Page Layout

When you print a document, it's frustrating to get a printed version that looks different from what you saw on the screen. Now, in Word for Windows, you can see on the screen exactly what your printer is going to deliver, saving you paper and time. Word offers two ways to look at the final printed page so that you can make corrections and adjustments before printing: Print Preview and Page View. In Print Preview, you see all of one or two pages at a time. In Page View, you see only part of a page at a time because the text and graphics are displayed at full size.

You can work with five views of a document:

- Normal editing view and Draft View for inserting, editing, and formatting text and graphics
- Outline View for organizing and structuring document contents
- Print Preview and Page View for previewing page layout and making final adjustments before printing

To choose a different view from the current view of the document, choose the Outline, Draft, or Page commands from the View menu or the Print Preview command from the File menu, as illustrated on the next page. To turn off a view, choose its command again.

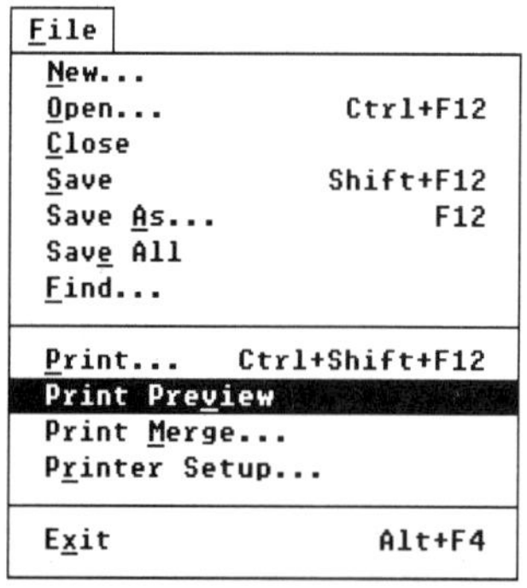

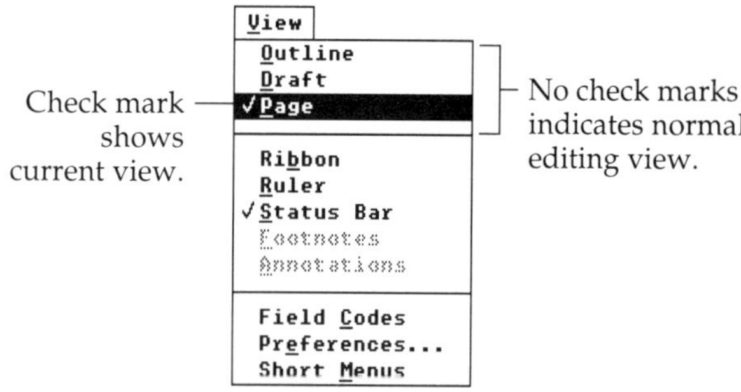

Normal editing view, Outline View, and Page View affect the current pane. Thus, you can see one of these three views in one pane and another view in the other pane. To give you maximum editing speed and legibility for all text, Draft View displays text in all windows in 12-point monospace font and graphics as empty boxes. Print Preview takes over the entire screen to display one document one or two pages at a time.

Print Preview and Page View give you a look at the final printed page so that you can make corrections and adjustments before printing. In Print Preview, the text appears in an illegible 4-point preview font, and graphics are similarly reduced:

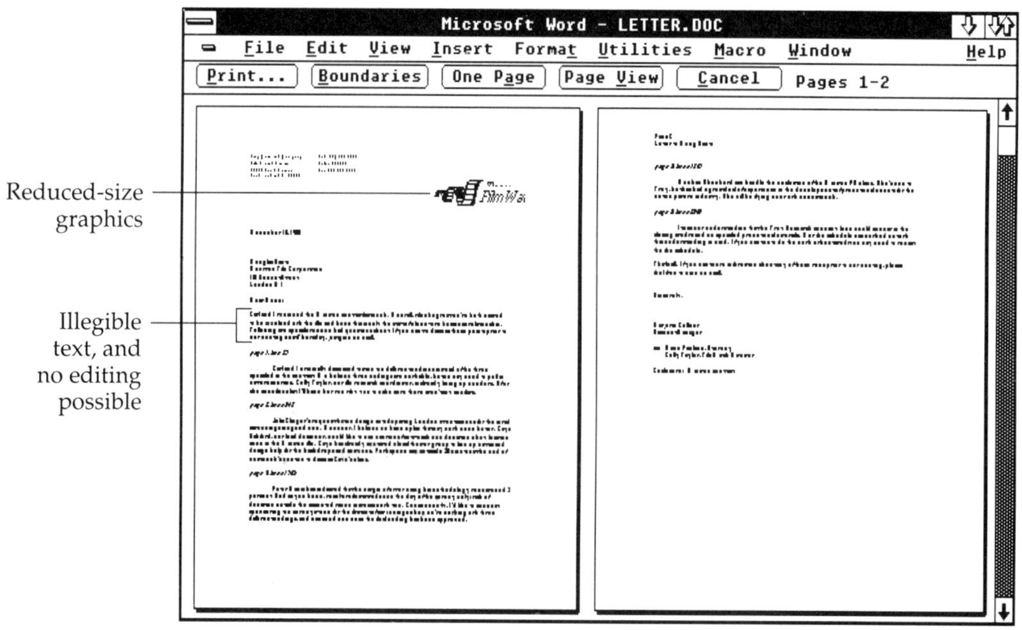

In Page View, none of the page elements are reduced:

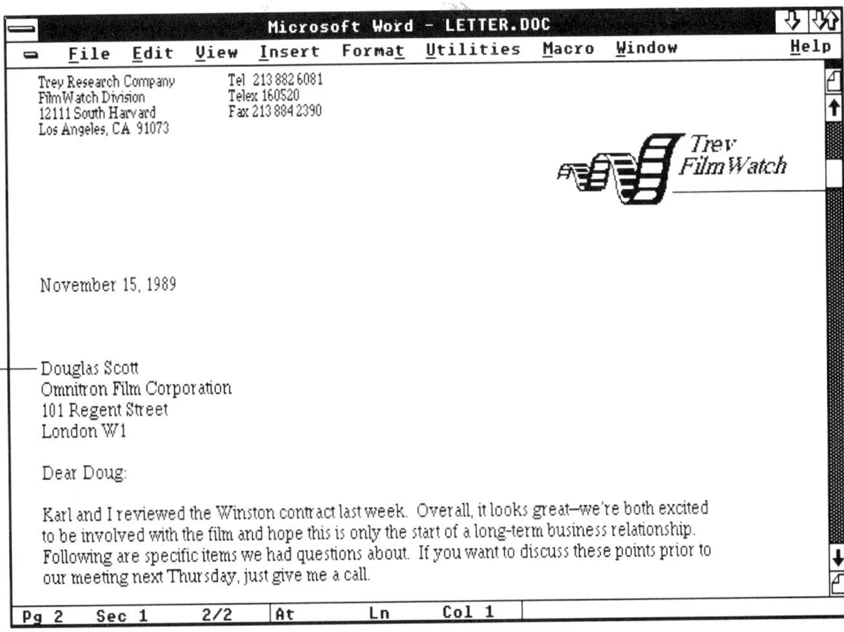

Full-size graphics

Full-size text, and editing possible

In both views, you see everything at its final position that Word will print except line numbers, which appear only in Print Preview.

TIP

How Fields Affect Previewing

In Page View fields appear as you set them. In Print Preview the Field Codes option in the File Print dialog box controls whether fields appear as their codes or their results. If field codes are showing when you're in Page View, the page breaks you see will not be the same as the breaks you get when you print the document.

To see the actual page breaks in Page View, turn off the View Field Codes command (Alt,V,C), and turn off the Show All option (Alt+ *) in the View Preferences dialog box. If field codes still appear in Page View, select the whole document by pressing Ctrl+5 (5 on the numeric keypad) and press the TOGGLE FIELD key combination (Shift+F9) until you see the fields' results. If field codes appear in Print Preview but you want to see field results, turn off the Field Codes option (Alt+O,Alt+L) in the File Print dialog box, choose OK, and then press the Esc key to cancel printing but to retain the new Field Codes setting. For more information about fields, see Chapter 8, "Fields: Facts and Functions."

Using Print Preview for a Quick Check of Whole Pages

In Print Preview, you can see one or two entire pages at one time. The text is small; Word uses the Preview font (4-point screen font) in Print Preview. You will not be able to read or edit the text or change character or paragraph formatting. You will, however, be able to see spacing and the positions of elements on the page. And you'll be able to move those elements, including margins, page breaks, headers, footers, and positioned objects (text, tables, and graphics to which you've assigned a specific position using the Format Position command). Word lets you scroll through the entire document, checking and adjusting page breaks and the positions of text and other elements. For information about how to make these changes, see "Moving Page Elements in Print Preview" later in this chapter.

The following illustration shows a document as seen in Print Preview and identifies the screen elements:

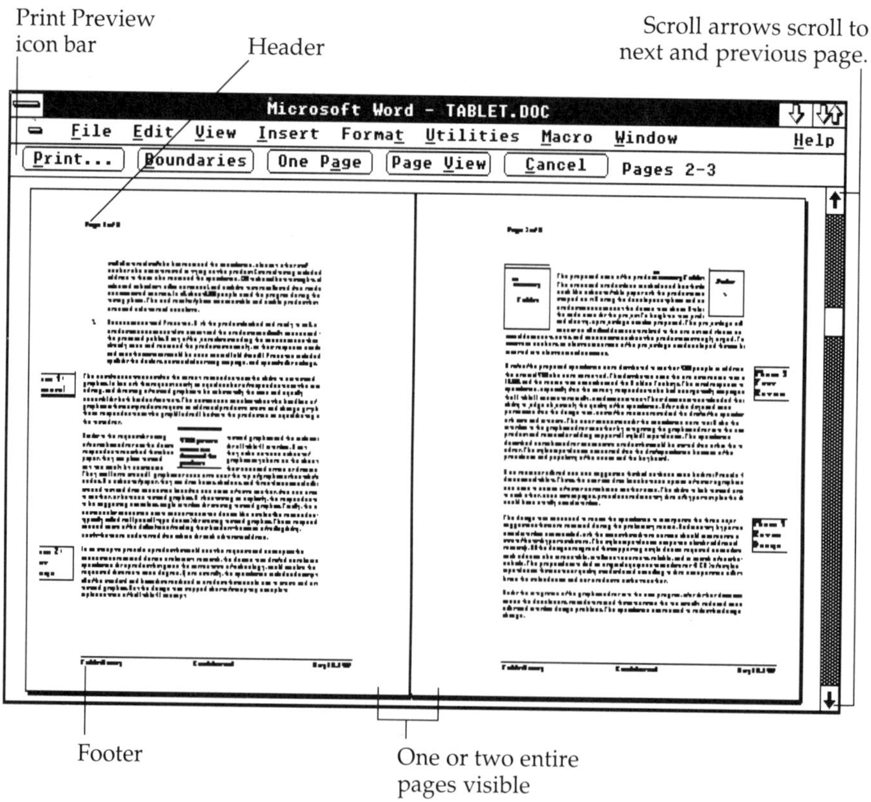

The Print Preview icon bar provides several major controls for the display:

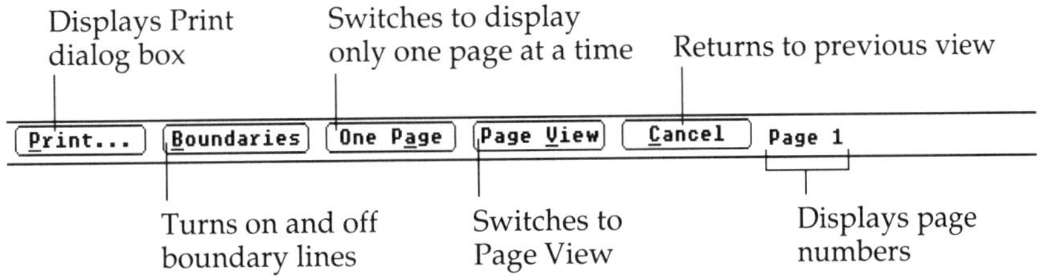

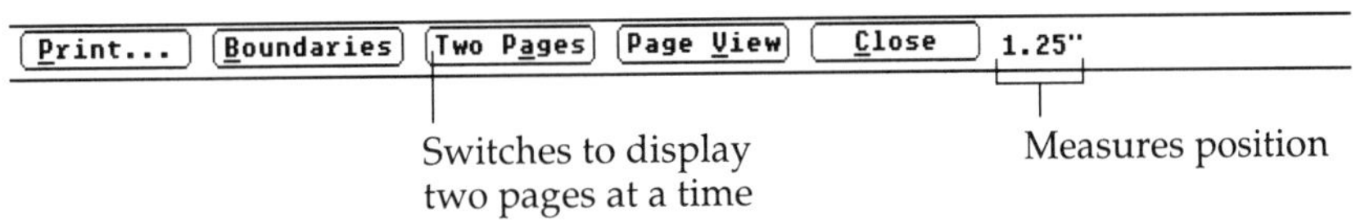

Word usually displays the current page number or numbers at the right end of the Print Preview icon bar. If you are moving an element, however, Word temporarily displays the current position measurement. See "Moving Page Elements in Print Preview" and "Changing the Position of an Object in Print Preview" later in this chapter for more information about moving elements and objects.

In Print Preview, many menu commands are grayed because you cannot edit or format text or graphics. None of the commands on the Edit, Insert, and Windows menus are available. On the Format menu, only the Document command is available. Only the Repaginate Now command is available on the Utilities menu, and only the Record and Run commands are available on the Macro menu. The Outline, Draft, and Page commands on the View menu are available for switching to a different view. None of the File menu commands for opening another

TIP

Getting a Larger Preview

If you have a full-page, high-resolution monitor, the text in Print Preview might be legible, and you might be able to see a whole page at one time in Page View. Via Windows, Word takes full advantage of the screen's display abilities. Throughout this chapter, the text and graphics describe an EGA-resolution monitor.

document are available, but all the commands that apply to the active document are available for saving, printing, closing, and quitting. And all the Help menu commands are available.

If you turn on the Mirror Margins option in the Format Document dialog box and display two pages at a time in Print Preview, Word displays pages in facing pairs—even-numbered pages on the left and odd-numbered pages on the right—as if bound in a book. If you also type a Gutter Margin measurement in the Format Document dialog box, Word adds the measurement to the inside margins (between the pages):

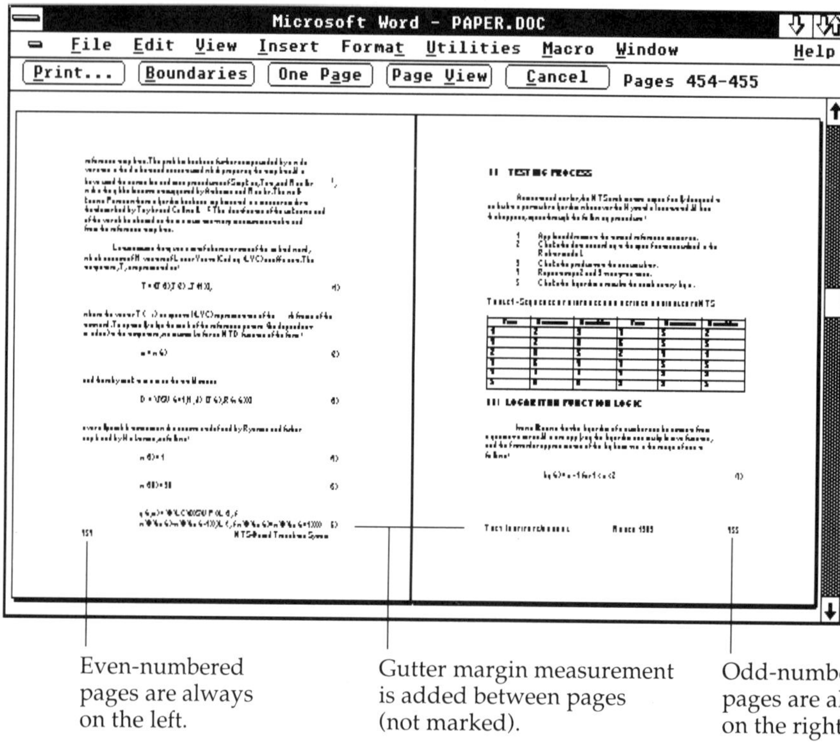

Switching into and out of Print Preview

To switch to Print Preview, Word lets you use either of two methods. You can choose the File Print Preview command (Alt,F,V) or, if you have the Format Position dialog box open to set position formatting, the Preview button (Alt+P) to see the effect of the position formatting you just set. Note that if the selected printer in the File Printer Setup dialog box is connected to None, you cannot switch to Print Preview.

To switch out of Print Preview, you can choose from a number of methods. Press the Esc key or the C key, which produces the same result as does choosing the Cancel (or Close) button on the Print Preview icon bar. This button and the File Print Preview command (Alt,F,V) return the window to the view it was in when you switched to Print Preview. You can also choose the Page View button (P) on the Print Preview icon bar, choose the View Page command (Alt,V,P), or double-click anywhere in the Print Preview window to switch to Page View. Or you can choose the View Draft command (Alt,V,D) or the View Outline command (Alt,V,O) to see those views.

Selecting Elements and Objects in Print Preview

When you first switch to Print Preview, you see the positions of document text and graphics and of the headers and footers, footnotes, and any line numbers. Word lets you turn on boundary lines that show you the positions and sizes of page elements and positioned objects on the page, as shown on the next page. Page elements are the margins and page breaks, which are represented by dotted lines. Positioned objects are the text, tables, and graphics to which you have assigned a specific position using the Format Position command, as well as the headers and footers, if any. Positioned objects are enclosed in dotted-line boxes. To see the boundary lines, click the Boundaries button on the Print Preview icon bar or press the B key.

TIP

Getting Back to Normal Editing View

Word contains no command or key that displays the normal editing view explicitly. Rather, normal editing view is the absence of any of the other four views. When you switch from Print Preview, Word displays the view you had just before you chose Print Preview. To display normal editing view after you switch from Print Preview, open the View menu (Alt,V) and choose the command with the check mark beside it. For example, if you see Page View after you switch from Print Preview, choose the View Page command.

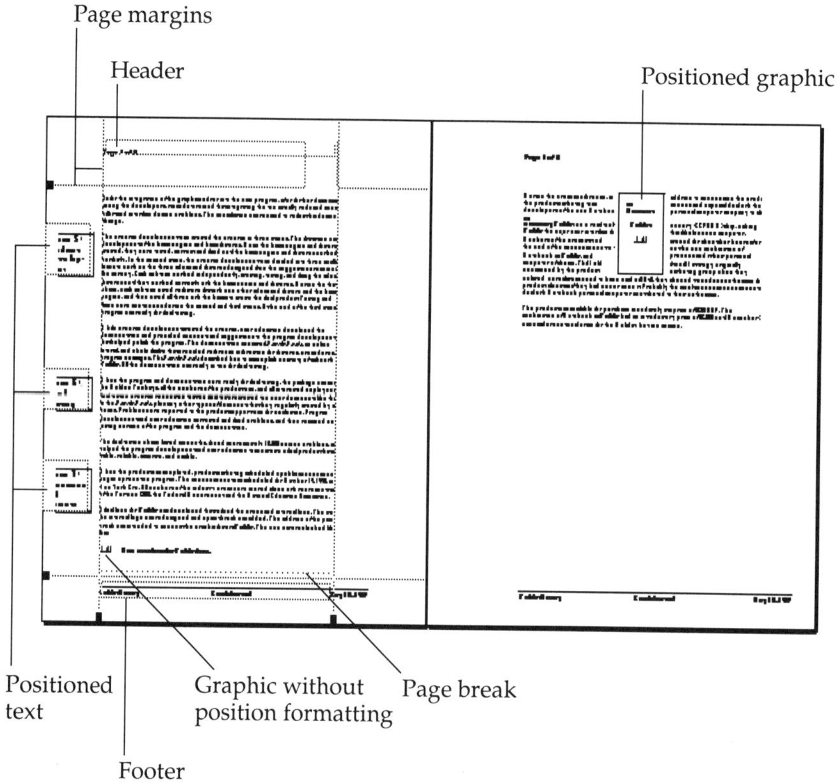

Note that text and graphics that are not positioned objects do not have boundaries.

After you turn on Boundaries, you can use the mouse or the keyboard to select the page elements or the positioned objects that you want to move.

To select a page element or a positioned object using the mouse, point to the element or the object. The mouse pointer becomes a cross hair (+) to indicate that the mouse pointer is properly positioned. To select a margin, position the mouse pointer on the appropriate black box at the left end of the top or bottom margin line or at the bottom of the left or right margin line. To select a page break, position the mouse pointer anywhere along the page break line. And to select a positioned object, position the mouse pointer anywhere within the dotted-line box. Move the mouse pointer off the selection spot to change the mouse pointer back to an arrow. The upcoming sections "Moving Page

Elements in Print Preview" and "Changing the Position of an Object in Print Preview" explain how to move page elements and positioned objects using the mouse.

To select a page element or a positioned object using the keyboard, press the Tab key. Word displays a cross hair on the black box for the left margin. Each time you press Tab, Word moves the cross hair to the next page element or positioned object in the following order: left margin, top margin, right margin, bottom margin, header, footer, page break, positioned objects in the order in which they appear in the file (that is, in the order in which you see them in normal editing view), and then back to the left margin. Pressing the Shift+Tab keys moves the cross hair to page elements and positioned objects in reverse order from Tab. To cancel selecting page elements and positioned objects using the keyboard, press the Esc key. See the upcoming sections "Moving Page Elements in Print Preview" and "Changing the Position of an Object in Print Preview" for more information about how to move page elements and positioned objects using the keyboard.

Moving Page Elements in Print Preview

Page elements in Print Preview are the page margins and the page break—all represented by dotted lines. To see the elements (and positioned objects), turn on the boundary lines by clicking the Boundaries button on the Print Preview icon bar or by pressing the B key. To move a page element using the mouse, select the page element (see the preceding section, "Selecting Elements and Objects in Print Preview") and drag the page element to the new position. Note the position measurement displayed at the right end of the Print Preview icon bar, as shown in Figure 14-1 on the next page.

When you drag a margin using the mouse, Word does not update the page format immediately, but the margin line shows its new position, as Figure 14-2 on the next page illustrates. By delaying reformatting when you drag margins using the mouse, Word lets you drag more than one margin without having to wait for reformatting. After you drag margins using the mouse, click outside the page box that shows the boundary lines. (You can also click in the page box for the other page when two pages are displayed.) Word then formats the pages with

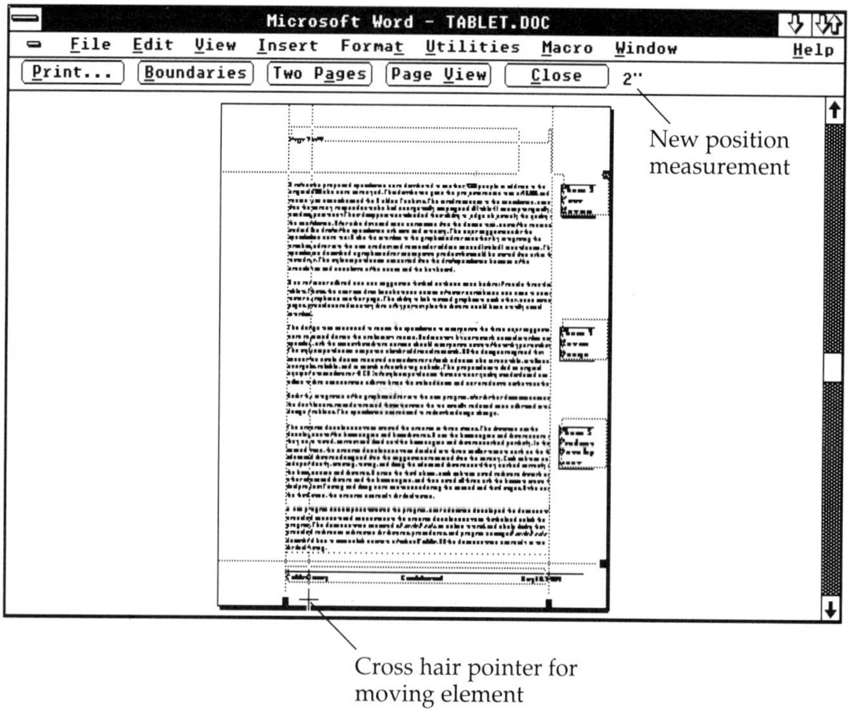

Figure 14-1. *Page element moved to new position.*

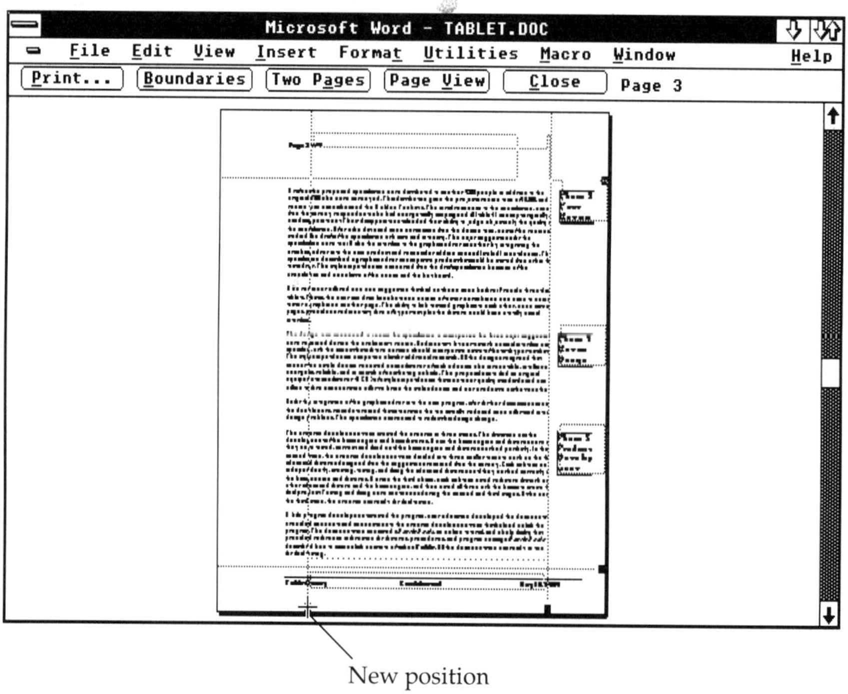

Figure 14-2. *Margin line shown at its new position.*

the new margins. When you drag the page break using the mouse, Word updates the pages as soon as you release the mouse button.

To move a page element using the keyboard, press the Tab key to first select the page element (see the preceding section, "Selecting Elements and Objects in Print Preview") and then press the appropriate arrow key to move the dotted line to the new position.

To move the left and right margins, press the left and right arrow keys. And to move the top and bottom margins and the page break, press the up and down arrow keys. Word does not reformat the page until you finish moving all the page elements and press the Enter key twice. The first time you press Enter, Word ends the special mode for moving page elements using the keyboard. The second time you press Enter, Word reformats the page. When you use the keyboard to move a page break, Word reformats the page the first time you press either Tab or Enter. To cancel the move of one page element and return that page element to its original position, press the Esc key instead of pressing

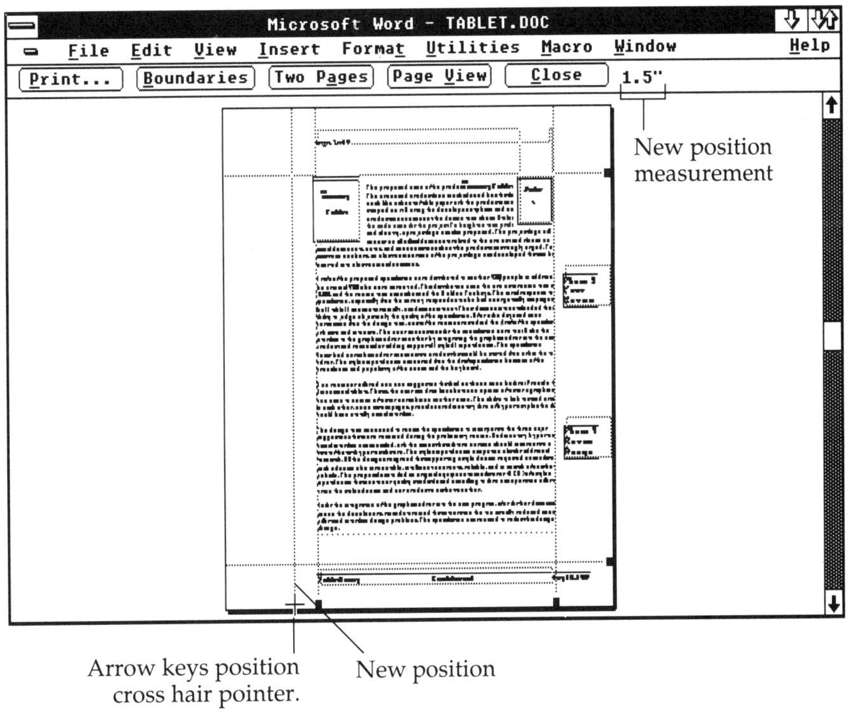

Enter to end the special moving mode. If you press Enter one time and then press Esc, Word reformats the page and then cancels Print Preview, returning to the view you were in when you switched to Print Preview.

Changing the Position of an Object in Print Preview

Changing an object's position in Print Preview is similar to moving a page element. You drag the positioned object to its new position using the mouse, or you press the Tab key to select the positioned object, press the arrow keys to change the position, and then press the Enter key twice to reformat the page. After you move a positioned object, Word waits to repaginate until you tell it to. This delay in repaginating gives you a chance to make all your changes before repagination begins so that you do not have to wait for repagination after each move.

Additional factors affect positioned objects. For text, tables, and graphics, you must first apply position formatting using the Format Position command before you switch to Print Preview. And you cannot use the mouse to move a header or footer across a page margin without using the Shift key, or use the keyboard to move a header or footer across a page margin without changing the margin measurement in the Format Document dialog box.

Assigning an Object Position Formatting

Word treats all text, tables, and graphics as characters to be printed consecutively—unless you apply position formatting to them (before you switch to Print Preview) using the Format Position command.

Before you can move text, a table, or a graphic within a page in Print Preview, Word needs to know whether you want to treat the element as an object that has a position rather than as a regular part of the text. To change text, a table, or a graphic from regular text to a positioned object, use the Format Position command (Alt,T,O) to assign it position formatting before you switch to Print Preview. The Format Position command is not available in Print Preview.

To position text or a table, select the paragraph or the table and apply position formatting to it. To position a graphic, insert the graphic in a paragraph (with or without text), select the paragraph, and then apply position formatting to the paragraph that contains the graphic.

When you choose the Format Position command (Alt,T,O), you see the following dialog box:

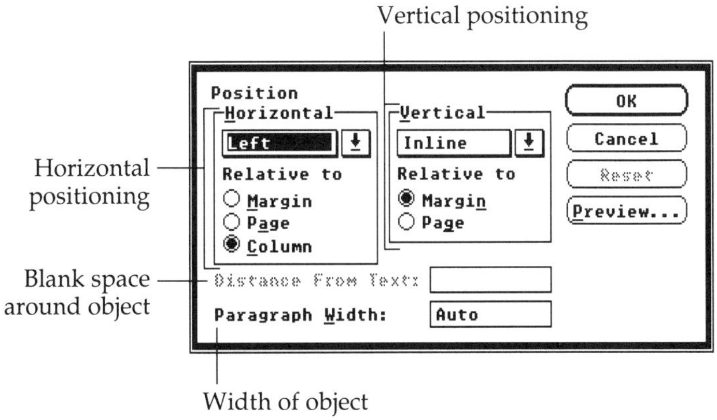

The Horizontal box under Position in the Format Position dialog box aligns the upper-left corner of the selected paragraph or table according to the option you choose under Relative to. The alignment choices in the Horizontal box are Left, Center, Right, Inside, Outside, or a specific measurement that you type. Inside means the inside edge, which is the left edge of all pages for which the Mirror Margins option in the Format Document dialog box is turned off. When the Mirror Margins option is turned on, Inside means the left edge of odd-numbered pages and the right edge of even-numbered pages. Outside means the right edge of all pages when the Mirror Margins option is turned off. When the Mirror Margins option is turned on, however, Outside means the right edge of odd-numbered pages and the left edge of even-numbered pages.

The options for Relative to under Horizontal specify from where the horizontal alignment is measured. Margin means the page margins. As a result, Left Relative to Margin means at the left margin. Page means the edge of the page. And Column means the edge of the column. If your document has one column, Column and Margin have the same effect. If your document has more than one column, Left Relative to Column means the left edge of the column in which the paragraph or table appears.

The Vertical box under Position aligns the upper-left corner of the paragraph or table according to the option you select under Relative to. The alignment choices in the Vertical box are Inline, Top, Center,

Bottom, or a specific measurement that you type. Inline means wherever the paragraph or table appears in the regular text of the document. The Relative to options—Margin and Page—apply to the top and bottom page margins and to the top and bottom edges of the page.

The Distance From Text box contains a measurement for an equal amount of blank space around all sides of the positioned object. The default measurement is 0.13" (9 points). Increase the setting if you want more blank space around the positioned object. Decrease the setting if you want the surrounding text and graphics to be closer to the positioned object.

The Paragraph Width box contains a measurement for the width of the positioned object. The default measurement is Auto, which means the full width of the area between the page margins (or of the column width in a document that has more than one column). Paragraph indents for a positioned paragraph are measured from the side boundaries of the Paragraph Width. The width of a table is set by the width of all its columns added together. For graphics in paragraphs by themselves, Auto means the width of the graphic, which is its original size adjusted by scaling.

If you want text to flow around a positioned object, you must leave at least 1" of width in which the flow-around text can fit. Type a measurement in the Paragraph Width box that allows enough room for Word to print the text between the side of the positioned object and the nearest margin or column boundary. The width of a positioned object combines the Paragraph Width measurement and the Distance From Text measurement in the Format Position dialog box. For a positioned object that has text around one side, the combined measurements for Distance From Text and Paragraph Width must be at least 1" narrower than the width between the margins or the width of the column. For a positioned object that has text around both sides, the combined measurements for Distance From Text and Paragraph Width must be at least 2" narrower than the width between the margins and the width of the column.

For example, if the Distance From Text measurement is 0.13" (the default) and you want text to flow around one side of the positioned object, type a measurement of 4.87" or smaller in Paragraph Width for a document whose width between margins is 6" (the default). If you want text to flow around both sides of a positioned object, type a measurement of 3.74" or smaller—in this case, you have 0.13" Distance From Text on both sides of the positioned object (0.26").

You need select only one of the settings in the Format Position dialog box to change text or a table into a positioned object. You can select any one of these settings, or any combination; as soon as you do, the Distance From Text box becomes available. The Distance From Text measurement is available only if you have changed one of the other positioning settings in the Format Position dialog box, such as the horizontal position, vertical position, or paragraph width.

Moving a Positioned Object

After you assign a position to an object, you can use the mouse or keys to drag the object to a new position in Print Preview. Using the mouse gives you a visual sense of the object's position on the page, but the mouse as well as the keys are only as accurate as your screen's resolution.

Using the Format Position command to move an object allows you to precisely control its exact position. Format Position can be as accurate as 1/20 point, which is 1/1440 inch, but this fine control is relevant only to printing on high-resolution printers, such as typesetting equipment. When you use the mouse or the keys to move an object, however, its position changes in jumps of about 0.06 inch. A distance of 0.06 inch is small, but some of the measurements that appear in the icon bar, such as 2.19", might not be typical measurements for you. Moving using the mouse and keys does, however, also allow you to move objects in 1/4-inch increments. Thus, you see 2.19", 2.25", 2.31", 2.38", 2.44", 2.5", 2.56", 2.63", 2.69", 2.75", and so on. To change either the distance between the object and surrounding text or the paragraph width, you must exit Print Preview and change those settings in the Format Position dialog box.

Moving Headers and Footers

You move headers and footers as you do other page elements and positioned objects. But Word contains a built-in safeguard to prevent you from inadvertently moving a header or footer across either the top or the bottom margin and into the regular text area. This restriction prevents you from accidentally printing headers and footers on top of your regular text.

If you do want to position a header or footer inside the regular text area, Word provides a special technique. Hold down the Shift key while you use the mouse to drag the header or footer. Shift acts as a margin release so that you can drag the header or footer into the regular text area.

To move a header or footer into the regular text area using the keyboard, first adjust the appropriate margin measurements in the Format Document dialog box. Choose the Format Document command (Alt,T,D), insert a minus sign in front of the measurement in the Top box (for headers) or in the Bottom box (for footers) under Margins, and then choose OK. Now, press the Tab key to select the header or footer, press the up arrow key or the down arrow key to position the header or footer, and then press the Enter key twice to reformat the page.

The minus sign in the Format Document dialog box sets the margin at a fixed position. Normally, Word adjusts the top and bottom margins to make room for headers and footers that are taller than the allotted vertical space (¼ inch by default). For example, if a header is three lines tall, Word starts printing the regular text farther down the page to leave enough room for the entire header. By adding a minus sign, you tell Word that you want the regular text to be printed starting at that position, even if the header or footer is taller than the allotted space or is positioned inside the regular text. Word then prints the header or footer in the regular text if that's where you set the header or footer position. When you hold down the Shift key and use the mouse to drag a header or footer into regular text, Word adds a minus sign to the appropriate margin measurement in the Format Document dialog box. For example, if you drag the header into regular text and then choose the Format Document command (Alt,T,D), you see the dialog box shown on the next page. Note the minus sign in the Top box under Margins.

To reinstate the margin restriction against dragging the header or footer into regular text, delete the minus sign from the Margins measurement in the Format Document dialog box.

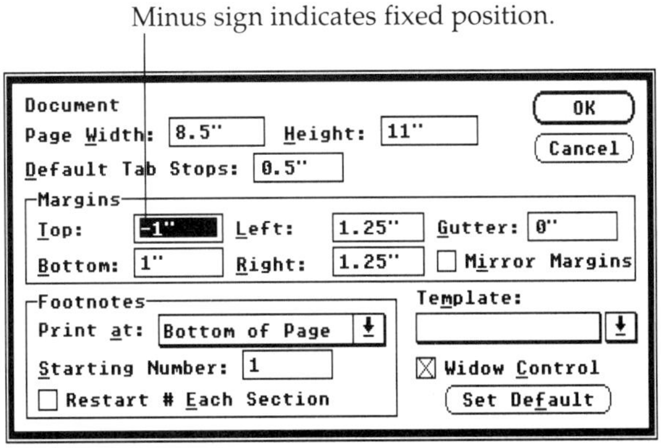

Using Page View to View Page Contents at Full Size

In Page View, you see headers, footers, and footnotes in place on each page, with positioned objects at their final positions and text wrapping around them. If your document is formatted in multiple columns, you see the columns beside each other. To switch to Page View, choose the View Page command (Alt,V,P) or choose the Page View button (V) on the Print Preview icon bar. To switch out of Page View to normal editing view, choose View Page again. When you're in Page View, the screen changes in a number of ways. First, a page icon appears at the top and bottom of the scroll bar:

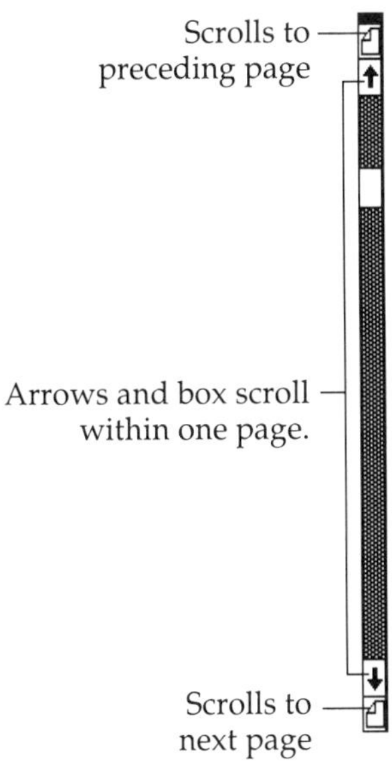

In addition, in Page View you can scroll the page vertically and horizontally and see a depiction of the edge of the paper. And the View menu shows a check mark beside the Page command. Also, if you turn on the Text Boundaries option in the View Preferences dialog box when you're in Page View, you see dotted outlines along the margins and around any text areas—and the margin corners show cut lines. If you double-click in a margin corner, Word displays the Format Document dialog box.

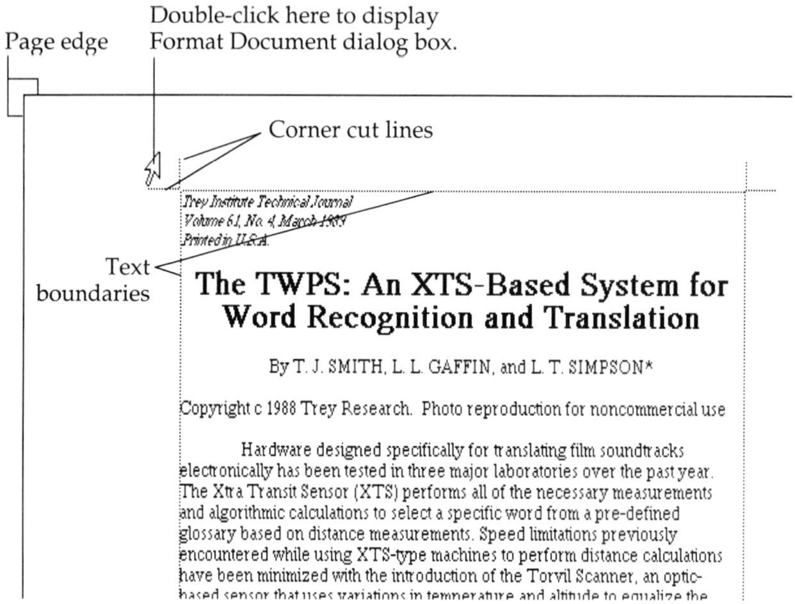

A text area is a rectangular area on a page that can be any size and that contains nonpositioned text, a table, or a positioned object. Word sets up text areas for the following text elements:

- Headers
- Footers
- Footnotes and footnote separators
- Each column of regular text
- Each positioned object
- Each line on both sides of a positioned object when the object is within a column

- Text on both sides of a positioned object when the object is between columns
- Each cell in each table

To see a text area, switch to Page View and turn on the Text Boundaries option (Alt+B) in the View Preferences dialog box. When Text

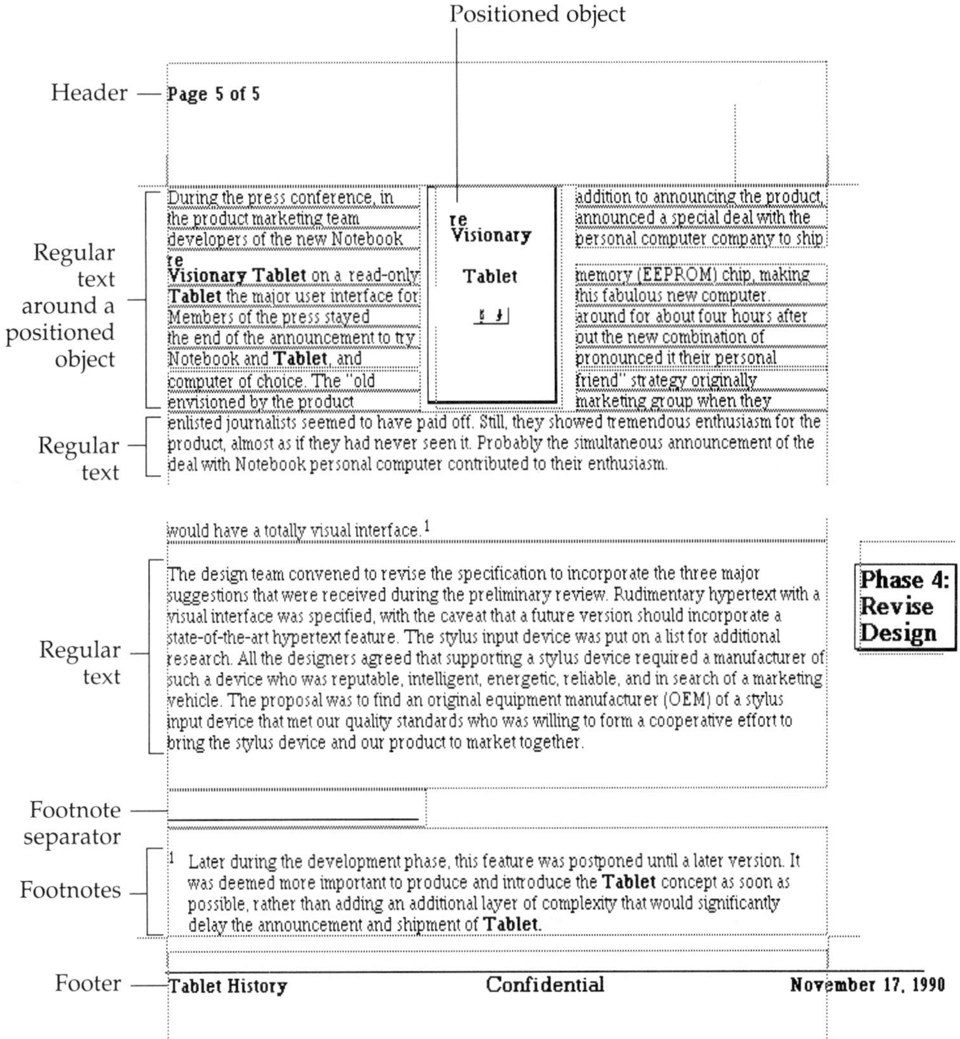

Boundaries is turned on, a dotted-line rectangle surrounds each text area except tables, as shown on the preceding page. To see boundaries in a table, turn on the Table Gridlines option in the View Preferences dialog box or a Borders option in the Format Table dialog box.

Editing Text in Page View

Editing text in a document is probably routine for you now. In Page View, editing text is basically the same as it is in normal editing view, with a few exceptions. These exceptions stem from the fact that text and graphics appear in text areas and that headers, footers, and footnotes appear where Word will print them. Before you begin editing in Page View, you should know how to move from one text area to the next.

Moving from One Text Area to Another in Page View

When you edit in Page View, you can move from one text area to the next using either a mouse or the keyboard. To use a mouse, you position the insertion point or make a selection. To use the keyboard, you use the Alt+down arrow keys and the Alt+up arrow keys. Alt+down arrow key moves the insertion point to the next text area. Alt+up arrow key moves the insertion point to the previous text area.

These keys move the insertion point to the beginning of the next or previous text area in the following order:

- Regular text areas in the order in which they appear in the file—that is, in the order in which you see them in normal editing view
- Table cells in the order in which they appear within regular text if the table is not a positioned object; if it is a positioned object, in the correct order for positioned objects
- Headers
- Footers
- Positioned objects in the order in which they appear in the file—that is, in the order in which you see them in normal editing view
- Back to the first regular text area

In Page View, you can edit text within any text area in the same way that you edit text in normal editing view. And you can scale and crop graphics as usual. As in normal editing view, however, you cannot edit text that's within a graphic. In some cases, your editing will make the size of the text or graphic larger than its text area. If the Background Pagination option is turned on in the Utilities Customize dialog box when you exceed the text area, Word repaginates the document. If Background Pagination is turned off, Word does not repaginate the document until one of the following happens: You choose the Utilities Repaginate Now command (Alt,U,P); you turn on Background Pagination; you position text, graphics, or a table; or the text and graphics exceed the size of the page. The page display might look messy or incomplete with Background Pagination turned off, until Word repaginates your document—especially if editing and formatting do not make the text exceed the size of the page.

You can also move elements around the page in Page View but not in the direct way using the mouse and keyboard that you can in Print Preview. Instead, you use the commands that you use in normal editing view—the Edit Header/Footer, Insert Break, Format Document, and Format Position commands. Of course, you can always switch to Print Preview, move the elements, and then switch back to Page View to edit or to see the text at full size and review the positions of elements and objects on the page.

When you insert and edit headers, footers, and footnotes in normal editing view, Word opens a separate pane. In Page View, all

TIP

Page Reformatting During Text Insertion

Note that if you type or insert text or graphics at the end of a text area—whether by pasting, copying, or moving—Word updates the display in the window so that you can see both the insertion point and what it is that you're typing or inserting. If you use the Insert Break command to insert a section break or if you delete a section break, Word updates the window. But Word does not update the window when you insert a page break.

headers, footers, and footnotes are seen on the page where they will appear when you print the document: headers in the top margin, footers in the bottom margin, and footnotes in the position that you select in the Format Document dialog box (the default position is immediately above the bottom margin). When you insert a header, footer, or footnote in Page View, Word positions the insertion point at the header, footer, or footnote position. Then all you have to do is type.

Note that in Page View you will not have the header/footer icon bar to help you insert the page number, date, or time in a header or footer. After you insert a header, footer, or footnote, you can edit it where it appears on the page. You do not have to choose the Edit Header/Footer command again to edit headers and footers. Nor do you have to choose the View Footnotes command to see and edit footnotes. Note, however, that you can use these commands to jump to headers, footers, and footnotes.

Layout Strategies for Perfecting Your Pages

Here you'll see how to use the Format Position command to experiment with your page layout. To see the results, switch to Print Preview or Page View. Then, in Print Preview, you can move the objects to polish the layout even further.

The following sections tell you how to position paragraphs, graphics, and tables on your document pages. Then, the discussion moves on to more complex operations—wrapping text around an object, changing the flow of text around an object, and overlapping two positioned objects.

Positioning and Setting Off Paragraphs

In Word, whenever you position any object—text, table, graphic, header, or footer—you are positioning a paragraph. A positioned paragraph is movable in Print Preview mode.

For example, you could position the first paragraph of a document in the left margin, where you might typically position a sidehead paragraph. Start by positioning the insertion point in the document's first paragraph. Next, choose the Format Position command (Alt,T,O). In the Format Position dialog box, type *0.75"* for the Horizontal Position, and choose the Page option for Relative to (Alt+A) under Horizontal. Then, in the Distance From Text box, type a number for the distance you want this paragraph to be from the nearest text—for example, *0.25"*. Type the width you want the paragraph to be in the Paragraph Width box—for example, *1"*—and then choose OK. Choose the Format Document command (Alt,T,D). In the Format Document dialog box, move to the Left box under Margins (Alt+L), type *2"*, and then choose OK. Next, choose the File Print Preview command (Alt,F,V). You see the positioned paragraph in relation to the whole page. Choose the Page View button (V) to see the text of the positioned paragraph at its full size:

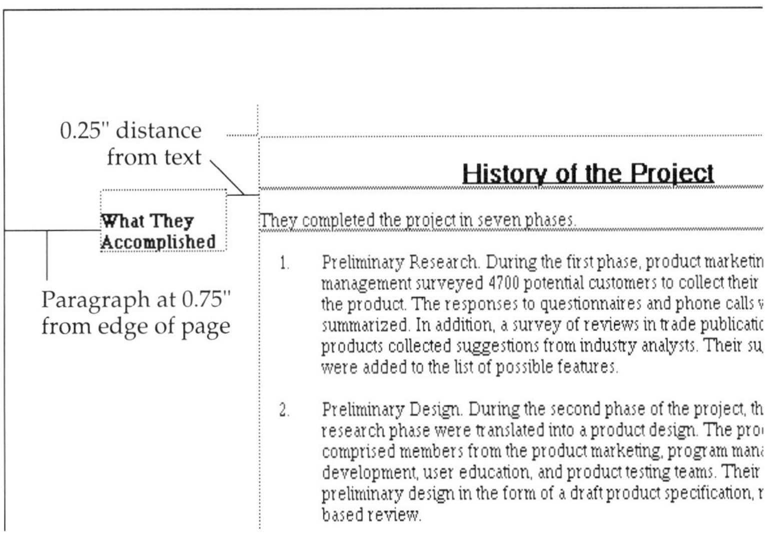

To make the paragraph you just positioned more visible and to separate it from the surrounding text, add a paragraph border. Choose the Format Paragraph command (Alt,T,P). In the Format Paragraph dialog box, select Box from the Border list (Alt+O, B) and Shadow from the Pattern list (Alt+E,S,S) and then choose OK. To see the whole page and the paragraph in position with its border, as shown on the next page, choose the File Print Preview command (Alt,F,V).

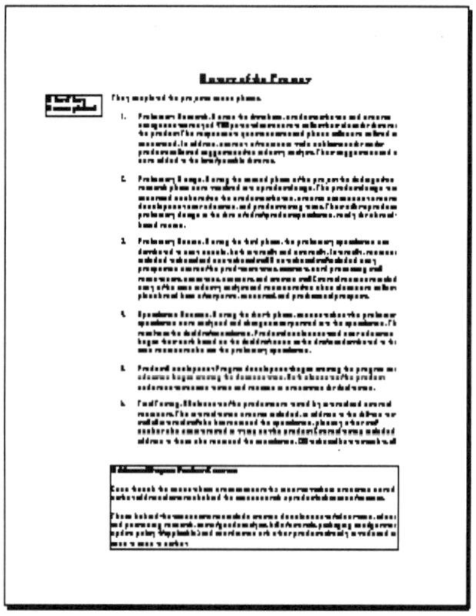

Move the paragraph to a different position if you want it elsewhere.

Positioning Graphics

Word treats a graphic as if it were a single character, like the letter A, for example. This arrangement allows you to type text on the same line as a graphic, which is handy if you want text to appear beside a graphic. But you can type only one line next to the graphic. Because Word positions paragraphs, both the text and the graphic are positioned as part of the same paragraph. To position a graphic by itself, you must put the graphic into its own paragraph. To surround a tall graphic with text along the graphic's entire height, you need to position the graphic separately from the text that surrounds it.

You follow the same procedure to position a graphic as you do to position a paragraph. In the Format Position dialog box, type the graphic's width in the Paragraph Width box.

Positioning Tables

Word lets you position a whole table or a number of rows from a table. To position a table, start by selecting the entire table. If you position the insertion point in a cell or select only some rows and not the entire table, Word positions only the row that contains the insertion point or the rows selected.

TIP

Getting Varied Borders on Different Sides of a Positioned Paragraph

The Format Paragraph command (Alt,T,P) gives you four different types of borders to choose from: Box, Bar, Above, and Below. For each of these types, you can also choose a Pattern. You get only one type of paragraph border, however, for each paragraph. But suppose you want a paragraph to have a thick top border and a thin bottom border, like the following:

Dogs extend
human
endeavors.

Figure 14-3.
Paragraph with different top and bottom borders.

To get a varied border, use Word's table facility. First, in normal editing view, Page View, or Draft View, select the whole paragraph. Next, choose the Insert Table command (Alt,I,T). In the Insert Table dialog box, type *1* in both the Number of Columns box and the Initial Col Width box. Then, choose the Format button (Alt,F). Select Thick (Alt,T) in the Top box and the Single option (Alt,B) in the Bottom box under Borders, and then choose OK. You now see a paragraph formatted like the one in Figure 14-3.

Now suppose you want to take this trick one step further and set up borders like the following:

Dogs extend
human
endeavors.

Figure 14-4.
Paragraph with two different top borders.

Position the insertion point in the table cell that you just inserted and formatted. Choose the Edit Table command (Alt,E,A). Choose the Row option (Alt+R), and then choose the Insert button (Alt+I). Now, choose the Format Table command (Alt,T,A), type *-4pt* in the Minimum Row Height box, select the Thick option (Alt+T) in the Top box and the Single option (Alt+B,S) in the Bottom box under Borders, and choose OK. You now see a paragraph like the one in Figure 14-4.

To position a table after you select it, follow the same procedure you use to position a paragraph. In the Format Position dialog box, type the width of the table in the Paragraph Width box.

Wrapping Text Around an Object

In magazines and brochures, you often see a sentence that's placed in the middle of the page—a "pull quote"—with the rest of the text positioned around it. You can create this same text wrap effect in Word:

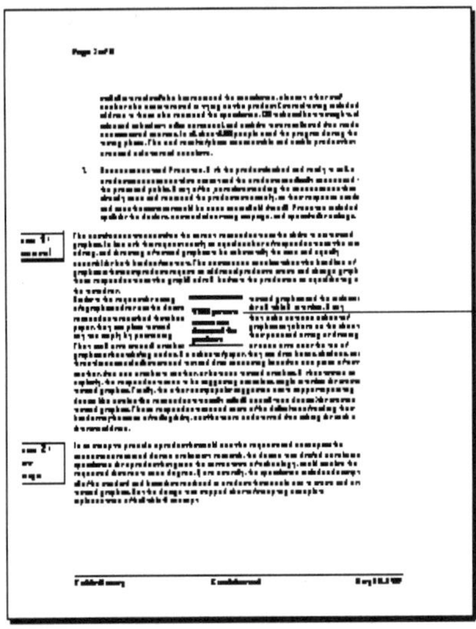

Positioned sentence with text flowing around it

First, position the insertion point anywhere in the paragraph that you want to position in the middle of the page. Choose the Format Position command (Alt,T,O). In the Format Position dialog box, select the Center option from both the Horizontal and Vertical Position lists. Type 2" in the Paragraph Width box, and then choose OK. Note that the paragraph width is important for text wrapping. The paragraph width must be narrow enough to leave sufficient space between the positioned object and the page margins (or the column boundaries if the document is formatted in more than one column). See the description of spacing in "Assigning an Object Position Formatting" earlier in this chapter. If you do not leave enough space, Word will not wrap text around the positioned object.

Choose the View Page command (Alt,V,P) if the window is not already in Page View.

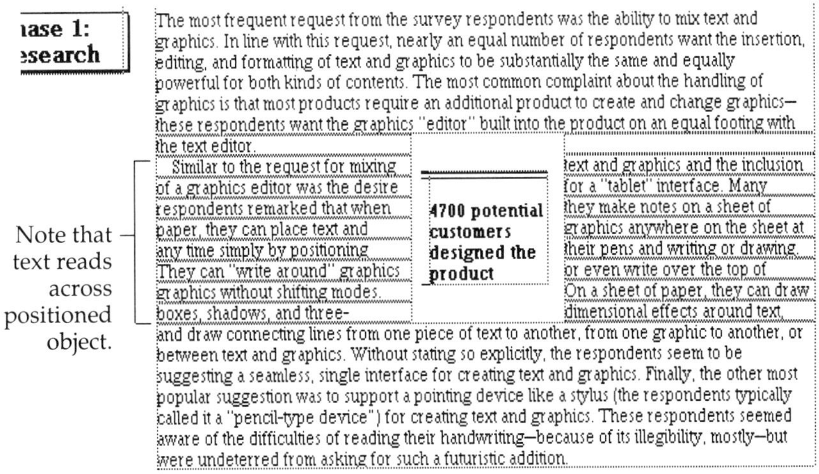

Figure 14-5.
Text straddles a positioned object.

Note that the text reads across the positioned object, with the first part of a line on the left and the second part on the right, back and forth across the object. Text straddles a positioned object when the text appears on both sides of the object.

Changing the Flow of Text Around an Object

If you prefer text to read down one side of an object and then down the other side rather than straddling it as shown in Figure 14-5, change the text flow. Position the insertion point at the beginning of the paragraph that's split by the positioned object. Then, choose the Insert Break command (Alt,I,B). In the Insert Break dialog box, choose the Continuous Section Break option (Alt+T), and then choose OK. Now, position the insertion point at the beginning of the first line that follows the paragraphs that are split by the positioned object. Choose Insert Break again, choose Continuous Section Break, and choose OK.

Position the insertion point anywhere between the two section breaks that you just inserted, and choose the Format Section command (Alt,T,D). In the dialog box, type 2 in the Number box under Columns and choose OK. Choose the View Page command (Alt,V,P) if the window is not already in Page View. The text now flows down one side and then the other side of the positioned object, as shown on the next page.

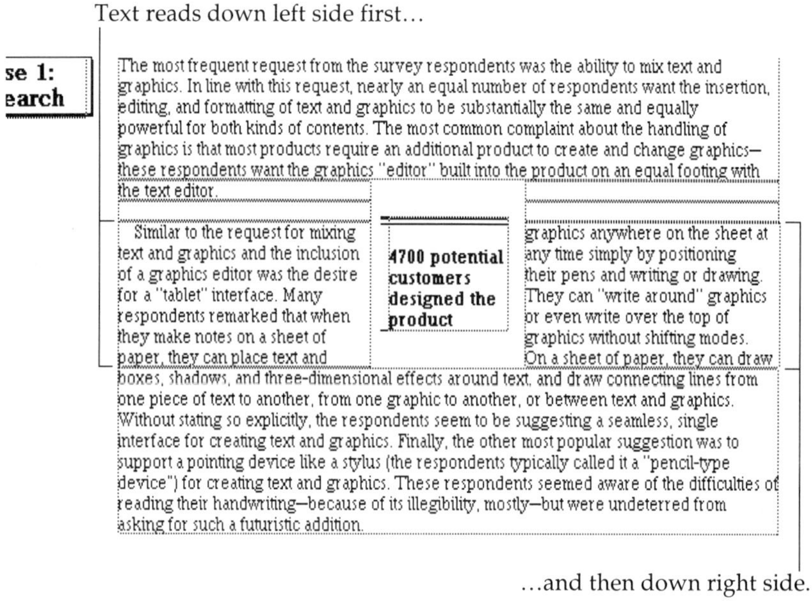

Note that if you insert text and graphics in the text area that surrounds the positioned object, the two columns extend below the positioned object, giving you two columns where you might want only one.

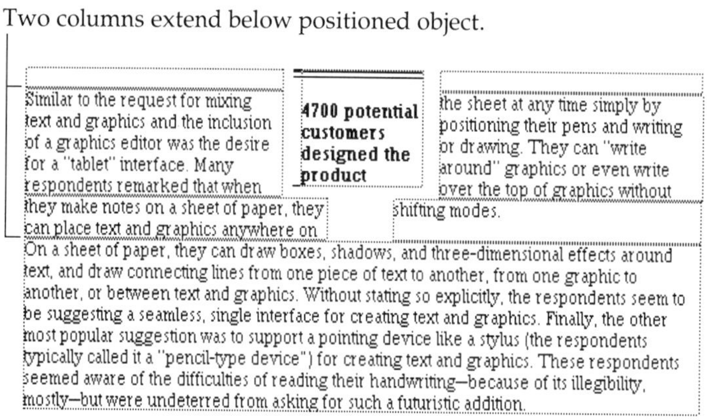

You must either delete some text or graphics or increase the height of the positioned object. In a similar fashion, if you delete text or graphics from the text area that surrounds the positioned object, you will not have sufficient text to surround the positioned object. Word uses the straddling method shown in Figure 14-5 in such cases, as shown at the top of the next page.

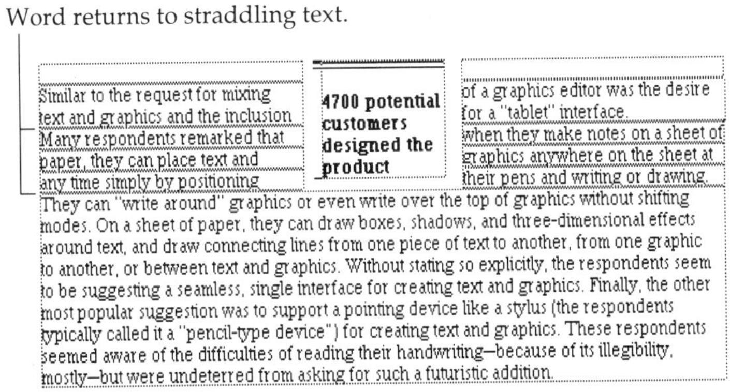

Either add text or graphics to the text area that surrounds the positioned object or reduce the positioned object's height.

Overlapping Two Positioned Objects

One of the most dramatic effects you can achieve with position formatting is to overlap two elements:

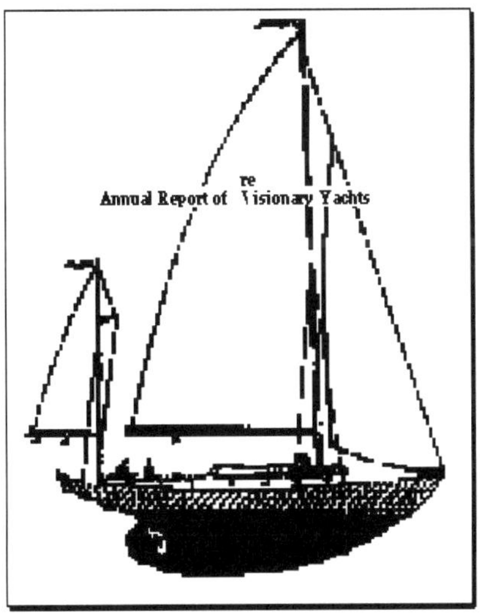

To achieve this overlapping effect, insert a graphic in its own paragraph in a Word document. Choose the Insert Picture command (Alt,I,P), select a graphic file name under Files (Alt,F), and then choose OK. Next, scale the graphic vertically until it's taller than the page. To do so, select the graphic and choose the Format Picture command (Alt,T,R). In the Format Picture dialog box, type a percentage in the

Height box (Alt,H) under Scaling that makes the graphic taller than the page. For example, if the original height of the graphic is 2.56", type *430* (11" divided by 2.56" is about 430%). In the Width box (Alt,W) under Scaling, type *430* again to prevent distortion of the graphic. Choose OK to scale the graphic.

Because this picture should fit the whole page, choose the Format Paragraph command (Alt,T,P). In the Format Paragraph dialog box, type *-1.25"* in both the From Left (Alt,F) and From Right (Alt,G) boxes under Indent and then choose OK. The paragraph that contains the graphic now spans the page. Position the graphic at the center of the page, and leave its width set to Auto. Choose the Format Position command (Alt,T,O). Under Horizontal in the Format Position dialog box, select the Center option, and choose the Page option for Relative to. Under Vertical, select the Center option, choose the Page option again for Relative to, and then choose OK.

Next, type some text in a paragraph that you want to overlap the graphic. Position that paragraph to the left or right of the page's center so that the position of the paragraph is not the same as the position of the graphic. For example, choose the Format Position command (Alt,T,O), and type *3"* for Horizontal in the Format Position dialog box. Under both Horizontal and Vertical, choose the Page option for Relative to. Type *3"* in the Paragraph Width box and then choose OK.

Now, switch to Print Preview to look at the first page. Note that the positioned text overlaps the graphic. Be aware that the positioned paragraph appears in the file after the graphic. If these objects appeared in the opposite order in normal editing view, the graphic would overlap and obscure the text. Note, too, that in Page View, the graphic always obscures the text, but in Print Preview, Word displays the positioned objects in their proper order. Thus, in Print Preview you can see the text overlapping the graphic.

Word also lets you use this overlapping technique to overlap text within a graphic. For best results, set the graphic and text to appear at a specific, measured position on the page.

Chapter 15

Merge Printing

Merge printing means combining two documents during printing. One document, called the main document, contains text and graphics that are the same for every document you print. If the final result is a form letter, for example, the main document contains the letterhead message and closing, which are the same in every form letter. The second document, called the data document, contains a table of text and graphics that are different for every document you print. Again, if the final result is a form letter, the data document contains the names and addresses of the people you will send the letter to, along with other information that's specific to each person. See Chapter 13, "Tables the New, Easy Way" for information about inserting and formatting tables. This chapter describes the basic steps you follow to set up a table in a data document.

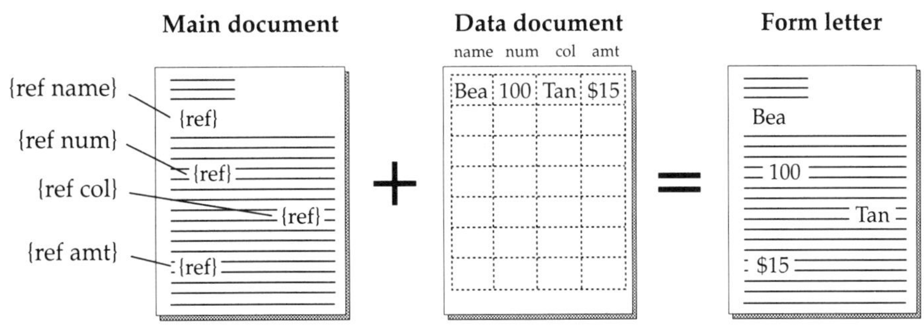

Understanding the Main Document

The main document in merge printing contains the text and graphics that are the same for all printed documents plus REF fields, which contain bookmark names, and a DATA field.

REF Fields and Bookmarks in the Main Document

Insert REF fields in the main document where you want the data to appear; the bookmark name identifies which information to put in place of each REF field. As explained in the Appendix in "Reference Fields: Text, Page Numbers, Styles, and Footnotes," you can insert either form of a REF field. The two forms of a REF field look like the following:

```
{ref bookmark}          or          {bookmark}
```

Provided the bookmark name is not the name of another field type, you can omit REF. The *bookmark* usually identifies text or graphics within the document that contains the REF field. During merge printing, however, a REF field takes its result from the data document.

The DATA Field in the Main Document

To tell Word which file is the data document, you insert a DATA field in the main document before the first REF field, as follows:

```
{data data-file-name}
```

The *data-file-name* can be the name of any document that Word can open. If you store the data document in a different directory from the main document, insert the pathname to the directory where you keep the data document. For example, for a data document stored in a directory named PLANS, which is a subdirectory of STRATEGY, insert the following DATA field:

```
{data c:\\strategy\\plans\\3yrplan}
```

Note that the path separator character, which is a backslash (\), must be typed two times because a backslash in a field tells Word to treat the following character as itself rather than as a special character. If you do not type the backslashes two times, Word looks for a file named strategyplans3yrplan.doc, which is not a valid DOS file name. Note also that the file name in the example field does not show a file-name extension. When you omit the file-name extension, Word looks for a file that has a .DOC file-name extension. If the file-name extension is not .DOC, type the extension. Or, if the file name has no extension, type only a period at the end of the file name.

As you'll read in the upcoming section, "Understanding the Data Document," the data-document table's first row, called a header record, usually contains the bookmark names that you use in the main document's REF field. You can put the bookmark names in a separate document, called a header document. This document is useful if the information for the data document comes from a separate database application, which will not contain your bookmark names. If you use a header document, the DATA field must also include that document's name:

```
{data data-file-name header-file-name}
```

You can also specify a pathname for the header document. Be sure to double the path-separator backslash characters, as explained earlier for data-file pathnames.

Example 1: Creating a Main Document for a Form Letter

The first and most popular use for merge printing is to produce form letters. We've all received form letters in the mail. Before merge printing technology was available, these letters were usually addressed to the impersonal "Occupant." Using merge printing, you can personalize your form letters to include names and other personal information, as shown in Figure 15-1 on the following page.

The form letter to Kelly Ceck shown in Figure 15-1 starts from a main document. That document contains the text and graphics that are the same in every letter plus the DATA field and the REF fields that contain bookmark names for the specific information you want to insert during merge printing. Figure 15-2 on the following page shows the main document that was used to create the form letter in Figure 15-1.

To create this main document, type exactly what you see in Figure 15-2. At the left field-character brace ({), press the INSERT FIELD key combination (Ctrl+F9) to insert the pair of field characters, type the field contents, press the End key, and then continue typing. Where you see a paragraph mark (¶), press the Enter key. By putting the DATA field on the same line as the NAME field, as in Figure 15-2 on the following page, you avoid adding an extra blank line at the beginning of the letter.

Kelly Ceck
2121 Camino Real
Weed OR 97000

Dear Kelly Ceck,

You may have already won one of our wonderful prizes. Imagine the surprise on your neighbors' faces when you drive your brand new 1990 Cadillac Coupe de Ville to 2121 Camino Real. Or, imagine going to your bank in Weed and finding an extra $10,000.00 in your account. These or other fabulous prizes may be yours already, Kelly Ceck.

All you have to do is return the enclosed prize form by **October 19, 1990.**

And while you have this package in your hands, why not browse through our fabulous merchandise. To order, just check the appropriate box on the prize form. Enter today and who knows, Kelly Ceck? Soon you too could be the proud owner of a 1990 Cadillac Coupe de Ville and be the envy of your neighbors in Weed.

Figure 15-1.
Sample form letter.

Fields for mailing address

{data maillist}{name}¶
{addr}¶
{city} {state} {ZIP}¶
¶
Dear {name},¶ — Personalized greeting
¶
You may have already won one of our wonderful prizes. Imagine the surprise on your neighbors' faces when you drive your brand new 1990 Cadillac Coupe de Ville to {addr}. Or, imagine going to your bank in {city} and finding an extra $10,000.00 in your account. These or other fabulous prizes may be yours already, {name}.¶
¶
All you have to do is return the enclosed prize form by **October 19, 1990.¶**
¶
And while you have this package in your hands, why not browse through our fabulous merchandise. To order, just check the appropriate box on the prize form. Enter today and who knows, {name}? Soon you too could be the proud owner of a 1990 Cadillac Coupe de Ville and be the envy of your neighbors in {city}.¶

Fields for personal touches

Figure 15-2.
Sample main document.

Understanding the Data Document

A data document contains information that you want Word to merge with a main document during merge printing. For example, if the main document is a form letter, the data document could contain customer names, addresses, and the names of the products or services those customers have bought.

Think of a data document as a table. Each column is a vertical list, headed by a label (bookmark name) that tells you what kind of information is in that column, as shown in Figure 15-3. Each cell in the first row of the table contains a bookmark name that matches the bookmark names in the REF fields of the main document. The other cells contain data items. Each row is a data record, which contains all the data items for one printed copy of the main document.

The next sections explain how you set up a header record and data records in data documents. To create a data document, choose the File New command (Alt,F,N) and then choose OK in the File New dialog box. Choose the Insert Table command (Alt,I,T), type *6* in the Number of Columns box, and then choose OK to insert the table. See Chapter 13, "Tables the New, Easy Way," for information about creating and formatting tables. You're ready now to set up the header record and data records.

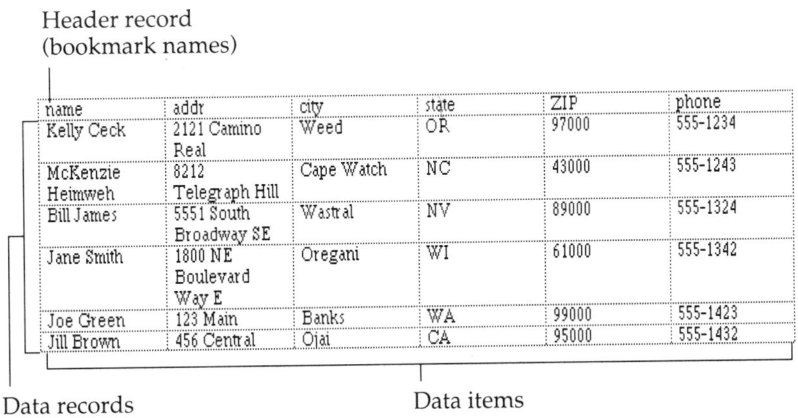

name	addr	city	state	ZIP	phone
Kelly Ceck	2121 Camino Real	Weed	OR	97000	555-1234
McKenzie Heimweh	8212 Telegraph Hill	Cape Watch	NC	43000	555-1243
Bill James	5551 South Broadway SE	Wastral	NV	89000	555-1324
Jane Smith	1800 NE Boulevard Way E	Oregani	WI	61000	555-1342
Joe Green	123 Main	Banks	WA	99000	555-1423
Jill Brown	456 Central	Ojai	CA	95000	555-1432

Figure 15-3.
Sample data document.

Example 2: Inserting the Header Record in a Data Document

In the Figure 15-3 example, the table's first row is the header record, which contains the bookmark names for each list. See the main document shown in Figure 15-2, and look for REF fields. (All the REF fields contain only the bookmark name.) In the first cell, type the first bookmark name in the main document (*name*). Do not insert a field. Press the Tab key to move to the second cell, and type the second bookmark name (*addr*). Press Tab to move to the next cell in the table, and type the next bookmark name (*city*). Repeat these steps for the other two bookmark names (*state* and *ZIP*). In the row's last cell, type *phone*. The table now looks like Figure 15-4.

A data document can contain much more information than you need for a single main document. To use only some of the data items, insert REF fields in the main document for only those data items you want. The header record must always be the first row in the data document table. The only time you can begin a data document with a data record instead of a header record is when you put the header record into a separate header document. A header document contains only a header record and nothing else.

Whether you use a header record in the data document or a separate header document, you must be sure that the bookmark names are in the same order as the information underneath them. If not, you'll get some strange results. For example, if you switch the name and city bookmark names, you might produce a letter that begins "Dear Weed," which might be humorous but not good business. After you insert the bookmark names to create a header record in the first row, you're ready to insert the data records.

Header record contains bookmark names.

name	addr	city	state	ZIP	phone

Figure 15-4.
Header record.

Example 3: Inserting Data Records in a Data Document

A data record is one row in a data-document table and consists of data items, one per cell. In addition, a data record contains information for each of the bookmark names in the header record. To add the data records to the data document shown in Figure 15-4, position the insertion point in the last cell and press the Tab key, which creates a new row. Now, type the data items for Kelly Ceck as shown in Figure 15-3. Remember to press Tab to move from one cell to the next. At the end of the row, press Tab to start a new row.

Complete the table to match the one in Figure 15-3. To save the data document and name it, choose the File Save command (Alt,F,S). In the File Save dialog box, type *maillist* in the Save File Name box and then choose OK. Fill in the summary information, if you want, and then choose OK. You can insert as many data records in a data document as you want. Usually, you'll insert as many data records as you want printed copies of the main document, even though during merge printing you can choose to print only some of the data records instead of all of them.

Setting Up a Data Document Without Using a Table

The examples in this chapter use tables to set up data documents because using tables makes it easier to set up the documents accurately. You can, however, use data-separator and record-separator characters instead of a table. You'll use separator characters if you extract your data records from a database file.

Outside a table, you must insert a separator character between data items to tell Word where one data item ends and the next one begins. You have several choices for separators: commas, tab characters, and quotation marks. You can use any mixture of separators within a data record. A paragraph mark inserted at the end of a data record acts as the separator between data records. If you are not using a table to set up a data document, try to use tab characters because they do a better job of visually separating the data items. For data records that will take up more than one line if tabs are used, switch to commas so that each data record will take up only one line rather than wrapping around to another line.

Because a data item can contain commas, you need to be able to tell Word when you're using a comma as a separator and when you're using a comma as a comma. The same is true for quotation marks and tab characters. To use a comma or a quotation mark as itself, type a backslash (\) in front of the comma or quotation mark. The following example requires the backslash (\):

Edmund G. "Jerry" Brown, Jr.

In a data record, you would enter this data item with backslashes in front of the quotation marks and the comma:

Edmund G. \"Jerry\" Brown\, Jr.

To include a tab character in a data item, you enclose the data item in quotation marks, as shown in the following example:

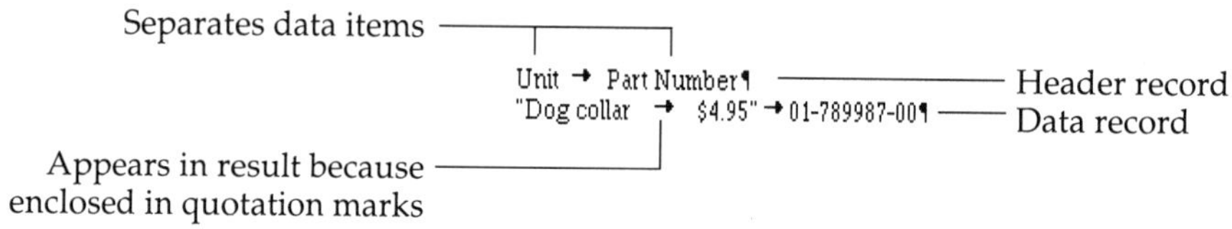

Here's one more point to remember about separators and data items: You can leave a data item blank. For example, if you keep customer records in a data document and a customer makes an inquiry about a product or service but hasn't yet bought anything, a data item for purchases would still be blank. To indicate an empty data item, type two consecutive separators with nothing between them, as shown in the following data record:

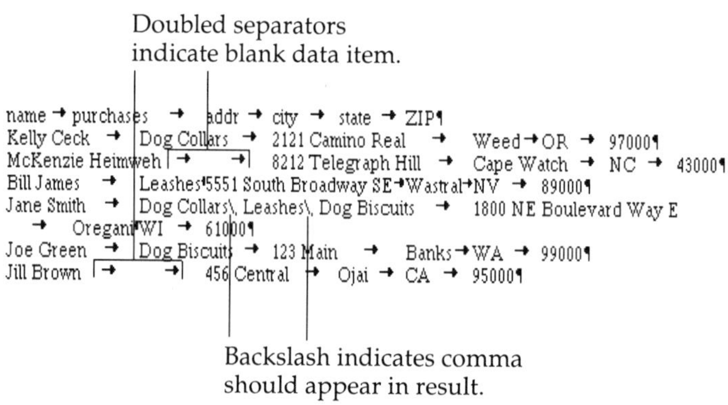

You must include separators between columns in every data record, even if some data items are blank. If you omit a separator, Word displays a message during merge printing to tell you that the number of fields (data items) does not match the number of names (labels) in the header record. Word then asks whether you want to continue. Choose No if you want to correct the situation before merge printing. To correct the error, count the separator characters in all data records to be sure you inserted all the necessary separators. If a data item is blank, you should see two separator characters together. Also, if a data item contains a comma or quotation mark, precede that character with a backslash (\). If a data item contains a tab character, enclose that data item in quotation marks. Choose Yes if you want to see what will happen if you merge print anyway. The worst that can happen is that you'll have some missing information or the wrong information in the wrong place in the document. Continuing to print will not affect other copies of the main document. You can fix the incorrect data record later and then print only that one data record by typing its number in the File Print Merge dialog box.

Even if you extract data records from a database, seriously consider converting the report to a Word document and inserting the data in a table. To do so, choose the File Open command (Alt,F,O), select the report file name, and then choose OK. When Word asks you to confirm converting the report file from Text format, choose OK. Select the entire contents of the report (Ctrl+5 on the numeric keypad), and then choose the Insert Table command (Alt,I,T). Choose the appropriate Delimited option under Convert From (that is, for the separator character between data items in the report), and then choose OK. To add a header record to the table, select the table's first row, choose the Edit Table command (Alt,E,A), choose the Row option (Alt+R), and then choose the Insert button (Alt+I). Now, type the bookmark names—one per cell in the new row—as explained previously in "Example 2: Inserting the Header Record in a Data Document."

You'll find some advantages to using a table for a data document. First, you do not have to worry about including separators. The table's cell boundaries act as the separators. When you use a table, you can use commas, tab characters, quotation marks, and paragraph marks freely, without having to type a backslash in front of them or enclose them in quotation marks. Also, being able to include paragraph marks means that you can have multiple paragraphs in a single data item, which is not possible outside a table. Finally, when you use a table, the data document is visually neat and therefore easier to read because each column has a specific width. The data item can fill many lines within a single cell, without causing a problem for merge printing. Although a single data item may fill more than one line outside a table, the appearance of the data document suffers badly when a data record takes up more than one line, and even more when a data item takes up more than one line.

Printing the Form Letters

After you create the main and data documents, you're ready to print your form letters. First, be sure your printer is connected and set up. See Chapter 1, "Setting Up, Starting, and Quitting," for information about setting up your printer. When the printer is ready, open or activate the main document. The data file can be either open or closed. Choose the File Print Merge command (Alt,F,M). Word displays the File Print Merge dialog box:

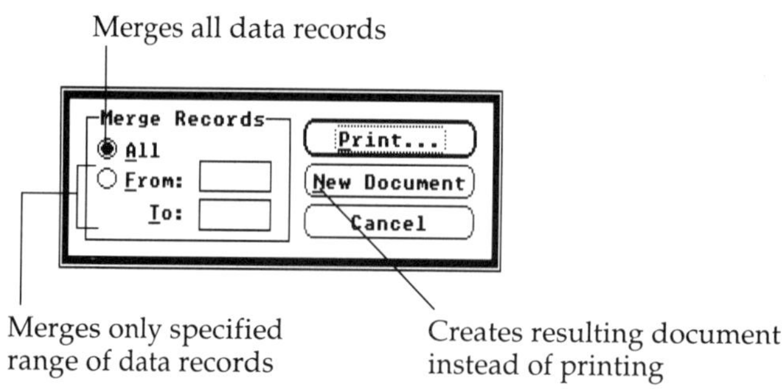

In the dialog box, choose OK to start printing the form letters.

When the data document does not contain information for a bookmark name, Word looks in the main document for the bookmark. If Word finds the bookmark in the main document, the result is the bookmarked text in the main document. If Word does not find the bookmark in the main document, the result of the field is the following message:

Error! Bookmark not defined.

If you see the error message as the result of a field, check the spelling of the bookmark names in both the main and data documents, correct any mismatches, and then try printing again.

Example 4: Address Labels

Using merge printing for address labels makes it easy to keep your mailing list up to date. You could keep your mailing list in a file that you print directly, rather than through merge printing. But if you use a regular file and delete or add addresses in alphabetic order, you must change the page breaks. By using merge printing, however, you need not worry about page breaks. And you can pull the names and addresses even from data files that can contain more than name and address information. As a result, you can maintain one data file for several different types of main documents, rather than maintaining numerous data files.

During merge printing, Word normally prints one document for each data record in the data file. For address labels, you want to print as many addresses per page as you have address labels. To do so, you insert a field that tells Word to use more than one data record. You insert a NEXT field and then insert additional REF fields and bookmarks, as the following section explains.

TIP

Merge Printing Without a Printer

The File Print Merge dialog box includes a New Document button. If you prefer to preview the form letters before printing them, if you do not have a printer connected to your computer, or if you want to print the form letters from another computer, choose the New Document button. Word puts the documents into a new file named Form Letters1. If you merge print to a document again during the same working session, Word puts the form letters from the second printing into a document named Form Letters2, and so on for all merge printing during the same working session. After Word puts the form letters into a new document, you can edit, format, save, and print the new document as you would any other document. Note that Word uses the section break (a character that looks like a row of colons stretching across the whole window) to separate the form letters within the document.

Using the NEXT Field in Merge Printing

The NEXT field tells Word to go to the next data record and use its data items for the REF (bookmark) fields that follow. For address labels, you insert a NEXT field between each set of REF (bookmark) fields that pull in the information for one label, as shown in Figure 15-5. By putting the NEXT field on the same line as the first REF (bookmark) field, you avoid adding an extra blank line.

Figure 15-5 illustrates that it's easiest to use a table to set up the main document for address labels, as the next section explains.

NEXT field means use next data record.

{data·address}{name}¶ {street}¶ {city},·{state}·{zip}×	{next}{name}¶ {street}¶ {city},·{state}·{zip}×
{next}{name}¶ {street}¶ {city},·{state}·{zip}×	{next}{name}¶ {street}¶ {city},·{state}·{zip}×
{next}{name}¶ {street}¶ {city},·{state}·{zip}×	{next}{name}¶ {street}¶ {city},·{state}·{zip}×
{next}{name}¶ {street}¶ {city},·{state}·{zip}×	{next}{name}¶ {street}¶ {city},·{state}·{zip}×

Figure 15-5.
Sample NEXT fields for mailing-label document.

Using Tables for Address Labels

For address labels, a table is an effective and easy way to set up a main document. You simply create a table that's a picture of a page of labels, with one cell for each label on the page.

Your Word package contains document templates that you can use to create a main document for address labels. The table on the following page describes the names and uses of these templates.

Name	*Use*
LBL15COT.DOT	1.5-inch labels in a single column, continuous feed
LBL1COLT.DOT	1-inch labels in a single column, continuous feed
LBL2COL.DOT	1-inch labels in two columns, sheet feed
LBL2COLT.DOT	1-inch labels in two columns, continuous feed
LBL3COL.DOT	1-inch labels in three columns, sheet feed
LBL3COLT.DOT	1-inch labels in three columns, continuous feed

The templates listed above use tables to set up a main document and to print the appropriate labels correctly. To use one of these templates, choose the File New command (Alt,F,N), select the appropriate template name in the Use Template list, and then choose OK. If you created a main document based on the LBL3COL.DOT template, for example, you would see the following document on the screen:

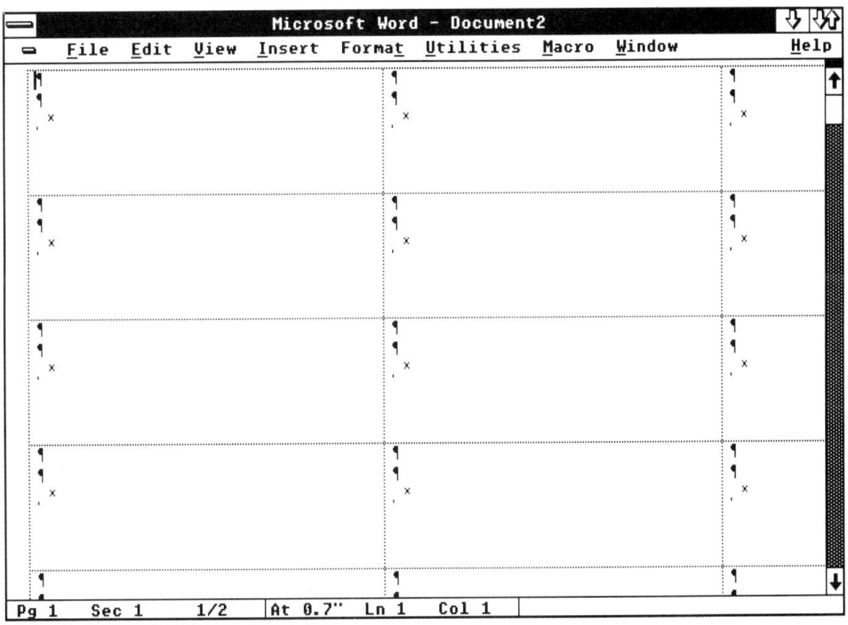

The important parts of this new document are the table and the fields in each cell. To see the fields, choose the View Field Codes command (Alt,V,C). The document on your screen now looks as shown on the next page.

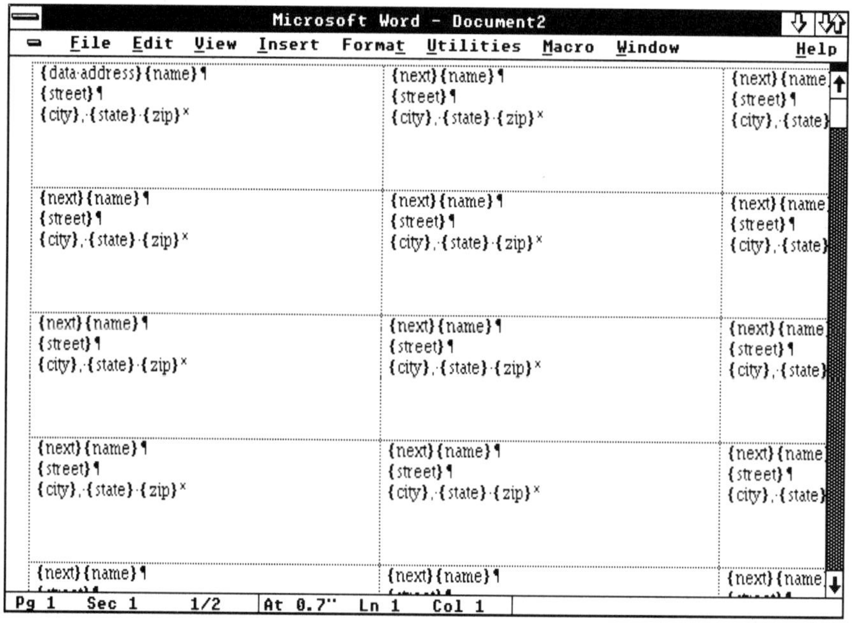

Make two adjustments to this main document. First, in the DATA field, change the name of the data file from "address" to the name of your data file. Second, select the whole table (Alt+5 [5 on the numeric keypad]) and choose the Format Table command (Alt,T,A). In the Minimum Row Height box, insert a minus sign in front of the *1"* entry and then choose OK. The –1" measurement for Minimum Row Height ensures that the cells will be exactly 1 inch tall and that text from one label will not spill over to the label below it.

Other adjustments you might need to make include setting a different row height and inserting additional REF (bookmark) fields in each cell. If your labels are 1½ inches tall, for example, you need to adjust the number in the Minimum Row Height box in the Format Table dialog box to –1.5". You'll also need to delete three or four rows at the bottom of the table to make the table fit on one page. To see whether one or more rows print on a second page, choose the File Print Preview command (Alt,F,V), choose the Two Pages button (A), and check to see if part of the table appears on the second page. To delete rows that print on the second page, choose the Cancel button (Esc), select the extra rows, choose the Edit Table command (Alt,E,A), and then choose the Delete button (Alt+D).

For business addresses that include a company name, you might want to add another REF (bookmark) field to each cell, as shown below:

Adds company name to result —

```
{data·address}{name}¶
{company}¶
{street}¶
{city},·{state}·{zip}¤
```

Some business addresses also include a building name and suite number:

Building name and suite number —

```
Ms. Roberta Ochre
Trey Research
1620 Research Bldg
1234 Fourth Avenue
Liberty, PA 10100
```

For addresses like the one shown above, you set up each cell to look like the following:

Adds building name and suite number —

```
{data·address}{name}¶
{company}¶
{building}¶
{street}¶
{city},·{state}·{zip}¤
```

After the address-label document is ready, prepare your address file if it's not already set up. This address file can be the same as the one created earlier in the chapter, as shown in Figure 15-3. You can also create a new address data document by following the steps you used to re-create the data document shown in Figure 15-3. To print address labels, use the File Merge Print command, as you did for the form letter in Examples 1, 2, and 3 earlier in this chapter.

A Brief Illustration of Advanced Merge Instructions

The NEXT field lets you produce address labels by printing more than one data record in a printed document. With the SKIPIF fields, you can exclude addresses (data records) that do not fit into the group to which you want to mail. You also might want to know on occasion which data record number was used in a specific merge document. The next sections include examples of these merge-printing options.

Example 5: Using the SKIPIF Field for Target Mailings

Mass mailings, such as form letters, can be sent to everyone on your mailing list, or they can be sent to specific portions of it. It's common to target a product announcement to a specific area, for example, or a political appeal to specific ZIP-code areas. For target mailings such as these, you can use the SKIPIF field during merge printing. The SKIPIF field allows you to give Word guidelines for skipping data records that do not match your selected group and for which you do not want to print letters.

The SKIPIF field is a combination of a SKIP instruction and an IF field. SKIPIF compares a data item with guidelines that you insert in SKIPIF. If the data item fits the guidelines in the SKIPIF field, Word skips the data record and goes on to the next one. If the data item does not fit the guidelines in the SKIPIF field, Word prints the data record. The following example shows you how to use the SKIPIF field for various target-mailing tasks.

You might want to exclude a particular ZIP code from your form-letter mailing. To do so, insert the following field at the beginning of your main document, immediately after the DATA field:

{skipif {zip} = *number*}

Then, when you're ready to create the address labels, you insert the appropriate ZIP code in this field where *number* is and merge print. Word prints form letters for all ZIP codes except the one that matches the number you insert in the SKIPIF field, as shown on the next page. You still need to set up the main document as you did in "Example 4: Address Labels" earlier in this chapter.

This example also demonstrates a case in which you would benefit from using an ASK or SET field to insert the ZIP code for which you want labels. For more information about using these two fields to insert the ZIP code, see "Using the ASK, SET, and FILLIN Fields in Merge Printing" later in this chapter.

The table on the following page lists variations on the above ZIP code example. If the target name in the field is more than one word, enclose the target name in quotation marks.

Target	*Code*
City	{skipif {city} = "*name*"}
State	{skipif {state} = "*name*"}
Region	{skipif {region} = "*name*"}

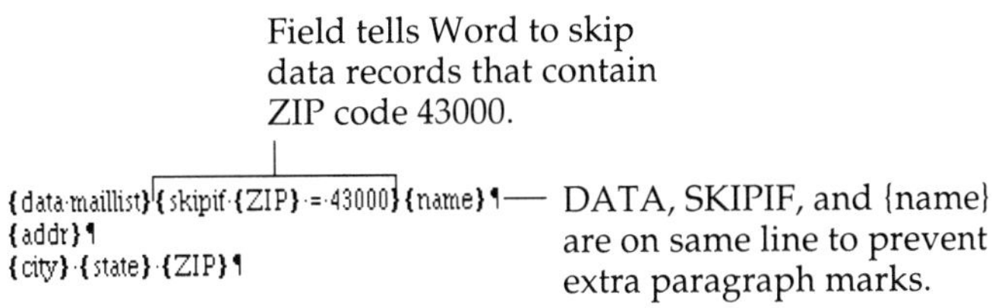

name	addr	city	state	ZIP	phone
Kelly Ceck	2121 Camino Real	Weed	OR	97000	555-1234
McKenzie Heimweh	8212 Telegraph Hill	Cape Watch	NC	43000	555-1243
Bill James	5551 South Broadway SE	Wastral	NV	89000	555-1324
Jane Smith	1800 NE Boulevard Way E	Oregani	WI	61000	555-1342
Joe Green	123 Main	Banks	WA	99000	555-1423
Jill Brown	456 Central	Ojai	CA	95000	555-1432

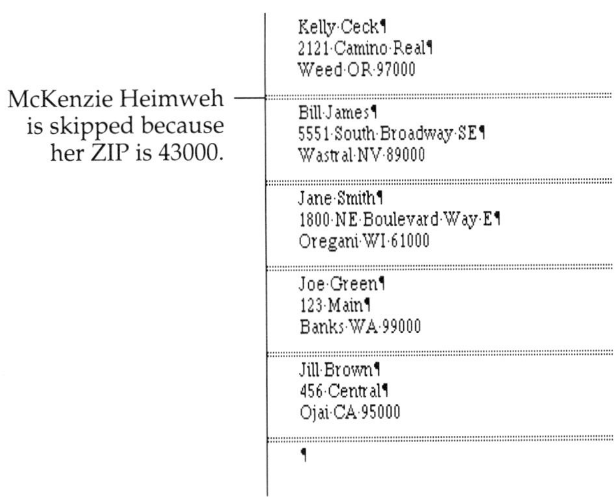

Using Other Operators with SKIPIF

To send mail to an area that includes several ZIP codes for a couple of cities, you might want to tell Word to exclude addresses in the several ZIP codes that are outside your target mailing. To do so, make use of the other operators in addition to the equal sign that are available with the SKIPIF field. The other operators are shown in the following table:

Operator	*Meaning*
>	Greater than
<	Less than
>=	Greater than or equal to
<=	Less than or equal to
<>	Not equal to

The following examples show some of the ways in which you can use these operators.

To exclude all addresses that are in ZIP codes from 11001 through 99999, use:

{skipif {zip} > 11000}

To mail to addresses that are in ZIP codes from 98000 through 99999, use the following SKIPIF field to exclude addresses with ZIP codes below 98000:

{skipif {zip} < 98000}

Using a MERGEREC Field to Keep Track of Records

At times you might want to know which data record Word used for a particular merge document. Word keeps track of the number of data records and invisibly assigns each a record number. The first data record after the header record is record 1. Other records are numbered consecutively through the data document, but you see no visible evidence of the numbers. You can, of course, include a number as a data item for your own use. To do so, simply add another column to the table in the data document.

For example, if the document printed incorrectly or if you want to change some information in a particular record, having the record number can be handy. The number helps you identify the erroneous record so that you can edit it. Or, if you're printing part of a data document by specifying a range of record numbers, you might want to know where you started and finished printing. By inserting a MERGEREC field in your main document, you tell Word to print the record number on each merge document. You might put a MERGEREC field in a header or footer, for example, where it would not distract the reader but would be easy to identify.

The result of a MERGEREC field is the data-record number from the data document. For example, the following illustration shows the record number in the footers of two resulting documents:

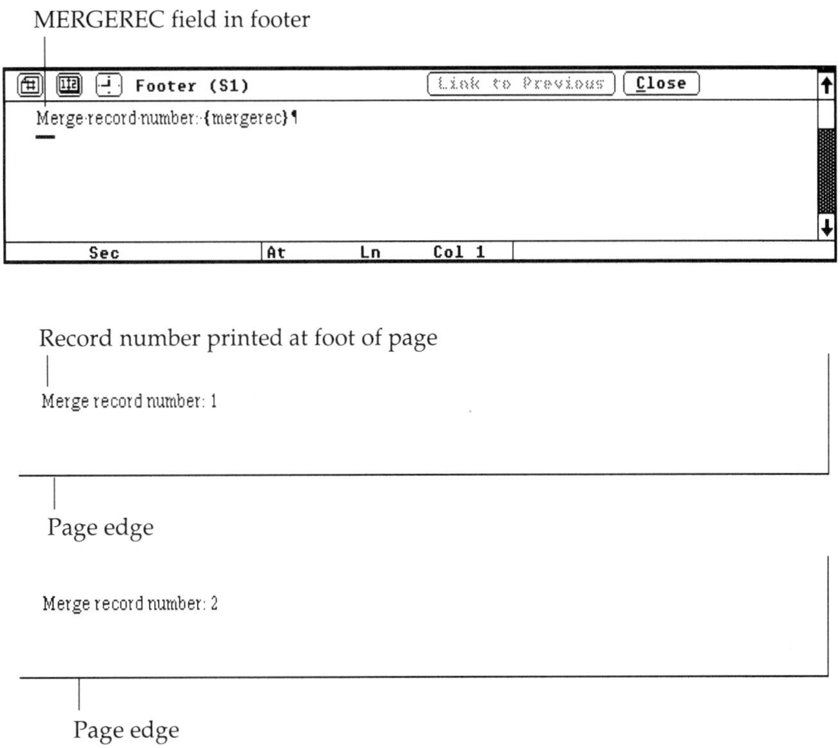

Nonmerge Instructions Are Also Useful in Merge Printing

You can use the fields that are described in this section in any document, whether or not you are doing merge printing. But keep in mind that using these fields can help you create snazzy merge documents!

Using the INCLUDE and IF Fields

The INCLUDE field inserts a document in another document. When you use merge printing, you can set up a main document to insert a whole document or only part of a document into each printed copy. You can also set up the main document to insert a whole document or only part of a document depending on to whom or to where the form letter is being sent.

Use the IF field to compare a data item with a guideline and then let merge actions depend on the outcome of that comparison. A comparison might verify whether a data item matches a guideline or whether it is larger or smaller than a guideline. For example, you might want to know whether an address ends in an odd or an even number. When you get the answer, you can tell Word to print the document according to guidelines such as the following:

> If the address number is odd, insert the first list of prizes. If the address number is not odd (that is, even), insert the second list of prizes.

In an IF field, this guideline looks like the following:

```
{if {=mod({addr}, 2)} = 1 odd even}
```

Guideline for evaluating each data record

The example in this section uses two fields and puts one field inside the other, which is called nesting. Using the form letter created earlier in this chapter in "Example 1: Creating a Main Document for a Form Letter," you could substitute the following opening for the letter:

```
You may have already won one of the following wonderful prizes:¶
¶
{include prizes {if {=mod({addr}, 2)} = 1 odd even}}¶
```

Field prints different prize lists for odd-numbered and even-numbered addresses.

The result of this set of fields is a table of prizes. One table is included for odd-numbered addresses and another for even-numbered addresses. Later in this section, you create the additional document you need for these fields.

The INCLUDE field in this example refers to only one document but to different bookmarks within that document. An INCLUDE field contains the name of a document plus the name of a bookmark when you want only part of the document. The document in this case, which is PRIZES.DOC, contains two tables. One table is marked by the bookmark "odd," and the other is marked by the bookmark "even." The PRIZES.DOC document could look like Figure 15-6 below.

Because the information is inserted in two separate tables, each with two columns and three rows as shown in Figure 15-6, the information appears in table format when it is printed in a form letter.

To create the PRIZES.DOC document, choose the File New command (Alt,F,N) and then choose OK in the File New dialog box. Choose the Insert Table command (Alt,I,T). In the Insert Table dialog box, choose OK to insert a two-column table. Type the text in the first cell (*Cadillac Coupe de Ville*), press the Tab key, and then type the text in the second cell (*Microwave Oven*). Press Tab to start a new row, press the Ctrl+O keys to open a blank line between rows in the table for better readability, type the text for the first cell as shown in Figure 15-6, press Tab, press Ctrl+O, and then type the text for the second cell. Repeat these steps for the third row of the table. (The open spacing will be set for you because Word copies the preceding row's formatting when you insert a new row.) After you fill in the table, press Alt+5 (5 on the numeric keypad) to select the whole table. Choose the Insert Bookmark command (Alt,I,M), type *odd* in the Insert Bookmark dialog box, and then choose OK.

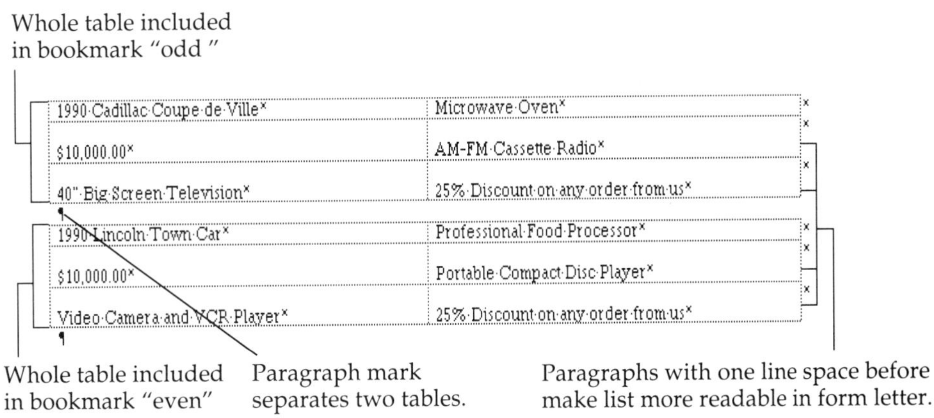

Figure 15-6.
PRIZES.DOC contains two tables, both marked with bookmarks.

To create the second table, press the Ctrl+End keys to move the insertion point to the end of the document, and press the Enter key so that you leave a paragraph mark between the two tables. This paragraph mark keeps the two tables separated. Choose the Insert Table command (Alt,I,T) again, and choose OK.

Using the same methods you used to fill in the first table, fill in the second table so that it looks like the second table shown in Figure 15-6. After you fill in the second table, press Alt+5 (5 on the numeric keypad) to select the whole table, press the INSERT BOOKMARK key combination (Ctrl+Shift+F5), type *even*, and then press the Enter key. Choose the File Save command (Alt,F,S), type *prizes* in the File Save dialog box, choose OK, fill in the Edit Summary Info dialog box with any information you want, and then choose OK.

Now, if you add the rest of the text from the original letter shown in Figure 15-2, your main document looks like the following:

```
{data maillist}{name}¶
{addr} {street}¶
{city} {state} {ZIP}¶
¶
Dear {name},¶
¶
You may have already won one of the following wonderful prizes:¶
¶
{include prizes {if {=mod({addr}, 2)} = 1 odd even}}¶
¶
Imagine the surprise on your neighbors' faces when you drive your brand new car to {addr} {street}.
Or, imagine going to your bank in {city} and finding an extra $10,000.00 in your account.¶
¶
All you have to do is return the enclosed prize form by October 19, 1990.¶
¶
And while you have this package in your hands, why not browse through our fabulous merchandise. To
order, just check the appropriate box on the prize form. Enter today and who knows, {name}? Soon
you too could be the proud owner of a new {if {=mod({addr}, 2)} = 1 "1990 Cadillac Coupe de Ville"
"1990 Lincoln Town Car"} and be the envy of your neighbors in {city}.¶
¶
```

IF field inserts name of car based on house number.

The IF field instructs Word to examine the data records for you and to insert the appropriate bookmark name in the INCLUDE field for an odd-numbered or an even-numbered address. To examine the parts of this IF field, first look at the {if {=mod({addr}, 2)} = 1 part of the field, which compares the result of a calculation with the number 1 to see whether the two numbers are equal. If the result of the calculation is 1, Word uses "odd" as the bookmark for the INCLUDE field. If the result of the calculation is not 1, Word uses "even" as the bookmark for the INCLUDE field.

In the field {=mod({addr}, 2)}, the ADDR field is a REF (bookmark) field, which is similar to the example shown earlier in the chapter in Figure 15-2. In this case, ADDR is not a bookmark for the whole street address; it's a bookmark for the house number only. The mailing list now looks like Figure 15-7:

New column in data document lists house number.

name	addr	street	city	state	ZIP	phor
Kelly Ceck	2121	Camino Real	Weed	OR	97000	555-1
McKenzie Heimweh	8212	Telegraph Hill	Cape Watch	NC	43000	555-1
Bill James	5551	South Broadway SE	Wastral	NV	89000	555-1
Jane Smith	1800	NE Boulevard Way E	Oregani	WI	61000	555-1
Joe Green	123	Main	Banks	WA	99000	555-1
Jill Brown	456	Central	Ojai	CA	95000	555-1

Figure 15-7.
Revised mailing-list table.

To add another column to the table, select the "city" column, choose the Edit Table command (Alt,E,A), choose the Column option (Alt+C) in the Edit Table dialog box if it's not already chosen, and then choose the Insert button (Alt+I). Type *street* in the new column's top cell, and then press the down arrow key to move down to the next cell in the new column. Press the MOVE key (F2), select the street name in the "addr" column (but do not select the house number), and then press the Enter key to move the street name to the new column. Repeat this step for each of the data records. When you finish, your table should look like the one shown earlier in Figure 15-6.

The Expression (=) field that contains the MOD instruction divides the house number by 2 and gives you the remainder of the division. Of course, if you divide an even number by 2, you get no remainder (zero). And, if you divide an odd number by 2, the remainder is always 1. As a result, if the remainder of dividing a house number by 2 equals 1, it's an odd-numbered address and the INCLUDE field becomes {include prizes odd}. If the remainder does not equal 1—that is, the remainder is zero, in this case—it's not an odd-numbered address and the INCLUDE field becomes {include prizes even}.

Note that near the end of the main document another similar IF field checks the house number and inserts the name of a car. This second IF field, however, includes the result text for odd-numbered and even-numbered addresses rather than inserting text from another file.

When you merge print with the revised MAILLIST.DOC data document, you see results for odd-numbered and even-numbered addresses like those shown in the following two illustrations:

Kelly Ceck
2121 Camino Real
Weed OR 97000

Dear Kelly Ceck,

You may have already won one of the following wonderful prizes:

1990 Cadillac Coupe de Ville	Microwave Oven
$10,000.00	AM-FM Cassette Radio
40" Big Screen Television	25% Discount on any order from us

Imagine the surprise on your neighbors' faces when you drive your brand new car to 2121 Camino Real. Or, imagine going to your bank in Weed and finding an extra $10,000.00 in your account.

All you have to do is return the enclosed prize form by **October 19, 1990.**

And while you have this package in your hands, why not browse through our fabulous merchandise. To order, just check the appropriate box on the prize form. Enter today and who knows, Kelly Ceck? Soon you too could be the proud owner of a new 1990 Cadillac Coupe de Ville and be the envy of your neighbors in Weed.

Letter to odd-numbered address has prize list and car name for odd addresses.

McKenzie Heimweh
8212 Telegraph Hill
Cape Watch NC 43000

Dear McKenzie Heimweh,

You may have already won one of the following wonderful prizes:

1990 Lincoln Town Car	Professional Food Processor
$10,000.00	Portable Compact Disc Player
Video Camera and VCR Player	25% Discount on any order from us

Imagine the surprise on your neighbors' faces when you drive your brand new car to 8212 Telegraph Hill. Or, imagine going to your bank in Cape Watch and finding an extra $10,000.00 in your account.

All you have to do is return the enclosed prize form by **October 19, 1990.**

And while you have this package in your hands, why not browse through our fabulous merchandise. To order, just check the appropriate box on the prize form. Enter today and who knows, McKenzie Heimweh? Soon you too could be the proud owner of a new 1990 Lincoln Town Car and be the envy of your neighbors in Cape Watch.

Letter to even-numbered address has prize list and car name for even addresses.

Example 6: Combining NEXT and IF for Selective Merging

You might occasionally want to create address labels for a particular group. For example, you might have a data file of friends' names and addresses but want to print address labels for only those friends who play soccer. To print this limited list, insert NEXT fields to tell Word to look at the next data record and IF fields to check the data record to see whether the friend plays soccer. The data file could include a column for soccer, with a Yes or No for the soccer data item in each data record:

IF field checks this data item and prints data records that contain Yes in this column.

name	addr	city	state	ZIP	soccer
Kelly Ceck	2121 Camino Real	Weed	OR	97000	No
McKenzie Heimweh	8212 Telegraph Hill	Cape Watch	NC	43000	Yes
Bill James	5551 South Broadway SE	Wastral	NV	89000	Yes
Jane Smith	1800 NE Boulevard Way E	Oregani	WI	61000	No
Joe Green	123 Main	Banks	WA	99000	No
Jill Brown	456 Central	Ojai	CA	95000	Yes

The main document you use includes NEXT and IF fields to check the data records for a Yes data item in the soccer column:

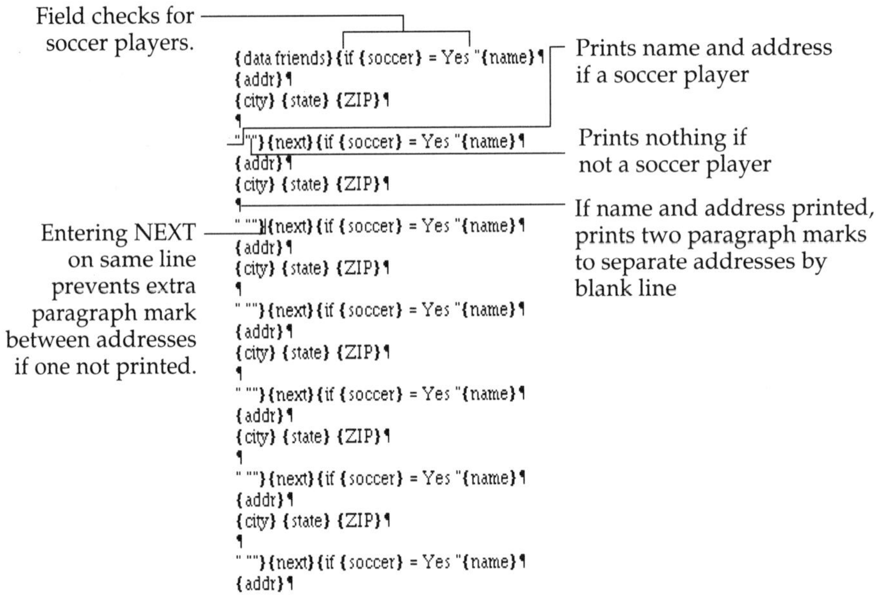

The following illustration shows the effect of the fields during merge printing:

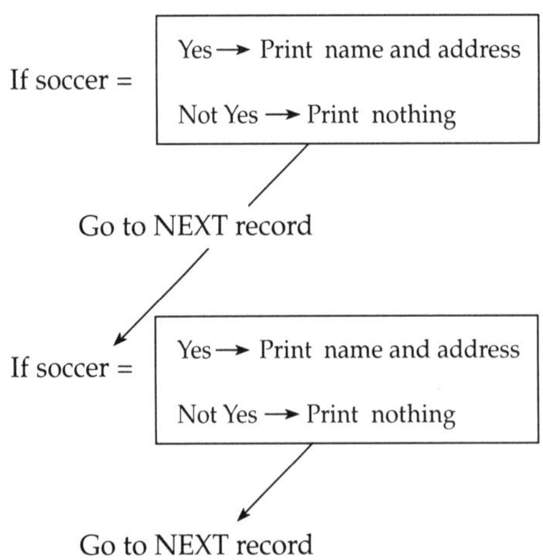

For each record in the data document, the IF field checks the soccer column's data. Word prints the name and the address from records in which "Yes" appears in the soccer column and skips records in which any other entries appear in the soccer column. In both cases, Word then continues to the next record.

The main document shown on the preceding page might look a bit odd, but the arrangement of fields serves an important purpose in the document that results from merge printing. The arrangement of fields and lines in the main document prevents Word from adding unnecessary paragraph marks to the resulting document. The first REF (bookmark) field ({name}) is on the same line as the DATA field so that if the first record is printed, Word will not insert a paragraph mark at the beginning of the document. The NEXT fields are on the last line of the preceding record's fields so that if the next data record is not printed, Word will not print an extra paragraph mark between addresses in the resulting document. The IF field checks the current data record to see whether the friend is a soccer player.

If "Yes" appears in the soccer column, Word prints that friend's name and address on three lines. The paragraph mark between the first set of quotation marks provides the line breaks. The final pair of paragraph marks after {ZIP} create a blank line between printed addresses. For friends for whom "No" appears in the soccer column, Word prints nothing. The two consecutive quotation marks with no entries between them tell Word to print nothing. The resulting document produced from these main and data documents looks like the following:

```
McKenzie Heimweh¶
8212 Telegraph Hill¶
Cape Watch NC 43000¶
¶
Bill James¶
5551 South Broadway SE¶
Wastral NV 89000¶
¶
Jill Brown¶
456 Central¶
Ojai CA 95000¶
¶
```

Two paragraph marks printed following each name

Using the ASK, SET, and FILLIN Fields in Merge Printing

The ASK, SET, and FILLIN fields can be helpful during merge printing because they give you a chance to insert information that you'll know only at the time of printing. For example, when you prepare the sweepstakes form letter that's used as an example in this chapter, the entry deadline date might be decided just before you print the letters.

Instead of having to edit the main document, you can insert one of these fields, and Word will use the date you type during merge printing. (As with the IF and INCLUDE fields, you can use these three fields at any time, whether or not you're merge printing.)

The ASK and FILLIN fields prompt you for information during merge printing. The SET field lets you set up a bookmark before merge printing begins. For merge printing, you'll usually be better off if you use the ASK field when you need prompting and the SET field when you do not. You can set up the ASK field to prompt you only one time or to prompt you before printing each copy of the form letter. Each FILLIN field in the main document prompts you before printing a copy of the form letter, so the FILLIN field is useful only if you want to be prompted to supply different information for every form letter. You have the choice of leaving the FILLIN field dialog box blank, meaning the FILLIN field in that case has no result. You can make use of this alternative to print or omit information during printing.

Note that after the FILLIN field is updated the first time, the proposed response is the response you typed the last time you updated the

TIP

The NEXTIF Field Uses the Current Record

Word contains a NEXTIF field that resembles a combination of the NEXT and IF fields. The NEXTIF field, however, checks the current record rather than the next data record. As a result, it's not useful in place of the NEXT and IF combination described in the example in this section because NEXTIF would tell Word to print the next record if the current data record showed "Yes" for the soccer column. So, even if McKenzie Heimweh were a soccer player, her name and address would not be printed because Kelly Ceck does not play soccer. The NEXTIF field looks at Kelly Ceck's soccer column, sees "No," and does not move to the next data record. Instead, Word prints Kelly Ceck's name and address seven times for each set of fields following a NEXTIF field. The NEXTIF field is useful only if a data item in the current record can be used to decide whether the next data record should be used or if the guidelines that you set up do not use any items from the data document.

FILLIN field. See the Appendix, "Field Types and Their Instructions," for information about how to set a default response for a FILLIN field. The ASK field can prompt you before every form letter, too, and you can use your response to the ASK field easily in several places in the form letter by inserting REF (bookmark) fields. The FILLIN field's result appears in only one place—at the location of the field. Each of the field examples below shows how you can set the entry-closing date for the sweepstakes using the ASK, SET, and FILLIN fields.

To use the ASK field to prompt you for the contest closing date, insert the following field:

```
{ask enddate "Type the contest closing date and then choose OK" \o}¶
```

The ASK field displays a dialog box in which you can type the date information—in this case, the closing date. If you use a plain ASK field, without the \o switch, Word displays the dialog box for each letter that prints. By adding the \o switch, you tell Word to display the dialog box only one time—before the first letter it prints—and then to use the same date for the rest of the letters. Using the \o switch in the sweepstakes example makes sense because you'd want the closing date to be the same in every letter.

Note that the ASK field does not have a visible result. The ASK field actually sets up a bookmark for the text you type in the dialog box. To use a date or some other information that you type in an ASK field dialog box, insert a REF field that includes the bookmark name in it, such as the following:

```
{enddate \@ "MMMM d, yyyy" \* charformat}
```

The result of this REF (bookmark) field is the date that you type in the ASK field dialog box. The date-and-time switch, which is shown as \@ "MMMM d, yyyy", tells Word how the date should look when it is displayed and printed. (For example, using October 19, 1990, "MMMM" tells Word to print the full name of the month, "d" tells Word to print the date, and "yyyy" tells Word to print the full year.) The formatting switch (* charformat) tells Word to make the result of the field the same text format as the first character in the field—the boldface "e"—so that the date will appear in boldface type.

The SET field performs the same action as an ASK field, except that a SET field does not display a dialog box to ask you for the bookmark text. You type the text in the field and enclose the text in quotation marks, as shown below:

```
{set enddate "October 19, 1990"}
```

The SET field is useful if you're using the bookmark name several times in all the documents and you want to set up the information before printing. Because the SET field does not display a dialog box, you do not have to attend to dialog boxes while the merge documents are printing. The one disadvantage of using the SET field is that the text you insert in the SET field is kept in the document, and you have to remember to change it during future printings. As is true of the ASK field, you must insert a REF (bookmark) field in the document where you want the text of the SET field to print. In this case, insert a REF (bookmark) field like the one shown for the ASK field where you want the ending date of the sweepstakes to appear in the form letters.

The FILLIN field displays a dialog box as the ASK field does, but instead of setting up a bookmark, the FILLIN field displays a result. Its result is what you type in the dialog box.

The following shows a FILLIN field that sets up the end date as the ASK and SET field examples do:

```
{fillin "Type the contest closing date and then choose OK" \@ "MMMM d, yyyy"}
```

The FILLIN field contains a message for the dialog box so that you know what to type. In this example, the field also contains a date-and-time switch to tell Word to display the date in the letter as "October 19, 1990" rather than as "10/19/90". Also, you can format the result of a

TIP

Formatting Results by Formatting a Switch

Word lets you format the date-and-time switch as an alternative to formatting the field type and inserting the * charformat switch in a field. For example, if you apply boldface formatting to the MMMM d, yyyy switch, the resulting date appears in boldface. In addition, if you apply a character format to only part of the date-and-time switch, only that part of the result uses that character format.

FILLIN field, as described for the ASK field, by using the * charformat switch or by formatting the date-and-time switch. The FILLIN field is handy for reminding you to insert specific information as you print the documents.

A document can contain as many FILLIN fields as you want. This field is useful during merge printing only if you must insert different information in various copies of the form letter and you do not know that information in advance. If you have the time, it's best to put the information that's different for each merge document in the data document. By putting the different information in the data document, you streamline the merge-printing process because you do not have to fill in a dialog box before Word prints each copy of the form letter.

Chapter 16

Mathematical Typesetting

Many mathematical, scientific, and research papers present proofs and results in mathematical form. Mathematical formulas typically include symbols and arrangements of characters that are unusual in documents outside the scientific realm. Because most word processors provide no means for printing mathematical formulas, mathematical typesetting—the ability to print mathematical formulas—has been an art shrouded in the mysteries of specialty typesetting companies.

Word for Windows, however, includes the tools you need to set up mathematical formulas on screen and print them on laser printers. Mathematical typesetting in Word gives you the ability to position numbers and text to create results such as those shown in the table on the following page.

To create the results shown in the table, you insert a Formula (EQ) field in your document where you want the result to appear. See Chapter 8, "Fields: Facts and Functions," to review the parts of fields and the procedures for inserting them. Coming up in this chapter, "Using Formula (EQ) Fields for Mathematical Typesetting" includes a quick review just prior to launching you into using the Formula (EQ) field. At the end of this chapter, "Formula (EQ) Fields for the Examples Shown at the Beginning of the Chapter" shows the codes you use to create the results shown in the table on the following page.

Type of Result	*Example*
Fractions	$9\frac{9}{139}$ A fraction consists of $\frac{\text{numerator}}{\text{denominator}}$.
Integrals	$\int_{n=1}^{2} x^2+4x$ $\int_{n=1}^{2} x^2+4x$ $\sum_{n=1}^{2} x^2+4x$ $\prod_{n=1}^{2} x^2+4x$
Roots	$\sqrt{29}$ $\sqrt[3]{43}$ $\sqrt[x-1]{\frac{1}{x^2+4x+9}}$
Arrays and matrices	$\begin{bmatrix} 1 & 2 & 3 \\ 2 & 3 & 1 \\ 3 & 1 & 2 \end{bmatrix}$ $\begin{array}{c\|c\|c} 1 & 2 & 3 \\ \hline 2 & \boxed{3} & 1 \\ \hline 3 & 1 & 2 \end{array}$
Equations	$r = \sqrt{\frac{A}{\pi}}$
Formulas	$f(x) = \frac{y^3+3y^2+7y+29}{\sqrt{\frac{a-b}{b^3-ab}}}$
Expressions	$\frac{1}{3}x^3 + xy^2$
Special effects	$\overset{re}{V}$ is a trademark of $\overset{re}{V}$isionary Manuals.

The examples shown above were printed on a PostScript printer. The rest of the mathematical formulas shown in this chapter appear as you see them on the screen. If you print the other examples shown in this chapter, you'll find that they look like the examples shown above and not precisely as displayed on your screen. To print mathematical formulas, you must use a Hewlett-Packard laser printer with at least 512 KB of memory or a PostScript printer. To see mathematical formulas on the screen, the Symbol font must be installed. Word's Setup program installs the Symbol font for you.

If you are running Word with Microsoft Windows version 3.0 and you are printing on any model of Hewlett-Packard LaserJet, you need to install the Windows 3.0 Symbol soft fonts. To do so, insert in drive A the disk that contains the Symbol fonts. For a 5.25-inch disk drive, insert the Conversions Disk. For a 3.5-inch disk drive, insert the Setup Disk. Switch to the new Symbol fonts directory by typing *a:*, pressing the Enter key, typing *cd \symbol\w3*, and then pressing Enter again. To copy the Windows 3.0 Symbol soft fonts from the disk in Drive A to your PCL fonts directory in drive C, type *copy *.pfm c:\pclfonts* and then press Enter.

This chapter assumes that you understand mathematical symbols and terms, so no attempt is made to explain them. The instructions and explanations of the procedures you use to typeset formulas, however, are aimed at nonexperts. This chapter shows many results and provides the instructions to achieve them. Because it's not possible within this book to display every possible formula, you'll need to synthesize the instructions in new ways to produce the results you want. Becoming proficient at mathematical typesetting means you'll need lots of practice using and combining special instructions.

Although you need to use a Formula (EQ) field to create results such as those in the preceding table, you can create formulas that consist of only symbols, superscripts, and subscripts with text formatting using the Format Character command. The Format Character dialog box lets you set the position and the font size for superscripts and subscripts. For example, the following expression uses only superscript and point-size text formatting:

$$(4n + 1)^{x^{4n+1}}$$

The expression in parentheses in this formula is set at 18 points. (A point is a typesetter's measurement equal to 1/72 inch.) The x exponent is set at a superscript of 12 points and a point size of 14 points. And the $4n + 1$ exponent of x is set at a superscript of 15 points and a point size of 8 points. Using text formatting in this case is easier than using a Formula (EQ) field, which would require you to type the following line to produce the same result:

```
{eq(4n + 1)\s\up12(x )\s\up15(4n + 1)}
```

Although using the Format Character command is usually easier than using the formula instructions for formatting superscripts or subscripts, often only a Formula (EQ) field can produce the results that you want.

Using Formula (EQ) Fields for Mathematical Typesetting

The Formula (EQ) field displays and prints a mathematical formula, expression, or equation. This field was specifically designed for mathematical typesetting. The procedures you follow in this chapter to insert fields use the INSERT FIELD key combination (Ctrl+F9). Between the field characters ({}) that Word inserts, you type the field codes, which are the Formula (EQ) field type followed by instructions for inserting, formatting, and positioning numbers, letters, and symbols:

{eq *instructions*}

After you type the field codes, position the insertion point anywhere inside the field and press the TOGGLE FIELD key combination (Shift+F9) to see the field result. A Formula (EQ) field does not calculate a result. It displays the characters and formatting associated with the field codes. You do not use the UPDATE FIELD key (F9) to see the result of a Formula (EQ) field. If you press F9 for a Formula (EQ) field, you'll hear a beep to remind you that Formula (EQ) fields cannot be calculated. Formula (EQ) fields are updated as soon as you make any change to their instructions.

TIP

Having It Both Ways: Seeing Codes and Results Simultaneously

You can set up your document window to show the codes and results of Formula (EQ) fields at the same time. First, split the window by choosing the Control Split command (Alt,hyphen,T) and then pressing the Enter key. In one pane, turn on the View Field Codes command. In the other pane, leave View Field Codes turned off. As you type and edit a Formula (EQ) field in the pane in which View Field Codes is turned on, the result appears in the other pane. Note that until you set up a valid formula, the field result will be the message "Error!"

Word includes 10 instructions that you can use in a Formula (EQ) field. Each of these instructions includes a backslash, a one-letter instruction, and parentheses that surround the formula's elements:

{eq \a(*elements*) }

Some instructions also have variations, which specify a symbol or a position or other formatting instruction. A variation modifies the instruction with which it's associated. Variations consist of a backslash and a two-letter variation instruction. You insert a variation between an instruction and its associated opening parenthesis:

{eq \a\ar(*elements*) }

If you want, you can insert spaces between the parts of the instructions. Note, however, that although spaces between instructions do not affect the result, spaces in the elements do.

Word lets you combine as many as all 10 of the possible instructions, and it lets you nest instructions and use an instruction more than one time in a field. Descriptions of these instructions are upcoming in this chapter in the section "A List of Formula Instructions and Variations." The section called "Cracking the Codes: Examples of Formulas with Their Codes Exposed," also later in this chapter, contains examples of the instructions at work, including examples that combine and nest instructions.

To acquaint you further with formulas, the next section gives you step-by-step instructions to show you how to build a formula one piece at a time.

Practice Building a Formula

Building a formula is like building a Chinese puzzle: You add one interlocking piece at a time to form a completed shape, such as a ball or a cube. If you misplace a piece, you do not get a correct result. This introduction to formulas is not meant to scare you but to alert you that learning to create formulas takes practice. After you learn how to build formulas, you'll be able to create a variety of effects with ease. The following example presents one way to build a formula. Other methods are possible, some of which you might find more convenient. But this example gives you a starting place, using the formula shown in Figure 16-1 on the following page.

$$z^3 = \sqrt[3]{\left[\frac{1}{\sqrt{x^2 + y^2}}\right]^2}$$

Figure 16-1.
Sample formula.

To create the formula above, first split the window into two panes (Alt,hyphen,T,Enter). Then, choose the View Field Codes command (Alt,V,C) to turn on field codes in the lower pane (referred to as the "codes" pane). Leave field results in the upper pane (referred to as the "results" pane).

Before you type the instructions, analyze the formula you want to create and list its parts. Then, list the levels and relationships in the formula's structure. For example, the formula shown in Figure 16-1 contains the following parts and relationships:

Part	*Relationship*
$z^3 =$	The cube of z, which is equal to the cube root of the squared fraction
$x^2 + y^2$	Binomial expression; can be set up without the Formula (EQ) field
$\sqrt{\quad}$	Square root of the expression $x^2 + y^2$—the denominator of the fraction; requires the Formula (EQ) field
1	The numerator of the fraction
$(\ )^2$	The parentheses that apply the exponent to the whole fraction
$\sqrt[3]{\quad}$	The cube root of the squared fraction

If you have not moved the insertion point, it should still be in the lower (codes) pane. If you have moved the insertion point to the upper (results) pane, position the insertion point in the lower pane (F6).

Type the formula instructions, one part at a time, as shown in the following paragraphs. Each instruction consists of a code and parentheses. For each part of an instruction, you type the code and the opening parenthesis first, which causes Word to display the message "Error!" in the results pane until you type the closing parenthesis. When all parts of an instruction are valid, the result appears.

Type the letter *z*, press the Ctrl+Shift+equal sign (=) keys, type 3, press Ctrl+Shift+equal sign again, type a space, type an equal sign, and then type another space. In both panes you see the following:

$z^3 =$

Now, type *x*, press the Ctrl+Shift+equal sign keys, type 2, and press Ctrl+Shift+equal sign again. Type a space, a plus sign (+), another space, and *y*. Next, press Ctrl+Shift+equal sign and type 2 again. In both panes you see the following:

$z^3 = x^2 + y^2$

You have not yet needed to use any formula instructions. From now on, however, you use the Formula (EQ) field to build the rest of the formula. Select the part of the formula that's on the right side of the equal sign ("$x^2 + y^2$"), and press the INSERT FIELD key combination (Ctrl+F9) to insert a field around the selected text. Then, type *eq* followed by a space. In the codes pane, you see the following:

z³ = {eq x² + y²}

In the results pane, you still see the results shown below:

$z^3 = x^2 + y^2$

Now you're ready to add the first Formula (EQ) field instruction, which draws the square-root symbol around the binomial. Be sure the insertion point is still positioned in front of "x^2" and type *\r(*, after which you see the message "Error!" in the results pane because the formula instruction is incomplete. Position the insertion point after "y^2," press the Ctrl+spacebar keys to turn off superscript, and type a closing parenthesis. In the codes pane, you see the following:

z³ = {eq \r(x² + y²)}

In the results pane, you now see the following:

$$z^3 = \sqrt{x^2 + y^2}$$

Next, you insert the instructions to create the fraction. Position the insertion point in front of "\r(" and type *f(1,* (including the comma). Again you see "Error!" in the results pane. Position the insertion point after "y^2)" and type another closing parenthesis. In the codes pane, you see the following:

z^3 = {eq \f(1,\r(x^2 + y^2))}

You see the following in the results pane:

$$z^3 = \frac{1}{\sqrt{x^2 + y^2}}$$

Now, insert the instructions to draw the parentheses around the fraction. Position the insertion point in front of "\f(1" and type *b(* without any following punctuation. Again, "Error!" appears in the results pane. Position the insertion point after "y^2))" and type another closing parenthesis. Then, press the Ctrl+Shift+equal sign keys and type 2. In the codes pane, you now see the following:

z^3 = {eq \b(\f(1,\r(x^2 + y^2)))^2}

In the results pane, you see the following result:

$$z^3 = \left(\frac{1}{\sqrt{x^2 + y^2}}\right)^2$$

Now, insert the instructions to draw the cube-root symbol. Position the insertion point in front of "\b(" and type *r(3,* (including the comma). "Error!" appears in the results pane. Position the insertion point after "y^2)))^2", press the Ctrl+spacebar keys to turn off superscript, and type another closing parenthesis. The codes pane shows the following codes:

z^3 = {eq \r(3,\b(\f(1,\r(x^2 + y^2)))^2)}

You see the final formula in the results pane:

$$z^3 = \sqrt[3]{\left(\frac{1}{\sqrt{x^2 + y^2}}\right)^2}$$

A List of Formula Instructions and Variations

The following sections explain each of the instructions and variations that you can insert in a Formula (EQ) field. You must precede each instruction with a backslash. For the instructions that have variations, you also precede the variations with a backslash. Whenever you see a backslash in a description or in an example, insert that backslash.

All instructions also contain parentheses, which you use to tell Word what elements belong to a particular instruction. If you cannot get a formula to display its result, you'll often find that you're missing a closing parenthesis. Try counting the left parentheses and then the right parentheses to be sure that the two numbers match. (Extra right parentheses and extra sets of parentheses appear in the result as parentheses.) Within the parentheses, use a comma to separate multiple elements. To insert a comma that you want to appear in the result, precede the comma with a backslash.

The instructions that follow appear in alphabetic order. The examples shown for each instruction and variation also show the codes that create that instruction and variation.

Array \a()

The array instruction positions a list of elements in a single vertical column that has centered alignment. For example, you can set up a column of numbers as shown in Figure 16-2.

1
2
...
3

Figure 16-2.
Sample array.

Note that the ellipsis (. . .) is centered in the column of numbers. To produce this result, you insert a Formula (EQ) field that includes the following instructions:

```
{eq \a(1,2, . . . ,3)}
```

Note also that elements, which are inside the parentheses, are separated by commas. A Formula (EQ) field displays its result on one line. If you type text before or after an array, the text aligns with the array's vertical center:

```
                            1
                            2
This is a simple array:  ...  More complex arrays are possible.
                            3
```

The height of the line on the page now equals the height of the array. That is, Word treats the result of a Formula (EQ) field as a single character.

Arrays are often enclosed in parentheses, brackets, or braces. The bracket instruction provides these and similar symbols. For more information about the bracket instruction, see the section called "Bracket \B()." Also see the examples of arrays in brackets in the section called "Cracking the Codes: Examples of Formulas with Their Codes Exposed" later in this chapter.

Variations for the array instruction align the array's elements, make the array more than one column, and set the space between the array's columns and rows. The array instruction has six variations: align left (\al), align center (\ac), align right (\ar), number of columns (\co*n*), vertical spacing (\vs*n*), and horizontal spacing (\hs*n*).

Align left \al

The align-left variation for the array instruction aligns the elements along the left edge of each column. Alignment variations are noticeable only when some parts of a column are wider than others. For example, the following array results from the align-left variation:

```
123
45
6
```

To achieve this result, insert a Formula (EQ) field such as the following:

```
{eq \a\al(123,45,6)}
```

Align center \ac

The align-center variation for the array instruction aligns the elements at the center of each column and is the default if you do not specify an alignment variation. An array that has centered alignment looks as shown in Figure 16-3 on the following page.

```
123
 45
 6
```

Figure 16-3.
Center-aligned array.

And the following shows the instructions for this array:

{eq \a\ac(123,45,6)}

Suppose, however, that you omit the align-center variation from this example and type the following instructions:

{eq \a(123,45,6)}

You would see exactly the same result as shown in Figure 16-3, above:

```
123
 45
 6
```

You use this variation for clarity when you're building several arrays—especially nested arrays—that have different alignments.

Align right \ar

The align-right variation for the array instruction aligns the elements at the right edge of each column:

```
123
 45
  6
```

To produce the above result, you insert a field such as the following:

{eq \a\ar(123,45,6)}

Number of columns \co*n*

The array instruction's columns variation sets the number of columns for the array. If you do not use this variation, Word sets up the array in one column. Figure 16-4 shows a three-column array:

```
123
231
312
```

Figure 16-4.
Three-column array.

To set the number of columns, you insert a column variation (\co) and follow it with the number of columns you want in the array. To create two columns, for example, you type *co2*. The Formula (EQ) field for the above three-column array looks like the following:

{eq \a\co3(1,2,3,2,3,1,3,1,2)}

Note that if the array includes more elements than the number of columns, Word creates new rows as needed. If the number of elements in the array is not an integer multiple of the number of columns, Word leaves blank spaces in the last row of the array, as shown in the following example, which includes seven elements in a three-column array:

```
123
231
3
```

The difference between the instructions for the above array and the one preceding it is the number of elements:

Former array: {eq \a\co3(1,2,3,2,3,1,3,1,2)}

Latter array: {eq \a\co3(1,2,3,2,3,1,3)}

To leave a blank in the middle of an array, omit an element between two commas. Be sure to include the correct number of commas. For example, you leave a blank in the middle of an array that's three columns by three rows, as in the following example:

```
123
2 1
312
```

The instructions for the above array look like the following, in which you'll see two commas in the middle of the list of elements:

{eq \a\co3(1,2,3,2,,1,3,1,2)}

Vertical spacing \vs*n*

The array instruction's vertical-spacing variation sets the amount of space between rows to the number of points you type. As you recall, the example in Figure 16-2 looks like the following:

```
1
2
...
3
```

You might want more vertical space between the numbers:

```
1

2

...

3
```

To increase the vertical space in an array, you insert a vertical-spacing variation (\vs) and follow it with the number of points of vertical space you want between the rows of the array. For example, for 3 points of vertical space you type *vs3*. The instructions for the above example, which has 6 points of vertical space, look like the following:

{eq \a\vs6(1,2,...,3)}

Horizontal spacing \hs*n*

The horizontal-spacing variation for the array instruction sets the amount of space between columns to the number of points you type. As shown earlier in this chapter, the example in Figure 16-4 looks like the following:

```
123
231
312
```

You might not want the columns to be crowded together, preferring instead more horizontal space between the columns:

```
1 2 3
2 3 1
3 1 2
```

To increase the horizontal space in an array, you insert a horizontal-spacing variation (\hs) and follow it with the number of points of horizontal space you want between columns. For example, you type *hs3* for three points of horizontal spacing. The above example has 6 points of horizontal spacing; its instructions look like the following:

{eq \a\co3\hs6(1,2,3,2,3,1,3,1,2)}

If an array has only one column, the horizontal-spacing variation sets the column width. In the example shown on the following page, an \hs12 instruction sets the column width, which determines the spacing between the array and the text that appears on its sides.

In the array $\begin{array}{c} a \\ b \\ \circ \\ n \end{array}$ we'll find ....

The following are the instructions for the above example:

In the array {eq \a\hs12(a,b,∘,*n*)} we'll find ....

(To insert a bullet character, press the Ctrl+F keys, type *symbol*, press the Enter key, turn on the NumLock key, hold down the Alt key, and type *0149* on the numeric keypad. Be sure to turn off NumLock and press the Ctrl+spacebar keys to return to the previous font.)

Without the horizontal spacing variation, the sentence text crowds the array, making it difficult to read:

In the array$\begin{array}{c} a \\ b \\ \circ \\ n \end{array}$we'll find ....

Box \x()

The box instruction draws borders around elements in a formula. Each element sits inside an invisible box that sets the element's height and width. The box instruction draws its borders along the sides of this invisible box.

If you use the box instruction without including any of its variations, Word draws a box:

$\boxed{A}$

To create this example, insert a Formula (EQ) field that looks like the following:

{eq \x(A)}

You can use the variations to draw top (\to), bottom (\bo), left (\le), and right (\ri) borders. If you use all four variations together, Word draws a box, exactly as it does if you use no variations.

Top border \to

The top-border variation draws a border along the top edge of the element. For example, an A that has a top border looks like the following:

$\overline{A}$

The instructions for the above example are as follows:

{eq \x\to(A)}

The top border is as wide as the element. To lengthen the border to match the element's width, add the letters PE after the A in the example:

{eq \x\to(APE)}

The result of those codes looks like the following:

$\overline{\text{APE}}$

Bottom border \bo

The bottom-border variation draws a border along the bottom edge of the element. For example, an A that has a bottom border looks like the following:

$\underline{\text{A}}$

To set up a bottom border for an A, insert the bottom-border variation:

{eq \x\bo(A)}

Like the top-border variation, the bottom border is as wide as the element.

Left border \le

The left-border variation draws a border along the left edge of the element. For example, an A that has a left border looks like the following:

|A

To produce this result, insert the following instructions:

{eq \x\le(A)}

The left border is as tall as the element. A border's height matches the element's height. Increase the point size of the A in the example above to 14 points so that the instructions look like the following:

{eq \x\le(A)}

Here's how the left border looks now:

|A

Right border \ri

When you use the right-border variation, Word draws a border along the right edge of the element. For example, an A that has a right border looks like the following:

A|

To create this example, you insert a Formula (EQ) field like the following:

{eq \x\ri(A)}

Like the left-border variation, the right border is as tall as the element.

The following example combines the left-border and right-border variations:

|A|

The instructions for the above result look like the following:

{eq \x\le\ri(A)}

Bracket \b()

The bracket instruction surrounds elements with parentheses, brackets, braces, or any other characters that you want to use. If you do not use a variation, Word draws a parenthesis on each side of the element:

$(n^2 + 1)$

You can produce this example as easily by typing the parentheses yourself outside a Formula (EQ) field. But outside a field, you must size the parentheses yourself. When you use the bracket instruction inside a Formula (EQ) field, Word matches the size of the parentheses to the element's size. Inside a field, you type the following:

{eq \b(n^2 + 1)}

Outside a field, what you type and the result you see are the same:

$(n^2 + 1)$

The difference in these examples between the parentheses the field draws and the parentheses you type is barely discernible. The difference between elements drawn by these methods becomes more obvious if the element is a tall one, such as a fraction or an array. For example, if you insert a Formula (EQ) field for a fraction but type the parentheses yourself, you would use the following instructions:

```
({eq \f(1,2)})
```

You would see the following result:

$$(\frac{1}{2})$$

This result is less satisfactory than the result created by the following instructions:

```
{eq \b(\f(1,2))}
```

These instructions give the following result:

$$\left(\frac{1}{2}\right)$$

In the same way, typing the parentheses around a Formula (EQ) field for an array such as the following gives the less satisfactory result shown below:

```
({eq \a\co2(1, 2,3, 4)})
```

$$(\begin{matrix}1 & 2\\3 & 4\end{matrix})$$

Using the following bracket instruction, however, gives a more satisfactory result:

```
{eq \b(\a\co2(1, 2,3, 4))}
```

$$\left(\begin{matrix}1 & 2\\3 & 4\end{matrix}\right)$$

You can set up brackets for either side or both sides of the element using the left-character (\lc), right-character (\rc), or both-characters (\bc) variations.

Left character \lc*c*

The bracket instruction's left-character variation draws the character you specify along the left side of the element. Notice that you must precede the character with a backslash, as in the following example Formula (EQ) field:

```
{eq \b\lc\{(\a\al(apple,banana))}
```

Notice also that the brace character inside the field is inserted by typing the left-brace key and not by typing the INSERT FIELD key combination.

When you include the above instructions, Word draws the following result:

$$\left\{\begin{array}{l}\text{apple}\\\text{banana}\end{array}\right.$$

Right character \rc*c*

The bracket instruction's right-character variation draws, along the right side of the element, the character you specify. Notice that you must precede the character with a backslash:

```
{eq \b\rc\}(\a\ar(apple,banana))}
```

The above instructions produce the following result:

$$\left.\begin{array}{r}\text{apple}\\\text{banana}\end{array}\right\}$$

Both characters \bc*c*

The both-characters variation draws along both sides of the element the character that you specify. Notice that you must precede the character with a backslash.

```
{eq \b\bc\{(\a\ac(apple,banana))}
```

From the above instructions, you get the following result:

$$\left\{\begin{array}{c}\text{apple}\\\text{banana}\end{array}\right\}$$

In the case shown above, the instructions specify only the left-side character. If you insert a parenthesis, bracket, brace, or less-than sign (<), Word inserts the opposite character at the end of the element so that you need not specify the right bracket character separately. If you use any other characters that can be considered a pair of opposites in the way that quotation marks are, you must specify the left and right characters separately using the left-character and right-character variations. Except for the left side characters of parentheses, brackets, braces, and less-than signs, the both-characters variation draws the same character at both ends of the bracketed elements. For example, suppose you insert a field that includes the following instructions:

{eq \b\bc\¦(\f(a,b))}

The result would look like the following:

$$\left|\frac{a}{b}\right|$$

Open and close apostrophes, open and close quotation marks, acute and grave accents, and forward-slash and backslash characters are examples of characters that you might want to pair as mirror opposites. The following examples show the instructions you type and the results you see for these paired characters:

Character Instructions	*Result*
Open and close apostrophes {eq \b\lc\‘\rc\’(\f(a,b))} For an open apostrophe, turn on the NumLock key, hold down the Alt key, and then type *0145*. For a close apostrophe, hold down Alt and type *0146*.	‘$\frac{a}{b}$’
Open and close quotation marks {eq \b\lc\“\rc\”(\f(a,b))} For open quotation marks, hold down the Alt key and type *0147*. For close quotation marks, hold down Alt and type *0148*.	“$\frac{a}{b}$”
Acute and grave accents {eq \b\lc\`\rc\´(\f(a,b))} For the grave accent (`), press the key on the keyboard. For the acute accent (´), hold down the Alt key and type *0180*.	`$\frac{a}{b}$´
Backslash and forward slash {eq \b\lc\\\rc\/(\f(a,b))}	$\backslash\frac{a}{b}/$

Displace \d()

The displace instruction moves an element horizontally by the number of points you specify. If the preceding parts of the formula become wider or narrower, you might need to adjust the displace measurement to produce the alignment you want. Word lets you use the displace instruction to move elements closer together or farther apart.

When you work with a proportional-space font, using the displace instruction is more reliable than using spaces. In proportional-space fonts, characters have different widths; the width of a space character is variable, depending on the surrounding text and its text formatting. Putting several spaces together compounds this problem.

The displace instruction has three variations: forward (\fo), which positions the element farther to the right; back (\ba), which positions the element farther to the left; and line between (\li), which draws a line between elements. If you do not use any variations, the displace instruction has no effect.

Forward \fo*n*

The displace instruction followed by the forward variation moves the elements that come after the forward variation to the right by the number of points you specify. This variation is handy when Word draws elements from instructions because often the spacing is cramped, as in the following example, which does not contain a displace instruction:

$$\sum_{0}^{1} x^2 + 2x$$

If you add a displace instruction that includes a forward variation of 3 points, you get the following result:

$$\sum_{0}^{1}\; x^2 + 2x$$

For the example above, the Formula (EQ) field looks like the following:

```
{eq \i\su(0,1,\d\fo3()x² + 2x)}
```

Note that although you must include the parentheses, you do not insert anything in them. And if you use the displace instruction by itself, you do not need to include the text inside the field. The instruction has the same effect with or without that text. When you use the displace instruction with other instructions, place the elements inside the field as necessary for those instructions.

Back \ba*n*

The displace instruction followed by the back variation moves the elements that come after the back variation to the left by the number of points you specify. Notice in the following instructions that the word "move" precedes the word "back":

```
{ eq move \d\ba60()back}
```

But in the result of these instructions, the back variation of 60 points puts "back" before "move":

back   move

The back variation is most useful when you also move up or down the element that follows as a way to prevent the overprinting of elements. If you want elements to overprint, however, it's easier to use the overstrike instruction than the displace back variation. The overstrike instruction is explained in "Overstrike \o()" later in this chapter. When you use the displace instruction in combination with a superscript instruction or subscript instruction, you can print pieces of text over or under other text. For example, the following instruction combines a displace back variation of 49 points with a subscript instruction of 12 points:

```
{eq Move back \d\ba49()\s\do12(down under)}
```

These instructions create the following result:

Move back
down under

The subscript instruction is explained in "Superscript or Subscript \s()" later in this chapter.

Line between \li()

Rather than displace elements, the line-between variation draws a line from the element that precedes it to the element that follows it. For example, the instructions below contain two line-between variations combined with the displace instruction's forward variations:

Follow the {eq \d\fo48\li()} to vector A{eq \d\fo6\li()}B

The following shows the effect of the line-between variation as used in the above instructions:

Follow the ________ to vector A _ B

Suppose you use the line-between variation in combination with a displace back variation and a subscript instruction, as follows:

{eq Move back \d\ba49\li()\s\do12(down under)}

Word produces a line between the elements that makes the result look similar to a fraction:

Move back
down under

In this case, however, the elements can be offset or aligned in various ways instead of merely centered one over the other as elements of a fraction are by the fraction instruction.

Fraction \f()

The fraction instruction puts a numerator over a denominator and separates the two with a horizontal line. The line is as long as the longer of the fraction's two parts. Both of the parts are centered horizontally in relation to each other, and the entire fraction is centered vertically on the text line. For example, suppose you typed the following instructions:

{eq \f(1,2)}

You would see a result that looks like a simple fraction:

$\frac{1}{2}$

You can use any text; numbers; or combination of letters, numbers, symbols, and other characters in the elements of a fraction. Word lets you make a fraction as complex as you want, such as the one in the example below:

$$\frac{\sqrt[3x^2-zy]{\frac{6x-z}{y^2}}}{\sqrt{\pi^2}}$$

The above example is the result of the following instructions:

{eq \f(\r(3x^2–zy,\f(6x–z,y^2)),\r(π^2))}

To insert a pi character, type the lowercase letter *p* in the Symbol font.

The fraction instruction has no variation.

Integral \i()

The integral instruction draws an integral symbol and positions the integral elements in relation to the symbol. This instruction takes three elements: The first is the lower limit, the second is the upper limit, and the third is the integrand. The following instructions show how to set up an integral:

{eq \i(*n*=0,1, x^2 + 1)}

The result of the above Formula (EQ) field is shown in Figure 16-5:

$$\int_{n=0}^{1} x^2+1$$

Figure 16-5.
Standard integral.

You can leave out any element as long as you hold its place with two commas inside the parentheses.

If you prefer to typeset the integral using an in-line format, use the in-line variation (\in). The integral instruction also has variations that substitute another character for the integral symbol: The summation variation (\su) substitutes an uppercase sigma (Σ), the product variation (\pr) substitutes an uppercase pi (Π), and the fixed-character (\fc) variation and variable-character (\vc) variation substitute any other character you want, such as a vertical bar.

In line \in

The in-line variation changes the position of the limits from above and below to the top-right and bottom-right of the integral symbol, as in the example below:

{eq \i\in(*n*=0,1,x^2 + 1)}

Then, instead of the result in Figure 16-5, you see the result shown in the following illustration:

$$\int_{n=0}^{1} x^2 + 1$$

Summation \su

The summation variation replaces the integral symbol (∫) with an uppercase sigma symbol (Σ) to create a summation. For example, if you add the summation variation to the instructions for the integral in Figure 16-5, the instructions look like the following:

{eq \i\su(*n*=0,1,x^2 + 1)}

The result changes from the one shown in Figure 16-5 to the following:

$$\sum_{n=0}^{1} x^2 + 1$$

Product \pr

Like the summation variation, the product variation replaces the integral symbol, but in this case with an uppercase pi symbol to create a product. Adding the product variation to the instructions for the integral in Figure 16-5 gives you the instructions shown below:

{eq \i\pr(*n*=0,1,x^2 + 1)}

The product variation of the integral instruction draws this result:

$$\prod_{n=0}^{1} x^2 + 1$$

Fixed character \fc*c*

The integral instruction's fixed-character variation replaces the integral symbol with the character you specify. Note that you must precede with a backslash the character you specify. To replace the integral instruction's standard symbol with another character, such as a vertical bar, add \fc\\| to the instructions for the result shown in Figure 16-5. Those instructions will then look like the following:

```
{eq \i\fc\| (n =0,1, x^2 + 1)}
```

The result will change from that shown in Figure 16-5 to the following:

$$\Big|_{n=0}^{1} x^2 + 1$$

The character will always be a specific height, which you assign by setting its point size in the Format Character dialog box on the ribbon or by pressing the POINT SIZE key combination (Ctrl+P). In the above example, the vertical bar is set at 24 points.

The in-line variation of the integral instruction is helpful when you use a substitute character, such as the vertical bar, that looks odd with the limits set above and below it. The following is one example:

$$\Big|_{n=0}^{1}$$

The above result is created by the following instructions:

```
{eq \i\in\fc\| (n =0,1, )}
```

The vertical bar is set at a size of 24 points.

Variable character \vc*c*

Like the fixed-character variation, the variable-character variation replaces the integral symbol with the character you specify. You must precede the character with a backslash. The character will be the same height as the integrand (the third element in the integral instruction).

Set the character's point size in the Format Character dialog box or on the ribbon; or press the POINT SIZE key combination (Ctrl+P), type a point size, and press the Enter key. In the following example, the integrand (x^2) is set at 14 points:

```
{eq \i\vc\|(n =0,1, x² + 1)}
```

The result of using the variable-character variation in these instructions is shown below:

$$\Big|_{n=0}^{1} x^2 + 1$$

To make the replacement character taller than the integrand, make the character itself larger by using the integral instruction's fixed-character (\fc*n*) variation.

List \l()

Although some formula instructions take only one, two, or three elements, the list instruction can insert a long list of items that become one element. Be sure to separate with a comma the elements in an instruction that work with more than one element. And if you want an element

TIP

Getting a Taller Variable Character

When you insert a variable-character (\vc*n*) variation in the integral instruction, you usually have to make the integrand bigger to make the variable-height character bigger. You can get Word to produce a taller symbol, however, without changing the size of the integrand. In many cases, you'll find that you need to insert a blank space before the third element in the parentheses (that is, before the integrand) to keep the integral from looking crowded. By selecting this space only and making its point size larger, you can increase the size of the symbol while leaving the visible portion of the integrand smaller.

Note that the same result can usually be achieved more easily by using the fixed-character variation and setting the symbol's point size in the Format Character dialog box. Using the fixed-character variation also makes it easier later, when you look at the instructions, to see how you accomplished the result.

to contain many items and commas, you must insert a backslash in front of the commas to make them appear in the result. This requirement can make the instructions look messy and confusing, however. For example, you might want a result that looks like the one shown below in Figure 16-6:

$\sqrt{a,b,c,d,e,f}$

Figure 16-6.
Result containing commas.

To achieve this result without using the list instruction, you would insert a Formula (EQ) field that looks like the following:

```
{eq \r(a\,b\,c\,d\,e\,f)}
```

But if you use the list instruction when you insert the elements and commas, you can omit the backslashes in front of the commas. The effect is a cleaner-looking instruction in which you can more easily see the elements. If you use the list instruction to create the result that's shown in Figure 16-6, the Formula(EQ)field looks like the following:

```
{eq \r(\l(a,b,c,d,e,f))}
```

The list instruction is most useful when the list of items is long. For short lists, it's usually as easy to type the backslashes.

Overstrike \o()

The overstrike instruction lets you print elements on top of one another to create custom characters that are not part of any Windows fonts. How you want Word to align the elements is your choice. Each element sits inside an invisible box that sets the element's height and width. The alignment variations position these boxes in relation to one another. The align-left (\al) variation aligns element boxes flush left with one another, the align-center (\ac) variation centers element boxes on one another, and the align-right (\ar) variation aligns element boxes flush right with one another. If you do not use any variation, the overstrike instruction centers the elements, as in the following example:

Ø

The above result is produced by these instructions:

```
{eq \o(0,/)
```

Align left \al

The align-left variation aligns the element boxes along their left edges. For example, the instructions shown below use the align-left variation:

```
{eq \o\al(stacked,Up)}
```

Overstrike and its align-left variation produce the following result:

Align center \ac

The align-center variation aligns the element boxes at their centers, as in the example produced by the instructions below:

```
{eq \o\ac(stacked,Up)}
```

Word uses center alignment if you do not specify an alignment variation. You use this variation primarily for clarity when you're building several overstrike instructions that have different alignments.

Align right \ar

The align-right variation aligns the element boxes along their right edges, as the following instructions dictate:

```
{eq \o\ar(stacked,Up)}
```

The following shows the result of the above instructions:

Radical \r()

The radical instruction draws the root symbol ($\sqrt{\ }$) around elements. Word draws the symbol as large as it needs to be to enclose all the elements inside the radical. You can set up a radical instruction for a square root or for multiple roots (cube root, fourth root, and so on).

Square-root \r()

To set up a square root, you insert only one element inside the parentheses in an instruction, as shown on the next page.

{eq \r(π)}

To insert the pi character symbol, type the lowercase letter *p* in the symbol font.

You see as a result the square root of pi:

$\sqrt{\pi}$

The element for a square root can contain more than one part, as shown in this example:

$\sqrt{a,b}$

The above example results from the following instructions:

{eq \r(a\,b)}

Notice that the comma is preceded by a backslash. Precede with a backslash any commas that you want to appear in the result, or put the commas inside a list instruction. If you do not use a backslash or a list instruction, Word sees two elements and displays a multiple root, as described in the next section, "Multiple roots \r(,)."

Multiple roots \r(,)

To set up multiple roots, insert two elements inside the parentheses. The first element is the root number (3 for a cube root, 4 for a fourth root, and so on). The second element draws the contents inside the radical symbol. The following result is the fourth root of 42:

$\sqrt[4]{42}$

The result shown above is drawn from the instructions below:

{eq \r(4,42)}

Both of a multiple root's elements can contain more than one part. For example, the following Formula (EQ) field contains a fraction instruction inside the parentheses for the radical instruction:

{eq \r(x–1,\f(1,2π²))}

And the result looks like the following:

$\sqrt[x-1]{\frac{1}{2\pi^2}}$

Superscript or Subscript \s()

The scripting instruction moves elements up or down from the baseline. For exponents and subscripts, it's usually more efficient to use the superscript and subscript text formats in the Format Character dialog box, as shown in the example included earlier in this chapter in the section called "Practice Building a Formula." Using the text formatting approach also shrinks the point size, which is the usual treatment for exponents and subscripts. When you want to move a character up or down by more than 63.5 points (the maximum Word allows in the Format Character dialog box), use a scripting instruction. Also, when you want to be able to see why an element moved up or down and by how many points, use a scripting instruction. Getting this information when you use text formatting is more difficult.

The two variations, up (\up) and down (\do), specify the direction in which to move the elements. Two other variations—ascender increase (\ai) and descender increase (\di)—provide additional space above superscripts and below subscripts. If you omit a variation, the elements move up by 3 points, which is also the default when you format superscript text using the Ctrl+Shift+equal sign keys. The following instructions omit a variation:

```
move{eq \s(up)}
```

And the result of the above instructions looks like the following:

moves up

Using the scripting instruction without variations is hardly worth the effort. You could get the same result by pressing the Ctrl+Shift+equal sign keys immediately before you type *up* for the up variation.

Up \up*n*

The up variation directs the scripting instruction to move its element above the baseline. The *n* is the number of points you want to move the element up. For example, these instructions contain an up variation of 12 points:

```
Baseline {eq \s\up12(\\Up12 variation)}
```

Notice the double backslash, which provides a single backslash in the result. From these instructions, you see the result shown below:

        \Up12 variation
Baseline

Down \do*n*

Adding the down variation to the scripting instruction moves the element down from the baseline. The *n* is the number of points you want to move the element down. These sample instructions move the element down by 12 points:

    Baseline {eq \s\do12(\\Do12 variation)}

The result looks like the following:

Baseline
        \Do12 variation

Ascender increase \ai*n*

Word adjusts line height to accommodate superscripts and subscripts. If you enclose a superscript, subscript, fraction, or complex radical with the box instruction (\x), however, you might find the space between the formula and the box to be less than you wish. To increase the space above a formula, use the ascender increase (\ai*n*) variation. (To increase the space below a formula, use the \di*n* variation, which the following section describes.)

The ascender increase variation enlarges space above a formula by the number of points that you type in place of *n*. For example, suppose you type the codes for the two following fields:

    {eq \x(X\s\up12(5.3496578))} Without the \AI variation

    {eq \x(X\s\up12\ai6(5.3496578))} With an \AI variation of 6 points

Word produces the following results:

5.3496578 X	Without the \AI variation

5.3496578 X	With an \AI variation of 6 points

Descender increase \ di*n*

To add space below a formula, add the descender increase (\ di*n*) variation to a subscript instruction. The *n* is the number of points that you want to increase space below the formula. To see the effect of the descender increase variation, insert the two following fields:

`{eq \x(X\s\do12(5.3496578))}` Without the \DI variation

`{eq \x(X\s\do12\di6(5.3496578))}` With a \DI variation of 6 points

The above codes produce the following results:

$\boxed{X_{5.3496578}}$ Without the \DI variation

$\boxed{X_{5.3496578}}$ With a \DI variation of 6 points

Cracking the Codes: Examples of Formulas with Their Codes Exposed

The following examples show you the variety of results you can create by using the Formula (EQ) field. For each example, you see both the result and the codes that create that result. By studying the results and their instructions, you can learn more about combining instructions to create almost any formula. To familiarize yourself further with mathematical typesetting in Word, try re-creating the results in the examples by imitating the instructions. Notice that in some examples, the instructions are longer than one line. Although the instructions can extend past one line, the result must fit on one line.

Example 1

$$\text{Speedup} = \frac{(s + p)}{\left(s + \frac{p}{N}\right)} = \frac{1}{\left(s + \frac{p}{N}\right)}$$

`Speedup = {eq \f(\b(s + p),\b(s + \f(p,N)))} = {eq \f(1,\b(s + \f(p,N)))}`

Note that if you want to include parentheses around an element, you need only insert the \b instruction; you do not have to specify the parentheses characters or indicate that you want them on both sides.

Example 2

$$\left.\begin{array}{l} F(N) = n - M(F(n-1)) \\ M(n) = n - F(M(n-1)) \end{array}\right\} \text{ for } n > 0$$

```
{eq \b\rc\}(F(N) = n - M(F(n - 1 ))\d\ba86()\s\do24(M(n) = n - F(M(n - 1))))\s\do12( for n > 0)}
```

For the displace instructions, you must guess by how many points you want to move an element up, down, forward, or backward and then adjust the numbers until the elements line up correctly. Remember that 1 inch equals 72 points and that one line is usually about 12 points. Note, for example, that the displace back variation specifies a back movement of 86 points, based on the character's point size of 10 points. If the point size were smaller, less displacement would be needed; if it were larger, more displacement would be needed.

Example 3

$$a_0 = \frac{1}{2\pi}\int_0^{2\pi} x \, dx = \frac{1}{2\pi}\frac{x^2}{2}\Bigg|_0^{2\pi} = \frac{1}{2\pi} \cdot \frac{(2\pi^2)}{2} = \pi$$

```
a 0 = {eq \f(1,2π) \i\in(0,2π, x dx = \f(1,2π) \f(x^2,2)) \i\in\fc\| (0,2π, = \f(1,2π)) · \f(\b(2π^2),2) = π}
```

To insert a pi (π) character, type the lowercase letter *p* in the Symbol font. And to italicize parts of the formula, select those parts in the codes and apply italic text formatting to them by pressing the Ctrl+I keys. The vertical bar that the fixed-character variation of the integral instruction draws is formatted as 30 points. The dot character that appears between the last two fractions is a period that is superscripted by 3 points and formatted as 14-point boldface.

Example 4

$$I = \sum_{i=1}^{N} \int_{x_j-1}^{x_j} f(x)\, dx = \sum_{i=1}^{N} \int_{-1}^{1} g_j(t)\, dt = \sum_{i=1}^{N} I_j$$

```
I = {eq \i\su(i = 1,N, )\i\in(x j-1,x j, f(x) dx) = \i\su(i = 1,N, )\i\in(-1,1, g j(t) dt) =
\i\su(i = 1,N, I j)}
```

Notice that the integrands for the summation uppercase sigmas are blank spaces. The in-line integral symbols thus appear to form the integrands for the summations.

Example 5

$$\frac{x_1 x_2 (\alpha - 1)}{x_2^1 + \alpha^3 x_2^2} \left[\alpha^2 x_{2'} - x_1 \right]^{T}$$

```
{eq \f(x₁x₂(α - 1),x\s(1,2) + α³x\s(2,2)) \s\up4(\b\bc\[(α²x₂' - x₁))\s\up8( T )}
```

To insert a lowercase alpha character (α), type the lowercase letter *a* in the symbol font. The x_2^1 and x_2^2 parts of the result are drawn by a scripting instruction that includes two elements in the parentheses: x\s(1,2) and x\s(2,2). Note that a \b\bc\[instruction draws the brackets in the result. The final superscript, the italic letter *T*, was formatted by pressing the Ctrl+I keys and including a superscript instruction of 8 points.

Example 6

$$\boxed{p_n(x_0 + sh) = \sum_{i=0}^{n} \Delta^i f_0 \binom{s}{i}}$$

```
{eq \x(p n(x 0 + sh) = \i\su(i = 0,n , Δ^i f 0 \b(\s(s,i))))}
```

Note that the box shown in the example above is created using the box (\x) instruction without variations. Much of this formula was formatted using the text formatting keys for superscript and subscript (Ctrl+Shift+equal sign keys and Ctrl+equal sign keys). To insert the uppercase delta character (Δ), type the uppercase letter *D* in the Symbol font. Notice again the use of two elements for the scripting instruction—this time inside a bracket instruction.

Example 7

$$p_n(x) = \sum_{j=0}^{n} f \quad [x_0, \ldots, x_j] \quad \prod_{i=0}^{j-1} (x - x_j)$$

```
p n(x) = {eq \i\su(j = 0,n, f )\d\fo12()}[x 0, . . . , x j]{eq \d\fo12()\i\pr (i = 0,j - 1, (x - xj))}
```

The preceding example is two formulas rather than one. Using two fields simplifies the codes by excluding the bracketed expression in the middle, which is easily created without using the Formula (EQ) field. You can choose to produce the entire result using one field. This formula is notable primarily because it uses both the summation uppercase sigma symbol (Σ) and the product uppercase pi symbol (Π) in the same formula. Notice also that this formula uses both the displace instruction and spaces to create spacing. Spaces were used in front of the integrands. The spaces can be formatted at a larger point size to make the sigma and pi symbols taller without also making their visible integrands taller.

Example 8

$$F^t AF - \lambda I = \left[\begin{array}{cc|cccc} \lambda_1 - \lambda & 0 & 0 & 0 & \cdots & 0 \\ \lambda_1 - \lambda & 0 & 0 & 0 & \cdots & 0 \\ 0 & 0 & B_{33} - \lambda & B_{34} & \cdots & B_{3n} \\ 0 & 0 & B_{43} & B_{44-\lambda} & \cdots & B_{4n} \\ \circ & \circ & \circ & \circ & & \circ \\ \circ & \circ & \circ & \circ & & \circ \\ \circ & \circ & \circ & \circ & & \circ \\ 0 & 0 & B_{n3} & B_{n4} & \cdots & B_{nn} - \lambda \end{array} \right]$$

```
{eq \s\do36(FtAF -λI =)\b(\a\ac\co6\hs12\vs4(λ1-λ, 0, 0, 0,···,0,λ1-λ, 0, 0, 0,···,0
)\d\ba149()\s\do70(\a\ac\co2\vs5( 0,     0,0,     0,o,   o,o,   o,o,   o,0,
0)\s\up1(\b\bc\[(\a\co4\vs4(B33-λ, B34,···,B3n,B43,B44-λ,···,B4n,o,o, ,o,o,o,,o,o,o,,o,Bn3,Bn4,···
,Bnn-λ))))))}
```

To insert a lowercase lambda symbol (λ), type the lowercase letter *l* in the Symbol font. This single Formula (EQ) field contains formatted letters and symbols without formula instructions followed by three array instructions. The left side of the equation uses a subscripting instruction of 36 points to position that side nearer the array's vertical center. The first array instruction draws the top two rows of six columns. This array instruction uses a horizontal-spacing variation of 12 points to provide sufficient width and a vertical-spacing variation of 4 points to provide sufficient height in which to fit the nested array instruction in brackets.

The second array instruction of two columns draws the third through eighth rows of the result's first two columns. The result of this array was positioned using the displace instruction with a back variation of \d\ba149(), a subscript instruction of \s\do70, and a vertical-spacing variation of 5 points. The third array instruction, which uses a superscript instruction of 1 point following the second array, draws the third through eighth rows of the third and sixth columns inside brackets and nested within the outer brackets around the whole array. This third array uses a vertical-spacing instruction of 4 points. To produce the blank column in the third array, type spaces between the commas.

Formula (EQ) Fields for the Examples Shown at the Beginning of the Chapter

At the beginning of this chapter, you saw examples of mathematical typesetting that Word can produce. The following table repeats those results with their Formula (EQ) fields shown beneath them:

Type of Result	*Examples*	
Fractions	$9\frac{9}{139}$	A fraction consists of $\frac{\text{numerator}}{\text{denominator}}$.
	9 {eq \f(9,139)}	A fraction consists of {eq \f(numerator,denominator)}.
Integrals	$\int\limits_{n=1}^{2} x^2+4x$	$\int_{n=1}^{2} x^2+4x$
	{eq \i(n=1,2,x^2+4x)}	{eq \i\in(n=1,2,x^2+4x)}
	$\sum\limits_{n=1}^{2} x^2+4x$	$\prod\limits_{n=1}^{2} x^2+4x$
	{eq \i\su(n=1,2,x^2+4x)}	{eq \i\pr(n=1,2,x^2+4x)}

(continued)

continued

Type of Result	***Examples***		
Roots	$\sqrt{29}$ **{**eq \r(29)**}**	$\sqrt[3]{43}$ **{**eq \r(3,43)**}**	$\sqrt[x-1]{\frac{1}{x^2+4x+9}}$ **{**eq \r(x-1,\f(1,x^2+4x+9))**}**
Arrays and matrices	$\begin{Bmatrix} 1 & 2 & 3 \\ 2 & 3 & 1 \\ 3 & 1 & 2 \end{Bmatrix}$ **{**eq \b(\a\co3(1 , 2 , 3,2 , 3 , 1,3 , 1 , 2))**}** $\begin{array}{c\|c\|c} 1 & 2 & 3 \\ \hline 2 & \boxed{3} & 1 \\ \hline 3 & 1 & 2 \end{array}$ **{**eq \a\co3(1,\x\le\ri(2),3,\x\to\bo(2),\x(3),\x\to\bo(1),3,\x\le\ri(1),2)**}**		
Equations	$r = \sqrt{\frac{A}{\pi}}$ r = **{**eq \r(\f(A,π))**}**		
Formulas	$f(x) = \frac{y^3+3y^2+7y+29}{\sqrt{\frac{a-b}{b^3-ab}}}$ f(x) = **{**eq \f(y^3+3y^2+7y+29,\r(\f(a-b,b^3-ab)))**}**		
Expressions	$\frac{1}{3}x^3 + xy^2$ **{**eq \f(1,3)**}** x^3 + xy^2		
Special effects	$\overset{\mathbf{re}}{\mathbf{V}}$ is a trademark of $\overset{\mathbf{re}}{\mathbf{V}}$isionary Manuals. **{**eq **V**\d\ba9()\s\up9(**re**)**}**is a trademark of **{**eq **V**\d\ba9()\s\up9(**re**)\d\ba3()isionary Manuals.**}**		

Appendix

Field Types and Their Instructions

This appendix provides some general information about fields and then goes on to describe Word for Windows' field types and their instructions. The descriptions of the fields are grouped according to their uses so that you can find fields that produce the effect you want in your document. In many cases, a short example illustrates the effect of the field type and its various instructions. You'll occasionally see a reference to an example that was used in another chapter in this book because the full effect of the field can be seen only in a more lengthy example.

For more general information about using fields in Word, see Chapter 8, "Fields: Facts and Functions," and Chapter 9, "Fields II: Creating Special Effects."

Field Syntax and General Information

A field consists of a matched pair of field characters ({ }), a field type, and instructions. The field characters form a field's boundary. Inserting a field using the INSERT FIELD key combination (Ctrl+F9) inserts both field characters together. When you select one field character, the opposite field character is also selected. You must delete both field characters and the field together; you cannot select and delete only one field character.

Field Type

The first item inside the field characters can be any of the following: the field type, a backslash, a blank space, or a bookmark name. The field type is the field's name, such as "date." You can precede a field type with an optional backslash, which has no effect on a field and, because it is unnecessary, is not used in any of the examples in this book. You can also precede the field type with as much blank space as you want—spaces, tab characters, paragraph marks, or newline characters. Preceding the field type with any of these characters has no effect on the field's result.

As mentioned, the first item in a field can be a bookmark name. Bookmark names are shorthand for REF fields, which are described in the later section "Reference Fields: Text, Page Numbers, Styles, and Footnotes." If, at the beginning of a field, you insert text that is not one of the field types, Word treats that text as a bookmark name. If you have not inserted a bookmark in the document that corresponds to the text in the field, the field's result is "Error! Bookmark not defined." For more information about bookmarks, see "Bookmarks" below.

Instructions

Many of the field types have additional instructions that define, refine, or modify the action initiated by the field type. For example, to insert another file in a document, the INCLUDE field type, which you use to insert another file in a document, needs the name of the file. The file name is the additional instruction for the INCLUDE field type. Instructions take different forms, depending on the field type. Instructions can be bookmark names, text, expressions, identifiers, switches, and fields (called nested fields).

Bookmarks

A bookmark name identifies a selection in a document. In Word documents, a bookmark is identified by a bookmark name. In spreadsheet files, a bookmark is called a "named range" and represents a group of cells. In many fields that get their results from another part of a document or from a different document, a bookmark name identifies the contents or the location that you want to use as the field's result.

Text

Text as part of an instruction can provide a file name, a bookmark name, an expression, a prompt, or formatting information. When you want to include more than one word as part of an instruction, enclose the text in quotation marks to indicate that the words are one element rather than several individual elements. Unless you precede the quotation marks with backslashes, they do not appear in the result.

A backslash that's inside instruction text indicates that the following character should appear in the result as it appears in the codes. The backslash is most often used to place quotation marks in a result. Use two backslashes in a row to place a backslash character in a result. To include a colon in the entry that appears in an index, precede the colon with a backslash. If you do not include the backslash, the colon indicates that the text following it is a subentry. For more information about using colons in Index Entry (XE) fields, see "Tables of Contents, Lists, and Indexes" later in this appendix.

Expressions

An expression is an arrangement of numbers along with mathematical and logical operators for a calculation that produces a number or a logical result (TRUE or FALSE). A number by itself is also an expression. See the description of the Expression (=) field in "Calculations and Comparisons" later in this appendix for information about the types of mathematical and logical operators that Word provides for building expressions.

Identifiers

Some fields collect information from other fields in a document. You use these "collector" field types repeatedly to create various different types of lists. To distinguish the fields from which information is to be collected for a particular list, you add a unique identifier to the field that collects the information and to the fields from which information is to be collected. Suppose you want to collect information from all fields that are identified by the letter "A." You insert the identifier "A" in the field that collects the information and in the fields from which information is to be collected. For examples of fields that use identifiers, see the descriptions of the SEQ field in "Numbering Fields" and the TOC and TC fields in "Tables of Contents, Lists, and Indexes."

Switches

Switches are instructions that affect the appearance of a field's result or affect the field's action. Some switches change the form of numbers (for example, to ordinal text, which uses "second" instead of "2"). Other switches change the form of the date or time information or identify the field or the source of information for the field's result.

Switches are divided into two major categories: field-specific switches and general switches.

Field-specific switches. Many fields have switches that affect their results. For example, the INDEX field contains a switch for adding a letter at the beginning of each of an index's letter sections. A field-specific switch is generally a single character following a backslash. The same character might appear in several fields but have a unique function in each field. See the descriptions of the field-specific switches that appear in each field's description. Each field can contain a maximum of 10 field-specific switches.

General switches. Word lets you use general switches to format the results of many field types. The effect of a general switch is the same in every field in which you can use the switch. Word offers three general switch types: date-and-time switches, numeric switches, and formatting switches. Date-and-time switches affect only fields that result in dates or times. Numeric switches affect only fields that result in numbers. Some formatting switches affect all the fields, but others affect only fields that result in numbers. Each field can contain a maximum of 10 general switches. For a full description of each of the general switches, see "General Switches" later in this appendix.

Nested fields

You can insert a field inside another field; this process ("nesting") can be carried out to 20 levels. The results of nested fields can provide the contents of instructions, such as text, a number, or a date and a time.

Note that if the result of a nested field is a table, the table is not displayed or printed as the result. A table can be a field's displayed result only if that field is not nested.

Date and Time Fields

Word can insert the current date or time, the last date on which a document was printed, the date on which a document was created, or the date on which a document was last saved.

The DATE and TIME fields insert their results in a default format, which they take from your WIN.INI file. Use the Windows Control Panel to set the format in your WIN.INI file. You can tell Word to print the date and time in other formats, which are controlled by special instructions (date-and-time switches) that you add to fields. For more information, see "Date-and-Time Switches" on the following page.

The Date Field

The result of the DATE field is either the date or the time when you or Word last updated the field. Printing the document also updates the DATE field.

The Time Field

The result of the TIME field is either the time at which you or Word last updated the field or the date on which it was updated. Printing the document also updates this field.

The Print Date Field

The PRINTDATE field's result is the date on which the document was last printed—it is not the date of the current printing. To print the current date in a document, either insert a DATE field instead of PRINTDATE or print the document a second time. The print date information appears in the Edit Summary Info dialog box's Statistics subdialog box.

The Creation Date Field

The CREATEDATE field's result is the date on which the document was created. The creation date information appears in the Edit Summary Info dialog box's Statistics subdialog box.

The Save Date Field

The result of the SAVEDATE field is the date on which the document was last saved. The save date information appears in the Edit Summary Info dialog box's Statistics subdialog box.

Date-and-Time Switches

You can add general switches for formatting the date and time when the default date and time formats are not appropriate. Or you might want both the date and the time in the result of a single date or time field. Then you use date-and-time switches to specify a picture of the date-and-time format for a field's result. If the field has no date or time in its result, these switches have no effect. The following list describes the date-and-time switches and provides simple examples of each one. All the examples can be used in all date and time fields, including using time pictures in DATE, PRINTDATE, CREATEDATE, and SAVEDATE fields and date pictures in a TIME field to specify results that display both the date and the time.

All date-and-time switches begin with \@. A date-and-time picture, which follows the \@, can combine any of the elements in the list below and must be enclosed in quotation marks.

Word lets you apply character formatting to the parts of a date-and-time switch as a means of formatting the result. For example, if you format as boldface the month portion of a date-and-time switch, the month will appear in the result in boldface. And if you apply character formatting to the entire date-and-time switch, Word will apply that formatting to the entire result.

Month

A month is represented by an uppercase "M." The "M" must be uppercase to distinguish months from minutes, which use a lowercase "m."

Picture	*Meaning*
M	Single-digit number for January through September (1–9); double-digit number for October through December (10–12)
MM	Double-digit number; January through September include a leading zero (01–09)
MMM	Three-letter abbreviation of month name (Jan–Dec)
MMMM	Full month name (January–December)

Day

A day is represented by an uppercase or a lowercase letter "d."

Picture	*Meaning*
d	Single-digit number for the first nine days of each month (1–9); double-digit number for the remaining days (10–31)
dd	Double-digit number; the first nine days of the month include a leading zero (01–09)
ddd	Three-letter abbreviation of the day of the week (Mon–Sun)
dddd	Full name of the day of the week (Monday–Sunday)

Year

A year is represented by an uppercase or a lowercase letter "y."

Picture	*Meaning*
yy	Last two digits of the year; the first 10 years of a century include a leading zero (00–09, 10–99)
yyyy	Full year number (1900–2032)

Hours

Hours are represented by an uppercase or a lowercase letter "h." An uppercase "H" represents a 24-hour clock. A lowercase "h" represents a 12-hour clock.

Picture	*Meaning*
h	12-hour clock; single-digit numbers for one o'clock through nine o'clock (1–9); double-digit numbers for the remaining hours (10–12)
hh	12-hour clock; double-digit numbers; the first nine hours include a leading zero (01–09)
H	24-hour clock; single-digit numbers for midnight through nine in the morning (0–9); double-digit numbers for the remaining hours in the day (10–23)
HH	24-hour clock; double-digit numbers; the hours for midnight through nine in the morning include a leading zero (00–09)

Minutes

Minutes are represented by the lowercase letter "m." The "m" must be lowercase to distinguish minutes from months, which use an uppercase "M."

Picture	*Meaning*
m	Single-digit numbers for the first 10 minutes of each hour (0–9); double-digit numbers for the remaining minutes in the hour (10–59)
mm	Double-digit numbers; the first 10 minutes of each hour include a leading zero (00–09)

AM/PM

The morning and afternoon hours of a 12-hour clock can be represented by the designation you set in your Windows Control Panel. In all of the following examples, substitute the designation you have set for the am/pm model. Word uses uppercase and lowercase in the result as you type it in the picture.

Picture	*Meaning*
a/p	Word uses "a" for morning hours and "p" for afternoon hours.
am/pm	Word uses "am" for morning hours and "pm" for afternoon hours.
A/P	Word uses "A" for morning hours and "P" for afternoon hours.
AM/PM	Word uses "AM" for morning hours and "PM" for afternoon hours.

'Text'

A date-and-time picture can also include text. Enclose the text in single quotation marks (').

Picture	*Result*
{date \@ "'Today is 'MMMM d, yyyy"}	Today is January 8, 1990

`Sequence identifier`

To include a sequence number as part of the date-and-time picture, enclose the sequence identifier in single back quotation marks (`). The sequence identifier will provide for the field's result the number of the nearest preceding SEQ field that has the same sequence identifier.

Picture	*Result*
{time \@"'Finisher '`fin_pos` ' finished at 'h:mm"}	Finisher 8 finished at 2:39

In a sheet of race results, the finishing position number could be generated by a SEQ field elsewhere in the document that included the identifier fin_pos. This TIME field can be updated at the moment the racer finishes. Note that the SEQ field can generate the finishing position number by using a sequence identifier (fin_pos). For information about how to use the bookmark-name option with a SEQ field, see "Numbering Fields: Pages, Sequences, Items, and Outlines" later in this appendix.

TIP

Default Time and Date Format Ahead of Time

The PRINTDATE and SAVEDATE fields depend for their results on printing or saving taking place first. The PRINTDATE field produces its result after you print the document at least one time, and the SAVEDATE field produces its result after you save the document at least one time. Until you print or save the document the first time, the field produces no print date or save date and instead substitutes the letter "X" for text and the number "0" (zero) for numbers as the field's result. For example, suppose you create the following field:

{printdate \@"ddd MMM-d-yy H:mm"}

The first time you print the document, Word displays the following as the field's result:

XXX XXX-0-00 0:00

After you print the document the first time, the date looks like the following:

Sun Dec-24-89 15:03

Other characters

You can include any other single characters without enclosing them in the single quotation marks that you need for text. For example, Word lets you include colons in time pictures and commas in date pictures.

Picture	*Result*
{date \@ "dddd, MMMM d, yyyy, h:mm AM/PM"}	Saturday, November 11, 1989, 11:11 AM

All commas and colons appear in the result. If you use hyphens or slashes (/) in the picture, these also appear in the result. Also notice that by applying small-capitals character formatting to the AM/PM part of the picture, you cause AM to appear in the result in small capital letters.

Fill-in and Glossary Fields

The FILLIN and GLOSSARY fields provide two ways to insert specific text. The FILLIN field prompts for the text that's appropriate to insert. The GLOSSARY field allows you to reuse the contents of a glossary entry at a specific position in a document. GLOSSARY fields are especially useful when inserted in a document template.

The Fill-in Field

The FILLIN field displays a dialog box that contains prompt text, a text box in which you type the text for the result, and OK and Cancel buttons. The result of the FILLIN field is the text that's typed in the dialog box. When you update this field, the field's last result appears in the dialog box as the proposed response. For example, suppose you inserted a FILLIN field such as the following:

```
{fillin "Type the name of the addressee for the letter"}
```

When you update this FILLIN field, you see the following dialog box:

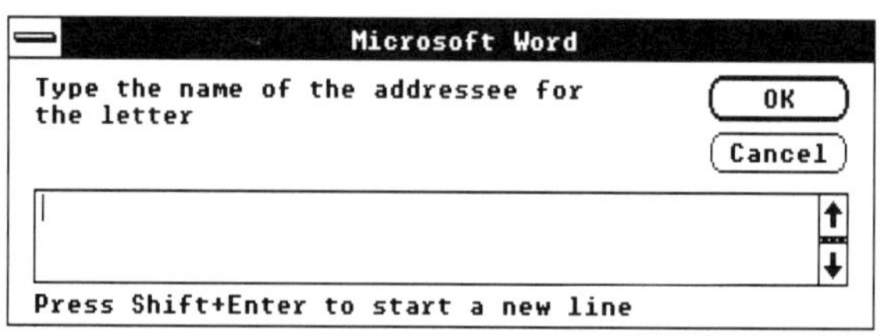

If you type *Elayla Surely*, that text is the field's result. The next time you update this FILLIN field, the dialog box looks like the following:

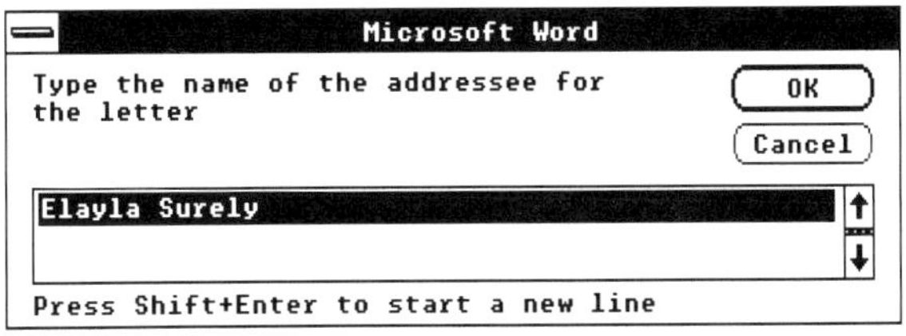

The FILLIN field has a field-specific switch, \d, which stands for "default." The default switch is followed by text that's enclosed in quotation marks. The text that follows the default switch is the proposed response that Word will display in the text box each time you update the field. For example, suppose you insert the following FILLIN field:

{fillin "Type the initials of the letter's author followed by a colon and your initials" \d "RE:ll"}

Every time you update this FILLIN field, you see the following dialog box, regardless of what you last typed as a response:

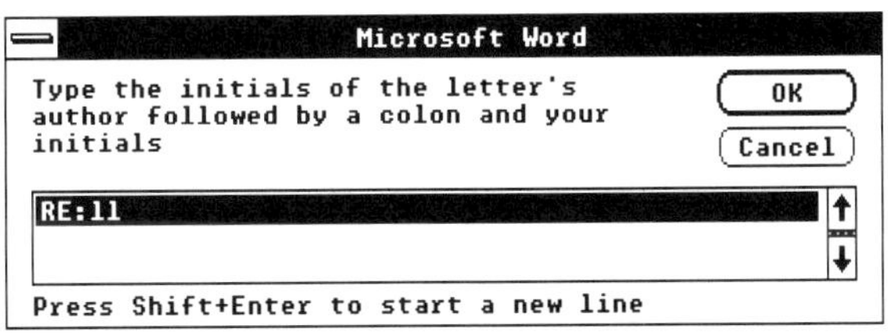

If you choose OK without editing the proposed response, the result of the field is the default response—RE:ll. If you insert the \d switch with an empty pair of quotation marks (\d ""), the text box is blank every time you update the FILLIN field.

You can also leave the text box blank or delete the proposed response to make the text box blank. A blank text box tells Word that the field has no result. For this reason, the FILLIN field can act as a manual conditional field, allowing you to decide whether you need the information in the document and to respond accordingly in the dialog box.

If you use the FILLIN field during merge printing, you can add the \o switch to tell Word that you want the field updated only one time during merge printing. That way you see the dialog box one time, type in the text box, choose OK, and then merge printing proceeds without further intervention. See the description of the ASK field under "Setting Up Bookmarks Using Fields" later in this appendix for an example of the \o switch.

The Glossary Field

The GLOSSARY field uses as its result the contents of the glossary entry you specify. For example, suppose you have a glossary entry named TRC that contains the following text and graphic:

Figure A-1.
Contents of TRC glossary entry.

You could insert the following GLOSSARY field:

{glossary TRC}

When you update the above field, you see the text and graphics shown in Figure A-1. If you later change the contents of the TRC glossary entry, you update this GLOSSARY field to insert the new contents in your document as the field's result.

Numbering Fields: Pages, Sequences, Items, and Outlines

You insert numbers for items and elements in a Word document—particularly for automatic numbers—using the PAGE, AUTONUM, AUTONUMLGL, AUTONUMOUT, and SEQ fields. The table on the next page describes what each of these fields does.

Field Name	*Inserts*
PAGE	Page numbers
AUTONUM	Sequential Arabic numbers
AUTONUMLGL	Legal numbers
AUTONUMOUT	Outline numbers
SEQ	Sequential numbers for items in lists, and cross-references to numbered items

Page Numbers

The result of the PAGE field is the number of the page on which Word prints the field. The page numbers appear by default in Arabic format. To change the format of the page number, select a page-number format in the Edit Header/Footer dialog box or add a formatting switch to the PAGE field. For example, to format page numbers as lowercase Roman numerals, insert a field such as the following:

```
{page \* roman}
```

The "* roman" switch has an uppercase counterpart, * Roman, which formats numbers as uppercase Roman numerals. For descriptions of all the formatting switches that you can use to modify the page-number format, see "General Switches" later in this appendix.

If you want page numbers that include the chapter number, insert SEQ fields in front of the chapter titles for the chapter numbers. Then, insert a SEQ field that contains a \c switch in front of the PAGE field, as shown in the example below:

```
{seq chapter \c}-{page}
```

In the above example, the \c switch in the SEQ field generates the current chapter number. In addition, if you want the chapter number to appear in uppercase Roman numeral format, add the "* Roman" formatting switch, as shown below:

```
{seq chapter \c \* Roman}-{page}
```

Automatic Numbering

Word contains fields that automatically number items in one of three different formats: Arabic sequence (AUTONUM), legal numbering (AUTONUMLGL), and outline numbering (AUTONUMOUT).

Automatically numbered items (Arabic sequence)

To number items using Arabic numbers and to let Word update the numbers automatically, insert the following field:

{autonum}

The result of this field is an Arabic number. When you number paragraphs using the AUTONUM field, Word counts all AUTONUM fields (from the nearest preceding paragraph) to which you've applied a heading 1 through heading 9 style. To omit a paragraph from the numbering sequence, omit (or remove) the AUTONUM field from that paragraph. For example, if you have four paragraphs, one of which should not have a number, insert AUTONUM fields as shown in the following example:

{autonum} Prepare the soil with deep cultivation. Cultivate the plot several times in various directions—for example, lengthwise, crosswise, and diagonally. Add fertilizer after the first cultivation pass so that it is worked in thoroughly.

Working fertilizer into the soil thoroughly provides several benefits. First, the fertilizer is spread evenly throughout the plot, which prevents "hot spots." Second, the fertilizer is spread deeply into the soil, which helps the plants send down long roots. A deep, strong root system can provide a better supply of nutrients to the plant. Third, you avoid the strong scent of fertilizer around the garden because it is masked by the smell of the soil. The aroma will be earthy but healthy and natural.

{autonum} Map out the beds for planting. Plan to plant taller plants on the side of the garden plot that is farthest from the sun, usually the northern side of the garden. Also, plant the tall plants toward the eastern side of the plot. Plant the lowest-growing plants at the southern and western sides of the plot.

{autonum} Plant vegetables in dense beds that are about six feet wide. You should be able to reach the middle of each bed from the walkway beside it. A few plants need more space, such as maize and squash. Seed these plants according to the directions on the package.

When you switch these AUTONUM fields to show their results, you see Arabic numbers as in the example on the following page.

1. Prepare the soil with deep cultivation. Cultivate the plot several times in various directions—for example, lengthwise, crosswise, and diagonally. Add fertilizer after the first cultivation pass so that it is worked in thoroughly.

   Working fertilizer into the soil thoroughly provides several benefits. First, the fertilizer is spread evenly throughout the plot, which prevents "hot spots." Second, the fertilizer is spread deeply into the soil, which helps the plants send down long roots. A deep, strong root system can provide a better supply of nutrients to the plant. Third, you avoid the strong scent of fertilizer around the garden because it is masked by the smell of the soil. The aroma will be earthy but healthy and natural.

2. Map out the beds for planting. Plan to plant taller plants on the side of the garden plot that is farthest from the sun, usually the northern side of the garden. Also, plant the tall plants toward the eastern side of the plot. Plant the lowest-growing plants at the southern and western sides of the plot.

3. Plant vegetables in dense beds that are about six feet wide. You should be able to reach the middle of each bed from the walkway beside it. A few plants need more space, such as maize and squash. Seed these plants according to the directions on the package.

The next example shows how automatically numbered items restart their numbering following a heading:

1. Heading Level 1
1. Body text paragraph
2. Body text paragraph
3. Body text paragraph

2. Heading Level 1
1. Body text paragraph
2. Body text paragraph
3. Body text paragraph
4. Body text paragraph

Automatic legal numbering

Legal and government documents often number paragraphs in hierarchical style, with each paragraph's number preceded by the numbers of all the superior levels. To use automatic legal numbering, insert the following field:

{autonumlgl}

The result for the second paragraph below a fifth-level heading (a paragraph to which the heading 5 style has been applied) is 1.1.1.1.1.2. The sequence of headings leading up to this number appears as shown on the following page.

{autonumlgl} Heading Level 1

{autonumlgl} Heading Level 2

{autonumlgl} Heading Level 3

{autonumlgl} Heading Level 4

{autonumlgl} Heading Level 5

{autonumlgl} Body text paragraph

{autonumlgl} Body text paragraph

1. Heading Level 1

1.1. Heading Level 2

1.1.1. Heading Level 3

1.1.1.1. Heading Level 4

1.1.1.1.1. Heading Level 5

1.1.1.1.1.1. Body text paragraph

1.1.1.1.1.2. Body text paragraph

Automatic outline numbering

Word lets you use the AUTONUMOUT field to insert automatic outline numbers for nine levels:

{autonumout}

The result of the AUTONUMOUT field for the nine levels is I.A.1.a)(1)(a)(i)(a)(i). The AUTONUMOUT fields for all paragraphs with the heading 1 style display the form for level 1, which is I. Each level in turn displays its own form. Body text always shows an automatic number in Arabic format. The following shows the field and result for nine levels and body text:

{autonumout} Heading Level 1

{autonumout} Heading Level 2

{autonumout} Heading Level 3

{autonumout} Heading Level 4

{autonumout} Heading Level 5

{autonumout} Heading Level 6

{ autonumout } Heading Level 7

{ autonumout } Heading Level 8

{ autonumout } Heading Level 9

{autonumout} Body text

I. Heading Level 1
A. Heading Level 2
1. Heading Level 3
a) Heading Level 4
(1) Heading Level 5
(a) Heading Level 6
(i) *Heading Level 7*
(a) *Heading Level 8*
(i) *Heading Level 9*
1. Body text

Numbers are displayed in the character-formatting style that's applied to the paragraph in which the automatic outline number appears.

Sequential Numbers

A sequence in Word is a numbered list of items. You can use SEQ fields to number various kinds of lists within a document and to refer to those numbers. The advantage of using SEQ fields instead of typing the numbers is that when you move, add, or delete items, Word updates the numbers for you. In addition, Word lets you intersperse sequences of chapter numbers, table numbers, illustration numbers, and chart numbers throughout a document. Then you can set up cross-references to a sequence number for a specific item in any of these sequences.

You can also use the SEQ field to number paragraphs in relation to a document's outline—that is, in relation to paragraphs to which you've assigned heading 1 through heading 9 styles. The following examples illustrate the various ways in which you might use SEQ fields.

Series of items

Word allows you to insert numbers for various series of items in a document. You identify each series with a name—for example, "photos." Each series is numbered independently of the others. As a result, Word allows separate sequences of photos, illustrations, charts, tables, and graphics. When you use the SEQ field to number a series of items, its syntax is as follows:

{seq *identifier*}

The *identifier* is the name you assign to the series. It must start with a letter; contain only letters, numbers, and underscores; and include 20 or fewer characters. Be sure not to start an identifier with a number because numbers indicate heading level styles.

Example	*Result*
Plate {seq pict}. Early cartoons by Picasso.	Plate 23. Early cartoons by Picasso.

The result shown in the above example assumes that in the document you've included 22 {seq pict} fields before this one. If you later want to refer to Plate 23 (or to whatever its current number is), you insert a SEQ field that contains a bookmark name after the identifier. The general syntax is shown below:

{seq *identifier bookmark*}

For Plate 23, you would insert a bookmark with a descriptive name such as "pic_ec" on the SEQ field that generates the plate number. Then you would insert the following SEQ field where you want the reference to appear:

{seq pict pic_ec}

This field's result is 23 (or whatever the current number is for this plate).

Note that the bookmarks you insert on a SEQ field must begin at or after the first field character and before the beginning of the next SEQ field that has the same identifier. A SEQ field with a bookmark name uses the sequence number at the first character of the text marked by the bookmark.

Paragraph numbering

To refer to automatic paragraph numbers, insert a number as the sequence identifier in a SEQ field, as the following shows:

{seq *number*}

The number can be any digit from 0 through 9. Use numbers 1 through 9 for paragraphs to which you've applied the corresponding heading 1 through heading 9 styles. Use 0 (zero) for paragraphs to which you've applied other styles. The paragraph referred to must contain an AUTONUM, AUTONUMLGL, or AUTONUMOUT field.

Example	*Result*
{seq 1}. Conclusions	5. Conclusions

The preceding example is based on the assumption that four other paragraphs come before this one. These paragraphs have the heading 1 style and an AUTONUM, AUTONUMLGL, or AUTONUMOUT field to generate the paragraph numbers.

Cross-references by item number

The SEQ field can refer to an item by number, even if the item is far away in the document. If the item is the nearest one preceding the SEQ field, you use one form of the SEQ field. If the item is far away from the reference, you use another form. For references that follow a SEQ field but precede any other SEQ fields, use the form of SEQ field shown below:

{seq *identifier* \c}

The *identifier*, as shown in the examples below, is the name you assigned to the series, or a number from 1 through 9. The \c switch (which stands for "current") tells Word that you want the result to be the number of the nearest preceding SEQ field that has the specified identifier.

Example	*Result*
As we saw in Table {seq table \c}, this year's earnings are disappointing.	As we saw in Table 3, this year's earnings are disappointing.
As described earlier in this section (Section {seq 2 \c}), selling requires extraordinary effort.	As described earlier in this section (Section 14), selling requires extraordinary effort.

The first of the above examples is based on the assumption that the preceding table in the document is the third one in a series of tables that include {seq table} fields. The second example is based on the assumption that the current section is number 14, as created by the fourteenth paragraph with the heading 2 style and the matching AUTONUM, AUTONUMLGL, or AUTONUMOUT field.

If the sequence item to which you want to refer is far away and another sequence item intervenes between the one you want to refer to and the point at which you want to insert a reference, use the *bookmark* form of the SEQ field, as the following shows:

{seq *identifier bookmark*}

Again, the *identifier* is the name you assigned to the series, or a number from 1 through 9. You must insert a bookmark at the item to which you want to refer. The result of this field is the result of the SEQ field that has the same identifier at or preceding the first character of the bookmark. Word searches from the beginning of the bookmark toward the beginning of the document until it finds a SEQ field that has the corresponding identifier. If Word does not find a SEQ field between the beginning of the bookmark and the beginning of the document, the result of the SEQ field is zero. When you use a bookmark name in a SEQ field, Word ignores any SEQ field-specific switches (\c, \r, or \n) that you insert in that field.

Example	*Result*
Chart {seq chart qtr1_reg_sales} shows First Quarter sales by region.	Chart 19 shows First Quarter sales by region.
See Section {seq 3 sect_10} for details.	See Section 10 for details.

The first of the two examples above is based on the assumption that the number for the chart is followed by the bookmark name "qtr1_reg_sales" and is generated by the nineteenth {seq chart} field in the document. The second example is based on the assumption that the section number is generated by the tenth paragraph in the document that has the heading 3 style applied to it and contains an AUTONUM, AUTONUMLGL, or AUTONUMOUT field. Also, this example assumes that the section number is marked by the bookmark "sect_10."

The SEQ field also provides a means to restart a numbering sequence. You can restart the numbering for illustrations, for example, at the beginning of each chapter. To reset a numbering sequence, use the following form of the SEQ field:

{seq *identifier* \r *number*}

Again, the *identifier* is the name you assigned to the series, or a number from 1 through 9. The \r switch tells Word that you want the result to be the number you insert after the \r switch and that you also want the result of the next SEQ field that has the same identifier to follow this number in the sequence.

Example	*Result*
See Plate {seq pict \r 8} for an artist's rendering of the new distribution center.	See Plate 8 for an artist's rendering of the new distribution center.
Section {seq 3 \r 1}: Troubleshooting	Section 1: Troubleshooting

Use the above field to restart numbering for a sequence of items anywhere in your document. Be aware that Word restarts numbering subsequent SEQ fields that have the same identifier from a SEQ field with an \r switch. For example, the result of the the next {seq pict} field after the one in the first of the above examples will be 9. To change this field's result, change the number that follows the \r switch.

Reference Fields: Text, Page Numbers, Styles, and Footnotes

Word provides several fields for inserting cross-references in a document. The REF field provides textual cross-references. You use the PAGEREF field to cross-reference page numbers. The STYLEREF field allows you to cross-reference headings. And the FTNREF field provides cross-references to footnotes.

Textual Cross-References

When you want to cross-reference title text (or any other text), use the REF field. This field refers to bookmarks within a single file.

{ref *bookmark*} or {*bookmark*}

The result of this field is the full text that's marked by the bookmark whose name you insert in the field. For example, if a report has a topic named "Current Budget Plans" marked with a bookmark named "CBP," you could insert a cross-reference such as the following:

See "{ref CBP}" for the amount allocated for R&D.

The result of the above cross-reference would be the following:

See "Current Budget Plans" for the amount allocated for R&D.

The advantage of using a REF field is that if the title changes, you need only to update fields instead of having to find all your cross-references and correct them.

Word lets you omit the REF part of the field and include only the bookmark name as long as the bookmark name is not the same as that of another field type. For example, if you have a bookmark named "subject," you need to insert a {ref subject} field to produce a result that shows the text of the bookmark rather than the text of the Subject box in the Edit Summary Info dialog box.

Page-Number Cross-References

When you want to cross-reference the number of a page on which a topic (or any other text) starts, use the PAGEREF field. This field refers to a bookmark within a single file.

{pageref *bookmark*}

The result of this field is the number of the page on which the first character that's marked by the bookmark whose name you insert appears. This field offers the same advantages as does the REF field. And PAGEREF is particularly useful in a document in which the page breaks change each time you print. Word updates this field during printing.

TIP

Page-Number References to Other Files

Word does not offer a field that will give you page-number cross-references when you've divided a document into several files. But, if you're willing to try a work-around, you can produce such references with little extra effort.

To start, insert a PAGE field next to the topic you want to cross-reference. Next, insert a bookmark on the PAGE field and then format the field as hidden text. The PAGE field updates during printing. Also insert a bookmark on the text you want to cross-reference.

In the document in which you want to insert the text and page-number cross-reference, insert an INCLUDE field such as the following:

{include *file bookmark* * charformat \!}

You can type a pathname as part of *file*. The \! switch is important. It tells Word not to update the field when importing it. Rather, you get the field's current result from the source file.

References by Style

The STYLEREF field lets you copy the text of paragraphs to which a particular style has been applied. One use of STYLEREF is to set up automatic dictionary-style headers. See Chapter 9, "Fields II: Creating Special Effects," for a description and an example of this use.

{styleref *style-name*}
{styleref *number*}

The results of the above fields are the text (with a maximum of the first 255 characters) up to but not including the paragraph mark of the "nearest" paragraph to which the *style-name* or the heading style of the specified *number* has been applied. The definition of "nearest" depends on where you insert the STYLEREF field. The following table lists the definitions of "nearest" that are associated with the various places in which you can insert the *styleref* field:

Field Position	*Definition of "Nearest"*
In text	From the position of the field, Word uses the nearest preceding paragraph that has the specified style. If no such paragraph precedes the field, Word uses the nearest following paragraph that has the specified style.
In footnotes and annotations	From the position of the footnote reference mark or the annotation reference mark, Word uses the nearest preceding paragraph that has the specified style. If no such paragraph precedes the field, Word uses the nearest following paragraph that has the specified style.
In headers and footers when printing	Word uses the first paragraph that has the specified style on the page on which the field is printed. If no paragraph on the page has the specified style, Word uses the nearest paragraph on the preceding pages back to the beginning of the document. If Word still cannot find a paragraph that has the specified style, Word uses the nearest paragraph on the pages following the current page, up to the end of the document.
In headers and footers when not printing	Word uses the first paragraph with the specified style in the section of the document that contains the STYLEREF field. If the specified style has not been applied to any paragraph in the current section, Word uses the nearest paragraph that has the specified style on the pages following the current section, up to the end of the document.

The STYLEREF field has one field-specific switch, the \l switch, which means "last."

{styleref *style-name* \l}
{styleref *number* \l}

The \l switch affects only STYLEREF fields that you insert in headers and footers. Elsewhere in a document, the {styleref} and {styleref\l} fields produce that same result. When you add the \l switch to a STYLEREF field, the result of the field is taken from the last paragraph on the current page. If the specified style has not been applied to any paragraph on the current page, Word uses the nearest paragraph on the pages following the current page, up to the end of the document.

Footnote References

The field below displays the number of the automatic footnote reference that's marked exactly by the bookmark:

{ftnref *bookmark*}

This field is useful for giving two footnote references the same number. Their numbers are kept synchronized regardless of the final position in the document and the number of the footnote reference mark to which the FTNREF refers. This field can also be useful for cross-referencing another footnote. The FTNREF field is also updated during printing.

In the table on the next page, the first example is based on the assumption that the bookmark name "masonry" has been inserted on the automatic footnote reference mark "4" because the footnote text applies to both sentences. If you moved the footnote reference mark "4" to before an earlier automatic footnote reference mark or to after a later one, the FTNREF field would result in the new number when the field was updated. You must format the FTNREF field yourself to give it the same format as an automatic footnote reference mark.

The second of the two examples on the next page is based on the assumption that you have inserted the bookmark name "Aber" on the automatic footnote reference mark that is currently number 8. The only difference from the first example is the form of presentation.

Example	*Result*
In his early years, Thomas Hardy studied architecture.[4] In his last novel, *Jude the Obscure,* the main character desires to study architecture but ends up as a lowly stonemason. {ftnref masonry}	In his early years, Thomas Hardy studied architecture.[4] In his last novel, *Jude the Obscure,* the main character desires to study architecture but ends up as a lowly stonemason.[4]
For an alternative explanation of these data, compare the theories of Abercrombie (see note {ftnref Aber}).	For an alternative explanation of these data, compare the theories of Abercrombie (see note 8).

Setting Up Bookmarks Using Fields

Bookmarks are used with a wide variety of fields as well as with the Edit Go To command and the GOTO key (F5). To insert a bookmark, you generally use the Insert Bookmark command or the BOOKMARK key combination (Ctrl+Shift+F5). You can, however, use fields to set up bookmarks. Unlike bookmarks that you insert using the command or the key combination, bookmarks that you set using the ASK and SET fields are not inserted on a text selection. Rather, bookmarks that you set using these fields are kept inside Word's memory without a corresponding selection in the document.

Most often, you use the ASK and SET fields during merge printing. (For information about using ASK and SET during merge printing, see Chapter 15, "Merge Printing.") You can, however, use these two fields at any time in any document. The ASK field prompts you to provide the contents for a bookmark. The SET field does not prompt you. Both fields show no result in the document. Typically, the contents of the bookmarks you set using these two fields will be used for the results of other fields that refer to bookmarks, such as REF fields.

The Ask Field

The field below sets a bookmark on the text that you type in response to the *prompt-text*:

{ask *bookmark "prompt-text"*}

When you update this field, a dialog box appears to display the *prompt-text* and to give you a text box in which to type the bookmark text. The ASK field is useful for setting a bookmark during merge printing. The dialog box appears for each document that Word prints.

{ask *bookmark "prompt-text"* \o}

This form of the ASK field displays its dialog box only while printing the first document during merge printing. Word uses the text you type in the text box for all the documents it prints. You can also insert a \d switch followed by text that's enclosed in quotation marks. The text that follows the \d switch is the default proposed response in the text box each time you update the field. If you insert the \d switch with an empty pair of quotation marks (\d ""), the text box is blank every time you update the ASK field. See the description of the FILLIN field under "Fill-in and Glossary Fields" earlier in this appendix for examples of the \d switch. This form of the ASK field is like the SET field, with one exception: The ASK field displays the dialog box to ask you for the bookmark text.

The Set Field

The field below sets the bookmark on the text you insert in the field:

{set *bookmark "text"*}

This field does not display a dialog box, so the SET field has no field-specific switches. The only way to change the text for the bookmark is to toggle the field display so that its codes show and then edit the text.

Tables of Contents, Lists, and Indexes

Word can collect several kinds of lists: tables of contents; lists of tables, photographs, graphics, graphs, or lists; and indexes. Word provides fields for collecting these lists and fields for identifying the items that you want collected into the lists. For tables of contents and lists of items, you use the TOC field to collect the list items and the TC field to identify the items to be collected. For indexes, you use the INDEX field to collect index items marked by XE fields.

Table of Contents

You collect a table of contents from heading styles or from TC fields.

In the Insert Table of Contents dialog box, choose the Use Heading Paragraphs option to collect the table of contents from headings. The Use Table Entry Fields option in the dialog box collects the table of contents from TC fields that have either no \f switch or an \f switch with a following "c." Word also lets you use the Insert Field command or the INSERT FIELD key combination (Ctrl+F9) to insert a TOC field for collecting a table of contents. Word applies styles toc 1 through toc 8 to the levels of the table of contents.

Standard table of contents from headings

The following forms of the TOC field collect a table of contents from paragraphs to which heading 1 through heading 9 styles have been assigned:

{toc}
{toc \o}
{toc \o *level-level*}

The {toc \o} form of the TOC field is the same form that the Insert Table of Contents command inserts when you choose the Use Heading Paragraphs option in the Insert Table of Contents dialog box. The \o switch tells Word to use the outline, which is the same as using the heading styles. The {toc} form is equivalent to {toc \o} because collecting the table of contents from the outline heading is the default.

When you collect a table of contents from heading styles, you can specify either in the Insert Table of Contents dialog box or by including a switch in the TOC field that Word collect only specific levels of the document outline. The {toc \o *level-level*} form of the TOC field limits the table of contents to paragraphs with a heading style that's in the specified range. If you want a table of contents collected from only those paragraphs with heading 1 and heading 2 styles, you insert the following form of the TOC field:

{toc \o 1-2}

As described in the upcoming section "Other Types of Lists," you can use a variation of this form of the TOC field to collect other types of lists in addition to tables of contents.

Standard table of contents from TC fields

The following two forms of the TOC field collect a table of contents from TC fields:

{toc \f} or {toc \f c}

The {toc \ f} form of the TOC field is the same field that the Insert Table of Contents command inserts when you choose the Use Table Entry Fields option in the Insert Table of Contents dialog box. The \ f switch tells Word to use fields. By default, the "c" means table of contents. Other letters can have other meanings, as the following section explains. If you use the Insert Table of Contents command and choose the Use Table Entry Fields option, Word collects all TC fields except those that include the \ f switch followed by a letter other than "c."

Table of Contents Entries

You can insert TC fields instead of using the heading styles. This method is useful when your document has few if any headings but you want to create a table of contents. This method is also useful if you want to collect such lists as a list of illustrations, a table of tables, or a table of photos. These fields do not show a result.

Regular table of contents entry

The form of the TC field shown below provides text for a table of contents entry:

{tc "*text*"}

If the text includes more than one word, it must be enclosed in quotation marks—otherwise, you may omit the quotation marks. Entries in this form will have the highest level in the table of contents.

Other list entry

The following form of the TC field provides text and identification for a list other than a table of contents:

{tc "*text*" \f *character*}

The *character* can be any single letter. Avoid using "c," however, because Word sees "c" as the signal for a table of contents. If you use the Insert Table of Contents command and choose the Use Table Entry

Fields option in the Insert Table of Contents dialog box, Word collects all fields that include no \f switch, or the \f switch followed by a "c." To use the forms of the TOC field that collect other types of lists from TC fields with the \f *character* switch, insert a TOC field using either the Insert Field command or the INSERT FIELD key combination (Ctrl+F9). The following table provides examples of the forms of the TC field you can use for various list entries. Word lets you use any identifying *character* you want in place of the suggested character shown:

Type of List	*Sample Form of TC Field*
Illustrations	{tc \f i "*text*"}
Charts	{tc \f g "*text*"}
Photographs	{tc \f p "*text*"}
Tables	{tc \f t "*text*"}
Lists	{tc \f l "*text*"}

Note that the only code difference among all the above fields is the character that follows the \f switch. Of course, the *text* for each field—even fields with the same character following the \f switch—is different, as appropriate for the entry in the collected list of entries.

Specifying level of entry

The form of the TC field shown below provides text and specifies the level of the entry in a table of contents:

{tc "*text*" \l *number*}

This form is useful if you are not using headings or if you are collecting another type of list and want to organize the list entries as major and minor entries. The *number* after the \l switch specifies which level you want this entry to have; the choices are 1 through 8. You can, of course, combine the \l switch with the \f switch to provide subordination in lists other than tables of contents—for example:

{tc "*text*" \f g \l *number*}

Other Types of Lists

To create other types of lists such as lists of illustrations, charts, or photos, you can use a specific heading style for the items and collect them using the {toc \o *level-level*} form of the TOC field. Word also lets you add an \f switch to the TOC field and then follow the switch with an identifying letter, as shown in the table on the preceding page.

{toc \f *letter*}

Before you can collect the list, you must insert TC fields to identify the list entries. These TC fields must contain an \f switch and the same following letter that you insert in the TOC field.

Limiting a table to part of a document

In the following example, the *bookmark* is set on the part of the document for which you want to collect a table of contents:

{toc \b *bookmark*}

For example, if you want to create a table of contents for a chapter in a book (for example, Chapter 10), select the chapter and insert a bookmark (for example, Ch_10). Then, at the beginning of the chapter, insert a field such as the following where you want to include the chapter table of contents:

{toc \b Ch_10}

You still need to format the entries using either TC fields or a heading style. If you use TC fields, add the \f switch to the example field—for example, {toc \f \b Ch_10}. If you use heading styles, you might want to specify the heading levels to collect—for example:

{toc \o 3-4 \b Ch_10}

As another alternative, you could designate one identifying letter for each portion of a document—"a" for the first portion, "b" for the second portion, and so on. You could insert the {tc \f *letter "text"*} form of the TC field within each portion. For example, in the first ("a") section, you could insert a field in the following form:

{tc \f a "*text*"}

In each subsequent section, you could change the letter that follows the \f switch. At the beginning of each section, insert a TOC field such as the following, which is an example for section "a":

{toc \f a }

This method eliminates the need to set bookmarks but might take slightly longer to collect the table of contents. The process is slower because Word searches the entire document instead of only one portion.

Lists with chapter-page numbers

If your document contains chapter-page numbers (for example, 4-1, 4-2, 4-3, and so on) and you want the page numbers to appear in that format in the table of contents, insert a TOC field such as the following where you want the table of contents to appear in the document:

{toc \s *sequence-name*}

To make this field generate chapter-page numbers, format each chapter as a separate section and set page numbering to start at 1 in the Edit Header/Footer dialog box. Start each chapter with a SEQ field that uses the same identifier—for example, "chapter":

{seq chapter}

Then, insert the TOC field as shown below:

{toc \s chapter}

The chapter sequence numbers will be in effect for the page where the table of contents entry appears. A heading such as "Sick leave" on page 4-23 in Chapter 4, therefore, would appear in the table of contents as follows:

Sick leave. 4-23

Word also lets you use the \s switch with all the forms of the \f switch, should you want a list of tables, a list of illustrations, or any other such list to show chapter-page numbers.

Separating chapter and page numbers in a table of contents. The default separator character between the sequence number and the page number is a hyphen, as shown on the following page. You can set this separator to any characters (up to three) that you want. The \d switch has an effect only if you also use the \s switch.

{toc \s *sequence-name* \d "*1-3 characters*"}

The above form of the TOC field changes the hyphen to the characters you insert after the \d switch. For example, if you insert "c_p" after the \d switch, the TOC field shown above would appear as follows:

{toc \s chapter \d "c_p"}

The result would appear in the table of contents as shown below:

Sick leave . . . . 4c_p23

Index

Word collects the entries for an index from XE fields. The Insert Index command, which you can use to insert an index, gives you a number of options: a normal index vs. a run-in index plus three choices for separating the index's letter sections from each other. A letter section consists of all the main-level entries that begin with a specific letter.

Standard index

The form of the INDEX field shown in the example below collects a standard (normal) index:

{index}

All of the main-level entries are flush with the left margin, and each subentry is indented one-quarter inch from the next higher level, as shown in the example below:

Birds
  chickadees, 27
  hawks
    black, 49
    red-tailed, 79

The formatting for the index entries derives from the index 1 through index 7 styles, which Word applies for you after collecting an index.

Run-in index

Word lets you opt for subentries that appear on the same line as their main entry rather than on separate lines. The following form of the INDEX field creates a run-in index:

{index \r}

If an entry is longer than one line, Word wraps the remainder of the entry's text to a new line. A colon separates a main entry in the index from all its subentries. Semicolons separate subentries from each other. The example for the preceding standard index would look like the following as a run-in index entry:

Birds: chickadees, 27; hawks; black, 49; red-tailed, 79

The value of a run-in index diminishes when the index contains more than two levels of entries because it's difficult to distinguish among the subentry levels.

Separating letter sections of the index

When Word sets up an index, the letter sections run together; the last entry beginning with A and the first entry beginning with B are not separated. This lack of separation can make it difficult to see where one letter section ends and the next begins. In the Insert Index dialog box, you have three choices: no separation between letter sections, a blank line, and the letter of the section. (For example, a "B" appears before the first entry that begins with the letter B.) Choosing one of these options in the Insert Index dialog box inserts one of the following forms of the INDEX field:

Option	*Field*
None	{index} {index \h ""} (Using quotation marks with no space between them is the same as having no \h switch in the field.)
Blank Line	{index \h " "} (Notice the space between the quotation marks. If this space appears by itself, Word leaves a blank line. If the space appears with any other characters within the quotation marks, Word treats the space as a regular space instead of as an instruction to leave a blank line.)
Letter	{index \h "A"}

Word lets you insert these fields yourself and use the \h switch to set up any kind of separation you want between the letter sections:

{index \h "*characters*"}

The *characters* can be any characters, as many as you want. If you insert a single letter or even five letters, you will see the appropriate letter combination at the beginning of each letter section. If you insert multiple copies of the same letter, multiple copies will appear. For example, suppose you insert the following INDEX field:

{index \h "AAAAA"}

Each letter section in the index will begin with five copies of the letter for that section—AAAAA, BBBBB, CCCCC, and so on. Even if you mix the letters, each letter section will use only its own letters. As a result, {index \h "wxyz"} still produces AAAA, BBBB, CCCC, and so on. You can, of course, mix letters with other characters. The field {index \h "<==>A<==>"}, for example, will insert <==>A<==>, <==>B<==>, <==>C<==>, and so on. If you want both a blank line and a letter, set up the INDEX field as shown below:

{index \h "¶
A"}

The first character after the initial quotation mark is a paragraph mark.

Limiting the index to part of a document

Word allows you to limit an index to certain pages within a document or to certain letters. For example, the *bookmark* shown below is set on the part of the document for which an index is to be collected:

{index \b *bookmark*}

Suppose you want to create an index for only one section in a book (for example, Chapter 19). You select that section, insert a bookmark (for example, "Ch_19"), and then insert the following form of the INDEX field at the section's end:

{index \b Ch_19}

If you want to create an index that includes a very large number of index entries and your computer has only 640 KB of memory, you might run out of memory trying to collect the index. In a case such as this, you can collect only part of the index at a time by inserting a \p switch in the field that tells Word to collect only a partial index:

{index \p *letter-letter*}

The *letter* characters you insert tell Word which range of letters you want to collect. For example, insert an INDEX field like the following to collect only those index entries that start with the letters A through M:

{index \p a-m}

You would then insert a second index field for the rest of the alphabet:

{index \p n-z}

To collect index entries for one letter only, make both characters the same letter:

{index \p l-l}

Unless your index includes more entries than you can collect in the amount of memory available in your computer or you need to index by letters or ranges for some other reason, you probably will not use this form of the INDEX field.

Index with chapter-page numbers

If your document contains chapter-page numbers (for example, 4-1, 4-2, 4-3, and so on) and you want the page numbers to appear in that format in the index, insert the following form of the INDEX field where you want the index to appear in the document:

{index \s *sequence-name*}

To make this field generate chapter-page numbers, format each chapter as a separate section and start page numbering at 1 in the Edit Header/Footer dialog box. Start each chapter with a SEQ field that uses the same identifier—for example, "chapter":

{seq chapter}

Then, insert the INDEX field as follows:

{index \s chapter}

The chapter sequence numbers will be in effect for the page where the index entry field appears. Thus, an index entry such as "Dog breeds" on page 8-32 in Chapter 8 would appear in the index as follows:

Dog breeds, 8-32

Separating chapter and page numbers in an index. The default separator character between the sequence number and the page number is a hyphen. You can set this separator to any characters (as many as three) that you want. The \d switch has an effect only if you also use the \s switch.

{index \s *sequence-name* \d "*1-3 characters*"}

This form of the INDEX field changes the hyphen to the characters you insert after the \d switch. For example, if you insert "c_p" after the \d switch, the INDEX field shown above would appear as follows:

{index \s chapter \d "c_p"}

And the result would appear in the index as shown below:

Dog breeds, 8c_p32

Separating index text from page numbers

When setting up an index, Word uses a comma followed by a space to separate the entry text from its page numbers:

Vacation, 49

If many of the entries for your index appear on multiple pages, you might want to change the comma to another character such as a tab character, a colon, or a hyphen because the page numbers are separated by commas in the index. To change the separator character between the entry text and its page numbers, use the form of the INDEX field shown in the following example:

{index \e "*1-3 characters*"}

The separator can be any characters (up to three), including a space or a tab character. For example, {index \e "   "} separates the index text from its page numbers by three spaces.

Separating page-range numbers

If you insert an XE field that includes an \r *bookmark* switch, you will see an index entry with the page numbers for the beginning and ending of the *bookmark*. (For information about inserting an XE field that includes an \r *bookmark* switch, see the upcoming section "Page-range entry.") These entries appear in the index like the following:

Vacation, 49-54

Word lets you change the hyphen that separates the two numbers of a page range to another character such as an en dash, a colon, or an underline. You use the following form of the INDEX field:

{index \g "*1-3 characters*"}

The page-range separator can be any group of single characters (up to three), including a space or a tab character.

Separating multiple page numbers

It's not unusual for a topic to appear on several different pages in a document. If you want to index each page on which the topic appears, insert an XE field with exactly the same text for each page. When collecting the index, Word puts duplicate text entries together as one entry followed by the numbers for all of the pages on which that topic appears. Word separates these multiple page numbers with commas, as in the following:

Absences, 23,29,47

Word lets you change the comma that separates the page numbers to another character such as a semicolon, a space, or a comma followed by a space. Use the form of the INDEX field that's shown below:

{index \l "*1-3 characters*"}

The characters that separate page numbers can be any group of single characters (up to three), including a space or a tab character. For example, the field {index \1 ", "} separates page numbers with a comma followed by a space.

Index Entries

The Insert Index Entry command inserts XE fields to create index entries. If you select text before you choose the command, Word uses up to the first 64 characters of that text as the index entry text. This is the simplest method that you can use to index text that is already in the document. Using this command lets you specify whether the page numbers for a specific entry in the index should be bold or italic or both. Word also lets you select a bookmark that includes an index entry if you want the page numbers to appear as a range—for example, as 12-15.

Each of the following topics describes a different form of the XE field. Although the different forms are described separately, you can use all of these variations in the field together at the same time.

Regular entry

The following form of the XE field provides text for an index entry:

{xe "*text*"}

If the *text* is more than one word, enclose it in quotation marks.

Boldface page-number entry

The \b switch as shown below tells Word to make the page number boldface for this entry in the index:

{xe "*text*" \b}

This switch is useful when an entry includes several page numbers and you want to indicate to the reader which entry is the most important.

Italic page-number entry

The \i switch tells Word to make this index entry's page number italic:

{xe "*text*" \i}

You'll find this switch useful when you want to draw the reader's attention to a particular entry. It's also useful if you have a cross-reference entry, which often appears in italic, as the following example shows:

Cursor, *see Insertion point*

See the upcoming section "Cross-reference entry" for information about the form of the XE field that in an index results in a textual reference rather than in a page number.

Page-range entry

The form of the XE field shown below tells Word to show the first and last page numbers included in the bookmark whose name you insert after the \r switch:

{xe "*text*" \r *bookmark*}

For example, review the following:

{xe "Long-term disability" \r disable}

If the bookmark "disable" covers pages 21–27, the entry will appear in the index as follows:

Long-term disability, 21-27

Cross-reference entry

The following form of the XE field tells Word to use the *text* that follows the \t switch instead of a page number:

{xe "*text*" \t "*text*"}

As shown in the section "Italic page-number entry" on the preceding page, a cross-reference entry might look like the following:

Cursor, see Insertion point

Word lets you type any *text* you want following the \t switch. If the *text* is more than one word, be sure to enclose it in quotation marks. And if you want the cross-reference text to appear in italic, add the \i switch to the XE field:

{xe "*text*" \t "*text*" \i}

The \b switch will make the cross-reference text bold in the index. For boldface, italic, and any other character formatting of the cross-reference text, apply the formatting directly to the cross-reference text in the XE field.

Multiple-level entry

Word allows you to create multiple-level entries for an index. You type the entry text for the first level, a colon, and then the entry text for the second level. For each additional level, you type a colon and then the text. Each entry must include all of its levels or Word will not be able to collect and sort the index entries correctly.

An index entry can have up to seven levels, as shown in the following example:

{xe "*text:text:text:text:text:text:text*"}

Because the colon tells Word that the following text represents another index level, you add a backslash (\) when you want to include a colon as part of a single entry. An entry such as {xe "Chapter 1: Feeding"} would normally appear in the index as shown on the following page.

Chapter 1
  Feeding, 43

By inserting a backslash in front of the colon, you tell Word that you want the colon to appear in the index entry, and that the text following the colon is not a subentry. Thus, the revised XE field would appear as shown below:

{xe "Chapter 1\: Feeding"}

In the index, the entry would now look like the following:

Chapter 1: Feeding, 43

In the same way, insert two backslashes in a row if you want to include a backslash in an entry:

{xe "WINWORD\\DOC"}

The backslash character tells Word to treat the next character as an actual character rather than as a part of the field instructions. If you were to type only one backslash in the above example, Word would treat the character that follows as a "D," and you would not see the backslash in the index.

Creating a Table of Contents or an Index for a Document That's in Multiple Files

Use the RD field when you want to create a table of contents or an index for a multiple-file document. RD stands for "referenced document," which means that the contents of the document are referred to rather than inserted in the document that contains the RD field. Word does let you use the INCLUDE field to collect a table of contents or an index for a document that's divided into several files. But the INCLUDE field's result is the text of the document you specify in the field. If the document is large, you could be trying to create a table of contents or an index for a document that is larger than the working environment can handle. The RD field opens the files and collects the entries but does not produce a result. Thus, the RD field gives you a means to deal with memory limitations.

To use RD fields to collect a table of contents or an index, create two separate documents that contain the fields shown on the next page.

{toc}	{rd *file-name*}
{rd *file-name*}	{rd *file-name*}
{rd *file-name*}	{rd file-name}
{red *file-name*}	...
...	{index}

Insert one RD field for each file that is part of the whole document. The table of contents appears where you inserted the TOC field, and the index appears where you inserted the INDEX field. Insert the TOC and INDEX fields wherever you want their results to appear in the document that contains the RD fields. After Word collects the table of contents and index, you can print the documents separately.

In the document that contains the RD fields, you can insert any or all of the forms of the TOC and INDEX fields described in this appendix.

Imported Contents: Files, Spreadsheets, Charts, Graphics

Documents can consist of imported contents. Importing is essential for information that must be changed using the application in which it was originally generated. Word contains fields for importing the contents of text files, spreadsheet files, charts, and graphics.

Importing Text Files

For a large document that you've divided into separate files, use the INCLUDE field when you want to create cross-references to the text of a topic title or to any other text.

{include *file-name bookmark*}

The result of the above field is the full text marked by the *bookmark* in the file whose name you insert in the field. If you omit the bookmark name, the result is the entire file. If a bookmark in an INCLUDE field contains a table or part of a table, the bookmark must be inserted in one of the following ways: The bookmark must include the whole table or a whole row or contents within a single cell but not a whole cell. The bookmark can be inserted on some of the rows of a table and extend to text or graphics outside the table.

The Insert File command inserts the contents of another text or spreadsheet file in the active document. If you leave the Link option turned off in the Insert File dialog box, Word inserts the contents of the file but does not insert a field. If you turn on the Link option in the dialog box, Word inserts an INCLUDE field. You can insert an INCLUDE field yourself using either the Insert Field command or the INSERT FIELD key combination (Ctrl+F9).

In the INCLUDE field, type the file name of any document format for which Word has a file-format conversion program. If you want to insert a file that is stored in a file format different from Word's, you must insert a \c switch in the INCLUDE field and follow the \c switch with the name of the appropriate conversion program in quotation marks. Choose the File Save As command (Alt,F,A), choose the Options button (Alt+O), and then drop down the File Format list (F4) to see the names of the available conversion programs. You must insert the \c switch in the INCLUDE field yourself. The Insert File dialog box provides no means for inserting the conversion program name in the field.

The text-file conversion programs shipped with Word convert the following file formats:

- DCA/RFT (Document Content Architecture/Revisable-Form Text for DisplayWrite and DisplayWriter)
- Microsoft Word for the PC, all versions
- Microsoft Works word-processing files
- MultiMate versions 3.3, Advantage, and Advantage II
- RTF (Rich Text Format—especially for Microsoft Word for the Macintosh)
- Windows Write
- WordPerfect versions 4.1, 4.2, and 5.0
- WordStar versions 3.3, 3.45, 4.0, 5.0, and 5.5

Along with the file name, you can specify a pathname to tell Word where the file is stored. Note that you must double the backslash (\) characters in the pathname. For example, if you keep a document named REPORT.DOC stored in the path named C:\WINWORD\DOC, the INCLUDE field will look like the following:

```
{include c:\\winword\\doc\\report}
```

Note that as long as the file-name extension is DOC, you can omit the extension. Include the file-name extension if it is anything other than DOC.

Importing Spreadsheet Files

In addition to the text-file conversion programs that are included in your Word package, Word has built-in converters for Microsoft Excel BIFF, Microsoft Multiplan file format and BIFF, and Lotus 1-2-3 WKS format. The built-in converters make it possible to open a file in any of these formats as a Word document. These converters also let you specify in an INCLUDE field a file that's in one of these spreadsheet formats—for example:

{include c:\\excel\\movcosts.xls}

The contents of the Microsoft Excel file will appear in the Word window, with a tab character between columns and a paragraph mark at the end of each row.

Using DDE Regular Links

Word allows you to set up a link to another Windows application that supports Dynamic Data Exchange (DDE). As of this printing, this feature includes Microsoft Excel. The easiest way to insert this field is to start Microsoft Excel and open the appropriate spreadsheet or chart file. Then, copy the spreadsheet or chart information to the Clipboard. In Word, choose the Insert Paste Link command to paste the Microsoft Excel information to your Word document. The Edit Paste Link dialog box gives you the option of inserting either a regular DDE link or an automatic DDE link. When you use a regular DDE link, the field starts Microsoft Excel and updates information from the spreadsheet or chart file when you update the field.

{dde excel *spreadsheet*}

The result of the above DDE field is all the data in the spreadsheet whose name you insert in the field. You can also insert part of a spreadsheet by specifying a range of cells:

{dde excel *spreadsheet range*}

The *range* can be a named range (a group of cells that you named in Microsoft Excel) or the cell references of a range. Cell references must be in R1C1 format. (Microsoft Excel requires this format for DDE requests.) The result of the above DDE field is the data from the spreadsheet range whose name or cell references you insert in the field.

{dde excel *chart*}

This DDE field's result is the chart that's in the chart file whose name you insert in the field.

When other Windows applications can put their information on the Clipboard in a format that supports DDE links, this field and the DDEAUTO field can also be used for those applications. In that event, the parts of the field are as follows:

{dde *application file place*}

The *application* is the name of the program. The *file* is the name of the file from which you want to get information. And the *place* is a marker for part of a file. A *place* is equivalent to a bookmark in Word documents and a named range in Excel spreadsheets. Depending on the application, the *place* might be optional, which is convenient if the file and application do not support such an item, as is the case with Microsoft Excel chart files.

When you insert a DDE field using the Edit Paste Link command, Word also adds a formatting switch instruction, * Mergeformat, to preserve any formatting you might apply to the field's result. By adding this formatting switch to the field, you can retain the formatting when you update the DDE field. When you look at a DDE field after inserting the field using the Edit Paste Link command, you see codes like the following:

{dde excel c:\\excel\\movcosts.xls * mergeformat}

Using DDE Automatic Links

When you use a DDE automatic link, the field starts Microsoft Excel and updates information from the spreadsheet or chart file whenever Microsoft Excel informs Word that new data is ready. A DDEAUTO field has the same structure and results as does a regular DDE field. The following examples show the only difference between the two fields—the addition of "auto" to "dde":

{ddeauto excel *spreadsheet*}
{ddeauto excel *spreadsheet range*}
{ddeauto excel *chart*}

When other applications support DDE, the form—like the DDE form—becomes the following:

{ddeauto *application file place*}

To insert a DDEAUTO field using the Edit Paste Link command, turn on the Auto Update option in the Edit Paste Link dialog box.

You can change any DDE field to a DDEAUTO field by inserting "auto" following "dde." You can also change a DDEAUTO field to a DDE field by deleting "auto" following "dde." To be certain that the changes will take effect, be sure to update the revised field.

Exactly as Word inserts the * Mergeformat switch in the DDE field when you use the Edit Paste Link command, Word inserts the same switch instruction in the DDEAUTO fields that you insert using the Edit Paste Link command.

Importing Graphics Files

Word provides a field that you can use to import the following graphics file formats:

- Tagged Image File Format (TIFF) files. Scanners are the major sources of TIFF files in Windows.
- Lotus PIC
- HPGL
- CGM Graphics
- AutoCAD ADI binary
- AutoCAD ADI ASCII
- Zenographics Mirage
- Video Show
- Micrografx Draw
- Windows Metafile

You must have the appropriate file (called a graphic file filter) that reads the graphics file into a Word document. And your WIN.INI file must contain an entry for each graphic file filter that you plan to use. Word's Setup program installs the graphic file filters that you select during the setup process and creates the proper entries in your WIN.INI file. For other graphic file filters that you acquire separately from the Word package, the entry in the [WWFilter] section of your WIN.INI file should appear as follows:

Windows Metafile=WMF.FLT, WMF

For examples of how a line for a graphic file filter in your WIN.INI file should look, open your WIN.INI file in Word, scroll to the [WWFilter] section, and study the lines already in the file. The graphic file filter must be stored in the same directory as is WINWORD.EXE or in the directory specified by the UTIL-PATH=entry in the [WWFilter] section of your WIN.INI file.

If you want to import different graphics file formats from a single product, be sure to make the name of the filter unique. For example, if you plan to import HGL, CHT, and INV formats from Hewlett-Packard graphics language, make the entries in your WIN.INI file something like the following:

HP Graphics Language Import=HPGLIMP,HGL
HP Graphics Lang Import=HPGLIMP,CHT
HP Graphix Lang Imp=HPGLIMP,INV

The Insert Picture command inserts a graphics file in one of the graphics file formats that are listed in the Insert Picture dialog box. You type or select the file name in the dialog box and then choose OK to insert an IMPORT field. If your printer driver is attached to "NONE," when you try to insert a picture, you see a message telling you that Word cannot read or display the file. Attach your printer drive to a port (for example, to LPT1:) or to a file name by using the Setup Connections command in the Windows Control Panel. (To attach a printer to a file name, first insert in the [ports] section of your WIN.INI file a line that contains a file name followed by an equal sign.) Select the appropriate printer in the File Printer Setup dialog box. Choosing the New Picture button in the Insert Picture dialog box inserts an empty picture frame and no field. You can also use the Insert Field command or the INSERT FIELD key combination (Ctrl+F9) to insert an IMPORT field:

{import *graphic-file*}

The result of the IMPORT field is the contents of the specified graphics file, which Word positions inside a picture frame in your document.

You can crop or scale the field's graphic result to the appropriate size and proportions. Using the Format Picture command, you can also add one of several border patterns to the graphic. By adding a formatting switch to the IMPORT field, you can retain the sizing, cropping, and border when you update the field. Use the * Mergeformat formatting switch. For example, if you insert an IMPORT field for the TIFF file YAWL.TIF, the field looks like the following:

{import yawl.tif * mergeformat}

Calculations and Comparisons

Calculations are handy in documents that contain numbers with which you want to perform arithmetic. Comparison fields evaluate one piece of information against another piece and then produce a result.

Calculations from Mathematical Expressions

To calculate numeric results, insert an Expression (=) field that contains a mathematical expression. Mathematical expressions consist of operands (numbers, bookmarks inserted in numbers, or fields that result in numbers) that are separated by operators (such as + or –) or functions (such as SUM or AVERAGE).

Operators and functions

The operators and functions in the following table can be used in Expression (=) fields. Word also lets you use some of the operators in IF fields. For information about using these operators and functions, see the next section, "Comparison by Condition."

Comparison by Condition

A comparison by condition consists of an IF field, which contains two expressions separated by an operator (see the following table for information about operators), and two resulting pieces of text or graphics. Use the IF field when your decision as to what text or graphics you will want to insert depends on the result of the comparison's evaluation.

The NEXTIF and SKIPIF fields also incorporate a comparison by condition. Descriptions of the comparison in the IF field in the following section apply to NEXTIF and SKIPIF, which are described in the upcoming section "Merging."

Sign	*Operation*	*Field Code Example*	*Sample Result*
+	Addition	{=1234+5678}	6912
–	Subtraction	{=1234–567}	667
*	Multiplication	{=123*456}	56088
/	Division	{=1234/56}	22.04
%	Percentage	{=12.34*8.2%}	1.012
^	Power	{=2^8}	256
^	Root	{=8^.5}	2.8
=	Equal to	{if {time \@ "AM/PM"} = "AM" "AM" "PM"}	At 9:00 AM, result is AM At 9:00PM, result is PM
<>	Not equal to	{if {=count(regions)} <> 5 "Send report request" {total_regions}}	If all five regions not reported (no expression in the bookmark) result is "Send report request." If all five regions reported, result is the total at "total_regions."
<	Less than	{if {amount} < 100 "Order canceled" "Thank you"}	If bookmark "amount" is fewer than 100, result is "Order canceled." If 100 or more, result is "Thank you."
>	Greater than	{if {profits} > 15% "Dividend declared" "Profits flat"}	If "profits" is greater than 15%, result is "Dividend declared." If "profits" is 15% or less, result is "Profits flat."
<=	Less than or equal to	{if {age} <= 64 "Expect excellence" "Please consider early retirement"}	If "age" is 64 or less, result is "Expect excellence." If "age" is 65 or older, result is "Please consider early retirement."
>=	Greater than or equal to	{if {sales} >= 1*10^6 "Congratulations" "Let's try harder"}	If "sales" is $1 million or more, result is "Congratulations." If less than $1 million, result is "Let's try harder."

(continued)

continued

Sign	*Operation*	*Field Code Example*	*Sample Result*
( )	Precedence alters order of calculation. Precedence order is ^; *, /; +, –. Within each rank, Word calculates left to right.	{=27^(1/3)} {=27^1/3}	3. 9.
ABS	Absolute value	{=abs(–2)}	2
AND	Logical AND—result is 1 if all expressions evaluate to TRUE; result is 0 (zero) if any expression evaluates to FALSE.	{=and({sales} >= 1*10^6,{=profits} >= 20%)}	If "sales" is over $1 million AND "profits" grew more than 20%, result is 1. If either or both are not true, result is 0.
AVERAGE	Average of expressions	{=average({jan},{feb},{mar})}	If "jan" is 255, "feb" is 526, and "mar" is 756, result is 512.33.
COUNT	Number of expressions	{=count({regions})}	If "regions" contains five expressions (totals), result is 5.
DEFINED	Reports on validity of expression—result is 1 if expression evaluates without error; result is 0 (zero) if expression contains an error, including an undefined bookmark.	{=defined(income)}	If "income" is a defined bookmark, 1. If not, 0.
INT	Integer value—truncates decimal fractions; result is largest integer that's less than value of expression.	{=int({profit_percentage})}	If "profit_percentage" is 12.345, result is 12. If "profit_percentage" is –9.6, result is –10.
MAX	Largest expression in the list	{=max({west},{east},{north},{south})}	If "west" is 1234, "east" is 1243, "north" is 1324, and "south" is 1342, result is 1342.
MIN	Smallest expression in the list	{=min({west},{east},{north},{south})}	If "west" is 1234, "east" is 1243, "north" is 1324, and "south" is 1342, result is 1234.

(continued)

continued

Sign	***Operation***	***Field Code Example***	***Sample Result***
MOD	Modulus—result is remainder of dividing first expression by second.	{if {=mod({date \@ "yyyy"},4)} = 0 "It's Leap Year!" "No Feb. 29"}	In 1989, result is "No Feb. 29." In 1988, result is "It's Leap Year!"
NOT	Logical NOT—result is 1 if expression evaluates to FALSE; result is 0 (zero) if expression evaluates to TRUE.	{=not({region_totals} = {month_totals})}	If "region_totals" does not equal "month_totals," result is 1. If "region_totals" equals "month_totals," result is 0.
OR	Logical OR—result is 1 if any of expressions evaluates to TRUE; result is 0 (zero) if all expressions evaluate to FALSE.	{=or({profits} = 20%,{sales} = 25%)}	If "profits" is 20% or "sales" is 25% or both, result is 1. If both are either more or less, result is 0.
PRODUCT	Multiplies expressions in list by each other, right to left.	{=product({net},{rate},{term})}	If "net" is $10,000, "rate" is 0.67%, and "term" is 36, result is $2,412.00.
ROUND	Rounds expression to specified number of digits—positive number for number of decimal places; negative number for number of places to left of decimal; fractions first rounded to nearest integer.	{=round({profits},2)} {=round({sales},–5)}	If "profits" is $123,456.7891, result is $123,456.79. If "sales" is $12,345,678.90, result is $12,300,000.00.
SIGN	Reports on sign of expression—result is 1 if expression is positive; result is –1 if expression is negative; result is 0 (zero) if expression is zero.	{=sign({profits})}	If "profits" is more than zero, result is 1. If "profits" is less than zero (a loss), result is –1. If "profits" is zero (none), result is 0.
SUM	Adds all expressions in the list.	{=sum({region1},{region2},{region3})}	If "region1" is 1234, "region2" is 1243, and "region3" is 1324, result is 5153.

The IF Field

The following IF field compares the first *expression* with the second *expression*, using the *operator* you insert:

{if *expression operator expression "true-text" "false-text"*}

If the comparison is true, the result of the field is the *true-text*. If the comparison is false, the result of the field is the *false-text*. An *expression* can be a REF (bookmark) field, which means that you can compare the information for a specific field and then print one piece of text or another, depending on the comparison's result.

{if *expression operator expression "true-text" "false-text"*}
{nextif *expression operator expression*}
{skipif *expression operator expression*}

Merging

Word lets you use print merge fields to combine a standard document, such as a form letter, with various pieces of information, such as customers' names and addresses, to create individualized letters. Creating form letters is only one use for Word's print merge feature. Other examples include address labels, rosters, league standings, contest results, and phone lists, and you can probably think of more. Any time you need to combine two documents, use the print merge fields to do so.

The print merge fields are DATA, NEXT, NEXTIF, SKIPIF, and MERGEREC. Some of these fields work only when you use the File Print Merge command. In addition, you cannot nest these fields. And, with the exception of the MERGEREC field, you cannot use the print merge fields in headers, footers, footnotes, or annotations. The other fields in this section are not limited to print merge documents, but they are described here to provide additional ways in which you can improve your control of merge printing.

See Chapter 15, "Merge Printing," for information about how to print merge documents. The following explanations describe only the print merge fields.

Bookmarks

To merge data into a document, you must insert a bookmark name inside a field. This process is the same as using REF fields and omitting the "REF." The bookmark fields identify what information you want and where you want to insert it in the main document.

In the data document, you type the bookmark names in the first paragraph. The bookmark names identify the information that's directly below them as the information that goes into the fields that contain the same bookmark names. Instead of typing the bookmark names in a paragraph, you can put the bookmark names in a separate file called a header file.

The Data Field

The DATA field below tells Word the name of the file that contains the text you want to merge into the document in which this field appears:

{data *data-file-name*}

The following field is similar to the field above, but it also tells Word the name of the separate file in which the bookmark names appear that identify the data in the data file:

{data *data-file-name header-file-name*}

The Next Field

During merge printing, Word normally prints one document for every paragraph of information in the data document. The following field tells Word to go to the next paragraph in the data document and use its information for the bookmark fields that follow the main document's NEXT field:

{next}

The Next If Field

The NEXTIF field combines the NEXT and IF fields:

{nextif *expression operator expression*}

If the comparison evaluates to TRUE, Word uses items in the next paragraph of information in the data document for the rest of the REF fields in the main document. If the comparison evaluates to FALSE, Word uses the current paragraph's information for the rest of the REF fields in the main document, and then goes on to the next paragraph of information when it's time to print the next merge document. If you are comparing a data item in the data document with another expression, be aware that Word compares the current record and jumps to the next record if the comparison evaluates to TRUE. If you want to compare a data item in the current record to decide whether to print the current data record, instead use a NEXT instruction followed by a separate IF instruction. See Chapter 15, "Merge Printing," for an example of using separate NEXT and IF instructions in combination.

The Skip If Field

The SKIPIF field combines an IF field with a skip instruction:

{skipif *expression operator expression*}

If the comparison evaluates to TRUE, Word does not print a merged document for the current data record and continues to the next paragraph in the data document. If the comparison evaluates to FALSE, Word prints a copy of the merged document using the data document's current data record.

The Merge Record Field

The MERGEREC field inserts the number of the data record that Word used in the current merged document:

{mergerec}

Document Information

Within a document, Word lets you print many kinds of information about that document. You usually print document information such as the file name or the operator's name only when you print drafts of your documents. Such information as the version number and author's name, however, are often also printed in a final document.

You can insert fields for every piece of information that appears in the Edit Summary Info dialog box and its subordinate dialog box, Statistics. For example, you can print the document's file name, who last worked on the document, and how many words the document contains. All of the fields you use to insert this information in a document get their results from the Edit Summary Info dialog box and the Statistics subdialog box. In some of the document information fields, you can type the result in quotation marks following the field type. The text you type updates the corresponding information in the Edit Summary Info dialog box. Use the Insert Field command or the INSERT FIELD key combination (Ctrl+F9) to insert these fields.

The Author Field

The result of the following form of the AUTHOR field is the name that appears in the Edit Summary Info dialog box's Author box:

{author}

The result of the form of the AUTHOR field shown below is the name you insert in the field:

{author "*name*"}

Word also inserts this name in the Edit Summary Info dialog box's Author box.

The Comments Field

The result of the following form of the COMMENTS field is the text that appears in the Edit Summary Info dialog box's Comments box:

{comments}

The text you insert in the field is the result of the form of the COMMENTS field shown below:

{comments "*text*"}

Word also inserts this text in the Edit Summary Info dialog box's Comments box.

The Create Date Field

The result of a CREATEDATE field is the date on which the document was created:

{createdate}

This date is shown in the Statistics subdialog box of the Edit Summary Info dialog box.

The Edit Time Field

The result of the EDITTIME field shown below is the total number of minutes the document has been open since it was created:

{edittime}

This number is shown in the Statistics subdialog box of the Edit Summary Info dialog box.

The File Name Field

The FILENAME field's result is the document's file name, which is shown in the Edit Summary Info dialog box:

{filename}

The Information Field

The INFO field gives the same result that you get if you insert a document information field using only *info-type*:

{info *info-type*}

The *info-type* is one of the other field types that result in document information. For example, {info author} gives the same result as {author}. Also, for any field (*info-type*) in which you can type the result to change the Edit Summary Info dialog box, you can also type the result when you use INFO in front of *info-type*. INFO is optional in every case.

{info *info-type* "*text*"}

The Keywords Field

The result of the form of the KEYWORDS field shown below is the text that appears in the Keywords box of the Edit Summary Info dialog box:

{keywords}

The following form of the KEYWORDS field has as its result the *text* you insert in the field:

{keywords "*text*"}

Word also inserts this text in the Edit Summary Info dialog box's Keywords box.

The Last Saved By Field

The name of the person who last saved the document is the result of the LASTSAVEDBY field:

{lastsavedby}

This name is shown in the Statistics subdialog box. To change the name of the person saving the document, change the Name box in the Utilities Customize dialog box and save the document again.

The Number of Characters Field

The NUMCHARS field's result is the number of characters in the document as of the last update of that number in the Statistics subdialog box:

{numchars}

Word updates the number in the Statistics subdialog box as you insert and delete text and graphics, when you print the document, or when you choose the Update button (Alt+U) in the Statistics subdialog box.

The Number of Pages Field

The result of the NUMPAGES field is the number of pages in the document as of the last update of that number in the Statistics subdialog box:

{numpages}

Word updates the number in the Statistics subdialog box as you insert and delete text and graphics if the Background Pagination option in the Utilities Customize dialog box is turned on. Also, Word updates the number when you print the document or choose the Update button (Alt+U) in the Statistics subdialog box.

The Number of Words Field

The NUMWORDS field's result is the number of words in the document as of the last update of that number in the Statistics subdialog box:

{numwords}

To update the number in the Statistics subdialog box, either print the document or choose the Update button (Alt+U) in the Statistics subdialog box. Until you update the number of words the first time, Word estimates the number of words by dividing the number of characters by 5.5. When you print the document or choose the Update button, the number shown is the actual number of words in the document. Then Word calculates a new character-per-word ratio. Word uses the new ratio to estimate the number of words for additional editing until the next update. Estimated word totals appear dimmed in the Statistics dialog box.

The Print Date Field

The result of the PRINTDATE field is the date on which the document was last printed:

```
{printdate}
```

This date is shown in the Statistics subdialog box and is updated after each printing. To show the current printing's date, use the DATE field.

The Revision Number Field

The result of the REVNUM field is the number of times the document was saved since it was created plus one, which is shown in the Statistics subdialog box:

```
{revnum}
```

TIP

Matching Version Number with Releases

A document that you publish in versions typically goes through many drafts and revisions before you release a version. As a result, the revision number is usually larger than the version number. It's easier in most cases to type the version number in the document than it is to use the REVNUM field to generate the version number. To match the revision number with a released version number, you need to trick Word. First, save the document for the last time when it is ready for final printing. Then, use the File Save As command (Alt,F,A) to save the document under a new name. Look at the revision number in the Statistics subdialog box of the Edit Summary Info dialog box. Then, save the document as many more times as needed for the correct version number. If it's the second version, save it one time; if it's the fifth version, save it four times.

The Save Date Field

The result of the SAVEDATE field is the date on which the document was last saved:

{savedate}

This date is shown in the Statistics subdialog box.

The Subject Field

In its following form, the SUBJECT field's result is the text that appears in the Subject box of the Edit Summary Info dialog box:

{subject}

The result of the form of the SUBJECT field shown below, however, is the text you insert in the field:

{subject "*text*"}

Word also inserts this text in the Subject box of the Edit Summary Info dialog box.

The Template Field

The result of the TEMPLATE field is the name of the template on which the document is based:

{template}

This template name also appears in the Statistics subdialog box. If the document is based on the default template named NORMAL.DOT, this field has no result. The Statistics subdialog box shows the template as "None."

The Title Field

In the form shown below, the TITLE field's result is the text that appears in the Edit Summary Info dialog box's Title box:

{title}

But the result of the following form of the TITLE field is the text you insert in the field:

{title "*text*"}

Word also inserts the text that you type in this field in the Edit Summary Info dialog box's Title box.

Mathematical Typesetting

The Formula (EQ) field, which you use for mathematical typesetting, does not calculate any values. It displays and prints a mathematical formula, expression, or equation. For information about this field and the topic of mathematical typesetting, see Chapter 16, "Mathematical Typesetting."

Button Fields

In Word, two button fields perform actions. The GOTOBUTTON field jumps to a destination in a document, and the MACROBUTTON field runs a macro.

Jumping Around in a Document from a Field

The GOTOBUTTON field provides a way to jump around in a document to specific places. You can insert various pieces of text anywhere in the document and then use this field to connect the pieces.

The field syntax is as follows:

{gotobutton *go-to-destination picture*}

The *go-to-destination* is any destination that you can use with the Edit Go To command or the GOTO key (F5). For a list of possible destinations, see "Moving Around Using the Edit Go To Command" in Chapter 2.

The result of this field is always the text or graphic that you provide as the *picture*. In this case, the text you provide for the result is not enclosed in quotation marks unless you want the quotation marks to appear in the result. The *picture* must fit within the width of one line, regardless of the line's length. You can apply any character formatting to the *picture*. And by putting this field in a paragraph by itself or in a single table cell, you can apply any paragraph and cell formatting. For example, you can add a border around the field, creating a buttonlike appearance. If you do not add any special formatting to the *picture* or the field, the *picture* appears in the document as regular text or as a regular graphic.

Word jumps to the destination that you've specified in the field when you activate the field. You can choose from two ways in which to activate a GOTOBUTTON field:

- Double-click the field using the left mouse button.
- Position the insertion point in the field, and then press the DO FIELD CLICK key combination (Alt+Shift+F9).

Running Macros from a Field

The MACROBUTTON field provides a way to run a macro from within a document. The macro you specify runs when you activate the field. And it runs in the same way all macros run, exactly as if you had chosen the macro using the Macro Run command.

The field syntax is shown below:

{macrobutton *macro-name picture*}

The result of this field, like the result of a GOTOBUTTON field, is the text or graphic that you provide as the *picture*. The text that you provide for the result is not enclosed in quotation marks unless you want the quotation marks to appear in the result. The *picture* must fit within the width of one line, regardless of the line's length. Word lets you apply any character formatting to the *picture*. By putting this field by itself in a paragraph or a table cell, you can apply any paragraph or cell formatting to the field. If you do not add any special formatting to the *picture* or the field, the *picture* will appear in the document as regular text or as a regular graphic.

To activate a MACROBUTTON field, you use either of two methods:

- Double-click the field using the left mouse button.
- Position the insertion point in the field, and then press the DO FIELD CLICK key combination (Alt+Shift+F9).

The MACROBUTTON field can run any macro or built-in command, which makes it possible to create some spectacular-looking actions and results. You can also use macro buttons to provide context-sensitive help information anywhere in a document.

Literals

A "literal" contains characters that represent only themselves. For example, if you yell "Go!" at the start line of a race, the racers start running. But if you talk about the letter combination "go," you talk about the literal characters "g" and "o" without the added meaning of the command "go." Word has two kinds of literals, and you have two means for inserting them: You use the QUOTE field for literal characters and the PRINT field for printer commands (called printer literals).

Literal Characters

The result of a QUOTE field with *literal text* as its additional instruction, as shown below, is the text you type between the quotation marks:

{quote "*literal text*"}

The *literal text* can be any text or a text result of a field. You can insert more than one piece of literal text in a single QUOTE field by enclosing each piece of text in quotation marks—for example:

{quote "*text-1*" "*text-2*" "*text-3*"}

Word converts numbers and the numeric result of a nested field to ANSI characters:

{quote 174}
{quote 0xae}

Both of the above forms of the QUOTE field display the ® character as the result. You can type the character number as a decimal number (174) or as a hexadecimal number, which must be preceded with 0x (0xae) to indicate to Word that the number is hexadecimal.

Using the QUOTE field is one way to insert ANSI characters that do not have corresponding keys on the keyboard. Note, however, that you can also insert the ANSI characters that do not have keys by turning on the NumLock key, holding down the Alt key, and typing a *0* (zero) followed by the ANSI character number. Whichever method you use, you need to know the ANSI character number. Appendix C of the *Microsoft Word for Windows User's Reference* contains a table of the ANSI characters. The table shows both the decimal and hexadecimal numbers for each character.

One way you might use the QUOTE field would be to construct a table of the ANSI characters and insert QUOTE fields to generate the characters.

Printer Commands

Use the PRINT field to send commands (control codes and PostScript instructions) to a printer:

{print "*printer-instructions*"}

Word does not format, translate, or check the syntax of the *printer-instructions*, which must be enclosed in quotation marks. By enclosing each set of printer instructions in quotation marks, you can insert more than one set of instructions in a single PRINT field—for example:

{print "*instructions-1*" "*instructions-2*"}

If you insert a PRINT field that contains PostScript instructions but print the document on a non-PostScript printer, the PostScript instructions are printed as plain text. You need to consult your printer manual for information about sending control codes and PostScript instructions to your printer. The following section describes the PostScript support that Word and Windows provide.

PostScript support

The descriptions in this section assume that you already understand PostScript programming. If you do not, first see the *PostScript Language Reference Manual* and the *PostScript Language Tutorial and Cookbook*, both by Adobe Systems, Inc., published by Addison-Wesley.

PRINT fields that contain PostScript instructions can appear anywhere in a document. When Word prints the document, the PostScript instructions are sent to the printer without translation. On each page, the printer first prints the results of any PRINT fields on that page that contain PostScript instructions. Then the printer prints the document's text and graphics for the page.

To send PostScript instructions to your printer, use the following form of the PRINT field:

{print \p *size* "*instructions*"}

The \p switch in the preceding field tells Word that the *instructions* are PostScript. The *size* instruction is part of the PostScript instructions and tells the printer the size of the PostScript effect and where it starts on the page. In the PostScript books published by Addison-Wesley and mentioned on the preceding page, the *size* is called a "group." The *size* instruction can be one of the following:

Size (Group)	*Meaning*
page	Current page (default); if you replace the *size* instruction with a pair of empty quotation marks (""), Word uses page size
para	Current paragraph (the paragraph that contains the PRINT field); the paragraph that contains the PRINT field must be at least 1 inch tall for the para size to print
pic	Next picture following the PRINT field but in the same paragraph as the PRINT field
row	Current table row
cell	Current table cell
dict	Definitions and procedures for one page

Use the "dict" group carefully. It is intended to define procedures to be used later on the same page. Word does not define any of the "wp$" variables (described in the following table) for the "dict" group. And Word does not alter the "drawing environment" (such as origin, clipping, and axes), so you should not "draw" using the "dict" group.

Each of the sizes (groups) recognizes specific variables, as shown in the following table. Enter all measurements in points, which is the standard unit of measure for PostScript. The y-coordinate space used for PostScript commands in Word is the same as normal PostScript. The graphics origin (0,0) is the lower-left corner of the drawing rectangle, and the positive directions are to the right and upward. Drawing takes place within a "clipping rectangle" (also called a "drawing rectangle"). The graphics origin is translated to the lower-left corner of the drawing rectangle.

Size (Group)	***Variable***	***Meaning***
All	wp$y	Drawing rectangle height of page, para, or pic
	wp$x	Drawing rectangle width of page, para, or pic
	wp$page	Current page number
	wp$fpage	Formatted page number (string)
	wp$date	Current date (formatted)
	wp$time	Current time (formatted)
	wp$box	Path containing the drawing rectangle
para and page	wp$top	Space before (para) Top margin (page)
	wp$bottom	Space after (para) Bottom margin (page)
	wp$left	Left indent (para) Left margin (page)
	wp$right	Right indent (para) Right margin (page)
para	wp$first	First-line indent
	wp$style	Style
page	wp$col	Number of columns on the page; the number varies depending on the section in which the PostScript appears
	wp$colx	Width of each column
	wp#colxb	Space between columns

The PostScript *instructions* must be enclosed in quotation marks if the instructions contain more than one word. The following illustration shows a PRINT field that contains PostScript instructions and the result of the PRINT field, which you can see only on a printed copy of the document.

```
{print \p page "/phrase {(opus fugit)} def
/left 64 def
/bottom {wp$y 2 div 30 sub} def
/Times-Bold findfont 30 scalefont setfont
/say {left bottom moveto phrase show} def
/retreat {gsave .02 .02 .98
{setgray say dx dy translate}
for grestore} def
/dx -1 def /dy .5 def retreat
/dx 1 def /dy -.5 def retreat
/dx -1 def /dy -.5 def retreat
/dx 1 def /dy .5 def retreat
1 setgray say"}
```

Word prints text and graphics in the same PostScript page as your PostScript commands. Do not use PostScript operators, therefore, that reset the PostScript environment. Avoid the following PostScript operators in the PRINT field:

- banddevice
- copypage
- framedevice
- grestoreall
- initgraphics
- initmatrix
- nulldevice
- renderbands
- showpage

General Switches

General switches apply to all fields that show a calculated result but do not affect fields that have no result (for example, TC) or fields that have a picture result (for example, GOTOBUTTON). Word provides three types of general switches: formatting switches, date-and-time switches, and numeric switches.

Formatting Switches

Applying text formatting to the source that supplies a field's result, to the first character in a field, and to the result itself provides one way to format a field's result. You can, however, also perform formatting changes such as capitalizing letters, changing the form of numbers, and controlling text formatting in results. The following list describes the formatting switches and provides simple examples for each. All formatting switches begin with *. Formatting switches must precede any other type of general switches in a field.

* Upper

The * Upper switch converts all letters in the result to uppercase.

Example	*Result*
{fillin "Type company's name" * upper}	MICROSOFT CORPORATION (source is Microsoft Corporation)

The source text can appear in any combination of uppercase and lowercase.

* Lower

The * Lower switch converts all letters in the result to lowercase.

Example	*Result*
{ref wp_family * lower}	word processing family of products (source is Word Processing Family of Products)

The source text can appear in any combination of uppercase and lowercase. See "* Cardtext" and "* Ordtext" later in this section for additional examples of * Lower.

* Firstcap

The * Firstcap switch converts the first letter of the first word in the result to uppercase.

Example	*Result*
{ref sect_title * firstcap}	Historical perspective (source is HISTORICAL PERSPECTIVE)

The source text can be in any combination of uppercase and lowercase.

* Caps

The * Caps switch converts the first letter of each word in the result to uppercase.

Example	*Result*
{set book_title "working with word" * caps}	No visible result; bookmark book_title is set to "Working With Word." When a REF field includes the book_title bookmark, the REF field's result will be Working With Word.

The source text can be in any combination of uppercase and lowercase. No letters other than the first letter of each word in the result change case.

* Arabic

The * Arabic switch converts numbers in the result to Arabic format.

Example	*Result*
On the {date \@ d * ordinal} of {date \@ mmmm}.... (The bookmark "condate" is inserted in the first DATE field.) Though the project was originally scheduled for the beginning of the month, it was {condate * arabic} days into the month before....	On the 11th of November.... Though...it was 11 days.... (Source is: On the {date \@ d * ordinal} of {date \@ mmmm}.... [The bookmark "condate" is inserted in the first DATE field.])

* Roman

The * Roman switch converts numbers in the result to Roman-numeral format. If the "R" in Roman is uppercase, the Roman numerals will be uppercase; if the "r" is lowercase, the Roman numerals will be lowercase.

Example	*Result*
{seq chapter * Roman}	IV
{page * roman}	vii

* Alphabetic

The * Alphabetic switch converts numbers in the result to letter format. Numbering proceeds from a to z; aa, bb, cc, to zz; aaa, bbb, ccc, to zzz; and so on. If the "A" in Alphabetic is uppercase, the letters will be uppercase; if the "a" is lowercase, the letters will be lowercase.

Example	*Result*
{seq appendix * Alphabetic}	F
{seq chromosome * alphabetic}	y

* Hex

The * Hex switch converts numbers in the result to hexadecimal format.

Example	*Result*
{=187 * hex}	BB

* Cardtext

The * Cardtext switch converts numbers in the result to cardinal text format.

Example	*Result*
{date \@ d * cardtext}	Twenty-One

Note that in the preceding result, the first letter of each word in the number is uppercase. Use the * Lower switch to make the first letter of each word lowercase:

{date \@ d * cardtext * lower}

For a description of the \@ d switch, see "Date-and-Time Switches" under "Date and Time Fields" near the beginning of this appendix.

* Ordtext

The * Ordtext switch converts numbers in the result to ordinal text format.

Example	*Result*
{date \@ d * ordtext}	Twenty-First

Note that in the result shown above, the first letter of each word in the number is uppercase. Use the * Lower switch to make the first letter of each word lowercase:

{date \@ d * ordtext * lower}

* Ordinal

The * Ordinal switch converts numbers in the result to ordinal format (numeral and abbreviation).

Example	*Result*
{date \@ d * ordinal}	21st

* Dollartext

The * Dollartext switch converts numbers in the result to the dollars-and-cents currency format. Dollars appear in cardtext format, and cents appear in Arabic format as a fraction of 100.

Example	*Result*
{=$109.95*8.1% * dollartext}	Eight and 91/100

* **Charformat**

Of the fields that display a result, most show the result using the text format of the paragraph in which the field occurs. Word lets you alter the text formatting of these fields by formatting the first character inside the field. For the REF, INCLUDE, GLOSSARY, and QUOTE fields, you need to add a * Charformat switch to direct Word to apply the first character's formatting to the result. These fields do not automatically apply the formatting of the first character inside the field because the source text can include formatting that you want to carry through in the result. And, while you edit the field codes, you might want to format them to make them distinctive or more readable. The * Charformat switch lets you override the formatting that Word gets from the result's source text and from the paragraph that contains the field.

Example	*Result*
{*glossary* disclaim} (without switch)	Information in this document is subject to change without notice and does not represent a commitment on the part of the company.
{*glossary* disclaim * charformat}	*Information in this document is subject to change without notice and does not represent a commitment on the part of the company.*

* **Mergeformat**

When you update a field, editing and formatting changes you made to the result are normally lost when the new result replaces the previous result. The * Mergeformat switch lets you hold on to formatting changes you made directly to the result.

Example	*Result*
{ref * mergeformat}	Our promise: Accurate books by skilled writers. (Field after first update)
	Our promise: The Best Books by the Best Authors. (Boldface applied to "Our promise:" and field updated)

Date-and-Time Switches

For information about these switches, see "Date-and-Time Switches" under "Date and Time Fields" near the beginning of this appendix. You can use date-and-time switches in any field, and not only in the specific date and time fields. If Word recognizes the result as a date or time, Word uses the date-and-time switch to format the result.

Numeric Switches

Fields can calculate numeric results, following the rules that apply to the Utilities Calculate command. For example, when you calculate numbers, the result of the calculation has as many digits and decimal places as the number with the most decimal places. For banks, such a result is not necessarily desirable. If an interest calculation results in a number like 123.456, what does the bank do with six-tenths of a cent? In situations like this one, you can add a numeric-picture switch to a field to format the result. Word lets you control the number of digits and the appearance of the currency signs, the thousands separator, and the decimal point. The switch is called a picture switch because you specify a pictorial representation of the way you want the resulting number to look. If the field includes no numbers in its result, numeric switches have no effect on the result. The following sections describe the numeric switches and provide simple examples of each.

All numeric switches begin with \#. The numeric picture, which follows the \#, can combine any of the elements explained below and must be enclosed in quotation marks.

0 (zero; required digit placeholder)

A 0 (zero) in a numeric picture indicates that under all circumstances you want a digit to appear at that place in the result. If the result does not include a digit that corresponds to the zero's position, Word displays a zero at that place. If the result has more digits to the right of a decimal point than zeros in the numeric picture, the digits are rounded, with 5 rounded to the nearest even number. If the result has more digits to the left of a decimal point than zeros in the numeric picture, the digits appear.

Example	*Meaning*
{=90/10 \# "0.00"}	A result of 9 appears as 9.00.
{=90/100 or \# "0.00"}	A result of .9 appears as 0.90.
{=4*3 \# "0.00"}	A result of 12 appears as 12.00.
{=20–7.445 \# "0.00"}	A result of 12.555 appears as 12.56.

(number sign; optional digit placeholder)

Word lets you insert a number sign in a numeric picture to indicate that you want to show spaces if the result does not include enough digits to correspond to the number signs. The number signs are especially useful when you want to set up the placement of decimal points and thousands separators but have them shown only if they are needed.

Example	*Meaning*
{=90+900–1 \# "#,###.##"}	A result of 989 appears as 989., with an extra space in front.
{=44950/36 \# "#,###.##"}	A result of 1248.61 appears as 1,248.61.
{=44950*2.000/3 \# "#,###.##"}	A result of 29966.667 appears as 29,966.67.

X (truncating digit placeholder)

An x in a numeric picture indicates the exact number of digits that you want to appear in the result. The result is not rounded; extra numbers are dropped from the result.

Example	*Meaning*
{=12*9+1 \# "xx"}	A result of 109 appears as 09.

Decimal point

A decimal point anywhere in the numeric picture indicates the number of digits that you want on either side of the decimal point. The decimal-point character that you type must be the decimal-point character that's set in the Windows Control Panel. In the U.S., this character is a period by default.

Example	*Meaning*
{=12345/10 \# "000.00"}	A result of 1234.5 appears as 1234.50.

Thousands separator

Position a thousands separator in the numeric picture to indicate how you want to group thousands in the result. If you insert a single thousands separator character, Word inserts as many thousands separator characters as are needed in the result. The character that you type as the thousands separator must be the thousands separator that's set in the Windows Control Panel. By default in the U.S., this character is a comma.

Example	*Meaning*
{=1000*1000 \# "00,000,000"}	A result of 1000000 appears as 01,000,000.
{=10^3 \# "00,000,000"	A result of 1000 appears as 00,001,000.
\# "####,.##"}	A result of 1000 appears as 1,000. followed by two spaces. A result of 10000000.00 appears as 10,000,000.00.

– (minus sign; negative sign)

Include a minus sign in the numeric picture to indicate that you want negative numbers in the result to include a minus sign. Positive numbers will have a space in the result at the minus sign's position in the numeric picture.

Example	*Meaning*
{=(7–32)*5/9 \# "–000"	A result of –14 appears as –014.
{=(–115)–(–460) \# "–000"}	A result of 345 appears as 345, with an extra space in front of the number.

+ (plus sign; required sign)

If you want positive numbers in the result to have a plus sign and negative numbers in the result to have a minus sign, include a plus sign in the numeric picture.

Example	*Meaning*
{=(–115)–(–460) \# "+000"}	A result of 345 appears as +345.
{=115–460 \# "+000"}	A result of –345 appears as –345.

Positive;Negative

You can create one numeric picture for positive numbers and another numeric picture for negative numbers. If the result is 0 (zero), Word uses the positive picture to format it. You use the positive;negative element in a numeric picture instead of the plus sign or minus sign when you want to include a symbol other than a simple plus or minus sign—for example, to show negative numbers in parentheses. A semicolon in the picture indicates that the switch contains more than one picture and also separates the positive from the negative parts of the picture.

Example	*Meaning*
{=42.25*108.1% \# "000.00;(000.00)"}	A result of 45.67 appears as 045.67.
{=325–330.6 \# "000.00; (000.00)"}	A result of –5.6 appears as (005.60).

Positive;Negative;Zero

Word allows you to create one numeric picture for positive numbers, another for negative numbers, and yet another for zero. You use the positive;negative;zero element in a numeric picture instead of the positive;negative element when you want to format a result of zero differently than positive numbers. Semicolons in the picture indicate that the switch contains more than one picture and also separate the positive, negative, and zero parts of the picture.

Example	*Meaning*
{=42.45*108.1% \# "00.00; (00.00); —0—"}	A result of 45.67 appears as 45.67.
{=–82.75/108.1% \# "00.00; (00.00); —0—"}	A result of –76.55 appears as (76.55).
{=(32–32)*5/9 \# "00.00; (00.00); —0—"}	A result of zero appears as —0—.

Note that the dashes in the zero part of the picture are em dashes (—). You insert them by pressing the Alt+0150 key combination when the NumLock key is turned on. If you want to use two hyphens instead of an em dash, enclose the hyphens in apostrophes, as shown below:

{=(32–32)*5/9 \# "00.00; (00.00); '--0--'"}

If you omit the apostrophes, a zero result appears as 0 with two spaces before and after.

'Text'

A numeric picture can also contain text, which must be enclosed in single quotation marks ('). Also, enclose the entire numeric picture in double quotation marks, as shown in the example below. The single quotation marks also distinguish the text from the part of the numeric picture that formats numbers in the result.

Example	*Result*
{balance \# "'Balance due: ' $#,##0.00"}	Balance due: $1,234.56 (Assume that the bookmark "balance" marks a number 1234.56.)

`Sequence-identifier`

To include a sequence number in a numeric picture, enclose the sequence identifier in single back quotation marks (`). The sequence identifier will provide for the field's result the number of the nearest preceding SEQ field that has the same sequence identifier.

Example	*Result*
\# "'Finisher `fin_pos` receives' $###,##0.00"	Finisher 3 receives $ 10,000.00.

For the above example, suppose you're using a sheet of race results. The finishing position number is generated by a SEQ field that includes the identifier fin_pos. This numeric switch could be used in a field that calculates the winnings for each position.

Other characters you can add to numeric switches

Word lets you include any other single characters you want without enclosing them in the single quotation marks you need for text. Examples include dollar signs, parentheses, thousands separators, and the degree symbol.

Example	*Result*
{=200+34.56 \# "$#,##0.00;(#,##0.0);==0=="}	$234.56 (positive result)
{=9000–16890.12 \# "$#,##0.00;(#,##0.0);==0=="}	(7,890.12) (negative result)
{=12–12 \# "$#,##0.00;(#,##0.0);==0=="}	==0== (zero result)

Index

Page numbers that are italicized indicate references to tables or figures.

SPECIAL CHARACTERS

A

D

E

F

I

K

L

M

N

O

P

S

T

U

V

W

X–Z

Russell E. Borland earned a bachelor of arts degree from Whitworth College, a master of arts degree from Portland State University, and a Ph.D. degree from the University of Washington. He has been a technical writer for Microsoft Corporation for eight years and currently resides in Kirkland, Washington.

The manuscript for this book was prepared and submitted to Microsoft Press in electronic form. Text files were processed and formatted using Microsoft Word for the Macintosh.

Interior text design by Darcie S. Furlan
Illustrations by Becky Geisler-Johnson
Principal typography by Lisa G. Iversen
Color separations by Wescan Color Corporation

Text composition by Microsoft Press in Palatino with display in Palatino Bold, using the Magna composition system and the Linotronic 300 laser imagesetter.